EAST EUROPEAN MONOGRAPHS, NO. CCCXCVI

DB
955.6
.H67
S25
1994
Jan. 1998

Published with the help of the
Charles Phelp Taft Memorial Fund,
University of Cincinnati

Contents

Preface

Mention the name "Admiral Horthy" to a group of scholars and the response is predictable and automatic: "Ah yes, the admiral without a navy." Miklós Horthy has long been an easy target for such light-hearted satire. Even during the interwar period, political pundits joked about the regent in a country without a king and the admiral who had no fleet. With the passage of time and frequent use such witticisms have become trite, yet they do in fact convey a hint of the many paradoxes and ironies that characterized Admiral Horthy's career.

That Miklós Horthy should have come to prominence in the first two decades of the twentieth century as a loyal naval officer of the Habsburg monarchy was certainly one of these ironies. Horthy came from the kind of Calvinist gentry family living in the heart of landlocked Hungary that historically had been hostile to the Catholic Habsburgs. Yet Horthy not only became a dutiful aide-de-camp to the venerable Emperor Francis Joseph, but during World War I so impressed the heir to the throne, Charles, that in 1918 he was appointed Commander-in-Chief of the Austro-Hungarian fleet. Horthy's tenure in the post was brief, for the war was soon over, the Habsburg Empire was collapsing, and the fleet had to be handed over to the new South Slav State. Deeply frustrated and embittered by these unexpected events, Horthy vowed that he would do everything in his power to restore the Habsburg monarchy to its rightful place in Danubian affairs. But only three years later, by a strange turn of events, it was Miklós Horthy who thwarted two attempts by Charles to regain his throne in Hungary.

When Admiral Horthy returned to his homeland in November 1918, he seemed almost a stranger. Though remarkably adept at learning foreign languages, he had been away from Hungary for so long that he now spoke Magyar with a pronounced German accent. At the age of fifty, it seemed that he would spend the last years of his life supervising the affairs of his modest country estate. No one, least of all Admiral Horthy himself, could have imagined that he would soon rise to great national prominence and be elected regent (*kormányzó*) in March 1920.[1] Even more unlikely was the thought that the "temporary" office of regent might last for an extended period of time. In fact, Horthy was to preside over Hungary as regent for twenty-four years, from 1920 to 1944, one of the longest tenures in power of any European head of state in the twentieth century. Here too the historian encounters an apparent paradox, for Horthy seemed to possess few qualities that would explain his longevity in office. He had no political experience. His intellectual abilities were modest at best. His perspective on political affairs and European diplomacy was extremely narrow and unsophisticated. Moreover, his election in March 1920 was accompanied by military intimidation and was strongly opposed by important segments of the population. Yet he not only survived for nearly two and a half decades without any serious challenge, but during World War II came to enjoy widespread popularity.

Although on paper Admiral Horthy had very extensive powers as regent, for the most part he ruled as a kind of constitutional monarch. In foreign affairs, for example, he generally preferred to leave the formulation of policy to his ministers. His role for many years was purely ceremonial. In any case, foreign diplomats and statesmen with whom he did speak frequently became convinced that he was poorly informed and pathetically simplistic in his views concerning international relations. But when the coming of the European crisis in the 1930s required the Regent's active participation in important negotiations, the results were sometimes quite unexpected. To the surprise of many Hungarian officials, the Regent was one of the few European statesmen to hold his own in direct talks with Adolf Hitler. Horthy's naive bluntness and his seemingly archaic code of honor proved to be useful weapons in several critical meetings with Hitler, who was unaccustomed to being challenged orally by the statesmen of lesser powers.

Perhaps the greatest paradox of Horthy's career was his relationship with the Jews of Hungary. His political career in fact began and ended in national crises that deeply involved the Jews. Horthy rose to power in 1919 in an outburst of violence against Jews and Communists known as the "White Terror." Through his participation in these events, Horthy gained an unsavory reputation abroad as a vicious anti-Semite, for a time perhaps the most notorious in all of Europe. Yet near the end of his career in 1944, when the Jews of Hungary were being sent to the gas chambers of Auschwitz as the last installment of Hitler's "Final Solution," it was Horthy who finally stepped forward to halt the deportations, thereby saving the lives of most of the members of the large Jewish community of Budapest.

Admiral Horthy's political career spanned a good part of the first half of the twentieth century, yet he was by no means a modern statesman. The most familiar image we have of him is the man on horseback, a throwback to an earlier age. His social and political views reflected a yearning for a Europe untouched by the doctrines of the French Revolution. His concepts of gentlemanly honor and chivalry had their roots in the Middle Ages. But even if Horthy was thus an anachronism, he was not completely unaffected by the powerful forces unleashed by World War I. Hungary proved to be a fertile breeding ground for one of Europe's most virulent radical right-wing movements. Frustrated by the outcome of the world war and appalled by the success of the Communist revolution in Russia and temporarily in Hungary, Horthy was at first strongly attracted to this Hungarian version of proto-fascism. With the passing of time, however, his traditional conservatism began to reassert itself. It makes little sense to call Miklós Horthy a Fascist, as did some of his opponents and some Marxist historians, but he did represent an interesting ideological hybrid, a blend of elements of nineteenth century conservatism and twentieth century right-wing radicalism.

Horthy's role in Hungarian history, particularly in the turbulent conditions of 1919–1920, is in several ways analogous to that of the White Generals in Russia. Of course, unlike such officers as Admiral Kolchak, General Denikin, and Marshal Mannerheim, Horthy was not a participant in the Russian civil war and the struggle against Trotsky's Red Army. But Hungary was the only other country besides Russia to experience a successful Communist revolution. The Soviet Republic of Béla Kun managed to survive for only four months in the spring and summer of 1919. In this period Admiral Horthy emerged as the most prominent figure in the Hungarian counterrevolutionary movement. Although he never engaged in direct combat with the Hungarian Red Army, Horthy did command an armed force that swept over the country in late 1919 in a campaign to eradicate all traces of bolshevism. In his staunch anticommunism, ambivalence about monarchy, and growing ambition to play a leading political role, Horthy did resemble the Russian White Generals. Unlike most of them, however, Horthy managed to come to power and to continue his crusade against communism until it culminated in the decision to join Germany in an attack on the Soviet Union in 1941.

No full-length scholarly study of Miklós Horthy has ever been written. Several flattering biographies appeared in the period between the world wars, including an authorized version written by Baroness Lily Doblhoff,[2] but they are of only limited value to the historian. In the 1920s several confidants of Emperor Charles wrote books in which Horthy was portrayed in scathingly negative terms as a breaker of oaths and a traitor to his monarch. This historiographical tradition was revived by the British historian Gordon Brook-Shepherd in his biography of Emperor Charles.[3] Biographies by Hungarian journalists and political activists in the Communist era after World War II tended to portray Horthy as a Fascist who came to power and maintained his position for so long solely through the application of force and terror.[4] Serious historians in the Communist era were usually reluctant to tackle a subject that bristled with controversy and touched on sensitive ideological concerns. Nonetheless, several Hungarian historians have done important work on aspects of Hungarian interwar history, notably Gyula Juhász, György Ránki, and Ignác Romsics.[5] Any historian who undertakes a study of Admiral Miklós Horthy also owes a great debt to those Western historians who have made an intensive study of Hungary in the era of the world wars, particularly C. A. Macartney, whose magisterial two-volume study is replete with keen insights and source material not available anywhere else.[6] Also valuable are the monographs of Mario Fenyő and Randolph Braham, and the short biography of Horthy written by Péter Gosztony.[7]

A major obstacle confronts the historian who embarks on a study of Admiral Horthy: the paucity of primary source materials. Miklós Horthy kept no diary. His memoirs, prepared by a man more than eighty years old and with an imperfect recall of events, are unreliable and largely uninformative.[8] A group of private papers and letters that survived the siege of Budapest was published in Hungary in the 1960s.[9] Although these "Horthy Papers" throw light only on certain topics, they do in some cases reflect his private musings and attitudes. On the other hand, the discouraging reality is that only a small handful of private letters written by Horthy in the period 1918–1944 has survived the vicissitudes of the war and its aftermath. Almost no letters or other material pertaining to Horthy's private life have become available.

An additional problem is the dearth of relevant memoir litera-ture. Of the major political figures with whom Horthy worked, only one of them, Miklós Kállay, was able to publish his memoirs.[10] Premature death, suicide, or imprisonment prevented such impor-tant Hungarian statesmen as Gyula Gömbös, Pál Teleki, and István Bethlen from placing pen to paper and providing accounts of events in which Horthy participated. On the other hand, the pa-pers or memoirs of certain lesser collaborators of Horthy, includ-ing Pál Prónay, Father Zadravecz, Géza Lakatos, Gyula Kádár, and Antal Vattay, have been published.

Because Admiral Horthy met frequently with foreign statesmen and military leaders, records of these conversations represent a significant historical source. Relevant documents have been un-covered for this study in published and unpublished collections in Great Britain, France, Germany, Austria, and the United States. In interpreting these documents, however, a caveat is in order. By nature a garrulous and friendly conversationalist, Miklós Horthy could be remarkably open and even indiscreet in his utterances. He simply lacked the guile, or indeed the common sense, of a statesman who instinctively knows that he must keep certain things secret and leave some ideas unspoken. He was truly the kind of person who "wears his heart on his sleeve." Since Horthy was apt to speak what was on his mind, he struck many people who met him as very sincere. On the other hand, his impulsiveness led him at times to voice some of his vulgar prejudices and darker impulses. Yet he rarely acted on these impulses or prejudices, since in most cases he was dissuaded from rash enterprises by his more moderate advisors.

The historian who attempts a study of Admiral Miklós Horthy is thus saddled with a number of handicaps, especially the dearth of pertinent historical records. Still, it is unlikely that important new documentary evidence relating to Horthy's career will be un-covered in the future. And even if there are notable gaps in the evidence, a detailed study of one of twentieth century Europe's most fascinating statesmen seems justified. After all, a historical figure who painted Francis Joseph's portrait, was tutored by the novelist James Joyce, gained an early reputation as one of Europe's most committed anti-Semites, thwarted the two restoration at-tempts of ex-king Charles, volunteered to serve as the organizer of a crusade to destroy the Soviet Union, contemplated fighting a duel with Thomas Masaryk, collaborated with and at the same time befuddled Hitler, defied Adolf Eichmann, and begged the forgiveness of Joseph Stalin certainly deserves the attention of historians.

I wish to express my profound gratitude to the many librarians and archivists in both Europe and North America who provided valuable assistance during my research trips. The staff of the Interlibrary Loan Office at Langsam Library of the University of Cincinnati was indefatigable in searching for often obscure books and articles. The late György Ránki encouraged me to embark and this project and facilitated my work in Hungary. Two scholars, Leslie Tihany and Ignác Romsics, have read the manuscript and offered invaluable suggestions and corrections. I am also grateful to Beth Rosenfeld for her careful and efficient editorial assistance.

The research for this study was supported by grants or fellowships from the following organizations: American Council of Learned Societies, University of Cincinnati Research Council, and the Charles Phelp Taft Foundation.

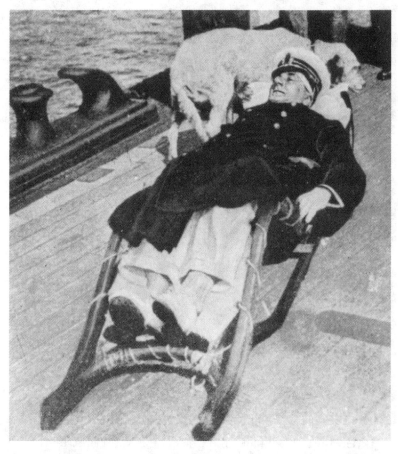

Admiral Horthy, wounded during the Battle of Otranto in 1917.

Horthy as Commander in Chief of the National Army
in Siófok in 1919.

The entry into Budapest, November 1919.

A 1919 poster, designed by Miltiades Manno, promoting
Admiral Horthy as the rescuer of the country.

Horthy presiding over the induction of a new member
of the *Vitézi Rend*.

Miklós Horthy in 1922.

At the hunt with Count Bethlen (right).

The Regent with Gyula Gömbös in the mid-1930s.

Horthy meets Benito Mussolini during his trip to Italy in 1936.

Horthy with Hitler at Kiel in 1938.

The Regent leads the procession into Kassa in November 1938.

"Family Group," a David Low cartoon from November 1940.
(Used with permission of Associated Newspapers/Solo.)

Horthy with Count Pál Teleki.

The Regent with István Horthy after his son's election as vice-regent in 1942.

The Regent with Miklós Kállay (to the immediate right of Horthy).

1

On the Road to Szeged: The Early Years

For Admiral Miklós Horthy, the train ride he took with his family in mid-November 1918 from Vienna to Budapest was a journey into a seemingly bleak and uncharted future. His splendid career as an officer in the Imperial and Royal Austro-Hungarian Navy was at an end. The political and social order that he, and so many of his contemporaries, had come to regard as immutable was collapsing all around him. His only thought was to escape to the security of his estate in Kenderes, a village in southeastern Hungary. Fifty years old at the time, he no doubt hoped to spend his remaining years as a country squire far removed from the political machinations of Budapest and Vienna. But this was not to be, for despite the fact that Admiral Horthy had spent most of his life outside of his native land, he was returning as Hungary's only well-known war hero. Before long many Hungarians were to regard him as the man on horseback who would rescue the country from chaos.

Twenty-six years later, in mid-October 1944, Miklós Horthy was to make the return trip by train from Budapest to Vienna and points westward. This journey was as gloomy and perilous as the first, for Horthy, who had served for nearly a quarter of a century as Hungary's head of state, had just been deposed. Under Hitler's orders, Admiral Horthy, an old and broken man, was being taken as a prisoner to Germany, a country itself only a few months away from catastrophic defeat in war.

The career of Miklós Horthy in the period between these two historic train trips, from 1918 to 1944, is the subject of this study. However, the first fifty years of his life must be examined briefly in order to gain a proper understanding of later events. Miklós Horthy was born

1

on June 18, 1868, in the small village of Kenderes in the heart of the Great Plain of Hungary about seventy miles east of Budapest. With an estate consisting of 1,437 hold (1,026 acres), the Horthy family belonged to the middle ranks of the landowning nobility.[1] For centuries the family had been associated with the Calvinist Church: at least one bishop could be found in the family tree. However, the Horthys were not prominent enough to be listed in a social registry of Hungarian noble families compiled in 1865.

Two aspects of Miklós Horthy's family life are worth noting. Although the Horthy side of the family was Calvinist, his mother's was Roman Catholic. This led to a compromise not uncommon at the time in Hungary: the father and six sons attended the local Calvinist church, while the mother raised the three daughters as Catholics. Miklós thus grew up in and became imbued with a spirit of religious tolerance.

Equally notable was the political orientation of the father. Ever since the sixteenth century, Hungarian political life had revolved around the struggle between two camps: the *labanc* and the *kuruc*. The former, consisting largely of the Catholic aristocracy from the western regions of Hungary, favored cooperation with the Catholic Habsburg dynasty. The latter, primarily Protestant noblemen from eastern parts of the kingdom, fiercely resisted Habsburg policies of centralization and Germanization. Periodic *kuruc* rebellions were suppressed but the Habsburg monarchs were never able to achieve lasting hegemony. The result was an uneasy stalemate that ended finally in 1867, one year before the birth of Miklós Horthy. In a political agreement known as the *Ausgleich*, Francis Joseph, the Habsburg emperor and Hungarian king, granted Hungary a high degree of autonomy. A sizable segment of the Hungarian nobility viewed this compromise with skepticism, but István Horthy, who was active in local politics, became one of its strong proponents. In recognition of his support, the king appointed him a lifetime member of the Upper House of the Hungarian Parliament, a remarkable accolade for a relatively unknown member of the gentry class. In return, István Horthy sent one of his sons, István Jr., to serve as an officer in the Imperial and Royal Army and another, Béla, to serve in the navy.

Like his brothers, Miklós Horthy was sent off at the age of eight to study in a Calvinist boarding school in Debrecen. Two years later he transferred to a school in Sopron. By all accounts he was a mischievous student with little aptitude for learning.[2] The one subject in which he showed promise was language study. In Debrecen he learned French from a tutor, and in Sopron he acquired a mastery of German, which was essential for most careers in public service. What career did István Horthy intend Miklós to enter? Although no definite evidence exists, one writer has made the plausible suggestion that, since his brothers had been assigned to all the other likely professions, Miklós must have been destined for the Calvinist ministry.[3] If so, fate intervened in 1882 when Béla Horthy was killed in a freak accident at the naval academy.

Miklós Horthy immediately expressed the desire to take his brother's place as a naval cadet, and an application was duly submitted. Since 612 boys were competing for only 42 places, István Horthy persuaded the Hungarian Prime Minister, Kálmán Tisza, to intercede with Francis Joseph, suggesting that Miklós would in effect be replacing his brother.[4] This strategy worked, for Miklós was admitted and began his four-year course of study.

Like other military schools in Austria-Hungary and Germany, the naval academy in Fiume on the Adriatic coast stressed iron discipline, esprit de corps, tactics, and rigorous physical training.[5] The cadets were imbued with the concept of *Ehrennotwehr*, the necessity of defending the honor of an officer, the officer corps, or the emperor himself.[6] The motto of the academy, "duty is more important than life itself," was reflected in all activity and instruction. The cadets were rigidly segregated from the outside world, and visits home were infrequent. As a result, an intense camaraderie developed, along with an insistence on loyalty to an officer's unit and to his oath to the emperor. In the curriculum the emphasis was on practical training to the detriment of the liberal arts. In addition, each cadet was inculcated with the Mahanist idea that the greatness of nations was directly related to the naval power they possessed. Although Horthy performed poorly when book learning was required and later admitted that "he was not one of the more zealous students,"[7] he did excel in several other important activities. While his peers were struggling to master Italian and Croatian, required languages for all naval officers, Horthy quickly gained the required fluency. Moreover, his physical agility and mechanical aptitude were outstanding. Only twenty-seven students survived the rigorous training: Miklós Horthy was one of them.[8]

Commissioned in 1886, Miklós Horthy entered a navy then only beginning to make the transition from sail to steam. Over the next two decades he progressed steadily in the ranks, overcoming any handicaps that blocked the way for a Protestant Hungarian in an officer corps that was strongly German and overwhelmingly Catholic. In 1913 he reached the level of line-ship captain (*Linienschiffkapitän*), the equivalent of colonel. In the Dualist era he was the only officer of Magyar origin to attain the rank of a flagship officer.[9] In the evaluation reports prepared by his superiors, Horthy was described as "very diligent" and "very capable in the essential practical skills." He was one of an elite group of some nine hundred officers to achieve the overall rating of "very good" (*sehr gut*).[10]

During periodic naval tours Horthy visited such far-flung lands as Borneo, New Zealand, India, Portugal, England, and Germany, thereby gaining at least a veneer of cosmopolitanism and, somewhere along the way, an elaborate tattoo that covered a large part of his body. Through contacts with British officers at various naval posts across the globe and a pleasant three-month sojourn in London, Horthy developed an "indelible sense of sympathy" for England, a country that seemed to exemplify the values and ideals that the Hungarian noble class had always cherished.[11] Wishing to add English to the languages he had mastered, Horthy took lessons in 1904 while stationed in the Adriatic port of Pola. His tutor was James Joyce, then an obscure writer who was dreaming of publishing his first great novel so that he could escape this "naval Siberia."[12] As always when it came to language study, Horthy was a quick learner. Soon he was speaking English well enough that he could move gracefully in society like an "English gentleman." Among the many British naval officers he came to know in the prewar period, one, Thomas Hohler, whom he met in Constantinople, was to play a significant role in Horthy's later rise to political power.

By the turn of the century, Miklós Horthy had become widely known in the Habsburg naval officer corps for his dutifulness, personal charm, and athletic prowess. At a military olympics held in 1896, Horthy won first prize in tennis and fencing, and third prize in cycling. He was also outstanding in equestrian sports.[13] Horthy and the woman he married in 1901, Magda Purgly, became fixtures in high society during extended stays in Constantinople and at the naval base in Pola. He found time for participation in a succession of hunts, polo matches, bridge parties, regattas, and charity dances. Horthy also became an accomplished pianist and singer. In Pola he came to know Franz Lehár, the band leader of the Imperial and Royal Navy who later became a renowned composer and musician. Years later Horthy recalled with fondness those times when he sang to Lehár's accompaniment on the piano. In the 1920s Lehár was to dedicate one of his parade marches to his former naval friend.[14]

During his tour of duty in Constantinople in 1908–1909, Horthy sent a series of reports to Vienna about civil disruptions in the Ottoman capital. These were read with interest in the Foreign Ministry, General Staff, and Defense Ministry.[15] It did not escape the notice of the naval leadership that Horthy possessed all the qualities of an *udvarképes* officer, that is, one who was capable of conducting himself properly at the imperial court. Thus, when in 1909 one of the coveted positions as aide-de-camp to the emperor became vacant, Horthy became a leading candidate. The major stumbling block was his Protestantism, for the aide-de-camps were expected to take part in many religious services of the Catholic Church. On the urging of his wife, Horthy asked the Hungarian Prime Minister, István Tisza, to intercede on his behalf. Their fathers had been political allies, and Horthy himself had met Tisza on several occasions while serving as an interpreter in Vienna. Perhaps because of Tisza's intercession, or perhaps because Francis Joseph wished to heal the wounds from a recent flare-up in his relations with the Hungarians, Horthy's application for the position was approved.[16]

Horthy's five years of duty as aide-de-camp were, in his own words, "the finest of my life."[17] Aside from having to be at his post by 4:00 A.M. to serve the early-rising emperor, Horthy found the duties to be far from onerous. The task of greeting and socializing with foreign dignitaries waiting to be received in audience was effortless for the gracious and polyglot Horthy, who now spoke six foreign languages (German, French, English, Spanish, Italian, and Croatian) with reasonable fluency. He also accompanied Francis Joseph on horseback at the hunt, on summer vacation, at the opera, and at numerous court activities. Although the aloof and laconic monarch spoke few words to his aides beyond "good morning" and "good evening," a bond of affection seems to have developed between him and the much younger Miklós Horthy. Having much free time on his hands, Horthy took up painting and secretly worked on a portrait of the emperor. The painting pleased Francis Joseph and remained one of Horthy's most cherished possessions in later years. What also remained with him was an admiration for the emperor/king's leadership style, which as regent of Hungary he would later strive to emulate.[18]

As aide-de-camp Horthy had the opportunity to meet and speak with the leading personalities of the Dual Monarchy, including Francis Ferdinand, then heir to the throne. It was an exhilarating experience to observe firsthand the inner workings of the Habsburg State, one of Europe's great powers. Horthy was present when some of the great issues of the day were being discussed and decided. He was also able to cultivate ties with István Tisza and other Hungarian politicians, such as István Bethlen, a count from Transylvania whose family was related by marriage to the Horthys. During these years, Horthy and his wife were frequent guests of Archduke Charles, the emperor's nephew, who at the time seemed to have little prospect of ever ascending the throne. When the emperor insisted that Horthy accompany him to Charles's wedding in 1911, he was the only person present who was not of royal blood. This early friendship between Horthy and Archduke Charles was to have important and, ultimately, tragic consequences in later years.

By coincidence Miklós Horthy's tour of duty at the imperial court coincided almost precisely with the years spent in Vienna by the young drifter Adolf Hitler. Of course, the two men moved in different worlds, but Horthy must have noticed some of the political and cultural phenomena that were making such a deep impression on the future German dictator. The Austrian legislature, the Reichsrat, was frequently the scene of violent obstruction and occasional pandemonium, a symptom of the growing Slav challenge to German ascendancy.[19] Such demagogues as Georg von Schönerer and Karl Lueger, the mayor of Vienna, were forming new political movements based in large part on popular resentment against the Jews. Artists and philosophers, like Gustav Klimt, Oskar Kokoschka, Sigmund Freud, and Arnold Schönberg, many of whom were Jews, were experimenting with radical new techniques that shocked the establishment throughout the Habsburg Empire.

It is difficult to determine what impression these developments in fin de siècle Vienna made on Miklós Horthy, since his life at the imperial court was to an extent isolated from the outside world. It is known, however, that as an amateur painter he was appalled at the unconventional techniques and subjects of the revolutionary movement known as the Viennese Secession.[20] Like most Habsburg military officers, Horthy remained aloof from the activities of political parties and movements. It seems that close association with Francis Joseph and the court merely strengthened in him a conservative political orientation that was characteristic of the upper classes throughout the Habsburg lands. Like others of his social background, Horthy harbored deep suspicions of social experimentation and democracy while extolling the virtues of social order, religion, and authoritarian government. As a result he viewed the Social Democratic party, the party of the workers, with contempt. When Horthy accompanied the emperor/king on a visit to Budapest in 1912, the imperial carriage was unable to proceed because the road was clogged by a demonstration organized by the Socialists against the Tisza government. Horthy found this to be a reprehensible political tactic and brazen disrespect for His Majesty.[21]

No direct evidence survives of Horthy's attitude toward Jews in this period, although later developments suggest that he probably shared some of the anti-Semitic attitudes prevalent in the officer corps. It is unlikely that he knew many Jews personally, although it is possible that had contacts with some of fairly large number of Jewish reserve naval officers. The most profound influence on Horthy in this respect was no doubt the emperor himself, who showed relative tolerance toward Jews and declared that he would permit no Jew-baiting in his lands. In fact, in prewar Austria and Hungary Jews enjoyed civil liberties and were provided many opportunities to excel in the world of finance, the professions, and the arts. Francis Joseph granted noble titles to a number of Jews who had made important contributions to economic life. Like his revered king, István Tisza, and most other prominent members of the conservative political establishment in prewar Hungary, Miklós Horthy seemed to recognize and appreciate the valuable role played by assimilated Jews in Budapest and Vienna.[22]

The assassination of Francis Ferdinand on June 28, 1914, not only brought to an end Horthy's halcyon days at the imperial court, but also set into motion forces that would eventually destroy the social and political order he regarded as natural and divinely ordained. But in terms of his personal career, the Great War was a boon to Miklós Horthy, for it catapulted him to the highest levels of the naval leadership. For the duration of the war the Imperial and Royal Navy was bottled up in the Adriatic Sea, a consequence of the decision by Italy, an ally of Austria-Hungary before the war, to join the enemy camp. Like his colleagues in the naval officer corps, Horthy regarded Italy's action as despicable and dishonorable, the worst kind of opportunism. He vowed that he would never again have anything to do with Italians, would in fact never again shake the hand of an Italian.[23] Italy joined the Entente powers, England and France, in sealing the Straits of Otranto and preventing easy access to the Mediterranean by the ships and submarines of the Central powers. As commander of the *Novara*, the fastest and most modern armed cruiser in the Habsburg Navy, Horthy was given the mission of towing a German submarine through the blockade. In May 1915, through a combination of good luck and a clever ruse, Captain Horthy carried out the assignment successfully and was awarded the German Iron Cross, third class.[24] It was largely this exploit that gained for Horthy the reputation as a bold and decisive officer. Buoyed by this success, Horthy pressed for further offensive action, but the ideas and initiatives he proposed could not be implemented because of the continuing success of the Entente blockade.[25]

For Horthy there thus followed a period of inactivity, broken in November 1916 by the sad duty of attendance at the funeral of Francis Joseph, whose long reign of sixty-eight years was finally at an end. A month later Horthy was in Budapest for the coronation of King Charles, who, as will be seen, held Horthy in high regard. Once back in Pola, Horthy requested authorization to attempt a breakthrough of the blockade at the Straits of Otranto. This was finally granted, and Horthy was placed in command of a flotilla involved in what came to be known as the Battle of Otranto, the greatest sea engagement in the Adriatic during World War I. The results of the battle were only a partial and ephemeral success in weakening the blockade, but Horthy's stature was greatly enhanced by the stories of his heroic actions that soon began to circulate. At the height of the battle, the *Novara* was under heavy fire from British cruisers. The second in command was killed by shell fire and Horthy received a severe leg wound. Though debilitated by his wound, Horthy continued for three hours to direct operations from a stretcher.[26]

Newspapers in Budapest and Vienna were soon printing photographs of Horthy and trumpeting him as the "Hero of Otranto." After the war, accounts of Horthy's exploits were embellished and grew to legendary proportions, which later led some more critical writers to attempt to debunk the myths of the "Horthy cult."[27] Nonetheless, the public acclaim of Horthy in 1917 was not artificially generated. Given the frustrating limitations under which the Habsburg Navy was forced to operate during the war, the commander of even a modestly successful naval engagement could find himself viewed as a glorious hero.

Enemy officers in the Battle of Otranto regarded Captain Horthy as an honorable and chivalrous adversary. Horthy made every effort to avoid unnecessary loss of life. When incapacitated enemy ships were encountered, an opportunity was given for all aboard to abandon ship and be taken prisoners on Austro-Hungarian vessels. Prisoners were treated courteously, and when several Entente officers died while "guests" on the *Novara*, Horthy arranged for a burial with full military honors and flowers.[28] Horthy thus espoused and practiced the kind of gentlemanly chivalry among aristocratic military officers during World War I that Jean Renoir later memorialized in his film *La Grande Illusion*.

After a period of recuperation in Kenderes, Horthy returned to active duty on February 1, 1918, as commander of the *Prinz Eugen*, one of the three largest battleships in the fleet. This was a major assignment for a mere line-ship captain. Horthy assumed command at a time when war weariness and discontent had reached dangerous levels. Word of a strike by harbor workers in Pola was sparking isolated disturbances among the sailors of the fleet. The *Prinz Eugen* was not immune: to protest the poor quality of the food, groups of sailors created a disturbance that threatened to get out of hand. Captain Horthy immediately summoned all sailors to the deck and announced his intention to maintain iron discipline. A petty officer who did not show proper respect for Horthy promptly received a sharp blow to the side of the head. When a sailor jumped in to aid the petty officer, Horthy shoved him forcefully down nearby stairs. The commander then dismissed his men with the warning that they should not be lead astray by agitators.[29]

Horthy's stern measures worked, for his ship was one of the few in the Habsburg fleet that did not experience a mutiny. This did not escape the notice of the young emperor, who was coming to the conclusion that the growing national and political discontent in the navy could be dealt with only by new, more vigorous leadership.[30] The action he took on February 27 was unprecedented: Miklós Horthy was promoted to Rear Admiral and named the new Commander in Chief of the navy. Passed over were the eighteen admirals who were senior in rank to Horthy, not to mention thirty line-ship captains. Word of Horthy's nomination "exploded like a bomb" in the naval officer corps.[31] Sensing that there might be resentment over the favored treatment of the fifty-year-old Horthy, Charles issued a pronouncement in which he explained that "the gravity of the situation makes it essential that younger men fill some of the high commands of the navy."[32]

When Admiral Horthy took over command the navy remained immobilized by the Entente blockade. Believing that continued inactivity only promoted rebelliousness among the sailors, Horthy ordered a renewed attempt to break out into the Mediterranean Sea. The futility of the operation soon became evident and Horthy was forced to call it off. In any case, the attempted mutinies of early 1918 were not repeated later in the year. In May Admiral Horthy was present at the execution of two sailors who had instigated the mutinies. He delivered a harsh speech to the assembled sailors, who were picked from all the major ships to witness the execution. Horthy praised those sailors who had died for their fatherland, but branded the two mutineers as traitors "who must be done away with, just as a doctor removes cancerous areas from the body of a sick man."[33] It was this speech and Horthy's reputation for ruthless discipline that led the leaders of antiwar groups, especially the Socialists, to regard him as one of the chief representatives of an oppressive regime that had brought four years of misery to the great masses of people.

By the end of the summer it was becoming clear that Danubian Europe was on the verge of cataclysmic changes. Bulgaria's withdrawal from the war was a prelude to the collapse of the Habsburg armed forces. On October 6 a South Slav council was established in Zagreb, the capital of Croatia. Ordinary soldiers began deserting their units and returning to their homes. It was only with the greatest effort that Admiral Horthy was able to contain the revolutionary spirit on the ships of the fleet. Several times during October he reported to Vienna that unless drastic measures were taken, an explosion was likely. Austrian and Hungarian sailors were deserting and soon only South Slavs would be on the ships. Emperor Charles procrastinated, hoping to find some last-minute solution that would preserve the empire of the Habsburgs. Finally, however, there was no option. On October 30 Horthy was instructed to hand over the fleet to the new South Slav State. As one final gesture of his esteem, Charles at the same time promoted Horthy to Vice Admiral.

October 31 was a sad day indeed for the Commander in Chief of the Habsburg fleet. Minutes before the ceremonial transfer of the fleet, Horthy telegraphed one last time to Charles, his Supreme War Lord: while the red-white-red flag of the empire still waved "proud and undefeated" over his ship, he wished to assure His Majesty of his "unshakable loyalty."[34] Horthy thereupon signed the papers of transfer on the flagship *Viribus Unitis*. As he debarked with the war flag under his arm, he could hear the cheers and the twenty-one gun salute as the South Slav flag was raised.[35]

On that same day momentous events were occurring in Hungary. King Charles appointed a new Prime Minister, Count Mihály Károlyi, the leader of a loose coalition of parties opposed to the war and in favor of major social and political reforms. At the same time irate revolutionary soldiers broke into the home of István Tisza, a hated symbol of the old order, and murdered him. By the next day, November 1, it was clear that Hungary was making a full break with the Habsburg dynasty and embarking on an independent national existence.

Reports of these dramatic events in Hungary must have caused Miklós Horthy grave concern. If his mentor, István Tisza, could meet such a horrible fate, his own safety was by no means assured. Thus his main objective now was to return safely to Kenderes with his family. First, however, he had to make a final report to his king and Supreme War Lord. A special train was secured by Horthy to transport naval officers and their families to Vienna. In fact, all across the Habsburg Empire high-ranking officers were now gravitating to the imperial capital. Many were confronted by a unique dilemma: they had spent their entire adult lives in the international milieu of the Habsburg officer corps and now found it difficult to switch their loyalty to one of the new national states. Some did not feel themselves to be Hungarians, Czechs, Croatians, or Austrians but simply subjects of the Habsburg monarch.[36] The problem was that the monarch no longer had any territory over which he ruled.

For Miklós Horthy this dilemma was not as acute as it was for some of his cohorts. It is true that less than a year earlier Horthy had scolded a journalist who suggested that the "Hero of Otranto" often turned his thoughts from the Habsburg Navy to his Hungarian fatherland, the home of his ancestors. "Remember," Horthy said, "that if my Supreme War Lord is in Baden [the naval headquarters] then my fatherland is also there."[37] Now, however, the Imperial and Royal Navy no longer existed. In Hungary Horthy could at least spend his days supervising the affairs of his estate. His spoken Hungarian might be a bit rusty, but it was still serviceable.

The final act of the dutiful commander of the navy occurred on November 8 at Schönbrunn Palace in Vienna. Neither Charles nor Horthy could contain his grief as the admiral reported that he had surrendered the fleet. With his body trembling and tears flowing, Horthy spontaneously raised his right hand and pledged that he would remain loyal to his king until his last breath. "I will never rest," he vowed, "until I have restored your Majesty to his thrones in Vienna and Budapest." Later that day Horthy described his audience with Charles as "the most tragic event of his life."[38] The next meeting, and the last, between ex-king Charles and Admiral Horthy would occur in March 1921 in quite different circumstances; strangely, Horthy was to use almost the same words to describe that meeting.

Horthy now journeyed with his family by train to Budapest. Embittered and disconsolate, he lamented the fact that everything on which he had based his ideals since his youth was now destroyed and betrayed. He wondered if it would be possible to "make something out of this chaos?" Echoing an idea that had already taken strong root in the officer corps, Horthy suggested that the most important task in Hungary was the liberation of the country from all alien racial elements, especially the Jews, who, he believed, had instigated the revolution that was now unfolding in Vienna and Budapest.[39]

Horthy was appalled at the state of affairs he observed in Budapest. The new government, a republic, had come to power on a wave of revulsion against the war and the discredited prewar regime. Count Mihály Károlyi, a maverick scion of one of the richest and best known aristocratic families in Hungary, hoped to rally all progressive forces in support of his program of democratic elections, land reform, and the maintenance of Hungary's territorial integrity on a federalist basis. Unfortunately, none of his major goals was to be achieved. The conditions were hardly auspicious. Hungary lacked a large urban middle class that could provide leadership and support for a democracy based on the West European pattern. Defeat in war had let loose nationalist forces that were tearing apart the thousand-year-old multinational Kingdom of Hungary. Pent-up grievances of workers and peasants were being expressed without any sense of social restraint. Budapest was inundated with refugees who were fleeing from those parts of Hungary under military occupation by neighboring countries. As one historian has aptly expressed it, the Károlyi government had "inherited a shipwreck and dreamt it had the wind in its sails."[40]

The problems of the new regime were exacerbated by its failure to form a reliable military force. Károlyi's Minister of Defense, Béla Linder, made the mistake of announcing that he "did not want to see any more soldiers," a statement that accelerated the collapse of the army and the erosion of military discipline. The decision to entrust military affairs to soldier councils dominated by Socialist activists further reduced the authority of officers.

For Horthy, who was blind to any fault of the old regime and incapable of appreciating even the good intentions of the new regime, these revolutionary changes had transformed Budapest into a strange, alien city. As he passed through the capital in mid-November he noticed only hooligan bands, terrorized citizens, closed shops, and harassment of military officers.[41] He was relieved to reach the safety of his estate in Kenderes: there, at least, the traditional social order had not yet been overturned. The Hungarian countryside still retained some characteristics of rural Europe in the late Middle Ages. Two-thirds of the land remained in the hands of the Roman Catholic Church and some two thousand aristocratic families. A small number of peasants owned land, but approximately three million worked on estates under conditions that in some ways resembled that of medieval serfs. The land hunger of the Hungarian peasants was not satisfied by the new government, although Count Károlyi did divide up one of his estates and distribute parcels to the local peasants. The government in Budapest, beset by a multitude of problems, simply did not have the time to draw up and implement a program of land reform.

Horthy spent the next few months supervising the affairs of the modest estate of 699 hold (500 acres) he had inherited. He was apparently well received in Kenderes, where his neighbors marveled at how quickly the returning war hero became a "model farmer" (*példás gazda*). In the newspapers he read with dismay of the advance of the Romanian, Czechoslovak, and South Slav armies and the military occupation of Slovakia, Transylvania, and a large part of southern Hungary. Such ancient cities as Kassa, Pozsony, Kolozsvár, and Temesvár, which Horthy and other Hungarian nationalists regarded as quintessentially Magyar, were now administered by nations that Hungarians had long regarded as culturally inferior. The government in Budapest seemed incapable of offering any effective military or diplomatic resistance to the dismemberment of the country.

For many months after the collapse of the old order in Hungary, those who opposed the revolutionary changes remained impotent. The landowners rarely strayed from the relative safety of their estates, and military officers tried to be inconspicuous, fearful of being insulted or even assaulted in the streets. Interestingly, even in the first days of the Károlyi regime some officers regarded Admiral Horthy as a possible leader of a counterrevolution. As early as November 1918, a rumor had circulated in officer circles in Budapest that Horthy would soon enter the capital with a contingent of sailors and "send the government packing."[42] When Horthy did journey unobtrusively to Budapest in early 1919, he met with a number of military officers opposed to the new government, including Captain Gyula Gömbös, president of the Association of Hungarian National Defense (Magyar Országos Véderő Egyesület), known by its acronym, MOVE. Deploring the poor organization of the counterrevolution, Gömbös urged Horthy to assume leadership of the whole movement. This Horthy refused, arguing that the plans outlined to him were bold but impracticable and that "it would be a long time before action could be taken."[43]

In the meantime, however, conditions in Budapest were becoming even more turbulent. Finally in March 1919, Károlyi, realizing that his effort to prevent the dismemberment of his country by pursuing a conciliatory policy toward the Western powers had failed, yielded power to the Social Democrats.[44] However, a radicalized majority of that party decided to join forces with the Communists. On March 21 a Hungarian Soviet Republic was formed with Béla Kun, a former prisoner of war in Russia who had become a fervent convert to bolshevism, as the leading commissar. Hungary thus became the second country in Europe to come under the direction of Marxist revolutionaries intent on building a dictatorship of the proletariat.

The Soviet Republic of Béla Kun lasted only 133 days, but this brief episode left an indelible imprint on the minds of Hungarians like Miklós Horthy. The program of Kun and his small cadre of fellow activists was, according to one historian, "a bizarre experiment of doctrinaire war communism."[45] Even while the new Hungarian Red Army was sent to try to evict the Czechoslovaks from Slovakia and the Romanians from Transylvania, the government in Budapest issued a constant stream of revolutionary decrees. The passion and intensity of the Hungarian Communists were akin to that of the Jacobins in the French Revolution. In their enthusiasm to cure the ills of Hungarian society, the young urban intellectuals who formed the nucleus of the Soviet government devised some ingenious plans. But these projects for social reform were overshadowed by a severe press censorship and a furious campaign against groups identified with the old regime. Whole categories of private property were confiscated by the state: horses, carriages, stamp collections, gold coins, jewelry, stocks, and bonds.[46]

In March 1919, a significant portion of Hungarian society may well have supported the new government on the theory that since Károlyi's pro-Western orientation had miscarried, a pro-Russian policy was the only remaining possibility for the preservation of Hungary's prewar boundaries. Many former officers agreed to serve in the Red Army because it seemed a potentially effective instrument to regain those territories occupied by Hungary's hated neighbors. In fact, there were some temporary successes in Slovakia, but the Allied powers in Paris remained hostile, and the tide soon turned against the Red Army. What little support ordinary Hungarians had given the Kun government in March quickly evaporated. By early summer a "popular counterrevolution" or "Magyar Vendée" had engulfed the Hungarian countryside.[47]

With the arrogance of urban intellectuals who, like Karl Marx, thought in terms of the "idiocy of rural life," Kun and his colleagues decided that the land reform demanded by the peasants should not be carried out by breaking up the estates, a procedure Lenin had shrewdly approved in Russia. Instead, it seemed more efficient to nationalize the estates, in some cases leaving them to be supervised by the same overseers who had been in place in prewar days. Their hunger for land unsatisfied and their traditional religious faith ridiculed by atheists from the city, the previously passive Hungarian peasantry now turned resoundingly against the revolutionary government. By June Hungary was on the brink of civil war between town and country.[48] The response of the Soviet leadership was to intensify the application of compulsion and terror that had been an implicit part of the government's program since the beginning. An unsavory gang of thugs known as the "Lenin Boys" inspired widespread fear with their *razzias* and the practice of seizing prominent citizens as hostages for ransom. In all, some five hundred Hungarians, the majority of them peasants, fell victim to the subsequent "Red Terror." Such brutal state-inspired terrorism had no precedent in recent Hungarian history.[49]

For Miklós Horthy the unfolding events of the Soviet Republic were like a horrible nightmare. Since Kenderes was on the fringes of the area firmly controlled by the Budapest government, Horthy and his family were for a long time untouched by the harassment or intimidation of the Budapest commissars, although one of his brothers, István, was imprisoned in Budapest for several months. However, occasionally on a Sunday afternoon Communist agitators did make their way from Budapest to Kenderes, where they urged the peasants to take action against their oppressors, the landowners, by seizing manor houses and land as property of the proletariat. Apparently the local peasants remained unmoved by these exhortations, which Horthy interpreted as proof that the farm workers were basically content with the traditional order. It is possible, however, that Horthy (or perhaps his wife) suffered some embarrassment or affront in a confrontation with one of these Communist agitators. No such incident is reported in his memoirs, but the vehemence of Horthy's lifelong crusade against bolshevism suggests that personal revenge may have been an important factor.

Horthy's loathing for the Communists increased with each fresh report from Budapest. Despite its claim to be a champion of Hungarian national interests, the Soviet Republic adopted a rigid inter-

nationalist stance that seemed calculated to offend national sentiments. The Hungarian national anthem was banned and the display of the national colors declared to be a crime. Statues of
national heroes were torn down in public ceremonies. Horthy was
particularly outraged when he learned that a famous statue of
Francis Joseph had been smashed to bits.[50]

In the isolation of his estate, Miklós Horthy pondered what had
occurred in Hungary since the end of the war. Politically unsophisticated and only superficially acquainted with European or
Hungarian history, Horthy struggled to make some sense of the
extraordinary, kaleidoscopic series of events. Like many other ordinary Hungarians, Horthy concluded that the Károlyi government and the Soviet Republic were virtually synonymous. Both
were horrible aberrations that brought only misery, suffering, and
terror to the country. By his ineptness the naive Károlyi had
served as a kind of "Jewish stooge" and had facilitated Hungary's
"slide down the slope of Bolshevik chaos."[51] Similarly, Social
Democrats and Bolsheviks seemed hardly distinguishable to Horthy. Both seemed perversely intent on attacking cherished national
symbols and the Christian churches. Their leaders were degener-
ates and riffraff who were unfit to manage the affairs of a country.

One other thing seemed quite clear to Horthy: the revolutionary
events in Hungary since November 1918 were part of a gigantic
Jewish conspiracy. Historians have in fact confirmed that Jews
held a remarkably large number of leadership positions in the Socialist and Communist parties of Hungary. Béla Kun and twenty
out of twenty-six of his commissars were from Jewish families,
although most would have agreed with Kun who proclaimed: "My
father was a Jew but I am no longer one, for I became a socialist
and a Communist."[52] Why so many young Jewish intellectuals
were attracted to the revolutionary movements in Hungary is still
a subject of scholarly debate, but for Miklós Horthy in the spring
of 1919 no special analysis was called for. As early as November of
the previous year he had suspected that Jews were somehow responsible for the loss of the war and for the revolutionary upheavals. Events of the past six months seemed to provide him with
ample evidence to support this belief.

One thing about the last year of revolution in Hungary continued to perplex Horthy. How was it that people who should know
better were persuaded to do incredible things? A count (Mihály

Károlyi) to give away his land? A military officer (Béla Linder) to preach pacifism? Sons of the richest Hungarian industrialists to have no respect for private property? University graduates to be willing to disown a thousand years of Hungarian history? Faced by such bewildering developments, Horthy could only conclude that communism was some sort of mysterious and diabolical force that had entered Hungary and spread like an invidious poison. Extraordinary efforts would surely be required to eliminate that poison from the body of the nation.

This was Horthy's frame of mind on May 9, 1919, when a messenger arrived at his home with news that counterrevolutionary groups were organizing in two cities, Vienna and Arad, which was located about seventy miles to the southeast of Kenderes. The leader of the Arad group, Count Gyula Károlyi (a conservative cousin of Mihály Károlyi), was requesting Horthy's support and participation.[53] The idea of enlisting Admiral Horthy in the struggle against the Soviet Republic had in fact occurred independently both to Count István Bethlen, president of a newly established Anti-Bolshevik Committee in Vienna and to ex-king Charles, now in Swiss exile. Horthy seemed to many prominent Hungarians to be a logical choice for commander of an armed force to rid Hungary of Bolshevism, since, as one of his admirers put it, Horthy was "the most prominent of the heroes left alive after the war."[54]

Before Horthy could decide what action to take, he learned that because of pressure from the Romanians the Arad government had been moved to the southern Hungarian city of Szeged, which was under French occupation. In late May he resolved to make the perilous fifty-mile journey to Szeged. Traveling part of the way by carriage and the rest by train, Horthy arrived unannounced in Szeged on May 30. For Count Károlyi, who was in the process of forming a Cabinet, the arrival of Horthy was a godsend. For several weeks there had been a good deal of wrangling in Szeged over the selection of a Minister of National Defense. Two likely choices, General Zoltán Szabó and General Sándor Belitska, were having difficulties in traveling to Szeged. Captain Gyula Gömbös, who had arrived as the representative of the Anti-Bolshevik Committee in Vienna, supported Horthy. Since, however, there were rumors that Horthy had been imprisoned or perhaps even executed by the Communists, a competition had developed among the officers of lesser rank in Szeged. In mid-May one of them, a colonel, was convinced he would soon be named Minister of National Defense.[55]

On May 30 Gyula Károlyi had no hesitation in asking Horthy to join his Cabinet and to serve as *fővezér*, or Commander in Chief, of the National Army soon to be assembled. As a Vice Admiral, Horthy was clearly the senior officer now residing in Szeged.[56] Moreover, he embodied the idea of continuity with Hungary's military past and, because of his close connections with the two most recent Hungarian heads of state, would bring to the provisional government a sense of legitimacy. Somewhat surprisingly, Horthy asked for a week's time to respond to Károlyi's offer. Károlyi agreed and left the portfolio of the Minister of Defense temporarily vacant. Horthy returned to Kenderes in order to discuss the matter with his wife. His main concern seems to have been the safety of his family, since they could not easily travel to Szeged. Yet if they remained in Kenderes they might be victims of retaliation by the Communists. An additional problem was posed by the Romanian Army, which was advancing westward and could be expected to impose harsh measures in occupied Hungary. Finally, a decision was reached. Horthy would join the Szeged government, and his family would abandon their estate and travel north to stay with friends in Debrecen.

During Horthy's one-week absence a mood of anticipation and optimism developed among the young officers who had assembled in large numbers in Szeged. To one of their spokesmen, Miklós Kozma, Horthy was a natural symbol of authority: "the hero of the *Novara*, victorious in many battles, the admiral who had never been defeated, who had crushed the sailors' mutiny—this was the man the officer corps needed."[57] The officers were thus jubilant when Horthy arrived back in Szeged on June 6 after riding horseback through the night to avoid the Romanians. He reported immediately to Count Károlyi, who was conducting a Cabinet meeting. Striding across the room in his trench coat and cap, Horthy made his dramatic announcement: "I couldn't sit in Kenderes listening to the grass rustling in the wind, when my poor fatherland lies in ruins. It has been a difficult inner conflict, but I have come. I accept the responsibility. I am at your command."[58] Horthy was immediately sworn in and introduced to his colleagues in the Cabinet, who were all anti-Communist but otherwise spanned the political spectrum from liberal to conservative. Horthy was to develop a particularly close friendship with the Foreign Minister, Count Pál Teleki, a geographer of European renown.

Admiral Horthy's chief task as Minister of Defense was to build a new National Army to be dispatched at the appropriate time for a march on Budapest and the liberation of Hungary from Communist rule. This project proceeded slowly in the summer of 1919, largely because of the ambivalent attitude of the French government. On the one hand, such French military commanders as Marshal Foch and General Berthelot dreamed of a grand military campaign to overthrow the Communist governments in both Hungary and Russia. Clearly a powerful Hungarian National Army would be a useful weapon in such a campaign. On the other hand, French liberal and democratic sentiments were offended by the "reactionary" and "pro-German" character of the Szeged government, what with so many aristocrats and an admiral who had close connections with the Habsburg dynasty. The result was that the local French commanders pursued toward the Szeged movement a policy that vacillated between strict and benevolent neutrality. A small army could be raised, but not by conscription. Only a limited amount of weapons was made available, although a few airplanes were brought in from Vienna and placed at Horthy's disposal. As a result, by mid-July the size of the National Army reached only about 5000, half of whom were officers. Recruitment among the landed peasants in the Szeged area proved disappointing.[59] Since the Hungarian Red Army numbered some 200,000, it was clear that Horthy's White Army (as many were now calling it, drawing a parallel with the White Armies in the Russian civil war) would not soon be combat-ready. Horthy did take steps to emphasize the "national" and traditional character of his army. The soldiers were equipped with braided caps named after István Bocskai, a famed Transylvanian prince. These Bocskai caps were ornamented with a white crane feather, which became the emblem of the Hungarian White Army.

There are indications that some of the higher-ranking army officers were a bit uncomfortable about having an admiral as their superior officer. Horthy disarmed his potential critics by his sincerity and self-deprecating humor, as can be seen in his instructions to the chief of staff, Colonel Kálmán Shvoy: "Do your work to the best of your abilities, because I know as much about land armies as the seat I'm sitting on."[60] Much of the organizational work was delegated to the energetic and efficient Gyula Gömbös, who served as secretary of state in the Defense Ministry. In mid-May Horthy joined Count Teleki on a diplomatic mission to Belgrade, where they assured the American Minister of their intention of ousting the Bolsheviks and establishing a truly representative government elected under a broadly democratic franchise.[61] Otherwise, Horthy's role was in large part ceremonial. He was the symbol of authority, responsible for maintaining discipline and inspiring confidence and optimism.

In both military and civilian circles Admiral Horthy's prestige and popularity rose day by day during the early summer of 1919. In the opinion of one observer of these events, Horthy's "splendid appearance, informal manner, knowledge of foreign languages, and comfortable anecdotal style" made a favorable impression and attracted to him a large retinue of supporters.[62] Another eyewitness recorded how he charmed "young and old alike" with his "scintillating spirit" and "warm conviviality." Long into the night he would play the piano and regale his company with tales of the sea, heroic episodes from the war, and humorous anecdotes about Hungarian peasants and their fear of the sea. Some stories brought tears to Horthy's eyes and to those of his companions.[63] Horthy was clearly a spellbinding raconteur. No one seemed to mind that he spoke Hungarian with a German accent, or that he occasionally used German and even English phrases when the correct Hungarian words did not come to mind. Perhaps this merely added to his image as a cosmopolitan gentleman.

Among the workers of Szeged, who in the early summer of 1919 conducted a twenty-day strike to protest the reactionary nature of Gyula Károlyi's government, Horthy's image must have been somewhat less exalted. No doubt there was some grumbling about the amount of time Horthy and his colleagues devoted to their recreations: daily swims and sailing on the Tisza River, horseback riding, socializing in the coffee houses, card games. As one local resident later wrote, "Never before had so much bridge been played in Szeged." Moreover, despite his earlier assurances to the American Minister in Belgrade, both publicly and privately Horthy made no effort to conceal his contempt for democracy. In a newspaper interview in July he declared that "the people have no aptitude for choosing or electing their own leaders." Democracy, he suggested, would work only if humans were demigods.[64]

Equally disturbing to proponents of liberalism and moderate socialism was the extremist right-wing spirit that seemed to pervade the National Army over which Horthy presided. This was an army top-heavy with young officers, most in their twenties, who like condottieri had flocked to Szeged from all corners of the old Kingdom of Hungary. The most prominent of them (Gömbös, Kozma, Ostenburg, Prónay) were captains. In social origin most of these officers were from the lower gentry, a group that in the turmoil of the postwar period was undergoing a thorough radicalization. Many had been forced to flee the Communist authorities or the new and often hostile administrations in Slovakia, Transylvania, and other fringe areas of Hungary. Deeply despondent and, in some cases, living in penury, these men were open to radical and violent solutions, to a venting of their rage against those they believed to be responsible for their personal plight and for the dismemberment of their country.[65] In Szeged the fury of these men acted as a catalyst in the formation of a powerful political force based on a fierce nationalism, anti-Semitism, anticommunism, militarism, and irredentism. Above all, the extreme rightist officers showed a propensity for violence and terror as a political weapon. The war experiences of these officers had inured them to violence and had made death a commonplace event.

Although the "Szeged idea," as the vaguely articulated ideology of the movement came to be called, was a new phenomenon in Hungarian political life, it in many ways paralleled the programs of early Fascist or national Socialist groups emerging in Central and Eastern Europe. In Hungary these radical right-wingers shared a broad set of basic political assumptions with the traditional conservatives, who in 1919 were to be found mainly in Vienna working under the tutelage of Count István Bethlen. But the proponents of the "Szeged idea" were distinctly more militant in their rhetoric and methods. Their nationalism was more intense and intolerant, their anti-Semitism more invidious and vulgar, their political methodology more open to demagoguery and the techniques of modern mass politics. Above all they showed a willingness to employ violence and terror as political weapons that was for the most part alien to those Hungarian conservatives who had retained some of Count István Tisza's limited commitment to liberal principles.[66]

To all appearances Admiral Horthy should have been in the

camp of the traditional conservatives, which in Szeged included such aristocrats as Gyula Károlyi and Pál Teleki. But the dramatic events of the past year had psychologically predisposed him to embrace the radical plans and ideas of the younger officers with whom he now came in contact. Later events would demonstrate that, despite the stern image he projected as a man of decisiveness, Horthy could sometimes be remarkably malleable: those who had the opportunity to explain things to him personally had a good chance of persuading him of the desirability and feasibility of their policies. In a political sense Horthy arrived in Szeged as a *tabula rasa*, a clean slate. Certainly his mind was filled with all sorts of political assumptions and prejudices, but he had formed no definite plan for action. It was thus significant that in the summer of 1919 such men as Gyula Gömbös and Pál Prónay had almost constant access to their commander and became his most trusted advisors. In the cafes and during staff talks Horthy's ears were filled with the emotional rhetoric and conspiratorial plans of the radical right-wingers. They assured Horthy that he was correct in his suspicion that the Jews, Communists, and Socialists were the cause of all of Hungary's misfortunes. What Hungary needed was a process of "purification": those peasants, workers, intellectuals, and others who had succumbed to the lure of the Communists would have to be punished. Their aim was to unleash in Hungary a "White Terror" that would be a just retaliation for Béla Kun's "Red Terror."

Gyula Gömbös seemed particularly adept at playing on Horthy's darkest impulses and frustrations. A German-Hungarian from a middle-class family of modest means, Gömbös had served as a general staff officer in Vienna during the war. However, even then his anti-Habsburg sentiments were well-known, for he publicly advocated the creation of an independent Hungarian Army. After the war Gömbös emerged as the chief spokesman for the myth that Hungary's defeat could be blamed only on incompetent statesmen and assorted traitors from within, especially the Jews. Through the efforts of Gömbös and his like-minded fellow officers, the new National Army was permeated by a rabid anti-Semitism, which found its expression in placards, pamphlets, newspaper articles, speeches, and a general call for the emancipation of Hungary from international Jewry.[67] Gömbös gained prominence in the atmosphere of intrigue and conspiracy that characterized the

Hungarian counterrevolutionary movement. In Szeged he quickly became Horthy's protégé and carried out much of the organizational work in the creation of the National Army. It seems, however, that the two men never became intimate friends. Perhaps Horthy was too sensitive to their differences in social origin, age, and rank. But Gömbös was able, for a time at least, to sharpen Horthy's resentment of the Jews. More important, he was perhaps the first to detect in Horthy a spark of political ambition, despite the admiral's repeated assertions that, as a military officer, he was aloof from political life. Throughout 1919 Gömbös was to work quietly but assiduously to fan that spark.

Another captain who had an important influence on Horthy in Szeged was Baron Pál Prónay, whose social background closely resembled Horthy's. It was Prónay who convinced Horthy in early June that the core of the National Army should be highly disciplined officer detachments.[68] As commander of his own detachment, Prónay was intent on launching a campaign to rid Hungary of the "Budapest spirit," which in his opinion comprised Zionists, Freemasons, Liberals, Communists, and other assorted enemies. His ideas and activity represented a strange blend of fanaticism, sadism, and paranoia. In Szeged he quickly set up an "interrogation center" in the basement of his headquarters where captured Communist couriers and other "undesirables" were brutally tortured. Prónay also began to experiment with a tactic that would bring notoriety to the officer detachments: assassinating political opponents, particularly Jews, and tossing their bodies into a convenient waterway, in this case the Tisza River. As the corpses of victims began to wash ashore, and rumors spread of Prónay's nefarious activities, moderate military officers became concerned and the liberal press in Szeged began to condemn these acts of violence as "White Bolshevism."[69] But nothing could be done, for it was clear that Horthy tacitly approved Prónay's methods. In fact, Prónay became Horthy's personal bodyguard and was thus constantly at his side during public appearances.

The decision to become a patron of Prónay and to sanction his murderous methods was a fateful one for Horthy. It reflected the profound horror that he felt for communism and the conviction, strengthened by his contacts with his extremist officers, that even the most violent methods were now justified in the campaign to eradicate the "Bolshevik poison." In this period Horthy began privately to speak the language of a Gömbös or a Prónay: "I am capable of anything," he told a colleague. "If necessary, I'll use strychnine poison and employ the basest methods. After all, our enemies have treated us like corpses to be desecrated."[70]

Admiral Horthy and his colleagues were emboldened in their plans by the general acceptance in right-wing circles of a "Christian national" (*keresztény nemzeti*) policy as the foundation stone of counterrevolutionary Hungary. The "Christian" element consisted of a commonly shared desire to curtail what was considered undue Jewish influence in society and enhance the prestige of the churches after the official atheism of the Kun regime. The strengthening of the Christian churches was considered desirable from the standpoint of restoring order and discipline to a society that had had a dangerous if brief experience with democratic and socialist ideas. But affirmation of the role of Christianity in Hungarian history had even broader implications. Historic Hungary was often referred to as the Kingdom of St. Stephen, and the crown of that famous king was regarded as a symbol of the inviolability of Hungary's traditional frontiers. In Hungarian Catholic circles this concept tended to lend a religious sanction to the campaign to regain Hungary's lost frontiers. Such novel ideas as national self-determination and ethnic rights could thus be more easily denigrated, and Hungary's Christian churches, both Catholic and Protestant, could rationalize their support for the campaign to restore Hungary's hegemony over millions of non-Magyars.[71]

Miklós Horthy proved to be adept at smoothing over potential difficulties between Protestants and Catholics in the counterrevolutionary movement. He worked closely with Count Pál Teleki, a fervent Catholic, and chose as the chaplain of the National Army a Franciscan friar, Father Zadravecz, who was of Slovak ancestry. In turn the Christian churches, both Catholic and Protestant, gave their approval to the National Army and its counterrevolutionary activities. Father Zadravecz was particularly zealous in promoting Horthy's cause. At frequent public ceremonies he blessed the efforts of the National Army as the instrument for the restoration of thousand-year-old Hungary, the "realm of the Virgin Mary."[72] As his two talismans Zadravecz carried a crucifix and a map of prewar Hungary. In Szeged Zadravecz also collaborated with Pál Prónay in the formation of a secret racist society, the Etelközi Szövetség, known more commonly as EkSz. Its purpose was to promote the "Szeged idea" and combat what Prónay and Zadravecz regarded as the insidious influence of freemasonry. Although Horthy was cautious enough to decline to become a member of EkSz, he supported its activities and declared himself receptive to the suggestions of EkSz members. Zadravecz reciprocated by assuring Horthy that he could always count on support from EkSz, since its guiding spirit was loyalty to him.

The full emergence of Admiral Horthy as the leading figure in the counterrevolutionary movement came on July 5 at a public meeting of MOVE. A suggestion by Gyula Gömbös that Horthy be acclaimed as honorary president of the organization was greeted with enthusiasm by the large group of officers and local dignitaries in the audience. Dressed in his admiral's uniform, Horthy then proceeded to deliver what would be the most powerful speech of his career. Speaking extemporaneously, Horthy reported that he had just come from a Cabinet meeting where he learned that the French government no longer had confidence in the "reactionary" government of Gyula Károlyi, which would have to be replaced by one more democratic. This, Horthy asserted, must not be regarded as the end of their effort to recover the Hungarian homeland. No foreign country could prevent the triumph of Hungarian nationalism, and he himself would support a new government only if it was Magyar and Christian in its orientation. Horthy ended his brief speech in a dramatic fashion: "Political adventurers should no longer be allowed to experiment on this martyred country, on the body of our beloved homeland. We must not tolerate this. Remain together, persevere, and we will attain our goal!"[73]

For a few moments there was a strange silence in the hall, for everyone was aware that a delegation of French officers was in attendance. Sensing this, Horthy turned to these officers and provided a summary of his remarks in French, asking them politely to report what he had said to the "gentlemen in Paris." This gesture removed all feelings of constraint felt by the Hungarians who had been enthralled by Horthy's patriotic words. A thunderous ovation soon enveloped the hall. Amid cries of "Long live Horthy!" the audience surged to the stage and several officers lifted Horthy on their shoulders. He was carried out to the street and the enthusiasm died down only when a French officer appeared, brandished a sword, and announced that such demonstrations were forbidden. As the crowd dispersed, many of those who had witnessed this event were now convinced that Horthy was the "coming leader of Hungary" and the "symbol of our future."[74]

In mid-July the Szeged government was in fact reorganized. Count Károlyi and Horthy were removed from the Cabinet and Gömbös was even expelled from Szeged. The new government, headed by Dezső Ábrahám, a liberal, was acceptable to the French but viewed with suspicion by the extreme right-wingers. From this point Horthy, who remained as Commander in Chief of the army, began to argue privately that the "resurrection" of Hungary would never be accomplished by the "politicians." He kept his contact with the Ábrahám government at a minimum and by the end of the month the National Army was acting as virtually an independent body.[75] Meanwhile, Horthy's optimism was no doubt increased by news report about the successes of the White Armies in the Russian civil war.

On July 31 word reached Szeged that Béla Kun's government had fallen and Romanian forces were about to occupy Budapest. This was the signal for action. French permission was obtained for the dispatch of the Hungarian Army into the territory west of the Danube river, known as Transdanubia. The first unit to leave Szeged was Prónay's officer detachment, which departed on horseback on August 4. What orders were given to Prónay and the other leaders of the officer detachments? Horthy had several options. He might have insisted that the only responsibility of the army was to maintain order while the government authorities and the courts decided what punishment was to be meted out to those who had acted improperly during the revolutionary period. This was the procedure advocated by traditional Hungarian conservatives like Count Bethlen and his colleagues in Vienna. The Szeged officers had a different view, which was colorfully expressed by Captain Miklós Kozma: "Both the red and the pink eras are over. . . . Those who for months have committed heinous crimes must receive their punishment. It is predictable . . . that the compromisers and those with weak stomachs will moan and groan when we line up a few red rogues and terrorists against the walls. Once before the false slogans of humanism and other 'isms' helped drive the country into ruin. This second time they will wail in vain."[76]

Admiral Horthy was in no mood to side with the "compromisers and those with weak stomachs." His decision to support his officers in their campaign to "cleanse" the nation seems to have been based on and justified by two historical analogies. Horthy had only a superficial knowledge of European history, but he now argued that the brutal suppression of the French Commune in 1871 represented a precedent for a similar action against the Hungarian Soviet Republic. Many atrocities and tens of thousands of deaths had occurred in the confrontation between the forces of the right and the left in France. A similarly bloody campaign could be expected in Hungary too. It would seem that the second historical analogy was made unconsciously, or perhaps atavistically, by Horthy and his officers. Four centuries earlier, in 1514, the greatest peasant rebellion in Hungarian history was put down with utmost savagery. In order to leave a lasting imprint on successive generations of peasants, the leader of the rebellion, György Dózsa, was placed on a red-hot iron throne and crowned with a glowing iron crown. Some of Dózsa's men, who had previously been starved, were forced to eat pieces of his roasted flesh.[77] The Hungarian officers of the White Army who departed Szeged in early August 1919 were eager to enact the kind of revenge that would, like the treatment of the rebels of 1514, survive in the memory of the nation for centuries to come.

Horthy's intentions were expressed in the instructions given by his chief of staff, General Károly Soós, to Pál Prónay, who was told to employ martial law to "reestablish law and order and to execute the ringleaders of the Soviet Republic." Those officials who had been deposed during the revolutionary period were to be reinstated. Two things suggest that Soós and Horthy sensed that they were sanctioning an extraordinary military campaign that might lead to excesses for which they would prefer not to be responsible. Apparently on Horthy's insistence, Prónay's orders were given to him only orally, not in written form. In addition, Soós added a final word of warning to Prónay: "Don't kill too many Jews, since that will create problems too."[78] However, since Horthy and Soós knew of Prónay's methods of torture and assassination in Szeged, the instructions given him could only be interpreted as a blank check for a campaign of terror.

2

The Making of the Regent, 1919–1920

As his "army of the crane feathers" advanced into Transdanubia, Admiral Horthy remained for a few days in Szeged, where he made his final break with the Ábráham government. On August 13 he departed by plane for Siófok, a town near Budapest that now became the headquarters of the National Army. This dramatic flight served further to embellish Horthy's image: the admiral who traveled by airplane to take command of the National Army. In Budapest, meanwhile, a right-wing government had been established by Archduke Joseph, a member of the Habsburg family, who now declared himself regent. The Prime Minister was István Friedrich, an engineer with little political experience who was mistrusted by the radical rightists because of his participation in the government of Mihály Károlyi. Horthy was formally installed as Supreme Commander of the army by Archduke Joseph on August 15. The gendarmerie and a 9000-man force assembled in Austria by Colonel Anton Lehár, the brother of the composer, now came under Horthy's jurisdiction.

While in Budapest Horthy also reported to the Interallied Military Mission that had recently arrived to assist in the restoration of order. Employing his impressive linguistic skills, Horthy quickly developed a rapport with these officers from the United States, Great Britain, France, and Italy. From the Mission he learned that the Friedrich government was not likely to be recognized by the Allies, since it offered little guarantee of "order and tranquillity."[1] Several days later the authority of the Budapest government was further weakened by word from Paris that the Entente would not tolerate the presence of a Habsburg archduke as head of state in Hungary. Joseph was thus forced to step down. Since the Szeged government had already disbanded, Horthy's Supreme Command in Siófok now loomed as a potentially significant factor in the shaping of the future Hungarian political system.

While Horthy was consolidating his position in Budapest, the National Army was moving relentlessly across Western Hungary, reestablishing law and order. Most units proceeded with discipline and restraint, but the special officer detachments, especially those of Prónay and Ostenburg, were responsible for a series of gruesome atrocities. In each town or village they visited, anyone suspected of having served the Soviet Republic in some capacity or having openly sympathized with the Communists was rounded up and subjected to "people's tribunals." Sometimes malicious accusations were made by villagers who blamed Jews for the miseries they had endured over the past year. Jews were in some cases apprehended even if no connection with Béla Kun's government could be proved. In many towns makeshift court martials were arranged and the accused were quickly executed by hanging or firing squad. At times, truly sadistic methods were employed. No precise data are available, but one plausible estimate suggests that Prónay's detachment alone was responsible for about three hundred deaths in August 1919. By the end of the year the victims of the "White Terror" probably numbered over a thousand.[2] Interestingly, a significant percentage of these were peasants on estates. This reflected the special concerns of the officers of the special detachments, who were mostly from the gentry class. Prónay declared that one of his major objectives was "to restore the formerly good relationship between the lords and servants on the great estates."[3]

Very quickly reports of a "White Terror" in Transdanubia appeared not only in the Budapest press but abroad as well. On August 22 the *Manchester Guardian* was informing its readers of the outbreak of pogroms against Jews in Hungary. Other Western papers published similar accounts. As a result, the Interallied Military Mission announced that it would investigate the reports of outrages in Transdanubia.

When these reports about a reign of terror in Hungary reached Horthy, his response was deeply ambivalent. On the one hand, at the time and in later years Horthy steadfastly denied that he had ever issued "bloodthirsty orders" or that any sort of "White Terror" had occurred in Hungary in 1919 and 1920.[4] He prided himself on being a proper, honorable commander whose officers acted in a disciplined, legal manner. It is true that Horthy is not known to have participated personally in any act of terror; nor, apparently, did he directly supervise the selection of victims. By remaining aloof from the bloody details of the military operations that he had approved, Horthy was able to convince himself that his actions were justified and that there was no "White Terror." At the most he would concede that some excesses were occurring, but that these were understandable reprisals by soldiers whose loved ones had suffered during the "Red Terror." "It goes without saying," Horthy said on one occasion, "that an officer should attack the murderer or violator of his sister and smash his skull. If he acted otherwise, we should have to expel him from the army." The Communists had "let hell loose," Horthy later asserted, and in restoring order his troops could not be expecting to be too "softhearted."[5]

On the other hand, Horthy felt compelled to honor the commitment that he had made in Szeged to his radical officers to support their plan for a "purification" of Hungary. He too wanted to eradicate bolshevism and was prepared to use an "iron broom" for this purpose. By thinking in terms of the suppression of the Paris Commune in 1871, he had created a rationalization for the execution of hundreds, perhaps thousands, of Hungarians. Once reunited with Gömbös and Prónay in Siófok, Horthy slipped effortlessly back into their world of conspiracy and extremist plans. In late August he told Prónay he should continue the "excellent job" he was doing, although he should be careful that the Allied Military Mission didn't arrest him.[6] For many months he found it difficult to express his growing unease or to intervene directly to put an end to the terror. The esprit de corps that had been ingrained in him since his days at the naval academy led him to stand by his officers and to view as blasphemous any public accusations made against the armed forces. The result was that well into 1920 Horthy tolerated the ruthless methods of the special detachments and offered official protection to their commanders.

Horthy's ambivalent attitude toward the "White Terror" was noticed by several of his contemporaries, including Colonel Lehár, who, after many private conversations with the Supreme Commander in 1919, concluded that Horthy had a dual personality. Lehár was perplexed to find that Horthy readily agreed with him that only legal procedures should be employed against those who were suspected of having committed crimes during the Soviet period, yet he continued to give free rein to the officer detachments. On one occasion Horthy even boasted to Lehár that he had under his command men who "with a cold smile will do away with anyone who stood in his way." Nor did Horthy try to hide from Lehár his contempt for those in Budapest who in late August were accusing the National Army of perpetuating a "White Terror." Employing the kind of vulgar language that he used when feeling most angered and frustrated, Horthy denounced the "shitty Jews" (*Scheissjuden*) who were prolonging the occupation of Budapest by the Romanians in order to prevent the entry of his army. When the time came he would have them hanged "till they rotted in the noose."[7]

In August it was not just the socialist press in Budapest that was critical of Horthy's army. Ferenc Schnetzer, Minister of Defense in the Friedrich government, insisted that the meting out of justice to those who had committed criminal acts during the revolutionary period was the responsibility of the civilian government. On August 16 he thus ordered Horthy to end the outrages of the White troops, including the people's tribunals and public hangings.[8] Horthy's response was strongly influenced by Gömbös, Kozma, and the other Szeged officers who thought the Budapest government "should go to hell."[9] Pointing out that Horthy commanded the only fighting force in Hungary, Prónay urged Horthy to break completely with the Friedrich government and establish a military government in a provincial city, perhaps Székesfehérvár or Szombathely. Horthy was not prepared to go that far, but he did decide to keep his distance from Friedrich's government. In all of 1919 he attended only one Cabinet meeting, and whenever possible he sought to usurp the government's authority and extend the authority of the Supreme Command. Recruits drafted into the army were required to take an oath of obedience to Horthy, not to the government.[10] Moreover, he issued a series of directives from Siófok in which he insisted that the courts were being "laughably soft" in their punishment of those who had supported the Communist regime. It was because of such misguided attitudes that on occasion his officers, in their "patriotic enthusiasm," had taken matters in their own hands. Such excesses could not be avoided unless it was clear that arrested Communists would receive their just punishment, even in cases in which "it is not possible to prove any ordinary crime against them."[11]

The Friedrich government was alarmed by the intimidating tone of Horthy's directives and by his refusal to rein in the special detachments, which continued their depravations, though more sporadically, in October and November. But the government was powerless to take action. Horthy's prestige increased steadily during this period as he crisscrossed Western Hungary in a grand tour that was meant to represent the formal liberation of each town by Horthy's army. In his travels Horthy both contributed to and benefited from a surge of Hungarian nationalism. His speeches were typically filled with nationalistic fervor and often ended with the words "Long live the Fatherland!" A striking feature of Horthy's tour was his appearance in each town riding a white horse, which was designed to link Horthy with Árpád, the military chief who was thought to have ridden a white horse when he led the Magyars into Hungary at the end of the ninth century. The ceremonies conducted in October in Székesfehérvár were typical.[12] Horthy and his entourage arrived on a train that stopped on the outskirts of the city. From there Horthy, in his admiral's uniform, led a unit of the National Army into the center of town, where he was greeted by the mayor and Bishop Ottokár Prohászka. Horthy delivered a brief patriotic speech in which he stressed the need for social harmony and discipline, for "only hard work can allow us to escape from this misery." The bishop then blessed the white flag of the army, and Horthy reviewed the troops from horseback. Such ceremonies in the cities and towns of Western Hungary no doubt convinced many that Horthy was a man of authority who could insure that the political turbulence of the past year would not soon return. That the Catholic Church gave its blessing to the National Army must have been reassuring to those who may have harbored doubts and concerns because of the reports of atrocities committed by military officers.

Far from being a political handicap, Horthy's staunch anticommunism won for him many adherents in the countryside, where a "popular counterrevolution" had been underway well before the arrival of the White Army.[13] Anti-Semitic feelings were sufficiently widespread that in some rural areas the violence of the special detachments against individual Jews was viewed with indifference or was even welcomed. Horthy's appeal was particularly strong among farmers of modest means, or smallholders, who were emerging as an important political force. Horthy regarded this social stratum as politically reliable (as opposed to the landless peasants or urban workers) and a suitable target for recruitment of soldiers. After receiving a delegation of smallholders at Siófok in early September, Horthy acknowledged their support by declaring that "the bayonets of the sons of the village must flash in the streets of Budapest." A month later at a meeting of the Small-holder party, István Nagyatádi Szabó, the leading peasant politician, declared that he had conferred with Miklós Horthy and approved his political views. Szabó even suggested that Horthy, because of his apolitical past, seemed singled out by fate to become regent of Hungary. This seems to have been the first public mention of the possibility of Horthy becoming the head of state.[14]

In this period further support for Horthy came from the officers of the Interallied Military Mission, who quickly came to regard this Hungarian admiral as a kindred spirit. They were impressed by his determined anticommunism and his general appearance as a well-mannered gentleman and an officer of European stature.[15] A repeated refrain in their reports from this period is the comment that Admiral Horthy "inspired confidence." The American delegate, General Harry Bandholtz, reflected these sentiments when he described Horthy as "an exceptionally straightforward honorable officer and gentleman who is imbued with a high sense of patriotism and who will do his utmost to have everything handled with moderation and dignity."[16] When the Military Mission sent an American officer, Colonel Yates, on an inspection tour of the National Army at Siófok, Yates was impressed by the discipline and order of the troops. Moreover, he found Horthy to be "an energetic, capable man" who would make "an excellent Governor-General of Hungary until the election."[17] It was this high estimation of Horthy that led the Allied Mission to conclude that Horthy's army could be relied on to maintain order in Budapest when the Romanians departed. The realization that the White Army was the only defense Hungary had against a resurgence of bolshevism seems also to have led the Allied officers to turn a blind eye to the surreptitious increase in the size of the army beyond the prescribed limits.[18] By October the army comprised about 30,000 soldiers. Strong support from the American and British officers greatly redounded to Horthy, for these two countries enjoyed widespread popularity in Hungary.

Horthy's role in the "White Terror" was minimized by the Allied officers, who in fact tended to accept the inevitability of at least some reprisals against those who had participated in the Soviet government.[19] With the apparent backing of the Allies, Horthy could now more easily confront his socialist and liberal critics in Budapest. One important group, however, remained to be mollified. Hungary's fortunes in the past had always been primarily in the hands of the aristocracy, who were deemed to have the requisite political wisdom and familiarity with Hungary's constitutional history. Returning from their temporary exile in Vienna and other havens, these Hungarian counts were preparing to resume their traditional role and restore the curious blend of conservatism and liberalism that had characterized the prewar regime. Many of them remained loyal to ex-king Charles and regarded Admiral Horthy as a popular, apolitical military man who could be relied on to assist in a Habsburg restoration. They were, however, alarmed by the extremist plans and anti-Habsburg attitude of Gyula Gömbös and others in Horthy's retinue. Of course, the aristocrats realized that the National Army was an indispensable tool in the restoration, but they feared that unchecked violence would tarnish Hungary's image abroad, perpetuate the state of lawlessness, and gravely complicate the task of establishing a stable, legitimate government.

These fears were expressed to Horthy in early October when a group of senior statesmen and government officials sought him out in Siófok. The delegation included Count Gyula Andrássy, Count Tivadár Batthyány, Count István Bethlen, and Ödön Beniczky, the Minister of the Interior in the Friedrich government. Acting as the spokesman for the group, Andrássy sketched the current foreign and domestic situation and pointed out that recent "military atrocities" were doing great harm to the country. The outrages committed by the special detachments had to be ended. During Andrássy's presentation Horthy became visibly agitated. When Bethlen began to speak in a similar vein, Horthy interjected: "What, are you turning against me too?" Bethlen explained that he had only one request: that the people's tribunals should be stopped because they eroded respect for the army. Horthy attempted, without apparent success, to justify the actions of his officers. Finally, Beniczky raised a sensitive question: "If the National Army enters the capital city, will there be a pogrom—yes or no?" Horthy's response was not entirely reassuring: "There will be no pogrom, but a few people will have to take a swim!" By way of explanation, Horthy read out an article from *Népszava*, the newspaper published by the Social Democrats in Budapest, in which the National Army was accused of committing atrocities. Those who write such articles, Horthy insisted, "will have to take a swim." After an uncomfortable silence, Beniczky asked for Horthy's promise to consult him before taking any action. This Horthy agreed to, and the conversation ended in a somewhat friendlier tone.[20]

Although Horthy seemed to bristle at the suggestions made to him, he was not unaffected by the confrontation with his prominent visitors. On later reflection he must have sensed that a man of his limited political experience and lesser social standing was not really in a position to challenge the judgment of Hungary's most respected statesmen. As Horthy pondered the advice they had given, there began to awaken in him certain conservative instincts that had been submerged over the past year. On several occasions he now tried to lessen the severity of the "White Terror" and to begin to dissociate himself from his extremist entourage. This was to be a slow, almost imperceptible process lasting several years, and Horthy may not have been entirely conscious of the path he was taking. Several cases are known of Horthy acting on petitions sent to him by individuals threatened by the special detachments. If a wife could penetrate the bureaucracy around Horthy and make a personal appeal on behalf of her husband, Horthy would usually respond favorably.[21] On one occasion while touring a prison where political suspects were held, Horthy recognized two of his former sailors and immediately pardoned them. These actions suggest that despite the image he projected of a stern, merciless commander, Horthy often acted out of sentiment. In his frequent speeches during his tour of Transdanubia in October, Horthy was also careful to avoid instigating violence against Jews or encouraging the "White Terror." It is worth noting that in his public speeches in this period he never once made inflammatory remarks about the Jews.

Finally, Horthy did attempt, albeit in oblique and convoluted ways, to express his concerns about the "White Terror" to the officers of the special detachments. Privately he pointed out to Prónay that the foreign press was publishing sensational stories about the "White Terror," and this did great harm to Hungary. In the same vein Horthy lamented the fact that so many Jewish corpses were being discovered in different parts of the country. Why not, Horthy suggested, stop these atrocities against insignificant Jews and concentrate on the more prominent ones? Such feeble protests were not very persuasive, but they did cause a perplexed Prónay to complain about his master's "timid conduct" and "pacifistic tendencies." Prónay tried to convince Horthy not to worry about foreign opinion. Now, when there were still enough soldiers "to finish the job," Hungary should complete the task of purification on the basis of the right of self defense of a Christian nation. Privately Prónay began to wonder who could be giving Horthy such bad advice? His wife? The Jew-loving aristocrats?[22]

The "bad advice" had been coming, in fact, not just from the conservative aristocrats but also from Sir George Clerk, an English diplomat who was sent to Hungary by the Supreme Council in Paris to serve as a midwife at the birth of a suitable coalition government in Hungary. Clerk was by no means predisposed to favor Horthy: he was known as a Slavophile who got on well with the leaders of the Successor States, those countries which were in the process of enlarging their territory at Hungary's expense. Eduard Beneš, the Foreign Minister of the new Czechoslovak state, had warned Clerk that Horthy was a reactionary and that his army represented a grave danger to the new order in Eastern Europe. Yet when Clerk met with Horthy in Budapest, he too succumbed to his charm. Clerk reported back to the Supreme Council that he had "complete confidence in Admiral Horthy's sincerity," and that he had received Horthy's assurance that his troops would be impartial and disciplined if they were permitted to enter Budapest. The socialist leaders in Budapest tried to persuade Clerk that they knew Horthy better than he did and that a strong government should be formed before the White Army entered the capital, but the English diplomat seems to have concluded that the left-wing faction in Hungary was weak and without significant popular support. Thus, Clerk's response was that he trusted Horthy, since "he is a gentleman."[23]

As Horthy's star was rising in November, that of István Friedrich was in a precipitous decline. Ironically, it was Friedrich far more than Horthy who appeared to the Western observers to be incorrigibly chauvinistic and anti-Semitic. When Friedrich rejected Clerk's proposal that Social Democrats be added to his Cabinet, Horthy showed a greater pragmatism by agreeing to meet with leaders of the Smallholder, liberal, and leftist parties. This must have been a distasteful prospect for Horthy, who had been excoriating some of these individuals as crypto-Communists, vowing to ban their newspapers once he entered Budapest.[24] In the resulting meeting, which was held in Clerk's residence on November 7, Horthy, for once in civilian clothes, was subjected to a barrage of complaints and accusations about the "White Terror" delivered primarily by Vilmos Vázsonyi, a respected liberal and the most prominent Hungarian Jewish politician, and by Ernő Garami, who represented the Social Democrats.[25] Horthy was greatly discomfited by the ensuing cross-examination, the like of which he had never before encountered. Quite agitated and struggling to maintain his composure, he made a poor impression on his inquisitors. His responses lacked continuity or real content and consisted primarily of certain memorized sentences or patriotic clichés that he repeated again and again in his accented Hungarian. One thing Horthy made clear was that he would "put to the sword" anyone who jeopardized discipline in the army or agitated for bolshevism. When questioned about the atrocities committed in Transdanubia, Horthy explained that these were the response of the "indignant nation." "In war," he insisted, "it could not be otherwise." To what war was he referring? "The war against the Bolsheviks," Horthy replied.

After a prolonged period of such inconclusive exchanges, a final question was posed. If Horthy was permitted to enter Budapest with the White Army, would there be a military dictatorship? Horthy's emphatic answer was that he would submit the National Army to the authority of the government. There would be no military dictatorship. Since this was the only statement made by Horthy that suggested a willingness to compromise, Vázsonyi and his colleagues quickly drafted a statement for Horthy's approval and signature. It stipulated that the National Army would be subordinated to the coalition government created with the aid of Sir George Clerk. A relentless campaign "to nip Bolshevism in the bud" would be continued, but the army would be under strict orders to respect civil rights. Horthy hesitated for a few moments, but then proceeded to sign his name to this declaration.[26] The meeting thus ended in a friendlier atmosphere.

The statement drawn up at the meeting of November 5 was prominently published the next day in the Budapest newspapers. In later years some of the participants were to express deep regret that they had failed to detect Horthy's insincerity and ulterior motives. Lajos Varjassy, a former Szeged liberal, later would call the agreement "one of the most serious errors committed in the course of Hungarian history."[27] But at the time there was a mood of cautious optimism among Hungarian Liberals and Socialists. To cement the understanding Sir George Clerk gave the Jewish community and the Socialists his own personal assurance that order and discipline would be maintained by Horthy's army. Momentarily dropping its guard, the *Népszava* warmly greeted the joint declaration of November 5 and declared that it had been signed by "trustworthy and responsible men."[28]

Such implicit praise by a newspaper that Horthy had vowed to ban must have been a source of some embarrassment to him and confusion in his entourage. Equally perplexing to the radical right-wingers was Horthy's willingness to make direct overtures to the Jews and the workers, a strategy that, in the light of later developments, was probably being recommended to Horthy by Count Bethlen. In early November Horthy received a delegation from the Jewish community of Budapest and for two hours listened patiently as they argued that the great majority of Jews had acted responsibly and patriotically during the war and revolutionary period. In a friendly but firm manner, Horthy assured his visitors that there would be no pogrom when his army entered the capital city. His only concern, which transcended all others, was the "rescue of the nation." It might be that in the course of the nation's recovery the Jews would still suffer injustice. But when Hungary was once again healthy, he would work to eliminate that evil too. In any case, they, as leaders of the Jewish community, should exercise a calming influence in Budapest, and report to him if any outrages were committed.[29] Horthy spoke in similar terms to a delegation of Christian Socialists who sought him out in Siófok. Warning that the workers must distance themselves from their traitorous and destructive leaders, Horthy promised that the government would endeavor to ease the plight of workers. An even more remarkable encounter with workers occurred on November 11 when Horthy participated in the formal "liberation" of Tatabánya, a mining town regarded as one of the strongholds of Communist activity. Despite the misgivings of his advisors, who feared for his safety, Horthy requested that he be allowed to speak to the miners in their canteen. Instructing the police to remain outside, Horthy made his way through a throng of workers to the canteen stage. He began by assuring the miners that he had mounted the stage not to emphasize his superiority but to be able to make eye contact with those to whom he was speaking. Horthy's brief speech was harsh but not without some conciliatory words. He acknowledged that among the miners "the red specter still lurked." He thus wished to emphasize that even the slightest effort aimed at restoring the Communist regime would be mercilessly suppressed. But he insisted that his objective was not to lower the wages of the miners. He would do his best to help "the poor workers and their families," but he thought it was not right that "precisely those who were the cause of the great devastation in Hungary should be the first to step forward with their very extensive demands." Horthy suggested that for the moment the only trustworthy group in Hungary was the peasantry, but he was convinced that within a short time "the misled industrial workers would return to the national idea and . . . take part in the work of national reconstruction." Horthy concluded by urging the miners to show their patriotism by forgoing strikes and producing the coal that Hungary badly needed, for "the destiny of the country was at stake." There could be no "hemming and hawing;" if the miners did not cooperate, the coal industry would be taken over by the National Army.[30]

Horthy thereupon left the canteen unmolested; indeed, an eyewitness reported that at least some of the miners seemed impressed by the admiral's performance. Scattered cries of "éljen!" (bravo!) were heard in the canteen. By seeking personal contact with the miners and projecting an image of a stern but sincere leader, Horthy perhaps persuaded some that he was not a monster intent on devouring the workers.

To mollify Prónay and the radical right-wing officers and to dispel the impression that he had capitulated to the forces of the left, Horthy publicly downplayed his negotiations with the leftist parties. "As far as the Social Democrats are concerned," he stated in an interview on November 12, "I have no dealings with them. . . . I order and they obey." Yet his cooperation with the Allied representatives and increasingly frequent consultations with Count Bethlen had led Horthy inexorably to a more moderate and conciliatory policy. He had, after all, given his gentleman's word to Sir George Clerk that he would support a coalition government and would subordinate himself to that government. This greatly distressed the radical right-wing officers, who had eagerly been awaiting the opportunity to extend the process of "purification" to what they regarded as "Red Budapest," hitherto the safe haven for Communists, Zionists, Freemasons, and other fellow travelers.

For some time Gyula Gömbös had been trying to persuade Horthy that the best solution to Hungary's political problems was not a restoration of the monarchy or a return to a traditional government of the discredited aristocrats but a military dictatorship dedicated to the "Szeged idea." The direction of the country would then be taken over by a "powerful and, when necessary, even a brutal hand." All administrative and military power would be concentrated in one person.[31] But Horthy had resisted Gömbös's blandishments. He continued to insist that, as a military man, he could have no political ambitions. Moreover, Horthy's loyalty to ex-king Charles, expressed so forcefully in November 1918, seemed to remain firm. On several occasions in late 1919 he gave private assurances that he would never abandon the King and that he would continue to wear his admiral's uniform as a symbol of his "Kaisertreue."[32] Yet Gömbös persevered, sensing that the tantalizing prospect of becoming a powerful national leader was not without its effect on Horthy. As the date for the entry of the National Army into Budapest approached, Gömbös devised a plan whereby a huge crowd of reliable supporters, drawn from the MOVE and other right-wing groups, would greet Horthy as he entered Budapest and stage a boisterous demonstration. Then Father Zadravecz would step forward and, on behalf of the Hungarian nation, "spontaneously" acclaim Horthy as *nádor*, or palatine.[33] But Zadravecz declined this responsibility, and Horthy preferred to proceed cautiously and in agreement with the Allied powers. This proved to be a shrewder strategy, for it helped set the stage for Horthy's elevation to the pinnacle of power only four months later.

In early November 1919, counterrevolutionary forces were on the march throughout Eastern Europe. General Anton Denikin's army was advancing on Moscow from the South. A White Army was poised on the outskirts of St. Petersburg. Admiral Horthy's entry into Budapest with his National Army on November 16 thus seemed just one part of the imminent suppression of communism in the two countries in which it had gained ascendancy. But Trotsky's Red Army was soon to turn the tide, and the fate of such officers as Admiral Alexander Kolchak and General Denikin would be sealed. Only Admiral Horthy, the one White General who had not actually engaged in combat with a Red Army, and Marshal Carl Mannerheim in Finland, were able to forge successful political careers on the basis of their exploits in the struggle against the Communist revolution.

Having staged practice runs in smaller cities over the past month, Gömbös was able to orchestrate the march into Budapest in a manner that would enhance Horthy's image as the "man on horseback" to whom the nation could and should turn for its salvation. All went well on that Sunday morning, except for the weather, which was "wet and cheerless."[34] Wearing his naval officer's cap and double-breasted navy jacket and solemnly astride his white stallion, Horthy led his troops toward Gellért Square, where the mayor of Budapest and other dignitaries offered a formal welcome. In his brief response Horthy made no attempt to conceal the bitterness and contempt that he and his officers felt for Budapest, which he called a "sinful city."[35] From afar he and his men had cursed the capital city, where "the filth of the country had collected" in the past year. Budapest had "dragged the Holy Crown and national colors in the dirt and clothed herself in red rags. The finest of the nation she had imprisoned or driven into exile." But the closer we have come to Budapest, Horthy said, the more prepared we are to forgive. "My soldiers . . . took up arms in order to restore order in the homeland. Their hands are open for a fraternal handshake, but they can also punish if necessary."[36] A brief address by Horthy later in the day from the steps of the Parliament building was equally stern and threatening. The reconstruction of Hungary, he declared, would take a long time unless the "poisonous elements" were quickly eliminated "from the soul of the nation." All Hungarians needed to join forces in a "holy cause" based on two pillars: the national ideal and Christian morality. "The days are over," he declared, "when any scoundrel can become Minister and any man of honor is executed."[37]

Although the mood in the workers' and Jewish sections of Budapest was quiet and dejected, along the path that Horthy's troops traveled through the city large crowds offered an enthusiastic welcome. According to a Western journalist, Admiral Horthy was greeted with the ringing of church bells and "a tornado of shouts and a waving of handkerchiefs."[38] The bridges, public buildings, and private houses were decorated with the national flag. A gypsy band played the national anthem as the procession made its way toward the Parliament building. The beginnings of a veritable cult of Horthy were evident in the posters that news vendors were selling. The most striking showed the steering wheel of a ship firmly grasped by two hands and the word "Horthy" at the bottom. Posters with photographs of Horthy were prominently displayed. In a similar vein, a leading Hungarian journalist expressed the nation's gratitude that the "God of the Magyars has brought you here!"

At midday an outdoor mass was celebrated by Cardinal János Csernoch, the Prince Primate, on the steps of the Parliament. In an ecumenical ceremony that followed, the regimental flags of the National Army were blessed by both Catholic priests and Calvinist ministers. The ceremonies concluded with a speech by Cecile Tormay, a noted anti-Semite, who greeted Horthy on behalf of the women of Hungary. She spoke of the Supreme Commander in religious terms. Hungary, she suggested, had suffered a "horrible, bloody Calvary." Mihály Károlyi had played the role of Judas Iscariot. Now Horthy and his army were carrying out the resurrection of the country.[39]

In Budapest the key question now was whether Horthy would in fact honor his pledge to restrain his radical officers and prevent outrages against the "poisonous elements" to which he referred in his bitter speech. The first signs were ominous. Although regular army officers were issued strict orders to avoid arbitrary actions and to act only "within the limits of lawful authority" so as to make a good impression on the Allies, the security detachments were authorized to make arrests. Horthy seems to have approved the "surveillance and investigation of destructive elements," by which was meant the ferreting out of any remaining Communists and the arrest of those who were regarded as "fellow travelers."[40] On November 16 over three hundred arrests were made in a well-planned rapid operation. Since most of the leaders of the Soviet Republic had fled months ago to Vienna with Béla Kun, those arrested consisted primarily of Socialists who had acquiesced in the Soviet Republic or had been public critics of the "White Terror." Among those seized were editors and journalists of the left-wing and liberal newspapers, including Béla Somogyi, the editor of *Népszava*. Many of those arrested were Jews, since Jews were to be found in journalism and in the other liberal professions, as well as in the Social Democratic leadership, in disproportionately high numbers.

These arrests were immediately protested by Sir George Clerk and the Interallied Military Mission, who warned that "any campaign against the Socialists at this time would have a most unfortunate effect in the capitals of the world." With some reluctance Horthy relented, and most of those who had been arrested were released. Clerk arranged for personal guards to be assigned to those prominent Social Democrats who felt most threatened. All in all, the Allied representatives in Budapest felt satisfied with the way in which the departure of the Romanians and the entry of the National Army had been carried out. In his report to the Supreme

Council in Paris, Clerk praised Horthy, who "showed himself the leader of an army which is really national and a servant of the State." The British diplomat noted the "extraordinary smoothness and absence of disorder" during the entry of Horthy's troops, which reflected the "complete hold which Admiral Horthy had over the forces under his command."[41] General Bandholtz, reporting that "there had been many arrests but fewer than expected," felt that the "whole proceedings have been rather dignified." He concluded that "Horthy's conduct throughout has been excellent." The London *Times* reported that "perfect order is reigning in Budapest," and the "fears of the Jews and other pessimists have hitherto proved groundless."

In recording these flattering comments about Admiral Horthy, the historian must also take into account the strong anti-Communist bias of most of the Western diplomatic and military representatives in Hungary. Clerk and Bandholtz shared Horthy's belief that those who played leading roles in the Soviet Republic should be punished. Hence Bandholtz was not surprised that there had been many arrests, but that the number had been smaller than one would have expected. As a result, these Western observers failed to note that an atmosphere of intimidation was in fact created in Budapest after the entry of Horthy's troops. The special detachments, quickly and ostentatiously setting up their headquarters in the most luxurious hotels, proceeded to patrol the streets in a menacing fashion and to harass and molest suspected Communist sympathizers in their apartments. For many months they were to remain a law to themselves, contemptuous of the civilian police. Arrests of those deemed "politically unreliable" continued at a steady pace and special camps designed to relieve the overcrowding of prisons soon contained tens of thousands of prisoners who had been detained over the past several months.[42] Street thugs associated with the Awakening Magyars, a radical right-wing group consisting largely of university students and former soldiers, were emboldened to harass and attack Jews in the streets. Soon even moderate Socialists who had refused to support Béla Kun's government felt so threatened that many fled to Austria. Among them was Ernő Garami, who had signed the November 7 manifesto on behalf of the Social Democrats.

These facts notwithstanding, it can still be concluded that Miklós Horthy felt constrained on the whole to honor the pledges he had made in the agreement of November 7. Certainly the special detachments were not upholding civil rights, as Horthy had promised, but the "White Terror," which continued to flare up sporadically in the countryside, was not extended in its full fury to Budapest. There the large Jewish community remained relatively secure, except for occasional verbal or physical attacks by marauding bands of Awakening Magyars. To use the analogy suggested by Horthy himself, what happened in Budapest in late 1919 and early 1920 was not comparable to the bloody suppression of the Paris Commune in 1871. In fact, Horthy's radical officers soon realized that they would not have a free hand to carry out the process of "purification" they had pursued in the countryside. Pál Prónay, who in this period was on a special mission in Austria, later lamented the fact that the punishment of Budapest that Horthy had threatened in his famous speech on November 16 was never really enacted.[43]

Once the festivities connected with the entry of the National Army had been completed, Sir George Clerk turned to the final goal of his mission: the creation of a coalition government that included representatives of the center and moderate left. Such a provisional Hungarian government would then carry out a "free, impartial, and democratic election," the results of which would be a legitimate government that would sign the peace treaty. But Clerk's efforts to achieve these results were thwarted by István Friedrich, who steadfastly refused to allow into his Cabinet any Social Democrat, Jew, or "any individual even remotely connected in the popular mind with the Communist regime."[44] Horthy proved far more pragmatic. At a series of meetings of Hungarian politicians convened by Clerk on November 17, 18, and 19, Horthy, who attended only as an observer, strongly cautioned those present against defying the Entente or even attempting to drive a hard bargain. Hungary needed immediate peace, and his small army would not be able to defend the country should there be a confrontation with the Peace Conference. "Without peace and without a loan," Horthy warned, there would soon be no money to pay the army, which would then simply fall apart.[45] Privately Horthy spoke even more forcefully on November 20: "If by this evening a coalition government is not formed, I'll have the whole group arrested and appoint a government that will be prepared to negotiate with the Entente."[46] Under the influence of Horthy's strong warning and the persuasive arguments of two respected statesmen, Count Albert Apponyi and Count Bethlen, the Hungarian politicians finally agreed on the composition of a coalition government, which was installed on November 24. The Cabinet contained two Social Democrats, but the Prime Minister, Károly Huszár, and most of the other ministers were vociferous rightwingers who shared Horthy's distaste for the left-wing and liberal parties.

A striking characteristic of these political maneuvers was the growing collaboration between Horthy and Bethlen. Horthy's conciliatory gestures toward the Entente and his willingness to approve the participation of the Social Democrats in the new government certainly did not find favor with his radical right-wing advisors. His newfound pragmatism seemed far more to reflect the advice of Bethlen, who already at this time apparently had a scheme for restoring a legitimate government through a "taming" of Horthy and his army. The close cooperation of Bethlen and Horthy in November 1919, was a foreshadowing of a political partnership that would dominate interwar Hungary.

A major task of the new government was the organization of the election of a new Parliament, which was scheduled for January 25. Since this election was to be on the basis of the secret ballot and almost complete universal suffrage, an unprecedented event in Hungarian history, the months of December and January were filled with feverish campaigning. Very quickly Horthy began to rue the concessions he had made to Sir George Clerk. It galled him, for example, that the trade unions and the Social Democratic party were holding public meetings at which speakers preached socialism and denounced the army. He reacted with revulsion to a report that at a Budapest cinema the screening of a newsreel showing the National Army's entry into the capital had been interrupted by "unpatriotic elements" who rose and sang the Internationale.[47] Horthy's deep-rooted aversion for democracy and his fear of a resurgence of bolshevism were fed by Gyula Gömbös and Miklós Kozma, the director of Military Intelligence, who kept supplying the Supreme Commander with reports of nefarious activities by the Hungarian Communists who were being held in protective custody by the Austrian government. Horthy was told, and apparently completely believed, that the Austrian government was on the verge of embracing communism and that the Czechoslovak government was pro-Soviet and encouraged the anti-Horthy activities of Mihály Károlyi in Prague. Finally, evidence was uncovered of an alleged Communist plot, hatched in Vienna, to assassinate Horthy by blowing up the Gellért Hotel, where the Supreme Command had its headquarters.[48] Given Horthy's feeling that he and the army he commanded were the only real obstacle to the triumph of the revolutionary spirit in Hungary, the assassination reports prompted him to remove some of the restraints he had been putting on his extremist officers for the past month. This backsliding was facilitated by the fact that Sir George Clerk had in December departed for Paris, confident that the fruits of his diplomatic mission would be a reasonably democratic government in Hungary.

In these circumstances Gyula Gömbös saw the opportunity to resuscitate his scheme for the creation of a military dictatorship under Horthy's direction. The first task of the new Parliament would presumably be the election of a regent or palatine. If the ground were properly prepared, Horthy could be elected and then proceed to direct the affairs of the country with a firm hand, relying for his support on the army. If the Parliament did not prove cooperative, a military coup d'état could still be carried out. In December the propaganda apparatus of the general staff was set in motion: films, posters, newspapers, and magazines proclaimed the need for a strong man at the helm, a "Hungarian Cromwell," to direct Hungary in its time of peril.[49]

Disillusioned by what he regarded as the ineptitude of the Huszár government, Horthy now seemed inclined to test the waters to see if Gömbös's plan for a military dictatorship might after all be feasible. When in late December General Bandholtz requested a report on the organization of the National Army, Horthy sent him a lengthy memorandum in which Hungary was described as being in a "chaotic state" and in need of a "thorough renaissance." The solution, Horthy suggested, would be a military dictatorship sanctioned by the Entente powers. The dictator would insure that a constitution would be written and the economy rebuilt in an atmosphere "free of class hatreds and party quarrels."[50] On January 9 Horthy elaborated on this theme during a visit to the full Military Mission. He argued that the Huszár government, which he had helped Sir George Clerk form, had turned out to be inept and incapable of governing. At a time when the nation was without coal, the Minister of Labor (a Social Democrat) was urging the miners to strike for higher wages. Though Budapest was daily on the brink of starvation, the Minister of Agriculture (a Smallholder) advised the peasants to hold out for higher prices. The upcoming elections would likely give an overwhelming majority to István Friedrich and his party. Friedrich, a "dangerous adventurer," would then disregard the Entente and appoint Archduke Joseph as king or president. Since the Entente would not likely tolerate a government of this kind, perhaps it would be best if he would go along now with those who had been urging him to establish a military dictatorship.[51]

Horthy's trial balloon was quickly punctured by the Allied officers, although the newly appointed British High Commissioner, Thomas Hohler, an old naval friend of Horthy's, showed some initial enthusiasm for the idea.[52] Of course, the Interallied Military Mission had for some time been nearly unanimous in its belief that Horthy would make an excellent elected head of state, and it was to this alternative that Horthy's attention was directed. In late August the British let it be known in Budapest that they would not object to the election of a notable Hungarian as palatine or even king. Although Horthy took this advice and, skillfully guided along by Gömbös, actively sought election as head of state, he nonetheless seems to have undergone a severe conflict of conscience. Horthy had always insisted that he had no political ambition and that Hungary's legitimate head of state was King Charles. Despite all the evidence to the contrary, Horthy insisted at the time and on many occasions in later years that he had never aspired for political power, that it had literally been thrust upon him.[53] It seems that he had somehow persuaded himself of the purity of his motives. This self-delusion may have contributed to Horthy's inner turmoil and increasing mental confusion in this period. Visitors began to notice his lack of concentration and a tendency toward incoherence. They noted that Horthy would listen attentively to his visitor, but would often respond in totally inappropriate ways, as if he did not understand what had been said. Quickly losing his trend of thought, Horthy would lapse into a series of anecdotes relating to his naval career. Sometimes he would talk uninterruptedly in this way for one or two hours, and the purpose of the meeting would have been long forgotten. Pál Prónay was perplexed by this development: was Horthy doing it deliberately, to avoid discussion of certain political matters? Was he playing a kind of joke? Or was this true mental confusion?[54]

However he rationalized his political ambition, Horthy moved forthrightly to gain election as head of state. The parliamentary election held on January 25, which the Social Democrats boycotted in protest of the repressive actions of the government, resulted in a relative balance of power between the two major parties, the Christian Union and the Smallholders, neither of which had sufficient strength to form a government. Both were right-wing in orientation, fully embracing the "Christian national" principle. Both favored monarchy as the form of government. The critical difference was that most members of the Christian Union were legitimists: they believed that Charles remained the legitimate king of Hungary and should be restored to power. Most of the affluent landowners identified with the Christian Union. By contrast, most members of the Smallholder party were free-electors, who argued that Hungarians were now free to choose as king anyone they pleased. Although the nucleus of the party, under the leadership of István Szabó, consisted of peasants owning small plots, many of those who supported the party were too rich to be called smallholders. In addition, the party became a convenient vehicle for those who, for a variety of reasons, found the Christian Union to be unacceptable. Thus, Gyula Gömbös and István Horthy, the Regent's brother, both ran for Parliament as Smallholders.

Although Admiral Horthy remained aloof from the political struggle, he privately had misgivings about both these parties. Earlier he had willingly accepted the support of the Smallholders, but he strongly opposed their call for extensive land reform. For most of his political career Horthy was to cling tenaciously to the idea that land reform could never work in Hungary. For Horthy this was a simple calculation: there simply was not enough land to distribute to each person who aspired to be a landowner. Each farmer would end up with a dwarf plot that would be inefficient and lead to disaster for the national economy. On this issue, at least, Horthy sided with the aristocratic landowners in the Christian Union. On the other hand, though he was a professed legitimist himself, Horthy had to take notice of the clear indications that the Allies would not tolerate a Habsburg on the Hungarian throne. Moreover, by early 1920 some of the most vocal critics of the "White Terror" were conservative aristocrats in the Christian Union.

On January 30 Admiral Horthy, speaking as Commander in Chief, issued a declaration in which he offered his interpretation of the agreement hammered out in November under the aegis of Sir George Clerk. The duty of the new Parliament, Horthy asserted, was to elect a head of state to whom the provisional government would transfer power and who would name a Prime Minister.[55]

That this head of state could not be a Habsburg was made clear on February 2, 1919, when the British and French governments stated their unequivocal opposition to the restoration of the Habsburg dynasty in Hungary. Very quickly there developed among Hungarian political leaders the consensus that a regency, for which there was suitable precedent in Hungarian history, should be established and maintained until such time as a king would be chosen. Horthy not only stated his approval of this compromise, but openly hinted that he would accept the office if it were offered. His previous ambivalence about seeking political power had been based in part on his earlier pledge to work for Charles's return to the throne. Now that the Allied veto had apparently foreclosed a return of the Habsburgs for the immediate future, Horthy could argue that it was his duty to accept election as regent. In that position he could preside over the recovery of his country and hold the reins of power until conditions were more propitious for the recall of Charles. Horthy's political ambition could thus be reconciled with his commitment to Charles and his previous image as a soldier aloof from politics.

Although during February other names were briefly mentioned, Miklós Horthy was clearly the only realistic choice as head of state. In many ways he represented the "link and the compromise" between the different factions in Hungarian society.[56] Since he had kept aloof from party politics, he gave the appearance of impartiality. On the question of the monarchy, he had straddled the fence, since his previous ties to the Habsburg dynasty were balanced by his association with Gyula Gömbös and the other notorious "free electors" in the officer corps. He was a Protestant who seemed to have the blessing of the Roman Catholic hierarchy. His candidacy seemed to be favored by the great powers who were determining the fate of Hungary at the peace conference in Paris. Moreover, Horthy enjoyed a degree of genuine popularity in the countryside, especially among landowning peasants, who saw in him the great war hero and a man on horseback who would lead Hungary out of its time of troubles. During January and February Horthy participated in a new series of "liberations" of towns that had suffered greatly during the Romanian occupation. He doubtless was viewed by many liberated Hungarians as their deliverer from oppression and the champion of national resurgence. Had a plebiscite been conducted on a democratic basis, Horthy would probably have been elected regent by a significant majority.

Support for Horthy was certainly not unanimous. The Liberals and Socialists were strongly opposed, fearing that his election would represent a triumph of the "Szeged idea" and the creation of a military dictatorship. Because of military censorship and the intimidation of the officer detachments, these fears could not be publicly stated in Hungary, but they found expression in Hungarian communities abroad. From the left-wing émigrés in Vienna there emanated a torrent of vituperative anti-Horthy newspaper articles and pamphlets. Here Horthy was depicted as the bloody architect of the White Terror, a butcher responsible for the death of thousands.[57] These attacks found their echo in various left-wing newspapers in the Western world, such as the *Manchester Guardian*, and even in anti-Horthy demonstrations by American-Hungarian workers in Cleveland and other American cities.

The most serious threat to Horthy's candidacy, however, came from a large group of traditional conservatives in the Christian Union party. Having observed the close cooperation between Horthy and Gömbös, they harbored doubts about the strength of Horthy's commitment to a Habsburg restoration. They worried, too, that the election of Horthy would give the officer detachments *carte blanche* to continue their murderous operations indefinitely. These concerns were increased when in early February Horthy traveled to Kecskemét, the scene of a bloody massacre of Jews carried out by Lieutenant Iván Héjjas's special detachment several months earlier. To the astonishment of even some of Horthy's supporters, he ostentatiously greeted members of the Héjjas detachment and visited the home of Héjjas's parents, where he gave a short speech.[58] That Horthy should have acted in such an indiscreet and politically damaging way suggests that he may well have dismissed reports about this massacre and other excesses of the "White Terror" as fabrications of the Jewish and Socialist press. Since he had no advisors among his officers who were likely to present him accurate reports about the activity of the special detachments, Horthy could blithely defend such officers as Héjjas or Prónay, unaware of the terrible impression this made on wavering delegates in Parliament. Even István Szabó, the leading peasant politician, who had been the first to suggest that Horthy was an ideal candidate for regent, now had his doubts, pointing out that "the people don't understand the purpose of this army."[59] Károly Huszár, the Prime Minister, voiced the concerns of many when he declared during a parliamentary debate that the government would not tolerate "individuals who use the slogan of Christianity to commit crimes that show they have no concept of morality, honor, decency, or legality."

Horthy's position was strengthened, however, by the inability of his opponents to agree on a suitable candidate. In fact, there was only one other individual of sufficient stature and popularity, Count Albert Apponyi, who at the time was serving as head of the Hungarian delegation at the peace conference in Paris. Apponyi had strong support among the legitimists in the Christian Union, and many Liberals and Social Democrats regarded him as more acceptable than Horthy. But the Smallholders had no enthusiasm for an aristocratic landowner who would almost certainly oppose land reform. Moreover, in the prewar period Apponyi had been the very visible sponsor of educational legislation that discriminated against Hungary's national minorities. For many political observers in Western Europe his name had become synonymous with intolerant Magyar nationalism.

It did not take long for pragmatic and politically aware Hungarians to conclude that there was no alternative to Horthy. Some critics might ridicule his poor command of the Hungarian language, but few could deny that he exuded an aura of authority and had served capably and even heroically during the war. One Budapest pundit observed that Horthy spoke Hungarian as badly as Francis Joseph, which was not such a bad thing, since at least there would be some legal continuity. Those of a more cynical bent predicted that even if Horthy were not elected regent, there would be the danger of a military coup d'état by his angry officer corps. Among conservative aristocrats there were those, like Count Bethlen and Count Gyula Andrássy, who quietly threw their support to Horthy, no doubt arguing that he could be controlled and his army tamed once the country returned to more normal conditions.[60] In the first week of February the Budapest newspapers published a flood of resolutions from county assemblies and councils supporting Horthy. Sensing that Horthy's election was now certain, various groups rushed to offer their endorsement, on the principle that the best strategy was to act quickly and enthusiastically rather than belatedly and grudgingly. Thus Jenő Polnay, the president of the National Association of Hungarian Jews, announced that his group favored the election of Horthy and asserted that patriotic Jews had never been and never would be involved in radical leftist and adventurous politics. On February

12 an editorial in *Az Est*, the leading liberal newspaper, described Horthy as "the embodiment of the Hungarian national idea." On the next day the Smallholders party, the largest in Parliament, voted its support for Admiral Horthy. In these circumstances Count Apponyi decided to yield gracefully and hope for the best. Privately he expressed his grave concerns about having a military commander as head of state, but he concluded that since Horthy had control over the only available military force, any other solution might result in civil war.[61] On February 15 he thus issued a public statement in which he threw his "vigorous support" to Miklós Horthy, "the only suitable candidate."

Just when it seemed that Horthy's election was a certainty, there occurred in Budapest an incident that confirmed the worst fears of his wary opponents. On February 17 two mutilated corpses washed up on the banks of the Danube River. They were identified as Béla Somogyi, editor of *Népszava*, and Béla Bacsó, one of his fellow journalists. The circumstances of the crime led to widespread suspicions that the special detachments were responsible. The news caused an uproar in Parliament, and the funeral several days later was turned by the Social Democrats into one of the largest mass demonstrations in Hungarian history. Like everyone else in Hungary, Miklós Horthy suspected that one of the officer detachments was responsible for the murder of Somogyi and Bacsó. Immediately he summoned Prónay and, in great agitation, demanded to know if he was involved in the incident. Prónay calmly answered that he was not, but he reminded Horthy that he and his entourage had for a long time wanted the "Jewish impostor scribblers" of the *Népszava* done away with. Why should anyone be reproached now that it was accomplished? Horthy replied with a pained expression: "Yes, but it should have been done in some other way, not like this!"[62]

For several months Béla Somogyi had in fact been one of the main targets of abuse when Horthy and his most trusted officers vented their frustrations and animosities in private discussions. Horthy had been particularly outraged by a series of articles that Somogyi published in *Népszava*, which he believed incited Communist terrorism. At a gathering of officers some time in late December, someone brought in a copy of a recent article by Béla Somogyi that had been banned by the military censors. The article must have been sharply critical of the officer corps, for it caused great consternation and outrage among those present. Someone suggested that the time had truly come for Somogyi to be tossed into the Danube. At this point Horthy pounded angrily on the table and declared: "This requires action, not just words!" One of the officers present, Captain Gyula Ostenburg, thereupon decided, on his own initiative, to plan and carry out the murder.[63]

By the time the murder actually took place, Horthy had apparently forgotten that he had instigated such a thing, if indeed he had ever intended his words to be taken literally.[64] When he learned that Ostenburg was responsible, Horthy upbraided him for the clumsy methods he had employed and for the poor timing, right before the election of the regent.[65] To minimize the harm that might be done to his candidacy, Horthy resolved to conceal his own knowledge of the crime and to protect Ostenburg and his officers from prosecution. In the direct aftermath of the murder of Somogyi, Horthy denied that the army was involved in any way and suggested that perhaps *agents provocateurs* or Freemasons were responsible.[66] He prevented the Minister of the Interior, Ödön Beniczky, from following up on evidence that implicated Ostenburg. In order to persuade his critics that he could be reasonable and conciliatory, Horthy went so far as to meet with two representatives of the moderate wing of the Social Democrats, Ferenc Miakits and István Farkas. He expressed his regret over the Somogyi murder and gave his pledge that everything would be done to track done and punish the assassins. He assured his visitors that he had "the best intentions" toward the workers, who should thus remain calm and cooperate in restoring prosperity to their unfortunate country. Miakits and Farkas listened politely to Horthy's words, and then asked if perhaps the special detachments would be disbanded. Horthy took note of their request, but insisted that he "reserved this decision to himself."[67]

Horthy's prevarications were sufficiently effective that most political observers in Hungary concluded that even though one of the special detachments was surely involved in the Somogyi/Bacsó outrage, Horthy himself was innocent. Some of Horthy's opponents in the Parliament tried to exploit the incident to discredit him, but to no avail. Horthy's impending election was now taken for granted. During the last two weeks of February the Parliament proceeded to discuss the provisions of the legislative act creating a regency. The result of these deliberations, Law I of 1920, was passed on February 28, 1920. The regent was to be elected by secret ballot and serve "as a temporary governor pending a definite settlement as to the exercise of the supreme executive power of the state." With certain exceptions, the regent was to have essentially the same powers formerly granted to the king. The regent would have sole authority to appoint and dismiss the Prime Minister, who did not necessarily have to be a member of the majority party in the Parliament. He would have extensive powers over military affairs as Supreme War Lord, although the military budget would have to be approved by Parliament. The regent was to be addressed as *Főméltóságú* (Serene Highness) and would be accorded "the same protection in criminal law as the king." On the other hand, the right to confer noble titles and certain ecclesiastical powers was denied to the regent.

Reflecting the lingering fears that Horthy and the officer corps might still at some point try to create a military dictatorship, the Parliament determined that the legislative body would still retain significant powers vis-à-vis the regent. Legislation would not have to be submitted to the regent ahead of time. The regent would be able to exercise a suspensory veto over legislation, but if passed a second time by Parliament such legislation would become law. Only the Parliament would be able to declare war or make peace. The regent would be able to dissolve Parliament only when it had been incapacitated for a long time. This was no doubt designed to prevent the regent from employing a tactic that had been favored by Francis Joseph, who had frequently adjourned the Hungarian Parliament and refused to recall it for long periods. Finally, the proposed law stipulated that the regent could be impeached by a two-thirds vote of Parliament.[68]

As this legislation began to take shape in the last half of February, the Minister of the Interior kept Horthy closely informed of the parliamentary deliberations. The Supreme Commander did not hesitate to express his concerns. At one point Horthy was informed that the regent would not have the "advowson" (*főkegyúri jog*), that is the right to appoint bishops. Misunderstanding the term and forgetting for a moment that the election had not yet taken place, Horthy blurted out: "What? I won't be able to grant pardons?"[69] Though reassured on this point, Horthy had strong misgivings about certain other provisions of the law, especially the limits placed on the power of the regent to adjourn or dissolve the Parliament. Privately he complained that since the current Parliament contained two major parties of roughly equal strength, the balance of power was held by a handful of liberal delegates. The regent, he argued, must have greater freedom of maneuver when deadlocks occurred in this kind of Parliament.[70]

On March 1, the day set for the election, Horthy's officers left nothing to chance. Prónay, Ostenburg, and the other special detachment commanders set up a military cordon around the Parliament building and several parliamentary delegates were refused admission, even as officers in uniform brazenly entered the building and milled about in the halls and galleries. When the Chief of Staff was later asked by irate officials of Parliament to explain the blatant military presence on March 1, he declared that he had received a report that an anarchist planned to assassinate Horthy.[71]

Despite the crude attempts at intimidation, the Parliament decided to proceed with the vote. The result was as expected: out of 141 votes cast, Horthy received 131, Apponyi 7. Even without the intervention of the special detachments Horthy would probably still have been elected, though the vote might well have been close.[72] Bishop Ottokár Prohászka then led a small delegation to the Gellért Hotel, where they found Horthy waiting in his white admiral's uniform. Prohászka formally reported the results of the election: "Hungary's Parliament has elected you Regent! Would it please you to accept the office of Regent of Hungary?" To the astonishment of the members of the parliamentary delegation, Horthy replied that he could not accept because the restrictions placed on the regent by Law I would so tie him down that he would be a mere figurehead who would be unable to govern properly. Unless changes were made, he preferred to remain as Commander in Chief of the army. He wanted greater discretion in dismissing Parliament, the right to approve legislation, and in general all the traditional royal prerogatives, especially in military matters.[73]

Horthy's demands, which Prohászka relayed to Parliament by telephone, caused great consternation. The initial reaction was a refusal to give in to what seemed blackmail. One angry delegate remarked that Horthy was acting "as if he were born to be king." Many free-electors suspected that Horthy wanted all the traditional royal powers because there was a plot to have Charles quickly assume the office after Horthy took the oath.[74] Yet it quickly became clear that to refuse Horthy would surely bring on the military coup d'état that everyone feared. Prohászka was thus empowered to inform Horthy that a legislative solution would be found to his concerns. Thus mollified, Horthy now proceeded by car to the Parliament building. Seated at his side was Pál Prónay, whose detachment was guarding the motorcade. Additional negotiations took place at the Parliament, at the conclusion of which Horthy received a written promise that a law expanding the powers of the regent would be passed in the near future. Although some of Horthy's demands were not specifically mentioned in this document, he nonetheless found it acceptable. The oath was thus administered, and Admiral Miklós Horthy became Regent of Hungary, an office that such illustrious Hungarians as Lajos Kossuth and János Hunyadi had once held. Would Horthy's regency, like that of Kossuth, last only a few spectacular months? Or would it, like Hunyadi's, be more durable and bring Horthy European renown? No one imagined that Horthy's tenure would be counted in decades, or that he would have to contend with the likes of Adolf Hitler and Joseph Stalin.

On March 1, 1920, some Hungarians peered into the future with great trepidation. They feared that Horthy's regency would bring military dictatorship and an even more furious "White Terror." The majority, however, were more optimistic. One did not have to belong to the radical right-wing camp to welcome Horthy's election. Gyula Kádár, a young officer with progressive political views, regarded it as a natural, favorable development. Ferenc Nagy, who would later become one of Hungary's most prominent peasant leaders, hoped that Horthy "would follow in the footsteps of Kossuth." Colonel Lehár, who had been revolted by the excesses of the "White Terror," rejoiced over Horthy's election because he thought that things would now begin to calm down and the special detachments would be curbed.[75] Even the Social Democrats hoped for the best. On March 2 *Népszava* published an editorial in which János Vanczák, who belonged to the right-wing of his party, extended to Horthy the "calloused hands" of the workers in a gesture of loyalty and conciliation.

How ironic, then, that it should be Pál Prónay who expressed the greatest misgivings on that March 1. After taking the oath of office, Horthy returned to the Gellért Hotel, where he was greeted jubilantly by his officers. In his excitement Horthy launched into a spontaneous speech that lasted an hour. The officers listened patiently, but, according to Prónay, the talk entirely "lacked logical content or a progression of ideas." He wondered if Horthy could in fact maintain his position and fulfill the role that so many had hoped for back in Szeged. His conclusion was tinged with fatalism: "what will be, will be."[76]

3

The Regent's Obsessions: The Treaty of Trianon and Bolshevism

The counterrevolution in Hungary was a river fed by many tributaries. All Hungarian counterrevolutionaries professed allegiance to the "Christian national" idea, but the specific objectives and methods of the various right-wing groups were by no means identical. Some, like Bishop Ottokár Prohászka, stressed the need for a moral revival, a campaign against Jewish and liberal cultural influence, and the restoration of the Church to its traditional place in society.[1] The extremist army officers looked forward to the establishment of a totalitarian dictatorship in which the military would play a leading role as the propagator of the "Szeged idea." A significant segment of the political establishment regarded the return of "normality" as synonymous with a restoration of Charles to the throne. Others saw the counterrevolution as a triumph of the true Magyar values of the countryside over the immorality and internationalism of Budapest, a theme that found powerful expression in a novel, *Az elsodort falu* (The Village Adrift), which was published just months before Horthy's election to the regency.

An infrequent reader of books, Miklós Horthy was probably unacquainted with Dezső Szabó's novel or with the other influential intellectual attack on liberalism published in this period, Gyula Szekfű's *Három Nemzedék* (Three Generations). Yet Horthy can nonetheless be seen as the embodiment of the counterrevolutionary spirit, for he was the only prominent Hungarian who could appeal to all right-wing factions and serve as the "link and compromise" among them. Once installed as regent, however, Admiral Horthy discovered that he would have to take a position on a variety of issues that sharply divided the conservative right and the

proponents of the "Szeged idea." This created an agonizing dilemma for Horthy, who proclaimed his dedication to the creation
of a "Christian national" Hungary but was incapable himself of
conceiving a specific program for achieving this objective. During
1920 he was thus the focal point of competing factions in an ideological struggle confined largely to the right wing of the political
spectrum. The gradual return of more normal conditions in 1920
did reawaken in him the traditional conservatism that he had im-
bibed in his formative years as a dutiful Habsburg naval officer.
Yet his extremist officers, who for most of 1920 still had easy access to the Regent, continued to try to translate his radical but private rhetoric into reality. Above all, Gömbös and Prónay
attempted to win Horthy over to radical plans for dealing with
what had become for him true obsessions: bolshevism and the
Treaty of Trianon. As a result Admiral Horthy followed a very
erratic course in 1920, trying somehow to please both Gömbös and
Teleki, both Prónay and Bethlen. Thus, Horthy seemed at times to
support alternate policies that were contradictory and irreconcilable. Some political observers concluded that the Regent was
playing a "double game."[2] Yet in his political naiveté Horthy
usually did not perceive the inconsistency of his positions and no
one in either right-wing camp was as yet bold enough to point this
out to him. Instead, each group hoped that the malleable Horthy
would eventually side with it.[3]

Horthy's first responsibility after his election was the naming of
a new Prime Minister. It was significant that his first thought was
to appoint István Bethlen, with whom he had been collaborating
for several months. Bethlen was one of the "Jew-loving aristocrats"
who were despised by Prónay and the more vociferous of the military officers. Leaders of the two main parties regarded Bethlen as
something of a maverick, for he had refrained from joining a political party and was not even a member of the Parliament. But
Horthy had tremendous respect and admiration for Bethlen,
whom he on later occasions would call the smartest man in Hungary. Perhaps Horthy subliminally recognized in Bethlen those
qualities of leadership that he himself lacked: political acumen,
clarity of vision, and diplomatic skill. In any case, Horthy must
have realized that, having rejected the idea of a military dictatorship, he had to entrust the direction of political affairs to someone
who would command respect both at home and abroad. Clearly
no one among the radical right-wingers had the traditional qualifi-

cations for high political office. Even the most talented of them, Gyula Gömbös, was a mere captain who, in any case, was *persona non grata* to the French as well as to the Hungarian legitimists.

In the spring of 1920, however, Bethlen apparently felt that conditions were not ripe for the program of consolidation he favored. Perhaps he also wished to avoid the damage to his prestige that might result if he were to be the Prime Minister responsible for carrying out such a distasteful assignment as the signing of the peace treaty. No doubt he advised Horthy that it would be better to find some interim figure. After consulting with leading politicians, Horthy thus named as Prime Minister a relatively unknown lawyer, Sándor Simonyi-Semadám. Given Simonyi-Semadám's lack of political stature, the nearly equal strength of the two rival parties in the Parliament, and the political anxiety over the nature of the peace settlement that was being fashioned in Paris, it is not surprising that for most of 1920 conditions in Hungary remained highly unstable. Contributing to the instability throughout Eastern Europe was a new "Red scare" brought on by the surprising success of the Soviet Army in repelling an attack by Poland. In the summer of 1920 a counterattack by the Red Army reached the suburbs of Warsaw. The possibility that the approach of the Red Army would spark a resurgence of bolshevism in Hungary gave renewed vigor and hope to the radical right-wingers, who, noting the Regent's more frequent consultations with aristocratic advisors like Count Bethlen and Count Teleki, were beginning to fear that Admiral Horthy was abandoning their program.

In the turbulent conditions of 1919 one other issue remained central to the concerns of many Hungarians: the possibility of a Habsburg restoration. Since Charles IV had not actually abdicated in November, 1918, but had merely "withdrawn from any participation in the affairs of state," the Hungarian legitimists regarded him as their reigning king who could reclaim his throne at an appropriate time. They had every reason to believe that Miklós Horthy would facilitate such a restoration. After all, Horthy had given a tearful pledge of loyalty to Charles in November 1918 in Schönbrunn Palace. From the time of his arrival in Szeged, Horthy had continued to wear his naval uniform to demonstrate that he remained a loyal officer of the King. Several times in late 1919 and early 1920 Horthy sent messages to Charles assuring him of his firm support. True, he did advise Charles to postpone any attempt at restoration until the peace treaty was signed, since an earlier move would harm Hungary's interests and alarm her neighbors. But, as Horthy assured a confidant of Charles in November 1919, as soon as the treaty was signed, the two-faced game would end and Hungary's crowned king could return to the throne.[4]

In March 1920 Horthy dutifully reported to Charles that he had been elected regent. He assured the ex-king of his continued loyalty, but pointed out that a premature return of Charles to Hungary would be a misfortune, since the peace treaty was still being negotiated and the National Army was not strong enough to resist a likely foreign intervention. Charles agreed to bide his time, trusting that Horthy, in his "prudence and wisdom," would pave the way for a restoration.[5] But the legitimists in Hungary were suspicious of the Regent, who frequently consulted Gyula Gömbös and seemed to surround himself with a clique of anti-Habsburg officers. The legitimists warned Horthy that Gömbös was an "evil genius" who had a plan for dethroning the Habsburgs and creating a national dynasty. These complaints Horthy merely brushed aside, arguing that Gömbös should not be taken too seriously for he had him "in the palm of his hand." Horthy's disingenuous argument that in any case he rarely saw Gömbös was met with skepticism by Aladár von Boroviczény and the ex-king's other supporters in Hungary.

Certain of Horthy's initial actions as regent increased uneasiness in the legitimist camp. To many Hungarians it seemed only natural that the regent reside in and govern from the otherwise unoccupied royal palace in Buda. Horthy even requested, and received, Charles's permission to move his family into the guest wing of the palace. Still, those who distrusted Horthy were afraid that the more accustomed the Regent became to the trappings of royal power, the more difficult it would be to dislodge him when Charles appeared to reclaim the throne.[6] Even more disturbing to the Hungarian royalists was Horthy's insistence that all soldiers take an oath personally to him. When some of the legitimist officers complained, Horthy insisted that this oath to him as "Supreme War Lord" did not supersede the oath that the officers had sworn to King Charles, the "Most Supreme War Lord." It was clear, however, that with the passage of time each new class of officers and soldiers would swear obedience only to the Regent, and that the army would fall even more under Horthy's influence. Thus, Horthy's action proved very controversial, and a few officers resigned in protest or took early retirement.[7]

Since both legitimists and free-electors agreed that the "royal question" should be postponed until after the signing of a peace treaty, it was foreign policy that became the focus of attention in the first months of Admiral Horthy's regency. When the preliminary terms of the peace treaty were presented to the Hungarian delegation in Paris on January 15, 1920, and made public in Budapest several days later, the reaction was one of profound shock and consternation. The victorious powers were planning a severe truncation of the old Kingdom of Hungary. Such cherished regions as Slovakia, Ruthenia, Transylvania, the Bánát, Croatia, and Burgenland would be lost to Hungary's neighbors. Cities like Kassa, Pozsony, Temesvár, and Kolozsvár, which had figured prominently in Hungarian history, would now appear on maps as Košice, Bratislava, Timisiora, and Cluj. To many Hungarians this amounted to a virtual death sentence for their nation: three days of public mourning were decreed and black flags were displayed all over Budapest.

Like virtually all politically conscious Hungarians, Miklós Horthy hoped that some way could be found to prevent the dismemberment of Hungary, which he regarded as not merely a blunder and a grave injustice, but as a crime against Western civilization. On several occasions in late 1919 and 1920 he lent his name to conspiratorial plans devised by his extremist officers to disrupt the status quo and regain territory lost through the peace treaty.[8] In the sacred cause of revision of an unjust peace settlement, Horthy now declared, even extraordinary methods were justified. The Magyars, who had traditionally been "honest and correct in their policies," were now forced to "conduct themselves like Balkan nations."[9]

It was this frame of mind that led Horthy to consider even the most preposterous of schemes. On one occasion he suggested that Transylvania would be infiltrated by a regiment commanded by his brother István, who would engineer a kind of St. Bartholomew Night in which all the "stinking Wallachians" would be killed. So fantastic were some of Horthy's ideas that at least one of his confidants wondered if perhaps the Regent was "pulling his leg."[10] Already in this period Miklós Horthy was exhibiting the tendency to "think aloud" and blurt out certain ideas and plans that even he, upon later reflection and after hearing the views of more moderate advisors, came to regard as unrealistic or undesirable.

The most spectacular example of Admiral Horthy's willingness to dabble in conspiratorial international politics came in 1920 when he approved plans submitted to him for cooperation with General Erich von Ludendorff and Bavarian right-wing extremists. The westward march of the Red Army in the late spring prompted the extremist Hungarian officers to intensify cooperation with their counterparts in Germany, especially with General Ludendorff, who despised the new Weimar government in Germany and looked to Horthy's Hungary as the vanguard of the counterrevolution in Eastern and Central Europe. This cooperation led to the plan for an alliance of anti-Communist groups whose ultimate aim was the eradication of all traces of bolshevism from the map of Europe. The idea seems to have originated early in 1920 with Gyula Gömbös and with another young General Staff officer, Tibor Eckhardt.[11] In mid-May a delegation representing Ludendorff and Bavarian right-wing extremists was invited to Hungary to begin clandestine negotiations with Gömbös and Prónay. On May 17 Horthy met secretly with the German delegation, which included Ludendorff's confidant, Colonel Max Bauer, and a remarkable political adventurer named Ignác Trebitsch-Lincoln.[12] Horthy was given the details of Ludendorff's scheme, which in certain ways paralleled plans secretly drawn up by the Hungarian General Staff in late 1919.

In this plan to create a "White International," Hungary was to provide monetary support and training facilities for a group of Bavarian, Austrian, and Hungarian putchists who at the appropriate time would topple the Austrian government and "cleanse" Vienna of all Socialist influences.[13] A joint Hungarian-Austrian-Bavarian military operation would then be launched against Czechoslovakia, which would be defeated and dismembered. In Prussia the Socialists would be swept from power and a military dictatorship would be established under General Ludendorff. As these operations were being launched, the White Armies in Russia would receive financial support in the form of counterfeit rubles manufactured in Hungary. All of this would be the prelude to a vast military crusade to crush bolshevism in Russia, in which Bulgaria and Turkey would be invited to join. Success in Russia would enable the "White International" to take revenge against the Entente powers and to redraw the map of Europe. As its reward for serving as the nucleus of the "White International," Horthy's Hungary would be restored to its prewar frontiers.

Horthy seemed enthusiastic about this fantastic plan and assured his guests that a German orientation would be the only possible one for Hungary. He requested, however, some time to consider his final response. What he did not tell his German visitors was that the Hungarian government had recently embarked on secret negotiations with France aimed at revising the peace treaty through diplomatic procedures. When informed by the Regent of the discussions he had had with Bauer and Lincoln-Trebitsch, Count Teleki, who had been named Foreign Minister in April, and Kálmán Kánya, the deputy Foreign Minister, reacted with great skepticism. They naturally regarded the idea of a "White International" as wildly unrealistic and potentially very dangerous for a militarily weak state like Hungary. Moreover, the Foreign Ministry rejected in principle the idea that delicate matters of state should be discussed by military officers and motley political adventurers.[14] Still, Horthy's prestige was so great that no one dared to suggest outright that the Foreign Ministry try to veto the clandestine negotiations with Ludendorff and his representatives. Instead, an effort was made by foreign policy experts, notably Kálmán Kánya, to minimize Hungary's role in the project. Thus, the Foreign Ministry apparently approved efforts to undermine the Socialist government in Austria and to poison relations between the Czechs and Slovaks, but rejected all proposals for military intervention. Kánya was intent on preventing any further direct contact between the Regent and the German conspirators.[15]

During the summer of 1920 Admiral Horthy thus became intimately involved in two sets of secret negotiations aimed at combating bolshevism and revising the Treaty of Trianon. The two initiatives, one diplomatic in nature, the other military and conspiratorial, were in almost all respects antithetical to each other. A leader less single-minded and determined might have been nonplused by the double game Horthy chose to play as he juggled his schedule so that meetings with German conspirators, Russian White Generals, and French diplomats would not only remain secret but would not overlap. As described below, Horthy gave his approval to a rapprochement with France, but, despite the misgivings of his Foreign Minister, it was the plans for a "White International" that truly stirred his blood. Colonel Bauer was thus informed by Gömbös on June 1 that Admiral Horthy agreed fully with Ludendorff's plan and that "we can get down to work."[16]

A Hungarian committee consisting of Prónay, Gömbös, and Tibor Eckhardt was formed to implement the scheme discussed on

May 17 and elaborated in the meantime. In the next few months plans were developed for the formation of volunteer "free corps" units drawn from the ranks of MOVE, the Awakening Magyars, and the special officer detachments. Sometime during June Horthy gave an audience to General Vladimir Biskupski, a spokesman for the White Russian monarchists. Horthy promised assistance to the anti-Communist forces in Russia, and in July, as the Red Army marched on Warsaw, 100,000 Hungarian crowns, which had been collected for a commemorative plaque to honor Admiral Horthy, were diverted to a fund to aid General Denikin's faltering White Army.[17] On July 16, despite the best efforts of Kálmán Kánya, Regent Horthy invited Colonel Bauer and Rudolf Kanzler, an emissary of the Bavarian Prime Minister, to meet him privately for lunch at the former royal summer palace in Gödöllő. Horthy assured his visitors of his continuing support of the "White International" and his eagerness to obtain weapons from Germany in exchange for grain shipments and cash payments. His guests returned to Germany with personal letters from Horthy to Ludendorff and to the Bavarian Prime Minister, Gustav von Kahr, as well as with an invitation to Ludendorff to travel to Hungary for face to face discussions with Horthy.[18]

In his reply to Horthy's letter, written on August 19 as the successful Polish counterattack (the "Miracle on the Vistula") was unfolding in Poland, Ludendorff politely declined the invitation to visit Hungary, citing the unfortunate repercussions should his presence in Hungary be discovered and publicized. He emphasized, however, the community of interests between Hungary and "order-loving elements" in Germany, and applauded Hungary's contribution to the struggle against the "Red peril in the East."[19] This exchange of letters between Horthy and Ludendorff represented the high-water mark in the effort to create a "White International." As the Red Army withdrew from Poland in the autumn of 1920, it became clear that bolshevism would be contained in Russia. It was equally clear, moreover, that the Russian civil war was about to end in a complete rout of the White Armies. As a result of these developments the program that had been approved by Horthy in June was never fully implemented. In any case, all hope of keeping the negotiations secret was lost in August when Trebitsch-Lincoln, fearing that his position in the counterrevolutionary movement was being undermined, fled Hungary for Vienna and Prague where he began selling incriminating documents connected with the German-Bavarian-Hungarian negotiations.[20] Soon the chancelleries of Europe and the newspapers of London and Paris were buzzing with all sorts of rumors about Hungary's role in a variety of sinister plots. Eduard Beneš, the Czechoslovak Foreign Minister, was so alarmed by the revelations in the documents supplied by Trebitsch-Lincoln that he ordered immediate military precautions.[21]

In these new circumstances the conservatives in the Hungarian Foreign Ministry felt that they were in a stronger position to wean the Regent away from the bellicose plans and political adventures of his radical right-wing officers. Deeply resentful of the intrusion of the General Staff into the realm of policy-making and fearful that implementation of the "White International" would plunge Danubian Europe into renewed warfare that could hardly redound to Hungary's favor, Pál Teleki and Kálmán Kánya now began to take a more forceful stand. Teleki, whom Horthy named Prime Minister in July, worked slowly but steadily to block implementation of the Ludendorff-Horthy plan. In September a ministerial council presided over by Teleki discussed and unanimously rejected a military plan for fomenting rebellion in Slovakia so that Hungarian and Polish troops could then intervene.[22] In October Teleki branded the idea of forging Russian rubles as neither feasible nor desirable. Indeed the Prime Minister was now prepared to take a firm stand against the foreign policy program of the radical right-wingers: "I regard the plan for offering support to Ludendorff through the MOVE and Awakening Magyars as unacceptable. Hungary is a constitutional state, which pursues its foreign policy through responsible officials and not social organizations."[23]

Like Teleki, Hungary's other prominent conservatives were convinced that Hungarian national goals could be promoted only through a long-term program rooted in traditional diplomatic methods and based on a European perspective.[24] The only realistic course was to accept the main features of the peace settlement, restore political, economic, and social stability, and work patiently for a program of treaty revision that could be sanctioned by one or more of the great powers. It seemed self-evident to them that Hungary on her own, or in cooperation with unreliable mavericks such as General Ludendorff or White Russian émigrés, would never be able to redraw the map of Danubian Europe. Since an unfavorable European diplomatic constellation had been the ruin of Hungary in 1919, only a more favorable one in the future could sweep away the hated Treaty of Trianon and restore Hungary to her former grandeur. These were the views of such statesmen as Count Bethlen, Count Teleki, and Kálmán Kánya, men whom Horthy apparently trusted and respected. After all, he had tried repeatedly in 1920 to persuade Count Bethlen to become Prime Minister. He had appointed Count Teleki first Foreign Minister and later Prime Minister.

Yet, while Horthy probably assured his conservative counselors that he fully agreed with their analysis of international affairs, he nonetheless found it difficult to dissociate himself completely from the plans of his Szeged officers, especially as the Red Army was advancing westward in the summer of 1920. Horthy might have reasoned that as long as conditions remained so unstable in Danubian Europe, it was best to have a "wild card" to play, should traditional diplomatic methods prove ineffective or should revolutionary outbreaks occur. In addition, he seemed perversely attracted to and fascinated by the kind of military adventures his Szeged friends presented to him. He found it difficult, not just in 1920 but even later in his career, to dismiss these ideas out of hand. Instead he would listen almost spellbound to the schemes of a Gömbös or a Trebitsch-Lincoln and then voice his immediate and enthusiastic approval. Histrionically banging his fist on his table so hard that the ink would fly from its container, he would inveigh against the ineffectiveness of Parliament and the incompetence of his diplomats. Yet once Horthy had time to contemplate such proposals and to consult with Bethlen or Teleki, he was invariably persuaded that such a policy would be foolhardy and dangerous. He would then summon Gömbös or Prónay and sheepishly declare that their plans had to be postponed, since, as he frequently phrased it, "if we move now, we will perish."[25]

Certainly Miklós Horthy, who for five years had served as an aide to the emperor of one of Europe's great powers, had a better appreciation than a Gömbös or a Prónay of the advantages to be gained in persuading one or another of the victorious great powers to champion the Hungarian cause. The United States was unlikely to continue active participation in European affairs. Italy was viewed with distrust because of what Horthy and many other Hungarians regarded as its perfidious behavior in the Great War. Germany and Russia were in shambles. Thus, only France and Great Britain remained as possible patrons. Of these two, Admiral Horthy's clear preference was for the latter, which he believed had been a "moral and civilizing force" in the world. Even before his election as regent, Horthy had approached his naval friend from prewar days, Thomas Hohler, and stated quite openly, and apparently sincerely, that Hungary would prefer an orientation toward London, since "it was in Great Britain alone that he and his country had complete confidence." Yet, as Hohler accurately put it, Britain had "little interest in this part of the world beyond the maintenance of peace."[26] Though rebuffed in this instance, Admiral Horthy was throughout his political career to retain a respect for British naval power and a hope that London would eventually see the justice of Hungary's cause and intervene in Danubian affairs on her behalf.

Since the British evinced no interest in championing Hungary's cause, the leadership in Budapest was desperate enough to test the sincerity of the French government, which in early 1920 had dropped strong hints that it was interested in a rapprochement with Hungary. In the spring and summer intensive secret negotiations were consequently conducted and the outlines of a major political and economic pact between France and Hungary were sketched.[27] Like many of his countrymen, Admiral Horthy viewed France as the one great power most responsible for the catastrophe that had engulfed Hungary at the end of the Great War. Yet Count Teleki and Count Bethlen both supported the negotiations with France, and Horthy was pragmatic enough to see that, in the current circumstances, this was Hungary's only hope for great power support. At first Horthy's attitude was reluctant and cynical: "I will accept even the dirtiest and filthiest hand if it will help us out."[28] In April, however, Horthy sent a private message to the French government in which he affirmed his support of a Franco-Hungarian rapprochement and suggested that, with French approval, he could quickly raise an army of 500,000 "courageous, united, and loyal men" to join in the struggle against bolshevism.[29] After meeting with the French Minister on May 18, only one day after his clandestine talks with Colonel Bauer and Trebitsch-Lincoln, Horthy became more enthusiastic and began to speak privately of how the French were going to assist in the restoration of much of "Greater Hungary," including Burgenland and most of Slovakia. The Regent even resigned himself to the possibility that Hungary would have to transfer control of Hungary's railroad network to a French consortium. Despite the misgivings of Prónay and the noisy opposition of the Awakening Magyars, Horthy acceded to French wishes and, as a gesture of good faith, authorized the Hungarian delegation at the peace conference to sign the Treaty of Trianon on June 4.

Hungarian disillusionment was thus all the greater when by early autumn, as the Bolshevik threat to Europe receded, it became clear that Paris was rapidly losing interest in Hungary as a possible pillar of French policy in Eastern Europe. A strong indication of the direction of French policy was the final refusal to accede to Horthy's request that the Hungarian Army, which by the spring of 1920 had grown to some 80,000 men, not be forced to demobilize in order to reach the 35,000 limit stipulated by the Treaty of Trianon. By September Hungary had become almost completely isolated on the international scene, the bête noire of Europe: no great power supported her cause; all her neighbors were hostile. Alarmed by sensational reports of Hungary's revanchist plans, Czechoslovakia, Romania, and the South Slav State had already begun to collaborate in a diplomatic alignment that would later be called the Little Entente. Only Marshal Joseph Pilsudski's Poland could be regarded as a state friendly to Hungary, but no significant help could be expected from that beleaguered country.[30] Horthy's "wild card" policy, the creation of a "White International," had made little progress and was, in any case, strongly rejected by the Hungarian Foreign Ministry. There seemed to be no alternative to submission to the dictates of the peace conference, for, as Teleki now argued, Hungary had "lost the war and lost it against a powerful world coalition." The Regent finally resigned himself to the situation. In early November he assured Thomas Hohler that "he intended to have the Treaty of Peace ratified and to keep law and order in the country to the best of his ability."[31]

Admiral Horthy's assurances to the British Minister were significant because for most of 1920 "law and order" had not been fully restored in Hungary. In the first few months of Horthy's regency, Hungarian domestic affairs remained turbulent, largely because the special detachments of Prónay, Ostenburg, and other officers continued their deprivations in Budapest. Ensconced in the most expensive hotels of the capital, which they had commandeered upon the entry of the National Army in November 1919, the special detachments remained, in the words of a moderate army officer, "arrogant, conceited, and impudent."[32] Claiming that they had special investigative powers granted directly by the Regent, the commanders of these detachments continued to usurp the powers of the police and to harass and intimidate Jews and others they suspected of left-wing sympathies. Young thugs, members of the League of Awakening Magyars, took advantage of the unsettled conditions to engage in plunder and extortion.[33] However, the number and severity of the acts of terror committed in this period were much reduced from the earlier phase of the "White Terror," and the press, Parliament, and the government were now in a stronger position to challenge the special detachments and their patron, the Regent.

In March, shortly after Horthy's election to the regency, Count Apponyi, head of the Hungarian delegation to the Paris Peace Conference, publicly denounced the persistence of what he called "White Bolshevism" in Hungary. He warned that until the "rule of law" was restored, Hungary's reputation abroad would remained tarnished and the Hungarian cause could not be effectively advanced at the peace conference.[34] In the Parliament frequent calls were made for an end to arbitrary and illegal arrests. Even Count Teleki, who like other conservatives had previously spoken out only privately against the special detachments, now joined Apponyi in publicly decrying the fact that atrocities were still being committed in Hungary. He urged that order, Christian morality, and Western culture be reestablished as soon as possible, for otherwise Hungary would not be able to advance its cause abroad with sufficient force.[35]

In the face of this barrage of criticisms, and a condemnation of the "White Terror" by a British labor delegation that had been invited by the Hungarian government to investigate the situation,[36] Miklós Horthy struggled to find a way out of his predicament. On the one hand he no doubt saw the validity of the arguments of such respected statesmen as Apponyi and Teleki, and fundamentally agreed with them that law and order had to be restored. Yet he could think of no easy way to break with his Szeged friends, whom he truly regarded as national heroes who had performed acts of courage in the anti-Bolshevik campaign.[37] Any decisive action on his part to demobilize the special detachments might so alienate Gömbös, Prónay, and the other radical right-wingers that they would turn violently against him and undermine his position as the link between the main rightist camps.

By June, however, the pressure on Horthy to take action against his Szeged cronies had become intense. On June 10, at a special audience with the Regent, the Cabinet demanded that measures be taken to disband the special detachments and establish constitutional procedures. Otherwise, the Prime Minister warned, he and his entire Cabinet would resign. It must also have been made clear to Horthy that in the ensuing government crisis it would be quite unlikely that Parliament would be able to pass the legislation, promised him earlier, that would enhance the power of the regent.

In these circumstances Admiral Horthy was prepared finally to comply with the demands of the government, albeit still with great reluctance. With his approval a decree published on June 13 abolished all special detachments, their investigative duties to be taken over by "reinforced police and gendarmerie."[38] This was a significant step in the restoration of civilian authority. Yet Horthy took certain steps to minimize the impact of this decree. Prónay was retained as his bodyguard, and his detachment and Ostenburg's were not disbanded but instead were dispersed throughout the army. Moreover, a nucleus of both detachments continued to exist and even to maintain quarters in Budapest's luxury hotels. Even so, these steps caused great consternation among the extremist officers, especially when they proved insufficient to forestall a trade boycott of Hungary declared by the International Federation of Trade Unions in Amsterdam on June 20. In the wake of this unexpected blow to Hungary's international prestige, Simonyi-Semadám's government, which only days earlier had suffered the disgrace of having signed the Treaty of Trianon, resigned.

In this period Horthy privately spoke in contemptuous terms of his Cabinet and expressed disgust with parliamentary government. But he was too committed to constitutional government to risk what would now amount to a coup d'état, which Prónay was again urging on him.[39] Instead he tried once again to persuade István Bethlen to become Prime Minister. For two weeks in July Bethlen did conduct intensive negotiations with the leaders of the two main parties. His intention was to smooth over party differences to such an extent that they would agree to merge and form a new "unified party." Bethlen discovered, however, that the situation was not yet ripe for the kind of compromise solution he was envisioning. He therefore declined to continue his efforts and recommended to Horthy that Count Teleki be authorized to form the new government.[40] That the Regent followed Bethlen's advice, even though Teleki had become one of the more outspoken opponents of the special detachments, reflected Horthy's growing realization that only experienced leaders like Count Bethlen or Count

Teleki could bring prestige to the office of Prime Minister and preside over Hungary's recovery from the catastrophes that had beset her. Shortly after he took office on July 19, Teleki saw to it that legislation was passed in Parliament expanding the power of the regent. Indeed, this may have been a quid pro quo in Horthy's nomination of Teleki as Prime Minister. Law XII of 1920 gave additional authority to the regent along the lines demanded by Horthy at the time of his election. The regent was empowered to dissolve Parliament, although provision had to be made for it to be reconvened within three months. In case of a direct threat to the security of the country, the regent and his ministers were given the authority to deploy troops beyond Hungary's borders. Finally, the regent was given the power to grant amnesty. In demanding the power of amnesty, Horthy was no doubt thinking of his Szeged protégés who might at some point face criminal prosecution. As it turned out, however, it also proved a useful weapon in appeasing the Regent's enemies on the left.

For his part, Count Teleki must have accepted the office of Prime Minister only after receiving some indication from Horthy, direct or indirect, that the Regent would support his moderate foreign policy and his intention of restoring constitutional government. This meant that the influence of the army and the remaining special detachments would have to be curbed. Teleki attempted to persuade the great powers that the Hungarian government was making every effort to restore order and stability and to refute the accusation that Hungary was an outlaw bent on destroying the European equilibrium. The first fruits of Teleki's policies came in late July when the trade boycott of Hungary was called off. Teleki realized, however, that Hungary's standing in the international community could be restored only if and when the Treaty of Trianon was ratified. As noted above, he was able to persuade the Regent that ratification of the treaty was unavoidable.

Horthy's support of a policy of accommodation rather than obstruction was significant because members of the Parliament were naturally wary of the opprobrium that might be attached to those who ratified a peace settlement that was regarded by virtually all politically aware Hungarians as a catastrophe of enormous proportions. Admiral Horthy sympathized with the Awakening Magyars who surrounded the Parliament building on November 17, ratification day, and angrily abused the deputies who had just voted to ratify the Treaty of Trianon. But Horthy was pragmatic enough to realize that Hungary had no other choice. He was convinced, however, that the peace settlement in Danubian Europe was patently unjust and unwise. He fervently believed that the day could not be far off when all the national flags in Hungary, which had been lowered to half-mast as a sign of national mourning, would be raised once again to celebrate the restoration of Hungary to her prewar frontiers. Horthy fully embraced the motto that now became embedded in daily Hungarian parlance: "Rump Hungary is not a country, Greater Hungary is Heaven."

Count Teleki's success in reviving Miklós Horthy's conservative instincts caused great dismay among the radical right-wingers. Prónay noted bitterly in his diary that the "Hero of Otranto" seemed to lack all determination and was under the sway of such "Freemasons" as Thomas Hohler and Hungary's "Jew-loving aristocrats." This greatly disheartened Prónay, who feared that the opportunity "to emancipate the country from the influence of Jewish international Freemasonry" had been lost.[41] Stung by the criticisms of his Szeged officers, Horthy gave private assurances that he was not abandoning them. The plans for the "Czech operation" were not being discarded but merely postponed. The "White International" was not dead: negotiations with Ludendorff and the Bavarians would continue, and in the spring of 1921 the Germans, Poles, and Hungarians would combine to drive the Czechs out of Slovakia. The special detachments had to be disbanded, but he would see to it that none of his friends would be prosecuted. After all, as he admitted candidly even to foreign diplomats, there was a bit of the Awakening Magyar in him as in all Hungarians.[42]

No matter how solemnly and sincerely Horthy sought to assure his Szeged friends that he would not forsake them, his metamorphosis from the radical right-wing military commander of the White Army in Szeged and Siófok to the cautious, conservative head of state in the Royal Castle of Budapest continued inexorably after the ratification of the peace treaty. True, the clandestine negotiations with the extremist German groups went on, with Horthy's approval, for several more years. But more and more the Szeged officers came to realize that the Regent's radical utterances were empty rhetoric. Sensing this, Prónay decided in December 1920 to try to force Horthy's hand by implementing the "Czech action" without informing the Regent ahead of time. Apparently he hoped that if he could create a *fait accompli*, Horthy would be able to ignore the warnings of his Foreign Ministry and give his approval to the operation. Specific plans were thus drawn up for the dispatch of Hungarian "free corps" into Slovakia on Christmas Day. Colonel Bauer was to arrange similar incursions into the Sudetenland. These actions, according to Prónay, would spark rebellion and cause the collapse of the Czechoslovak state. However, since the Hungarian conspirators seemed incapable of maintaining secrecy, both Budapest and Prague were soon buzzing with rumors of a German-Hungarian scheme to invade Czechoslovakia. Apprised of Prónay's scheme, Count Teleki declared that he would take no responsibility for it and would in fact warn the Czechoslovak government of what was afoot.[43]

In the circumstances, the Regent had to summon Prónay and urge him to call off the operation. "What are you trying to accomplish, you clumsy oaf?" Horthy asked him. "This will bring the country to ruin." Such an operation, he insisted, was bound to fail since Prague already knew about it. The Hungarian currency would plunge. As chief of state he could not take responsibility for a plan that was doomed to failure. In any case, Horthy insisted, he and his Chief of Staff had a plan to be implemented in the following spring, by which he would "purge the *Felvidék* [Slovakia] of Czechs."[44] Prónay had no choice but to accede to Horthy's request, but his disappointment with the Regent was even further deepened.

Ironically, Horthy's plan for driving the Czechs out of Slovakia in the spring of 1921 was every bit as preposterous and irresponsible as Prónay's. It called for the massacre of Czech soldiers in their barracks by the timely opening of cyanide gas cylinders. "In five minutes," Horthy had told an incredulous Colonel Lehár in November, "all the Czechs will be done for" and Slovakia will be ripe for Magyarization.[45] When the Regent and his Chief of Staff presented to the Cabinet in early 1921 a revised plan (minus the cyanide gas attack) for fomenting rebellion in Slovakia so that Hungarian paramilitary units could be dispatched to "restore order," the plan was rejected. The Foreign Minister, Gusztáv Gratz, was now bold enough to declare that such "adventurous military plans" were "doomed in advance to failure." Reflecting the frustrations that many of the moderate conservatives had experienced in the past year as they were forced to accommodate themselves to military interference in domestic and foreign policy-making, Gratz asserted that "to play *va banque*, to risk the whole country in the interests of a plan for the realization of which, according to my conviction, there is very little hope, would be a policy with which I could not identify."[46] In fact, Count Teleki and Gusztáv Gratz were now in the position to reaffirm the fundamental principle that only the Foreign Ministry was empowered to formulate policy affecting Hungary's international relations. That this was now the case in Hungary was reflected in the decision made by Teleki and Gratz, precisely in this period, to seek a rapprochement with Czechoslovakia. In the late winter and early spring negotiations conducted by high-level delegations from each country made considerable progress in reducing tensions and in reviving the natural trade patterns that had existed in Danubian Europe before World War I. Even the delicate matter of territorial concessions by Czechoslovakia was broached, although Eduard Beneš insisted that this could be realized only after a period of normal, friendly relations between the two countries.[47]

That Regent Horthy approved the idea of a rapprochement with Czechoslovakia clearly reveals his remarkable capacity for blithely making abrupt shifts and turns in his foreign policy views. Over the past two years he had sanctioned a series of aggressive plans aimed at the destruction of Czechoslovakia; almost overnight, however, he became euphoric about the prospects for a diplomatic arrangement with Prague that would result in the return of at least some of Hungary's lost territories. On March 7, 1921, he exultantly told Colonel Lehár that within a few days he hoped to be entering Pozsony (Bratislava).[48] One can understand why Lehár and, indeed, most of those in whom Horthy confided in his first year as regent eventually came to the conclusion that he was hopelessly naive and that many of his utterances, especially those that related to hopes and plans for overturning the peace settlement, could not be taken seriously.

It was during the ministry of Count Teleki that certain patterns of government emerged that in fact would characterize most of the twenty-four years of Admiral Horthy's tenure as regent. For the most part Horthy did not immerse himself in the process of policy-making, whether foreign or domestic. He had an aversion to written reports and rarely studied or composed position papers or other government memorandums, preferring instead to have his ministers report orally to him. Although Horthy seldom gave specific instructions to his ministers, he was of course consulted on major issues and had the opportunity to state his personal views. His ministers quickly learned, however, that the Regent's spontaneous and informal opinions on a given subject would in many cases be immoderate, bellicose, or hopelessly naive. Yet once things had been carefully explained to him by Count Bethlen or Count Teleki, even Horthy himself seemed eventually to realize that the ideas and schemes that flowed so easily from his lips could for the most part not be implemented. In almost all cases, therefore, he ended up deferring, however reluctantly, to his Prime Minister.

Only rarely in the 1920s did Horthy convene the Cabinet for a so-called Crown Council, at which matters of vital importance would be considered in his presence. Much of Horthy's time in his first year as regent was instead devoted to ceremonies and rituals that were designed to restore faith in and obedience to the government and to promote the ideals of "Christian nationalism." On his now familiar white steed Horthy carried out the "liberation" of those towns and cities, including Szeged, that were newly evacuated by the Romanians, South Slavs, or the French. He ceremoniously visited hospitals, re-opened schools, and presided over frequent military parades. A self-styled "itinerant preacher,"[49] he crisscrossed the country and gave speeches warning his countrymen that only through hard work and discipline could Hungary regain its former prosperity and grandeur.

Only in a few areas of special interest to him did Admiral Horthy take the initiative in the formation of policy. In the tradition of Emperor Francis Joseph, Regent Horthy took very seriously his title of Supreme War Lord and regarded the armed forces as his special preserve. Appalled at the idea that, according to the terms of the Treaty of Trianon, the army would have to be reduced to 35,000 volunteer soldiers and that the General Staff would have to be disbanded, Horthy seized every opportunity in 1920 to try to persuade British and French representatives and the general public in the West of the unfairness and foolishness of these restrictions. On several occasions, both public and private, he argued that the Czechs and the Romanians were totally incapable of defending the Carpathian Mountains from possible incursions by the Red Army. The Romanians, he asserted, were unreliable fighters because they preferred "bloodless wars." The Czechs were pro-Communists. Only the Hungarians possessed the proper martial spirit and traditional fighting skills to fulfill their key role in Danubian Europe as defenders of Western Civilization. How could the Entente in good conscience allow Hungary to become a third-rate power?

When such arguments proved unavailing, Horthy showed no compunction about actively supporting various subterfuges for evading the military terms of Trianon. One such program designed to foster military discipline and provide a kind of paramilitary training for Hungarian boys came to be known as the Horthy *Levente*.

In a more general sense, Admiral Horthy was intent on restoring the Hungary of his youth, a country unsullied by what he regarded as the pernicious ideas and institutions that had briefly triumphed during the revolutionary period. As its first act in 1920 the Hungarian Parliament had declared null and void all legislation introduced by the Károlyi or Kun governments. With the Regent's full support and inspiration, Parliament approved legislation in March 1921 that provided the legal framework for "the more effective defense of the state and the social order." In practice this meant the suppression of the Communist party and other left-wing activity deemed by the government to be subversive. Horthy's yearning to return to an idyllic past and to revive the concept of gentlemanly honor also led him to insist on the reintroduction of dueling as a method for resolving disagreements among officers. Horthy is not known ever to have participated in a duel, although, as will be seen, on one occasion during his regency he seriously considered issuing a challenge to someone whom he deemed to have insulted him. Nonetheless, Horthy's support for dueling ensured its survival in Hungary throughout the interwar period, at a time when in most European countries it had long been prohibited as an irrational, archaic custom. Hungary's reputation as a country that was regressing towards a primitive past was further enhanced by the reinstatement of corporal punishment and public floggings as a penalty for certain criminal offenses.[50]

The solution to two of the most contentious problems in the Hungary of 1920 also reflected the Regent's influence. Like a great many of his countrymen, Admiral Horthy believed that Hungary had a "Jewish problem" that demanded some solution. Widespread revulsion over the excesses of the revolutionary governments facilitated the open expression of anti-Jewish sentiments that had been muted in the more tolerant atmosphere of prewar Hungary. The fact that most Jews had had no connection with and no sympathy for Béla Kun's government, as leaders of the Jewish community had tried to explain to Horthy on several occasions, was simply disregarded in the growing hysteria. Jews were now routinely excoriated as a kind of multifaced enemy: the fanatical Communist, the grasping capitalist, the war saboteur, the alien intruder. Many Hungarians deeply resented the highly visible presence of Jews in the professions and in economic life. Indeed, though Jews represented only 6 percent of the population in 1920, they were disproportionately represented in the medical profession (59.9 percent), law (50.6 percent), journalism (34.3 percent), and high finance (61.7 percent).[51] For many Hungarians, Regent Horthy among them, this was an intolerable situation, and the question to be answered was not whether the Jews should be punished for their alleged crimes against the nation, but what form the punishment should take.

In Count Teleki the Regent found a willing collaborator in the search for a solution to the "Jewish problem." Teleki, otherwise one of the most humane and moderate statesman of interwar Hungary, shared Horthy's disdain for the Jews. In an analysis in part drawn from his areas of scholarly expertise, geography and ethnography, Teleki argued that a large number of those Jews who had immigrated to Hungary in the last half of the nineteenth century were "unassimilated, nationless, and even antinational." They had come to predominate in the press and literature, where they promulgated a "militant cosmopolitanism" that was injurious to the "national ideal."[52] A staunch supporter of the rule of law and the precepts of Christian morality, Teleki had denounced the violent and illegal measures against Jews that occurred during the "White Terror." He likewise regarded as unthinkable the ultimate solution, already being bruited about in radical right-wing circles, of expelling the Jews from Hungary. Instead he won the Regent's quick approval and strong support for a legislative act aimed at reducing the influence of Jews in Hungary's intellectual and cultural life. Agitation for such legislation was particularly pronounced among university students and faculties, who sought, sometimes violently, to prevent the enrollment of Jewish students as Hungarian universities reopened in 1920 after the revolutionary upheavals.

The *numerus clausus*, passed by the Hungarian Parliament in September 1920, stipulated that enrollment of students of various "races and nationalities" in Hungarian universities was to be limited to their percentage in the general population. Thus, the Jews, who were not specifically mentioned in the legislation, could henceforth not constitute more than 6 percent of university student bodies.[53] Since Jews had represented more than 25 percent of the prewar student population, the *numerus clausus* was a severe blow to their future educational advancement. In later years, as will be seen, the *numerus clausus* was not strictly enforced, but Hungary's adoption of Europe's first postwar anti-Jewish legislation gained for Admiral Horthy an unsavory reputation as one of Europe's most prominent anti-Semites. Such notoriety did not embarrass Horthy; indeed, on several occasions later in his career, he would speak with a kind of pride of how he had been the first statesman in Europe to take action against the Jews.

Regent Horthy took a special interest in one other policy issue that agitated Hungarian political life in 1920: land reform. In every East European country the peasants emerged from the World War I with the expectation that they would be rewarded for their great war sacrifices by grants of land. This land hunger was particularly strong in Hungary, where 36 percent of the land was in the form of large estates owned by only 2,400 individuals. Hungary's aristocratic landowners firmly resisted the idea that any of their holdings, their private property, should be taken from them and distributed. Yet political realities dictated that some form of land reform, however superficial, be introduced.

The largest party in Parliament, the Smallholders, led by István Nagyatádi Szabó, was nominally in favor of extensive land reform. However, the Smallholders were a heterogeneous party in which few sympathizers could be found for the most impoverished sector of Hungarian society, the three million landless farm servants. Moreover, Nagyatádi Szabó, though appointed Minister of Agriculture in August 1920, possessed neither the political experience nor the personal charisma to battle successfully with the Hungarian magnates, who by this time had regained much of the self-confidence and aura of authority they had lost in the revolutionary period. As a result, the land reform act passed in December, dubbed the "Nagyatádi Act," provided for only a modest distribution of land and left the large estates virtually untouched. The approximately one million acres of land offered for distribution did make possible a substantial increase in the number of land-owning peasants, but the dwarf farms thus created were destined to be inefficient because of the poor quality of the land distributed and the difficulty of competing with the large estates.[54]

The "Nagyatádi Act" of 1920 and subsequent minor extensions of the land reform ensured that Hungary would remain "the homeland of the great landowners." As far as Miklós Horthy was concerned, this was both logical and natural. As noted above, he regarded it as a fundamental truth that there simply was not enough land in Hungary to satisfy the land hunger of all the peasants. The vigorous economic expansion and apparently efficient agricultural production in Hungary during the decades before the Great War seemed proof enough to Horthy that Hungary could regain its prosperity only by restoring prewar conditions in the countryside. Yet he was not averse to the strengthening of that group of enterprising peasants known in Hungary as smallholders and in Russia as *kulaks*. Horthy must have sensed that some of his strongest political support had come from the smallholders, whose leader had been the first to propose publicly that Horthy be elected regent. Horthy later had his differences with Szabó, but the Regent continued in the sincere belief that the smallholders represented a reliably "patriotic, upright, and conservative" social group in Hungary.[55]

It was this conviction that prompted Admiral Horthy not only to approve the land reform of 1920 but also to establish an organization, the *Vitézi Rend* (Order of Heroes), that made possible further, albeit modest, distribution of land.[56] The Order of Heroes was one of the few innovations of the interwar period that can be attributed directly to Miklós Horthy, who conceived it as a way of rewarding those Hungarians who had performed heroically in World War I or in the anti-Bolshevik campaigns. Only Christian men with Magyar names and an "unblemished record of patriotism" were eligible. Those selected were bestowed the title *vitéz* and were awarded plots of land of about 20 acres, called "heroes' estates." Each "hero" received in addition a house, stable, two horses, and a cow. The "hero" was inducted into the order by Horthy in a solemn ceremony akin to the dubbing of a knight in the Middle Ages. Like a medieval lord, the Regent touched the shoulder of his vassal with a sword, and the "hero" swore an oath of loyalty to his Commander in Chief. During Horthy's regency over 21,000 men were to be honored as "heroes," most of them of peasant origin. Of course, as a form of land reform the impact of the "heroes' estates" was negligible, but the *Vitézi Rend* served a useful propagandistic purpose in projecting an image of the Regent as a benefactor of the common people. The "heroes" and their families (for both title and land were hereditary) became the staunchest and most loyal of Horthy's supporters. By contrast, Hungary's aristocrats were disdainful of the Order of Heroes. Only with the greatest reluctance were they persuaded to donate land to be distributed to such "parvenus."[57]

By the end of Horthy's first year as Hungary's head of state, it was becoming clear that earlier fears that he would be the pawn of radical right-wing military officers had been unfounded. It was the authoritarian system of the Dualist period, rather than a totalitarian dictatorship based on the "Szeged idea" to which he was being guided by Teleki and Bethlen. This implied a pluralist political system in which considerable expression of political opinion would be permitted in Parliament and the media. British diplomats in Budapest, especially Thomas Hohler, urged Horthy on several occasions in 1920 to emulate Britain and open the "exhaust pipes" so that parliamentary and socialist extremists could have their say. The "noise and smell" might be an annoyance, but the common sense of the people would prevail.[58] Horthy sometimes found the "noise and smell" of parliamentary debate extremely distasteful. More than once in 1920 he privately berated members of Parliament and threatened to sweep the whole group of politicians away and establish a dictatorship.[59] But Horthy was too respectful of Hungarian political traditions to give serious thought to governing without Parliament. Moreover, like many Hungarians of the nobility, he took pride in the importance that an unwritten constitution and an independent Parliament had played in both British and Hungarian history. He insisted, however, that political stability could be attained only when electoral procedures ensured the political hegemony of a consolidated "Christian National" party. As early as November 1920, Horthy was developing a plan for a new franchise that would result in a reliable Parliament and would make possible the creation of a new Cabinet with Count Bethlen as Prime Minister.[60]

A pluralist political system in interwar Hungary implied some accommodation with the forces of the left. Of course, for Horthy the *sine qua non* of any regime over which he presided was prohibition of the Communist party. Towards the more moderate left, however, Admiral Horthy proved much more open, especially as the bitter memories of 1918–1919 began to fade. Though he had a distinct aversion to democratic and socialist ideals, he nonetheless was pragmatic enough to see the value in grasping the "calloused hands" of the workers that had been offered to him shortly after his election to the regency. His message to the workers, repeated many times in speeches, was that as long as they worked hard and refrained from strikes, he would listen to their grievances with a favorable ear. Perhaps these words had mainly a propagandistic purpose, but in July 1920 Horthy did have an unpublicized meeting with Ferenc Miakits, the leader of the Social Democratic party, at which he suggested that once the regime was consolidated, he would make sure that the Socialists would have substantial representation in the Parliament. Although Miakits had his doubts about Horthy's ability to fulfill this pledge, he seemed to be persuaded of the Regent's sincerity.[61] Another gesture to Horthy's political enemies was made at Christmas in 1920, when, using his newly legislated power, he issued a general amnesty of those who had committed political crimes in the past two years. This measure, to be sure, was largely designed to protect from prosecution those extremist officers who, in the grip of what was euphemistically termed "patriotic enthusiasm" (*hazafias felbuzdulás*), had committed outrages during the "White Terror." But also included were a significant number of individuals who, because of suspected sympathies for or participation in the Hungarian Soviet Republic, had been incarcerated in the notorious detention camp of Zalaegerszeg or various prisons. The Regent's gesture was a signal that the harshly repressive and extralegal methods of 1919–1920 would not become a permanent feature of the emerging Hungarian government.

All in all, Miklós Horthy had managed to navigate the turbulent waters of 1920 with considerable success. Despite his lack of political sophistication, his remarkable malleability, and his bungling, naive attempts to support the "White International," Horthy had been able to project a public image of a confident, determined leader in whom the Hungarian people could place their trust. Sporadically and almost inadvertently, Horthy had begun to distance himself from the radical right-wing officers without totally alienating them. He had continued the shrewd policy, initiated even before his entry into Budapest in November 1919, of maintaining personal ties with representatives of the workers and of the Jewish community, who would bitterly protest against the government's repressive acts yet would somehow leave an audience with the Regent with a favorable impression of Horthy's apparent sincerity and sympathy. And he had continued his close collaboration with István Bethlen, to whom he intended to entrust the reins of government in the near future.

The fact that after one year of Admiral Horthy's regency Hungary had made significant progress in recovering from the traumatic events of 1919 did not escape the notice of foreign political observers. Among British and American diplomats, especially, there was a growing tendency to view as exaggerated Horthy's reputation as a rabid anti-Semite and champion of the "White Terror" and to discredit the accusations against him made by Ignác Trebitsch-Lincoln and others.[62] More and more Horthy was seen as a sincere, honorable leader, a bit old-fashioned and rigid in some of his views, but nonetheless a reliable opponent of communism and an admirer of the Anglo-Saxon world. In the words of a British diplomat in Budapest, Admiral Horthy was really "our creation" and was "far and away the best man to consolidate the internal political situation in Hungary."[63] Even those with no reason to admire the Hungarian Regent, nonetheless marveled at his apparent success in guiding Hungary in its return to normality. Eduard Beneš, no friend of Horthy or Hungary, concluded in late 1920 that the Regent was an adroit statesman whose regime was more solid than many had assumed.[64]

Within Hungary, however, a significant segment of the political community viewed with considerable misgiving the growing popularity and prestige of the Regent. The loyal supporters of ex-king Charles, including dignitaries of the Roman Catholic Church and some of the most prominent and affluent landowners, were alarmed by the dilatory and ambiguous way Horthy had been responding to royal messages and directives. From his villa in Prangins, Switzerland, where he was living in exile, Charles was quietly and secretly making preparations for his return to Hungary and restoration to the throne, despite the commitment he had made to the Entente to refrain from such activities. Heeding the Regent's advice that nothing be done that might jeopardize Hungary's position as the peace treaty was being drawn up, Charles had bided his time but was prepared to move forward with dispatch on June 4, 1920, when the Treaty of Trianon was signed. On that day Gyula Bornemissza, the Hungarian Minister in Switzerland, delivered to Regent Horthy a letter from Charles.[65] Asserting that he remained Hungary's legally crowned king who had abdicated "none of his rights," Charles expressed his resolve to take part in the "rehabilitation of the country." He thought it unlikely that the Western powers would attempt to prevent his restoration; in any case, he had received statements of support from the French government. Thus, he intended to exercise his sovereign rights "as soon as possible, perhaps during this year." Praising Horthy for the "energy and circumspection you displayed in the past," Charles asked him to make appropriate preparations and to inform him of the most appropriate time to reclaim the throne.

Charles's resolve to reclaim his throne in the near future created a crisis of conscience for Miklós Horthy and set the stage in Hungary for a prolonged and rancorous political debate with fateful consequences in 1921. The balance of power between the legitimists and the "free-electors" in Hungary was a precarious one. Probably a substantial majority of politically conscious Hungarians could be counted among the "free-electors", who believed that Hungary was legally and constitutionally free to choose its own king, whether he be a member of the Habsburg family or of some other European dynasty. This was the viewpoint of most of the Smallholder delegates in Parliament, some of whom were viscerally anti-Habsburg and preferred a "national king" of Magyar origins. But those who regarded Charles as their reigning "Catholic, apostolic, and historical" king, though relatively small in numbers, nonetheless wielded important influence and firmly believed that their position was grounded in constitutional law.[66] In the ranks of the legitimists could be counted many of the prominent aristocratic statesmen of Hungary, most of them Roman Catholics whose estates were located in the traditionally pro-Habsburg areas of western Hungary: Apponyi, Andrássy, Sigray, Pallavicini. In the army most of the younger officers seemed to share Gömbös's distaste for the Habsburg dynasty, but the officer corps of 1920 and 1921 still consisted largely of veterans of the "*kaiserlich and königlich*" army. For many of these officers, including Colonel Anton Lehár and Gyula Ostenburg, the oath of loyalty taken to their new commander, Admiral Horthy, did not supersede their oath to King Charles, from which they had never been formally released. Legitimist sentiment was also strong in the Roman Catholic hierarchy, from village priests to Father Zadravecz, now the chaplain of the army, to Pope Benedict XV, who in August privately expressed his sympathy for Charles's aspirations to regain the Hungarian throne.[67]

Somewhere between the militant Habsburgophobia of Gyula Gömbös and the zealous legitimism of Count Gyula Andrássy and Count Antal Zichy was a middle ground to which some pragmatic Hungarian statesmen gravitated. Such was the case with István Bethlen, who argued that a premature attempt to solve the regal question in Hungary would only poison Hungarian political life and throw Danubian Europe into renewed turmoil. After all, he argued, a Habsburg restoration could hardly be viewed as having ramifications only for Hungary. The victorious Entente had placed a prohibition on the restoration of the Habsburg dynasty in Austria or in Hungary. In addition, the leaders of the Successor States were likely to regard a Habsburg restoration in Hungary as merely a prelude to an attempt to claim the throne in Vienna and reconstitute the Habsburg Empire in its former frontiers. For these reasons, Bethlen recommended that the regal question be put into abeyance until conditions were more propitious for its solution.[68]

As was often the case in 1920, Admiral Horthy found Bethlen's analysis of this issue to be compelling. But unlike Count Bethlen, Horthy could hardly approach the problem in a purely dispassionate way. For the Hungarian Regent the issue was not only a very controversial political problem but also a wrenching personal dilemma that forced him to try to reconcile what seemed to be the conflicting claims of personal honor and political responsibility. The fervent and tearful pledge he had made to Charles in November 1918, and the realization that he had never been formally released from his oath of loyalty, weighed heavily on Horthy's conscience.[69] For Horthy, and for many Hungarians of his generation, the breaking of an oath by a gentleman was a grievous transgression and a serious mark of dishonor. Thus, during 1920 Horthy was very defensive about accusations that he was abandoning King Charles. "You can spit in my face," he told Count Anton Sigray, "if I am anything but the most emphatic legitimist."[70] Some of Charles's supporters remained unconvinced. They noted uneasily that the Regent was living in the royal palace, bestowing titles, and in general acting more and more like a man who hoped to usurp the throne. When, however, in September 1920, rumors about the Regent's alleged ambitions began to spread, and a delegation of EkSz members, headed by Father Zadravecz, visited Horthy to determine his intentions, he melodramatically denied that he had any aspirations to become king of Hungary: "Even if the whole country, young and old, were to kneel down along the banks of the Danube and beseech me to become king, I would reach for a revolver rather than the crown."[71] In a speech on October 17 Horthy spoke in similar terms, insisting that his fondest hope was to see Hungary once again prosperous and powerful under its crowned king. Like Count Bethlen, however, he insisted that conditions were not suitable for an immediate solution to the problem. Any rash, poorly thought-out move would only aggravate the situation.

By the fall of 1920 Miklós Horthy had apparently concluded that any attempt to restore Charles IV to the Hungarian throne would have to be postponed indefinitely. Unlike the ex-king and some of his advisors in Switzerland, who had deluded themselves into believing that the majority of Hungarians longed for the return of a Habsburg king, Regent Horthy could not be oblivious to the indications that Charles was by no means as beloved in Hungary as Francis Joseph had been, and that anti-Habsburg sentiments had been intensified in the wake of a lost war and a humiliating peace settlement. The increasingly bitter exchanges between "free-electors" and legitimists in the Parliament and in the press during October and November suggested that a restoration bid by Charles might cause severe civil disruptions and possibly civil war. An even more important consideration in Admiral Horthy's thinking was the veto of a Habsburg restoration imposed by the victorious great powers and the threat of retaliation by Hungary's new neighbors, especially Czechoslovakia and Yugoslavia, who feared the repercussions in Danubian Europe of a Habsburg monarch again on the throne in Budapest and perhaps in Vienna as well.

As an Anglophile who even before his election to the regency had argued that Hungary had no alternative but submission to the dictates of the Entente powers, Horthy found it psychologically impossible to defy Britain by actively working to restore Charles IV to the throne. On several occasions in late 1920 he assured British diplomats that he would not engage in any "Habsburg intrigues," for he regarded the return of any Habsburg to the throne of Hungary "to-day and for a long time to come" as out of the question and a disaster for his country. In one such conversation he asserted that, in his opinion, ninety-five percent of the nation would never willingly take Charles back, and since the great powers and the Little Entente were opposed, it was "nonsense talking about the question."[72] Horthy's inclination to postpone the question indefinitely was strengthened in February 1921, when an acrimonious debate in Parliament between "free-electors" and legitimists shattered an attempt Prime Minister Teleki was making to merge the two largest parties and create a unified government party. On February 6, in an attempt to quell the growing agitation, Thomas

Hohler issued a statement to the Hungarian press in which he warned that the Entente powers would not tolerate a Habsburg restoration in Hungary. This was reaffirmed a week later in a formal resolution of the Conference of Ambassadors in Paris.

These circumstances must be considered when evaluating the judgments of Horthy's political enemies and some historians who would later assert that personal ambition and vanity were the major determinants in Horthy's reluctance to work energetically to fulfill the fervent pledge he had made to Charles in November 1918.[73] It is certainly true that Horthy shunned participation in any secret planning for a restoration attempt, despite the fact that he had exhibited real enthusiasm for equally risky and unrealistic enterprises, such as the "White International." Treaty revision was an objective to which Horthy made a total emotional commitment; the restoration of Charles was not. He also showed no inclination to quell the anti-Habsburg sentiment that had developed in the General Staff. No doubt Horthy savored his first year as a head of state residing in the royal palace. He must have been gratified by the flattering comments about his leadership qualities made by his admirers and political manipulators like Gömbös. Horthy appears to have taken great pride in fulfilling the role of a captain who rescues his ship from near disaster and guides her safely toward port. In the near future who better than he could be trusted to make sure that the Hungarian ship of state continued along the right course? There is also some evidence that Horthy had doubts about the leadership of Hungary's ex-king. In one conversation with Colonel Lehár in late September 1920, he described Charles as "incompetent" and suggested that his son, Otto, might be a better choice in the future.[74] Thus, behind Horthy's emotional and unwavering protestations of loyalty to Charles during 1920 one detects a certain sense of relief that for the time being international conditions precluded a Habsburg restoration.

If Miklós Horthy is to be ascribed some responsibility for the unfortunate events that were soon to unfold in Hungary, it must be because of his failure to inform Charles in a direct and frank manner of how unfavorable conditions were in Hungary for any restoration attempt. He was simply unable to find a satisfactory solution to the crisis of conscience in which he found himself. How could he, for example, convey to Charles his conviction that ninety-five percent of the population did not favor his return? A shrewder statesman might have found a diplomatic way of disabusing Charles of his illusions. But Admiral Horthy lacked such skills, and resorted instead to procrastination and formulary recitations of his devotion to the legitimist principle. Thus, Horthy never responded in writing to Charles's letter of June 4. He never challenged Charles's assertion in that letter that his restoration would be viewed favorably by the Western powers.

Regent Horthy remained similarly silent when he received a second letter from the ex-king. In that communication, dated November 9, Charles gave assurances that he would rule Hungary as a constitutional monarch and that he had no intention of using his Hungarian throne as a springboard for gaining "sovereign power in any other country."[75] Charles instructed the Regent to make public his letter and thereby calm those in Hungary who feared that a Habsburg restoration would imply the eventual resurrection of the Dual Monarchy. Instead, however, Horthy suppressed the letter, no doubt fearing that its publication would merely exacerbate the situation and be counterproductive. Since, as in the previous case, he once again failed to respond in writing to this communication from Charles, Horthy provided no explanation for his refusal to carry out the ex-king's instructions. Admiral Horthy's ambiguous conduct convinced many of the legitimists that he could no longer be counted on as a trustworthy servant of the King. Yet despite their warnings, Charles remained confident that Horthy, whose rise to power he claimed to have engineered from afar, would never break his oath of obedience and loyalty. No doubt he regarded it as a sign of the Regent's essential goodwill that late in 1920 Horthy approved the appointment of two prominent legitimists, Count Sigray and Colonel Lehár, to the most important political and military posts in West Hungary, a region traditionally regarded as most sympathetic to the Habsburgs and thus a potential launching area for a restoration attempt. Buoyed by excessive optimism, largely ignorant of the true political situation in Hungary, and convinced that the great powers would place no obstacles in his way, Charles went forward with secret planning for his return to Hungary.[76] The stage was thus set for a dramatic confrontation between the King and the Regent, whose views on the timing and prospects of a Habsburg restoration had become irreconcilable.

4

The Regent and the King in 1921

On Easter weekend in 1921, March 26 and 27, political life came to a standstill in Hungary. The National Assembly was not in session, its members having dispersed to their homes throughout Hungary. The diplomatic corps was enjoying a brief respite from the affairs of state, many of them guests at the grand estates of the Hungarian aristocracy. Regent Horthy planned a quiet holiday with his family in the royal palace. Hoping to take advantage of this political inactivity, Charles IV chose precisely this weekend to carry out his plan of appearing unannounced in Hungary, persuading Horthy to hand over power, and regaining his throne.

Charles embarked on his attempt to regain power with an optimism undiminished by the warnings of many of his supporters, and of Regent Horthy himself, that conditions were not yet propitious. So confident was the ex-king in the success of his enterprise that he chose not to inform any of the Hungarian legitimists of his plan. With his young wife, Zita, Charles had come to believe that the mere news of his appearance in Hungary and the willingness of the Regent to hand over the reins of government would revive in the Hungarian people the former affection for and obedience to their monarch. The resulting ground swell of support for a Habsburg restoration would make an impression on the great powers. At worst, Italy and Great Britain would be neutral. Moreover, Charles's secret negotiations with the French Prime Minister, Aristide Briand, had led him to believe that the French government would offer support if he managed to carry out a *fait accompli* in Hungary.[1] In the circumstances Hungary's neighbors might make a lot of noise, but would not intervene militarily.

Shorn of his moustache and armed with a forged Spanish passport, Charles thus departed his Swiss villa and arrived undetected on March 26, Holy Saturday, in the Hungarian town of Szombathely. There he made his way to the palace of Count János

Mikes, a Catholic bishop and prominent legitimist. The astonishing news quickly spread among local legitimists and by the early hours of March 27 Charles had at his service a small privy council, including József Vass, Horthy's Minister of Education, and Colonel Lehár. The latter, assured by Charles that his restoration attempt had support "from the highest level" in the West, placed himself and his soldiers at the disposal of His Majesty.[2] Lehár warned, however, that the enterprise involved significant military risks, especially if the army was not united or if civil disturbances occurred. He thus insisted that Charles regain the throne not in a "march on Budapest," that is, a revolutionary putsch, but through legal means and in cooperation with Regent Horthy. Charles preferred not to dwell on the military risks.[3] But he did agree that Count Teleki, the Prime Minister, who by coincidence was spending the weekend at the nearby estate of Count Sigray, be summoned to join in the deliberations.

Roused from his sleep at 2:00 A.M., Teleki at first feared horrible news: perhaps there had been a coup d'état and Horthy had been assassinated. When he was informed by Bishop Mikes of the true reason for his early morning journey, Teleki's fear turned to consternation. As he appeared before his former king, Teleki could only mutter "too soon, too soon," and urge Charles to return immediately to Switzerland, for otherwise civil war would likely break out in Hungary and the Little Entente countries would intervene.[4] Charles replied that there was no turning back at this point for the die had been cast, *"alea iacta est."* In the circumstances, Teleki, who was clearly under great psychological strain, finally agreed with the others that the only possible course of action now was for Charles to travel to Budapest to confer directly with the Regent. Charles was confident that Horthy would be "absolutely loyal" and would do nothing that would tarnish his honor as a military officer. Count Teleki and Colonel Lehár were cautiously optimistic, but recommended that Horthy be offered some inducements to guarantee his cooperation. It was decided that, at the appropriate time in his conversation with the Regent, Charles would offer to confer on him the title of prince and to award him the Order of Maria Theresa, an honor that Admiral Horthy had long coveted.[5]

All who participated in these discussions realized the need for rapid action. Accordingly, Teleki left by car for Budapest at 6:30 that Easter Sunday morning. His task was to inform the Regent of the imminent arrival of Charles and, by implication, to prevent him from consulting with Gömbös or other advisors who were hostile to a Habsburg restoration. Accompanied by Count Sigray, Charles departed one hour later. However, the car in which Teleki was traveling somehow took a wrong turn along the way and arrived in Budapest much later that day. Some political observers, noting that the road from Szombathely to the capital was straight and should have posed no difficulty for the Prime Minister's experienced chauffeur, later speculated that Teleki had had second thoughts and decided to use the excuse of a "wrong turn" to relieve himself of the necessity of choosing sides.

Charles's arrival at the royal palace early that afternoon was thus totally unannounced. Unaware of the momentous events that had been unfolding, Miklós Horthy was just sitting down to an Easter dinner with his wife. The first attempt of his aide de camp, László Magasházy, to draw him away from the table met resistance from Magda Horthy, who insisted that her husband should at least be allowed to finish his soup without distraction. Once the first course was completed, however, Horthy withdrew and received the startling news. The Regent had little time to collect his thoughts and no opportunity to phone Bethlen or Gömbös for advice: he had to grapple with the situation on his own. One of Horthy's bodyguards, sensing the gravity of the situation and hoping to embolden Horthy, solemnly declared: "The Guard will be faithful until death to the Regent. In the name of the Magyar nation we ask the Regent to remain true to the oath he has taken to the nation."[6]

Within minutes Horthy was embracing Charles and leading him into the regent's (formerly the king's) office. There then ensued an emotional, two hour discussion that Horthy would later describe as "the most difficult moments in my entire life" and a "thoroughly odious" experience.[7] The conversation between the thirty-four-year-old ex-king and the fifty-four-year-old regent began inauspiciously. Charles thanked Horthy for serving as regent but declared that the time had come for him to "hand over power to me," to which Horthy promptly replied: "This is a disaster. In the name of God, Your Majesty must leave at once and return to Switzerland, before it's too late and the Powers learn of your presence in Budapest."[8] Charles replied that there was no turning back for he had "burned his bridges." Sensing that the flustered regent was undergoing a wrenching crisis of conscience, Charles, speaking in

German, proceeded over the next two hours to use every possible argument and inducement to break down Horthy's resistance. He reminded him of the tearful pledge of loyalty he had made at Schönbrunn Palace in November 1918. He pointed out that Horthy, like all other Habsburg officers, had never been released from his sworn oath of obedience to the monarch. Is it possible, Charles asked, "that you would disobey a command of your King?"[9] Unnerved by these arguments, Horthy's responses became disjointed and vacillating as he searched for some way out of the dilemma in which he now found himself. He acknowledged the pledge of loyalty he had sworn two and a half years earlier, but pointed out to Charles that in the meantime he had pledged before the National Assembly to serve the Hungarian nation. Furthermore, the army was now loyal to the Regent, Charles would never be able to form a Cabinet, and, besides, the majority of Hungarians opposed him. Thus, the timing was very bad; it would take many years to prepare things properly. Why had Charles not given him advanced warning, as he had promised in one of his letters?

Shocked by Horthy's recalcitrance, Charles attempted methodically to rebut each of these points. It was he, the King, who had the ultimate responsibility to the nation, not the Regent. As for forming a government, Sigray, Teleki, and Vass had already agreed to serve. If, Charles added with emphasis, Horthy did not submit to his Supreme War Lord and hand over power, it would be a case of "simple revolution."[10] Shaken by Charles's words, Horthy began to flounder and raise trivial objections: Where would Charles live in the Castle? What would happen to him when he was no longer regent? Believing that Horthy's resolve was weakening and that the time was opportune to employ a tactic previously discussed with his advisors, Charles assured him that he need not worry about his future position, for he would remain the King's "right-arm man." Once restored to the throne, he would bestow on his faithful admiral the title of Prince of Otranto and Szeged. Moreover, he would recognize Horthy's great military exploits by conferring on him the Order of Maria Theresa and the Order of the Golden Fleece.[11]

Forgetting for a moment the issues at hand, Horthy expressed delight at the prospect of such honors, especially the Order of Maria Theresa, for which he had been nominated in the last months of the Great War.[12] When, however, Charles asserted once again that the Regent must now hand over the reins of government, Horthy reverted quickly to his previous position: "There is not even a one-half percent possibility that Your Majesty will succeed." The country was in a critical position, he argued, and catastrophe threatened at any moment. It was not a good time, Horthy suggested, to discuss the conferring of such honors on him.[13] In despair, Charles finally declared that they had reached a deadlock. What did Horthy propose to do, arrest him? When Horthy thereupon turned red with shame and answered in the negative, Charles pointed out that the only other logical solution was for the Regent to hand over power. But Horthy refused to budge from his position, and even gently reproached his visitor for acting in such a precipitous manner. "Why didn't Your Majesty wait for a few years?" he asked. In the meantime he could have laid the groundwork and there would have been no need to proceed in such a "stealthy way."[14] Charles brushed aside this objection and responded: "I stick by my position. I'll give you five minutes to think it over."

Noting Charles's apparent exhaustion, Horthy took advantage of this break in the conversation to arrange for a servant to bring a dinner, which both men proceeded to eat. In the meantime Horthy was able to gather his thoughts and ponder the likely consequences if he indeed were to announce that he had yielded power to the former king. Surely the friendly relationship that Horthy had helped to establish with Great Britain would be totally undermined, for he would be breaking promises that he had quite recently made to British diplomats. Moreover, there would be the risk of severe political disruptions, since the Smallholders, the largest party in the National Assembly, would be unlikely to accept a restoration without the most vigorous opposition. The resulting political chaos and possible turmoil in the officer corps would tempt Hungary's neighbors to take action. This was Horthy's worst nightmare: the occupation of the country by Romanian, Czech, and South Slav troops. It is quite likely that, in addition to these political and diplomatic calculations, a measure of personal ambition and vanity also influenced Admiral Horthy as he groped for a solution to the harsh dilemma that now confronted him. As Hungary's head of state over the past year he had guided the country through some very difficult times. Should he now take the enormous risk of turning over the government to the former king, perhaps undoing much of the constructive work that he, Teleki, and Bethlen had done? Was it likely that Charles, who had not been particularly effective in dealing with the deepening crisis in the last months of his reign, would be a better leader for Hungary than the current head of state, who had the confidence of the Entente and strong support in the National Assembly?

As Charles and Horthy resumed their political discussion, the Regent thus solemnly declared: "Your Majesty, I must choose between my loyalty to the dynasty and to my nation. I choose the nation, and will not hand over the government, because in twenty-four hours this unfortunate country would be occupied and partitioned."[15] At this point Charles felt compelled to use his final trump card. He had hoped for success without having to reveal the fact that his restoration attempt had the apparent backing of the French government. Indeed, he had pledged to Briand that this would remain "absolutely secret." Now, however, he decided to tell the Regent that he had assurances from a "prominent statesman" in the West. Pressed for more specific information, Charles reluctantly agreed to give Horthy the name, "if you promise to keep the secret." He thereupon wrote the name "Briand" on a slip of paper and passed it to the Regent.[16]

Horthy's reaction was skeptical, especially when Charles admitted that he had not personally conferred with Briand. Hungary's negotiations with France in 1920 had left Horthy and his colleagues deeply embittered and convinced that French statesmen were perfidious and untrustworthy. Horthy thus quickly searched through his files to present to Charles written evidence that the French Minister in Budapest and French representative at the Conference of Ambassadors had publicly joined with their British colleagues in firm opposition to a Habsburg restoration. Charles was unmoved and reiterated that his support came from the highest level. Whether because his resolve began to weaken or because he wished merely to find a way to persuade Charles to leave Budapest, Horthy now suddenly took a different tack. He would be willing to cooperate with His Majesty, but needed several weeks to arrange things in Budapest. In the meantime Charles should consider marching on Vienna with Colonel Lehár's troops. "Your Majesty would conquer 'good old Vienna,'" Horthy declared, "and we would have our dear Austria-Hungary again."[17]

Charles seemed uninterested in this proposal. Instead he seized on the Regent's suggestion that he needed several weeks to make preparations in Budapest. Charles agreed to return to Szombathely but issued a warning: "Today is March 27. Three weeks from now is April 17. So, Horthy, if you are not in Szombathely on that day, I will be in Budapest on that date."[18] But Horthy was unyielding. Three weeks was too short. The Entente representatives would get wind of what was happening, and it would be the downfall of the country. No, it would be best if Charles simply returned as soon as possible to Switzerland. Sensing that he now had no other choice, Charles thus agreed to return to Szombathely and discuss with Lehár the idea of a march on Vienna. In the meantime the Regent would remain in the capital as the "King's General." If foreign diplomats came to protest, Horthy should declare that Charles was on his way out of the country. But, Charles warned, if the march on Vienna could not be carried out, he would remain in Szombathely and wait three weeks for Horthy's summons.

After two hours the ex-king and the regent had thus achieved a fragile *modus vivendi*. Yet, as events would demonstrate, the two men had quite different interpretations of what had been agreed upon. The wish being the father to the thought, Regent Horthy believed that his unexpected visitor had agreed to leave the country, either to march on Vienna or simply to return to Switzerland, and not to return again without written notice.[19] By contrast, Charles assumed that, whether or not a military move against Vienna was made, Horthy would strive in the next three weeks to facilitate the restoration. In the meantime he would remain in Szombathely. Perhaps because the two men were eager to bring to an end what had been a traumatic experience for both of them, neither seemed inclined, as they prepared to part, to put their agreement in writing or even to enunciate it in clear terms. Instead, they were able to conclude their discussions in a friendly tone. In parting Charles presented Horthy the Grand Cross of the Order of Maria Theresa. Horthy accepted the medal, but when Charles asked if he was pleased, the admiral could only reply: "How could I be happy about anything at a moment like this." He would only be happy, Horthy declared, "when he could jubilantly lead His Majesty through the streets of the city."[20]

At this point Horthy's main concern seemed to be to arrange for Charles to leave the capital as unobtrusively as possible. Perhaps it would still be possible to conceal from the press and foreign diplomats the fact that the ex-king had attempted a kind of coup d'état. Claiming that the King's life might be in danger, Horthy insisted that Charles leave the Castle by a rear entrance. Without informing Count Sigray, Magasházy guided Charles to a chauffeur-driven car and sent him off on his own to Szombathely. This proved even more grueling than his morning journey, for the car was an open one and neither Magasházy nor Horthy had thought to provide Charles a heavy coat. He thus shivered through the long ride, which was interrupted by repeated car trouble, and arrived in Szombathely suffering from lack of sleep and a severe cold.

Meanwhile, once Charles had left the Castle, the Regent discovered that his wife and a large group of people were waiting anxiously in the hallway outside his office. In addition to Sigray and Teleki, who had finally arrived, Bethlen, Gömbös, Prónay, Ostenburg, several Cabinet ministers and assorted members of Horthy's retinue had broken off their Easter Sunday activities to learn firsthand of the momentous events. Speaking with deep emotion, Horthy gave a brief summary of what had transpired and announced that the King was already on his way back to Szombathely and would soon leave the country. As the Regent finished his account, Gömbös, to the annoyance of Sigray, gave an impromptu speech in which he lauded Horthy for the great deed he had done to the save the Hungarian nation. Horthy thereupon conferred with Teleki and Bethlen, and it was decided that the Prime Minister should return to Szombathely to facilitate Charles's departure from the country.

Horthy then spent the rest of the evening recounting his two-hour ordeal to a stream of curious visitors. With each retelling, his words seemed to become more melodramatic and his emotions more strained. He told of how he had had to "get down on my knees" in order to persuade Charles to abandon his plans. He spoke of the King's "pitiable" physical condition and the way he had had to literally "push him out" the back door in order to insure that he could leave Budapest safely.[21] Yet it was clear that the Regent was still deeply troubled by the course of action he had chosen. From time to time he broke down and wept bitterly. "I, the old soldier," he told Count Lajos Windischgraetz, "have broken my oath!"[22]

Before retiring that night, Horthy, or someone acting on his behalf, took one other step: a telegram, somewhat clumsily and undiplomatically worded, was sent to Colonel Lehár in Szombathely. Lehár was instructed, "in the interest of the Fatherland," to make every effort to "transport Charles across the border before the night is over."[23] This telegram caused consternation among the royalists in Szombathely, especially when Charles arrived at 5:00

A.M. after an exhausting, trouble-plagued trip. Charles immediately discussed with Lehár Admiral Horthy's proposal to march on Vienna. Neither of them thought such a plan was practical, and Charles informed his entourage that he had no intention of leaving Hungary. He had departed from Budapest because he feared for his safety, yet he still believed in the essential loyalty of the Regent. His return to Szombathely had eased the situation for Horthy, who would now, as he had promised, be better able to prepare the transfer of power in the capital.[24] In his stubborn optimism Charles believed that he could now accomplish by an exchange of telegrams what he had failed to achieve face to face on the previous day. Lehár was instructed to telephone the Regent's office and ask that Horthy be summoned to the Hughes telegraph machine for an important message. At 7:30 A.M. Charles had the following telegram dispatched: "Taking into account the changed conditions, I demand that you immediately submit yourself to my command. I have no doubts, my dear, faithful admiral, about your response."[25]

Charles had indeed chosen his words well, for this straightforward command seemed to greatly discomfit the Regent, who had been convinced the night before that the crisis would soon be ended by the King's imminent departure from Hungary. In his response Horthy begged Charles to withdraw his order, for a transfer of power would mean "catastrophe for our country." In desperation he asked the King to grant him a few hours to consider the matter. By the afternoon he would be better able to respond. This Charles agreed to do. Horthy and Teleki then exchanged messages on the Hughes machine, communicating mostly in English with the apparent intention of maintaining confidentiality. "I cannot oppose my king," Horthy lamented, "but pushed into a conflict of conscience I shall be obliged to resign; that is why I ask for the withdrawal of the order." Horthy then repeated his suggestion that Charles leave the country quickly, before the public and Parliament demanded his expulsion. "I am afraid they will demand arrest," Horthy said, "which I will not carry out."[26]

In compliance with Horthy's wishes, Teleki now informed Lehár and other government officials in Szombathely that no orders issued by Charles were to be obeyed. At the same time, he let it be known that the Regent had mentioned the possibility of resignation. This raised the spirits of Charles and his entourage. At Charles's request Teleki then sent a return telegram to Horthy in which he expressed the ex-king's thanks for the Regent's loyalty and suggested that should he resign, the King's choice for a successor as military commander of Budapest would be Field Marshal Géza Lukachich.[27]

In Budapest, meanwhile, the vacillating Regent summoned, in turn, the British, Italian, and French envoys. Any inclination he had momentarily had to resign and yield to Charles was quickly discarded as the Entente representatives asserted that their governments remained opposed to a Habsburg restoration. To Maurice Fouchet, the French High Commissioner, Regent Horthy posed a direct question: Had Briand, as Charles claimed, given his private support to the ex-king's bid for power?[28] Fouchet, who in February had been informed by Briand that France would give no support to the Hungarian monarchist movement or a Habsburg restoration, reaffirmed the Entente declaration of February 20, 1920, and agreed to join his colleagues in composing a diplomatic note along these lines that could be sent to Charles in Szombathely.[29] However, the French diplomat was too cautious to give a categorical response to Horthy's direct question, preferring first to consult with his superiors in Paris.

Horthy's renewed determination to thwart Charles's bid for power was stiffened by the other Entente diplomats in Budapest, especially by his old naval friend, Thomas Hohler, who praised the Regent for his actions on Easter Sunday and declared that the Habsburgs had always looked only to their own dynastic advantage and never to the good of Hungary.[30] All through the late afternoon of Monday, March 28, unfolding events suggested to Horthy that the only course open to him was to arrange for Charles's departure from Hungary and safe arrival in some neutral country. Now that news about Charles's presence in Hungary was spreading through the country and across Europe, the Little Entente countries reacted with great alarm. The Czechoslovak and South Slav envoys declared that a Habsburg restoration would be a *casus belli* for their countries.[31] Even such a staunch legitimist as Count Gyula Andrássy now told Horthy that the restoration attempt had clearly miscarried and that the King had to be persuaded to leave the country.[32]

Horthy now resolved to take more forceful action. Bethlen and Andrássy, two of the most respected elder statesmen of Hungary, were dispatched to Szombathely, along with bodyguards from Prónay's detachment, to make a personal plea for the King's departure. Finally, around 8:00 that evening Horthy telegraphed to Szombathely and announced his firm decision: Charles must leave Hungary as soon as possible. Counts Bethlen and Andrássy would arrive early on the 29th to ensure that his orders were obeyed.[33] In a separate telegram to Teleki the Regent pleaded in unpolished English for understanding of his difficult position:

> I never seeked [*sic*] my position, and I am very tired of it, but till I am here I must also respect my oath to the nation. I had resigned Sunday, but I knew if I do so and do not give to Szombathely strict orders we die of it. I can swear that I have no aspirations for me at all, only to go home quietly, and I never will have any. I must protect the interests of this poor, ruined country. I would be sorry if his Majesty would not see my behavior as absolutely correct. I can assure him that he never had a treueren [more faithful] subject than me.[34]

Over the next several days a war of nerves developed between Charles and Horthy. Despite the personal pleas of Hungary's most eminent statesmen, Charles remained adamant: he would not leave Hungary unless it became clear that his presence would precipitate a war. Charles was apparently still hopeful that Horthy's "struggle of honor and conscience" would lead him to fulfill his oath of loyalty to his king. "I can't have been so dreadfully mistaken" about Horthy, Charles declared.[35]

Yet none of the proposals the King put forward in the next few days were acceptable to Horthy. One such idea was for Charles to remain unobtrusively in the country and designate Horthy his "royal governor." Then, when things had calmed down, Charles would be able to assume the reins of government. But day by day the protests of the Little Entente, especially Czechoslovakia, became more menacing and the potential for a major European crisis increased.[36] Horthy launched his own counterattack against the King already on March 30. To the army he issued a proclamation in which he explained his reasons for remaining in office and expressed his gratitude for the "unified and loyal manner" in which the soldiers had honored their oath to him. Without mentioning the restoration attempt of Charles, Horthy declared that "any abrupt change in government would threaten the very existence of the State."[37] Responding to urgent requests from leaders of the Smallholders party, Horthy convened the National Assembly on April 1. After a brief debate in which legitimist delegates remained silent, a resolution was unanimously passed praising the Regent's conduct in the current crisis and stressing the need to adhere to the present constitution.

Although ordinary Hungarians, workers and farmers, had reacted to the news of Charles's presence in the country with calm and even indifference, the anti-Habsburg political camp was becoming more boisterous each day the King's stay was prolonged. By April 1 there were calls for the arrest of Charles and his expulsion from the country. This Horthy refused to do: "No! I will not lift my hand against my crowned king. I would rather put a bullet through my head than to harm a single hair of his head."[38] Instead the Regent and his advisors sought patiently to disabuse the King of his belief that France was benevolent and military action by the Little Entente was unlikely. On April 2 Fouchet, the French High Commissioner, finally received from Paris a formal response to his request for guidance on March 28. Briand instructed him to inform the Hungarian government that France categorically denied any connection with or support for Charles's putsch.[39] This information was immediately conveyed to the royal party in Szombathely, but at first Charles refused to take notice of it and was inclined instead to trust more favorable information about French intentions that he was obtaining through various pro-Habsburg intermediaries.[40]

By April 3, however, even Charles had to concede that his audacious enterprise had miscarried. After several days of silence, Briand had been forced publicly to disclaim any connection with the restoration attempt. Most of Hungary's prominent statesmen were urging the King to leave. The Hungarian officer corps had apparently remained loyal to the Regent. Reluctantly Charles now agreed to depart, but only on the condition that he be allowed to promulgate a manifesto to the Hungarian nation and that he and his aides be given safe passage back to Switzerland. These conditions being granted, Charles and his entourage left Hungary by train on April 5. The Swiss government agreed to allow Charles once again to take up residence there, but only under more stringent limitations on his political activity.

In his manifesto, which was published in the Hungarian press on April 7, Charles explained that he had returned to Hungary because he "firmly believed that only under the leadership of the legally crowned king could this sorely tried country regain its inner peace and legal order." He had become convinced, however, that his assumption of power at this time would subject the nation to "serious and intolerable trials." Thus, he was leaving the country in the hands of those whom the Parliament had given serious responsibilities. However, in the fervent conviction that Hungary needed its king, he would continue to "devote all my strength and time, my blood if necessary, to my country, which I will never desert and to which I will never be disloyal."[41]

Despite the diplomatically worded allusions to the Regent in his manifesto, Charles left Hungary with a deep antipathy toward Horthy, on whom he and his advisors now placed the total blame for the failure of the restoration attempt.[42] In making Horthy the scapegoat, however, Charles remained a prisoner of the illusions that had inspired him to return to Hungary and claim his throne. He persisted in his belief that the great powers would not oppose his restoration, despite the hostility shown by Great Britain and Italy in the crisis. He continued to trust in Briand, even though the French government had failed to make any public statements of support. Moreover, Charles remained convinced that the Hungarian people truly yearned for his return, notwithstanding the fact that the Parliament had voted unanimously to support the Regent. In the minds of Charles and Zita, the only obstacles to the natural reunion of the monarch and his subjects were Horthy, Gömbös, and a clique of Habsburgophobes in Budapest. Yet during the "Easter Crisis" no popular demonstrations of support of Charles occurred in Hungary, except on a small scale in the traditionally royalist counties of West Hungary. Certainly Charles was given respectful treatment in Szombathely, and most army officers preferred to remain "on the fence" and await the outcome of the crisis, but the general attitude of ordinary Hungarians toward their former king was the kind of polite indifference normally shown to visiting European dignitaries. The Hungarian writer, Dezső Szabó, observed at the time that ordinary people showed more concern about the temporary rise in the price of eggs and meat than they did about the return of their former king.[43]

In the aftermath of the Easter Crisis the consensus among European statesmen was that Charles, in failing to understand the political realities of postwar Europe, had become an embarrassing anachronism. Much more stringent restrictions on political activity were now stipulated for Charles's renewed exile in Switzerland. By contrast, Horthy's conduct in the crisis was generally viewed as statesmanlike.[44] Lord Curzon, the British Foreign Minister, who had previously shown little sympathy for Hungary, now instructed

Hohler to commend the Hungarian government for its firmness during the Easter Crisis. "The history of the whole incident," Horthy was told, "has given a favorable impression of the good political sense of the Hungarian Government and people."[45]

Although, as will soon be seen, the Easter Crisis had by no means settled the royalist question in Hungary, it did provide the Regent with an unexpected opportunity to implement a political strategy that had been gestating in his mind over the past year. Horthy had the greatest respect for Pál Teleki as a Hungarian patriot and a scholar, but already by the end of 1920 he had concluded that as a government leader Teleki was too weak and irresolute (*puhakezű*) to bring about the consolidation of the counterrevolutionary regime.[46] Teleki's ambiguous conduct during Charles's restoration attempt no doubt also troubled Horthy. Finally, when on April 6 Teleki authorized publication of Charles's manifesto to the Hungarian nation, despite the protests of Smallholders in the Cabinet, the Parliament was the scene once again of vituperative and stormy exchanges between the legitimists and "free-electors." Under the circumstances, Count Teleki tendered his resignation.

Most Hungarian political observers assumed that the Regent would show his confidence in Teleki and reappoint him. After all, since the end of the war the country had already had ten prime ministers and a certain continuity now seemed desirable. But Teleki himself had no desire to continue in office; indeed, on several occasions in previous months he had asked Horthy to relieve him of his duties and to appoint Bethlen in his place.[47] Horthy was now even more convinced that Count Bethlen was indeed the only Hungarian statesman capable of extricating the country from its time of troubles. In one respect Horthy's naming of Bethlen as Prime Minister on April 14 was unorthodox, for Bethlen belonged to neither of the two major parties in Parliament. For many, however, this merely enhanced Bethlen's stature in the current crisis, since it meant that he could more easily play the role of mediator among the warring political factions. And it was not only Admiral Horthy who recognized the aura of authority that Bethlen, who was nicknamed "the steward" (*a gazda*), seemed to possess. On the day on which he became Prime Minister, Count Bethlen conducted a private news conference with a group of reporters. So thoroughly did the new Prime Minister dominate the meeting that not a single journalist dared to question him. Recognizing that an important political turning point had been reached, one journalist whispered to his colleague: "An era of authority and consolidation has now begun in Hungary."[48]

In his maiden speech to Parliament on April 19 Count Bethlen struck a similar chord. "The revolution is now at an end!" he declared in his opening words. Bethlen made it clear that the revolutionary excesses of both the right and the left had to be taken "off the streets." What was needed was a compromise between "unbridled freedom and unrestrained dictatorship." Bethlen professed support for democracy, not in the form of a "wild hegemony of workers and peasants," but in a system that ensured the "leadership of the intelligent classes." As a gesture of conciliation to the Liberals and Social Democrats, Bethlen suggested that he intended "at the proper time" to restore civil liberties, including freedom of the press. Moreover, he insisted that he was opposed "to every kind of noisy anti-Semitism."[49] In stating these general principles Bethlen adumbrated his strategy for restoring the quasi-liberal prewar regime in which Hungary's ruling elite had created a symbiosis with the Jewish industrialists and financiers who had come to dominate Hungary's economic life.

Little documentation has survived that throws direct light on the private discussions between the Regent and Count Bethlen in 1921. Later in the 1920s Bethlen told one of his confidants that he rarely consulted Horthy on political matters, for he alone was responsible for policy-making.[50] Yet it is clear that in the two years leading up to Bethlen's appointment as Prime Minister, the two men held frequent private discussions and reached an agreement on certain fundamental political goals and strategies. Certainly they concurred in the belief that the proposals of the Smallholders (and even of some proponents of the "Szeged idea") for additional land reform had to be defeated. For political and economic reasons, the great landed estates would have to be left basically intact. Horthy also approved Bethlen's idea of creating a new "government party" that would be ensured dominance in Parliament by a revision of the current electoral law, which both men regarded as too democratic.[51] Finally, Bethlen apparently persuaded Horthy of the need to end anti-Jewish excesses and to reforge the prewar alliance with the Jewish financial establishment. This implied the eventual restoration of civil liberties and the neutralization of the organizations of the radical right-wing, which would be necessary in any case to revive Hungary's prestige abroad and permit the reintegration of the country into Europe's political and economic life. What Bethlen alluded to in his maiden speech in Parliament must also have been made clear to the Regent beforehand: Hungary, surrounded by the hostile Little Entente, lacking any benefactors among the great powers, and gravely weakened militarily and economically by the war and revolutions, was totally incapable of conducting an active irredentist program. Bethlen insisted that the first priority was the achievement of national unity, a drawing together of all the energies of the nation and the rejection of extremist, disruptive movements of any kind, whether emanating from the left or the right. In short, Hungary needed "a policy of realism, not one of adventures."[52]

That Miklós Horthy embraced a program potentially so inimical to the "Szeged idea" demonstrated the great faith he had in the abilities of István Bethlen. Indeed, he now spoke of Bethlen as "a man of providence" who was uniquely qualified to restore Hungary to its former glory.[53] In the aftermath of the Easter Crisis it may also be that Admiral Horthy for the first time began to realize that his tenure as head of state might indeed last many years. Perhaps he now reasoned that close association with Count Bethlen was the best way for him to enhance his image abroad as a responsible statesman and to erase lingering public memories of his unsavory role in the "White Terror." Horthy was thus willing to give his imprimatur to Bethlen's strategy for coopting and neutralizing the radical right-wingers. When, later that summer, a querulous Pál Prónay expressed alarm over the program of the new Cabinet, Horthy responded by affirming his unbounded faith in his pragmatic Prime Minister, who "would dance a bit to the left, then right, and then left again." "Don't worry," Horthy assured Prónay, "our time will come."[54]

In forming his Cabinet, Bethlen for the most part chose conservative but not openly legitimist aristocrats with expertise in political and economic matters gained during government service in prewar Hungary. Many had been political allies of István Tisza. Horthy's suggestion that Gyula Gömbös be offered the position of Deputy Minister of the Interior was gently rebuffed by Bethlen, who apparently argued that such an appointment would be controversial and that Gömbös's services would be better employed in other ways. In any case, such a move would surely have infuriated the legitimist aristocrats whom the Prime Minister was now intent on wooing, for Bethlen proceeded in the first months of his prime ministry to attempt to construct his "Party of Unity" on the basis of cooperation with the Christian National party. This must have perplexed Horthy, for the legitimists, ensconced mostly in the Christian National party, seemed to be his most bitter political enemies, whereas the Smallholders had been has most reliable support during the Easter Crisis. But Bethlen probably reasoned that in the current international climate a second restoration attempt was precluded; surely even Charles and his entourage had to realize this. Thus it did no harm to appear conciliatory to the legitimists, even while privately the Hungarian government was assuring the Successor States that if Charles appeared again in Hungary he would be arrested. Using the well-honed skills of a consummate politician, Count Bethlen intended to exploit the Smallholders' fear of a restoration and the legitimist aristocrats' fear of extensive land reform. In the end there would be no additional land reform and probably no restoration, the Smallholders' control of Parliament would be weakened, and Bethlen would be able to build his new coalition on reliable segments of both of the leading political parties.[55]

Admiral Horthy acquiesced in Bethlen's convoluted strategy, though he now openly described Charles as too "rash" and of weak character. "I have always been a legitimist," Horthy said privately, "but after these events King Charles's return to the throne is totally and forever impossible."[56] Nonetheless, Bethlen proceeded with his strategy and the Regent made an effort to cooperate. Using Gusztáv Gratz as a liaison, Bethlen reestablished contact with Charles in Switzerland and hinted that he had come to the conclusion that only an eventual legitimist restoration would solve Hungary's problems. Although Charles and his entourage remained skeptical, arrangements were made for Gratz to meet with the Regent. Their five hour discussion at Gödöllő in mid-July did seem to pave the way for a rapprochement between the ex-king and the Regent. Horthy promised to reestablish direct contact with Charles by means of a personal letter. In addition, the Hungarian government would take steps to ease the growing financial plight of the ex-king.[57]

This discussion set the stage for an important conference on August 22, at which Gratz and Count Andrássy conferred with Bethlen and Horthy. The two emissaries of the ex-king seemed to agree with Bethlen that Charles should be warned of the perils of any untimely actions to regain his throne. To reassure Charles, it was decided that the Regent would send a letter in which, among other things, he would promise that no legislative steps would be taken to dethrone the King and that preparations would in fact be made for his eventual restoration. To complaints that the Hungarian press was one-sidedly antiroyalist, Horthy replied that articles sympathetic to Charles would only alarm the Little Entente and the great powers. Gratz and Andrássy left the meeting only partially satisfied. Count Bethlen, who at several points stressed that he was a legitimist, had made a good impression, but Horthy had seemed much cooler and reserved.[58]

Horthy's letter to Charles, delivered by Gratz on September 4, proved unsatisfactory. Referring to Charles's recent restoration attempt as "your Easter visit," Horthy asserted that diplomatic complications made a restoration "impossible for the time being." Nonetheless he assured Charles that "nothing could be farther from my mind then to cling to my present position, or to expand this position in any way." Indeed, he looked forward to the day when he could be "released from this seat of tribulation."[59] Both Gratz and Andrássy were disappointed in the tone and content of the letter, which lacked some of the specific assurances that had been made at the August 22 conference.

As expected, Charles was unimpressed by Horthy's letter, since it provided no guarantees that the Regent had had a true change of heart and would actively promote a restoration. "Is this a letter," he asked, "that an admiral would write to his sovereign, whom he promised to serve even in exile?"[60] Charles's disgust for Horthy was deepened when a highly embarrassed Boroviczény conveyed a request that Horthy had made of Gratz: would Charles please inform the Curate of the Maria Theresa Order that it was the Grand Cross medal that His Majesty had conferred on him in March and not the (less prestigious) Knight's Cross medal that the commission had originally recommended? Such tactless, indeed impertinent, behavior by Horthy must have strengthened Charles's growing conviction that in his bid to reclaim the throne he could not trust the Regent. From this point Charles seems to have come to the firm conclusion that the Hungarian government represented an illegal, revolutionary challenge to his authority.[61]

Although the meetings between Charles's representatives and the leaders of the Hungarian government had been kept secret, rumors of a second restoration attempt repeatedly surfaced in Budapest and throughout Europe during the summer of 1921. This merely intensified the concern felt by the Hungarian radical right-wingers over the course of events since Bethlen's appointment. Bethlen's gradual loosening of censorship had emboldened the critics of the right-wing extremist military officers both in the press and in Parliament. Annoyed and frustrated, a group of Szeged veterans and leaders of EkSz, including Gömbös, Prónay, and Zadravecz, demanded an audience with Horthy.[62] Their complaints were numerous: an "impudent tone" was being permitted in the newspapers; the legitimists were continuing their "poisonous activities," especially in the officer corps; the jostling of political parties had intensified. Despite being warned about this, the Regent had done nothing. Instead of heeding the advice of his loyal friends, he had allowed "ambitious meddlers" to swarm all around him. When the delegation appeared in the Regent's office on July 7, Horthy, sensing the ominous mood, greeted his visitors with mock trepidation: "My, what dangerous company!" To which Zadravecz replied: "Yes, but loyal!" Anticipating his friends' displeasure over recent developments, Horthy began by deploring current conditions, but he insisted that his hands were tied and he was powerless to act. For example, he would like to arrest legitimists like Count Andrássy or Bishop Mikes. But "I can't catch anyone. They all operate so cleverly that I'm not able to seize them by the throat."[63] Still deferential to Horthy, Prónay and Gömbös were unwilling to state their views boldly. Instead of declaring that Bethlen himself was the "ambitious meddler" to whom they were alluding, they insisted in more general terms that unless a vigorous policy were soon implemented, all would be lost. The audience thus ended inconclusively.

In the coming weeks Bethlen's plan for neutralizing the power of the officer detachments was facilitated by a political scandal into which Prónay blundered. Infuriated by continuing exposés in the National Assembly of atrocities committed during the "White Terror," Prónay sent an insulting public letter to István Rakovszky, president of the Assembly and an outspoken legitimist. Prónay's indiscretion caused a political uproar that prompted Bethlen to recommend to the Regent that Prónay's detachment be separated once and for all from the National Army. Horthy reluctantly agreed. Summoning Prónay and his officers, he announced that the detachment had to be temporarily separated from the army, for otherwise there would be complications and Hungary's prestige would suffer abroad. Prónay was indignant. He and his men would leave not only the army but the country, because they did not want to continue to be the target of Jewish attacks. With tears welling up in his eyes, Horthy tried to console his Szeged comrade: "Don't do that, Pali. Trust me. You're too pessimistic. . . . But you must realize that your actions vis-à-vis Parliament . . . created a critical situation for the government and for me too."[64] Prónay suspected that Horthy's tears were contrived, but agreed nonetheless to confer with Bethlen, who persuaded him to accede to the Regent's wishes and accept a government post as Inspector of the Gendarmerie.

Before the summer was over, however, Count Bethlen found it expedient one final time to exploit the power of the special detachments. Although the Hungarians had been unsuccessful, whether through diplomatic negotiations or clandestine military plots, in undoing any of the territorial provisions of the Treaty of Trianon, one opportunity remained in 1921. It had particularly galled the Magyars that even Austria, regarded like Hungary as one of the defeated countries, should be permitted to join in the dismemberment of the Kingdom of St. Stephen. A small strip of territory in western Hungary, known as the Burgenland, was assigned by the peace conference to Austria, despite a significant Hungarian population in and around the town of Sopron. As the date for the formal occupation of the territory by Austrian troops neared in the late summer, a wave of indignation swept through Hungarian society.

Although his plan for revision of the Treaty of Trianon involved a patient, long-term strategy in which Hungary would first recover its strength and then seek great power support, Count Bethlen saw in the Burgenland issue an opportunity for a minor revision of the peace treaty that would boost the national spirit of the Magyars and enhance the prestige of the Horthy regime. Accordingly, the Hungarian Cabinet approved a plan that involved disseminating propaganda and fomenting disturbances in the disputed territory.[65] The Hungarian government would then appeal to the great powers for a more equitable territorial settlement that would not so inflame Hungarian national sentiment. To implement this plan, which may have been patterned after a similar strategy recently employed successfully by Germany in Upper Silesia, Bethlen was willing to take certain domestic risks. Though his intention was to reduce and eventually eliminate the power of the special detachments, he calculated that this was one last opportunity to harness their "patriotic enthusiasm" in a legitimate national cause. In addition, he was willing to allow the existing political and military authorities in that part of Hungary, notably Count Sigray and Colonel Lehár, to play leading roles in the resistance to Austrian occupation. Both men were, of course, widely regarded as loyal followers of King Charles, and Bethlen was warned that he might be creating conditions in western Hungary that would set the stage for another restoration attempt. But the Prime Minister was confident that he could walk the tightrope and achieve a diplomatic success without dangerous domestic complications.

Through these tactics Count Bethlen succeeded in bringing the issue of the Burgenland to the attention of the great powers and achieving a compromise settlement. According to the terms of an agreement made in mid-October under the auspices of Britain and Italy, Hungary ensured that all paramilitary units would be withdrawn from Burgenland and all agitation ended by October 23, at which time an internationally supervised plebiscite would be held in Sopron and the immediate surrounding area.

Since this was the first time that Hungary's demand for a plebiscite in a disputed territory had been granted by the great powers, the agreement was greeted with great satisfaction by Hungary's political establishment and heralded as a diplomatic triumph for a country that since 1918 had experienced only humiliating defeats in the international arena. The prestige of his government greatly enhanced, Count Bethlen moved quickly to win a domestic victory as well. The leaders of the military detachments, most notably Prónay, were asked by Bethlen and Horthy to show "sober moderation and patriotic self-denial" and evacuate the area by October 23. Satisfied that the situation in western Hungary was now under control, Bethlen renewed his political discussions with Count Andrássy and in a major speech in the city of Pécs on October 21 was able to make the dramatic announcement that he had reached agreement with the leaders of the Christian National party on the creation of a unified government party. In carefully chosen words Bethlen asserted that in Hungary "the exercise of royal power is not just a right but a necessity." No one who advocated dethronement of the Habsburg dynasty would be welcome in the unified party. Equally unwelcome, however, would be those who planned a royalist putsch. Hungary's problems, he declared, could only be solved "with patience and honorable efforts," for any other approach could lead to civil war.[66]

Count Bethlen's overture to the moderate faction of the legitimist aristocrats on October 21 was embarrassingly ill-timed, for on the previous day Charles IV had landed surreptitiously in western Hungary after a daredevil flight from Switzerland in a Junkers monoplane. Ironically, the forces that Bethlen had unleashed to create disorder in Burgenland had now backfired against him. Rejecting the Prime Minister's call for "sober moderation," Colonel Lehár, Ostenburg, and other legitimist officers had decided to take advantage of their presence in traditionally pro-Habsburg western Hungary to facilitate a second restoration attempt. In a message sent by courier to Charles in mid-October they called on the ex-king to seize the favorable opportunity and reclaim his throne before October 23. "The domestic political situation," they asserted, "is such that when His Majesty enters Budapest no sort of opposition is to be expected. To the contrary, the restoration will be greeted everywhere with jubilation."[67] Unaware of the fact that some of Hungary's most prominent legitimists, including Count Andrássy and Count Apponyi, had no knowledge of the invitation that Lehár had dispatched, and would surely have disapproved of it as dangerously misleading, Charles imagined that this was the long-awaited cry for help from the Hungarian nation. "The Hungarians need me," he now declared.[68] After his plane landed on the estate of a legitimist aristocrat, he quickly made his way to Sopron where he formed a new government, with Colonel Lehár as Minister of Defense and a highly skeptical and disheartened but dutiful Andrássy as Minister of Foreign Affairs. This time Charles had no intention of searching for a compromise with Regent Horthy, whose government he considered illegitimate.

Thus, as Bethlen was making his speech in Pécs on the afternoon of October 21, a group of armored trains was being equipped in Sopron. This royal armada was guarded by Ostenburg's troops, who apparently were told that communism had erupted in Budapest and that the Regent had called for the King's help in the "restoration of order." In a stirring mass ceremony, the battalion took the traditional Honvéd oath of loyalty to "Charles of Habsburg, King of Hungary and King of Bohemia."[69] The royal armada departed late on the morning of October 21 for the capital city, some 120 miles away. Unfortunately for the royalist cause, this "march on Budapest" proceeded more in the fashion of a ceremonial excursion in the countryside than a rapid and relentless military advance. At each village station time was taken to have the local garrison and public officials take the oath of loyalty and to allow groups of loyal peasants to chant "long live the King!" and to pay homage to the royal couple. Ten hours were spent in traveling from Sopron to Győr, a distance of only 50 miles. The operation thus gave the comforting appearance of "one long triumph,"[70] but it allowed time for Admiral Horthy to launch a counteroffensive.

A report of the King's return to Hungary, sent by the Entente Mission in Sopron, seems to have reached the government in Budapest only late on the 21st. The news greatly discomfited Admiral Horthy, who was shocked to learn that both Lehár and Ostenburg had gone over to the King. Count Bethlen, no doubt all the more resolute because of his bitterness over the apparent duplicity of the legitimist political leaders, presided over a Council of Ministers meeting at 9:30 in the morning of the 22nd. Here it was decided that the restoration attempt would be opposed by force if necessary, and that the assistance of the great powers would be urgently requested.[71] Horthy immediately issued a military proclamation in which he announced that the government refused to hand over power to King Charles, because to do so would mean the destruction of the country. "I expect," he declared, "that every member of the National Army will be true to his oath to me and will unquestioningly carry out all orders."

The response to Horthy's exhortations was not encouraging, for many officers, especially those of the older generation, hesitated to take sides, preferring to adopt a "wait and see" attitude.[72] Most of those whose units were stationed in towns along the path of the royal armada found it impossible (or perhaps, in some cases, inexpedient) to be disloyal to the former king who had suddenly appeared in their midst. Perhaps some recalled the famous words from a poem ("Fóti dal") of the nineteenth century poet Mihály Vörösmarty:

A legelső magyar ember a király
Érte minden honfi karja készen áll!
(First among all the Magyars is the king
For him the arm of every patriot is ready!)

Whatever their motives, the officers and soldiers of the garrison of Győr took the oath of loyalty at about the time Horthy was issuing his military proclamation on the morning of the 22nd. Later in the day the important town of Komárom also capitulated. Even more disconcerting was the unwillingness of the highest military officers in Budapest to assume command of the government's forces. Sándor Belitska, Minister of National Defense, preferred not to assume that responsibility until the situation had been clarified. Others who were approached reacted with equivocation: one declined because of sickness, another couldn't be located, still another requested that he be retired. When, finally, General Pál Nagy agreed to take command, Horthy was concerned enough about his loyalty to find it necessary to assign Gyula Gömbös to him as a representative of the government.[73] In his attempt to mobilize various units to serve under General Nagy, Regent Horthy encountered other unpleasant surprises. Of the twelve commanders of battalions outside of Budapest, only two reported that they could reach the capital ready for combat by October 23. Even more alarming was the suspicion that the garrison in Budapest was not reliable. Its commander was now dismissed because of his royalist sentiments, but Horthy and Bethlen must have feared that the garrison would be neutral at best if actual fighting broke out. Even Pál Prónay, who remained with his gendarmerie detachment in western Hungary, was straddling the fence. Perhaps still smarting from the humiliation he had suffered earlier in the summer, he now informed Horthy that he would like to help out, but his men could not be transported to Budapest for several days.[74] All of this took its toll on Admiral Horthy. When, later on the morning of the 22nd, he received the Entente diplomatic representatives in a delegation, Horthy gave the impression that he was "by no means as certain of himself as he had been last Easter." He spoke now of the difficulties of his position being "almost too great to deal with." Though he insisted that he would do everything in his power to thwart Charles's restoration bid, he expressed concern because a "Hungarian does not like to fight against another Hungarian soldier."[75]

With Thomas Hohler as their spokesman, the three Entente ministers tried to stiffen Horthy's resolve and spur the Hungarian government to vigorous action. In a note that was quickly drawn up and handed to the Hungarian Foreign Minister, it was declared in "most categorical" terms that the Entente powers remained opposed to a Habsburg restoration. More ominous was the blunt message from the Czechoslovak, Yugoslav, and Romanian ministers that Charles's restoration would be regarded as a *casus belli*.[76] In these desperate circumstances Horthy and Bethlen hoped that somehow Charles could still be dissuaded from attempting to enter Budapest. When István Rakovszky, whom Charles had designated as his Prime Minister, telephoned Bethlen and demanded the immediate capitulation of Budapest, Bethlen responded by citing the grave danger of military attack by Hungary's neighbors. Rakovszky was unmoved, declaring that His Majesty's Cabinet would deal with that issue. Bethlen insisted that at least nothing be done until a letter from the Regent had been read by Charles. That letter, now hastily drafted, was sent by courier to the royal train. In it Horthy pleaded one final time for understanding of his difficult position. He argued that the prospects for a restoration had not only not improved since the previous spring, but had actually deteriorated. "If Your Majesty entered Budapest with armed force," Horthy warned, Hungary's neighbors would attack, bolshevism would erupt, and "Hungary would cease forever to exist."[77] But Horthy's words had no effect, for Charles, determined not to be deflected from his mission, refused even to read the Regent's letter.

In this bleak situation late on the 22nd only the inimitable Gyula Gömbös had some success in organizing a military resistance. From the ranks of the MOVE, the Awakening Magyars, and students from the University of Budapest, he was able to assemble a volunteer battalion of about 400–500. This ragtag force of untrained and poorly equipped volunteers was to be used to bolster the meager regular army units in Budapest until reinforcements arrived on the 23rd or 24th. This news temporarily lifted the Regent's spirits; when he met the Entente ministers again late in the day he declared that he almost welcomed the opportunity to clarify the situation "once and for all." He was determined to remain in Budapest and repel Charles, who had broken his promise to inform him beforehand of any restoration plans. Perhaps through his personal influence he could prevent bloodshed, but civil war, and a possible eruption of bolshevism, seemed all but inevitable. Horthy pleaded for the help of the great powers in restraining Hungary's neighbors and in persuading Charles to abdicate and remove himself to some far-off place of exile.[78]

On Sunday morning, October 23, Hungary seemed on the brink of civil war. The armed forces loyal to Charles were now on the outskirts of Budapest, only 20 minutes of clear track from the suburban rail station of Kelenföld. Martial law had been declared in Budapest. Reports were being received that Czechoslovakia had begun to mobilize. In a telegram to the Foreign Office in London, Thomas Hohler concluded, on the basis of information from the Hungarian Foreign Minister, that "all is lost" and that Charles might make a victorious entry into Budapest by the afternoon.[79] The most prominent of the "free-electors," István Nagyatádi-Szabó, was sufficiently alarmed to seek protection on a British monitor temporarily docked in the Danube at Budapest.[80] At an early morning meeting with General Nagy, the Regent was given the discouraging news that "the soldiers don't want to use their weapons," and that if the royal forces were to launch an attack, the defense would collapse. Gyula Gömbös expressed dismay at the tendency among military and civilian officials to respond to orders of resistance with what he called *általános ámenkázás*, that is, pious platitudes instead of action.[81]

The first glimmer of hope for the Horthy government came shortly after 9:00 A.M., when General Pál Hegedűs, who had been authorized by Charles to proceed to the Front and win over the pro-Horthy military units stationed there, arrived at the Kelenföld station and was persuaded to proceed to Budapest for direct consultations with the Regent and Prime Minister. Hegedűs had in fact been playing something of a "double game" since the arrival of Charles two days earlier. Though he took the oath of loyalty to the King, Hegedűs also discreetly informed the Entente mission in Sopron of Charles's arrival in Hungary. Like many other Hungarian officers, Hegedűs was attempting to straddle the fence and refrain from making a final commitment to either Charles or Horthy. He was taken immediately to the Royal Castle, where Admiral Horthy proceeded to describe the situation in the same terms he had used in his letter to Charles on the previous day. If, Horthy pleaded, Hegedűs could not convince the king of the dire consequences of a restoration in the present unfavorable conditions, he should at least suggest that His Majesty accept an offer of safe passage to Budapest so that he could become acquainted firsthand with the domestic and foreign impediments to a Habsburg restoration.[82]

As General Hegedűs went off to confer with the Prime Minister, Horthy decided that in the desperate circumstances his personal intervention at the Front was needed to inspire the troops. He thus made his way to Kelenföld with Gyula Gömbös and around 10:30 am gave a rousing speech to the largely volunteer force guarding the rail station. Suggesting that "our poor king has been led astray" by his military and political advisors, Horthy urged the assembled soldiers and students to hold their position, for if the royal forces triumphed, the old Austria-Hungary would be restored and Hungary would again be the underdog. Gömbös thereupon exhorted the volunteer students to fight the King's army, which, he claimed, consisted mostly of "Austrian and Czech adventurers."[83]

The personal intervention of Horthy and Gömbös apparently emboldened the soldiers and students, for throughout the morning there was sporadic fire in the direction of the royal forces from an artillery unit that had remained loyal to the government. More important, sometime before noon an advance contingent of Ostenburg's detachment was fired upon as it approached the Kelenföld station. This minor skirmish (in which the government forces counted fourteen dead, the Ostenberg detachment, five) was to be the only significant military engagement during Charles's second restoration attempt. However, when word reached the royal rail armada that fighting had broken out, the effect was dramatic. Most of the officers who had joined the ex-king's enterprise, including Colonel Lehár, had hoped that the march on Budapest would be a bloodless victory. Now, however, civil war was a definite possibility.

Meanwhile, after his brief meeting with Regent Horthy, General Hegedűs had been taken to Count Bethlen, who employed even more forceful arguments to convince him that the King's actions were a "mad enterprise" that would plunge Hungary into disaster. Thomas Hohler, who at Bethlen's request joined the discussion, informed Hegedűs that England "would never recognize Charles and would never permit the return of a Habsburg in view of the very eventuality with which we are now faced, namely war." He warned that if royal troops were to enter Budapest, within a week the capital city would be occupied by the Czechs.[84] Hegedűs, who like others in Charles's entourage had trusted in the King's assurances that his restoration to the throne would be supported by the great powers, was greatly disturbed by this new information. Sensing the hopelessness of the King's position and wishing to protect himself in all eventualities, Hegedűs now made an abrupt about-face. Denying that he had sworn an oath of loyalty to Charles or that he had accepted the command of the royal forces, he now offered his services in the arrangement of an armistice.

By noon on October 23 the tide was clearly shifting in Admiral

Horthy's favor. Favorable news came even from an unexpected quarter, when an emissary from the Hungarian Social Democrats informed the government that, despite secret offers made by emissaries of Charles, his party would oppose a Habsburg restoration and the workers would remain quiet in the current crisis.[85] When Hohler saw Horthy again shortly after noon, the Regent seemed over his "mental crisis" and "fully confident and determined." Horthy reported that "real fighting" had occurred at the Front, but he was confident that the situation was now in hand and that the bulk of his officers had decided that their duty to country came before their oath to the King. In any case, he suggested, many of the officers and soldiers who were supporting Charles were actually Austrians, and Hungarian soldiers were more willing to fire on them. His major concern was the Little Entente, whom he hoped the great powers would be able to restrain.[86]

On the afternoon of the 23rd, when General Hegedüs arrived back at the royal military headquarters just east of Kelenföld, the prospects for a successful restoration of Charles to the Hungarian throne had considerably dimmed. As word spread of the morning skirmish and of the possibility of an armistice, the mood in the Hungarian officer corps became increasingly pro-Horthy. Particularly disillusioned were those officers who had taken the oath to Charles in the belief that the "march on Budapest" would be largely ceremonial and that Regent Horthy had actually welcomed the King's return. Others were dismayed when they discovered that earlier rumors of the eruption of bolshevism in Budapest had been untrue.[87] Most observers, perhaps even Charles himself, now realized that an armistice could only favor the current government. Yet when General Hegedüs reported on his conversations in Budapest and on the Regent's determination to stand at the head of his troops and resist His Majesty to the bitter end, Charles agreed reluctantly to armistice negotiations. Perhaps the King would have preferred one last military gamble, but his officers complained that the troops were too fatigued and his political advisors warned that if Horthy's offer of a cease-fire were rejected, it would appear that "only Charles was bent on further bloodshed."[88] A truce was thus arranged until the following morning, at which time talks were to be held at the town of Biatorbágy by emissaries from both sides.

By 8:00 on the 24th, the time set for the parley, the military advantage had swung decisively to the government side. Anticipating the demands of the Entente powers to be drawn up later that day in Paris, Horthy and Bethlen composed harsh terms and appointed a stern negotiator, Kálmán Kánya, to represent the government. Charles was called on to order his troops to lay down their arms and turn over all war material. The king's personal safety would be guaranteed if he submitted his abdication in writing. In return all supporters of the restoration attempt, "except agitators and ringleaders," would be granted an amnesty.[89] As Charles stood reading these severe terms in the small train station at Biatorbágy, shots rang out and a stray bullet from an unknown source hit the royal train. The king was quickly bundled into the train, which began slowly to move westward. Indignant over the stiff peace terms and what appeared to be a treacherous attack by Horthy's troops, Lehár and Ostenburg now called frantically for a "last stand" and a "fight to the last drop of blood." But Charles was resigned to his fate. He ordered the train to stop and from his compartment window he shouted: "Lehár! Ostenburg! Stop and come back here! I forbid any more fighting. It's all quite senseless now. . . ." He thereupon dictated a surrender order.[90]

The Hungarian government now moved with dispatch to restore domestic stability and to defuse the growing international crisis that Charles's presence in Hungary had precipitated. To the chagrin of the legitimists, such prominent supporters of Charles as Count Sigray, Count Andrássy, and Gusztáv Gratz were promptly arrested, and the King and Queen, who had found temporary safe haven on the estate of Count Móric Esterházy, were placed under military custody in a monastery at Tihany. Charles complied with all requests made of him except for one: he would not abdicate the throne. Until preparations could be made by the Entente powers to transport the royal couple to a remote place of exile, the situation in Hungary thus remained parlous. Even when it became quite clear that Charles's restoration attempt had miscarried, Czechoslovakia and Yugoslavia refused to demobilize the army divisions they were deploying on the borders of Hungary. Eduard Beneš, the Foreign Minister of Czechoslovakia, clearly intended to exploit the crisis to deal a crushing blow to nationalist and irredentist sentiment in Hungary and perhaps even to topple the Horthy regime.[91] On October 29 he presented an ultimatum threatening an invasion if Hungary did not comply with his demands, which included dethronement of the Habsburgs, Little Entente participation in the disarmament of Hungary, and willingness on the part of the Hungarian government to reimburse Prague for the cost of Czechoslovakia's mobilization.[92]

Admiral Horthy regarded these demands as outrageous and demeaning, coming as they did from the leader of a state he considered to be an artificial creation of an unjust peace treaty. His first instinct was to mobilize Hungary's army and resist any invasion. But Thomas Hohler, speaking on behalf of the Entente powers, advised against such action and the Regent relented, although he pointed out the heavy responsibility he would bear should an invasion take place against a defenseless Hungary.[93] Count Bethlen, acutely aware of Hungary's military weakness, likewise urged restraint, but pointed out to the Entente representatives that the government would likely be accused of cowardice, since Hungarians who had supported Charles were fired upon but invading Czechoslovak and Yugoslav troops were not. Besides, what guarantee was there that Hungarian territory occupied by Czechoslovakia would ever be evacuated? On November 1, when an invasion of Hungary seemed imminent, Bethlen informed Hohler that Hungary placed itself entirely in the hands of the great powers and would conform to their decisions. He gave an assurance that the Hungarian Parliament would soon pass legislation that would exclude all Habsburgs from the Hungarian throne.[94] At the same time Regent Horthy summoned the officers of the special detachments and urged that all insurgents be evacuated from western Hungary. If demobilization did not occur immediately, he would personally lead the National Army to Burgenland to accomplish it. Otherwise there was a risk that all of Hungary would be occupied by her hostile neighbors.[95]

Count Bethlen's desperate diplomatic maneuver, Admiral Horthy's plea to the military officers, the departure of Charles and Zita on November 1, and a stern British and French warning to Eduard Beneš now combined to defuse the crisis. The final chapter of the dramatic confrontation between the Habsburg King and the Hungarian Regent occurred on November 3, only hours after a British gun boat, the *Glow-worm*, and its royal passengers left Hungarian waters. In Budapest Count Bethlen presented to the Parliament a legislative bill that nullified the Pragmatic Sanction of 1723. Passed on November 6, this legislation amounted to a dethronement of the Habsburg dynasty, although Hungary remained a monarchy and a Habsburg could conceivably be elected king in the future. The physical strain of the restoration attempt and the psychological blow of the dethronement soon took their toll on Charles, who was forced into exile on the Portuguese island of Madeira in the Atlantic Ocean. Month by month his health deteriorated, and on April 1, 1922, he died at the age of thirty-four. By that time Count Bethlen had gained mastery over the political parties in Budapest and was well on his way to fashioning a new regime to be presided over, for the indefinite future, by Regent Miklós Horthy.

5

In the Bethlen Era, 1921–1931

Shortly after the death of Charles IV in April 1922, a memorial service was held at the Matthias Church in Budapest, where Charles and other Habsburg monarchs had been crowned. To the surprise of many, Miklós Horthy appeared among the mourners, and when the time came for him to walk through the church to touch the symbolic "tomb of state," the huge crowd grew completely silent.[1] Having discharged this final duty to his former king, the Regent returned to his offices in the Royal Castle that would never again house a king of Hungary.

After the failure of the second restoration attempt, those who had challenged Horthy's authority were in complete disarray. Indeed, the Hungarian royalist movement was never to recover its former influence. The legitimists were to place their hopes in Otto, Charles's eldest son, but it was clear that the ten-year-old heir to the vacant Habsburg throne would not play any active role in politics for many years. Also stymied were the left-wing Hungarian émigrés in Prague and Vienna who had anticipated that Horthy would be toppled during the restoration attempt and a more liberal and democratic regime established. British restraint of the Czechoslovak government and the decision of the Hungarian Social Democrats to refrain from any seditious activities during the October crisis had dashed these hopes.[2]

Admiral Horthy's victory over his opponents did not, however, immediately clarify the nature of the regime over which he was presiding. Only one thing seemed certain: Horthy's "temporary" position as regent was secure for the indefinite future. Already on November 3, 1921, János Csernoch, Hungary's Prince Primate, sent Horthy a private message urging him to remain in office because he and all Catholics were loyally behind him. Csernoch may even have hinted that he would be happy to place the crown of St. Stephen on Horthy's head if in time a coronation seemed the appropriate solution to Hungary's political dilemma.[3] But, true to his earlier promises, Horthy showed no interest in such a prospect. Instead he turned once again to Count Bethlen, "the steward," to implement the political program the two men had agreed on over the past year: creation of a unified, dominant government party; introduction of a new, less democratic franchise; and restoration of fiscal and financial stability.

István Bethlen responded with a dazzling display of political skill and pragmatic maneuvering that resulted within six months in the laying of a firm foundation for the interwar regime. Almost no documentary evidence survives of the confidential exchanges of the Regent and his Prime Minister in this period, but it seems clear that Bethlen was given a free hand to proceed as he deemed necessary, with the understanding that when called on Horthy would intervene to exert his personal influence and prestige. Bethlen moved rapidly and boldly, in his search for a new partner to help checkmate the Smallholders and their plans for further land distribution. On December 21, after two weeks of behind-the-scene negotiations, Bethlen made the startling announcement that he had concluded a political pact with the Social Democrats.

Although Count Bethlen hoped to restore as much as possible of the prewar Hungarian political system, he was realistic enough to take into account the growing literacy and political consciousness of the "people." The traditional ruling class would be restored to the helm, but a benevolent attitude would be shown toward the workers, who, Bethlen argued, should be "forgiven their sins" and gradually integrated into the political nation. If Hungary aspired to rejoin the European state system and attain international respectability, a secure niche in the political system had to be provided to its moderate Socialists. In strictly political terms, a small Social Democratic contingent in Parliament would pose no threat to the government party, and might even provide a useful counterweight to those Smallholders avid for more radical land reform. Regent Horthy was amenable to Bethlen's plan, although he probably did not fully understand the nature of what Bethlen called a "guided democracy."[4] Throughout this period he continued privately to disparage Socialists as mere stalking horses for bolshevism, but he was pragmatic enough to maintain contact with and receive in audience representatives of the right-wing of the Social Democratic party. In addition Horthy was gratified by the attitude of the workers and trade unions during the Sopron plebiscite and the restoration crises. In a proclamation issued on October 25 he had commended the "patriotic conduct of the workers of Budapest, who refrained from anything that would threaten the maintenance of order."[5]

Bethlen's rapprochement with the Social Democrats, which was announced in December 1921, proved to be the catalyst in the rapid dissolution of the Smallholders party. Bethlen was able to convince Nagyatádi Szabó to merge his party with the nonlegitimist wing of the National Christian Union to form a new "Party of Unity." Nagyatádi-Szabó was elected president of the new party, but real power and authority were clearly in the hands of István Bethlen, who had brilliantly engineered the capitulation of the largest party in the Hungarian National Assembly. As part of the newly merged party, the Smallholders were gradually to lose their distinctive identity. As Bethlen and Horthy had intended, those who had been calling for a second installment of land reform were now effectively silenced. Once this political reality was recognized, the Roman Catholic hierarchy and even many legitimist estate owners became strong, if quiet, supporters of the government.

The final step in the consolidation of the Horthy regime was the introduction of a new, more restricted franchise. On this issue, too, Bethlen and Horthy held similar views. Convinced that maintenance of the liberal franchise on which the 1920 elections were based would have further destabilizing effects on traditional society, they had been searching for some time for a way to return to the more restricted voting procedures of the prewar period. Horthy's private comments on this issue reflected his intense suspicion of and distaste for democracy. The problem, he declared, was that the masses were ignorant and liable to be misled by demagogues. Since in the last resort he was responsible for the welfare of the country, he did not dare "leave it to the hazard of an election to decide who shall administer it." He much preferred to do all that was possible in accordance with existing laws and Hungarian traditions to "get the very best and wisest men I possibly can to direct its destinies." He was also concerned to limit the franchise to the "right" people without resorting to an education qualification, which would give an advantage to the Jews and to workers over the peasants.[6] These were the considerations that led Horthy to favor the reintroduction of the open ballot in rural areas, and indeed this was the key element in the new franchise bill presented to the National Assembly by Bethlen in February 1922. The proposed franchise reduced the percentage of the population eligible to vote (28 percent versus 40 percent in 1920), and 80 percent of the voters would be denied a secret ballot.[7] This form of voting had in prewar elections made it possible for the government party to exert considerable coercion and to manipulate elections to insure a comfortable majority in the legislature. Alarmed by this prospect, opponents of Bethlen and Horthy, notably embittered legitimists, protested vociferously and managed through various obstructive tactics to prevent adoption of the franchise bill before expiration of the National Assembly in mid-February.

At this juncture Count Apponyi publicly implored the Regent to call the new elections on the basis of the 1920 franchise, but Bethlen responded with yet another clever, if devious, maneuver. Citing the complexity of the problem, he had the Regent announce that he was establishing a commission of prominent jurists to study the legal and constitutional issues connected with the franchise. This commission, over which Horthy himself presided, quickly did its work and conveniently concluded that the 1920 franchise had no legal validity and that the Regent had the authority to establish the ground rules for the election of a new Parliament. Horthy thereupon proceeded to promulgate Bethlen's franchise by executive decree, and the election was scheduled for late May and early June. The election of 1922 was a landmark in the establishment of the Horthy regime. In his capacity as both Prime Minister and leader of the Party of Unity, or the government party,[8] Count Bethlen was able to hand-pick most of the candidates of the government party. To insure that all went according to plan and to prevent any major defections from the ranks of the radical right-wingers, Gyula Gömbös was designated vice president of the government party and was entrusted with the task of "organizing" the election. The result was as expected: of the 245 seats at stake, 143 were captured by the Party of Unity. In this and in subsequent elections the "potent trinity of landlord, gendarme, and village notary" assured safe majorities for the regime.[9]

The core of the government party consisted of civil servants in the middle and upper echelons and of owners of medium to large estates, but the whole spectrum of right-wing opinion was represented, from advocates of the "Szeged idea" to finance capitalists from Budapest. The common denominator was that most of these delegates were beholden to Count Bethlen as party leader and the dispenser of patronage. By design the opposition parties garnered approximately one-third of the seats in the Assembly. The secret ballot in urban areas and Bethlen's tacit support resulted in the election of a substantial bloc of Social Democrats. Administrative pressure and coercion succeeded in excluding from the Assembly the most vociferous critics of the government, including the most fanatical anti-Semites and many recalcitrant legitimists. But Bethlen had not attempted, or perhaps thought it counterproductive, to deny seats to the most prominent of the legitimists. In the National Assembly they, along with other members of the opposition, were to have the opportunity to express grievances and engage in free-wheeling political debate. In the end, however, as events would demonstrate, the solid majority enjoyed by the government party insured that the policies of Bethlen and Horthy would always prevail.

Many Hungarian nationalists applauded Bethlen's success in restoring political stability because they anticipated that the government would now be able to pursue a vigorous foreign policy aimed at a rapid revision of the hated Treaty of Trianon. They were thus quite disappointed with the patient and cautious program introduced by the Prime Minister starting in 1922. Certainly Count Bethlen shared the yearning of most of his countrymen for a restoration of a great and powerful Hungary playing its traditional role as the dominant power in Danubian Europe. But in contrast to his more impulsive colleagues, Bethlen saw the true implications of Hungary's defeat in the Great War. Surrounded by the hostile Little Entente, confronted by a powerful alignment of great powers supporting the territorial status quo, and enormously weakened militarily and economically by the war and revolutions, Hungary, in Bethlen's view, was totally incapable of conducting an active, dynamic foreign policy. This was the blunt message he had tried to convey to his countrymen in his maiden speech to Parliament in 1921.[10]

Bethlen's scheme for Hungary's recovery involved a patient, long-term effort by a united nation in which disruptive, extremist movements of any kind, whether emanating from the left or the right, were suppressed. Above all, Bethlen believed that Hungary must once again project to the rest of Europe an image of a *Rechtsstaat*, a country in which constitutional procedures were adhered to and ordinary citizens could rely on the police and an independent judiciary to guarantee their personal security and civil liberties. Count Bethlen hardly fit the mold of a typical nineteenth-century European liberal, but he did believe that an authoritarian state of the kind he was fashioning could and should tolerate a reasonably free exchange of ideas in the press, the political arena, and cultural life.

During 1922 Bethlen took further steps to demonstrate that the excesses of the "White Terror" would no longer be tolerated and that Hungary was evolving toward a more open, pluralistic political life. A new press law further eased censorship, to the dismay of military censors who as early as mid-1921 had already classified more than half of Budapest's newspapers, including the prestigious German language *Pester Lloyd*, as "destructive" and "Jewish-liberal" in spirit.[11] By prosecuting members of the League of Awakening Magyars who had bombed a meeting where a democratic group was meeting, Bethlen made it clear that "patriotic enthusiasm" would no longer be an acceptable excuse for terrorist acts or open defiance of the government.[12] At the funeral of the nine victims of the bombing outrage, all of whom were Jews, the Regent was represented by his Commander in Chief, General Pál Nagy. By these actions Count Bethlen also intended to demonstrate to observers both in Hungary and throughout Europe that the symbiotic relationship between Hungary's Jewish community and the traditional political establishment was being restored. Bethlen regarded discrimination and violence against Jews as vulgar acts of "the gutter" that tarnished the honor of the Hungarian nation and unleashed the greed and resentments of the masses.[13] There was also the pragmatic consideration that the regime could hardly expect to rely on the valuable financial expertise and entrepreneurial talents of Jews who otherwise felt insecure and alienated from Hungarian society.

In Bethlen's view the achievement of domestic political stability would thus facilitate the country's economic recovery as well. Count Bethlen held no doctrinaire economic views, but simply assumed that the industrialists, bankers, and estate owners who had helped create a relatively prosperous Hungary before 1914 should be relied on to restore that prosperity.[14] Heeding the advice of experts from the financial community, most of them Jews or converts, Bethlen also concluded that Hungary's economic recovery could be sustained only through a major infusion of capital in the form of long-term loans from the Western powers. Such loans could be obtained, however, only if the great powers were persuaded that Hungary was a stable country that intended to pursue a "policy of fulfillment" of the peace treaty.

Given his own predilection for foreign policy adventures and his close association with proponents of the "Szeged idea," Miklós Horthy had some reservations about his Prime Minister's cautious and moderate policies. But such was Horthy's respect for "the steward" that he endorsed the "policy of fulfillment" and the re-establishment of the traditional economic system in which Jews played a major role. By the summer of 1922 Horthy and Bethlen had apparently come to a tacit understanding concerning policy-making. The Prime Minister now had almost complete freedom to formulate policy without even consulting the Regent, who insisted on being involved only with military matters within his sphere of interest as Supreme War Lord.[15] Certainly Bethlen always took pains to avoid the impression that he was abusing his special relationship with the Regent. From time to time he reported to Horthy on the general state of affairs and, with his remarkable powers of persuasion, managed to assuage any doubts or concerns that his critics might have planted in the Regent's mind. As time passed and Bethlen's policies proved successful, such consultations became more infrequent, and Bethlen could even boast to his closest colleagues that he alone was responsible for making Hungarian policy.[16] Nonetheless Bethlen always remained properly deferential to the Regent, who of course had the power at any time to dismiss a Prime Minister who no longer enjoyed his confidence.

Since Bethlen's program for Hungary's economic reconstruction required close cooperation with the Western great powers, he sought in various ways to reintegrate his country into the European system and gain some measure of international respectability. A necessary first step was admission to the League of Nations, which, after some resistance from Hungary's suspicious neighbors, took place in September 1922. As Count Bethlen's program began to unfold in 1922, however, murmurs of discontent became audible in the camp of the radical right-wingers and in military circles. Virtually all of the Prime Minister's initiatives and strategies were branded as mortal sins in the catechism of the Szeged movement. Making deals with the crypto-Communists in the Social Democratic party? Coquetting with Jewish capitalists? Prosecuting such fine patriots as Iván Héjjas? Allowing the Jewish journalists once again to spread their poison? Rubbing elbows with the inferior Czechs, Romanians, and Serbs at the League of Nations? Not surprisingly, such diehard Szeged veterans as Father Zadravecz and Miklós Kozma made every effort to gain Admiral Horthy's ear to present their litany of complaints about the government's policies. Surely, they reasoned, the man who had rallied the counterrevolutionary army in 1919 and had been elected honorary president of EkSz would not knowingly approve the perfidious policies of the current Prime Minister.

Count Bethlen endeavored to separate Horthy from the extremist right-wingers by closely supervising those who were allowed an audience, but the Regent insisted on receiving his Szeged friends warmly and listening sympathetically to their grievances. Indeed, throughout his political career Horthy was to display an uncritical favoritism toward those with whom he had shared the camaraderie and exhilaration of 1919: to have been at Szeged was to have slept on Mount Parnassus. For this reason Horthy's responses in 1922 to the complaints of Kozma and Zadravecz were a bit embarrassed and ambiguous. He could find no easy way to explain his great confidence in Count Bethlen and his willingness to give him *carte blanche* to carry out Hungary's reconstruction. Instead Horthy resorted to procrastination or prevarication, claiming that he was being muzzled and was not free to speak his mind.[17] But when pressed on the most controversial matters, he retreated more and more to the language and arguments with which he had been primed by Bethlen. For Father Zadravecz one very disquieting development was Horthy's increasing willingness to break with the more fanatical of the radical right-wingers. When asked to intercede in Héjjas's favor, Horthy declined on the grounds that his former officer was a sadist. As for Prónay, if he were to request an audience, "I wouldn't receive him or talk to him."[18]

For much of 1922 the mood in the Szeged camp was thus one of profound disenchantment and dejection. Father Zadravecz concluded that Horthy had undergone a "lamentable metamorphosis" from a straightforward military man to a cautious politician. In the army officer corps there was considerable bitterness toward Count Bethlen, who, it was said, had isolated the Regent in the Royal Castle and surrounded him with Liberals, Jew-lovers, and Freemasons.[19] It was left to Gyula Gömbös to find some way to break the spell Bethlen had cast over the Regent and to champion the cause of the radical right-wing. No direct evidence survives of the conversations between Gömbös and Horthy in this period, but there are indications that Gömbös forcefully expressed his dissatisfaction with Bethlen's policy toward the Jews and his "passive" foreign policy.[20] Horthy resisted any suggestion that he dismiss Bethlen and tried to mediate between the two protagonists, but Gömbös's frustration and impatience led him to go public with his complaints. In the summer of 1922 he announced the formation of a "League of Race-Defenders" and began to circulate a "white paper" in which many of Bethlen's policies were denounced. The chief thrust of the document was the accusation that the Prime Minister's favoritism toward the Jews and his "policy of fulfillment" of the Treaty of Trianon were totally inconsistent with the fundamental principle of "Christian nationalism."

When Gömbös was accused of destabilizing the government party, he hinted that he had the Regent's approval for his actions, and rumors soon spread of a growing estrangement between the Regent and the Prime Minister.[21] But Bethlen had no intention of making substantial changes in the long-term program on which he had embarked. In any case, he was confident that if it came to a real political confrontation with Gömbös, he would retain the support of the Regent and a large majority of the government party. After all, Gömbös was a mere army captain whose political immaturity, conspiratorial flamboyance, and impetuosity caused much uneasiness in the conservative establishment that was once again in control of Hungary's political fortunes.

In the first months of 1923 Count Bethlen's government was put to a severe test. The occupation of the Ruhr by French troops in January created great political unrest and agitation not only in Germany but also in Hungary, where rumors quickly spread that the Little Entente countries were planning a similar intervention to force Hungary to comply with the reparation clauses of the Trianon Treaty. In this turbulent atmosphere extremist students in the League of Awakening Magyars organized public demonstrations in which the government was denounced for its "spineless" foreign policy and Bethlen was accused of practicing a "Manchester liberalism." Ignoring such protests, Bethlen traveled in May to Paris, London, and Geneva to work out the details of his plan for Hungary's economic stabilization. By contrast, Gömbös decided that the time was propitious for a resuscitation of the plan for a "White International," which had been vetoed by the Hungarian Foreign Ministry in 1920. In the intervening years low-level contacts had been maintained between the Bavarian and Hungarian radical right-wingers, and the unfolding international crisis of 1923 prompted the Germans once again to seek the support of Horthy's

Hungary. In February Ludendorff sent Horthy a message suggesting that they reestablish the old line of communication. Adolf Hitler, then an obscure but rising figure in German right-wing politics, proposed through a Hungarian intermediary that he travel incognito to Hungary to have personal discussions with Regent Horthy.[22]

Neither Ludendorff nor Hitler ever made it to Budapest, but Horthy, whose enthusiasm for the "White International" had apparently been stimulated anew by Gömbös, did meet behind his Prime Minister's back with several of the Hungarians who were in contact not only with the fledgling National Socialist party in Bavaria but also with Benito Mussolini's Fascist government in Italy.[23] As a result the conspirators, including a lawyer by the name of Ferenc Ulain, gained the impression that Horthy tacitly approved their activity and would support them openly if they could create a *fait accompli*. Once he learned of these indiscretions by the Regent, Bethlen immediately chastised Gömbös and ordered that all clandestine contacts with the German conspirators be ended. No doubt he explained once again to Horthy why the making of foreign policy had to be left to the professionals of the Foreign Ministry and not to immature amateurs. Tension between Bethlen and Gömbös was heightened in the early summer of 1923 by the revelation that Hungary would be required to accept very stringent terms in order to secure an international loan and postponement of reparation payments. This news led to new and more strident attacks on the government by the radical right-wingers, who excoriated Bethlen for his "sellout" of the nation's vital interests. Horthy managed for a time to arrange another uneasy truce between Bethlen and Gömbös, but he was growing increasingly exasperated by the Race Defenders, some of whom were now calling for far-reaching social reforms, including more radical land reform. Gyula Gömbös himself was ambivalent about this "populist" element of the "Szeged idea," but many of those attracted to the League of Race Defenders were intensely suspicious of both Jewish capitalists and Hungarian noblemen and were prepared to build a mass political movement by offering social reforms to benefit the peasantry and even the workers.

For several months Gyula Gömbös had complied with Horthy's personal plea that he try to resolve his differences with Bethlen within the framework of the government party. Making no headway and convinced that Bethlen's policies were leading to disaster,

Gömbös finally announced, in August, that he was resigning from the government party and forming the Party of Race Defenders. Joining him were several prominent Szeged veterans, including Tibor Eckhardt, Ferenc Ulain, and Endre Bajcsy-Zsilinszky. Abandoning his previous restraint, Gömbös now openly attacked Bethlen for his "philo-Semitism" and demanded the elimination of the "excesses" of capitalism and parliamentary government. Gömbös's bold move precipitated a new round of vociferous street demonstrations by the Awakening Magyars and sparked rumors that he planned some sort of coup d'état on the pattern of Mussolini's "march on Rome."

Convinced now that his old Szeged friends were too "politically immature" and that they had broken faith with him, Admiral Horthy acted resolutely.[24] Shortly after Gömbös launched his new party the Regent summoned representatives of the Awakening Magyars and solemnly declared that he was determined to maintain order in Hungary. "I will order that all troublemakers be fired on," he declared, "and if the trouble is caused by right-wingers, for me the only difference will be that I will issue the order with a heavy heart, while I would enthusiastically order fire on left-wing troublemakers." In words spoken to Miklós Kozma but clearly meant to be passed on to Gömbös, Horthy now reaffirmed his complete confidence in Bethlen, who, he asserted, was free to pursue his policy without having to explain every little step. He and the Prime Minister had agreed on a grand foreign policy of the "possible," the details of which he could not divulge since no one in Hungary could keep a secret anyway. As for Gömbös, it would be better for him to work within the government party to influence it to move more to the right.[25]

Horthy's attitude was a bitter disappointment to Kozma and the other Szeged veterans, who concluded, more in sadness than indignation, that the "Hero of Otranto" had become a "puppet" who now spoke "in the words of others."[26] In any case, Gömbös was not about to alter his new course, and in fact continued to be involved in conspiratorial planning for a coup d'état to be carried out jointly by radical right-wing groups in Munich and Budapest. During August 1923 Gömbös and his colleagues met secretly with several emissaries of Ludendorff and Hitler, who planned a seizure of power in Munich in November.[27] The German conspirators managed to stage their so-called Beer-Hall Putsch on November 8–9, but there was no parallel action in Hungary. The Hungarian police, having infiltrated the League of Awakening Magyars, were able on November 7 to make a dramatic arrest at the Hungarian-Austrian border of Ferenc Ulain, who was carrying with him detailed proposals for fantastic plots to be hatched in cooperation with the Bavarian rightists. It remains unclear whether a coup d'état had actually been planned to take place in Budapest on November 8.[28] In any case, Gyula Gömbös was able to avoid implication in any of the plots, and the crackdown now ordered by Bethlen focused mainly on suppression of the Awakening Magyars and strict enforcement of a ban on political and irredentist activity by military officers.

Regent Horthy had even stronger reasons now to dissociate himself from the radical right-wing underworld that had proved so irresistible a temptation to him over the past four years. Certainly he was alarmed to learn of the plans to topple Bethlen's government, even though the conspirators apparently assumed that the Regent would remain in power. Horthy's alarm must have turned to chagrin when he received a detailed memorandum from Ferenc Ulain, whose first act once in prison seems to have been to draw up a long report on his activities for the Regent.[29] In his account of his dealings with the Bavarian radical right-wingers, Ulain reported that Hitler and Ludendorff had absolutely no confidence in the Bethlen government but retained the highest "respect and esteem" for Horthy. Ulain strongly implied that his surreptitious actions over the past year had been approved beforehand by Horthy, and that he was reporting in writing to him now just as he had done in person earlier in the year.

Count Bethlen managed to prevent the Regent's role in this affair from being mentioned at Ulain's trial, and Horthy, properly chastened, seemed finally prepared to sever all remaining ties with right-wing adventurers like Ulain. For the duration of the Bethlen era Horthy received in audience only visitors approved beforehand by the Prime Minister. For several years Gömbös himself was to be *persona non grata* at the Royal Castle, although, as will be seen, Horthy refused to impose complete ostracism on a Szeged comrade to whom he owed so much. Moreover, both Horthy and Bethlen were willing to offer government jobs to prominent radical right-wingers who would cease their oppositional activities and become docile members of the government party. This tactic, which Bethlen had initiated soon after he became Prime Minister in 1921 and which had co-opted such important Szeged veterans as Miklós Kozma and Zsigmond Endre, was so successful that by 1924 Gömbös's Party of Race Defenders was neutralized as a political factor. Gömbös remained in Parliament as a forceful champion of radical right-wing principles, and he and Tibor Eckhardt did continue their efforts to stir up public sentiments against the Jews. Thus in 1925 they organized a World Congress of Anti-Semites that attracted to Budapest many of Europe's most virulent radical right-wingers. But the anti-Jewish hysteria that had gripped Hungarian society in the first tumultuous years of the postwar era had largely dissipated by this time. Moreover, Bethlen was not averse to using the time honored methods of government coercion to stymie the efforts of the Race Defenders to increase their representation in Parliament. After a by-election campaign in 1925 in which his party had made a poor showing, Gömbös wrote to Bethlen to complain about official harassment of his party colleagues: "If we had been left-wingers, I don't think these narrow-minded measures would have been instituted. . . . You know best of all that the application of force is my own style . . . but in this case I regard it as a blunder."[30]

The political consolidation of the Hungarian regime was greatly facilitated by the successes of Count Bethlen's economic policies. A successful floating of bonds in London during the summer of 1924 made it possible for Hungary's budget to be brought quickly into balance. The inflation (in part government-sponsored) that had flared in 1923 started to subside and industrial production began a steady improvement.[31] By the mid-1920s Western bankers, noting the strength of Hungary's new currency (the *pengő*) and the growing stability of the Horthy-Bethlen regime, were beginning to view Hungary as a desirable field for investment. The modest trickle of capital that had entered Hungary in 1924 soon became a substantial current. To be sure, only about a third of this capital was wisely invested, and much was used for conspicuous consumption,[32] but the foreign loans and high world wheat prices made it possible for the Hungarian economy to return to prewar levels of production and for the country to enjoy a modest prosperity. In the process Hungary took on the largest per capita foreign debt of any European country, but so long as the international economy was stable and grain prices remained high, the gamble seemed worth taking. Even Bethlen's most vociferous critics on the right who had opposed his policies as a "sellout" of Hungarian interests were silenced by the success of his economic policies. Abroad, especially in Britain, there was growing admiration for the way in which Bethlen (and by implication Horthy) had guided Hungary toward economic and political stability. The prevailing view among British policymakers was that the Horthy government was, after all, a "British creation" and the best that could be hoped for in a part of Europe where democratic traditions were not strong. The Horthy regime might not be "perfect," but Hungary's leaders were straightforward and Hungary was "one of the few places in Central Europe where an honest attempt to grapple with the situation is being made." It was felt that any attempt to impose liberal and democratic reforms in Budapest might boomerang and result instead in a victory for Gyula Gömbös.[33]

The strength of the Horthy regime was severely tested in 1925 and 1926 by two crises. Both cases were fueled by revelations of sordid and illegal activities that Horthy and Bethlen had condoned in the immediate postwar period. In February 1925 the Budapest newspaper *Újság* published two articles in which Ödön Beniczky, the former Minister of the Interior, revealed the hitherto unpublished findings of the investigations he had conducted in 1919 and 1920 of the atrocities committed by the special detachments, including the assassination of the Social Democratic journalists Somogyi and Bacsó. Beniczky thereby made public the conclusions that he had reached privately at the time: the murders of Somogyi and Bacsó had been perpetrated by members of the special detachment commanded by Count Ostenburg and the Regent had known of and had covered up this crime.[34]

Beniczky's revelations unleashed a political storm. Calling this Hungary's "Matteotti affair," a similar political scandal in Italy several years earlier, Horthy's critics declared that the government had been thoroughly discredited and that Bethlen should draw the consequences and resign. In June 1925 the Social Democrats introduced in Parliament an amendment to Law I of 1920 that would have replaced the regency with a Council of Three elected by the Parliament. The Regent's personal reaction to these developments is not known, though he must have been furious. In any case, he and Bethlen were able to weather the storm, largely because the government party remained loyal and disciplined. No attempt was made to offer a specific rebuttal to Beniczky's charges, which, though largely accurate, probably struck many political observers as based mainly on circumstantial evidence. Instead, pro-Horthy demonstrations were organized by government loyalists in different parts of Hungary, and legal action was taken against Beniczky for the crime of "insulting the regent" (*lèse régent*). Beniczky was convicted and sentenced to three years in prison, although he was released after only three months. The newspaper *Ujság* was banned.

By the summer of 1925 the Horthy-Bethlen regime seemed impregnable. Count Bethlen was sufficiently confident of his position to submit for parliamentary approval the franchise law that Horthy had issued by decree in 1922. Just when it seemed that the passage of the electoral law was signaling the beginning of a more tranquil political era, a second, more serious scandal erupted. Once again an earlier collaboration with the radical right-wing came back to haunt Horthy and Bethlen. At some point in 1921 or 1922, Count Bethlen had authorized a surreptitious plan for the forging of Czechoslovak, Yugoslav, and Romanian currency in order to finance Hungary's revisionist activities and in general to weaken the economies of the Little Entente countries.[35] This plan was carried out with the cooperation of the Hungarian Cartographical Institute (under the direction of Count Pál Teleki) and of Imre Nádosy, Chief of the Hungarian National Police. At some point, however, without the direct knowledge of Horthy or Bethlen, the project became enmeshed in the conspiratorial activities of the Hungarian and German right-wing extremists and was expanded to the counterfeiting of French francs. When some of the forged francs were discovered in late 1925 and traced to Budapest, a major international scandal seemed about to erupt. The enemies of the Horthy regime, both at home and abroad, imagined that the opportunity had finally arrived to bring to power a more democratic and progressive government. But, despite some tense moments as French detectives pursued their investigation in Hungary, Horthy and Bethlen managed in the end to emerge relatively unscathed from the scandal. Once he had withstood the initial tidal wave that had threatened to engulf him when the crisis first erupted, Bethlen was able to pursue a very effective tactic of "divide and rule." He warned Vilmos Vázsonyi, spokesman for the Liberals and the most prominent Jewish politician in Hungary, that if his government were to be toppled, its likely successor would be a radical right-wing one that would sponsor virulent anti-Semitic legislation. By contrast, the legitimists and extreme right-wingers were urged to restrain their attacks on the government, for if Bethlen were to be severely weakened or even forced to resign, the only beneficiaries would be the forces of the left. These arguments carried the day in London and Paris as well, for despite initial expressions of indignation not even France found it expedient in the end to push for a new government in Budapest.[36]

As the forged francs scandal drew to its conclusion in the summer of 1926, the domestic critics of the Horthy regime were enveloped by a mood of futility and frustration. Bethlen's triumph seemed even greater when the European powers, with Great Britain and Italy taking the lead, decided to terminate the financial control of Hungary by the League of Nations that had been imposed as one of the conditions for implementation of the League-approved reconstruction plan. Bethlen now seized the opportunity to put into place the final building block of the political edifice he had constructed. Through most of its history Hungary's Parliament had consisted of two chambers on the English pattern. Only the lower house had been reconstituted in 1920, and Bethlen had hesitated to restore the upper house for fear that it would be dominated by staunch legitimists. By 1926, however, such a danger seemed remote, and Bethlen's conservative instincts prompted him to advocate an upper chamber as a "safety brake" against a more volatile lower chamber that might someday fall under the sway of more demagogic leaders.[37] The proposal had the added advantage of further ingratiating Bethlen to Horthy, who remained irked about the fact that the law establishing the regency had not empowered the head of state to grant titles of nobility. Of the 244 members of the new Upper House, the Regent would name 40 who would be lifetime delegates. The others would be members of the Habsburg family, leading dignitaries from the realms of organized religion and economic life, and elected representatives from the universities and professional groups.

This was the last measure approved by the Parliament elected in 1922, for Horthy now prorogued the session and set new elections for December 1926. At this juncture, Count Bethlen, apparently enervated by the difficult political struggles of the past five years and the strain of the forged francs scandal, tendered his resignation. In a private letter to the Regent, he expressed "an irresistible desire to rest."[38] He thanked Horthy for his support and for allowing him to work freely "even when you might have felt that I was not quite on the right path." Political and economic consolidation had now been achieved, Bethlen declared, and his withdrawal from the government would cause only minor disruptions. Others could now carry on "with ease," since his policies were approved by the "overwhelming majority" of the country. After a year or two he would be rejuvenated and could return to serve his country once again.[39]

Was Bethlen serious about resigning? Perhaps, but the self-congratulatory tone of his letter suggests that his ulterior motive might have been to plant even more firmly in Horthy's mind the notion that his brilliant Prime Minister was indispensable. In any case, Horthy, declaring that his confidence in Bethlen had not wavered, refused to accept the resignation and persuaded Bethlen to stay on. The Prime Minister proceeded to organize the new elections with his accustomed vigor. The results were a major victory for the government party, which increased its representation from 143 to 170 delegates. Of course, some of this can be attributed to the fact that since the previous elections Bethlen had been able to "fine tune" the techniques of manipulating the vote. But it is noteworthy that even in those urban areas where the voting was secret the government party had unexpected successes, and in all areas the parties on the extremes of the political spectrum faltered.[40] The Party of Race Defenders was nearly eliminated from parliamentary representation: only Gömbös was able to retain his seat, perhaps at Horthy's insistence. The Social Democrats lost eleven of their twenty-five seats, all in the cities where the secret ballot was in place.

A truly free election based on universal suffrage would doubtless have produced quite different results in 1926, but the impressive victory of the government party did reflect growing admiration for the achievements of the regime that Bethlen and Horthy had fashioned. The modest prosperity that Hungary was beginning to enjoy affected not only the capitalists and estate owners, but also the broad middle class and, to a certain extent, even the workers. Unemployment fell to low levels and the average standard of living for factory workers rose to the general Central European level.[41] The great social scandal of the Bethlen era was the continued misery of the "three million beggars," the landless peasants working in medieval-like conditions on the great estates. But even among the peasants the government had won support from those whose hunger for land had been temporarily satisfied by the admittedly modest land reform. Some 400,000 formerly landless Hungarians had gained a tenuous foothold as "smallholders."[42]

Certainly an important factor in the growing prestige of the regime was Miklós Horthy's willingness to accept the role that Bethlen had assigned him. Horthy was to be a head of state who on paper possessed enormous powers, but who in practice remained aloof from everyday political problems and played an almost exclusively ceremonial role in the government. By 1926 it was clear to most Hungarians that Horthy had not only reconciled himself to this role but would play it with grace and dignity. Those who had feared that, once ensconced in power, Horthy would demand to be crowned king or would establish a military dictatorship, found their fears allayed. Remaining true to the public promises he had made in 1920 and 1921, Regent Horthy rejected all suggestions that he be crowned king and establish a Horthy dynasty. When a delegation of dignitaries headed by Count Gedeon Ráday approached Horthy in August 1922 with proposals of this kind, he thanked them for their expression of confidence but asserted that he could not in good conscience "stretch my hand towards the crown."[43] All but the most embittered legitimists gradually came to adopt a more pragmatic, and in some cases even sympathetic, approach to Admiral Horthy and his regime. Typical was the view of Count Albin Schager, the leading Austrian monarchist, who in 1925 declared privately that legitimists had no interest in overthrowing Horthy. Indeed, he asserted, Danubian monarchists should be relieved that the man at the helm in Hungary was a conservative who remained "unwaveringly legitimist-minded."[44]

Although Horthy was adamant in his refusal to consider a formal coronation, he was not averse to being treated with the deference normally shown only to monarchs. No doubt Bethlen had insisted on this from the start, shrewdly calculating that the Magyars, however divided they might be over the ultimate disposition of the crown, yearned for a ceremonial head of state who would be a symbol of unity and authority. Bethlen and his colleagues were careful always to show proper deference to the Regent. All but his closest friends addressed Horthy, even in private, as *főméltóságú* (Your Serene Highness). Certain ceremonies or procedures were revived, or in some cases invented, that would enhance Horthy's image as a constitutional monarch. Starting in 1924 Horthy found his time more and more taken up by the kind of royal duties that Francis Joseph had carried out with such grave responsibility in the last decades of his reign. Nearly every morning he met patiently with a stream of petitioners and promised to look into their grievances. However, unlike Francis Joseph, whose custom it had been to remain seated behind his desk when visitors approached, Horthy rose to greet them and shake hands, a practice that enhanced his image as a "man of the people."

As head of state Miklós Horthy found himself spending countless hours signing proclamations and decrees, dedicating bridges, opening new hospitals, visiting schools, inducting new members into the Order of Heroes, and traveling the country to give what became a stock speech on the need for hard work, discipline, and devotion to traditional values. He fulfilled these functions with a pleasing combination of courtly etiquette and patriarchal benevolence. From the mid-1920s on, Regent Horthy formally opened each new session of the Parliament in a manner reminiscent of the king's traditional "speech from the throne."[45] Well versed in the rules of protocol and fluent in most European languages, Horthy also presided with ease at diplomatic receptions and dinners. During the 1920s almost every visiting dignitary in Budapest was granted an audience with the Regent. Many of them remarked on the Regent's bluff, healthy, and robust appearance. He was, as one American diplomat noted, "a typical sea dog."[46] Everyone was impressed by Horthy's polyglot skills, charm, and gallant manner. Indeed, those who met Admiral Horthy, whether friends or foes, foreigners or Magyars, were almost inevitably won over by his gracious and friendly manner.[47] Some were made uneasy by Horthy's crude political views or were astonished by his lack of discretion, but virtually everyone agreed that the Regent was "sincere, not a sneaky, fawning opportunist."[48] Moreover, for all his prejudices and chauvinistic attitudes, Horthy could on some contentious issues, such as religion, seem remarkably tolerant. He regularly attended both Catholic and Protestant church services, and often declared that belief in God was the important thing, not what church a person belonged to.[49]

The seeds of a "Horthy cult" that Gyula Gömbös had planted in 1919 came to full flower during the Bethlen era. School textbooks and children's books glorified Horthy as the "Hero of Otranto" and the liberator of Hungary from Bolshevik tyranny.[50] Sycophantic public officials praised Horthy as "our gloriously governing Great Lord" and compared him to Prince Árpád, the founder of the country. The feast day of Horthy's namesake, St. Miklós, was declared a national holiday. Each year two key dates in Horthy's career, March 1 (election to the regency) and November 16 (entry into Budapest) were commemorated in lavish ceremonies. Postage stamps bore the Regent's stern but benevolent visage. Newsreels, which in Europe and North America had always shown a fascination for royalty, frequently depicted Regent Horthy as a dignified monarch presiding over a variety of neo-Baroque ceremonies, parades, and other extravaganzas. This constant adulation and flattery was not without its effect on Admiral Horthy. He became very sensitive to personal sleights or to what he deemed lack of respect for the office of the regency. Once while traveling by car in the town of Csaba, Horthy spotted on the sidewalk a worker who had not joined the other spectators in showing respect for the Regent by taking off his hat. Horthy ordered his chauffeur to stop, leaped from the car, and scolded the culprit, who was immediately descended upon by the police.[51] Public criticism or ridicule of Horthy was treated as *lèse régent*, as Ödön Beniczky discovered in 1925. In a typical year, 1928, twenty-seven unfortunate Hungarians were convicted of insulting the Regent. They were fined or sentenced to prison terms of up to three months.[52] The only forum of Horthy's Hungary where public criticism of or discourtesy toward the Regent were possible was Parliament, where raucous debate was not just permitted but seemed the order of the day. The Regent's critics, confident in their immunity as delegates in Parliament, delighted in referring to Horthy as the "temporary head of state" or derisively calling him "Miklós Hunyadi," a reference to János Hunyadi, regent of Hungary from 1446 to 1453. Socialist delegates criticized the pomposity of the regime, complained about the cost of the Regent's special train, the Turán, and lamented the fact that Hungary had become "an operetta-like country that has a monarchy without a king."[53]

These manifestations of continued hostility toward the Regent and the artificial and forced nature of the government-sponsored "Horthy cult" must be balanced by other evidence that the substantial public support enjoyed by Admiral Horthy in 1919 and 1920 grew steadily during the Bethlen era. Many Hungarians must have been gratified by the dignified way in which the Regent comported himself. Although he performed many public functions, Admiral Horthy managed to remain largely out of the public light. He and his family avoided vulgar public displays, and, although he cherished his many medals and honors, Horthy rarely displayed them and regularly wore only one, the Order of Maria Theresa. The Horthys lived fairly unostentatiously. The guest quarters they occupied comprised only 9 rooms of the 814 in the cavernous Royal Castle. Most of the Castle thus remained eerily empty throughout the Horthy era, which had been true during the Dualist period as well, for Francis Joseph had made only infrequent visits to Budapest. The Regent's salary was modest by the standards of the day: it allowed for a lifestyle commensurate with that of a high-level ambassador.[54] The staff and servants provided for the Regent represented only a minimal level of service. Moreover, Horthy made no effort to use his political authority or connections with wealthy financiers to accumulate a fortune. It apparently never occurred to him that he should plan for all eventualities by stashing away funds in a foreign bank account.

Miklós Horthy's public stature was also enhanced by the exemplary nature of his family life. His wife was widely admired for her modest and dignified manner. The absence of even the hint of scandal in their marriage must have pleased many Hungarians who read with dismay about the improprieties of members of the royal family in neighboring Romania. The three surviving Horthy children (one daughter, Magdolna, had died in 1918) also avoided bringing any discredit on the family, although Miklós Jr. served a brief prison term in 1924 for participation in a duel.

By the late 1920s even some of Horthy's most vociferous critics on the left had to concede that their worst fears had been unwarranted. The Soviets might continue to use Horthy as the "horrible example" of what to expect if the "Whites" ever returned to Russia,[55] and the *Manchester Guardian* might insist that the lot of a political prisoner was "considerably worse" in a Hungarian jail than a Russian jail,[56] but most disinterested political observers had to grant that Admiral Horthy had not established a military or totalitarian dictatorship. He preferred the traditional methods of conservative, authoritarian government. Though in theory he possessed great power, he chose to remain largely aloof from policymaking and administration. For most of the Bethlen era he met occasionally with Cabinet ministers to discuss current issues, but for the most part this was a formality and he seldom tried to dictate policy. As one perceptive observer of that era has observed, Admiral Horthy had the power to do a good deal of mischief but fortunately he took an interest in only a few public issues.[57] On one thing he was indeed unyielding: communism should never again be permitted to infect Hungarian society. The Hungarian police kept a close surveillance of left-wing groups and were quick to pounce on any that showed radical tendencies. Thus, when in 1925 Moscow dispatched two former members of Béla Kun's government to attempt to revive the Communist movement in Hungary, they were quickly arrested. Yet it is characteristic of the quasi-liberal nature of the interwar Hungarian legal system that the two defendants, Mátyás Rákosi and Zoltán Vas, were given a formal public trial at which they were represented by a group of Hungary's most prominent bourgeois lawyers. Rákosi and Vas were given long prison sentences, but in open court they were allowed to make closing statements in which they vilified Horthy and his regime.[58]

Confident that communism had been all but extinguished in Hungary, Admiral Horthy was willing to approve, or at least tolerate, the pluralist system that Bethlen had put in place. Horthy's personal preference might have been, as in his Szeged days, to ban all newspapers and journals except those that supported "Christian National" principles. But Count Bethlen insisted that it was not possible, or even desirable, for a government to exercise total control over political or artistic activity. Thus, a relatively open expression of political ideas and thought was to be found in the numerous newspapers and small journals that were published in the Bethlen era and the 1930s. Editors who flirted too openly with Marxist ideology were indeed hounded by the censors or the police, and certain kinds of publications were frequently banned or were heavily censored, but in Budapest, at least, a very broad range of political opinions could find an outlet. Private organizations and associations of all kinds were permitted, including the Freemasons and a Hungarian chapter of the Fabian society.[59] There was an active artistic life, especially in music and theater, and significant advances were made in science and mathematics.

Some left-wing Hungarian artists and intellectuals, like the painter László Moholy-Nagy and the film theorist Béla Balázs, found the atmosphere in their native land too oppressive or stultifying and pursued their work as émigrés. But others, such as Béla Bartók and the poet József Attila, managed to defy the prevailing philistinism in Horthy's Hungary and produce artistic works of lasting importance.[60] A fairly free-ranging debate of social, intellectual, and political issues was conducted by urban intellectuals in such "unlicensed but tolerated" journals as *Szép Szó*. Many writers and scholars gravitated to a very active populist movement, which embraced dissidents from all sectors of the political spectrum.

Known as "village explorers," they managed in journals like *Válasz* and *Tanú* and a variety of pamphlets and books to expose the misery and penury in which Hungary's landless peasants, the "three million beggars," lived. Gyula Illyés's *People of the Puszta*, one of the great masterpieces of Hungarian literature, was a later product of this social and political ferment.

A man of limited intellectual interests and conventional cultural preferences, Miklós Horthy paid little attention to most of these activities on the fringe of Hungarian society and political life. He had once tried to read the Social Democratic *Népszava* as a kind of *Kriegsspiel* (war game) but had quickly abandoned the effort as a waste of time.[61] Occasionally he read books that came to his attention, mostly memoirs and right-wing tracts. He probably knew nothing about such obscure publications as *Szép Szó* and *Válasz*. Perhaps he was aware of the work of the "village explorers," but he is unlikely to have read any of their works. Why should he read a book like *People of the Puszta*? After all, he was a country gentleman who had a firsthand knowledge of rural Hungary and the contented peasants on his estate. For his musical entertainment Horthy preferred the classical repertoire. Had he been in the audience at the Budapest premiere of one of Bartók's more challenging works, he might well have been tempted to contribute to the crescendo of boos from the baffled and indignant audience. No one, it seems, informed the Regent of the latest developments in the cinema; thus the revolutionary Soviet film *Battleship Potemkin*, which depicted in heroic terms a naval rebellion in 1905, was granted a license and was presumably quietly shown in Budapest in the late 1920s.[62] All in all, Regent Horthy remained happily oblivious to all these manifestations of political and social pluralism. Count Bethlen had effectively shielded him from contact with such Szeged cronies as Gömbös, Prónay, and Zadravecz, who remained appalled by the regime's tolerance of the "nefarious" activities of socialists, fellow-travelers, decadent artists, Freemasons, and sundry other despicable elements of society.

Although the general tenor of Horthy's Hungary was rigidly conservative and, on some issues, even obscurantist, Admiral Horthy himself felt no compulsion to stand in the way of any and all reforms. Indeed, outside the realm of land reform, to which he long remained rigidly opposed, there is no record of his objecting to or vetoing any progressive social measures put forward by his ministers during the interwar period.[63] During the Bethlen era certain notable reforms in health insurance and education were in fact implemented. On many controversial social issues Horthy managed to keep an open mind, perhaps because he remained largely ignorant of the terms of the debate. As a result, on rare occasions, usually as a favor to a friend, Admiral Horthy even took the initiative in fostering progressive reforms. Cecile Tormay, one of Horthy's main supporters in 1920, later became the champion of a unique right-wing, nationalist feminist movement that developed in Hungary during the 1920s. Frustrated by the stubborn resistance of the University of Budapest to the admission of female students, Tormay took her case directly to the Regent, whom she won over to a clever solution. Horthy gave his consent to the enrollment of females in the army student battalions, a right-wing group that had been given a priority rating for admission to the university. Administrators and faculty objected to this subterfuge, but Horthy remained adamant and the Faculty of Philosophy at the University of Budapest was open for the first time to women.[64]

Perhaps the most dramatic aspect of Horthy's metamorphosis in the 1920s was his approval of Bethlen's more tolerant policies toward the Jews. Bethlen had never been enthusiastic about the *numerus clausus*. Thus, it was not only to appease his foreign critics or satisfy his allies in the financial community, but also out of personal conviction, that he worked step-by-step during the 1920s to blunt the effect of this discriminatory legislation. By the end of the decade the *numerus clausus* remained on the books but its provisions had been mitigated by court decisions and amendments. As a result, by the early 1930s Jewish students represented over 12 percent of the university student population, twice that stipulated by the original *numerus clausus*, though substantially lower than the prewar rate. Bethlen's modification of the anti-Jewish legislation came too late to prevent a significant "brain drain" of young Jewish scientists and mathematicians like Leó Szilárd and János Neumann, who were to forge remarkable careers in the West. But it meant that, ten years after the Hungarian Parliament passed Europe's first postwar restrictions on the number of Jews admitted to higher education, Hungarian Jews continued to be disproportionately represented in such professions as law (56 percent), medicine (40 percent), and journalism (36 percent), figures that were essentially unchanged from before the war.

Bethlen's willingness to act on what he called the "legitimate grievances" of the Jews was publicly decried not only by Gyula

Gömbös and his fellow Race Defenders but also by such advocates of "civilized anti-Semitism" as Count Pál Teleki. What prompted Admiral Horthy, who often boasted about his role in inspiring the *numerus clausus* in 1920, to support his Prime Minister's more tolerant policies? Once again, almost nothing is known of the arguments that Bethlen used to persuade Horthy, but it is likely that he endeavored to strengthen Horthy's view that the assimilated Jews of Hungary were by and large "good indigenous types,"[65] that is, patriotic Hungarians long resident in Hungary who were making useful contributions to society. Admiral Horthy's willingness to embrace this view was enhanced by the fact that at some point in the mid-1920s, for apparently the first time in his life, he came to know certain Jews as individuals. Perhaps through Bethlen's initiative several of Hungary's leading industrialists and bankers, who were either Jews or Jewish converts to Christianity, became the Regent's regular bridge partners. Horthy enjoyed the company of these men. Perhaps he was awed by their great wealth; perhaps, as Budapest pundits suggested at the time, he sought their company because they allowed him to win consistently at the bridge table. In any case, Horthy developed feelings of friendship and even affection for such men as Ferenc Chorin and Leó Goldberger, whom he came to rely on as his economic "brain trust." In Horthy's mind these men were not Jews at all; they were patriots like him, men of his generation who were indispensable to the welfare of the country.

Yet despite his association with prominent Jews and his approval of Bethlen's tolerant policies, Regent Horthy continued to regard himself as, and privately to speak the language of, a convinced anti-Semite. This seemed to be a function both of his incorrigible garrulousness and his inability to free himself from the rhetoric on which his regime was based, especially the constant emphasis on the use of the term "Christian" in an anti-Jewish context. It is symptomatic that when in 1922 Horthy met with the visiting Secretary General of the American YMCA, he is said to have greeted him with the words: "I am delighted to meet the head of such an important anti-Semitic organization."[66] This story might be apocryphal,[67] yet it does capture the earnest but ill-informed and often naive nature of Admiral Horthy's extemporaneous remarks on social and political matters. Here was a man who truly "wore his heart on his sleeve." Horthy's mind was filled with an odd and amorphous collection of right-wing ideas, vulgar prejudices, and stock anecdotes that he had picked up over the years from colleagues and from a desultory reading of books and newspapers. In conversation these ideas came tumbling forth unimpeded by the normal restraints of discretion, diplomacy, or common sense. Horthy had never made any attempt to submit his pet theories to rigorous analysis; on most issues his mind was closed, for he felt that he had long ago discovered the truth. He thus showed few inhibitions about expressing the most bizarre and even obnoxious ideas. A visitor might find himself subjected to a discourse on the importance of eugenics, the evil "Elders of Zion," or the dangers of racial contamination.[68] Certain stories and anecdotes became his favorites; they appear often in the accounts left by visitors to the Regent's office in the Royal Castle, and their constant repetition seemed to strengthen Horthy's belief in their validity and pertinence.

So it was with Horthy's views on the Jews. Many a visitor was surprised to receive from the Hungarian Regent a lecture on the alleged dangers that Jews posed for European civilization.[69] As Horthy explained to visitors on several occasions in the interwar period, the Jews were "a people whose hand was against every man and a people whose only God was Gain." Under the malicious direction of the "Elders of Zion," Jews exploited other people's misfortunes, fomented trouble, committed sabotage, and in general paved the way for bolshevism.[70] It was the Jews who were responsible for the horrors that Russia had experienced. They welcomed wars because they always managed to avoid fighting and were in a better position to amass great fortunes. Horthy illustrated these ideas with a story he often repeated:

> In peacetime if a Jew is poor and steals he is taken to prison and punished; this the Jew does not find agreeable. Therefore the Jew goes up to one man and points out another saying: "that man has many things which he has no right to, go and kill him and take the things which he has and which really are yours." Then the first man being greedy does as the Jew suggests. The two men have a struggle, one is killed and the other grievously wounded; then the Jew helps himself to what is in the pockets of both as they lie there helpless and goes on his way rejoicing a rich man where before he was poor.[71]

Admiral Horthy did admit that in peacetime in a well governed state like England the Jews could hold responsible posts and have a real stake in the welfare of the country. But, he insisted, things were different in Central and Eastern Europe, where the Jews monopolized economic life. How unpleasant it was for him to visit Hungarian factories and be welcomed at each one by what seemed to be the same six Jews. The Christian population played hardly any role in economic life, for the Jews always managed to kick them out. When in 1922 the Hungarian crown depreciated rapidly in value, Horthy could only conclude that this was the work of the "Elders of Zion," who, having failed to establish bolshevism in Hungary, now were seeking to establish their hegemony by undermining the economy.[72]

Admiral Horthy seemed not to notice the contradiction between his privately expressed anti-Semitic prejudices and the relatively tolerant official policies of his regime. Perhaps, as a fervent Anglophile, he was unconsciously making the point that Hungary, which was believed by most Magyars to resemble England in its parliamentary and constitutional traditions, was as well governed as England and thus, unlike other countries in Eastern Europe, could allow its talented Jews to make important contributions to society. Perhaps when he spoke with contempt of Jews he was thinking only of left-wing intellectuals and the so-called Galician Jews, the largely unassimilated Orthodox Jews living primarily in rural areas. Of course, these were the kind of Jews that Horthy never actually encountered or met formally. In any case, by the end of the 1920s Horthy seemed prepared to continue for the indefinite future the tacit alliance between Hungary's conservative political establishment and the community of assimilated Jews. He was happy to continue to socialize with Jewish bankers, honor Jews who had contributed to Hungary's spectacular performance in the 1924 and 1928 Olympics,[73] and even appoint prominent Jews to the Upper House of Parliament. Horthy's ambivalence about the Jews was apparently imparted to his children as well. According to Miklós Horthy, Jr., his parents often spoke disparagingly of Jews, and it was made clear that the marriage of one of the children to a Jew was inconceivable.[74] Yet the Horthy children were also exposed to more tolerant attitudes. As adults, both of Horthy's sons gained a reputation as philo-Semites, and Miklós, Jr., was to play a key role in World War II as a liaison between the Regent and the Jewish leadership.

A second subject on which his guests often heard Regent Horthy pontificate was the danger of communism. Of all European statesmen of the interwar period he was perhaps the most intransigent and unyielding in his hostility toward the Soviet Union. His experiences during the Hungarian Soviet Republic had left an indelible imprint on his thinking. Foreign diplomats often remarked on Horthy's obsession with communism; as one British observer aptly put it, the Hungarian Regent seemed to have "Bolshevism on the brain."[75] He placed his greatest trust in those whom he knew to be staunchly anti-Communist: "So long as a friend is opposed to communism, he is a real friend, and I make no other demands on him."[76] In private conversation Horthy used the strongest language to describe communism: it was a cancer to be excised, a poison to be removed from the system, a vile mafia run by the scum of society. Moscow, he was convinced, was the center of a conspiracy whose immediate goal was the overthrow of all existing institutions. In Horthy's view the Bolsheviks ruined everything; even animals were not spared. During the Hungarian Soviet Republic, he asserted, an incredible number of stags, boars, and other wild game had been slaughtered, truly a grievous offense in the eyes of an avid hunter like Horthy. Although he had very little accurate information about conditions in the Soviet Union, Horthy was convinced that all sorts of outrages were being committed there. He found particularly abhorrent the decline of morals among the youth, who, he believed, were encouraged to practice free love in coeducational schools.[77]

Given these strong views, it is not surprising that Admiral Horthy's one major intervention in policy-making during the Bethlen era involved the Soviet Union. For the first few years of the 1920s the Soviet Union had been treated as a pariah by the European diplomatic community. By 1924, however, several great powers, including Germany and Italy, had resumed diplomatic and economic ties with Moscow. The new Labour government in Great Britain seemed poised to follow suit. These changes prompted István Bethlen to pursue a more pragmatic policy aimed at emulating Weimar Germany, which had gained certain economic advantages and enhanced its freedom of maneuver in international affairs by establishing relations with Soviet Russia. Noting that the USSR was the only great power that had not recognized the validity of the Treaty of Trianon, Bethlen authorized secret negotiations in Berlin for a normalization of relations between Budapest and Moscow. By September the terms of political and economic agreements had been arrived at, but when the draft treaties were presented to the Regent, he responded negatively. Under Bethlen's prodding Horthy did agree that he might give his reluctant approval to the publication of the terms of the tentative agreements if the government regarded it as absolutely "necessary for diplomatic reasons," but he declared that "he could not imagine the content of any such agreements that would gain his final approval." Moreover, "no one could force him to receive a Soviet envoy in audience."[78] Bethlen proceeded to win the approval of his Cabinet for the treaties, but when the Regent's hesitations became publicly known, the opponents of diplomatic recognition of the Soviet Union were emboldened. The debate in Parliament dragged on for weeks. In October, when it was learned that the new Conservative British government had repudiated the trade agreement negotiated several months earlier by the Labour government, the ratification of the Soviet-Hungarian agreement was postponed indefinitely.[79] Only in 1934 would Hungary finally resume diplomatic relations with the USSR, the last European country to do so.

With this one exception, Admiral Horthy refrained from direct interference in the making of foreign policy in the Bethlen era. In general, although he occasionally read works of European history, he made no great effort to study the intricacies of contemporary international problems. He rarely read Foreign Ministry memorandums or the reports of Hungarian diplomats abroad. He had learned early in life certain "truths" about Danubian and European affairs and these opinions were virtually unaltered by the passage of time. All of this did not, however, make him hesitant or cautious about privately voicing his strongly held and sometimes eccentric opinions. Foreign diplomats, especially those newly arrived in Budapest, were quietly informed that the Regent "speaks back and forth and one should not attribute political significance to what he says." Journalists were required to submit the copy of any interview so that any sensational utterances could be judiciously deleted.[80]

No one, not even Count Bethlen, found a way to muzzle the Regent. Horthy seemed to relish any opportunity to expound his views on the hated Treaty of Trianon, the duplicity of Hungary's neighbors, the heroic qualities of the Magyars as the defenders of Western Civilization, and a myriad other issues. The problem was that during the course of such monologues, which often lasted an hour or more, Horthy was apt in his excitement to let slip certain states secrets or to make highly indiscreet statements. For example, during a conversation with the Austrian Minister in July 1922, Horthy spoke openly about plans he had had to send Hungarian troops into Austria in 1919 and defended those who had participated in the Burgenland insurrection of 1921 as his "best friends."[81] On several occasions in the 1920s Horthy expressed to diplomats his concern about the spread of labor unrest in Great Britain. In the wake of the coal strike of 1926 Horthy suggested to the British military attaché that his government would have done itself and the world "an inestimable service" if they had simply shot the leader of the miners, A. J. Cook.[82]

Foreign dignitaries, journalists, and diplomats often left an audience with Admiral Horthy quite perplexed. On the one hand, visitors were virtually unanimous in concluding that the Hungarian Regent was a charming, sincere, and honorable gentleman. The view of W. Athelstan Johnson, a British envoy in the early 1920s, was typical: "No one can leave the admiral's presence without feeling that ethically speaking he is absolutely honest and sincere," a man with "seemingly impregnable walls" of "personal rectitude."[83] Yet there was at the same time a belief that in his political and social views Horthy was an anachronism, a man who would have been more comfortable as a nobleman in pre-1848 Austria or a nineteenth-century English country squire. Admiral Horthy, it was said, appeared incapable of adjusting to the realities of the twentieth-century world. That he never appeared in public except in his Habsburg naval uniform and had his office decorated in a distinctly nineteenth-century Austrian style convinced many a visitor that the Hungarian Regent was truly living in the past. Many were struck by how stubbornly and rigidly Horthy held to his beliefs. The French Minister, reporting in September 1921 on a conversation with the Regent, lamented that Horthy is "a man who closes his ears to all reasoning and is quite inflexible."[84] Thomas Hohler, the one foreigner who knew the Hungarian Regent best, probably spoke for many of his colleagues when in a report to the Foreign Office he described Horthy as "a man of sterling honesty but of no great cleverness: he has no suppleness of mind, and when he gets hold of an idea, it crystallizes within him into a principle."[85]

In his attitudes toward the various national groups in Europe Horthy certainly showed scant "suppleness of mind." Like so many of his contemporaries in East Central Europe, Horthy attributed to each nationality certain more or less fixed characteristics.

For Horthy the essential truth of these stereotypes was demonstrated by one or two appropriate anecdotes that he told and retold many times during his career. That the Czechs were by nature cowards was shown by an alleged incident in 1919 when the sound of a bugle announcing the approach of a Hungarian officer frightened two Czech regiments into a hasty, unordered retreat.[86] Since, in Horthy's way of thinking, the Slovaks were not a distinct nation but merely "misled Magyars," it stood to reason that the Czechoslovak state was a hopeless, artificial creation. Horthy had a similar attitude toward Yugoslavia, though he had a relatively favorable view of the Croatians as "fine sailors" and the Serbs as "good soldiers." The problem was that these two nations could never live together: a South Slav State was thus "a purely geographical concept." Moreover, the Croatians could not survive as a nation on their own, since they were not a "state-building" people like the Magyars.[87] The Romanians Horthy dismissed contemptuously as "a mixed race of Balkan shepherds, gypsies, and deported Roman convicts." Moreover, they were inveterate bribe-takers and had throughout their history "cheated and betrayed" every one of their allies. How could one trust a people whose bureaucracy was so thoroughly corrupt?[88]

Indeed, of all the peoples of Eastern Europe only the Poles (and, to a lesser degree, the Bulgarians) met Horthy's high standards. The Poles were traditional friends of the Magyars. Under the leadership of Marshal Pilsudski, whom Horthy greatly admired, the Poles had held off the Red Army. They, like the Magyars, were a "state-building people" who possessed the will, discipline, and fighting spirit to serve as the advance guard for Christian Europe against incursions from the East.

Among the great powers Admiral Horthy reserved his greatest respect and admiration for Great Britain. Like many upper-class Hungarians, he believed that England and Hungary shared a remarkably similar historical tradition of constitutional government and parliamentary practices. Fancying himself to be something of an "English gentleman," Horthy always sought out the company of British officers. He enjoyed immensely his brief visit to London in 1895, and later found such men as Thomas Hohler and Reginald Gorton to be most congenial companions. The myth of Britain as the only great power capable of pursuing a disinterested policy aimed at achieving fairness and justice in European international affairs was fully accepted by Horthy and many of his countrymen.

As a naval officer steeped in the teachings of Alfred Mahan, Horthy was convinced that sea power was the key element in military conflict, as the results of the Great War had seemingly demonstrated. Moreover, he thought that Britain was a striking example of the maxim that all successful countries need a thriving overseas trade.[89] He thus believed that Hungary should make every effort to ally with, or at least not to alienate, Great Britain, which would surely emerge victorious from any future war. Moreover, it struck him that both England and Hungary were essentially conservative states whose common interest in combating bolshevism would inevitably draw them together in a coordinated approach to European affairs. During the 1920s Horthy made it a point to receive in audience all visiting British dignitaries and to express his feelings of friendship and emphasize his belief that their countries shared a common destiny. It was his fervent hope that Britain would eventually be drawn into continental affairs and be persuaded to lead a campaign of peaceful revision of the peace treaties and an anti-Bolshevik crusade.

Admiral Horthy also had a generally favorable view of the other "Anglo-Saxon" great power, the United States of America, although his knowledge of American society and history was very limited. He did, however, have the highest regard for American technology and arranged for his son István, who had studied engineering at the Technical University in Budapest, to spend a year as a worker in the Ford Motor Plant in Detroit. Horthy also cultivated close ties with American diplomats and economists stationed in Budapest, notably John Montgomery, Royall Tyler, and Nicholas Roosevelt.[90] Yet Horthy had no inkling of the vital role that the United States was poised to play in world affairs. Like most of his contemporaries in interwar Europe, he tended to regard America's intervention in World War I as an aberration not likely to be repeated. Nonetheless he greatly valued American economic advice and loans and believed that Hungary's cause would receive a significant boost if prominent Americans could be persuaded to become champions of the campaign for revision of the Treaty of Trianon.

Germany, the one great power most likely to take an active interest in the revision of the peace settlement in Eastern Europe, evoked in Admiral Horthy a strong ambivalence. On the one hand, he found many Germans to be overbearing and arrogant. He disliked their boorish manners and their eternal refrain of "deutsch" and "Deutschland." As a Habsburg naval officer he had been an honorary member of every German club in the port cities he visited, but, so he later claimed, had never set foot in any of them.[91] On the other hand, Horthy did feel a special affinity for the nationalist right-wing in postwar Germany, especially for the military officers prominent in its leadership. This helps explain his ready collaboration with General Ludendorff in the early 1920s, later secret contacts with General Hans von Seeckt, and a continuing friendship with Admiral Wilhelm Canaris and General Werner von Blomberg. Like these German officers, Horthy viewed the Weimar government with contempt and looked forward to the eventual emergence of an authoritarian right-wing regime, a more compatible partner for Hungary. In a letter in 1925 to Marshal Paul von Hindenburg upon his election as president of the German Republic, Horthy suggested that the resurgence of such a Germany would signify a "better and more beautiful future" for Hungary as well.[92] With like-minded Germans Horthy spoke often in the 1920s of the existence of a unique German-Hungarian community of fate. This almost mystical bond, as Horthy described it, had been forged by the common shedding of blood by their valiant soldiers fighting "shoulder to shoulder" in World War I and sealed by the scandalous peace treaties imposed on the two countries.[93] In May 1927, during a conversation with a visiting German politician, Horthy openly spoke of a future German-Hungarian effort to achieve territorial revision. "Certain things cannot be suppressed," Horthy asserted, "such as the recovery of great nations and the fulfillment of the elementary needs of life." Among the latter he mentioned Hungary's need for an outlet to the sea, which could not be forever denied to her, and Germany's absorption of Austria, which was inevitable.[94]

Although Count Bethlen approached foreign policy problems in a far more pragmatic and unemotional way, he by and large shared Admiral Horthy's views and objectives. Both men believed that the postwar settlement in East Central Europe was artificial and transitory. Hungary, they believed, was predestined by geography and the exemplary leadership qualities of the Magyars to play the leading role in Danubian Europe. According to Bethlen's "grand plan," which Horthy supported, Hungary would cling tenaciously, if at first unobtrusively, to her demands for the revision of the Treaty of Trianon and the restoration of its rightful place of dominance in Danubian Europe. Eventually, Bethlen believed, a more favorable European diplomatic constellation would arise and Hungary would have some "trump cards to play."[95] Until that point, however, Hungary had to avoid impetuous acts and forge a policy predicated on the realities of its exposed position and commensurate with the extent of its economic recovery.

Like Horthy, Bethlen was an Anglophile and would no doubt have been delighted to enlist Britain's support as the champion of Hungary's revisionist cause. In 1919 he had even suggested that Hungary might become Britain's "continental Gibraltar."[96] But he was above all a realist who by the mid-1920s had to concede that the British government was wedded to the status quo and the concept of collective security. Still there remained good reasons for Bethlen and Horthy to ingratiate themselves with the English political and economic establishment. In no other European country were there so many manifestations of sympathy for Hungary. Regent Horthy was particularly gratified by the campaign of Lord Rothermere, publisher of the *Daily Mail*, who in 1927 began advocating revision of the Treaty of Trianon.[97] Bethlen too welcomed such support, but it was clear to him that pro-Hungarian utterances by mavericks like Lord Rothermere or by members of the pro-Magyar contingent of the House of Lords carried very little weight in the arena of international relations. The best that could be hoped was that when the critical time came for a transformation of Danubian Europe, British public opinion would push the British government toward a policy of benevolent neutrality.

As early as 1921 Count Bethlen had intimated to his colleagues that only a rejuvenated Germany friendly to Hungary could provide the "favorable diplomatic constellation" for a successful revision of the Trianon Treaty.[98] In the short run, however, Bethlen was willing to pursue a pragmatic policy of smaller steps aimed at reducing Hungary's diplomatic isolation. When the plan to establish ties with Moscow was stymied by Horthy's intransigent anticommunism, Bethlen decided instead to attempt to undermine the Little Entente by wooing Yugoslavia. This was an initiative that Regent Horthy found more compatible with his personal beliefs. Accordingly, during a speech on August 29, 1926, at a ceremony commemorating the four hundredth anniversary of the Battle of Mohács, Horthy dropped strong hints that Hungary was prepared to reestablish the "old friendship and understanding" with her neighbor to the south.

Hungary's interest in and negotiations for a rapprochement

with Yugoslavia had unexpected repercussions. Seeking to counter France's position of strength in Eastern Europe by staking out an Italian sphere of influence in Danubian Europe, Benito Mussolini suddenly stepped forward and suggested the possibility of closer relations between Italy and Hungary. Admiral Horthy still bore resentment toward Italy for what he considered that country's perfidious behavior in World War I, but he was quickly persuaded that an agreement with Italy would greatly facilitate Hungary's emergence from isolation. The talks with Belgrade were thus quickly abandoned, and on April 5, 1927, Italy and Hungary signed a Treaty of Friendship and Cooperation. This was a major diplomatic triumph for the Horthy regime. Over the next ten years Italy aided Hungary's surreptitious military rearmament and Mussolini offered his strong, if somewhat boisterous, support for the campaign to revise the Treaty of Trianon. Above all, the pact with Italy demonstrated that Hungary, though weak and reduced to the status of a pawn, could still play a role on the diplomatic chessboard.[99]

In 1927 the signing of the pact with Italy and the departure of the Inter-Allied Military Commission seemed to signal a new era in which Hungary would have greater freedom of maneuver to pursue its revisionist program. In his letter to the Regent one year earlier, Bethlen had suggested that "in about four or five years Trianon might be liquidated."[100] He now became more outspoken in his public statements, declaring in a speech in March 1928 that what Hungary needed was not merely a general revision of the peace settlement, but "different frontiers." In what for him was an uncharacteristically militant tone, he added that "frontier questions are not merely a matter of justice and law, they are usually questions of power." The Hungarian leadership now began to give increasing attention to military matters, a subject in which Horthy claimed special expertise.

In contrast to his general indifference toward most domestic issues, Admiral Horthy insisted throughout his regency that, as Supreme War Lord, he was entitled to play the leading role in the administration and development of Hungary's armed forces. On numerous occasions he complained to Western diplomats and officers about the baleful effects of the ban on universal conscription in Hungary, arguing that "we can never have a voluntary army even if we try for twenty years."[101] Working closely with his trusted advisors in the Regent's Military Bureau (*Kormányzó Kato-*

nai Irodája), he promoted a number of paramilitary organizations designed to maintain a martial spirit in Hungarian society, including the paramilitary Horthy *Levente*. Although Horthy had great faith in Bethlen's diplomatic skills and shared his hope for the eventual formation of a European great power constellation favorable to Hungarian interests, he was realistic enough to sense that the Little Entente countries would never make territorial concessions to a militarily weak Hungary. Thus preparations had to be made for war, or at least the threat of war at some point in the future. Admiral Horthy by no means shared the euphoria of some Europeans in the late 1920s who believed that war could and should be outlawed. When Hungary was invited in 1928 to sign the Kellogg-Briand Pact, which required a pledge to "renounce the resort to war as an instrument of national policy," Horthy's private response was very skeptical and negative. He declared that he was opposed in principle to such a pledge, and insisted that if Hungary had to be a signatory for diplomatic reasons, she should do so without haste or enthusiasm.[102] Hungary finally did adhere to the pact, as did almost all European countries, including the Soviet Union.

What role would Hungary play in a future European war? To help answer that question Horthy in 1928 solicited the thoughts of Colonel Károly Mayer-Csekovits, one of the foremost military thinkers and writers in interwar Hungary.[103] Horthy agreed with Mayer-Csekovits in his conviction that in any future war Hungary would have "a role to play" and that measures should be enacted to strengthen national discipline and a martial spirit. Participation in a future conflict could not be avoided because, in Horthy's opinion, the Little Entente intended to seize any favorable opportunity to partition Hungary. Yet for the foreseeable future Hungary's strategic position was far from favorable. Her neighbors had an enormous edge in aircraft and manpower. "With only a force of 2 to 300,000," Horthy asserted, "you cannot defeat a force of 2 to 3 million soldiers who, to boot, are better armed." It was clear that Hungary needed to gain powerful allies, since "the fate of small countries does not depend on the part their armies will play, but merely on the side on which they fight."

Although Gustav Stresemann and the other statesmen of the Weimar Republic were cool to overtures from Budapest in this period, Bethlen and Horthy were able to establish a close working relationship with a number of conservative German military officers. It was with these more congenial Germans that they spoke most candidly (and, in the circumstances, theoretically) of their most secret military concerns and aspirations. In 1927 General Hans von Seeckt, the recently retired Chief of the German Army Command, was invited to Budapest for consultations on the logistical and administrative problems that the rebuilding Hungarian armed forces would face. Horthy and Bethlen bluntly informed him that Hungary was resolved to attack Czechoslovakia at some point in the future and, if possible, destroy it, The goal was the reannexation of Slovakia, where Czech rule had not taken strong roots.[104] In 1929 Horthy met with General von Blomberg and a delegation of high-ranking officers and suggested that in compensation for a settlement of the Corridor question in Germany's favor, Poland should be allowed to swallow up Lithuania.[105]

What territorial changes did Admiral Horthy and Count Bethlen eventually hope to make in Danubian Europe once a "favorable diplomatic constellation" was created or, should diplomatic methods fail, a successful war was waged?[106] Like most Hungarians, Horthy dreamed of a complete restoration of the Kingdom of St. Stephen as it had existed before the Great War. However, Count Bethlen was, not surprisingly, more pragmatic than the Regent in sensing that in the new conditions created by the war and its aftermath, Croatia and Burgenland could not be reincorporated into a Greater Hungary, and Transylvania would have to be granted some sort of autonomous status. Both men seemed to agree, however, that Slovakia should be directly reannexed and a common border established with a friendly Poland to the north. Those parts of western Transylvania and northern Yugoslavia (including the Bánát) with large Magyar populations would also have to be recovered and formally annexed. For Horthy, who was more influenced by emotional and symbolic considerations, two goals were paramount: the destruction of Czechoslovakia, whose leaders he despised[107]; and the securing of an access to the sea through Croatia, which he regarded as perhaps Hungary's most fundamental need.[108]

In the late 1920s Hungary's armed forces were, of course, still encumbered by the severe terms of the Treaty of Trianon and thus very far from ready to participate in any kind of military operation. An additional concern for Regent Horthy in this period were the frequent reports of demoralization in the Hungarian officer corps. The officers were grumbling about the chronically low pay, limited opportunities for advancement, and what they perceived to be a general indifference to their concerns on the part of the government. Convinced that ultimately only Hungary's military leadership would be able to rescue the nation, Horthy searched about for someone who could carry out a reinvigoration of the officer corps.[109] His attention was called to Gyula Gömbös, who was once again "respectable" (*szalonképes*) and, given the élan and efficiency with which he had helped to build the National Army in Szeged, seemed ideal for the task. Perhaps Horthy also sensed that a reconciliation with Gömbös would in part restore his pivotal role as the link between the two main right-wing camps. Count Bethlen relented to the proposal, apparently calculating that Gömbös, humbled by his years in the political wilderness, would now play the role of a docile civil servant. Taking no chances, Bethlen did insist that Gömbös provide written promises that he would confine his activity strictly to military matters and would refrain from any political statements without the prior approval of the Prime Minister.[110] Gömbös seemed willing to oblige on all counts. He gave the requested assurances, formally disbanded the Party of Race Defenders, and in September 1928 was appointed Under Secretary of State in the Ministry of Defense, the same position he had held in 1919.

Gömbös proceeded with his accustomed vigor to instill a new spirit of confidence and efficiency in the officer corps. The prewar cadre, including the Minister of Defense, Károly Csáky, resented the upstart captain and his brash manner, but younger officers regarded Gömbös as their champion. The Regent was pleased with Gömbös's apparent success in cleaning the "Augean stables" in the armed forces.[111] In October 1929 Gömbös was named Minister of Defense; four months later Horthy promoted him to the rank of general. During this period Gömbös seems to have honored his promise to restrict his official activities to the military sphere. However, he now once again had easy access to the Regent's office in the Royal Castle, and he naturally supplied Horthy with information that enhanced his own stature. Thus, it seems that frequent consultations between Gömbös and Horthy led to a renewal of the cordiality and mutual trust that had characterized their relationship before 1923.

When, in March 1930, Hungarians were called on to celebrate the tenth anniversary of the Regent's election, the triumvirate of Horthy, Bethlen, and Gömbös that had been largely responsible for the creation of the postwar regime seemed to be once again working in harmony. The series of parades, balls, speeches, operas, and commemorative ceremonies in the spring of 1930 provided a major impetus to the "Horthy cult." A bill introduced by Bethlen and passed without dissent in Parliament enumerated the virtues and accomplishments of the Regent. In recognition of his services to the nation the name "Horthy" was now given to a new bridge over the Danube River, to a laboratory for cancer research, and to several hospitals and schools. To mark the ten-year jubilee a new five *pengő* coin was issued with a portrait of Horthy and the date of his election. All the religious denominations, including the Jews, held commemorative religious services. Typical of the adulatory speeches was that given by Bishop László Ravasz, spiritual leader of the Reformed (Calvinist) Church, who asserted that Horthy had restored to the Magyar nation its self-confidence and pride. The Regent, he declared, "embodies Hungarian defiance, Hungarian will, and Hungarian hope; for that reason every Hungarian sees in him the realization of his own ideals."

In an effort to soften Horthy's image as an unforgiving autocrat, it had been announced in late 1929 that in conjunction with the Regent's ten-year jubilee a full pardon and amnesty would be granted to a large number of political prisoners, including those convicted of *lèse régent*. Among those affected were several prominent Social Democrats, including Ernő Garami, who had lived in exile for the first decade of the postwar regime. They now returned to their native land, vowing to carry on the struggle against the Horthy regime. Yet even the *Manchester Guardian*, which since 1920 had maintained a sharply critical attitude toward the Hungarian government, could concede that this gesture was "an important step in the liquidation of the counter-revolution in Hungary." Admiral Horthy, the writer for the *Guardian* asserted, had shown "splendid tenacity" in his efforts to "put the clock back." He had found his country in dissolution and had restored to it "a tradition and a purpose," though it was a pity that it was not "done in a better cause."[112] The report on the ten-year anniversary of the Horthy regime in the *London Times* presented a more flattering portrait. Horthy was there described as "a lucky man, perhaps, but one who has deserved his luck."[113]

Even as the church bells were pealing throughout Hungary in celebration of Horthy's ten-year jubilee, and Count Bethlen was declaring that Horthy "would remain in office to the end of his life,"[114] the ominous rumbles of an expanding economic earthquake could be detected. The shock waves from the stock market crash on Wall Street in October 1929 had been fairly slow in reaching Eastern Europe, but by the spring of 1930 world grain prices, the strength of which had fueled Hungary's recovery, were beginning to decline rapidly, a signal of the coming catastrophe. For a time Bethlen and his economic advisors were able to stave off the worst by relying on what had been the second important prop of the Horthy regime, foreign loans. Reparations payments were renegotiated and Hungary proceeded to borrow abroad more in 1930 than in any other previous year. But the advance of the depression seemed inexorable, and Hungary's economic experts, like their counterparts everywhere in Europe, were unable to devise any effective countermeasures. Month by month industrial production plunged and by the fall of 1930 unemployment reached 20 percent. In Budapest more than 100,000 were out of work. Since the modest social reforms that Bethlen had sponsored did not include unemployment insurance, the misery of those who lost their jobs was acute.

The onset of the Great Depression opened fissures in Hungarian society and political life that had been papered over in the brief period of prosperity of the late 1920s. The Social Democrats, perhaps emboldened by the return of their more radical colleagues from exile, inspired a series of strikes which culminated in Budapest on September 1 in the biggest and most hostile such demonstration in Hungary since February 1920. Clashes between the police and the demonstrators led to a near riot in which one person was killed and 300 were wounded.

Even the seemingly monolithic government party seemed to be cracking under the strain. In October, a group of dissidents representing agricultural interests seceded from the party and formed the Independent Smallholders party. The bitter complaints from opposition members about government corruption and extravagance, never totally absent in the Parliament even in the most tranquil days of the Bethlen era, now became more persistent and menacing. Sensing that opportunities to whet his ambitions were at hand, Gyula Gömbös now began once again to meddle in political affairs. In November he made a speech in Kecskemét that contained derogatory comments about the Jews. Whenever possible he bypassed Bethlen and endeavored to revive the Regent's former sympathy for radical right-wing solutions. In this effort he now had considerable success, for Admiral Horthy was appalled by the strikes, demonstrations, and terrorist actions that the forces of the left had unleashed in response to the deepening economic crisis. Horthy was particularly annoyed that the leaders of the September 1 demonstration were precisely those who had been able to return from exile on the basis of the amnesty he had proclaimed only months earlier. Horthy had always retained a fundamental distrust of the Social Democrats and had given only lukewarm support to Bethlen's more tolerant policies. On several occasions in the 1920s he had complained privately that the socialists were trying to undermine some of his pet projects, such as the Horthy *Levente*.[115]

Although it would be going too far to assert that by early 1931 Horthy had lost confidence in his Prime Minister, he was clearly disappointed that Bethlen, whom he regarded as a political genius, seemed to be floundering in the growing crisis. Also irritating and embarrassing to the Regent was the more or less open way in which Bethlen was engaging in an extramarital romantic affair.[116] In the more stable and prosperous years of the late 1920s Horthy had been content to remain aloof from policy-making and to give Bethlen an entirely free hand; now, however, he complained to a confidant that he was "tired of being a rubber stamp."[117] Horthy's displeasure was reflected in several initiatives he took in 1930. On one occasion he requested that Cabinet ministers send reports on their activities to the Regent's Cabinet Bureau. Bethlen was deeply offended by this unprecedented meddling of the Regent in government affairs, and told a friend that if this kind of thing happened again, he would resign. Another confrontation occurred when, upon the resignation of the Foreign Minister, Bethlen proposed as his successor Sándor Khuen-Hederváry, an experienced diplomat with whom he had an excellent rapport. However, Horthy preferred his trusted friend, Gyula Károlyi, who, he remarked privately, was the only politician left in Hungary who dared to state his opinions to Bethlen. In the resulting test of wills, which Miklós Kozma termed "a struggle of two equal forces," it was the Regent who in the end had his way.[118]

Perhaps egged on by Gömbös, Horthy decided further to reassert his authority by calling a Crown Council at which matters of special concern to him would be discussed. Such a Crown Council had not been summoned for more than eight years. The agenda for the meeting was drafted by Horthy himself. Several of the topics selected for discussion were precisely those that were being publicly bruited by the resurgent radical right-wing groups and Szeged veterans, an indication that Gömbös may have assisted Horthy in his initiative.

Regent Horthy opened the Crown Council of February 20, 1931, by declaring that in such difficult times it was more desirable than ever that the head of state work in close cooperation with the government.[119] He wished to participate in the "difficult work" that lay ahead. After warm but somewhat perfunctory praise for Count Bethlen's accomplishment over the past decade, Horthy launched into a recitation of his complaints. Echoing an opinion that was commonplace among the radical right-wingers, Horthy asserted that the Budapest police had not acted firmly enough during what he sarcastically dubbed the "promenade of the unemployed," the demonstration of September 1, 1931. That deplorable incident, Horthy declared, had done substantial harm to the reputation of Hungary and had endangered the public order, especially since several of the ringleaders were members of Parliament. For that reason he recommended, among other things, that martial law be declared to prevent further outrages and that steps be undertaken to limit the parliamentary immunity of those who took part in such events.

In response Bethlen agreed that the police had treated the Socialists leniently, but he pointedly rejected each of Horthy's proposals. The implementation of preventive martial law was, he asserted, "neither desirable nor necessary." Such a step would harm Hungary's name abroad at a time when the goodwill of the great powers was necessary to ensure additional loans. In any case, legislation already existed to meet the concerns expressed by the Regent. All the Cabinet members who spoke supported Bethlen's position, except Gömbös, who agreed with Horthy that the response of the authorities on September 1 had been inadequate and had failed to reassure public opinion. If the Social Democratic ringleaders had been arrested on the spot, he argued, it would have sent a clear message to the middle classes, who feared "left-wing terror" and were concerned not about the legality of repressive action but whether such repression was successful.

Horthy put before the Crown Council two other issues that had been troubling him. In language redolent of contemporary radical right-wing attacks on the government, Horthy bemoaned the continued "infiltration" into Hungary of illegal Jewish immigrants. It was amazing, Horthy noted, that whenever Communists were arrested in Hungary they always seemed to be Jews, as was true in a recent case of railroad sabotage. Moreover, he regarded it as especially galling that Hungarian businesses should have so many foreign Jews as managers. Despite existing legislation, Jews continued to flood into the country, especially from the east and northeast. He also raised the question of whether new legislation was needed to empower the government to move more forcefully against newspapers that harmed the national interest. On both these issues Bethlen assured the Regent that adequate laws already existed. Over the past decades many foreign Jews had been deported and over fifty papers had been banned. Thus, what was needed was not new legislation but the fullest and most rigorous application of existing statutes.

Although none of the Regent's proposals relating to political or social affairs was approved by the Crown Council, and Bethlen's attitude during the discussions might have struck some observers as patronizing, the opportunity to speak his mind apparently temporarily appeased Horthy. It was clear to the assembled ministers that the relationship between Horthy and Bethlen was no longer completely harmonious, but over the next few months, as Hungary plunged even further into economic crisis, Bethlen's authority seemed undiminished. On May 11 the *Kreditanstalt*, Austria's central bank, collapsed, sending shock waves throughout Danubian Europe. Through bank holidays and a variety of emergency measures to balance the budget, the Hungarian government managed to prevent a similar collapse in Hungary. Then, with characteristic aplomb, Bethlen gained the Regent's approval for the election of a new Parliament. Despite the increasing political turmoil and pervasive economic misery in the country, Bethlen managed to engineer the usual victory for the government party in the June elections. After this show of strength, Bethlen turned his attention to the negotiation of a new international loan. On August 13 it was announced that the loan had been arranged, the funding to be supplied mostly by France. It now seemed possible that, despite the continuing torrent of abuse aimed at the government by the opposition in Parliament, Count Bethlen might after all survive the gravest crisis of his premiership.

Yet behind the scenes a quite different story was unfolding. Though the precise timing is difficult to determine, at some point in the early summer István Bethlen decided that he must resign. Not only had his health deteriorated, but he knew that the process of *szanálás* (economic rehabilitation) that the government would have to fulfill would be unpopular and would intensify the "wave of hate" that had been directed at him. Within a short time, he feared, it might sweep away not only him personally but the entire regime.[120] Indeed, it is possible that Bethlen called new elections in June precisely because he intended to resign in the near future and wished to ensure that a majority of Parliament would remain loyal to him whoever his successor might be.

There are several indications that Bethlen intended that his departure from the government would be brief and that Horthy would recall him once the economic crisis had run its course. In a memorandum presented to the Regent at the time of his resignation, Bethlen recommended that the new Prime Minister be an economic specialist, a kind of "financial dictator," who had no connections with the present government or any political parties.[121] Such an individual could carry out his difficult economic mission above the political fray; indeed, Bethlen argued, the new Prime Minister should not deal at all with political questions.

Unlike the previous occasion in 1926 when Bethlen had offered his resignation, Admiral Horthy apparently made no effort now to persuade his friend to stay on. Moreover, Horthy was cool to the idea of a "financial dictator," especially when Bethlen suggested the name of a prominent financier, János Teleszky, who was a converted Jew. Horthy's response was: "My dear István, so long as I sit in this chair, a Jew will never be Prime Minister in Hungary. You can't ask that of me."[122] After extensive consultations with his other advisors and leaders of the political parties, Horthy decided not to follow the course that his Prime Minister of ten years had set out for him. Instead, the Regent persuaded his somewhat reluctant friend, Count Gyula Károlyi, to form a new government. Horthy's actions in August 1931 represented an assertion of the kind of political independence and initiative that he had rarely shown in the past decade. In this way the Bethlen era came to an inglorious end. Although István Bethlen would play a vital role in Hungarian political life for many years to come, and in time would once again become the Regent's must trusted advisor, he would never again hold political office in the Hungarian government.

6

From the Depression to the Anschluss, 1931–1938

Admiral Horthy's decision to jettison István Bethlen, the man to whom he owed much of his own political prestige, reflected both the desperation he felt as the economic crisis persisted and his growing conviction that only a "strong hand" at the helm could prevent revolutionary outbreaks. Perhaps already in August 1931 Horthy had been tempted to entrust the government to Gyula Gömbös, but in addition to the likely domestic political uproar such a radical step would have caused, there were international factors that had to be kept in mind. France, which seemed at the time to be escaping the worst ravages of the depression, loomed as the economic arbiter of Europe for years to come. Moreover, earlier in 1931 the French Minister in Budapest had hinted that France was unhappy with its Little Entente treaty partners and was willing to turn instead to a Danubian policy based on a strengthened Hungary.[1] In the circumstances it seemed inadvisable to hand the reins of government to Gyula Gömbös, who, because of his harsh anti-French statements over the years, was distinctly *persona non grata* in Paris.[2]

For this reason Gyula Károlyi, who was generally regarded as a Francophile, seemed a much safer bet. In addition, the Regent had the highest regard for the man who had made possible his initial entry into national politics. Their friendship, forged in Szeged in 1919, had deepened later when Horthy's daughter, Paulette, married one of Károlyi's sons. Horthy might have reasoned that Károlyi's simple, almost puritanical, life-style would make it easier to blunt opposition criticism of government extravagance, which had contributed to the undermining of Bethlen's position. It was Károlyi's habit, for example, to walk to work each day rather than make use of the government car and chauffeur that were provided to high officials. On the other hand, in his political and economic policies Gyula Károlyi could hardly be distinguished from István Bethlen. He had no plan to cope with the financial crisis other than to continue to follow the orthodox prescription of deflation demanded by the League of Nations and Hungary's creditors in the West. Thus, Károlyi and his Cabinet were to be virtually helpless bystanders to Hungary's continued slide into an economic chaos now exacerbated by a growing worldwide tariff war.

By late 1931 the political temperature in Hungary was nearing the boiling point. Strikes and demonstrations of various kinds became commonplace. Turmoil in the countryside gave rise to a variety of millenarian movements and sundry right-wing extremist groups.[3] Sensing that the time was ripe to resume agitation in Hungary, Moscow dispatched several Communist activists to Hungary with the mission of instigating terrorist outrages. The most spectacular result was the dynamiting of the Vienna express train just outside Budapest in September 1931, in which sixty-three passengers were killed. The two agents responsible were apprehended, court-martialed, and immediately executed.

These developments put a considerable strain on the government party, especially on those members representing rural interests. Károlyi, who had little experience with party politics, was unable to contain the growing discontent and prevent the disruptive activity of various splinter groups. One ominous manifestation of the unprecedented nature of the crisis occurred in August 1932, when the Minister of Agriculture, Emil Purgly, was defeated in a parliamentary by-election conducted under the open ballot. This was a severe jolt to the government not only because the victor, Tibor Eckhardt, was the leader of the major opposition party, the Independent Smallholders, but also because the defeated candidate was the brother-in-law of the Regent.[4] Eckhardt had been a cofounder of the Party of Race Defenders and was now prepared to work behind the scenes with Gömbös to promote reforms based on the "Szeged idea," including restrictions on "Jewish finance," land reform, and even abolition of the secret ballot.

By 1932 in Hungary, as the historian C. A. Macartney has suggested, the "demand for a Fascist regime led by Gömbös was certainly widespread."[5] The electoral successes of the National Socialist party in Germany gave an additional fillip to the Szeged camp in Hungary. Yet Gömbös was acutely aware that his support within the government party, where a Bethlenite majority was firmly entrenched, was negligible. In order to triumph he needed to win over the Regent, a task for which he had gained excellent training during 1919 and 1920. Gömbös had the knack for stirring Admiral Horthy's deepest fears and ambitions: all he needed was direct and continual access to the Regent's office and the absence of a powerful countervailing force. After August 1931, Gyula Károlyi was unable to exert the same kind of influence on Horthy as Bethlen had. As a result Gömbös made considerable progress in persuading the Regent that radical change was imperative. He may also have revived in Horthy a fear of a Habsburg restoration. A flurry of activity among Hungary's legitimists did in fact occur when Archduke Otto celebrated his eighteenth birthday in Belgium.[6] Gömbös clearly wanted the Regent to recall what a staunch ally he had been in the struggle against Charles and his supporters in 1921.

Gömbös's strategy seemed to work: in April 1932 Horthy apparently hinted strongly to him that he would be Károlyi's successor.[7] Gömbös thus proceeded with alacrity to plan for his assumption of power; by September he and his colleagues in the radical right-wing movement had drafted a grandiose reform program containing exactly 100 points, parts of which were sent to the Regent for his perusal.[8] In another clever move, Gömbös also apparently informed Horthy that a bill strengthening the powers of the Regent vis-à-vis Parliament would be given high priority on his legislative agenda.

Yet Horthy bided his time through the tumultuous summer of 1932, and in the end it was the beleaguered Károlyi who took the initiative. Frustrated by his opponents in the government party who seemed intent on making him an object of public ridicule, Károlyi submitted his resignation on September 21. The day before, sensing that events were moving in his direction, Gömbös had forwarded to the Regent a copy of a recent book by Hjalmar Schacht, who at the time was regarded as Adolf Hitler's most influential economic advisor. In an accompanying letter Gömbös declared that in drawing up his economic program he would emulate Schacht, who was taking the "sober middle course" between extreme right-wing doctrines and orthodox capitalism. The prerequisite to any plan of national renewal, however, was the restoration of political confidence, to be achieved, if necessary, "by radical means."[9]

Miklós Horthy probably did not understand the nuances of the economic debate to which Gömbös referred in his letter, but he was now in complete agreement with the proposition that more "radical means" were required to ensure political stability. He made only a perfunctory attempt to persuade Károlyi to stay on. In any case, the international situation no longer favored the Francophiles in Hungary, since France's plans for European economic cooperation had just been defeated by Germany and Italy at the Lausanne Conference. Like his counterpart in Germany, Marshal Hindenburg, who three months later would appoint Adolf Hitler Chancellor of Germany, Horthy was now willing to gamble on entrusting the government to a right-wing extremist whose ideological affinities were clearly with Mussolini and Hitler. Immediately after Károlyi's resignation, Horthy proceeded, in his customary fashion, to consult with his advisors, party leaders, and other prominent dignitaries. From the scattered remarks that have survived from these conversations, however, it is clear that Horthy had already made up his mind and was merely seeking to build support for that decision. He told Károly Rassay, leader of the Liberal party, that "Gyula Károlyi is my best friend," but "you must see that in our difficult times a stronger hand is needed."[10]

Unaware of the Regent's plan, many Hungarian political observers anticipated that Count Bethlen, who still commanded the loyalty of a majority in Parliament, would now make a triumphal return. Bethlen, who in early September had publicly urged Károlyi to resign, clearly expected to be called back to power. But quite quickly he must have sensed what was in the wind, for when Horthy received him in audience on September 23 and asked him what he thought of the appointment of Gömbös as Prime Minister, Bethlen made no attempt to dissuade him but merely responded: "One might try the experiment."[11] Bethlen insisted, however, that certain constraints be placed on Gömbös so that the more radical parts of the Szeged program could not be implemented. Though clearly more willing than Bethlen to gamble on a "turn to the right," Horthy shared the view of the conservative establishment that Hungary's fundamental political traditions must not be violated. No record of the discussions over the following week among Bethlen, Horthy, Gömbös, and other interested parties has survived, but, as Gömbös later explained to his colleagues, he "had to make concessions to Bethlen, the Party, and the Regent."[12] Gömbös reluctantly agreed to the ground rules finally stipulated by Horthy. As Prime Minister he would, for the foreseeable future, have to work with the existing Parliament: no new election would be called.[13] Furthermore, no anti-Jewish legislation or additional land reform would be proposed.

The formal appointment of Gyula Gömbös as Prime Minister on October 1, 1932, caused a considerable stir both in Hungary and abroad, but of course few observers were aware of the severe restrictions that had been placed on his freedom of maneuver. Gömbös now had his foot in the door, but as he surveyed the head table he found that all the choice seats were still occupied by Bethlen and his supporters. Gömbös discovered that he was not able even to select his own Cabinet, for Horthy had apparently granted Bethlen the right to veto appointments he opposed. Thus, no ministers with identifiable ties to the Szeged movement were selected. Gömbös was able to assemble a group of quite talented ministers, two of whom, Béla Imrédy and Miklós Kállay, would later become Prime Minister, but he could not rely on his Cabinet to support his more radical plans. In an indirect way, however, Gömbös's Cabinet did reflect the distrust the Szeged camp felt toward the magnates: it was the first such body in Hungarian history (excepting Béla Kun's) that did not contain a single titled nobleman.

Conspicuous by its absence in the ambiguously worded program Gömbös announced in October was any reference to the "Jewish question." Having pledged to the Regent that he would not initiate any anti-Jewish legislation, the original Hungarian "Race Defender" now decided to attempt to turn this apparent liability into an advantage. In a stroke of breathtaking opportunism, Gömbös established contact with leaders of national Jewish organizations and with prominent Jewish financiers. In the secret negotiations conducted by intermediaries, Gömbös offered assurances that his government would not undertake programs detrimental to Jewish interests. Startled by Gömbös's apparent change of heart, the Jewish leaders agreed to sign a personal agreement in which they "recognized and approved Gömbös's progressive policy."[14] The public first learned of this astonishing development on October 11, when in his inaugural speech as Prime Minister Gömbös declared: "I say openly and sincerely to the Jews that I have revised my point of view. Those Jews who acknowledge a common fate with the nation I regard as my brothers, just like my Magyar brothers." Gömbös went on to praise Jewish war heroes and those who assimilated fully into Hungarian society.[15]

Perhaps with an eye to currying favor with the Regent, Gömbös thus embraced the attitude to the Jews that Admiral Horthy had often expressed privately during the 1920s and would continue to cling to through World War II. No doubt Gömbös would have acted differently had his hands not been tied by Horthy, but it must be recorded that the four years of the Gömbös era proved to be relatively tranquil for Hungary's Jews.[16] Indeed, to the uninformed observer, it might have seemed that Gömbös had scant success in promoting the "Szeged idea." In whatever direction he turned, the *vezér* (a title he now adopted, in imitation of the Duce in Italy and the Führer in Germany) encountered roadblocks that he dared not circumvent. Although in October 1932 Bethlen did yield his place as leader of the government party, Gömbös commanded the allegiance of only a small minority of party members. Nor could he hope to win significant support in Parliament for any radical proposals, since the traditional conservatives there feared, and rightly so, that Gömbös would have preferred, like Mussolini in Italy, to ignore the legislature and rule in dictatorial fashion.

Only one piece of major legislation was passed in Gömbös's first year in power. In accordance with his promise to Horthy, Gömbös submitted to Parliament a bill that empowered the Regent to dissolve Parliament and prorogue it indefinitely, rather than for the thirty days stipulated when the regency was established in 1920. Even this stirred up the suspicions of the Bethlenites, who feared that a strengthened regency might be exploited by Gömbös to promote his personal ambitions. Gömbös denied that he aimed to establish a dictatorship, but he did declare at a Cabinet meeting in June 1933 that he hoped that the Regent would "take over the role of Parliament."[17] In July, however, the bill was discussed and approved in Parliament without opposition, for no one wished to take a public stand against legislation that fulfilled a long-standing desire of Admiral Horthy.

It must not have escaped Horthy's notice that in the ten years of the Bethlen era the Prime Minister had shown no inclination to strengthen the regency, whereas it took Gyula Gömbös less than a year to push through the legislation. A slight easing of the economic crisis during 1933, due largely to certain international developments rather than any initiatives taken by the Gömbös government, may also have convinced Horthy that in appointing Gömbös he had made the right choice. Horthy must also have been gratified that he could now more freely express his opinions on various public issues without fear of a condescending response from Count Bethlen. At the first Cabinet meeting of the new government, Horthy presided over the proceedings and made frequent contributions to the discussions. He suggested that there was a need for more efficient legal procedures in cases of sedition and for well-written and translated propaganda materials. He also expounded at length on one of his pet projects, the developing of Budapest as a major shipping center on the model of Liverpool, England.[18]

In this period Horthy also apprised his Prime Minister of his views on a variety of issues, including the threat of "mental degradation" of the Hungarian people.[19] Too many of the "valuable elements of the nation," Horthy argued, were practicing the "single-child system" (*egyke*), or worse, were having no children at all. Thus in the schools a feebleminded student was typically found to have many siblings, while a talented student came most often from a one-child family. Horthy suggested that vigorous steps be taken to counteract the "one child system" and to prohibit marriages in which one of the partners had tuberculosis, syphilis, or certain other debilitating diseases. Furthermore, citing the practice of sterilization and other measures adopted in some parts of the United States, he recommended that steps be taken to reduce the number of "undesirable elements," such as the sick, criminals, imbeciles, and "shirkers."

Whenever possible, Gömbös followed up on Horthy's suggestions, although sterilization was never introduced in Hungary. Gömbös also refrained from introducing, or even permitting discussion of, legislation that would likely incite Horthy. Thus, when Béla Imrédy, Minister of Finance, proposed at a Cabinet meeting that a study be made of the problem of the inefficient distribution of land in Hungary, Gömbös quickly interjected that this was impossible because the Regent would strenuously oppose any additional land reform.[20] Gömbös was very careful to please the Regent because he knew that he could never implement his full program until he had persuaded Horthy to remove some of the restrictions he had imposed on his Prime Minister.

Given the affinity that Gyula Gömbös felt for Italian fascism, it was to be expected that in his foreign policy he would set as a first priority the cultivation of the Italian-Hungarian partnership that Bethlen had instituted. This policy had the Regent's full support, for he had by this time been able to overcome the revulsion he had previously had for Italy because of its "perfidy" in World War.

Indeed, Horthy admired what Mussolini had accomplished in Italy and regarded him as a "great statesman."[21] Shortly after his appointment as Prime Minister, Gömbös visited Rome and savored the opportunity to consult with the Duce, whose reputation as a successful European statesman was at its zenith. Mussolini was quite willing to continue and expand the close ties with Hungary that had been forged in the Bethlen era. The prestige of the Gömbös government was enhanced, and the value of the friendship with Italy was seemingly demonstrated, when Italian economic assistance gave a boost to Hungary's wheat imports in 1933. Mussolini's call in July 1933 for a great power conference to discuss a revision of the peace treaties seemed also to raise the possibility of an early success for Hungary's revisionist campaign.

Gömbös had long believed that "the axis of European policy will lead from Rome to Berlin,"[22] and that Germany and Italy would eventually be the nucleus of a powerful grouping of ideologically compatible states with which Hungary would link up. For this reason he made a special effort to cultivate ties with Adolf Hitler after the latter's ascension to power in 1933. Hitler was prepared to cooperate with Hungary on certain issues, but Gömbös's efforts to draw Italy and Germany together initially met with little success. Hitler refused to disinterest himself in Austria, the annexation of which he had listed as a first priority in his book *Mein Kampf*. For the Hungarian government this was not in principle an obstacle to a friendly relationship with Germany, since most Hungarian leaders believed that the *Anschluss* of Austria to Germany was inevitable. On this issue Horthy and Bethlen concurred with Gömbös, who told a confidant that Austria could not survive in the long run because it lacked sufficient "national strength, self-assurance, and racial confidence."[23] But the Hungarians felt obliged to placate Mussolini, who in this period regarded Austria as in the Italian sphere of interest and was determined to resist German expansionism to the southeast. Thus in March 1934, Hungary joined with Italy and Austria in forming the Rome Pact, which strengthened economic and political ties among the signatories.

In the circumstances Gömbös devised a new strategy to cope with the fact that the Rome-Berlin axis that he had envisioned seemed for the time being unattainable. Hungary, he declared, would pursue a policy that "south of the Danube is based on Italy and north of the Danube on Germany."[24] Hungary would be left to play the leading role in the "Carpathian region," gaining back territory from Czechoslovakia with the help of Germany, and from Yugoslavia and Romania with the assistance of Italy. This naively optimistic formula seemed perfectly reasonable to Horthy, who, however, dropped strong hints to the German diplomats in Budapest that he personally regarded his country's connection with Berlin as taking precedence over that with Rome. Thus, the German Minister reported to his superiors that the Regent was "by far our most reliable friend here."[25]

In the first two years of the Gömbös government, Admiral Horthy played a somewhat more active role in the conduct of foreign policy than he had in the 1920s. However, while others fretted over assorted plans for European economic recovery, the fate of Austria, or disarmament negotiations at the League of Nations, Horthy felt obliged to take the initiative in dealing with the one international problem he continued to regard as the most pressing: the Bolshevik threat. In late 1932, shortly after the formation of the Gömbös government, Horthy decided the time had come to organize an international crusade against the Soviet Union. There are indications that Horthy had been toying with this idea for many years; in a sense the roots of such a plan could be traced back to the days of the "White International." But Horthy was emboldened to take pen in hand and compose a draft of his plan only when a disapproving Count Bethlen no longer peered over his shoulder to monitor his activities.

Writing in German, Admiral Horthy addressed a memorandum to the heads of state of all major European countries, as well as the Emperor of Japan and the President of the United States.[26] He seems to have devoted considerable time to this project, composing a draft in pencil and then a more polished version in ink. He began by explaining that in the current economic crisis it was the duty of each statesman to "contribute all within his powers to save mankind." It was his conviction, however, that even if solutions could be found to such evils as unemployment and overproduction of goods, and even if the League of Nations should agree on terms for a general disarmament, peace and prosperity would still be beyond reach so long as "a dangerous purulent abscess like Soviet Russia is tolerated on the body of mankind." He, as Hungary's head of state, felt not only duty bound but also uniquely qualified to rally the forces of civilization, for his country had felt "the horrors of the Soviet regime on her own body."

Admiral Horthy then proceeded to paint a portrait of the Soviet Union as a "satanic power" that for fifteen years had been conducting "a war of annihilation against the whole world." Citing as supporting evidence a book of Maurice Paléologue, a former Foreign Minister of France,[27] Horthy described how the Communists had expended the great treasure of the Russian Empire in a worldwide campaign of agitation and terrorism. In Russia itself they had imposed despotism and enslaved the peasants, in whom an "ineradicable hatred" had been kindled. Russia, once one of the most flourishing countries in Europe, had become "a cemetery, an abode of misery." And to what end?

> The Communists fight with the catchword: "Equality!" Where is "Equality?" In misery and slavery. A power that intends to destroy civilization by turning the Ten Commandments inside out, ignores moral concepts, and considers slavery the ideal and liberty a sin, must be wiped out. The world underestimates the peril; conditions are becoming worse every day. Flames dart high, once here, another time there. We must take the initiative before it is too late.[28]

Yet, Horthy warned, instead of uniting against Soviet Russia, the West was "assisting the enemy in building up its peace and war machinery to its full extent." This was done partly to stimulate export trade, partly because some countries were already overrun with Communists. But how can one do business with a government that "not only ignores the sanctity of the given word but even derides it?" In concluding, Horthy suggested that he would prefer a radical solution to this problem, but, in light of the likely diplomatic difficulties, was willing to start with smaller steps, such as a trade boycott of the Soviet Union, prohibition of Soviet dumping of trade goods, and suppression of Communist parties as had been done in Hungary.

Even as he composed his memorandum, however, Miklós Horthy seemed to have sensed that his was indeed a quixotic project. "I am making this attempt without much hope for success," he wrote, "rather in order to calm my conscience. Somebody has to begin." He saw himself as a voice crying in the wilderness, virtually alone in recognizing the nature of the threat that communism posed to civilization. Yet he imagined that world leaders, noting his promise that their responses to his letter would be held in the strictest confidentiality, would allow him to collate their ideas and entrust him with the responsibility for the anti-Soviet enterprise. In the end Admiral Horthy did not dispatch his memorandum to the twenty-three heads of state for whom it was intended.[29] Perhaps Hungary's new Foreign Minister, Kálmán Kánya, a protégé of Count Bethlen, gently dissuaded him; if so, Horthy must have relented only with reluctance, for the project remained very much on his mind and moved him to action at a later point.

Admiral Horthy's desire to isolate and destroy the Soviet state ran directly counter to the general trend in international relations. By the end of 1933 every major Western country, including the United States, the final holdout, had established formal diplomatic relations with the USSR. Even Regent Horthy had to admit that this placed Hungary in an awkward diplomatic position and at a trade disadvantage. When the issue was discussed at a Crown Council in December 1933, Kálmán Kánya proposed that diplomatic ties be established with the USSR on the basis of the agreement reached in 1924. The Regent reluctantly agreed, and despite his previous insistence that he would never grant an audience to a Communist diplomat, Horthy did receive the Soviet envoy who arrived late in 1934. In a cool and abrupt manner, Horthy advised him that relations between their countries would be restricted to commercial and economic matters.[30]

Despite the fanfare accompanying journeys undertaken by Gömbös to Berlin, Rome, and, in 1934, Warsaw, Hungary's strategic position remained essentially unaltered in this period. The grim reality was that Hungary was almost completely encircled by the Little Entente countries, which differed on many international questions but maintained unanimity in their resolve to oppose any revision of the Treaty of Trianon. One way Hungary could disrupt the unity of the Little Entente was by achieving a rapprochement with one of its members. Since Berlin was advocating this approach, and Hungary had taken a similar initiative in the mid-1920s, Admiral Horthy decided in the summer of 1934 that he would make another effort to reach an understanding with Yugoslavia. With the Romanians and the Czechs it was, Horthy believed, impossible to do business, but the Serbs were an adversary "to whom one could hold out a hand without blushing."[31] Accordingly, Horthy sent a friendly message to King Alexander and proposed that they work for improved relations. Ever optimistic, Horthy seems to have had in mind an agreement whereby Belgrade would agree to a "slight rectification" of the frontier in which that part of Yugoslavia north of the Danube River, namely the Voivodina, would be returned to Hungary.[32] King Alexander was interested enough to send his aide-de-camp to meet with Horthy in September,[33] but the attempted rapprochement was abruptly aborted just weeks later when King Alexander and the French Foreign Minister were assassinated by a Macedonian terrorist in Marseilles, France. An investigation of the assassination produced some evidence of Hungarian complicity: the accomplices of the assassin, members of the Ustasha, a Croatian separatist group, had trained for a time at a secret camp in Hungary and had received some financial support from Budapest.[34] Italy and Germany had also promoted the activities of the Ustasha, but, because of international factors, the League of Nations focused its investigation into the incident on hapless Hungary, which found itself almost completely isolated in European affairs. Undaunted, Gyula Gömbös attempted to exploit this highly unfavorable development in foreign affairs to promote his domestic program. The "siege mentality" that gripped many Hungarians during the international crisis in late 1934 made it somewhat easier for Gömbös to urge a general rallying of public support for the government.

Hoping to take advantage of the heightened sense of national unity, Gömbös began to move more forcefully to break the shackles that restricted his political maneuvering. Using his political ally, Tibor Eckhardt, as a mouthpiece, Gömbös increased the attacks on Bethlen and the "reactionary forces" in the government party. Indoctrination of youth in radical right-wing ideas was pushed more vigorously in a student organization known as the *Turul*. Gömbös's supporters, though not the Prime Minister himself, urged that the secret ballot be introduced, albeit with certain restrictions that would have provided significant advantages to Eckhardt's Independent Smallholders and the radical right-wing dissidents in the government party. Now on the defensive, Count Bethlen argued in Parliament that the secret ballot would lead inevitably to either "dictatorship or revolution."[35] On this issue, at least, the Regent stood firm with Bethlen. He refused to approve the abolition of the open ballot in the countryside and regarded Eckhardt's public advocacy of such a change as sheer demagoguery.[36]

By early 1935 Gömbös's relentless efforts were alarming the moderate conservatives, including several Cabinet members, who protested to the Prime Minister that his government was moving toward a Fascist dictatorship. Two ministers, Miklós Kállay and Béla Imrédy, resigned and warned that the thousand-year-old

Hungarian constitution was in danger.[37] Gömbös welcomed these defections, for it allowed him to replace those who resigned with his supporters. Even more advantageous to the promotion of his program was the sudden resignation in January of twenty-two senior military officers in protest of the League of Nations report condemning Hungary in connection with the Marseilles assassinations. Ever since his appointment as Minister of Defense in 1929, Gömbös had been filling the lower ranks of the officer corps with men sympathetic to the Szeged program.[38] Now he had the unexpected opportunity to make similar changes at the highest level. At the risk of alienating Horthy, who regarded such senior appointments as his own prerogative, Gömbös proceeded to install at the highest levels of the military leadership a cadre of officers who were strong proponents of the "Szeged idea" and were imbued with the notion that the National Army had an important political mission to fulfill. Finally, on January 24, 1935, Gömbös made a provocative speech at Szolnok in which he condemned the "old men" who were obstacles to the reform program of the government.[39]

Stung by this criticism, Bethlen and his allies responded in kind and a true political donnybrook seemed about to erupt. At this juncture Admiral Horthy decided to intervene as peacemaker, as he had on several occasions in the early 1920s. Gömbös and Bethlen were summoned to a joint audience at which their political differences could be reconciled. To prepare the ground for their joint meeting, the Regent met separately with each of the antagonists several days earlier. Nothing is known of the meeting between Horthy and Bethlen, who had not had personal contact for more than two years. It is known, however, that Gömbös once again requested the authority to hold new parliamentary elections. Horthy's response was that "he would think about it," which, given his previous refusals, hinted at an important change in his position.[40] At the joint audience on February 9, the Regent's mediation brought about an apparent compromise. Gömbös, it seems, agreed to dissociate himself from Eckhardt's oppositional activities, end the radical right-wing indoctrination of the youth, and continue to work with the existing Parliament until the end of its mandate. For his part, Bethlen indicated that he was not opposed outright to all elements of the reform program of the government.[41]

The joint audience thus ended in apparent harmony. In the next two weeks Gömbös acted in such a contrite and conciliatory fashion that political observers believed that he had been chastised by Horthy and that Bethlen had won a clear victory.[42] This particular political crisis, however, was to have a completely unexpected denouement, for behind the scenes Gömbös was preparing a political sensation that was worthy of István Bethlen at his finest a decade earlier.

At some point in late February or early March, Gömbös finally persuaded Horthy to dissolve Parliament and hold new elections. Few of the decisions Horthy made in his twenty-four-year regency had as great an impact on Hungary's political life as this one, yet, unfortunately, almost no documentation has survived that illumines his frame of mind and motivations. For once, however, Horthy's memoirs might offer a valuable insight into his thinking. There he was to write that he agreed to permit new parliamentary elections in 1935 out of loyalty to Gömbös, for after all a "Premier must have his majority."[43] No doubt Horthy continued to share the concern of the traditional conservatives about Gömbös's dictatorial tendencies, and he surely resented the way in which his Prime Minister had overstepped the bounds in appointing replacements for the military officers who had resigned. But Horthy might well have reasoned that, in the difficult circumstances, Gömbös had done as well as could be expected in his two-year tenure in office. Perhaps there was something in Gömbös's argument that the Bethlenites were reactionaries blocking needed reforms that had broad public support.[44] Could he in good conscience tie his Prime Minister's hands vis-à-vis Parliament for the indefinite future? After all, Gömbös had shown his loyalty to Horthy by quickly guiding through Parliament the legislation expanding the Regent's powers.

Whatever his precise motivation, Admiral Horthy apparently acted entirely on his own in making this momentous decision. Fearful that Horthy would change his mind and withdraw his written authorization, Gömbös moved swiftly. On March 4 he tendered his resignation. Two hours later Horthy reappointed Gömbös and approved a new Cabinet. Only then was the public informed that new elections would take place. István Bethlen, appalled by this turn of events, immediately complained that the Prime Minister had reneged on the promise that he had made in the joint audience to work with the current Parliament until the end of its mandate. To this Gömbös responded blandly that any obligations made by the previous government were now null and void, for a new government was in place and Parliament had been dissolved. Bethlen rushed off to plead his case with the Regent, but his arguments were in vain. It may be that the malleable Horthy wavered as he listened to the grave warnings of "the steward"; perhaps already at this point he began to regret that he acted so hastily in acceding to Gömbös's request. But the written authorization for new elections that Gömbös now had in his pocket could not easily be revoked: there was no turning back.

Nothing was left for Count Bethlen but to admit temporary defeat and to devise a new strategy. His first step was to resign from the government party and to assume the mantle of the unofficial spokesman for the opposition in Parliament. Some of his supporters also departed the government party in protest, but, at Bethlen's urging, a small core remained to serve as a possible Trojan horse. The elections, duly held in March, were exceedingly rancorous; complaints about police coercion and the brutality of the gendarmes came not only from the anti-Gömbös camp, but also from none other than Tibor Eckhardt, who was dissatisfied with the number of seats Gömbös had allotted to his party. The election results, as expected, provided Gömbös and his reconstituted government party with a solid majority of 170 out of 245 seats. This victory, however, was marred by the actions of Tibor Eckhardt, who was so angered by what he considered to be perfidy on the part of the Prime Minister that he challenged Gömbös to a duel, which, in typical Hungarian fashion, was duly conducted but left both participants unharmed.

Gömbös could afford to be elated over the electoral victory despite the unpleasantness with Eckhardt, who now reconciled with Bethlen and took the bulk of the Independent Smallholder party into opposition to the government. For Gömbös the essential thing was that he now had a reliable majority of supporters in Parliament to complement the radical right-wing cadres that he had been building up in the officer corps and the civil service. Indeed, had Gyula Gömbös succumbed in April, 1935 to the fatal disease that would take his life one and one half years later, his legacy to Hungary would have been essentially the same. He had injected the "spirit of Szeged" into the main arteries of Hungarian political and military life. For the next decade, as C. A. Macartney has written, the "voice of Szeged claimed to determine decisions of policy, and the representatives of Szeged carried them out."[45]

Yet the casual observer of the Hungarian political scene in the year following the April 1935 elections might not have concluded that any such major transformation had occurred. To be sure, Gyula Gömbös became more audacious in his public statements of admiration for the totalitarian systems of Fascist Italy and Nazi Germany. But he did not immediately put forward any far-reaching legislation to implement the "one party, corporative state" of which he spoke so glowingly. In proceeding cautiously at first, Gömbös may have been wary of alarming Hungary's financial community, whose support would be needed when the time came for the government to embark on a massive program of rearmament. Gömbös thus continued to honor the commitment he had made to Jewish leaders, and to the Regent, that he would not initiate discriminatory measures against the Jews. But there is strong evidence that by the end of 1935 he was poised to take more dramatic steps to implement the Szeged program.

In September 1935 Gömbös again journeyed to Germany, where he received the same advice that he was given during his first conversation with Hitler in 1933: Hungary should focus its territorial claims on its neighbor to the north. Gömbös nonetheless now drew the optimistic conclusion that "although Hitler had promised him revision only against Czechoslovakia, . . . Hungary would end up by getting everything back with Germany's help."[46] Gömbös was profoundly impressed by the dynamism and vitality of the National Socialist regime. He found the leaders of the Nazi party to be "a group of exceptionally gifted, able, and resolute men."[47] He quickly developed a rapport with Hermann Goering, to whom he bore some physical resemblance. During one exuberant conversation with Goering, Gömbös apparently solemnly promised that within two years he would introduce in Hungary a political system based on radical right-wing, totalitarian principles. Among other measures, he would regulate the position of the Catholic Church and deal with the "Jewish question."[48]

Gömbös's statement to Marshal Goering was in no sense a binding agreement, but it did indicate that his public hints about the need to emulate the Fascist dictatorships were an adumbration of a concrete program he was determined to implement in the near future. Moreover, since even the most confidential matters rarely remained secret in interwar Hungarian political life, the rumor soon spread among members of the anti-Gömbös coalition that the Prime Minister had made far-reaching promises to the Nazi leaders. This merely confirmed the suspicions of Count Bethlen, who during 1935 had made several speeches in which he warned against Gömbös's dictatorial ambitions, his "flirting with the principles of National Socialism" and his apparent intention to form dangerous groups akin to S.A. and S.S. units.[49] Bethlen and others in the conservative camp were not averse to cooperation with Nazi Germany in achieving territorial revision, but they strongly resisted the notion, now fully embraced by Gömbös, that to cooperate in the international arena with Hitler's Germany and Mussolini's Italy, it was necessary that Hungary also be governed in a totalitarian fashion. Ferenc Keresztes-Fischer, who had earlier resigned in protest from Gömbös's Cabinet, spoke for many in the conservative camp when he asserted privately that though he was an advocate of an authoritarian system and an opponent of socialist and liberal tendencies, he nonetheless deplored what was happening in Germany. Everything had its limit, he declared, and the "suppression of all personal freedom" that was occurring in Germany could not last.[50]

The informal anti-Gömbös coalition that was beginning to coalesce by the end of 1935 attracted some unusual bedfellows. Joining the Bethlenites were monarchists who found the drift to radical right-wing dictatorship highly inimical to their cause; a few Szeged veterans and Race Defenders such as Tibor Eckhardt and Endre Bajcsy-Zsilinszky, who for a variety of reasons had turned against Gömbös; and, for obvious reasons, the Social Democrats and Liberals. Yet Bethlen, now in the unaccustomed role of the underdog, realized that Gömbös could be dislodged from his newly won position of dominance only if the Regent could be persuaded to withdraw his support from his Prime Minister. Every effort was thus made to shake Horthy's confidence in Gömbös. However, though Horthy apparently soon came to rue his decision to tilt in Gömbös's favor, he resisted the idea that he should quickly reverse himself, for this would damage his image as a decisive head of state. Through late 1935 he thus remained aloof from the political process, observing the increasingly rancorous debate among the main factions, but abstaining from any direct intervention. Perhaps by this time Horthy had come to sense the nature of his role as the vital link between the extreme and the conservative right. By maintaining a delicate balancing act between these opposing camps, Horthy found that his own authority and role in policymaking were enhanced and an equilibrium in domestic politics maintained.

One advantage enjoyed by the anti-Gömbös forces seemed eventually to tip the scales in their favor. Most of the members of Horthy's family and of his so-called camarilla (the group of elder statesmen in which he often confided) were hostile to Gyula Gömbös and sympathetic to István Bethlen. The Regent could not fail to notice, for example, that his brother István, a cavalry general whom he had appointed a member of the Upper House of Parliament, made several anti-Gömbös speeches in the summer of 1935. At one session that Gömbös himself attended, István Horthy spoke of Bethlen's unsurpassed leadership qualities and declared that he had no confidence in the current Prime Minister.[51] One tactic employed by the traditional conservatives in Horthy's retinue proved particularly effective. Beginning in late 1935 Horthy was frequently warned by General Lajos Keresztes-Fischer, the head of the Regent's Military Bureau, by his brother, and even by his wife that Gömbös would never be satisfied with being simply the "leader" (*vezér*), but would eventually aspire to be the "chief leader" (*fővezér*), in other words that he would try to usurp the Regent's power.[52] In a newspaper article Tibor Eckhardt even suggested that if the Regent were to die suddenly, Gömbös would proclaim himself both Regent and Prime Minister, with unlimited power.[53]

Regent Horthy's growing suspicions about Gömbös's ultimate political goals must have been strengthened by the rumors, surely passed on to him, that his Prime Minister had spoken of his plans for a radical remaking of the Hungarian government with Marshal Goering, whom Horthy despised. An important indication that Horthy was beginning to turn against Gömbös was his willingness to consider a reconciliation with Count Bethlen. The two men had been estranged since the stormy session early in the year when Bethlen had protested in vain against the Regent's decision to authorize new elections. At that time the furious Bethlen is said to have reproached Horthy bitterly: "I told you that Gömbös was no gentleman. You will see, you will go the way of King Charles."[54] These words must have rankled Horthy at the time, but subsequent events seemed to suggest that "the steward" had been right after all. In December Horthy made the first overture by inviting Bethlen to a hunt, a recreation the two men had shared many times in the 1920s. Early in 1936 an evening of bridge, arranged by the two wives who hoped to facilitate their husbands' political reconciliation, provided the opportunity for two hours of private discussions between Horthy and Bethlen.[55] The former atmosphere of trust and easy rapport was now reestablished, and Bethlen must have argued persuasively that the time had come for the Regent to nip in the bud Gömbös's aspirations for dictatorial power.

Yet Admiral Horthy bided his time, especially when it was discovered in early 1936 that Gömbös was suffering from a kidney disease that gradually sapped his strength in the coming months. The swiftly changing European diplomatic scene may also have prompted Horthy to hold off on any destabilizing changes in Hungary. In fact, in October 1935 the Regent had been called on to make what seemed at the time a critical decision concerning Hungary's foreign policy. Mussolini's invasion of Ethiopia in 1935 had led to the possibility that the League of Nations would impose sanctions on Italy because of its unprovoked aggression. The question of whether to vote in favor of sanctions provoked a vigorous debate in the Hungarian Cabinet. Gömbös, of course, argued that Hungary must remain faithful to Italy, its only reliable friend among the great powers. Kálmán Kánya pointed out that by any standard Italy had indeed launched an unprovoked war. A decision to vote against sanctions might irrevocably destroy British goodwill toward Hungary. When the rest of the Cabinet sided with the Prime Minister, Gömbös and Kánya called on the Regent for a final decision. Realizing that his position lacked support among the ministers, Kánya offered his resignation. After some deliberation, Horthy offered a Solomon-like judgment: Hungary would vote against sanctions but Kánya must nonetheless remain as Foreign Minister.[56] This proved to be a shrewd decision, for it turned out that Great Britain preferred to avoid the imposition of severe sanctions and was actually searching behind the scenes for some compromise that would appease Mussolini.

For Hungary and the countries of East Central Europe, the most important repercussion of the Ethiopian crisis was Mussolini's decision to seek a rapprochement with Germany, which had adopted a strongly pro-Italian position in the crisis. With Mussolini's tacit support, Hitler was able to carry out the remilitarization of the Rhineland in March 1936. This daring gamble, which the Western powers countered with strong diplomatic protests but no military action, profoundly altered the European balance of power. Above all, it signaled to the countries of East Central Europe that Germany would before long reassert its traditional influence in that part of the continent and might in fact resume its historic *Drang nach Osten.* Admiral Horthy was impressed by Hitler's achievement. He told the British Minister in Budapest, Geoffrey Knox, that he was by no means a Germanophile, but he had nothing but admiration for the way in which Hitler had torn up the Locarno Treaty.[57]

The upheaval in international relations caused by the Ethiopian War and the Rhineland crisis prompted Admiral Horthy to believe that the time had come for him to make known his views on the restructuring of the European state system. When in 1932 he had acted on a similar impulse and drawn up a statement of his beliefs and proposal for action, he had decided in the end not to dispatch it to the various heads of state. Now, four years later, Horthy was determined to carry through, although this time he intended to send a letter only to King Edward VIII of England, who, as Prince of Wales, had twice visited Hungary and met Horthy. It is significant that in pleading Hungary's case Horthy should turn first to Great Britain. His hopes for securing British support had been lifted several months earlier when Austen Chamberlain, the former Foreign Minister, visited Budapest and tried to stiffen Hungarian resistance to German pressure. From his conversation with Chamberlain, Horthy had gained the impression that Britain's leaders understood Hungary's territorial claims to be just in principle. Hungary, Chamberlain had urged, should pursue a patient and moderate policy. When the "right moment" came, England would step forward and offer her support.[58] Thinking perhaps that the "right moment" was now at hand, Admiral Horthy sent off on May 16, 1936, a rambling six-page letter, a document that provides important insights into his thinking at a critical juncture in interwar European history.[59]

Writing avowedly with the knowledge and approval of both Gömbös and Kánya, Horthy declared that he wished to present his views on possible solutions to "the crisis of the League of Nations." He then proceeded to draw the familiar picture of the injustices and indignities that Hungary had suffered at the Paris Peace Conference and subsequently at Geneva. Yet, Horthy argued, Hungary had never done anything to justify the harsh punishment meted out to her. In a quick review of Hungarian history, Horthy rejected as baseless the accusations that the national minorities had been persecuted in the Kingdom of Hungary or that his country bore any responsibility for World War I. The peace treaties, Horthy asserted, had "by their economic, military, and territorial decisions led Europe to the edge of the abyss." Unless a "just peace" were created in Europe, it would be useless "to dream of an effective League of Nations, much less world peace." Bad peace treaties, Horthy averred, "are always the fundamental causes of new wars." The League had been a dismal failure. The French, who were always able to "juggle the paragraphs," were able to defeat any attempt to right the wrongs of the peace treaty. His country had been dealt an enormous injustice in the "dictated peace treaty of Trianon," yet it was poor Hungary that had to defend itself against unjust accusations in connection with the Marseilles assassinations. Meanwhile the Successor States, especially Romania, were oppressing their Magyar minorities, ignoring their responsibilities under the League covenant, and building powerful armies, while Hungary remained disarmed and defenseless, its capital city only eight minutes by airplane from the border of its hostile neighbor to the north.

As a solution to the crisis in which Europe now found itself, Horthy suggested that a new European Congress be established to revise the peace treaties and eliminate the distinction between the "satisfied" and the "desperate" states. This was the procedure he and his countrymen preferred, because Hungary was pursuing territorial revision "always and exclusively by peaceful means." Once the injustices of the peace settlement had been eliminated, the way would be cleared for the most dangerous task: the liquidation of bolshevism. The continuing danger of communism was being underestimated, Horthy insisted. Some states, like Czechoslovakia, were even facilitating the expansion of evil Soviet influence. In its eternal quest for ice-free ports, Russia had its eyes on northern Finland, Sweden, and Norway, from which it would establish itself on the Atlantic coast and "destroy the world." With its 116 nationalities, Russia was *too big* and could only be ruled by the use of terror. Those states that at the twelfth hour had freed themselves from the Bolshevik yoke, like Hungary, Poland, Germany, Italy, and Austria, should, with the help of Japan and under the leadership of England, join together "to free the world of this plague and break Russia into its constituent parts."[60] Everyone, Horthy ended, trusted in England's leadership, and the Hungarians did so unconditionally.

The diplomats of the British Foreign Office, which was asked to pass on Horthy's letter to the king, were unsure exactly how to respond to what one official described as "a very wild production."[61] The Regent's proposals seemed naive and unrealistic, but he was, after all, head of state of an important, if small, European country with which Great Britain had developed a very friendly relationship in the postwar period. It is not known if King Edward, who was entangled in a delicate private affair that would lead to his abdication only months later, actually read the letter, but eventually a response signed by the king was sent off to Budapest; it was polite but brief and noncommittal. Horthy did not follow-up on the matter, and the whole episode was conveniently forgotten. But the Regent's initiative is nonetheless important as a reflection of his basic ideas toward European affairs, some of which were shared by influential members of the Hungarian political establishment. His "cry from the heart" for British sympathy was consistent with his long-held view that Great Britain, with its powerful navy, remained the strongest of the great powers and the arbiter of Europe's destiny. The bloc of friendly states he projected (which of course omitted France, Soviet Russia, and the Successor States) and the idea of a European conference to revise the peace treaties were consistent with the thinking of Hungary's Foreign Minister, Kálmán Kánya, though not with that of Gyula Gömbös, who had little faith in the Western powers. Nor was Horthy's appeal to the anticommunism of the king and his countrymen an outlandish one. There were many in British society who regarded Soviet Russia as a greater menace than Nazi Germany, and perhaps even a few who, in certain circumstances, would have supported an anti-Soviet campaign of the kind Horthy outlined. The Regent's mistake was in thinking that this might be the attitude of the British government and the Foreign Office, and that as a prelude to a move against the Soviet Union, Britain would take the lead in a major remaking of the map of Europe to Hungary's advantage.

In his letter to King Edward, Admiral Horthy was careful to avoid too strong an expression of his hatred for the Successor States. Yet it is clear from other evidence that Horthy's frustration and humiliation were mounting in this period. At one point in late 1935, in fact, Horthy became incensed by articles in the Prague press in which the Hungarian government was denounced as criminal and the Hungarian Regent was referred to as a "bloodthirsty Admiral." Such insults were more than Horthy could bear. Taking pen in hand he began to draft a letter to Thomas Masaryk, the President of Czechoslovakia, to demand a formal apology. If no apology was extended, Horthy wrote, he would insist on obtaining satisfaction with arms, that is through a duel. Recognizing that Masaryk was "an ailing old man," (Masaryk was eighty-seven at the time, Horthy sixty-seven), Horthy stated his willingness to allow Eduard Beneš to take his place. All the better, Horthy suggested, since it was Beneš to whom the Magyars owed "all the misfortune and insults we have tolerated so far." Yet even as he drafted the letter, Horthy seemed to realize the impracticality of his idea, for his hand-written draft ends in mid-sentence with the acknowledgment that Masaryk might consider this a "medieval solution."[62]

Even Horthy had to recognize that, despite his personal concept of honor and gentlemanly conduct, dueling would hardly be a way to settle international disputes. Yet he was not about to abandon his belief, so firmly held since 1919, that Czechoslovakia must be destroyed. Although Horthy had tried to assure King Edward that Hungary would pursue its irredentist program only through peaceful means, he continued to believe that military force was the only way to deal with such a vile enemy as Czechoslovakia. In this regard, the reemergence of Germany as a great power under Adolf Hitler's leadership buoyed Horthy's spirits. Like many politically aware Hungarians, he hoped that Hitler would eventually pursue a Bismarckian policy, that is one that relied on the Magyars to exercise hegemony in Danubian Europe. He hoped, too, that Germany and Britain would avoid the problems that had bedeviled their relationship before World War I. With the dramatic increase in Germany's prestige and power in 1936, Horthy's curiosity about and desire to meet with Hitler also grew. It seems that in early 1935 Horthy wrote to Hitler to express interest in a meeting. In his response Hitler suggested that Germany and Hungary were united in the struggle for the "emancipation" of their countries and the "reparation of the injustice committed against them." The German leader approved the idea of a personal meeting with Horthy but only when international conditions were suitable.[63]

In the summer of 1936, when Berlin and Vienna signed a "Gentleman's Agreement" that temporarily defused the "Austrian question" along lines that the Hungarians had long been advocating, the way was cleared for Horthy and Hitler to meet. Horthy had already planned to make a brief visit to hunt game in Austria for a few days in August, his first journey abroad as Hungarian head of state. Arrangements were made for the Regent unobtrusively to cross the German frontier near Salzburg and spend a few hours with the German Chancellor at his retreat in Berchtesgaden. Accounts of the actual meeting with Hitler are sparse, but insights into Admiral Horthy's frame of mind on the eve of his visit can be gained from the memorandum he drew up on topics likely to be discussed.[64]

Like his letter to King Edward, Horthy's memorandum of August 1936 stressed the need for a thorough revision of the peace treaties and for combating bolshevism. But Horthy's bitterness and hostility toward Hungary's neighbors were here more forcefully and candidly expressed. Czechoslovakia was a "cancerous tumor" that had to be excised, preferably by a joint attack of Germany, Hungary, Poland, and Austria. There were, Horthy wrote, indications that Britain would accept this solution, and that even France and Russia would refrain from interference. Hungary was not striving for war, since, Horthy conceded, a "lost war would wipe Hungary off the map." Yet sooner or later the time of confrontation would arrive, and it was best to prepare for that contingency. The Serbs and Romanians, in Horthy's opinion, were untrustworthy nations who would inevitably oppose those, like the Magyars and Germans, who tried to revise the peace settlement. None of the Successor States, least of all Czechoslovakia, could be relied on to oppose Russian bolshevism or Pan-Slavism, which for all practical purposes were "one and the same."

These were the ideas and arguments, so typical of the worldview Horthy had expressed during his political career, that the Hungarian Regent brought with him to Berchtesgaden for his first meeting with the Führer.[65] No record was kept of the initial one-hour conversation that the two men had *"unter vier Augen"* (with no one else present) in Hitler's study, but later evidence suggests that Horthy and Hitler quickly confirmed that they shared a contempt for Czechoslovakia and a strong hostility to Communist Russia. Horthy was no doubt pleased to hear the Führer declare that a conflict between Soviet Russia and the "authoritarian-bourgeois governments" was inevitable.[66] Hitler, it seems, was a gracious host, allowing his garrulous guest to hold the floor and even asking for his advice: "What would you do, Your Highness, if you had to set Germany's course?" Horthy apparently did not hesitate to suggest that Germany refrain from entering into a naval competition with Great Britain. One should be careful, he argued, not to underestimate or provoke a country like England, which possessed enormous reservoirs of strength. It would be best, Horthy added, for the new Germany to forge an alliance with Britain, thus avoiding the mistakes made by Germany's leadership before World War I.[67]

Joining Hitler and Horthy for the duration of their three hour conversation were Konstantin von Neurath, the Foreign Minister, and General Blomberg, Minister of Defense, with whom Horthy had long been in friendly contact. In the course of their wide-ranging conversation, Horthy repeated the offer he had made several times in the past to serve as a mediator between Italy and Germany, but Hitler explained that the relationship between the two countries had already improved greatly and would doubtless become even more intimate in the future. Thus, Hungarian assistance was not needed. As for the Austrian question, Horthy urged that Germany be patient, since the *Anschluss* was inevitable in any event. He had observed that the older generation in Austria had "mental inhibitions," but the youth, who "had an almost unanimous will for *Anschluss*," would get their way in the end. When asked about Hungary's relations with the Little Entente countries, Horthy responded "very pessimistically." On the prospects for a rapprochement with Yugoslavia, which the Germans had been recommending to Budapest over the past two years, Horthy must have sensed that it would not be advantageous to speak in the harsh terms of his memorandum, in which he had roundly condemned the Serbs and termed Yugoslavia "a purely geographical concept."[68] Instead, Horthy remarked that this was a delicate matter that required the proper psychological preparation. Nonetheless, he hoped that an understanding would slowly be achieved.

This meeting proved to be by far the most cordial and pleasant of the six that Hitler and Horthy would have in the coming years. Like so many other statesmen who had met Horthy, Hitler formed a favorable impression. In later years, even when he became greatly annoyed at Hungarian policy, he would at times still speak almost respectfully of Horthy's courage, charm, and aura of authority. Horthy, he later declared, was "a bull of a man . . . and without doubt the bravest man in the Austrian Navy."[69] Horthy's initial reaction was similar. Hitler, Horthy later recalled, seemed to be "a moderate and wise statesman." Though uneducated, he had employed a "remarkable memory" to amass considerable knowledge. What's more, he had proved to be a "delightful host" who asked many questions and by no means dominated their conversation.[70] Admiral Horthy must have been aware of the concerns that some Hungarians, among them Count Bethlen, had expressed in the past two years about the German dictator and the excesses of the Nazi system. But the man with whom he conversed and drank tea in the spectacular setting of the Obersalzberg seemed well-mannered and reasonable. Moreover, such trustworthy representatives of the conservative German military tradition as General Blomberg seemed to have no compunctions about cooperating with the Nazis.

Curiously, Horthy formed this initially positive view of Hitler at precisely the same time that he finally decided that he must dismiss Hungary's would be dictator, Gyula Gömbös. The fate of Gömbös seems not to have been a topic of discussion at Berchtesgaden, though Hitler must have inquired about the health of the European leader who had honored him with the first visit after his coming to power. At some point in August (whether before or after the visit to Germany is uncertain), Horthy decided to request his Prime Minister's resignation. The only explanation Horthy ever offered for this decision was his growing realization that those advisors whom he most trusted were "increasingly estranged" from Gömbös, with whom, in any case, he found it more and more difficult to work.[71] Precisely what combination of the factors already mentioned finally tipped the scales against Gömbös is impossible to determine, although Horthy's growing suspicion that he might be fancying himself the future Regent of Hungary may have been decisive. In short Admiral Horthy finally concluded that Bethlen was correct after all: Gömbös was not "a true gentleman."[72] Accordingly, Horthy summoned his Prime Minister to his summer residence at Gödöllő to carry out his delicate task. But, Horthy later recalled, he quickly realized that "here was a man whose days were numbered." Taking pity on a dying man, Horthy decided not to mention resignation but instead to urge Gömbös to accept an invitation of the German government to go for treatment at a Munich hospital specializing in kidney disease. They agreed that Kálmán Darányi, the Minister of Agriculture, should serve as Acting Prime Minister in Gömbös's absence.[73]

Gömbös's death on October 6, 1936, opened a new phase in Hungary's interwar political history. Ever since 1921 everyday political affairs had been dominated by the influential leaders of the two main right-wing camps, Bethlen and Gömbös, both of whom had known and worked with Miklós Horthy even before he became the country's head of state. Now, however, Gömbös had passed from the scene and none of his possible successors among the radical rightists possessed anything like his prestige, popularity, and access to the Regent. On the other hand, no one, not even "the steward" himself, proposed that István Bethlen be appointed Prime Minister again. Bethlen's open condemnation of Germany made such an appointment inadvisable. Bethlen remained, of course, a powerful influence on the government, but Admiral Horthy's stature seemed even greater now that the political triumvirate that had dominated Hungarian politics for over a decade had dissolved.

In appointing a successor to Gömbös, Regent Horthy followed the now familiar procedure. Leaders of all the significant political parties (with the exception of the Social Democrats and the right-wing fringe groups) and Horthy's traditional advisors were consulted. Given Horthy's apparent aim of avoiding domestic turmoil by finding someone acceptable to both the major right-wing groups, the field of candidates was extremely small. A consensus quickly formed that only Kálmán Darányi, the Acting Prime Minister, was suitable. Darányi was a chameleon-like politician who had demonstrated a knack for ingratiating himself with leaders of all the right-wing camps. Before his departure for medical treatment in Germany, Gömbös had advised the Regent that Darányi be appointed as his successor and had urged his followers to support this decision.[74] Yet Bethlen also favored Darányi, for he was convinced that he had fundamentally conservative instincts and was entirely free of any dictatorial ambitions. Horthy must have shared this opinion, for in appointing Darányi he apparently gave him written authorization to dissolve Parliament if he deemed it necessary. This option, so desperately coveted by Gömbös for the first two years of his premiership, was in fact never exercised by Darányi.

Regent Horthy set certain tasks for his new Prime Minister, including a reestablishment of the "old order" in political life, suppression of the more boisterous elements on both the right and the left, and maintenance of friendly relations with Great Britain as well as Germany and Italy.[75] On one other matter Horthy and Darányi apparently reached a tacit agreement. Just as had been the case with the appointment of Teleki in 1920 and of Gömbös in 1932, the new Prime Minister quickly declared his intention of introducing legislation that would strengthen the authority of the regent. Horthy's dissatisfaction with the limitations placed on the regent's power had not been quelled by the additional legislation passed in 1920 and 1933. By 1936 another factor had to be taken into account. The regency had been designed as a temporary expedient. Though in good health, Miklós Horthy was now 68 years old. What would happen in case of his incapacitation or untimely death? In the legislation establishing the regency no provision had been made for a successor. Horthy had begun contemplating this potential problem as early as July 1934, when he privately suggested a procedure for selecting his successor: he would draw up beforehand a list of three men he considered suitable successors. The Parliament would then choose from that list.[76]

By late 1936 and early 1937 the idea of a further extension of the Regent's powers had gained widespread support. Even Bethlen, who had in the past quietly expressed his reservations about such measures, now declared publicly that most of the rights once enjoyed by Hungarian kings should be granted to the regent. It struck some observers that after seventeen years as head of state, Horthy had become a king in all but name. In November 1936 Horthy made an official state visit to Italy, where, in the words of a Hungarian diplomat, he was celebrated with "pomp that far exceeded what would be expected" for a Hungarian head of state.[77] Horthy was accorded similar "royal" treatment in subsequent state visits to Austria and Poland.[78] Foreign visitors to the Royal Castle in this period felt themselves to be in the presence of one of Europe's most distinguished elder statesmen. Joseph Davies, making a diplomatic tour of Europe in 1937 as President Roosevelt's emissary, had an extended conference with Horthy, whom he found to be filled with "vigor and confidence." The Hungarian Regent was, Davies reported, "one of the exceptionally strong and able men I have met in Europe."[79]

Given Horthy's enhanced stature, neither he nor his Prime Minister apparently anticipated any problems when, in the spring of 1937, Darányi presented to Parliament draft legislation for strengthening the regency and regulating the process of succession. No significant opposition developed to most provisions of the bill, but many delegates were alarmed by the possible implications of the proposed procedures for determining Horthy's successor. The legislation, which Horthy had helped draft, authorized the regent to nominate three candidates, whose names would be kept secret until his death. The Parliament would then be able to add other names to the list of candidates, but only through a somewhat cumbersome process that would have required a large number of delegates to declare publicly that they were not satisfied with the late regent's choices. Some members of Parliament, especially the dwindling but still vocal band of Habsburg loyalists, were outraged by what they regarded as a cynical maneuver to facilitate a secret plan to found a "Horthy dynasty." They suspected that Horthy would nominate his oldest son, István, and two other candidates he knew would be unacceptable to Parliament. Others feared that Horthy was being used by a clique of military officers who aimed to abolish Parliament and set up a military dictatorship.[80] Moreover, even among Horthy's supporters in Parliament there was some concern that the proposed changes encroached too much on the legislature's traditional role in selecting the head of state.[81]

The unexpectedly stormy debate over the proposed legislation in June 1937 greatly disturbed Horthy, who regarded as a grave insult any intimation that his motives were less than honorable. He professed surprise that anyone would fail to see that, after seventeen years as head of state, he was uniquely qualified to judge "what . . . qualities a regent requires in these hard and complicated times." The purpose of the proposed legislation, Horthy asserted privately, was not to promote any particular candidate, but to enable him to eliminate from consideration "persons whom I consider unsuitable for nomination."[82] Horthy's assertions of innocence notwithstanding, it seems probable that already in 1937 he had formed the opinion, on which he would act more forcefully in 1942, that his son István was in fact the person best qualified to be his successor.[83] In this period the only other person mentioned by Horthy as a possible successor was Gyula Károlyi, who, however, was only three years younger than Horthy himself.[84]

To quell the uproar in Parliament, Admiral Horthy was prepared to have the draft legislation withdrawn from consideration, since, he now argued, he had "neither demanded nor urged" an extension of his powers.[85] But in the meantime Darányi had been working behind the scenes with party leaders to find a compromise. An amended bill was submitted and on July 1, 1937, was approved unanimously by the Lower House. According to the terms of this legislation (Act XIX: 1937), the regent was no longer liable to impeachment; in effect, Horthy was made regent for life. His ability to prevent the enactment of legislation to which he was opposed was enhanced, although the new provision fell short of an absolute veto. The most significant change from the first draft of the bill involved the Parliament's role in the procedure for creating the list of candidates for the succession to the regency: names could now be added through a secret ballot, thus making it easier for members to expand the regent's list without having to take a public position. Although Horthy made no public statement about the legislation, and in fact proceeded to place the names of three acceptable successors (Bethlen, Károlyi, and Darányi) in a sealed envelope, privately he expressed unhappiness with the compromise that had been reached, which, in his opinion, rendered his role insignificant.[86] Ultimately, however, this controversial legislation made little difference, since Horthy later found another way to promote the candidacy of his son and, in any case, he was to outlive the institution of the regency by more than a decade. Moreover, Horthy never found it necessary to make use of his expanded powers.

Nonetheless this episode revealed that despite Horthy's immense prestige and the unique role that he played as the linchpin of Hungarian political life, his power had definite limits. Any attempt on his part to tamper with the traditional prerogatives of Parliament was likely to be met with the same alarm and resistance that Gyula Gömbös had encountered. This was especially true in 1937 because of fears that the radical right-wingers, frustrated by Gömbös's failure to make any substantial progress toward the establishment of a totalitarian regime, would stage a coup d'état and abolish Parliament. It was in connection with rumors of such a coup d'état that the name of one of the alleged conspirators, Ferenc Szálasi, first came to the attention of the broader Hungarian public.[87] Szálasi had in fact had no connection with the rumored conspiracy, but by the spring of 1937 he was beginning to be viewed by many as Gömbös's successor as titular head of the radical right-wing movement. A former military officer who had resigned in 1935 to pursue a political career, Szálasi was a spokesman for a new generation of right-wing extremists who had not been at Szeged. The program he espoused, known as "Hungarism," added strong currents of messianism, populism, and mystical nationalism to the traditional elements of the "Szeged idea." Even in the kaleidoscopic world of interwar Hungarian politics Szálasi must be regarded as *sui generis*. Totally convinced that providence had destined him to be the future leader of a totalitarian Hungarian state, he brushed away many early setbacks, including two unsuccessful attempts to win a seat in Parliament. His efforts to propound his political philosophy in a book and some pamphlets proved fruitless, for his prose was highly convoluted and virtually unreadable. Yet many were impressed by his single-mindedess, unpretentiousness, and sincerity. Through personal contact Szálasi was thus able to build a small cadre of followers, many of them young military officers, who believed deeply and fanatically in him and his political mission. For a long time the number of formal members of his party, known by various names over the years but most familiarly as the Arrowcross, remained quite small, but a much larger percentage of the population identified with his message and regarded him as an exemplary patriot. In addition, Szálasi's strident attacks on Hungary's capitalist establishment and his calls for economic justice resonated strongly among the workers, many of whom had grown disillusioned with the Social Democrats.[88]

At some point in the late summer or early fall of 1936, Regent Horthy must have been apprised of and become curious about Szálasi and his activities, for shortly after Gömbös's death he apparently instructed the head of his Military Bureau to make inquiries into this former officer and his activities. Lajos Keresztes-Fischer consequently summoned Szálasi to the Royal Castle and listened, with interest and perhaps even sympathy, to his analysis of the political situation.[89] After their two-hour talk Keresztes-Fischer asked Szálasi to submit a written statement that he could pass on to the Regent, who might then be willing to grant him an audience. The memorandum later submitted by Szálasi, whose party at the time counted less than a thousand members, was audacious in tone.[90] Szálasi argued that Hungary was faced by a severe crisis that the Regent could resolve only by drastic measures. The nation, Szálasi suggested, "believed in, trusted, and agreed with the Regent." However, Horthy was making the mistake of confiding in the likes of Bethlen, Eckhardt, Darányi, and Rassay. If he wished to avoid the fate of King Charles, the Regent must join forces with those who represented the true interests of the nation, that is with Szálasi and his movement of national renewal. Then Horthy and Szálasi, with the help of the army, would impose a "new order." The only solution, Szálasi claimed, was "the Regent at the head of the nation and with the nation."[91]

Keresztes-Fischer passed on Szálasi's memo to the Regent, who, however, found Szálasi's prose to be impenetrable. Horthy later showed the memorandum to Darányi, who gently urged the Regent to make sure that the military officers not interfere in policy-making. Any fears Darányi might have had that Horthy might be tempted by Szálasi's offer were unwarranted. More worrisome to the conservative establishment, however, was the extent of Szálasi's influence in the army officer corps. He was on particularly close terms with General Jenő Rátz, whom Gömbös, as the last of his key appointments, had named Chief of Staff in September 1936. Rátz subscribed to the idea, which was anathema to the older generation of officers trained in Habsburg days, that the military should play an active role in the political life of the country. He frequently consulted with Szálasi and, on one occasion, suggested that the two men work in tandem: Szálasi to mold the "new nation" and Rátz to mold the "new army."[92]

General Rátz and most of the younger officers were imbued with the notion that Hungary could achieve her cherished national goals only by armed conflict in cooperation with Hitler's Germany. To prepare for this eventuality, however, Hungary had to embark on a massive rearmament and sweep away all Jewish and Socialist influences. Rátz expressed his ideas in a series of memorandums that he presented to the government in the spring and summer of 1937. With some urgency he proposed a massive program of military rearmament and modernization. This was necessary, he argued, because by 1940 the Axis powers would enjoy a two-year advantage over the Western Democracies and would seek an "armed solution" of their problems. Hungary, by virtue of her geographical position and irredentist goals, would inevitably become involved. But, Rátz added, military rearmament would not succeed without a simultaneous moral and political rearmament. Thus he also proposed such measures as a reduction of Jewish influence and a more just division of the national wealth.[93]

Through most of 1937 Darányi and his colleagues remained cool to Rátz's initiatives, especially since his proposals seemed suspiciously similar to those Szálasi had made in his memorandum to the Regent. Kálmán Kánya, who was adamantly opposed to allowing military officers to encroach on the making of foreign policy, was loath to adopt any strategy that committed Hungary unalterably to the Axis powers.[94] Experts in the Finance Ministry were skeptical about the country's ability to carry out the rearmament envisioned by Rátz, especially since talk of anti-Jewish legislation was likely to cause alarm among leading bankers and industrialists. Meeting resistance elsewhere, Rátz managed to gain access to the Regent in June to plead his case. Horthy, it seems, was sympathetic, at least to the idea of rapid rearmament. He promised that he would pressure the government to give the matter serious consideration, and went so far as to summon a group of Jewish financiers to discuss the funding of rearmament. During that meeting Horthy urged his guests to show their patriotism and keep constantly in mind that the ultimate source of their fortunes was the Hungarian soil.[95]

Before long some details of these behind-the-scene maneuverings reached the attention of political observers, albeit in exaggerated form. During the summer of 1937 accusations were made, notably by Tibor Eckhardt, that Rátz and military officers in the Regent's Military Bureau were plotting with Horthy to carry out a coup d'état and establish a military government à la Pilsudski's Poland.[96] Concern about political meddling of the military officers, the increased popularity of Szálasi and the Arrowcross movement, and the threat of Nazi German expansionism was so widespread in Hungary by October that a unique attempt was made to bridge the political differences of some of the oppositional parties. The one thing that united the monarchists, Social Democrats, Liberals, and Independent Smallholders was the firm conviction that Hungary's independence had to be protected from attacks by the radical right-wing, whether launched from abroad or within. Accordingly, on October 10 representatives from most of these parties held a rally at Körmend in western Hungary and declared that the best course for troubled Hungary was a return of a king to the throne. To the surprise of many observers, Tibor Eckhardt and Károly Rassay announced their support for and confidence in Otto of Habsburg. The Social Democrats welcomed the cooperation of all anti-Nazi groups and hinted that in an emergency they too would support the reinstitution of monarchy. Few of the speakers at Körmend could have believed that a Habsburg restoration was possible in Hungary in the foreseeable future. The rally had mainly symbolic importance: it demonstrated that a significant segment of Hungarian society was alarmed about recent developments and realized the dangers of a close association with Nazi Germany.[97]

Admiral Horthy's reaction to the Körmend rally is not recorded. Certainly he too was an opponent of the introduction of Nazi ideas and institutions into Hungary. He had finally turned against Gömbös in part because of the suspicion that he aimed to establish a

Nazi-style dictatorship. On the other hand, Horthy remained strongly opposed to a Habsburg restoration and had come to regard Archduke Otto as a potentially dangerous, if remote, rival. Knowing that Hitler and Goering bristled at the very mention of the Habsburgs, Horthy had been careful to give assurances in this regard. He had told Neurath in 1936 that the "role of the House of Habsburg was played out," and no "Habsburg would ever ascend the throne of the Kingdom of Hungary again."[98] If, however, Horthy was merely unsympathetic to the political strategy adopted by the participants at the Körmend rally, he was positively outraged by what happened at an Arrowcross rally held on November 28 in Debrecen. There some of the more impetuous leaders of the movement proclaimed Hungary to be a national kingdom with Horthy as king. Leaflets were distributed emblazoned with the words "Long live King Miklós I."

What prompted this bizarre action, which Szálasi had not authorized, is unknown, but the impact on the Regent was far-reaching. When apprised of the Arrowcross rally by General Vilmos Röder, Minister of Defense, Horthy was so agitated that it appeared he might have a stroke. He declared that his worst enemy could not have done anything more harmful to him personally, for any Hungarian who aspired to be king of Hungary was in fact a traitor.[99] In a speech delivered shortly thereafter, Horthy deplored the fact that "reckless" people had used his name in an unauthorized and despicable manner. He proceeded to affirm what he had declared publicly seventeen years ago: he would not allow the person of the Regent to be brought up in connection with the throne.

Perhaps the most important result of this affair, however, was the strong aversion Admiral Horthy now developed for the Arrowcross and its leaders. Szálasi glumly noted in his diary that "from that day forward the Regent regarded with antipathy both Szálasi and all his initiatives."[100] Typically undaunted by this setback, Szálasi intensified his efforts to gain an audience with the Regent. He remained convinced that if just once he could talk personally with Horthy, he would immediately persuade him of the efficacy of his plans.[101] But Horthy had indeed decided that he wanted nothing to do with this would-be dictator. His contempt for the Arrowcross movement was deepened when in late 1937 he was informed by his conservative advisors of rumors that Szálasi's men were slandering his son István and plotting assassination attempts against members of his family. Szálasi did not help his cause when, in late 1937, he proclaimed to more than one visitor that in 1938 he would end up in power in the Royal Castle or in the prison on Markó Street.[102]

The tumultuous political events in Hungary during 1937 were capped in November by an important development in German-Hungarian relations that remained hidden from public view, unlike the boisterous activities of Szálasi and his followers. During a visit to Berlin, Darányi and Kánya were surprised to discovered a new mood of friendship and cordiality toward Hungary, a sharp contrast to the recriminations over the past year. Hitler now spoke candidly of his intention of redrawing the frontiers of Danubian Europe in the near future. The Hungarians need not fear this, Hitler declared, for he was giving his personal pledge that in the course of German expansion not a single Hungarian town would ever be touched. Moreover, "swastika propaganda" would no longer be directed at Hungary. The Hungarian delegation noted with great interest the strong hints of Hitler and Goering that in the not too distant future Germany would preside over a dismemberment of Czechoslovakia. Hitler assured his visitors that he supported Hungary's claims to the recovery of all of Slovakia. He wanted a "strong Hungary" and a common German-Hungarian border along the Carpathians. Goering even suggested that although for the present Hitler did not approve of aggressive action against Romania, he did not in principle oppose Hungarian territorial aspirations in the East. The realization of these goals simply had to be postponed until a later date.[103]

As word of the results of the Berlin visit spread in the Hungarian political establishment, those who had been agitating for a rearmament program were greatly emboldened. Even the more moderate and cautious Hungarian leaders, like Kánya, had to concede that the country had to make preparations for the crisis in Danubian Europe that now seemed only a few years away. Of course, Kánya remained intent on maintaining a firm neutrality between Great Britain and Germany and avoiding participation in a war on Germany's side. But no Hungarian statesman, least of all Admiral Horthy, believed Hungary could or should remain neutral if Czechoslovakia began to disintegrate under German pressure or internal disorder. Upon learning of the nature of the conversations Darányi and Kánya had had in Berlin, Regent Horthy could hardly contain his excitement. After consulting with General Rátz he summoned the Austrian military attaché, René

Eberle. Horthy began by referring to the friendly ties between Austria and Hungary "now and in the future," and then proceeded to speak openly of a partition of Czechoslovakia. The Slovaks, Horthy suggested somewhat implausibly, felt less threatened under Hungarian rule, since the Hungarian language stood in sharp enough contrast so that the purity of the Slovak language could be maintained. The Czechoslovak state, Horthy insisted, had no "justification for existing," and if it were to be dismembered, the Austrians could only gain from it. Thus, it would be a good idea for Vienna to participate in such a military operation, particularly in light of the possibility that German troops might in any event use Austrian territory as a transit area. Previous "binding agreements" would preclude this possibility.[104] That Horthy was not acting completely on his own was demonstrated several weeks later when General Rátz suggested to the Austrian Minister in Budapest, Eduard Baar-Baarenfels, that Austria join Hungary and Germany at the "consultation table" to plan a joint march into and a partition of Czechoslovakia.[105]

The Austrian leadership had no intention of following up on the proposal of Rátz and Horthy, which they regarded as an "insane plan" that had apparently not been thought out well beforehand.[106] Officials of the Hungarian Foreign Ministry, who were appalled to learn that the Regent and Chief of Staff had been infringing deeply on their sphere of responsibility, informed Vienna that the idea of joint Austrian-German-Hungarian planning for an attack on Czechoslovakia did not conform with official Hungarian policy.[107] Darányi or Kánya may have cautiously chastised the Regent for his unauthorized initiative, but it is clear that Horthy's exuberance over the prospect of a dismemberment of Czechoslovakia was, for the moment, sweeping away the inhibitions he had felt about full cooperation with Nazi Germany. Although in his conversation with the Austrian Military Attaché Horthy had spoken as if Austria would remain an independent state for the foreseeable future, just a week later he told the German Minister in Budapest that he assumed Austria would become a part of the German Reich not in "twenty or thirty years, but very soon." Moreover, the Germans could rest assured that he would never permit any policy that would involve Hungary in a pact with Austria and Czechoslovakia.[108] A month later, in a conversation with Ernst-Wilhelm Bohle, director of Germany's *Auslandsorganisation*, Horthy expressed his hatred for the French, whom he termed a "filthy people," and lamented the alarming signs of decadence he detected among the youth of England. He was determined to stand by Germany in all circumstances, "through thick and thin."[109]

Regent Horthy was not alone in responding enthusiastically to the news that Hungary was likely to reap great rewards from a German move against Czechoslovakia. The Berlin visit served as a spur to Chief of Staff Rátz and the group of restless army officers who were convinced of the necessity of modernizing Hungary's military establishment in preparation for the coming conflict. On the basis of information obtained from German sources, the Hungarian General Staff estimated that 1940 or 1941 was Hitler's target date for action. This allowed time for Hungary to prepare if rearmament was begun immediately. Thus Rátz now pressed even more forcefully for approval of his rearmament plan. When he encountered continued foot-dragging by the more cautious members of the Hungarian Cabinet, Rátz expressed his frustration by tendering his resignation. But Horthy convinced Rátz to stay on so that they could work together to find some solution to the problem.[110]

By the end of 1937 a substantial number of Hungarian military officers were sufficiently disgusted with the civilian leadership that they began to call for a military putsch. In late December General Rátz was urged to "proclaim a military dictatorship on a Fascist or National Socialist basis."[111] Rátz was unwilling, however, to take such a drastic step unless the Regent gave at least his tacit consent. To this end Szálasi and Rátz persuaded General Károly Soós, a senior officer with impeccable credentials as a Szeged veteran, to intercede with the Regent. During two audiences in early January 1938, Soós advised Horthy of the restless mood in the officer corps and handed over a memorandum in which he reported on the concerns and aspirations that had been expressed to him during a fact-finding mission that he had conducted over the past weeks.[112] According to Soós some of Horthy's finest officers, and the nation's "best sons," were deeply disillusioned by the failure of successive Hungarian governments to proceed in the spirit of the original Szeged program and the reforms that the "poor, departed Gyula Gömbös" had planned. Instead, Hungary's civilian leaders, though professing full support for a "Christian, national" policy, remained lamentably lenient toward the Jews and irresolute in dealing with the threat posed by the left. Kálmán Kánya's direction of foreign policy was neither decisive nor vigorous enough. Though his motives were no doubt honorable, General Röder, the

Minister of Defense, was flirting with Jewish bankers when, by all rights, he should be steadfastly promoting the interests of the National Army, which of course was "a Jew-free institution *par excellence.*"

Soós emphasized the urgency of the situation. Europe, he asserted, was on the brink of a renewed conflict, a "total war," in which Hungary would have to fight in order to achieve its cherished national goals. What was needed was a clear orientation toward Hungary's "true friends," the Axis powers, and a demonstration that Hungary would be a "valuable ally" willing to cooperate "come life or death." With war likely to erupt by 1941 or 1942, Hungary needed to create a "powerful combat-ready" army. It was the hope of the officer corps, Soós concluded, that Horthy would facilitate this by boldly sweeping away the ineffective civilian government and establishing an authoritarian right-wing government based on the military and the "Szeged idea." Hungary might be able to return to more traditional government in the future, but in the current critical times radical measures were necessary.[113]

For the most part Admiral Horthy listened carefully and respectfully to Soós's presentation, but his reaction was skeptical. When, for example, Soós pointed out that right-wing, authoritarian governments were now in place not only in Italy and Germany but also in Romania and Yugoslavia, Horthy retorted that the desired changes and reforms could be attained in Hungary "in the framework of the current constitution." When Soós suggested that the Regent consider whether the time had come to give greater freedom of political maneuver to the various radical right-wing groups, Horthy warned that such an action would be fraught with dangers. The Regent's most emotional response came when Soós gingerly mentioned that he had had the opportunity to meet Ferenc Szálasi and was impressed by his "sparkling idealism, imposing conviction, and powerful determination." Szálasi's program, Soós declared, was essentially the same as "our original Szeged program." If Horthy would only grant Szálasi an audience and speak with him personally, he would no doubt discover that Szálasi was in fact one of the Regent's most convinced adherents. But Horthy would hear nothing of this. The very mention of the name "Szálasi" seemed to enrage him. He shouted that he would not speak with a person like Szálasi who wanted to usurp the regency and who hatched assassination plots against his family.

General Soós was thus forced to report to Rátz and Szálasi that his intervention with the Regent has been a "total failure," and since Horthy had declared that he did not wish to discuss these matters with Soós again, there seemed to be no sense in pursuing the matter.[114] No doubt Soós was confounded by the change that had occurred in Horthy in his eighteen years as Regent. The Horthy of 1919 would have responded enthusiastically to such a presentation, even if he might in the long run have been unable to implement the changes that were being proposed. But after nearly two decades of service as the constitutional head of state, Horthy had grown decidedly more cautious and statesmanlike. He was convinced now, more than ever, that military officers should not mix in politics. His respect for Hungary's constitutional and parliamentary traditions had grown deeper under the tutelage of Bethlen and his conservative advisors. Moreover, he must have sensed that any scheme to overthrow the government would ultimately affect his own authority, for he had become an integral part of the political establishment.

Although Horthy rejected the more radical proposals of the officer corps, his continued vigorous support to the push for rapid rearmament finally yielded results in early 1938 when Béla Imrédy, the president of the Hungarian National Bank, was brought into the discussions. Widely admired as a brilliant economist with moderate political views and pro-Western sentiments, Imrédy expressed the willingness to assume responsibility for raising the funds to pay for a major expansion of the military forces. Although he strongly opposed the idea of a military dictatorship, Imrédy believed that some political concessions had to be made to appease the restless military officers and "take the wind out of the sails" of the right-wing extremists. Thus he proposed that a five year program of accelerated military rearmament be accompanied by new legislation to restrict Jewish influence in the economy and to ameliorate conditions for Hungary's agricultural proletariat. These measures, he argued, would be mild enough to be accepted by at least a part of the Jewish community, while still strong enough to prevent any further growth of the Arrowcross movement.[115] Since Darányi had also come to believe that a compromise solution of this kind was needed, and Admiral Horthy had no objection, a comprehensive program along these lines was now hammered out and announced by the Prime Minister in a speech on March 5, 1938, in the city of Győr.

This Győr program, designed to prepare Hungary militarily for participation in a war that the Hungarian General Staff estimated would erupt in four or five years, was thus launched only days before the first of the crises that would propel Europe to the brink of war later in 1938. The first tremor of the new crisis had occurred already in late January when the world learned that Hitler had shuffled his political and military leadership. Among those officers forced to resign was General Blomberg. This episode, which was followed by rumors that Hitler had intimidated the Austrian Chancellor during the latter's visit to Germany, caused increased uneasiness among those Hungarians who saw the possible rewards of collaboration with Hitler but at the same time feared that Germany might be an unreliable and indeed even dangerous ally. Even Horthy, who had regarded Blomberg as an effective brake on Nazi extremism, now expressed some misgivings.[116] In an eloquent speech to Parliament in early February, Count Bethlen spoke for many of his countrymen when he warned that "if our political system is subjected to a *Gleichschaltung* in the form of right-wing ideas, we will become Germany's slaves, not her friends, and in that case an independent Hungarian foreign policy will be once and for all at an end."[117]

Hungarians had little time to ponder Bethlen's words. On March 12 German troops entered Austria and the next day Hitler announced that the land of his birth would now be absorbed into the Third Reich. Hungary suddenly discovered on its western border a powerful, expansionist great power. For those Hungarians, foremost among them the Regent himself, who in the past few months had rather glibly informed the Germans that the *Anschluss* was inevitable and natural, the rapid development of events could only have a sobering effect.

7

The Coming of War

Although long expected by many Hungarians, the Austrian *Anschluss* of March 1938 occurred so rapidly and effortlessly that the psychological impact was nonetheless profound. Despite government instructions to the press to refrain from sensationalist headlines and stories, and the almost nonchalant attitude evinced by Darányi and Kánya in their official statements, most perceptive observers had to agree with Count Bethlen, who would later declare that since 1921 there had been no international event as important for Hungary's future.[1] There were many signs of uneasiness among anti-Nazi groups and in the financial community. By contrast, the right-wing extremists were jubilant, for it seemed that Hitler's triumph gave credence to Ferenc Szálasi's slogan, proclaimed in January, that "1938 is Ours!" On March 13 a large crowd of Arrowcross loyalists and other pro-Nazi Hungarians assembled at the German Tourist Office in Budapest, where they lustily cheered and saluted a huge portrait of Hitler that was on display.[2]

Miklós Horthy may have felt a tinge of nostalgia at the passing of the "old Austria," but he had long ago concluded that an independent Austria lacked a *raison d'être*. Yet when, even after several weeks, a mood of anxiety continued to grip the country and radical right-wing exuberance continued unabated, Horthy decided that he must take the initiative to calm the nation. On April 3 he thus delivered a talk to his countrymen for the first time in a live radio broadcast. In this short, meandering speech, Admiral Horthy spoke with the same sincerity and affable manner that had so impressed his many visitors over the years at the Royal Castle. The effect, one imagines, was similar to the reassuring fireside chats of President Roosevelt in the United States.

In his speech Horthy managed to touch on most of his pet theories and customary nostrums: the need for hard work and national discipline, the importance of overseas trade and naval power, the

207

impossibility of extensive land reform, and the role of Hungary as the defender of Western, Christian civilization.[3] Horthy's main purpose, however, was to persuade his countrymen that there was no basis for the "unrest and excitement" that had occurred in recent days. The union of Austria and Germany, he asserted, was merely a case of "an old friend who had been dragged by the peace treaties into an impossible situation," joining with "another old friend and comrade in arms." Rather than being alarmed by imaginary threats, each Hungarian, he suggested, would do best to trust in his government and take up his share in the reconstruction of the country. Those subversive elements who persisted in spreading "mendacious rumors" or were tempted to "fish in troubled waters" would be punished severely.

What most struck informed observers about the Regent's speech were his sharp, if indirect, criticisms of Szálasi and the schemes for establishing a military dictatorship that he and his officer friends had been floating in the past few months. Horthy condemned those who believed that military officers should be drawn into political affairs. An army that was engaged in politics, he asserted, was "not only worthless but harmful too." Horthy added that Hungarians were "freedom-loving people" whose liberty was safeguarded by the constitution. There was no place in Hungarian society for anyone who would "appoint himself savior of the world" and through "adroit demagogy" mislead the masses.

Both in Hungary and abroad Admiral Horthy's speech was well received and widely praised. It was, in the words of a Hungarian diplomat, "reassuring, moderate, and gentlemanly."[4] Of course, Ferenc Szálasi by no means shared that sentiment: he noted in his diary that the Regent's address had made "the worst possible impression."[5] Nor were the rapidly growing ranks of the Arrowcross party about to heed Horthy's warnings. Throughout the spring the right-wing extremists continued their agitation and, almost as if to spite the Regent, put forth the very kind of programs for extensive land reform and social welfare that Horthy had denigrated as "demagogy" in his speech.[6]

In the spirit of Horthy's April 3 speech a regulation was implemented later in April that required military officers to sign an oath to eschew political activity of any kind. This action, however, was accompanied by an inexplicable initiative launched at the same time by the Prime Minister, Kálmán Darányi. Although Horthy had made it quite clear over the past months that he detested

Szálasi and wanted to crush the Arrowcross movement, Darányi decided, without consulting Horthy, that the best strategy was to attempt to "tame" Szálasi and absorb his movement into the government party. Darányi had apparently come to the conclusion that Szálasi's blending of populism and traditional right-wing radicalism was genuinely popular in Hungary, even among the workers and poor farmers . In the long run government efforts to repress such a movement would likely be ineffective, especially if, as now seemed likely, the principle of secret balloting was to be extended to Hungarian elections even in rural areas. Accordingly, Darányi extended feelers to Szálasi, who responded favorably. By late April a tentative deal had been worked out. In exchange for a promise from Szálasi that his party would observe constitutional norms and play the role of a "loyal opposition," Darányi offered to allot the Arrowcross party a small number of seats in Parliament and to suspend police supervision of the movement. Moreover, if Szálasi would only provide a written pledge that he would not seek to come to power by means of a putsch or a military coup, Darányi would endeavor to facilitate a reconciliation with the Regent.[7]

Although a majority of the members of the government party would probably have approved of Darányi's initiative as a logical step in the strategy of "taking the wind out of the sails" of the Arrowcross movement, Count Bethlen and his allies in the Parliament were shocked to learn of the Prime Minister's machinations. When Darányi rejected as unfounded Bethlen's warnings about the dangers of flirting with totalitarian and demagogic movements, "the steward" immediately reported to the Regent on the activities in which his Prime Minister had been secretly engaged. Shocked that Darányi should have acted in a manner so inconsistent with the spirit of his speech of April 3, Horthy summoned him and demanded an explanation. The Regent was unimpressed by Darányi's arguments. He declared that he did not trust Szálasi's pledge of constitutional behavior, and that in any case he would not negotiate with anyone who spoke and acted in such a dictatorial fashion.[8] Recognizing that he had lost the confidence of the head of government, Darányi now offered his resignation, which Horthy accepted, although he insisted that this should occur only after the two legislative acts promised by the Prime Minister in his Győr speech had been guided through Parliament.

By April 1938 a strong consensus had developed in Hungary's political establishment for passage of the first of these measures, an anti-Jewish law that reinforced the concept of quotas that had first been used in the *numerus clausus* of 1920. Those Hungarians defined as Jews (religious affiliation rather than race being the determining factor) were to be limited to a 20 percent representation in the professions. Capital and property owned by Jews was not to be touched and the restrictive measures were to be phased in over a five-year period. It was a sign of the rightward shift of Hungarian political opinion in the wake of the *Anschluss* that the Jewish Law of 1938 passed without any overt pressure exerted by Germany and with only minor opposition from some Bethlenites and left-wing delegates. Most members of the government party, even if they had reservations, felt that to oppose such a measure was tantamount to political suicide.[9] After all, even the leaders of the Christian churches gave their approval, going so far as to argue that the law would be advantageous to patriotic Jews because it would succeed in disarming the real anti-Semites.[10] In these circumstances it was not surprising that Admiral Horthy, who had always spoken proudly of his role in establishing the *numerus clausus* in 1920, should voice no objections. Privately he remarked that it wasn't such a bad thing to frighten the Jews a bit, because otherwise they became too insolent. On the other hand, he did not favor too drastic measures, because the Jews were needed to carry out the planned rearmament. Besides, if the government moved too openly and forcefully, the Jews would simply leave the country and transfer their wealth abroad.[11]

The second important legislative act put forward in conjunction with the Győr rearmament program was a franchise law that extended secret voting to rural areas. Here too opinion in the political establishment had shifted away from the political assumptions on which Bethlen had established his system in the 1920s. Many of the "Gömbös orphans" and others on the extreme right believed that a properly administered secret ballot could be used to harness powerful popular sentiments to implement the Szeged program. The Bethlenites remained concerned that under a secret ballot the will of the people might be translated by right-wing demagogues into hostility not only toward the Jews but also toward the aristocrats, and thus to the plundering not only of Jewish capital but also of the estates of the big landowners. Admiral Horthy retained his wariness of the democratic process, but was willing to accede to what seemed now to be the will of the great majority of the government party. He reasoned that if in any future elections there were to be too strong a swing to the left, he would simply exercise his newly won right to dissolve Parliament and call for new elections. This was his "safety valve."[12] Horthy had not yet recognized what a more astute political analyst like Bethlen had already observed: namely, that the forces of the left had been considerably weakened in Hungary, and that the most likely beneficiary of the secret ballot would be the exponents of the "Szeged idea.".

Having accomplished his mission of gaining approval in Parliament for the new legislation, Darányi complied with the Regent's wishes and formally resigned on May 10. Horthy was intent on finding a new Prime Minister who would fully share his own views on certain critical issues. Political realities required that he be someone capable of winning the approval of the right-wingers of the government party, who were clearly in the ascendancy. By the same token, he would have to be acceptable to the Germans and in a position to ride Hitler's coattails to gain territorial revision, if this could be achieved without risk of war. On the other hand, he would have to be someone with pro-Western sentiments who would maintain Hungary's ties above all with Great Britain. Finally, the new Prime Minister would be expected to move vigorously to suppress the Arrowcross movement. Later events would demonstrate that no Hungarian was capable of performing such an intricate juggling act. But Béla Imrédy, whom Horthy appointed on May 13, seemed at the time to have the proper credentials. Certainly Imrédy was one of the few Hungarians of stature who enjoyed a favorable reputation in London, especially in financial circles where he had many friends. Yet, because of his role in facilitating the passage of the Győr program he was acceptable even to the more radical elements of the government party. Imrédy's devout Catholicism was also a factor in his favor, for the new Prime Minister would be serving as a host to the pope and many cardinals who would be attending the Eucharistic Congress scheduled to be held in Budapest in June.[13]

Imrédy's first actions as Prime Minister showed that he had learned at least one lesson from Darányi's downfall. He immediately made a public condemnation of the Arrowcross and issued an order prohibiting civil servants, many of whom were attracted to the extremist right-wing parties, from joining political organizations. Police surveillance of Szálasi was intensified. In the late spring of 1938 there occurred an incident that provided a pretext for an even more severe crackdown. The people of Budapest awoke one day to find the streets inundated with leaflets that seemed clearly of Arrowcross provenance. The leaflets bore the inscription "Long Live Szálasi!" on one side, and "Rebecca, get out of the Castle!" on the other. The latter was a reference to the Regent's wife, who, according to a scurrilous rumor that had been circulating for some time in certain extremist right-wing circles, had a Jewish branch in her family tree.[14] Nothing could have been better designed to infuriate Admiral Horthy and turn him even more forcefully against the Arrowcross movement. It seems unlikely that Szálasi, who called the leaflet "a filthy forgery,"[15] would have planned or approved this self-defeating operation, and it is even possible that the incident was masterminded by the chief of the Hungarian political police, József Sombor-Schweinitzer.[16] In any case, Szálasi was arrested, tried and convicted of subversive activities, and given a three-year prison sentence that he began to serve in August 1938.

In his foreign policy program Béla Imrédy was also careful to adhere to the guidelines that the Regent had stipulated. Horthy's enthusiasm for all-out cooperation with Germany in a future military campaign against Czechoslovakia had diminished considerably in the aftermath of the *Anschluss*. The so-called weekend crisis in late May, in which the Western great powers protested strongly against what appeared to be German military maneuvers aimed at Czechoslovakia, also had a profound effect on the Hungarian leadership.[17] Horthy remained convinced in this period that England, because of its great navy and "immeasurable financial and material resources," was still the world's strongest power.[18] He continued to hope that cooperation with Germany would lead to the recovery of some of Hungary's lost territories, and was particularly eager to exploit the situation should Germany decide to "settle accounts" with Czechoslovakia. But for Horthy and others of his generation like István Bethlen and Pál Teleki, the memory of Hungary's ignominious defeat in the last war was still too deeply etched in memory to dismiss lightly the dangers inherent in any collaboration with a Germany led by the unpredictable Adolf Hitler.

Admiral Horthy thus lent his support to the "free hand" policy that the Foreign Minister, Kálmán Kánya, pursued in the summer of 1938. Kánya attempted to carry out a pragmatic policy that would preserve the country's freedom of maneuver no matter how the current European crisis developed. Thus, at the same time that he was assuring the Germans that Hungary remained hostile to

Czechoslovakia, Kánya initiated negotiations with the Little Entente countries for a nonaggression pact.[19] He, Imrédy, and Horthy informed representatives of the Anglo-Saxon powers that Hungary's policy was entirely pacific and neutral. Budapest would maintain its freedom of action and refrain from any action that would disturb the European peace. If a military conflict did erupt over Czechoslovakia, Hungary would "play a lone hand" and would resist being dragged into war as an ally of Germany. Of course, if Czechoslovakia did break up, the Hungarian government naturally expected that its just territorial claims would be honored.[20]

During the summer of 1938, as European tensions seemed temporarily to subside, Regent Horthy presided over a series of state ceremonies and commemorations that were designed, in part, to reaffirm Hungary's adherence to traditional values and constitutional government and to proclaim the glories of the thousand-year-old Kingdom of Hungary. The Eucharistic Congress in May served admirably to emphasize the role of Hungary as an important center of Catholicism. The absence of a delegation from Germany tended to point up the essential incompatibility of National Socialism and a thriving Christian Church. Among the events in celebration of the 900th anniversary of the death of St. Stephen was a tour through the country of a special train in which the embalmed right hand of Hungary's first king was exhibited. Implicit in these events was a message intended for both the Hungarian people and foreign observers: the Kingdom of Hungary possessed sufficient historical roots and moral strength to resist absorption by the Third Reich. It must not be overlooked, of course, that ceremonies of this type conveniently served the revisionist cause as well, for they were reminders of Hungary's former grandeur in her pre-Trianon borders.

Although all through the summer of 1938 the focus of European attention remained on Czechoslovakia, Hungarian policymakers did not suspect that a crisis was imminent. Horthy, Imrédy, and Kánya thus had no reason to believe that a forthcoming state visit to Germany, which had been arranged many months earlier, would bring any major surprises. In early August, however, alarming reports began to reach Budapest from the German General Staff that Hitler had been in a warlike mood since the "weekend crisis" and was intent on an immediate confrontation with Prague.[21] More specific information was obtained from Helmuth Groscurth, who arrived in Budapest on August 20 as a secret emissary of Wilhelm Canaris, the Director of Military Intelligence in Germany, and General Ludwig Beck, the Chief of Staff. Beck and Canaris were intent on preventing Hitler from plunging Germany into a dangerous conflict. Granted an immediate audience with the Regent, who had known Canaris as a fellow naval officer in the Great War, Groscurth reported that Hitler was determined to settle accounts with Czechoslovakia by the "end of September or beginning of October." Hitler's decision seemed "irrevocable," despite the fears of his generals about the possible intervention of Britain and France, the generally pacific mood of the German people, and the inadequate supply of raw materials.[22]

This disturbing report on the eve of his departure to Germany prompted Horthy to make an immediate inquiry into Hungary's readiness for war. The response from General Rátz, who was now Chief of Staff, was not encouraging. The Hungarian Army was still in a very low state of readiness. Hungary possessed no guns of large caliber, few aircraft, and ammunition for only two days. Conditions were thus not favorable for either an offensive or defensive war.[23] The question of how to proceed was then discussed at a hastily assembled council of Horthy's advisors, which included Imrédy, Kánya, Bethlen, and Eckhardt.[24] Hungary was now apparently confronted with the one development its leaders had most dreaded: an early war over Czechoslovakia brought on by blatant German aggression. France, and probably Britain, would intervene, and Hungary would be placed in the most perilous of positions, open perhaps to an unprovoked attack by Romania and Yugoslavia. Particularly troubling was the realization that Hitler's own Director of Military Intelligence and Chief of Staff secretly opposed the Führer's plans. In these circumstances it was decided that if, during the visit to Germany, Hitler raised the question of a "settling of accounts" with Prague, the Hungarians, while indicating a general determination to proceed against Czechoslovakia "at the proper moment," would emphasize that "the autumn of this year is not very suitable, as our preparations are not far enough advanced."[25] Of great significance was Horthy's determination not only to reject any German offer to join in an attack, but also to attempt to dissuade Hitler from embarking on a military adventure in the current unfavorable situation.[26]

On August 21 the Hungarian party thus embarked on its journey to Germany with a certain trepidation that was not necessarily eased by the "fantastic welcome" that Joseph Goebbels, the German Propaganda Minister, had arranged.[27] As the Hungarians made their way by train toward the first destination, the Baltic port of Kiel, they were greeted at each station along the way by enthusiastic, cheering crowds of Hitler Youth. In Kiel, and later in Berlin, Horthy was feted in royal fashion.[28] The German newsreel recorded all the pomp and glitter: a huge military parade, a naval review, the christening of a new cruiser by Magda Horthy, and lavish entertainment that included a spectacular performance of circus animals.[29]

Only on the second day of the visit, August 23, did the time come for political discussions. The Hungarian party was taken on a cruise to the German island of Heligoland, where Kánya and Imrédy were closeted with the German Foreign Minister, Joachim von Ribbentrop, and Horthy met alone with Hitler. This was to be one of the most dramatic personal encounters of Miklós Horthy's career.[30] Hitler wasted no time in polite banter. Directly at the outset of the conversation he informed his visitor that he had decided to solve the "Czech problem" by military action in the near future. His plans called for Poland and Hungary to join in this operation. If Hungary cooperated and attacked Slovakia, she would of course keep that territory. As he had said back in November, Germany made no claim to any territory that had been a part of the thousand-year Kingdom of Hungary.

Although he must have felt strong conflicting emotions, Admiral Horthy refused Hitler's offer. He explained that Hungary was simply not ready for a military conflict. On the basis of information Hungarian general staff officers had obtained earlier from their German counterparts, the Hungarian government had assumed that the time for a confrontation with Czechoslovakia would come only in three or four years. Hungary's rearmament was based on that timetable. Moreover, if Hungary were to attack Czechoslovakia today, it would take England ten years to forgive her.

Hitler was no doubt taken aback by Horthy's negative response, which must have seemed to him completely incompatible with the very hostile attitude toward Czechoslovakia that the Hungarian Regent had exhibited during their first meeting in 1936. In response he offered to help remedy any military deficiencies of the Hungarian Army, and pointed out that if the confrontation with Czechoslovakia were put off for five years, England would by then be "armed to the teeth" and even less willing to forgive.[31] Hitler's surprise, however, quickly turned to extreme annoyance as Horthy rambled on with a lecture about why the planned military operation should not be undertaken at all. England, he pointed out, would certainly intervene, and, because of her superior naval strength, would triumph in the end. "You can mobilize in five days," Horthy said, "and put thirty Army corps here and forty there, while England will take perhaps five months to mobilize, but in the end she will inevitably win."[32] When Horthy persisted in this fashion it was, as a Hungarian diplomat later related, like waving a "red flag to a bull."[33] Hitler was unaccustomed to having his strategy questioned by anyone, let alone by the regent of a minor European country. In great irritation he interrupted his guest in mid-sentence and shouted: "Nonsense! Shut up!"[34] Horthy, who was not about to permit anyone to treat the Hungarian head of state in such an undignified way, promptly broke off the conversation.

Despite the firm stand he had taken, Horthy seems to have regretted that the conversation with Hitler had ended so unpleasantly. He did not wish to foreclose the possibility of moving jointly with Germany against Czechoslovakia at some point in the future. In his conversations with German officials over the next two days, Horthy seemed filled with "a wild hatred of the Czechs." He asked Goering if the campaign might be postponed until the spring, when the Hungarian Army would be in a better position.[35] He implied that he did not approve his Foreign Minister's policy of accommodation with the Little Entente.[36] Horthy thus wavered a bit, but he did not budge from his basic position, especially after one of the dissident German officers, General Walther von Brauchitsch, contacted him and warned again of the danger of a European war. Meanwhile, Kánya, Imrédy, and Rátz also stood their ground in their conversations, even though Hitler pointed out to them that "he who wanted to sit at the table must at least help in the kitchen."[37]

On the 25th Horthy and Hitler had a second private meeting, but this proved to be short and unproductive. Having learned that Horthy had been approached by one of the concerned German officers, Hitler reproached the Hungarian Regent and informed him that in Germany he alone made policy. Horthy's rejoinder that this was "a truly dangerous policy" ended any possibility of a meaningful conversation.[38]

As the Hungarians departed for Budapest, Hitler privately expressed his disgust over the attitude of the Hungarians, who seemed incapable of steeling themselves for action and preferred to sit around "listening to gypsy music."[39] For their part the Hungarians returned home fearful that Europe was on the brink of war. Quietly both Paris and London were warned of the belligerent attitude of the German leaders. Horthy seemed baffled by the turn of events. He remarked to the German Minister on the irony that he, "who for years had desired nothing more ardently than a speedy realization of Hungarian revisionist aims, was forced to sound a warning note owing to the international political situation."[40]

As the crisis deepened day by day and Hungarian irredentist groups began to demand that the government pursue a more active policy, Admiral Horthy remained cautious and even projected himself as a European peacemaker. On September 1 he agreed to receive in audience George Lansbury, the famous British pacifist and Labour party leader, who happened to be passing through Budapest. Lansbury was greatly impressed by Horthy's "hearty and genial manner" and his expressions of admiration and respect for Great Britain. He found Horthy depressed over the thought that Europe once again stood at the brink of war. The responsibility for the current crisis, Horthy argued, rested not with Hitler's Germany, but with Czechoslovakia and France for imposing "cruel and devastating" peace terms after World War I. Why, Horthy asked, would London ever contemplate going to war in defense of the "absurdities" of the peace treaties? He "hoped and prayed" for peace, but feared that if fighting erupted Hungary would be dragged in. As a possible way to avoid the "inferno of slaughter" into which Europe was about to be swept, Horthy suggested that he and Lansbury attempt to arrange a meeting of the five great powers, to be chaired by President Roosevelt. Lansbury, who had long believed that European war could be avoided only by a general conference of the great powers, did prepare a draft letter along these lines for Horthy to sign and deliver to the American president, but on the advice of Neville Chamberlain the letter was never sent.[41]

Although Horthy played no role in the negotiations, it was in fact a meeting of the leaders of the major powers (minus the United States and Soviet Russia) that ended this first phase of the Czechoslovak crisis. During September Hitler renewed his effort to persuade the Hungarians to join him in crushing Czechoslovakia, that "Soviet aircraft carrier in the heart of Europe." But Horthy,

Imrédy, and Kánya felt compelled to heed London's call for restraint and moderation. Stymied in his plan for a rapid military solution to the "Czech problem," Hitler reluctantly agreed in late September to attend a four-power conference in Munich to work out a diplomatic solution. The Germans were in no mood to champion Hungary's territorial claims. In fact, Hitler was now privately berating the Hungarians as "spineless dogs" who had prevented him from "laughing in Chamberlain's face."[42] Yet Neville Chamberlain, too, saw no reason to add to Czechoslovakia's humiliation by insisting on the immediate session of Magyar-inhabited areas to Hungary. Instead, largely at Mussolini's urging, a protocol was added to the Munich Agreement in which it was stipulated that the problems of the Polish and Hungarian minorities of Czechoslovakia would be dealt with by the great powers only if they were not settled through bilateral negotiations in three months.

Horthy and his colleagues were ambivalent in their reaction to the Munich Agreement. On the one hand, an unwanted and probably disastrous war had been averted; on the other hand, Hungary's claims had been virtually ignored. Germany, which had acted in a bellicose manner, had been rewarded with the immediate cession of territory; Hungary, which had taken at face value British promises that their claims would be the "focus of attention" at "the appropriate time," was faced with the unenviable task of negotiating a settlement with a delegation of Slovak nationalists. The rather fulsome letters of gratitude that Horthy dispatched to Hitler, Goering, and King Victor Emmanuel gave no hint of the frustration and disappointment that he and many Hungarians felt.[43]

On the eve of the negotiations with the Slovaks, Admiral Horthy decided to make yet another appeal to the British sense of "fair play." On October 8 he wrote a letter to Neville Chamberlain, not in his official capacity as chief of state, but as "a simple Hungarian, who loves his country above all."[44] Horthy called Chamberlain's attention to the promise that his late step-brother, Austen, had supposedly made during a visit to Budapest several years earlier: "Keep quiet now . . . when the right moment comes, England will help you." The "right moment" had now come, Horthy insisted. Would the British Prime Minister accept this promise as his brother's legacy and assist Hungary in her time of need? Chamberlain's response of October 28 acknowledged that Hungary had "legitimate grievances" but was otherwise noncommittal.[45] In fact, the dominant mood in the British government by this time was a growing aversion for the whole tangle of Danubian politics. In the Foreign Office the conclusion had been reached that any British initiative to support the "beastly" Hungarian government would be futile, since Danubian Europe had now definitely fallen into the German sphere of influence.[46]

In the circumstances it was not surprising that Hungary should join the other small countries of East Central Europe in a rather unseemly scramble to curry favor with Berlin. When the negotiations with the recalcitrant Slovaks ended in deadlock, Horthy on October 13 dispatched a letter to Hitler announcing that the Hungarians had decided on a partial mobilization of the armed forces.[47] At the same time Horthy agreed to a rather abrupt *volte face* in Hungarian policy toward Germany. Kálmán Darányi, one of the few prominent Hungarians who was still in Hitler's good graces, was sent to Berlin with the message that the Hungarians had had a change of heart.[48] They were now ready to follow Germany's example and support their claims with military force if necessary. Hitler was unsympathetic: the German Army was being demobilized and the best season for a military campaign was past. Besides, "Once I offered you all of Slovakia. Why didn't you take it then?" He then proceeded to lecture his guest on Hungary's past sins, especially the obstructionist policies of Kánya during the Munich crisis. Hitler was, however, somewhat mollified by Darányi's declaration that he had been sent also to clear up the misunderstandings that had arisen in German-Hungarian relations. Hungary, he declared, was now prepared to join the Anti-Comintern Pact and sign a long-term trade pact. Hitler responded by suggesting that he would see what he could do to mediate the Hungarian-Slovak problem.

After two weeks of confused diplomatic wrangling, Hungary's claims were arbitrated by Ribbentrop and Count Ciano at a meeting in Vienna. This first Vienna Award established a new frontier between Hungary and Czechoslovakia that was based, to a much greater extent than the Trianon settlement, on the ethnic principle. News of the Vienna Award was greeted with great jubilation in Hungary, although Regent Horthy reflected widespread public sentiment when he grumbled about the fact that two cities with strong historical connections to Hungary, Pozsony (Bratislava) and Nyitra (Nitra), remained in Slovakia. The Hungarian occupation of the "liberated" territory took place in appropriately splendid fashion. A huge gathering of prominent Hungarians, including the whole Parliament, formed the procession that entered Kassa, the most cherished of the cities regained by the Award. Characteristically astride a white stallion, Admiral Horthy received a tumultuous welcome from the local Magyars. His brief speech on this occasion was filled with the usual patriotic platitudes, although as a small gesture of conciliation Horthy, speaking in Slovak, assured the Slovak minority the free use of their language. But the general mood of the Hungarians taking part in this great celebration was far from moderate. On the signs and placards welcoming Horthy to Kassa were many jingoistic calls of "On to Transylvania!" and "Get the rest back, too!"[49]

In early November the clamor for additional territorial revision was widespread in the Hungarian political and military establishment. Even the normally circumspect Count Bethlen spoke publicly of the need to establish a common border with Poland, using military force if necessary.[50] In this heated atmosphere a plan was devised for a military seizure of the Czechoslovak province of Ruthenia, a small part of which had been granted to Hungary under the Vienna Award. Regent Horthy hinted at what was afoot in a conversation with the German Minister on November 15. Referring to the "untenable conditions" that were developing in "Carpatho-Ukraine" (Ruthenia) and the possibility of the spread into that province of bolshevism, Horthy suggested that Hungarian troops might have to march in and remain until the population had been guaranteed the right of self-determination.[51] Despite subsequent warnings from both Berlin and Rome that Hungary seemed to be blundering into a military fiasco, those Hungarians responsible for the planning of the operation plunged ahead in the hope that the Axis powers would accept a *fait accompli* if it were created quickly and smoothly. Emulating German propaganda methods, the Hungarian government launched a lurid press campaign that focused on alleged "Macedonian conditions" in Ruthenia. On the basis of a formal military order issued by Regent Horthy, units of the Hungarian Army were poised to attack on November 20. Then, at the very last moment, there arrived a severely worded joint German-Italian demarche in which serious misgivings were expressed about the Hungarian incursion into Ruthenia. Ribbentrop declared that the Hungarian action would "discredit the Axis powers, whose award Hungary had unconditionally accepted three weeks ago."[52]

In the face of this Axis veto, the Hungarians had no recourse but to back down and call off the military operation. For Horthy this was a grave humiliation. His personal order as Supreme War Lord had to be rescinded because of pressure from a foreign power. Over the next few months Horthy remained in a distinctly anti-German mood. Reflecting views that were now widespread in Hungary, even in military circles, Horthy complained bitterly that Hitler had become the patron of the Czechs and Slovaks. In this somewhat jaundiced view, Hungary's failure to recover all of Slovakia and Ruthenia was due to German malevolence. Ribbentrop had, he believed, favored the Slovaks in the Vienna Award and, by seizing a small area of strategic importance near Bratislava, Hitler had broken his solemn promise never to annex any former Hungarian territory. Horthy's disgust for the Nazi regime was no doubt increased in early December when Admiral Canaris visited Budapest and declared privately that some of the leading Nazi figures were "pure Bolsheviks."[53]

That the events of the Munich crisis and its aftermath should have created in Horthy such antagonism toward Germany is perhaps surprising. That those events did not shake his faith in Great Britain is even more remarkable. The British government had shown scant interest in Hungary's territorial claims and had by its actions suggested that Danubian Europe belonged in the German sphere of interest. Yet Horthy's disappointment in the failure of London to play the assigned role of a champion of Hungarian territorial revision did not diminish his Anglophilia. This can be seen quite clearly in the conversation Horthy had in early December with the Hungarian Minister in London, György Barcza, before the latter's return to his post. In a histrionic manner Horthy declared that if Britain did not triumph in the current struggle with Germany, it would mean the disappearance of all independent countries and human freedom. In other words, it would result in the end of Europe and of all that makes life worthwhile. If he had to choose, Horthy added, he would infinitely prefer that Hungary fall under British rather than German domination. England's shrewd and tactful policies made it possible for everyone to prosper. By contrast, the Germans were violent and inhumane. He wanted the British Foreign Office to know that he remained a "most sincere and enthusiastic partisan of England," and would do whatever he could so that London would look favorably on Hungary.[54]

Barcza was somewhat perplexed by Horthy's performance, for

Imrédy had just told him that the only correct policy for Hungary was one based on firm ties with Germany. How could that be reconciled with what the Regent had just told him? Horthy replied that, yes, Imrédy was now pro-German and the current international situation required that Hungary be friends with the Germans. Nevertheless, he stood by everything he had just said.

Horthy thus accepted the growing pro-German orientation of Hungarian foreign policy as a temporary strategic necessity, but neither emotionally nor ideologically was he comfortable with such a policy. His naive hope was that somehow through personal, private diplomacy he could continue to foster friendly British-Hungarian relations.[55] By contrast, Béla Imrédy was prepared now to pursue a pro-German policy with strong conviction, for he had undergone a dramatic political metamorphosis at the time of the Munich crisis. During his visit to Germany, Imrédy had been profoundly impressed by Hitler and by the dynamism of the Nazi system.[56] The results of the crisis convinced him that Great Britain could no longer be relied on and that Hungary could gain territorial revision only on the side of Nazi Germany.[57] Like Horthy, Imrédy had no special liking for the Germans, but unlike the Regent he was prepared to act forcefully and pragmatically on his new evaluation of the European balance of power. In October Imrédy thus initiated a series of steps, already described, to persuade Berlin that Hungary had indeed turned over a new leaf.

Admiral Horthy was prepared, for the time being at least, to sanction the major reorientation of Hungarian foreign policy that Imrédy was engineering. What jeopardized Imrédy's position, however, was his attempt to complement that policy with appropriate domestic measures that would lead to what he would later call a "gentlemanly Fascist dictatorship." Already at the time of his visit to Germany, Imrédy, like Gömbös before him, sought to ingratiate himself with the Nazi leadership by indicating that he too planned a "general rebuilding of the state" and further measures against the Jews.[58] In a speech in the town of Kaposvár on September 4, Imrédy spoke in general terms of his intention of promoting a "miraculous revolution" that would involve an expansion of social welfare measures and additional land reform. Imrédy couched his words in such a way that many now believed that he was prepared to don Gömbös's mantle and assume leadership of the Szeged camp. Whereas he had in early 1938 emphasized the need to "take the wind out of the sails" of the radical right-wing, it now appeared that he intended to join the extremists on board and position himself at the helm.

Imrédy's attempt to implement his new program, however, unleashed a political storm that remained largely hidden from public view because attention was riveted at the time on the unfolding crisis over Czechoslovakia. During a Cabinet meeting in early October and in later private conversations, Imrédy hinted strongly that he considered traditional parliamentary procedures too cumbersome. To achieve the needed reforms Hungary's government had to be "streamlined." This language, so reminiscent of that used several years earlier by Gyula Gömbös when he had tried to introduce elements of a Fascist dictatorship, caused alarm bells to ring for the conservatives in the government party.

Although several conservative Cabinet members had alerted the Regent to the brewing controversy, Horthy seemed largely unaware of the real issues at stake. This stemmed partly from his own growing inattentiveness to the details of political life and partly from the fact that Imrédy had apparently thought it unnecessary to consult with the Regent before he embarked on his program of reforms. When, on November 15, Imrédy tendered his resignation as was customary for a Prime Minister after the conclusion of important developments (in this case, the incorporation of the newly recovered territories in southern Slovakia), Horthy quickly reappointed the government. He continued to trust in Imrédy's abilities and, in any case, did not wish to create a government crisis on the eve of the proposed military intervention in Ruthenia.

Emboldened by his reappointment, Imrédy now elaborated on his plans to bypass parliamentary procedures, which were not "sufficiently fast or flexible." He began also to stress that more stringent measures against the Jews were necessary, since the legislation of 1938 was too tentative and mild.[59] In response Bethlen resolved to take up the gauntlet and thwart what he regarded as the Prime Minister's dictatorial plans. On November 22 Bethlen and over sixty dissidents announced their dissatisfaction with Imrédy and withdrew from the government party. On the following day there occurred an event unprecedented in Hungarian political life in the Horthy era. On a procedural vote Bethlen was able to muster a majority against the government. Stunned by this vote of no confidence, Imrédy had no option but to submit his resignation. Only now did Admiral Horthy realize the depth of dissatisfaction with Imrédy. Although he did not immediately accept Imrédy's resignation, on the basis that he needed time to examine his options, Horthy was sympathetic to the dissidents, whom he called "the finest men" in Parliament.[60] He gave Bethlen the impression that he would accept the advice of the dissidents. But when he sounded out the two men he considered suitable successors to Imrédy, Horthy discovered that neither Pál Teleki nor Ferenc Keresztes-Fischer was willing at that point to take on the responsibility of the premiership. Indeed, both recommended that Imrédy be reappointed, for to do otherwise would antagonize Germany and perhaps provoke a "right-wing insurrection" in the streets. In the end Hungary might be left with a Nazi regime installed by the Germans. Teleki shared the concerns of the dissidents about Imrédy's possible dictatorial ambitions, but he sympathized to an extent with his reform proposals, especially further measures to deal with the "Jewish question." In Teleki's opinion Imrédy would be able to gain majority support in the current Parliament for his reforms, which, once enacted, would have a calming effect on public opinion. If Imrédy in fact proceeded to act in a dictatorial fashion or flirted with the Arrowcross, the Regent could always dismiss him.

Seeing no other way out, Horthy summoned Imrédy on November 27 and, in the course of a two-hour discussion, informed him that he could continue as Prime Minister. In light of later developments, it does not seem likely that the two men discussed the details of the reforms Imrédy planned to implement. Horthy did, however, demand assurances that Imrédy would take additional steps to curb the activity of the right-wing extremist parties. It also seems likely that Horthy gave some warning about avoiding any activities that might be interpreted as dictatorial or unconstitutional.[61]

When Horthy made public his decision late on the 27th, he justified it by asserting that Imrédy's reform program apparently had popular support and the backing of a majority in Parliament. The greatly disheartened dissidents complained bitterly of Horthy's "broken promise" and his "unconstitutional" action. Bethlen was furious at Horthy's unexpected change of mind, which must have brought back painful memories of the Regent's backing of Gömbös in early 1935.[62]

Events over the next few months, however, demonstrated that Admiral Horthy's analysis of the situation was essentially correct.

The new anti-Jewish law, introduced by Imrédy on December 22, had substantial support in Parliament, including many members of the Smallholder and Christian parties that a month earlier had joined the Bethlenites in voting no confidence in Imrédy. The minority of delegates who opposed the legislation, including István Bethlen and Gyula Károlyi, raised a variety of economic, humanitarian, and political objections. They protested in particular against the introduction for the first time of a racial definition of a Jew similar to that of the infamous Nuremberg Laws. Imrédy declared that the law was designed to ensure that the capital and resources of the country should be largely in Christian hands. In the professions and industry the previous quota for Jewish representation was to be reduced from 20 percent to 6 percent, and a variety of other discriminatory measures were to be instituted.[63]

For unknown reasons Imrédy had not bothered to consult beforehand with the Regent about the anti-Jewish law. Perhaps he assumed that as a self-proclaimed anti-Semite Horthy would welcome any additional measures against the Jews. Perhaps Imrédy felt that his position was now sufficiently secure that he could govern in the Bethlen style, that is without bothering to bring the Regent into the details of policy formation. In fact, there is no evidence that Imrédy had political discussions of any sort with Horthy in late 1938 or early 1939. Horthy's growing frustration with the seeming arrogance of his Prime Minister apparently led to his curious decision to summon Imrédy's wife, who was widely regarded to be a kind of "power behind the throne." In a long conversation on December 10 Horthy hinted strongly to Mrs. Imrédy that he was not satisfied with her husband's performance. The Prime Minister's failure to take strong measures against the Arrowcross, for example, a ban on their newspaper, left the unfortunate impression that the government was weak and "cowardly." Although Horthy claimed to be in agreement with his Prime Minister about most things, he nonetheless went on to express serious reservations about the reforms that Imrédy was planning. He declared that land should not be taken from Hungary's landowning class, because "it was they who kept things in hand in the villages." Nor would he allow the Jews to be treated brutally, for it was they who carried on business and trade in Hungary. Such men as Lipót Aschner and Leó Goldberger (two of Horthy's bridge partners) performed a real service for the country. Horthy seemed unimpressed by Mrs. Imrédy's argument that her husband should be trusted because he realized now that it was impossible to govern in the old way, that is, moving a bit to the left and then a bit to the right.[64]

On the "Jewish question," which now loomed so important in Hungarian political life, Miklós Horthy had traveled a considerable way from the strident anti-Semitism he had exhibited in his Szeged days. It is notable that Count Teleki, with whom Horthy had fashioned the *numerus clausus* in 1920, remained a proponent of strong measures against the Jews. It was he who wrote the preamble to the second anti-Jewish law. Horthy continued to share with Teleki a belief in the need for "civilized anti-Semitism," but he was increasingly ambivalent. In the wake of the outburst of violence in November against German Jews known as "the night of the broken glass," Horthy privately deplored such actions as "brutal" and "inhuman." Perhaps he was influenced by Admiral Canaris, who during his December visit in Budapest declared that every honorable German was ashamed of the "brutal persecution of the Jews."[65] It seems likely that Horthy's continued socializing with prominent Jewish industrialists, which was sharply condemned by radical right-wingers,[66] contributed to his uneasiness about embracing extensive new anti-Semitic legislation.

When in early 1939 Horthy finally was apprised of the draft of the second anti-Jewish law, he immediately declared that he could not support it in that form.[67] Although Horthy expressed this view to a number of people, he stated his objections most forcefully to the British and American Ministers at a diplomatic luncheon on January 12. The Regent had, for reasons to be described below, worked himself up into a virulent anti-German mood in early January. To the amazement of the Western envoys, Horthy launched into a long and loud sermon on the sins of the Nazis and their imitators in Hungary. After denouncing the treatment of Jews and dissidents in Germany, he declared that he would not permit the anti-Jewish law to become law in its present form, since it was "inhuman and harmed patriotic Jews long resident in the country who were as much Hungarian as he was." Horthy did admit that given the general trend of international politics some action would have to be taken against the Jews, especially the "undesirable" Jews who had entered the country since World War I, but he would insist on certain amendments to the proposed legislation.[68]

Horthy's outburst before Montgomery and Knox was not simply an attempt to ingratiate himself with the Western great powers. In this period he also expressed his reservations about the proposed anti-Jewish legislation to the German Minister in Budapest, although he was careful in that case to use practical and economic rather than moral or humanitarian arguments.[69] Horthy reminded Otto von Erdmannsdorff that he was a convinced anti-Semite and agreed that the "Jewish problem" must be solved, but he nonetheless believed that one must not move too hastily or radically against the Jews. The Jews, he pointed out, occupied an extraordinarily powerful position in the economy, but in many cases there were no non-Jewish Hungarians to take their place. One could not, he argued, "butcher a cow but at the same time continue to milk her."

Horthy's growing disenchantment with Imrédy could only have been increased early in 1939 when the Prime Minister announced the launching of the Movement of Hungarian Life, a new political party that featured grotesque uniforms and assorted quasi-Fascist paraphernalia. This was too much for Bethlen, who declared that "no responsible Hungarian statesman could blunder in this way."[70] In mid-January Bethlen and his allies sent to the Regent a long memorandum in which the complaints about Imrédy's alleged demagoguery and dictatorial tendencies were resurrected. Horthy was warned that "the Jewish Bill does not serve Hungarian interests, but aims at satisfying base passions with the intent of propping up the position of a weak government in the eyes of irresponsible elements, irrespective of how much this success costs the country." Yet the dissidents did not call for the immediate dismissal of Imrédy. Rather Horthy was advised to allow the Prime Minister to gain passage of suitably amended versions of the anti-Jewish law and land reform proposal. Only then, when popular passions had subsided, would it be safe to drop Imrédy, appoint a suitable successor, and hold elections.

It would seem likely that Regent Horthy would have sought to discuss his disagreements directly with his Prime Minister, but there is no surviving account of any such conversation in January 1939. There are indications, however, that when Horthy informed Imrédy that he would veto the anti-Jewish law if passed in its present form, Imrédy responded by requesting a dissolution of Parliament and new elections in which the focus of campaigning would be the "Jewish issue." Horthy agreed with the Bethlenites that an election held on such a basis would stir up vulgar passions and grave disorder. In late January Admiral Horthy was thus confronted by a perplexing dilemma. He was now resolved to get rid of Imrédy at the earliest opportunity, for he no longer trusted him. Imrédy had failed to suppress the Arrowcross movement and had acted in a deceitful and unreasonable manner. Yet there seemed to be no way to jettison Imrédy without sparking a political crisis with unforeseen consequences.[71]

At this juncture there occurred a bizarre event that demonstrated some of the absurdities of Central European political anti-Semitism. In early February Bethlen presented to the Regent information obtained by Imrédy's opponents that seemed to indicate that one of his great-grandmothers had been Jewish. Asked to investigate, Ferenc Keresztes-Fischer reported a few days later that the documentation seemed genuine. This, Horthy quickly realized, was the pretext he needed for dismissing Imrédy, since the Hungarian government would be humiliated if the world were to discover that the Prime Minister who was sponsoring anti-Semitic legislation had a Jewish relative, however remote, in his ancestry. On February 11 Horthy summoned Imrédy and upbraided him for acting unconstitutionally by presenting to Parliament the proposed legislation on the Jews and land reform without first consulting the Regent.[72] No doubt Horthy hoped that Imrédy would realize that he had lost the confidence of the Regent and would now resign. When, however, Imrédy gave no indication of doing so, Horthy handed him the documentation relating to his family tree and said: "Well, what is this?"

The evidence, which later proved to be dubious at best, must have seemed superficially convincing, for upon perusing it Imrédy fainted and had to be revived on the Regent's sofa. Horthy did offer Imrédy a way out: "If you tell me this information is false, I will throw the documents in the wastepaper basket."[73] But the stunned Prime Minister replied that "I think this is true," and offered to resign. On the next day Imrédy gave a frank public explanation of his resignation: not only had he lost the confidence of the Regent, but a trace of Jewish blood had been found in his ancestry.[74]

In his memoirs Miklós Horthy was to write that he dismissed Imrédy in February 1939 because of his "rabid anti-Semitism" and his sponsoring of an unacceptable anti-Jewish law.[75] This, however, was at best a half-truth. Certainly Horthy had expressed strong misgivings about the proposed anti-Semitic legislation, but, as will be described below, he would soon allow Imrédy's successor to guide through Parliament an amended version of the very same legislation. Rather, Horthy turned against his Prime Minister primarily for other reasons, both personal and political. After his "conversion experience" during and after the Munich crisis, Imrédy seemed, in Horthy's eyes, to have become far too boastful, arbitrary, and deceitful. It was hard for Horthy to understand how a man well known for his pro-Western sympathies could suddenly become so infatuated with Nazi Germany, or how a Prime Minister who had had Szálasi imprisoned could later act so leniently toward, and even imitate, the Arrowcross party. It seems that Horthy, probably unconsciously, exaggerated his disagreement with Imrédy over the proposed anti-Jewish law as a way of expressing his growing distrust of and alienation from his Prime Minister. In effect he was saying: "I agree that in the circumstances measures of this kind must be taken against the Jews, but I have no confidence that Imrédy will do this in a honorable, Hungarian way."[76]

In the new circumstances brought on by Imrédy's downfall, Admiral Horthy was able to prevail on Count Teleki to accept appointment as Prime Minister. That Teleki approved Imrédy's anti-Jewish law and most other parts of his reform program seemed not to deter Horthy in the slightest. The important thing was that he trusted Teleki implicitly and had no fear that this Prime Minister would develop dictatorial ambitions or pander to the Arrowcross. Horthy thus did not object when Teleki, who in some respects was an even more radical anti-Semite than Imrédy, proceeded to guide the second anti-Jewish law through Parliament.[77] To satisfy Horthy and the spokesmen of the Christian churches, a few amendments were made to the draft proposal, including an expansion of the category of Jews who would be exempt from legal discrimination because of their contributions to the nation.[78] Horthy apparently was then satisfied that "the patriotic Jews long resident in the country who had helped to make it prosperous and who were as much Hungarian as he was" would not be deprived of their livelihood.[79] The second anti-Jewish law was approved by strong majorities in both houses of Parliament in May 1939.

The thing that truly united Admiral Horthy and Count Teleki in 1939 was their common view of the European crisis and the proper goals of Hungarian foreign policy. Like Horthy, Teleki was convinced that the Western Democracies would triumph over Germany in any military conflict. Teleki was realistic enough to acknowledge that some sort of cooperation, or at least the appearance of cooperation, with Hitler's Germany was unavoidable, since Hungary's room for maneuver was very small indeed. It was his aim, however, to pull Hungary back from the brink of a complete German orientation and maintain good relations with Great Britain.[80]

This policy received strong backing from Regent Horthy, whose bitterness toward the Germans had reached new heights in early January when an incident on the Slovak-Hungarian border erupted into a few days of full-scale warfare. Convinced that the Germans had become the patrons of the Slovaks and had instigated the event as "part of a deep-laid plot" against Hungary, Horthy vented his anger in a conversation with the British and American envoys. Hitler, he exclaimed, was a "madman" who was bringing the world to chaos. He had sent his agents into Ruthenia to foment anti-Hungarian feeling and to pave the way for German expansion in that direction. Asked what he would do if Hitler provoked a war, Horthy responded that "as long as he had the breath of life he would keep Hungary neutral." And to the question of what Hungary would do if German troops entered the country, Horthy replied bombastically: "We would fight them to the last ditch and start a European war!"[81]

The British envoy thought it not implausible that in a crisis Admiral Horthy might lead the charge against "eighty million [Germans] on his white horse," but he thought it unlikely that the Hungarian government or people would follow him.[82] Certainly the official policy of the Teleki government seemed to give no hint of a move away from the German orbit. On February 23, 1939, Hungary joined the Anti-Comintern Pact, followed two months later by withdrawal from the League of Nations. Horthy tried to minimize the importance of these steps, privately insisting, for example, that Hungary would never go to war for the other signatories of the Anti-Comintern Pact, least of all for Japan. At the same time Teleki gave his assurance to London that he would never do anything to "injure the interests of Great Britain."[83]

With Horthy's support the Teleki government attempted over the next two years to "straddle the fence" between the antagonistic, and soon to be warring, European camps. What greatly complicated this policy, and eventually doomed it to failure, was the inability of the Hungarians, above all Admiral Horthy himself, to show any restraint in the pursuit of additional territorial revision. Count Teleki was one of the few prominent Hungarians to realize that the long-term strategic interests of the country might dictate a moderation, or even temporary postponement, of the campaign to revise the Treaty of Trianon. It was a fundamental principle of

Teleki's political thinking that, in carrying out its revisionist policy, Hungary must strive to minimize any cooperation with Nazi Germany and solicit the support, or at least benevolent neutrality, of the Western powers. He reasoned that in the long run it would be difficult, perhaps impossible, to keep any territorial gains that bore the stigma of having been abetted and approved by Hitler.

These considerations came into play in the spring of 1939 as the Hungarians continued to search for a way to create a common border with Poland. Teleki strongly favored the annexation of Ruthenia, but he hoped to achieve this in a way that emphasized Hungary's independence of action. In principle Admiral Horthy supported this approach, but when on March 12 Hitler sent word that he intended to overrun Bohemia and suggested the time had come for Hungary to seize Ruthenia, Horthy was so excited that he quickly sent off to the German leader a somewhat pompous handwritten letter. "I cannot express how happy I am," he wrote, "for this headwater region is, in fact, for Hungary—I dislike using big words—a *vital question.*" Horthy indicated that a frontier incident would be staged and the Hungarian action would be launched in a few days. "I shall never forget this proof of friendship," he added, "and Your Excellency can at all times ever rely steadfastly on my gratitude."[84] A few days later Horthy issued a military order that called on the army to march "forward to our thousand-year-old frontier, to the rampart of the Carpathians, there to stretch out your hands to your Polish comrades."

The Hungarian occupation of Ruthenia was carried out quickly and with very little fighting. Every effort was made to suggest that this was an independent Hungarian action, not tied directly to the parallel German aggression in Bohemia. The press attributed this latest revisionist triumph to the magnificent leadership of Regent Horthy, who was glorified as the "expander of the country." Many Hungarians, unaware of the behind-the-scenes diplomacy, even believed that their government had created the common border with Poland as an act of defiance of the Germans. Teleki did nothing publicly to dispel this illusion, but Horthy dispatched an exuberant, one might say obsequious, letter of gratitude to Hitler in which he assured the German leader that he would never forget "this proof of friendship."[85]

Hoping to take advantage of the national euphoria over the recovery of Ruthenia to restore more stable political conditions, Teleki now moved forcefully against the Arrowcross party. This greatly pleased Horthy, whose indignation against Szálasi and his supporters reached new heights after an incident at a Budapest opera house on March 15. Just as the performance began, a group of young men shouted slogans demanding justice for Szálasi. The irate Regent rushed from his box, slapped the demonstrators in the face, and denounced them as traitors to their country. The audience responded to this spectacle with a loud ovation for Horthy.[86]

Admiral Horthy could take satisfaction in this sort of personal victory over the Arrowcross, but the elections held in May under the newly instituted universal secret ballot demonstrated that the radical right-wing had made substantial inroads in Hungarian society. The Arrowcross party, which, through a clever reorganization, managed to evade the government ban, joined with four other extremist parties allied to it to garner 25 percent of the vote. The left-wing, pro-Western parties suffered devastating losses, which were only partly due to the loss of the franchise that some Jews had suffered under the recent anti-Jewish law. In "Red Budapest" the radical right-wing parties outpolled the Social Democrats by a two-to-one margin. The old cadre of moderate conservatives disappeared almost entirely from Parliament; István Bethlen and Gyula Károlyi remained on the political scene only because Horthy appointed them lifetime members of the Upper House. The government party retained a comfortable majority, but within the party there was a perceptible shift to the right. Indeed, it is probably fair to say that only about one-third of the delegates were fully committed to Teleki, who managed to maintain party discipline only because it was clear that he had the strong support of the Regent.[87]

It is unlikely that Teleki could ever have gained a parliamentary majority to support the schizophrenic foreign policy that he and Regent Horthy conducted over the next two years. To be sure, Hungary's "official" policy in the spring and summer of 1939, pursued with apparent gusto by the new Foreign Minister Count István Csáky and constantly trumpeted in the daily press, seemed not to deviate from the pro-Axis course that had been set in November 1938. Moreover, the Hungarians were loath to do anything that might jeopardize their chance for territorial revision in Romania. On several occasions in this period Horthy spoke of worsening conditions in Transylvania and the possibility of a Hungarian attack.[88] General Henrik Werth was authorized to work up contingency plans for an attack on Romania, and Csáky toyed with different plans for snatching Transylvania.[89] But even the most ardent Hungarian irredentists saw the need for caution as the European crisis deepened, especially after Great Britain's guarantee of the independence of numerous states, including Romania.

Teleki and Horthy now embarked on a private diplomacy aimed at convincing the Western powers that, despite appearances to the contrary, Hungary had not fallen into the Nazi German orbit. On a number of occasions in the spring of 1939 Horthy assured the British and American Ministers in Budapest that his country would play "a strictly Hungarian political game" and would refrain "from rushing headlong into situations which in the past had cost it so much." He remained convinced that, if war came, Great Britain would triumph, since in the final analysis "those nations that cannot hold command of the seas will be choked to death." Hungary would thus strive to remain neutral and refuse to cooperate with the Germans, "whom most Hungarians detested." Of course, Horthy insisted, Hungary could not be expected to refuse Axis help in to the recovery of her lost territories if such help entailed no significant obligations. If war came, however, Hungary would hold back and then "like jackals feed on the carcasses of the losers." But if Germany should be foolish enough to commit military aggression against Hungary, his country would resist to the last shepherd.[90]

In late April Horthy began to receive reports from military sources in Germany that Hitler planned to make Poland his next victim. Even the most vocal of the pro-German Hungarians found it difficult to make a case for cooperation with Berlin in an attack on Poland. Like most of his countrymen, Admiral Horthy harbored strong feelings of friendship and sympathy for the Poles. In Horthy's thinking the issue was thus one of national honor: Hungary could not abet an attack on an old friend. In the intensive Cabinet deliberations over this issue some argued that sentiment should not be allowed to obscure the military reality. Germany was likely to remain the dominant power in Central and Eastern Europe for the indefinite future, and it would be unwise to incur Hitler's ire. But Horthy and Teleki insisted that this was one issue in which the country could and should remain neutral, especially since Hungary had no territorial claims on Poland. The decision was thus made that Hungary would not agree to participate "directly or indirectly in an attack on Poland."[91]

As the European crisis intensified in the early summer of 1939, Admiral Horthy sought, as he had in the previous September, to play the role of peacemaker. During the Munich crisis Horthy had devised a plan for an international conference to be presided over by President Roosevelt. Now he resolved to revive that plan for a conference, this time with the Pope presiding.[92] Teleki saw no reason to discourage Horthy, and, when sounded out, the Vatican had no objection to a Protestant head of state making such a proposal. In his speech opening the new session of the Hungarian Parliament on June 14, Horthy thus called attention to the perilous conditions in Europe and warned that "war would lead to a complete annihilation of our civilization." This calamity could be averted if the Pontiff, as "the most unselfish moral authority in the world," summoned the great powers to a conference at which all the problems threatening the peace of Europe would be discussed. The decisions made at this meeting would then be imposed on the smaller countries of Europe.[93]

Horthy's motives in making his proposal were not entirely altruistic, for he imagined that such an international conference would effect a major revision of the postwar treaties and "justice for Hungary" would finally be achieved. It apparently did not occur to him that for the British and French much larger issues were now at stake. Nor did Horthy consider the possibility that the Poles would not welcome his proposal, predicated as it was on the assumption that Poland would make, or be forced to make, substantial territorial concessions at such a conference.[94] In any case, Horthy's proposal went almost entirely unnoticed. The only person who seemed to take the idea seriously was the British pacifist, George Lansbury, with whom Horthy had sought to collaborate eight months earlier.[95]

Hungary's straddling of the fence in the summer of 1939 would have been made easier if Italy had provided some support. But Mussolini was pursuing an erratic course, at times wary of the Germans and intent on remaining aloof from war; at other times convinced of Germany's invincibility and ready to march wherever Hitler led. In July he was in one of his more bellicose moods. He warned Teleki that Hungary could not hope to remain neutral if war broke out, and suggested that Budapest reaffirm in writing its commitment to the Axis. Teleki attempted to do so in a letter to Mussolini and Hitler, dated July 22, in which he declared that if war occurred Hungary would align its policy to that of the Axis, so long as her sovereignty would not be infringed. Yet this statement, however much hedged, struck Horthy, and probably Teleki himself, as too strong. At the Regent's insistence, and over Csáky's objections, a second letter was composed and sent along as a kind of addendum to the first. Here it was stated that "Hungary could not, on moral grounds, be in a position to take armed action against Poland."[96]

This rather awkward diplomatic initiative, which actually reflected quite accurately the schizophrenic nature of Hungarian policy, pleased neither of the two recipients. Indeed, Hitler, who had not been planning any role for Hungary in the attack on Poland, was furious at this Hungarian impertinence and incredulous that any government would evoke moral factors to explain its policy. Count Csáky, who was sent to Berlin to try to explain away the fiasco, was subjected to a long and unpleasant lecture from the Führer, who reminded his guest that Hungary could not hold on to its present frontiers, let alone win additional territory, if Germany were defeated in war.[97]

The Hungarian government continued to straddle the fence as the European crisis moved toward a crescendo in August. On August 23 came the completely unexpected announcement that Germany and Soviet Russia had signed a nonaggression pact. Hitler privately gloated that this news would shock the whole world, but he surely gave no thought to what the reaction might be in Budapest. Yet no one could have been more surprised and appalled by this news than Miklós Horthy, for whom anticommunism was a litmus test of a right-thinking statesman. When German forces attacked Poland on September 1 and the second great European war of the twentieth century was unleashed, Regent Horthy was thus all the more determined that his country should remain aloof from the struggle.

8

Armed Neutrality, 1939–1941

The way in which Hitler had provoked into war in September 1939 no doubt strengthened Admiral Horthy in his view that the Germans were "buffoons and brigands."[1] Even in the company of pro-German Hungarian military officers Horthy now spoke openly of his admiration for England. The Germans, he argued, would find many obstacles blocking their ambitions. After all, in the words of the Hungarian proverb, "trees don't grow to reach the sky" (*a fák nem nőnek az égig*).[2] He was intent now on giving Count Teleki full support in fashioning a policy of armed neutrality. The two men were convinced that if the war took its full course the Western powers would triumph, but what form that victory would take could not be foreseen. Their hope was that the German leaders would soon come to their senses and seek a compromise peace; their fear was that a long, enervating war would leave Germany so weakened that the Soviet Army would find no resistance to its westward advance. The future course of the war was highly uncertain. What role would Italy play? Would Hungary's neighbors, Romania or Yugoslavia, eventually take sides? Given all the imponderables, it seemed imperative that Hungary be a cautious observer of unfolding events, ready to defend itself if danger threatened, but also prepared to respond opportunistically to any unexpected developments.

No formal declaration of neutrality was ever made by Budapest, and a reader of the Hungarian press after the outbreak of the war and through the entire period of the "phony war" over the next seven months could easily have reached the conclusion that Hungary's sympathies lay with Germany. But Teleki gave private assurances to the British that Hungary would indeed strive to remain neutral, even if circumstances made it impossible to proclaim this loudly.[3] In any case, it did not take long for the Germans to discover the ambiguities of Hungarian policy. Despite the fact

237

that the campaign in Poland seemed to be going well without any Hungarian participation, on September 9 Ribbentrop made an urgent request for permission to transport troops and supplies over the Hungarian railway through Kassa in southern Slovakia. As compensation for this cooperation, Hungary would receive a small oil-rich region in southeastern Poland.[4]

This unexpected request was discussed by Teleki, Foreign Minister Csáky, Chief of Staff Werth, and Minister of Defense Károly Bartha at an emergency meeting presided over by the Regent. Csáky and the two military leaders seemed tempted to accede to the German request. After all, Poland was all but defeated and such a small contribution by Hungary to the campaign could hardly be thought significant. Yet such arguments were apparently not introduced, since it was obvious that Horthy would not consider any action that would be inconsistent with his concept of national honor. As Horthy later put it, he "would sooner have died on the scaffold" than permit Hungarian territory to be used for such a dastardly purpose.[5] A decision was thus quickly reached and was shortly thereafter endorsed by a unanimous vote of the Cabinet: the German request would be denied, and Hungary would regard it as an unfriendly act if the Wehrmacht nonetheless tried to force the issue. Horthy suggested that the Germans be informed that he was having the railways and bridges mined and was prepared to have them blown up if necessary.[6]

This defiance of the Germans had more symbolic than practical importance, since Poland was on the verge of collapse anyway. It did, however, provide one important service to the Poles. By keeping Wehrmacht forces at a distance from the Polish-Hungarian frontier, the passage of Polish war refugees into Hungary was facilitated. As a result, in the last days of the German invasion more than 70,000 Poles sought haven in Hungary, where they were welcomed and treated virtually as honored guests. Most of the refugees were soldiers and officers who eventually made their way to France and Great Britain. Both at the time and after the war Admiral Horthy took great pride in Hungary's "honorable" behavior and the assistance it provided the Allied war effort.[7]

The Germans naturally showed no understanding for Horthy's concept of national honor and took deep offense at Hungary's almost ostentatious display of benevolent neutrality toward Poland. Among his cronies Hitler sharply denounced the "Horthy clique" as "friendly to the Jews, hostile to the Germans, and infinitely egotistical."[8] To show his displeasure Hitler ordered an immediate embargo on the shipment of arms to Hungary. This made a deep impression on Hungarian General Staff officers, the majority of whom had been eager for the army to join with Germany in the Polish campaign. Discontent among the officers spread rapidly and found expression in complaints that Teleki and Ferenc Keresztes-Fischer were hopelessly pro-British. The grumbling about Horthy intensified: it seemed inappropriate that he should continue to play bridge with his Jewish friends twice a week during the current crisis. At a Cabinet meeting in early October General Werth threatened to resign in protest of the "zigzag course of the government." The officers even dropped hints to Erdmannsdorff and the German military attaché that they would welcome German pressure to overthrow Teleki.[9]

At some point in October Werth reported directly to the Regent on the increasingly negative attitude of the officers toward the government and the need to placate the Germans. Horthy was not about to turn against Teleki and Keresztes-Fischer, for he regarded them as his most trusted advisors. Nonetheless, he shared with the military officers an admiration for the military achievements of the Wehrmacht in the Polish campaign and saw the need to restore an amicable relationship with Germany so that the arms embargo could be quickly lifted. Horthy decided to undertake a bit of personal diplomacy. In early November he sent off to Hitler an assortment of Hungarian fruits and an accompanying letter that was meant to clear up misunderstandings and even give helpful hints to the German leader on his future political strategy.

The Regent's discursive letter of November 3 contained the usual litany of complaints about Hungary's unfair treatment at the Paris Peace Conference and refutations of accusations that Hungary had oppressed her minorities.[10] Then, without referring to Hungary's policy during the Polish campaign or the German arms embargo, Horthy expressed surprise that the relationship between the Germany and Hungary had recently deteriorated. He reminded Hitler that the Hungarians had always been "loyal comrades-in-arms" and had remained "true friends" even when the whole world turned against Germany after World War I. Since Hungary's attitude had not changed in recent days, he could only conclude that German leaders had been misled by "falsely colored reports and mendacious accounts" by Arrowcross members and other "contemptible individuals" who were trying to drive a wedge between the two countries. He assured Hitler that the Hungarians remained "a grateful and reliable people" who realized their debt to the German nation and would support the German war effort with all the foodstuffs that could be spared. He himself was prepared to help out in any way: "If you should, perhaps, some day wish to make use of my services in some other way, in absolute secrecy, for very confidential negotiations, I shall always be available—except for Easter." Here Horthy seemed to be suggesting that he would be a suitable mediator between Germany and the Western powers.

In his letter Horthy could not resist making an indirect criticism of the Nazi-Soviet Pact. Claiming that he had reliable confidential information about and special insight into the nature of the Soviet regime, Horthy warned that Russia would be an unreliable partner. Following the principles set down by Lenin, Stalin would try to embroil other countries in the war and, when others had exhausted themselves, intervene with the Red Army and win "the final victory of world revolution."

Hitler's response to the Horthy's letter is not recorded. By 1939 he surely was no longer surprised to receive such unconventional missives from the Hungarian Regent. It is possible, in fact, that Hitler found Horthy's letters diverting, in a sense even flattering. After all, what other European statesman thought it appropriate, or worthwhile, to send personal letters to the German Führer on a regular basis? Who else but Admiral Horthy would compose and handwrite his letters in a quaint, somewhat archaic, German style? Who would think to try to lecture Hitler on the evils of communism and the true nature of Soviet policy? Certainly Hitler found unconvincing Horthy's rather feeble attempts to attribute the friction between Germany and Hungary to misunderstandings and the malicious activity of the Arrowcross. Nor did he have any use for Horthy's services as a mediator in the war, least of all at Easter time in 1940, when the Wehrmacht was poised for a massive invasion of France and the Low Countries. Yet Hitler somehow found it impossible to abandon all hope that Horthy would in the long run be a useful collaborator. Over the next several years he would often rant about the corrupt "Horthy clique," but only in the last months of the war, after Horthy had caused him considerable aggravation, did he turn definitively against him.

Hitler's strategy in late 1939 and 1940 required stable conditions in Southeastern Europe and a steady flow of Romanian oil and

Hungarian grain to facilitate his campaign in the West. For this reason he agreed in December to lift the arms embargo on Hungary in exchange for certain economic concessions rather reluctantly offered by Teleki. At the same time the Germans insisted that Hungary refrain from any further revisionist activity against Romania. Count Teleki was inclined, for his own reasons that have already been outlined, to put the question of further treaty revision "on ice," but irredentist sentiment among politically aware Hungarians did not abate with the outbreak of the war. The idea that, in one way or other, Transylvania must be regained before the end of the war was soon widespread in the officer corps. More importantly, Horthy himself seized on this idea, especially as the recovery of territory from Romania could, in his mind, be linked with the kind of grand crusade against Bolshevik Russia that he had long advocated.

In separate conversations with the American and British envoys in Budapest during November, Horthy expressed his belief that the Soviets planned soon to seize the province of Bessarabia and continue their imperialist drive toward the Turkish Straits.[11] He hinted strongly that the best response to this threat would be a reconciliation of Germany and the Western powers and a joint campaign of all European states against the Soviet Union. Horthy warned, however, that Romania was not qualified militarily or politically to "resist the threats or embraces of Russia." The Romanians were neither honest nor loyal nor steadfast. Hungary, by contrast, "was predestined by history and geography to hold at bay alike the insidious propaganda of the Comintern and the immense forces which the Soviet government could put into the field." By seizing Transylvania and setting up a military frontier on the Carpathians, Hungary would thus truly be serving the interests of European civilization. To be sure, Romania had numerical superiority and new fortifications built, to his regret, "with French advice and English money," but Horthy still expressed confidence that his army of "half-trained, poorly equipped, but stout-hearted peasants" could "push the Romanian army off the Carpathian ridges at any time."

Count Teleki certainly agreed with the Regent about the desirability of building a European anti-Soviet bloc and persuading the Western powers to rely on an expanded Hungary as a bulwark against the Communist East.[12] As a native Transylvanian, he yearned for the day when that province, or a large part of it, would be returned to Hungary. He was willing to ply the British and Americans with maps and statistics to try to win them over. But nothing that happened in the opening months of the war altered his conviction that Germany would lose the war, and that any territorial gains made with Berlin's assistance would be nothing but "withering laurels." Privately he argued against a policy of "immediate successes," one which demanded "everything back, no matter how, with whose help, or at what cost."[13] Teleki was gravely apprehensive about the unbridled irredentism prevalent in the officer corps, for, as he complained to a confidant at the end of 1939, the Regent "believes everything the soldiers tell him."[14]

Although, as events would demonstrate, Admiral Horthy would not always agree with the General Staff on major policy questions, he did share the officers' admiration for the early successes of the German *Blitzkrieg*.[15] He continued to believe that the Western powers would be the ultimate victors, and he deplored the way that the Germans acted like "an elephant in the porcelain shop." But, as he told György Barcza late in 1939, one had to recognize that, unlike the English, the Germans were natural, if perhaps brutal, soldiers. Hungary should continue to avoid joining the war on Germany's side, but Hungary would be foolish to pass up opportunities for treaty revision made possible by German victories. Attempts at peaceful revision had always left Hungary empty-handed. It was clear, Horthy now concluded, that "without force there is no success, and without courage there are no results." Horthy brushed aside Teleki's argument that any territory gained without the sanction of the Western powers would be lost forever at the peace conference. On several occasions he argued privately that once the lost provinces were regained, no one would ever be able to wrest them away again. His splendid army would see to that.[16]

Hungary's policy of armed neutrality had not yet been put to a severe test by March 1, 1940, the twentieth anniversary of Miklós Horthy's election to the regency. In recognition of the gravity of the European crisis, there were no lavish ceremonies and festivities of the kind that had marked the ten-year jubilee in 1930. Instead, Horthy quietly received in audience a procession of foreign envoys who brought with them flattering tributes to one of Europe's most durable elder statesmen. King George and President Roosevelt sent signed photographs.[17] The kings of Norway, Sweden, and Denmark conferred on him the insignia of their highest orders of knighthood. Those who met with Admiral Horthy in these days found a seventy-two year old man who, it was generally agreed, had "aged well" and retained his "vigor of speech and gesture."[18] His continued regimen of physical exercise through swimming, tennis, and hunting had clearly contributed to Horthy's excellent health. At this point his mental faculties also seemed largely unimpaired.

Horthy's twenty-year tenure as Hungary's head of state cannot, however, be said to have brought him political wisdom or a more sophisticated understanding of European diplomacy. He had, it is true, learned to be somewhat more discreet when dealing with foreign statesmen, and, as will be seen, on certain subjects like land reform he was not totally incapable of adjusting to new realities. But, for good or bad, Horthy's old personal habits, idiosyncrasies, and ingrained patterns of thought had remained largely unaltered by the passing years. In normal times this would be of little import, since elderly heads of state usually yield to reality or the gentle persuasion of their advisors and withdraw from an active role in political life. This was by no means true of Regent Horthy in 1940; indeed, some of the most trying experiences and most difficult decisions of his political career were yet to come.

Miklós Horthy's rise to political prominence in the postwar period had been based in large part on the unique position he came to occupy as the "link and the compromise" between various Hungarian political factions. During World War II Horthy would continue to play this role. Indeed, it was largely through his mediating influence that an uneasy equilibrium was maintained in a society that might otherwise have been torn apart by ideological conflicts. By 1940 Horthy's prestige and popularity in Hungary were immense. No public opinion polls can be cited to document this assertion, but there is a good deal of indirect evidence. The country had shaken off the last traces of the Depression and, thanks in large part to war-related production and substantially increased trade with Germany, was enjoying an economic boom. Almost full employment had been attained and food was in plentiful supply. Hungary truly was, as one British visitor noted at the time, an "island of plenty."[19] The great surge in nationalist feelings that had accompanied the recovery of southern Slovakia and Ruthenia also redounded to Horthy's favor, for he was widely hailed as the man responsible for these successes, the true "expander of the country."

Because Horthy was himself ambivalent about so many fundamental issues confronting the Hungarian nation, he was able to retain the support of widely disparate groups. Fanatical irredentists, cautious pro-Westerners, pro-German army officers, and even many Hungarian Jews could imagine that when the time for great decisions arrived, Horthy would take their interests into account. Unfortunately, Horthy played this mediating role almost inadvertently and not on the basis of a conscious, well-thought-out strategy. He lacked the political acumen to detect the inconsistencies in some of the policies he supported. Thus he was able to convince himself that Hungary could proceed to regain her lost territories by almost any means, even with German help, and still not damage her standing with the likely victors in the war, the Anglo-Saxon powers. After all, as he boasted privately in early 1940, the fact that he was a sincere Anglophile was well known in London and helped account for his popularity in Great Britain.[20]

That by the spring of 1940 many in the British political establishment had come to appreciate Admiral Horthy as one of the few East European statesmen who remained friendly to their country can not be gainsaid. The British Minister in Budapest, Sir Owen O'Malley, became an ardent admirer of Horthy and reported to his superiors that so far as the British government was interested in the preservation of Hungarian independence and neutrality, "they can have no better friend than Admiral Horthy."[21] In the British Foreign Office there was little support for Hungary's revisionist plans, but it was thought useful to encourage Horthy and Teleki in their policy of armed neutrality. One way to do this was to flatter the Hungarian Regent. Thus, Alexander Cadogan told Barcza in March 1940 that Horthy "was one of the most popular and most respected of Europe's leading figures" and was "especially sympathetic to the British because they honored in him the chivalrous sailor and gentleman."[22]

A striking public expression of British admiration for Regent Horthy appeared in a *London Times* editorial at the time of his twenty-year anniversary. There Horthy was commended for the forthright and statesmanlike manner in which he had dealt with the many crises of his regency. The tributes that he now received were thus "hard-earned and thoroughly deserved." The editorialist even showed some understanding for Hungary's territorial claims, and suggested that the time would no doubt come when the great European conference that Horthy had proposed in his

June 1939 speech would be convened. If Horthy's government continued its policy of forbearance in its just quest for treaty revision, the Hungarians would have a "still better title to be heard later than they had already."

One can perhaps understand how these words of praise could convince Horthy that the British understood and sympathized with his policies. Yet he completely failed to recognize that the popularity he enjoyed in London would be undermined if he abandoned the "forbearance" for which he was lauded. On several occasions György Barcza tried, in vain, to convince Horthy that just because he continued to affirm his sincere Anglophilism did not mean that he could act with impunity in pursuing territorial revision. Horthy took no heed of such warnings; nor, apparently, did he consider that a David Low cartoon that appeared in the *Picture Post* late in 1940 might in fact be a better reflection of his standing in British society. There a diminutive Horthy, in naval uniform, is depicted posing for a family photograph with Hitler and an assembly of his collaborators, including Stalin, who is represented only by a boot with the name "Joe" on it. Above this ragtag group is the heading "Europe United for the Axis."[23]

Admiral Horthy regarded it as a grave insult to be portrayed as a crony of Hitler and Marshal Ian Antonescu, the Romanian leader, let alone of Joseph Stalin. Had he not, in March 1940, warned the British Minister of a likely German attack in the West and described Hitler as "mentally abnormal"? Had he not, on the same occasion, lamented the possibility that "such a frightful disaster to humanity and particularly to the flower of Europe's youth should be about to flow from the mad prepossessions of a single man...."[24] In fact, however, Horthy was to be dazzled by Germany's military successes as the spring campaign in the West unfolded. He was particularly impressed by the shrewd strategy that Hitler employed to outfox the British and occupy Denmark and Norway.[25]

These German successes emboldened General Werth to compose a memorandum he submitted to the Regent and Prime Minister in mid-April. Hitler's successes in Scandinavia, Werth asserted, demonstrated the invincibility of the Wehrmacht. The time had come for Hungary "to abandon its policy of neutrality and nonintervention and to take a stand with Germany in this struggle." Only in that way could Hungary's thousand-year frontiers be recovered.[26]

Count Teleki was infuriated by Werth's memorandum, which

he regarded as an unwarranted interference of the Chief of Staff in a governmental matter beyond his sphere of authority. In a letter to Horthy dated April 18, Teleki noted sarcastically that Werth's position was understandable, since as a Schwab, "a non-Magyar," he could not be expected to understand the great problems of preserving the independence of the country or the "dangers of German penetration."[27] A German victory, Teleki warned, was by no means certain, and for that reason it would be a mistake to make a "total and spiritual" military commitment to Berlin. "We have carried off our policy well up to now," he declared. "Let's not jeopardize our position here at the last moment." At the same time Teleki implored Horthy to rein in the General Staff: "See to it that the soldiers don't mix in politics!"

Werth seemed undaunted by this criticism; in early May he submitted another memorandum in which he reiterated his earlier arguments and strongly urged that Hungary sign a military and political alliance with Germany. A highly irritated Teleki thereupon informed Horthy that he would immediately resign if Hungary were to form an alliance with Hitler's Germany.[28] Horthy's response, if any, to these sharp exchanges between his Prime Minister and Chief of Staff is not known. In any case, Teleki's position seemed increasingly untenable in May and early June as German forces moved relentlessly into France. Italy entered the war on June 10 and Paris was occupied by the German forces a few days later. These events were greeted with jubilation by many Hungarians, even by some in the liberal camp.[29] Few mourned the defeat of France, which had always been regarded as the great power most responsible for Hungary's humiliating treatment after the Great War. Reflecting this sentiment, and implicitly acknowledging that he had not anticipated such a rapid and complete German victory, Teleki declared publicly in mid-June that "the Europe of Versailles and Trianon" had finally been dismantled. He even evoked the memory of Gyula Gömbös, suggesting that his dream of a new Europe had now been realized.[30]

In the opinion of many influential Hungarians, however, the course of events had thoroughly discredited Teleki and his pro-Western policies. In June there were many public calls for his resignation. Among those who privately urged Horthy to drop his Prime Minister was Bálint Hóman, the Minister of Culture. Hóman, a distinguished historian, called on the Regent to "draw all the consequences from the new European conditions" and make a total commitment, both in foreign and domestic policy, to Nazi Germany.[31] But Horthy refused to bow to these pressures and to the political reality that Teleki's support in Parliament had seriously eroded. When Teleki offered to resign, Horthy urged him to stay on. Apparently he believed that, so long as Britain remained unbeaten, it would still be possible for Hungary to cling to its armed neutrality. In any case, the list of acceptable successors to Teleki was short. Horthy wanted nothing more to do with Béla Imrédy, who had managed to escape the opprobrium of the previous year's events to emerge as the spokesman for the extremist right-wing forces. Those few politicians whom Horthy knew well and still trusted, such as Ferenc Keresztes-Fischer, Gyula Károlyi, and István Bethlen, were fashioned from the same political mold as Teleki.

Count Teleki agreed only with reluctance to continue on as Prime Minister, for he realized that Horthy was likely to be more receptive than ever to the advice of the military leaders. General Werth now lost no opportunity of reminding the Regent of how needlessly alarmist and pessimistic the Prime Minister had been in the spring.[32] On the critical issue facing Hungary in the summer of 1940, however, Teleki was largely at one with his critics. In late June Soviet Russia used a threat of force to compel Romania to cede Bessarabia and other territory. There immediately arose a great clamor in Hungary for the "liberation" of the Magyars of Romania, who, as Horthy himself put it, were "impatiently pounding on their prison bars. . . ."[33] Teleki agreed that conditions might now be propitious for a successful confrontation with Romania, which had recently renounced her British guarantee. He no doubt hoped it would be possible for Hungary to achieve territorial revision in Romania without alienating Britain or abandoning neutrality in the war.

To alert the Germans to Hungarian intentions, Horthy now wrote again to Hitler in early July.[34] Here he repeated, in typical rambling fashion, the familiar arguments in favor of Hungary's recovery of Transylvania. He suggested that it would be to Germany's military advantage that Hungary control the Carpathian ridge, since "sooner or later Germany and Russia will have to settle accounts." But Hitler desired above all that there be stability in the Balkans while he attended to the situation in the West. The Hungarians were thus sternly warned that if they provoked a conflict with Romania, there would likely be dire consequences.

On the other hand, if Budapest would show patience and restraint, in time a peaceful solution could likely be worked out and Hungary's claims would be recognized. A similar message was received from Rome and even from London.[35]

Although the pressure on the Hungarian government from the General Staff to take military action was enormous, Teleki and Horthy eventually agreed to accept Axis arbitration of the dispute. The resulting second Vienna Award, signed and announced on August 30, 1940, fully satisfied no one but Hitler, who welcomed a temporary stabilization of the situation and sensed that he could in the future pit Romania and Hungary against each other in a continuing struggle to win Germany's favor. Although the newly drawn Hungarian-Romanian frontier conformed more closely to the complex ethnic makeup of the area than that devised by the peacemakers in 1919, Hungary was clearly the beneficiary of this second Vienna Award. Territory containing 2.5 million inhabitants, two-fifths of them Romanians, was recovered by Hungary, while 400,00 Magyars remained in Romania.

The stage was now set for Regent Horthy once again to mount his white stallion and pose as the glorious "expander of the country." Over the course of a ten-day period in early September, Horthy led the National Army into such treasured former Hungarian cities as Szatmárnémeti and Kolozsvár. Yet amid the jubilation of the "liberated" Magyars and the great acclaim showered on Horthy and Teleki, there were disquieting signs. So poor was the general appearance and discipline of the Hungarian troops in Szatmárnémeti that Horthy publicly upbraided Werth and other officers on the reviewing stand.[36] Nor was Teleki completely satisfied by the way things had worked out. Privately he told close friends of his fear that the recovery of Northern Transylvania would end up a "Pyrrhic victory" for Hungary.[37]

Teleki's despondent mood had led him already on September 1, two days after the Vienna Award, to write a letter to the Regent in which he once again suggested that he be relieved of his duties as Prime Minister. In the letter and a lengthy accompanying memorandum, Teleki complained bitterly that Hungary really had two governments, the legal one and an unsupervised military government that had spread to "practically all branches of civil administration."[38] He reproached himself for allowing the soldiers to become so powerful that they had created a "military dictatorship from below." On several occasions, Teleki argued, most notably in the events leading to the second Vienna Award, that the Chief of Staff had interfered in matters of foreign policy and had placed the Prime Minister in an awkward position. This was a violation of the constitution that greatly harmed Hungary's interests. It was clear, Teleki concluded, that in the final analysis he himself must be held accountable for allowing the situation to deteriorate to this point. Despite his misgivings over many months and his feelings of inadequacy, he had remained in his position out of loyalty to the Regent. Now, however, he no longer felt "strong enough to tackle these tasks in such an obscure and uncertain situation."

From the notations he made in the margins of the memorandum, it is clear that Admiral Horthy carefully studied the arguments of his Prime Minister and agreed with at least some of them. Yet it is unlikely that Horthy understood the implicit message of Teleki's communication: it was in fact he, as Regent and Supreme War Lord, who had failed to restrain the military officers. It was he who had failed to heed Teleki's repeated warnings that the soldiers were mixing too much in politics. But Teleki failed to make these points directly, and Horthy's response was merely to insist that Teleki stay on and to promise that he would patch things up. In late September, after the celebrations over the latest success of territorial revision had subsided, Horthy presided over a meeting of Teleki, Werth, and Bartha. Declaring that he wished to strengthen the position of the Prime Minister vis-à-vis the Minister of Defense and Chief of Staff, Horthy directed that certain, rather minor, changes be implemented.[39] These hardly touched on the central concerns expressed in Teleki's memorandum, but Teleki seemed temporarily satisfied, especially as Horthy seems also to have promised that he would stand with his Prime Minister even if he had to adjourn Parliament.[40]

Although Teleki remained intent on carrying out his policy of armed neutrality, he now concluded that he must make further concessions to Germany, both as a token of gratitude for the Vienna Award and as a further appeasement of the right-wing extremists in the government party. He hoped that the British and Americans would recognize that with Germany exercising hegemony on the European continent, Hungary had little room for maneuver. In order to preserve Hungary's tenuous neutrality, he would have to take responsibility for certain policy initiatives that he and his colleagues found personally repugnant.[41] Already as part of the Vienna Award, Hungary had agreed to grant extensive rights to the German minority, whose leaders were now fervent supporters of Hitler. In a new trade agreement Hungary promised an increase in the shipment of foodstuff and raw materials to Germany. Teleki also announced plans for further land reform and a new anti-Jewish law that would be "clear, radical, and simple, without the complications and loopholes" of previous measures.[42] The most fateful step came in November 1940 when, after several months of negotiations, Hungary formally adhered to the Tripartite Pact. Although the agreement involved few additional concrete obligations, it did trumpet Hungary's acceptance of and participation in the "New Europe" that the Axis powers had created. This was the first foreign policy initiative of the Teleki government that was sharply criticized by the moderate and left-wing opposition. Count Bethlen was to describe it as a "fatal blunder" and Hungary's "first step on the road to ruin."[43]

Teleki persuaded Horthy to approve one additional gesture to the radical right: the amnesty and release from prison of Ferenc Szálasi. Exactly what prompted Teleki to propose this is uncertain, since there is no evidence that Berlin had demanded this particular concession. It may be that he felt that Szálasi would become a rival of Imrédy and thus further splinter the radical right-wing movement. Horthy approved this tactic only with reluctance and ambivalence. His animosity toward the Arrowcross party had been intensified by the discovery in August of a bizarre plot masterminded by two members of the Arrowcross delegation in Parliament. According to their plan, Horthy was to be ambushed while being driven to his estate in Kenderes. He was to be kept prisoner and forced to appoint Szálasi Prime Minister. Those who resisted the creation of a Hungarist state, like Ferenc Keresztes-Fischer and even Horthy himself, were to be executed.[44] It must have been galling to Horthy that the two main conspirators managed for a time to escape prosecution because of their parliamentary immunity. Equally alarming to Horthy was Szálasi's decision, only weeks after his release on September 18, to foment a miners' strike as a prelude to a nationwide general strike. The strike turned out to be the largest ever organized during Horthy's regency.

That the extreme right-wingers apparently aimed to supplant the Social Democrats as the main instigators of labor unrest must have seemed to Horthy a particularly ominous development. In musing over recent events, Horthy found it incongruous that his government should be making concessions to the Arrowcross while at the same time proposing harsh new measures against the Jews. He expressed his concerns on this and related issues in a rare personal letter to his dear friend "Bóli" on October 14.[45] Horthy reminded Teleki that he had always been an anti-Semite and had never had contact with Jews.[46] He considered it intolerable that in Hungary "every factory, bank, large fortune, business, theater, press, commercial enterprise, etc., should be in the hands of the Jews" and that the Jews should be the image of Hungary that was projected abroad. Nonetheless, since a major task of the government was to raise the standard of living, it was impossible in a year or two to eliminate the Jews. That process would require a generation. In the meantime any attempt to replace the Jews by "incompetent, mostly unworthy loud-mouthed elements" would merely lead to bankruptcy.

One particularly striking passage in Horthy's letter provides an insight into his attitude toward the Jews at the time and in coming years:

> I have perhaps been the first loudly to profess anti-Semitism, yet I cannot look with indifference at inhumanity and senseless humiliations when we still need them. Moreover, I consider for example the Arrowcross men to be by far more dangerous and worthless for my country than I do the Jew. The latter is tied to this country from self-interest, and is more faithful to his adopted country than the Arrowcross men, who . . . with their muddled brains want to play the country into the hands of the Germans.

Horthy professed to find agents of Szálasi and Imrédy everywhere in Hungarian society, from the state tourist bureau to the management of the bauxite industry.[47] It was a mistake, Horthy suggested, to try to win over an enemy by giving him a good job. After all, "petting a pig will not turn it into a gazelle."[48] Over time these untrustworthy Arrowcross men should be removed; otherwise they were likely to sabotage all the "energetic and proper measures" of the government. If the right-wing extremists persisted in their seditious activities, such as harmful strikes, the government should invoke martial law, suppress the Arrowcross, send Szálasi back to prison, or, if necessary, "put them all up against the wall."[49]

In his letter Horthy also complained about the government-financed press, which he regarded as "scandalously bad" and "nauseating." The constant and coarse attacks on and belittling of the

Anglo-Saxon countries were unnecessary and unchivalrous. So far the British and American governments had shown understanding for the grave situation in which Hungary found itself, but this would not last. "We do not know what the future has in store," Horthy warned, "and it would be a great evil if one day we were called to account for these attacks."

Having unburdened himself to Teleki in this way, Horthy concluded his letter by expressing the utmost confidence in his friend. "There is no one I trust more than you," he wrote. The country relies on your unselfish work, self-sacrifice, and "unique and exceptional abilities."

Although Horthy's more drastic ideas for suppressing the Arrowcross were not implemented, and no major effort was made to purge radical right-wingers from key positions, over the next two years Szálasi and his party did not in fact pose a serious threat to the social and political order. By the end of October the miners' strike was suppressed by army troops and no similar large-scale strikes were to occur for the duration of the war. Endemic infighting among the no less than eight different right-wing factions and Szálasi's bitter personal rivalry with Imrédy prevented the creation of a powerful, unified right-wing radical party. One important repercussion of this was the German government's decision not to champion Szálasi, who appeared to their agents to be too erratic and unreliable. Of course, the Germans remained highly suspicious of Teleki and Horthy,[50] but they decided to avoid any destabilizing moves in Danubian Europe. "For the moment," Hitler declared privately, "it is necessary to dissemble with Hungarians, as we need their railroads. But the moment will come when we shall speak clearly."[51]

These developments afforded Teleki a period of several months in late 1940 and early 1941 to strengthen his internal political position and to find ways to persuade the British that Hungary had not become a German puppet. Teleki, Horthy, and other pro-Western Hungarians were heartened by Winston Churchill's speech in the House of Commons on September 6. "Personally," Churchill declared, "I have never been happy about the way Hungary was treated after the last war." The British Prime Minister went on to suggest that Britain would not oppose territorial changes that took place "with the free consent and goodwill of the parties concerned." The British Minister in Budapest later reaffirmed Churchill's statement, but warned that London's attitude would inevitably be influenced "by the degree and manner in which the various countries concerned have withstood the pressure of the Axis and endeavored to maintain a neutral attitude."[52]

In searching for ways to demonstrate that Hungary remained committed to neutrality, Teleki rejected Horthy's suggestion that something be done about the harsh anti-British tone of the Hungarian press. He believed that this was a relatively harmless way of appeasing the Germans. After all, few people outside Hungary read the Budapest newspapers anyway, and the British and the Americans were sophisticated enough to realize that the press did not reflect the government's true policy. In late 1940 and early 1941 Teleki seized on two other projects that he hoped would reassure the British government. One was the improvement of relations with Yugoslavia, which Teleki termed Hungary's last "window to the West." Regent Horthy showed genuine enthusiasm for this idea. In a conversation with the Yugoslav Minister on November 18, he expressed his great sympathy and respect for the Serbian people, who "always fought heroically, openly, and honestly." Horthy suggested that in the current European crisis Yugoslavia and Hungary (joined perhaps by Bulgaria) could best defend their interests by forming an alliance. The Hungarian government would not, Horthy continued, take part in any action or make any demands that would "render good neighborly feelings between Hungary and Yugoslavia impossible in the future." Furthermore, no country would ever force Hungary to make war against Yugoslavia.[53]

Negotiations between Budapest and Belgrade proceeded rapidly, especially when it became clear that the German government supported such a rapprochement as a way of drawing Yugoslavia closer to the Axis. The resulting pact, signed on December 12, 1940, called for "constant peace and eternal friendship" between Yugoslavia and Hungary. No direct mention was made of Hungary's territorial claims, although vague language was inserted to suggest that such problems would be considered at some point in the future when more normal conditions prevailed. The British government privately lauded this pact of "eternal friendship" as a contribution to stability in Danubian Europe.

London also looked with favor on a second initiative launched by Count Teleki in this period. Teleki's faith in an eventual victory of the Western powers remained unshaken by the events of 1940, although he now concluded that the war would be long and drawn out. Admiral Horthy, however, had become less vocal in his prediction that Britain was sure to win the war. He continued to express his admiration for the British Navy and his preference for a British victory, but he now suggested that the outcome of the war was uncertain. Perhaps the best to be hoped for was a limited British victory that would destroy the Nazi state but would leave Germany strong enough to hold off the Bolshevik threat from the East. In the meantime Horthy continued to insist that he would never agree to any German demand, such as the granting of military or air bases, that was inconsistent with Hungarian sovereignty.[54] It was to prepare for just such a contingency that Teleki now embarked on preparations for a Hungarian government in exile that could gain recognition from the Western powers should Hungary become the victim of German aggression. This would help prevent the debacle of World War I, when all the East European peoples hostile to the Magyars were represented in London, Paris, and Washington, but Hungary was not. Teleki had begun to explore this idea already in early 1940, but had placed it in abeyance when Hitler's attention turned westward.[55] The plan was resurrected later in the year with the encouragement of Sir Owen O'Malley, the British Minister in Budapest.

Sometime late in 1940 Regent Horthy presided over a meeting of his close political advisors, including Bethlen, Kánya, and Eckhardt, to discuss Teleki's proposal.[56] They decided that if Germany made unacceptable demands on Hungary, Horthy would appoint a government that would function in exile and would then himself resign. Bethlen would fly to London and serve there as the new Prime Minister. György Barcza would be Foreign Minister and Tibor Eckhardt, who had made a lecture tour of America earlier in 1940, would be the representative of the Hungarian government in Washington. Exactly what Horthy would do after he resigned remained unclear. O'Malley urged him to consider moving with loyal troops to Szeged, whence he could, if necessary, enter Yugoslavia and travel to join Bethlen in London. But Horthy refused to commit himself on this matter. He seemed reluctant to consider the idea of his leaving the country in such circumstances; perhaps it seemed to him too much like a captain abandoning his ship. Indeed, there are hints that, for whatever reason, Horthy had reservations about other parts of the plan. He apparently opposed the idea that Bethlen or Eckhardt should depart the country before a real emergency arose. When, at the urging of Teleki and Bethlen, Eckhardt nonetheless left on his mission early in 1941, he did so without any instructions or authorization from Horthy.[57]

The response in London to the Hungarian plan was favorable. In the Foreign Office Barcza was told that if Horthy and his Cabinet flew to England, His Majesty's government "would be honored and pleased, and would recognize them as a Government." In early March 1941 Count Teleki could thus take some satisfaction in the fact that, against almost impossible odds, he had managed to recover much of Hungary's lost territory, to preserve Hungary's neutrality, and to take out an insurance policy with the Western powers should Hungary be bullied by Nazi Germany. Apparently he had even received a promise from the Regent that Werth would soon be forced to resign as Chief of Staff.[58] His hope now was that Hungary could conserve its strength and resources until the end of the war, when chaotic conditions might prevail in Eastern Europe. Above all, Teleki cautioned, Hungary must not allow its youth and its army to be exploited in the interests of any other country.[59]

Miklós Horthy certainly agreed in principle with Teleki's strategy, but he found it difficult to reconcile himself to the notion that a moratorium should now be called in the quest for territorial revision. The shibboleth of "justice for Hungary" had become such an obsession with him that he seemed incapable of showing self-restraint. On several occasions during the autumn of 1940 Horthy had grumbled about the unfairness of the second Vienna Award and had voiced a determination to recover the rest of Transylvania at the first opportunity.[60] He had even urged Hitler to intercede with the Italians to see if Fiume might be returned to Hungary.[61] When Mussolini hinted that the Hungarians would do well to suppress their appetite for more territory, Horthy had quickly sent off a letter to the Duce in which he insisted that the Hungarian nation could not renounce the idea of further revision. "There is no human force," he wrote, "that can persuade the Hungarians to renounce their future."[62]

The fundamental difference of opinion between Horthy and Teleki on further territorial revision had tragic consequences in March 1941. On March 25 a coup d'état by pro-Western military officers toppled the Yugoslav government, which had just announced its intention of joining the Anti-Comintern Pact. In Budapest the significance of this event remained unclear until March 27, when the military attaché, Döme Sztójay, arrived from Berlin with an urgent message from Hitler. With great enthusiasm Sztójay informed Regent Horthy and Teleki that Germany intended to punish Yugoslavia by launching a major military operation in which

Hungary was invited to participate. Hitler had made it clear that Hungary would naturally regain her former territories, including the Bácska, Bánát, and perhaps even Croatia. Furthermore, since the Führer knew that the Regent had his heart set on a free port on the Adriatic, he would use his influence with the Italians to see if something could be worked out in Fiume.[63]

As Hitler had no doubt anticipated, Horthy reacted to this message with unrestrained enthusiasm. He immediately composed a letter in which he offered Hungary's unconditional participation in the planned invasion.[64] Teleki was aghast that Horthy was offering to cooperate "body and soul" with the Germans, for, as he complained to a friend, the Regent had "told me thirty-four times that he would never make war for foreign interests, and now he has changed his mind."[65] He attempted to point out to Horthy that if Hungary joined Germany in a military attack on Yugoslavia, she would "lose face before the whole world." After all, only three months earlier Hungary had signed a treaty of "eternal friendship" with Yugoslavia. Horthy saw things differently: Hungary would be dishonored and humiliated if she did not move. Employing a pithy Hungarian proverb, he declared that "the skin would burn off my cheek, if I did not take advantage of the opportunity to liberate Southern Hungary."[66]

Teleki and László Bárdossy, who had recently become Foreign Minister, managed to persuade Horthy at least to sleep on the matter. But on the morning of the 28th Horthy's enthusiasm seemed hardly diminished. Teleki repeatedly insisted that Hungary's honor was at stake: "We cannot stab in the back those people to whom we have sworn friendship." No doubt he pointed out that only a few months earlier Horthy had assured the Yugoslav Minister that no country would ever be able to force Hungary to make war against her neighbor to the south. But the Regent was adamant: "Yes, but the people to whom we swore friendship are no longer there."[67] After prolonged discussions along these lines, Horthy finally, albeit grudgingly, yielded ground. Although he insisted that a positive response had to be sent to Hitler, he agreed to the deletion from his letter of those passages Teleki deemed to be "dangerous."[68]

In that letter, which Sztójay presented to the Führer later on the 28th, Horthy declared that he felt "fully and wholly united with Germany."[69] The destinies of their countries were linked, Horthy asserted, and he was firmly resolved that his country should "stand by the German Reich in unalterable loyalty and to the extent of its strength." Moreover, the "territorial claims to which Your Excellency was kind enough to refer . . . exist and await their fulfillment." It is true that nowhere in his letter did Horthy specifically agree to join in the military attack on Yugoslavia. He merely asserted that he welcomed staff discussions between the High Command of the Wehrmacht and the Hungarian Army Command. Horthy also hinted (and here one detects Teleki's influence) that Hungarian participation in a military operation might be constrained by the threat to Hungary from Russia and Romania.

Despite strong misgivings, Teleki had agreed that Horthy's letter would be delivered by Sztójay even before the Hungarian Cabinet met to discuss the situation. This proved a serious miscalculation, for the gloss that Sztójay put on the Regent's letter left the impression in Berlin that Hungary had made a full and enthusiastic commitment to join in the attack. The excitement among German and Hungarian officers over this apparent renewal of the traditional "comradeship of arms" was profound.[70] Joint war planning now proceeded apace, and in Budapest General Werth began to push for an immediate mobilization of the army and a full participation in the forthcoming attack. He interpreted Horthy's letter as a complete acceptance of Hitler's offer and hinted darkly that he could not take responsibility for the consequences should the soldiers once again be denied the opportunity to test their mettle in battle.[71]

Struggling to slow his country's plunge toward disaster, Count Teleki did his best to counteract the baleful influence on the Regent of Werth and "that Nazi" Sztójay.[72] At a Cabinet meeting later on the 28th, Teleki discovered, however, that most of his colleagues supported at least a limited participation in the attack on Yugoslavia. To his dismay even the pro-Western faction in Parliament, including Bethlen himself, believed that Hungary could not pass up this opportunity to regain the *Délvidék*, the former southern provinces of the Kingdom of Hungary.[73] At the conclusion of the Cabinet meeting, Teleki's growing frustration and despair led him to announce his intention to resign, but his colleagues insisted that the country needed his services. He agreed only with great reluctance to stay on, hopeful that something could still be salvaged from what he called this "dreadful situation." Perhaps the Regent, who in the meantime had been approached by others who feared the consequences of full military cooperation with Hitler's Germany, might still moderate his view.[74]

The issues at stake in the crisis and the various policy options open to Hungary were extensively discussed at a meeting of the Supreme War Council on April 1.[75] Regent Horthy, who presided over the session, began by recounting the events of the past few days and declaring that the purpose of the meeting was to determine how Hungary would participate in the "liberation of the *Délvidék*." No one took issue with Horthy's assumption that the issue of whether to participate had in fact been decided. The Foreign Minister, László Bárdossy, did point out the dire consequences for Hungary if the Anglo-Saxon powers won the war, but he insisted that this opportunity to liberate fellow Magyars had to be seized.[76] For diplomatic reasons, however, he urged that certain limits be placed on Hungary's participation. Above all, Hungary must wait until Yugoslavia had collapsed internally and a "power vacuum" had been created. Then the Hungarian-Yugoslav Treaty of Friendship would be void and the Hungarian Army could be dispatched to protect the Hungarian areas of the former Yugoslavia. Bárdossy urged, however, that this "pacification" operation should extend only to territory that had belonged to Hungary's thousand-year kingdom and not beyond.

The two military leaders present, generals Werth and Bartha, opposed the setting of any limits on Hungarian participation. Werth argued for a full mobilization and a campaign with unlimited military objectives. Bálint Hóman, the Minister of Culture, agreed. This war, he asserted, would not be won by the United States and Great Britain, but by either Germany or Soviet Russia. In the circumstances Hungary really had no choice: she must stand firmly on Germany's side.

Count Teleki was the last to speak. He made no attempt to oppose Hungarian military action, but he did rebut the arguments put forward by Werth and Hóman. He warned against the facile assumption that the Anglo-Saxon powers had lost the war. On the contrary, they still ruled the world's seas and possessed vast resources. For this and other reasons Hungary should proceed cautiously and in a manner that would be deemed "correct" by not only Hungarian but also world opinion. Teleki thus offered support for the limited military operation outlined by Bárdossy and opposed the full mobilization recommended by Werth. He insisted further that Hungary join the military operation only a few days after the initial German attack and that Hungarian troops remain under Horthy's command. When the issue was put to a vote, seven of those present supported Hungary's participation in the "pacification" of Yugoslavia as proposed by Bárdossy and reluctantly supported by Teleki. Four voted for full and unlimited cooperation with Germany.

It was Admiral Horthy's responsibility as Supreme War Lord to interpret and act on the advice of the War Council. Given the enthusiasm with which he had greeted Hitler's offer of the 27th, Horthy might have been expected to side at this meeting with the minority in favor of an all-out military campaign. But in the intervening days Horthy had had time to ponder matters and give due consideration to the views of the civilian advisors he most respected. His initial impulsiveness had faded and he was now more receptive to the call for a traditional "Hungarian caution" that several of the members of the Supreme War Council sounded. In his concluding words Horthy declared that he could not approve a premature or unlimited military intervention that would dishonor Hungary and drag her into the European war. Hungary's participation in the campaign, he insisted, must be limited to the liberation of fellow Magyars, and must take place only after Croatia had declared its independence and Yugoslavia thus ceased to exist. He instructed Teleki and Werth to come to an agreement on the size of an appropriate military force and present him with a proposal.[77]

The results of this critical meeting of the Supreme War Council, which ended late on April 1, represented a minor victory for Teleki, since Horthy had decided against the more ambitious plans of General Werth. But this did not lessen Teleki's deepening depression, for he continued to fear the consequences of even a limited Hungarian role in the attack on Yugoslavia. He would have preferred that Hitler's request for cooperation be turned down completely, but, as he wrote to a friend on April 2, no one seemed to share this view: "[M]y situation is extremely difficult, because the Regent, the army, half of the government, and the parliamentary majority are against me . . ."[78] The intensive German-Hungarian staff talks made it certain that German troops in large numbers would soon be pouring through the country; indeed, advance units were arriving already on the 2nd. Teleki was likewise uneasy about the virulent propaganda campaign in which the Hungarian press now began to engage. He did not believe the sensational reports of increasing violence against the Magyar minority by the Yugoslav authorities.

Teleki clung to one last hope: perhaps the British would after all show understanding for Hungary's dilemma. A telegram from György Barcza that arrived late on April 2 showed this to be a delusion. Barcza reported that if Hungary, for whatever reason, joined in the German attack, she could expect to find herself at war with not only Great Britain but, in time, with the United States and Soviet Russia. Moreover, in the English-speaking world Hungary would become notorious as a country that violated treaties and attacked its friends in the back.[79] For Teleki, who had been struggling "to find a way out and to save face," this was devastating news. Only three weeks earlier he had assured the British that as long as he was alive and at the head of his government, he would never comply with demands that were "incompatible with the honor and sovereignty of the country."[80]

Early on the morning of April 3, Ferenc Keresztes-Fischer arrived at the Royal Castle in great agitation. He informed Horthy that Pál Teleki was dead. During the night he had shot himself and had left a note addressed to the Regent. One can imagine the deep emotion with which Admiral Horthy read Teleki's suicide note:

> We have become breakers of our word—out of cowardice—in defiance of the Treaty of Eternal Friendship based on the Mohács speech.[81] The nation feels this, and we have thrown away its honor. We have placed ourselves on the side of scoundrels, for there is not a word of truth in the stories of atrocities against the Magyars or the Germans. We shall become the despoilers of corpses, the most abominable of nations! I did not restrain you. I am guilty.[82]

Horthy's reaction to the suicide of one of his best friends was somber but composed. Neither at the time nor later did he concede, or perhaps even realize, that he bore at least some responsibility for the events that had led Teleki to his tragic fate. Certainly the members of Count Teleki's family grasped the meaning of the suicide note. When Horthy came to pay his condolences, they were conspicuously unfriendly to him and refused even to shake his hand.[83]

This horrible turn of events did not lead Horthy to reconsider his commitment to join in the attack on Yugoslavia. Acting on the advice of Kánya, Keresztes-Fischer, and Bethlen, he moved already on April 3 to appoint László Bárdossy as Teleki's successor. Bárdossy expressed some reservations about taking on the task, for he had been abroad in the diplomatic service for the past ten years and was practically unknown in domestic political circles. This, however, was seen by Horthy as an advantage, for it meant that he could proceed more impartially and without getting embroiled in party politics. Bárdossy was, in Horthy's opinion, very well suited for the most urgent task, which was to carry out and gain international acceptance of the plan for Hungary's recovery of the *Délvidék*.[84]

Horthy's determination to implement the decision of the Supreme War Council can be seen in his conversation later on the 3rd with Sir Owen O'Malley, who had come to express his sympathies and inquire about Hungary's plans. Horthy recapitulated the events of the past few days and tried to justify Hungary's role in the impending operation against Yugoslavia by referring to "the sacred duty of restoring the frontiers of Hungary" and to his country's need for an access to the sea. He brushed aside the British diplomat's suggestion that the time had come to resist the Germans and put into operation the plan for a Hungarian exile government in London. It was clear, Horthy argued, that his country could expect no help from Britain. Besides, the war would likely end in a deadlock, which meant that his country had to be careful not to take any action that would anger Berlin and lead later to savage German reprisals against Hungary. Greatly disillusioned by Horthy's attitude, O'Malley uttered a harsh indictment: If the Regent "entered into such a corrupt bargain with Germany or in any way acted as a Hungarian jackal to the German lion against a State with which he had just signed a treaty of eternal friendship, his country could expect no indulgence, no sympathy, and no mercy from a victorious Britain and United States of America and that he personally . . . would be covered with well-deserved contempt and dishonour." Horthy was oblivious to O'Malley's protests and suggestions: "It's no use talking to me. I've made up my mind."[85]

This bitter exchange with O'Malley suggests that Admiral Horthy had finally resigned himself to the impossibility of maintaining the diplomatic balancing act that he and Teleki had performed for the past two years. Yet he still could not bring himself to join wholeheartedly with the Germans, despite the urgent pleas of his military chiefs. Late on April 3 he dispatched to Hitler a letter in which he gave a straightforward account of the events of the past few days.[86] Teleki, he wrote, blamed himself for not protesting strongly enough against a policy that would turn Hungarians into "despoilers of corpses." He thus fell victim to a "conflict of conscience which is felt also by the entire nation." In the circumstances Horthy asked that Hungarian troops be assigned only those tasks that would be "reconcilable with our conscience."

In his letter to Hitler, Horthy suggested that he shared some of the moral qualms that had led to Teleki's suicide, but events would soon demonstrate that it did not take much to ease his conscience. Once the German attack on Yugoslavia began on April 6, retaliatory air strikes were made by Yugoslav and British planes on German positions in Hungary. By Horthy's skewed logic, this was an unprovoked attack on Hungary, especially as some bombs were dropped on Szeged and Pécs, where no German troops were stationed. Moreover, the Hungarian government claimed that the primary mission of the enemy bombers, which was thwarted, was to drop bombs on Budapest during Teleki's funeral service.[87] Hungarian military plans now proceeded apace, and when, on the 11th, Croatian nationalists proclaimed the independence of their province and the anticipated "political vacuum" had been created, Horthy gave the signal for the Hungarian attack. In an Army Order calling on the soldiers to hurry to the aid of their kinsmen in the south, Horthy declared that the "God of the Magyars and every thought of the nation are with you." Since the Wehrmacht had already shattered most of the front-line Yugoslav forces, Hungarian troops met little resistance. Within three days slightly more than one-half of the southern areas lost through the Treaty of Trianon was recovered, although the Germans kept under their military control one province, the Bánát, which Hitler had specifically promised to Hungary.

In the aftermath of this new revisionist success, Admiral Horthy expressed no lingering remorse over the death of death of Pál Teleki or the abandonment of the policy of armed neutrality. There is no recorded response by Horthy to the British breaking of diplomatic relations on April 8. His delight in the revival of the German-Hungarian "brotherhood in arms" seemed genuine.[88] Most striking was the tone that Horthy used during a conversation with György Barcza, who returned to Budapest in mid-April after the Hungarian Legation in London had been closed. In their conversations over the previous two years, Horthy had always emphasized that he wished to remain neutral and on good terms with Great Britain, which would emerge victorious. Now, when Barcza warned that Germany was bound to lose the war and Hungary would once again be punished for having chosen the wrong side, Horthy replied with some irritation that this was not so. Despite everything he remained pro-English, but his personal preferences no longer mattered. The reality was that the Germans "had mastered the art of war," while by contrast the English "committed blunder after blunder." It was thus in Hungary's best interests to stand firmly with the Germans, who "were winning the war" and would dominate Europe.[89]

Having fully abandoned the policy of armed neutrality and embarked on military cooperation with the Germans, Horthy now felt emboldened to proffer to his ally advice on the best strategy for conducting the war. His musings on the future course of the war, recorded in an incomplete draft of a letter to Hitler in mid-April, suggest that Horthy, despite his sharp exchange with Barcza, continued to regard the British as a formidable opponent.[90] Horthy began his draft letter by denying that he had any intention of influencing the Führer's war plans. Nonetheless, out of loyalty to Germany he wished to suggest an idea that was so secret and sensitive that he would never talk or write about it anywhere else, not "even in my eventual memoirs." Actually, what Horthy had in mind was hardly new or unexpected. "It is my opinion," Horthy wrote, "that there will be no happiness, peace, or tranquillity so long as this immense Russia under Soviet power, which can be governed only with terror, . . . continues to exist." The Wehrmacht, Horthy suggested, was capable in "a matter of weeks" of destroying "red communism, the greatest of all threats" to civilization. If Germany were to accomplish this great deed for mankind, "history would bless her for centuries to come."

On the other hand, Horthy cautioned against an invasion of England, which would be "fraught with a thousand dangers." Even if successful, the result would be inconclusive, since the war would then be managed from Canada and the United States and would be continued by the powerful Royal Navy. Far better, Horthy suggested, to move against Russia while continuing the struggle against Britain with airplanes and submarines. Once the "inexhaustible mineral wealth" of Russia was in German hands, "one could hold out forever."

Horthy intended his letter to Hitler to contain a restatement of Hungary's claim to the whole of Transylvania and the Bánát, but before he had finished the draft he decided that he could best argue his country's case in a personal conversation. On his initiative a meeting was thus arranged and took place on April 24 in Hitler's headquarters in a railroad car at Mönichkirchen in southern Germany. No detailed record of this conversation has survived, but it clearly transpired in a convivial atmosphere, even though Hitler showed no inclination to grant Horthy's wishes with respect to the Bánát and Transylvania. According to a German account, the Hungarian Regent was in an exuberant mood and "talked on and on" about his favorite subjects. In discussing Germany's military successes in the Balkans, Horthy asserted that Greece had been defeated because it was a democracy, where "the votes of two idiots count for more than that of one wise man."[91] But Horthy's impassioned call for a military campaign against Soviet Russia evoked no response from Hitler, who merely noted that relations with the Soviet Union were "entirely correct."[92] Although plans for Operation Barbarossa were by this time at an advanced stage, and June 22 had been designated as the launch date for a German invasion of the USSR, Hitler was understandably reluctant to pass this information to the indiscreet Hungarian Regent.

Horthy thus returned home disappointed about his apparent failure to persuade Hitler to adopt his strategy. Yet within just a few weeks Hungarian military officers were receiving from their German counterparts strong hints about the impending attack on Soviet Russia. As was his habit, General Werth moved quickly to try to persuade the government to join wholeheartedly in the German campaign. In a series of memorandums that he submitted to the Prime Minister in May and early June, he argued that Hungary would best serve its interests by taking the initiative of proposing a political and military alliance with Germany. Fearful that Hungary would be left out unless she voluntarily offered his participation, Werth argued that Hungary's revisionist program and her reputation as a pioneer in the anti-Bolshevik struggle would be threatened if she did not take a resolute stand on the side of Nazi Germany.[93]

Werth was dismayed by the negative response of Bárdossy, who refused even to consider the question unless the Germans made a formal request for assistance through diplomatic channels. But he was truly astonished to learn that Horthy also urged caution. Werth was apparently so certain that he would have the Regent's backing that he had not even bothered to send his memorandums to Horthy, who in early June was at his home in Kenderes, recuperating from a minor illness. Apprised by Bárdossy of the rumors of an impending German attack on Russia, Horthy greeted the information with enthusiasm, and no doubt took satisfaction in the thought that he had played some role in bringing Hitler to his senses. Nonetheless Horthy apparently saw little to be gained by an expenditure of the nation's resources and manpower on the plains of Russia, even if, as General Werth confidently predicted, victory was assured in less than six weeks. Moreover, he thought it absurd that tiny Hungary should declare war on a major power, especially one against which Hungary had no territorial claims. Thus, Horthy seemed content to sit back, hold on tightly to the newly recovered territories, and applaud as Germany performed this splendid deed on its own. Perhaps he also calculated that if Germany required assistance from Hungary, Hitler would have to make a formal request, at which time Hungary would demand suitable compensation, such as the fulfillment of the promise to hand over the Bánát.[94]

Given his record over the past two decades as perhaps Europe's main proponent of a grand crusade against Bolshevik Russia, and his stated willingness to organize and perhaps even lead such a campaign, it remains a mystery why, when it was clear that his cherished hope would finally be realized, Horthy reacted with such prudence and calculation. Perhaps this was a reflection of a lingering resentment toward and suspicion of the Germans. Why, he might have wondered, had Hitler not given him a hint of what was afoot during their conversation in late April? Surely the plans for the attack on Russia were fully developed by that time. Horthy's cautious attitude might also have been prompted by his growing disillusionment with General Werth. He was apparently greatly offended when Werth circulated his most recent memorandums to members of the Cabinet without even discussing the matter beforehand with the Regent.[95] In any case, Horthy's cautious response to the unexpected news from Germany was consistent with that of his Prime Minister, most of the Cabinet, and the advisors in his camarilla.

When on the morning of June 22 the German Minister appeared at the Regent's office to deliver a letter from Hitler announcing the commencement of the great campaign against Russia, Horthy was appropriately ecstatic. He, the "old crusader against bolshevism," for twenty-two years had longed for this day. Hitler's decision would surely bring peace, he declared, because the Anglo-Americans would have to recognize that Germany, once in control of Russia's vast resources, would be invincible.[96] Horthy did not, however, give any indication that Hungary was prepared to join in the campaign. In fact, over the next several days he seemed to go out of his way to make himself inaccessible to German officials who might be bearing requests for assistance.[97] When on the 23rd Werth got hints from his contacts in Germany that any help that Hungary could give in the campaign would be appreciated, he and Bartha had to travel to Kenderes in order to consult with Horthy. The two officers pleaded their case: Hungary's good standing with Germany would be damaged if she did not join in; the Russian campaign would be over in the matter of weeks; Romania and Slovakia were eagerly rallying to the campaign; Horthy's reputation as a staunch anti-Bolshevik would be tarnished if Hungary did not take part. Horthy was unmoved by these arguments, and merely replied that he still failed to see any national interest that would be served by such a decision. Werth and Bartha thereupon disclaimed any responsibility for the consequences should Hungary remain inactive. They argued that prowar sentiment was so strong in the officer corps that there was the danger of military coup d'état that would oust the Regent.[98]

Admiral Horthy's view was shared by a strong majority of the Hungarian Cabinet, which, at meetings on the 23rd and 24th, decided to sever diplomatic relations with the Soviet Union, but not to volunteer any substantial military assistance to Germany. However, events took a totally unexpected turn on the morning of June 26, when Werth and Bartha appeared before the Regent, who was now back in Budapest, to report with great excitement that Russian planes had conducted a bombing raid on the city of Kassa (Košice). Twenty-six civilians had been killed. Incensed by what seemed to be a dastardly, unprovoked Russian attack, Horthy agreed that Hungarian reprisals were in order. On the spot he ordered that appropriate retaliatory measures be initiated. Horthy then conferred with Bárdossy, who in these new circumstances had become convinced that Hungary had no choice but to enter the war against the USSR. Horthy apparently expressed no curiosity about why the Soviets should have launched such a self-defeating bombing attack, and Bárdossy, for his part, saw no need to inform the Regent about a friendly message that the Soviet Foreign Minister, Vyacheslav Molotov, had recently given the Hungarian Minister in Moscow.[99] Bárdossy and Horthy quickly agreed that decisive action was now in order, but, there may have been a misunderstanding about how Bárdossy would proceed. It seems that Horthy believed Bárdossy would take the matter before the Cabinet for discussion, and then report back to the Regent before any final action was taken. But Bárdossy had gained the impression that Horthy was fully in support of a declaration of war on the Soviet Union. He thus proceeded to summon the Cabinet, which after brief deliberations voted to enter the war. Without consulting the Regent again or bringing the matter before the Parliament, Bárdossy immediately drafted and had issued a communiqué that stated that because of "an act of unprovoked aggression by Russia," Hungary "considers a state of war to have come into being between herself and the USSR."[100]

Some months later, when Admiral Horthy's enthusiasm for the war had greatly diminished, he began to complain that on June 26, 1941 Bárdossy had presented him with a *fait accompli*.[101] Many years later Horthy would assert in his memoirs that his decision to approve a declaration of war against the Soviet Union had been taken because some pertinent facts had been withheld from him. Bárdossy had failed to inform him both of the friendly overtures from the Russians and the possibility that the Kassa bombing had been a German provocation, perhaps with the connivance of Hungarian officers.[102] This, however, would seem to be *ex post facto* rationalization. Even if Horthy had known of these extenuating factors, it seems unlikely that he would have been persuaded to put the brake on Hungary's headlong rush to war. Certainly, in the circumstances of late June 1941, he would have been unlikely to put any credence in promises made by the Soviet Foreign Minister. As for the rumors that the Kassa bombing was a conspiracy arranged by the German and Hungarian military officers, Horthy would likely have dismissed them as preposterous and a calumny of the Hungarian officer corps.[103]

There is no reason to doubt the sincerity and enthusiasm to be found in the letter Horthy wrote on June 28th to Hitler announcing that, because of "murderous attacks on Hungarian territory," he had had war declared on Soviet Russia. "I count myself happy," he declared, "that my army can take part , shoulder to shoulder, with the glorious and victorious German Army in the crusade for the elimination of the dangerous Communist horde and for the preservation of our culture."[104] On that day the first Hungarian units crossed the frontier into Soviet Russia and Horthy's Hungary had, at last, enlisted to fight in Hitler's war.

9

Hungary's Supreme War Lord, 1941–1943

It is one of the more curious facts of Miklós Horthy's career that when the opportunity finally arrived for him to play an active role as Supreme War Lord in wartime, he proceeded with great circumspection and little apparent enthusiasm. On June 29 he issued from Kenderes a proclamation informing the Hungarian people of the imminence of "an important transformation" of Europe and urging all citizens to preserve "order and brotherly love." For the next few months, however, Admiral Horthy maintained a kind of sibylline silence: there were no fiery calls to vanquish the hated Bolsheviks or bellicose statements of any kind. Horthy's seeming unease in his new role reflected a growing regret that he had allowed his country to be swept into this war. Certainly during July he watched with great satisfaction as the Wehrmacht made its impressive advances eastward. But there were also disquieting developments that belied his earlier prediction that Hitler's turn against Soviet Russia would so discomfit Britain and the United States that they would settle for a compromise peace. Horthy doubtless took notice when that other anti-Communist of long standing, Winston Churchill, offered Britain's full support to Stalin's war effort. Churchill's meeting with President Roosevelt on August 14 and the issuance of the Atlantic Charter must have suggested to Horthy that the Anglo-Saxon powers were forming a powerful coalition against Nazi Germany.

It is significant that shortly after the meeting of Roosevelt and Churchill became publicly known, at a time when Nazi Germany's power in Europe was nearing its apogee, Horthy deemed it desirable to make a friendly gesture to the American Minister, Herbert Pell, who had recently replaced John Montgomery. Horthy invited Pell to the summer residence at Gödöllő and stressed, as he often had with Pell's predecessors, his friendly feelings toward and sympathy for the United States and England.[1] At the same time, Horthy did not hide his admiration for Germany and its "faculty for organization," which he described as "even superior to that of America." Horthy asserted that the Soviets, who had lost nearly five million soldiers, were "practically beaten," even though the Germans had, in his opinion, not sent their best troops or officers on this campaign. Hungary itself had sent very few soldiers. Nonetheless, Horthy conceded that he could not foresee a quick end to the wider war. He hoped for some sort of compromise peace, but he thought a "rapid or a fair solution of the present mess would be difficult to reach, because of the terrific force of hatred both in England and in Germany." This was unfortunate, since the Germans were "tactless and humorless" and unfit to dominate Europe. Worst of all was the Gestapo, which was as bad as the OGPU, the Russian secret police.

At this point in mid-August 1941, Admiral Horthy still remained confident that Russia would soon be defeated, although, as Pell put it in his report, the Regent seemed to appreciate "the need of an anchor to windward." But his confidence about an easy victory in the East was soon to receive a jolt. On August 26 Horthy received from Bárdossy a long letter in which the Prime Minister bitterly complained that Chief of Staff Werth was once again attempting to insinuate himself into political and diplomatic affairs.[2] Werth, he reported, had submitted a memorandum to the Cabinet in which he criticized Hungary's "puny" participation in the war and proposed that the government volunteer a massive new contribution. Only through total mobilization, Werth argued, could Hungary realize its cherished national goals, including the restoration of her "millennial frontiers" and the deportation of the non-Magyars and the Jews.[3] Although Bárdossy, as will be seen, was not in principle opposed to an increase in Hungary's military effort, he was infuriated that Werth continued in such a brazen fashion to infringe on his, and on the Regent's, prerogatives. He now declared the situation to be intolerable: the Regent must choose between his Prime Minister and Chief of Staff.

A year earlier Horthy had responded to similar complaints from Count Teleki with temporizing measures. Despite Werth's brash ways and propensity for political machinations, Horthy had hesitated to force his resignation, in part, no doubt, because in 1939 and 1940 the Chief of Staff's predictions about the invincibility of

German arms had proven to be uncannily accurate.[4] For the past several months, however, Horthy's patience had worn thin as Werth again and again sought to influence policy without even consulting the Regent. It must also have occurred to Horthy that Werth's most recent memorandum was submitted precisely six weeks after the start of a war that he had predicted would in fact be over in six weeks. Even so, Horthy, who had always been reluctant to dismiss military leaders who were, like Werth, efficient and competent officers, might not have taken action had it not been for the intervention of his older son, István.

Thirty-seven years old at the time, István Horthy was an engineer who served as Director of the Hungarian Railways. He had previously played no major role in political affairs. However, he had in the past year become the target of strong abuse from radical right-wingers, who branded him a "Jew lover" and an enemy of Nazi Germany.[5] It was true that István Horthy had fostered friendly ties with many Jews and, according to the scandalmongers, had had romantic dalliances with the daughters of rich Jewish financiers. Moreover, he made no secret of his affinity for the West, especially for the United States, where he had spent a year studying the auto industry. He shared his father's personal revulsion for the Nazis and their Hungarian imitators. In his views of the war István Horthy was greatly influenced by the opinions of General Ferenc Szombathelyi, whom he met in Szeged in August 1941. An apolitical officer of German background, Szombathelyi was a rarity among his fellow officers in his skepticism about the chances for a rapid German victory in Russia. At young Horthy's request, Szombathelyi drafted a memorandum in which he suggested that on the vast Russian plains there would be no *Blitzkrieg*. Rather, the war would be "a long, drawn out, and bloody struggle, the result of which was completely uncertain." Since a complete German victory was unlikely, Hungary would do best to conserve its power in order to be able deal with the smaller wars with its neighbors that would be likely at the end of the larger war.[6]

István Horthy was so impressed by Szombathelyi's arguments that he presented the memorandum to his father and urged him to act on it. Although Admiral Horthy was himself not yet convinced that Germany could not win the war, he had the highest regard for the opinions of his eldest son, whom he considered a true genius. Horthy now resolved not only to reject Werth's call for a total mobilization and formation of a new Hungarian Army but in fact to reduce Hungary's participation in the war.[7] In late August Horthy dismissed Werth and appointed as his successor General Szombathelyi, who was by no means the obvious candidate for the post in terms of seniority or experience.[8] When in early September Hitler invited the Hungarian Regent and Chief of Staff to consult with him at the "Wolf's Lair," his military headquarters, it was thus Szombathelyi and not Werth who accompanied Horthy. Moreover, to the Führer's further surprise, the Hungarians brought with them a request that they be permitted to withdraw the bulk of their forces from the Eastern Front. Horthy explained that the main Hungarian fighting force, a Mobile Corps, had lost much of its equipment and could hardly be of help to the Germans on the broad expanses of the Ukraine.[9] There was some heated discussion of this request, but Hitler seemed willing to placate the Hungarian Regent, no doubt because he believed that his war in the East was all but won. The two sides agreed to a compromise: portions of the Hungarian Mobile Corps would return to Hungary, but four infantry brigades would remain in the Ukraine as occupation troops.[10]

By early December 1941 it seemed that Moscow would soon be taken by German troops and that Soviet Russia was indeed on the brink of defeat. At the time the only Hungarian military unit active at the Front was a lone bicycle battalion. Admiral Horthy could take satisfaction in the thought that little Hungarian blood had been spilled to achieve this objective for which he had ardently yearned over the past two decades. Hitler was sufficiently satisfied with Hungary's military contributions that he awarded Horthy the large gold cross of the Order of Holler to convey his gratitude.[11] Yet even minimal participation in Hitler's war had its baleful consequences for Hungary. The launching of "Operation Barbarossa" was accompanied in Germany by even more violent rhetoric against the Jews and "Judeo-communism." This emboldened Hungary's radical right-wingers who for many months had been clamoring for new, more effective measures against the Jews. Sensing that it would be expedient to make some gesture to Hitler and his Hungarian supporters, László Bárdossy initiated a third anti-Jewish law that was approved by the Hungarian Parliament in August. This legislation, which was opposed by the leaders of the Christian churches, banned marriage between Jews and non-Jews and adopted a definition of a Jew that conformed much more closely to the German model.[12]

It was also in August 1941 that Hungary's leaders got their first inkling of the fate of Jews in German-occupied territory. Acting on a plan submitted by a group of General Staff officers and then Chief of Staff Werth, the Hungarian government approved the deportation to German-occupied Poland of some 18,000 Jews who had sought refuge in Hungary. Once handed over to S.S. units, the Jews were quickly and methodically massacred. When reports reached Budapest of this horrible atrocity, the Minister of the Interior, Ferenc Keresztes-Fischer, expressed his indignation and insisted that no further deportations take place.[13]

Miklós Horthy's role in and attitude toward these anti-Jewish measures in the summer of 1941 remain unclear. Although he later accused Bárdossy of introducing new anti-Semitic legislation without his approval, he did not actively oppose the third anti-Jewish law when it was being debated in the Parliament. Although there is no direct evidence that Horthy specifically approved the plan to deport Jews, there is no reason to believe that he would have raised objections. Over the years he had often in private derided the so-called Galician Jews, whom he regarded as aliens who could never be properly integrated into Magyar society. It is certain, however, that neither Horthy nor his colleagues suspected in August 1941 that Jews handed over to the Germans would be machine-gunned on the spot. Indeed, reports describing this atrocity must have had a profound impact on Horthy and his advisors, for from this point on the Hungarian government refused to consider any further deportation of Jews. It is also noteworthy that until the German occupation of Hungary in 1944, Regent Horthy adamantly resisted demands that he dismiss Keresztes-Fischer, who soon came under furious attack from right-wing extremists disgusted with his relatively tolerant and humanitarian policies toward the Jews.

If, as the historian John Lukacs suggests, the "turning point of the entire war" came in early December 1941,[14] this was especially true for Horthy's Hungary. In the first days of the month Admiral Horthy became seriously ill and a rumor spread that the seventy-three-year-old Regent had cancer. Although the rumor proved false, grave events occurred during the two weeks the Regent was incapacitated. On December 6 when, as usual, Hungary celebrated the Regent's name day, Great Britain and the Commonwealth countries finally took the inevitable step of declaring war on Hungary. Then came the attack on Pearl Harbor and Hitler's decision to show his solidarity with Japan by entering the war against the United States. Prime Minister Bárdossy, wishing to curry favor with Berlin and to avoid being the only ally of Germany to stand aloof, announced on December 12 that Hungary and the United States were now at war. Bárdossy had acted with such haste that he did not bother to seek explicit approval from the Cabinet and the Regent.[15] When Horthy returned to his desk later in December, he thus had to deal with new circumstances that, for a man of sincere Anglo-American sympathies, were highly unpalatable. His displeasure with the actions of his Prime Minister was evident in his words to the departing American diplomat Howard Travers: "Remember that this so-called declaration of war is not legal, not approved by Parliament, not signed by me."[16]

More bad news arrived at the end of December in the form of a letter to Horthy from Hitler.[17] Blaming bad weather and the fanaticism of Red Army soldiers who "fought with an Asiatic indifference to the loss of life," Hitler tacitly acknowledged that the *Blitzkrieg* had not succeeded in Russia. A spring campaign would be necessary in order to deal the final annihilating blow against the Red Army. He earnestly hoped that Hungary would be prepared to make a major military contribution to this "world-historic" campaign that would prevent Europe from being engulfed by the "dark barbarism" from the East. Hitler expressed a willingness to do as much as he could to provide the new Hungarian force with modern equipment.

On January 5 German Foreign Minister Ribbentrop arrived in Budapest to take part in a hunting party with the Regent, but his main objective was to persuade the Hungarians to accede to Hitler's request and order a general mobilization. During his conversations with government leaders, which at times became quite heated, he warned that a Hungarian refusal to cooperate would have an incalculable effect on Hitler, who was "just but passionate." Moreover, Ribbentrop added, there was an obvious connection between the size of Hungary's military contribution and the realization of its territorial objectives. There was no need, he added, for Hungary to feel threatened by Romania, since Antonescu had already promised to send his entire army to the Eastern Front.[18]

On January 10, the date of Ribbentrop's departure, Horthy composed a letter to Hitler in which he explained Hungary's intentions. Here one finds repeated at great length the derogatory assessments of other national groups and the highly tendentious description of Hungarian policy that Hitler would have been familiar with from previous letters from the Hungarian Regent.[19] Asserting that Hungary was "firmly resolved" to take part in the German spring offensive, Horthy nonetheless proceeded at great length to argue that Hungary could provide the greatest service to the Reich by maintaining order at home and holding off the Pan-Slav forces that secretly hoped for a Russian victory. In Horthy's view, none of the other countries in East Central Europe and the Balkans could be trusted. The Romanians were turncoats who would end up fighting against the Germans, as they did in World War I. Even the Slovaks and Bulgarians would defect to the "Anglo-Saxon-Bolshevik Alliance" if the opportunity presented itself. Only Hungary, which throughout its history had remained true to its allies and was attached to Germany by "unbreakable bonds of loyalty, friendship and devotion," could be relied on. But Hungary had to defend itself against the hate-filled and bloodthirsty Slovaks, Croatians, and Romanians, who had formed a second Little Entente aimed at reinstating the Trianon frontiers. As a responsible head of state, he had to keep some of his soldiers at home to guard against all contingencies. Despite these problems and the need to conserve manpower to ensure efficient agricultural production, Hungary would send as many troops to the Front as possible. He stressed, however, the absolute necessity of equipping these units with the necessary armaments, since "troops poorly and insufficiently armed are inferior in the face of an enemy equipped with modern and powerful weapons, and not even good morale can change this."[20]

Although Horthy's letter could be interpreted as an indication that the Hungarian government would attempt to make only a token contribution to Germany's spring offensive, the reality proved quite different. After intense wrangling between German and Hungarian military leaders, in which Horthy himself apparently took no part, it was agreed that Hungary would form a new military force of approximately 200,000 soldiers, which was about two-thirds of what Ribbentrop had suggested. This so-called Second Army would be equipped by Germany and would be sent to participate in the great spring offensive.[21]

Miklós Horthy gave his support to this fateful decision, which would lead one year later to one of the greatest military disasters in Hungarian history, despite the warnings he had been receiving from Count Bethlen and other conservative advisors that "this war is not ours and we have nothing to gain from it." Horthy had apparently agreed with General Szombathelyi's analysis of the war in August 1941, as well as with that of General Béla Miklós, who returned from the Eastern Front in November and told the Regent that this was "a long and bloody war, the outcome of which is uncertain."[22] Yet when the difficult decision had to be made in January 1942, Horthy did not dare to risk a confrontation with Hitler. Several factors must have influenced him. Both Bárdossy and Szombathelyi, despite the latter's skepticism about the prospects for a rapid victory, favored substantial concessions to Germany.[23] They could offer no viable plan of action based on a negative or dilatory response to Hitler's request. Given Ribbentrop's thinly veiled threat, Horthy probably also feared that if he provoked Hitler's wrath, Hungary would not only lose any chance to recover the Bánát but might also find its claim on northern Transylvania called into question. Finally, Horthy had a very compelling reason for wishing to remain in the Führer's good graces, because it was precisely in this period that he was preoccupied with a personal project to which he assigned the highest priority and which might be jeopardized if German-Hungarian relations soured.

In late 1941, even before his illness in December, Admiral Horthy began to worry once again about the fate of the regency in the case of his death or incapacitation. He had never been happy with the procedures that Parliament had approved in 1937. His fondest hope, of which he had never spoken to anyone outside his family, was to find a way to ensure that his son István would succeed him as Regent. With this in mind Horthy now returned to an idea, with which he had briefly toyed four years earlier, of having Parliament create a new office of Deputy Regent that would carry with it the right of succession to the Regency. Although he later denied that he had set in motion the series of events to be described below, it is clear that Horthy, encouraged by his wife and certain members of his entourage, intended from the start to promote the candidacy of his son István and thereby establish a kind of family dynasty based on the regency.[24]

Not only did Miklós Horthy sincerely believe that his elder son was the best qualified man in Hungary to succeed him as regent, but he had convinced himself that Hungary's political establishment would defer to his judgment in this matter After all, he reasoned, who knew better than he the qualities needed for success as

Hungarian Regent? It was true, of course, that István Horthy was handicapped by a complete lack of any political or military experience and by a reputation of being a libertine playboy.[25] But Admiral Horthy was so enamored of his elder son that he chose to ignore these liabilities and to emphasize István's brilliant mind and great managerial skills. Furthermore, the list of three suitable candidates that, in compliance with the legislation of 1937, Horthy had placed in a sealed envelope was now outdated. Kálmán Darányi had since died, Count Bethlen was too closely identified with the anti-Nazi camp, and Gyula Károlyi was nearly as old as Horthy. Archduke Albrecht, the one Hungarian who openly coveted the post of regent, was totally unacceptable not only to Admiral Horthy but to many other Hungarians who were appalled by his close identification with the radical right-wing movement and his willingness to curry favor with the Germans.

Horthy seems first to have mentioned his plan to two of his closest friends, Gyula Károlyi and Móric Esterházy. They must have warned him to expect an adverse reaction from the Catholic Church, which would likely oppose the idea of having another Protestant in the office of regent. Horthy's next step was thus to request a meeting with Cardinal Justinián Serédi, Hungary's Prince Primate. In their conversation on November 16,[26] Horthy at first spoke somewhat elliptically: he who owns a house naturally desires to pass it on to his children after his death. When Serédi failed to react to this, Horthy was more explicit in hinting that he wished to pass on the regency to his son, whom he regarded as much more intelligent and able than himself. Cardinal Serédi, who had grave reservations about the elevation of István Horthy to the highest political office in the land,[27] nonetheless felt uneasy about interfering too directly in political matters. He did make clear his strong opposition to an eventual crowning of István as king. Beyond this, however, he simply warned the Regent that the idea of having his son elected deputy regent would be highly controversial and would probably be accepted by the Hungarian nation only if it was regarded as the only way to avert civil war or intervention by a foreign power. Horthy replied that only "scoundrels" would fail to see that the country was in a time of grave danger and that it would be best to settle the issue of succession while he was still alive.

Undaunted, a few days later Horthy sent to Bárdossy a letter in which he expressed his desire to "settle the question of succession" so that the transfer of power after his retirement or death would occur "without a hitch or excitement and an electioneering campaign."[28] The legislation of 1937, Horthy asserted, failed to solve the problem. He instructed Bárdossy to move quickly to prepare a new law that would provide for the election of a deputy regent by the two Houses of Parliament. The deputy regent, who would be vested with the right of succession, would have time to become acquainted with the responsibilities of the job and, Horthy added, "would be of help to me, too." Horthy suggested that he was prepared to waive his right to nominate candidates, but he insisted on reserving the right of confirming the election of the deputy regent, since he felt uniquely qualified, after more than twenty years of service, to judge who was qualified.

Nowhere in his letter to Bárdossy did Horthy mention his son's name, but Cardinal Serédi quickly spread word of the Regent's real intentions and members of the Regent's entourage began actively to promote István Horthy's candidacy. Soon Budapest was buzzing with rumors of the imminent establishment of a "Horthy dynasty." Although there were some Horthy loyalists in Parliament who enthusiastically embraced the Regent's plan, most deputies were deeply ambivalent or vigorously opposed. Some were prepared to give the Regent the benefit of the doubt and place the blame for this unfortunate development on other members of the Horthy family, especially the so-called female camarilla.[29] As in 1937, however, the predominant sentiment was that Horthy had overstepped the bounds of propriety and was making a thinly disguised bid to establish a dynasty.

Bárdossy, who himself had strong misgivings about Horthy's plan, thus confronted a difficult task in carrying out his assignment. István Horthy, himself, seemed extremely reluctant to take on a political role and was going along only out of filial loyalty. Almost everyone Bárdossy consulted, even those who shared István Horthy's pro-Western sentiments, voiced objections of one sort or another. The Catholic legitimists feared that Horthy's maneuvers were designed to transform the regency into a Protestant, national kingship. Arrowcross zealots complained bitterly that Horthy's son was compromised by his association with "the filthiest Jewish circles."[30] Army officers bemoaned his hostility to Nazi Germany and his lack of military experience. Nevertheless, most delegates found it politically and psychologically impossible to defy the Regent directly and openly. Cardinal Serédi lamented that "the whole case has been presented in a manner as if those who opposed the bill and the candidate . . . were enemies of the country and the Regent."[31] In any case, there was no agreement in Parliament about any alternate solutions to the problem of succession or on a candidate other than István Horthy. Archduke Albrecht had eagerly declared his availability and sought Germany's support, but his candidacy was doomed when Hitler decided that Germany should take no position on this question so long as Admiral Horthy was still alive.[32]

During January of 1942 a compromise solution was emerging from the intense discussions and negotiations of the previous weeks. The legislation proposed by Horthy would be enacted and István Horthy would be elected, but the office of deputy regent would not carry with it the automatic right of succession. On February 9 Bárdossy presented to the Lower House a bill that embodied these principles, fully expecting it to be approved without complications or debate. He, and most of the deputies, were thus shocked when Béla Imrédy rose and delivered a long speech in which he expressed the reservations that many of his colleagues felt. He deplored the haste with which the bill was being considered and the fact that the election would be by acclamation rather than by ballot. It concerned him, Imrédy continued, that whoever was elected deputy regent would be virtually assured of becoming regent. In an obvious allusion to István Horthy, he asserted that for such an important post the nation needed a man who had a high degree of military knowledge and experience and "can see the spirit of the new Europe in its reality. . . ." Hungary was lucky to have just such a leader in the current Regent, but it was incumbent on Parliament to take great care in its selection of a successor.[33]

Imrédy's audacious speech had little effect except to deepen Admiral Horthy's contempt for his former Prime Minister.[34] The legislation was duly passed by a large majority in both Houses and on February 18, 1942, in an elaborately staged ceremony, the Parliament, meeting in joint session, elected István Horthy by acclamation. There are indications, however, that Miklós Horthy was not entirely satisfied with the outcome, since his son's succession to the regency was not assured. Thus his mind turned immediately to a search for ways to promote István Horthy's image as a gallant Hungarian who, contrary to the complaints of Imrédy and others, did possess military skills and experience. It was apparently General Szombathelyi who put forward the idea of allowing the Deputy Regent, an experienced pilot, to join an air force unit for a tour of duty near the Eastern Front.[35] There were obvious dangers in such a plan, but István Horthy was eager to demonstrate his patriotism and to put off for a time the boring daily routine of his new office. Miklós Horthy thus relented, and amid great publicity the Deputy Regent flew off to the Front in May.

On February 24 Admiral Horthy wrote to Hitler informing him of his son's election, which he deemed a reflection of the will of the people since neither he nor his son had desired this solution. The Führer did not for a moment believe Horthy's assertion of political innocence, but he had no objection to this development. Indeed, later he was to express admiration for Admiral Horthy's "very neat plan" for bolstering his son's reputation as a warrior in the anti-Bolshevik struggle. This would, Hitler suggested, win support for him and eventually "grace him with the glory of the crown of St. Stephen."[36] Certainly Hitler's attitude would have been quite different if, like Joseph Goebbels, he had been shown the many German intelligence reports detailing the anti-Nazi and pro-Jewish sentiments of István Horthy. Goebbels wrote in his diary on February 2: "Horthy's son is a pronounced Jew-lover, an Anglophile to the bones, a man without any profound education and without any broad political comprehension; in short, a personality with whom, if he were Regent of Hungary, we would have some difficulties to iron out."[37] And even the active network of German agents in Hungary had not uncovered one incident that revealed the extent of young Horthy's pro-Western sympathies. In December 1941, shortly before the departure of the American diplomatic mission from Hungary, István Horthy had appeared at the legation to bid farewell. In a conversation with the First Secretary of the Legation, Howard Travers, he expressed the sympathy for the Allies that both he and his father felt. He regretted that he was not able to leave Hungary for the West in order to take part in the war against Germany.[38]

Admiral Horthy's actions in early 1942 thus represent a kind of paradox. On the one hand, he used his great prestige to overcome objections from powerful right-wing and pro-German factions to set up as his likely successor a man (who happened also to be his son) who was distinctly anti-German and friendly to the Jews. Even though nepotism rather than ideological preference was apparently his main motivation, the practical result was the same. Yet at the same time Horthy made a significant concession to the

Germans in the form of a new Hungarian Army to be sent to fight on the Eastern Front. Horthy's continuing ambivalence and the contradictory nature of his statements were noticed by Count Ciano when he visited Hungary in mid-January 1942: "The Regent repeats every other minute his conviction that the Axis will emerge victorious from the war, but from his way of speaking there is implied—and often clearly appears—a deep-seated bias which amounts to hostility towards the Germans." Horthy's suspicions about the Germans were reflected in the hope he expressed to Ciano that at the end of the war Italy would continue to exercise an effective influence in Danubian Europe. That, he said, would be the best guarantee of "the political and moral independence of the Hungarian people."[39]

It was only in late February, after the election of the Deputy Regent, that Admiral Horthy had the opportunity to assess fully the events of the past six months. He was not happy with what he found. Despite his own reluctance to get involved in Hitler's war, Hungary was in the process of sending a large army to fight on the plains of Russia. Although he had often stated his admiration for the Anglo-Saxon powers, Hungary was now at war with Great Britain and relations with the United States had been broken off. His plan to have his son appointed Deputy Regent had been only partly implemented, since there was no automatic right to succession.

Lacking the capacity for any significant self-criticism, Horthy, as was his custom, assumed others were responsible for this sorry state of affairs, even though it is clear that his own complicity was significant. By Horthy's simple calculations, the blame could be placed only on his Prime Minister who had inexplicably begun to pursue "an un-Hungarian policy."[40] It is true that, like Béla Imrédy before him, Bárdossy had determined after taking office that only a forthright policy of cooperation with Hitler's Germany and concessions to the powerful radical right-wing in Hungary made sense, given Hungary's geopolitical situation and the likely outcome of the war. Bárdossy did not proclaim such a policy openly, but his initiatives in proposing new anti-Jewish legislation and widening Hungary's participation in the world war were clear indications of his new orientation. As early as October 1941, an informal anti-Bárdossy clique headed by Ferenc Keresztes-Fischer had formed and the Regent was presented with complaints and accusations against the Prime Minister,[41] among them that Bárdossy in reality opposed István Horthy's candidacy for the deputy regency and worked behind the scenes to make sure that the legislation did not contain the right of succession.

This alone might have tipped the balance against Bárdossy, but it was a further misunderstanding between the Regent and his Prime Minister that led to a final confrontation. At some point in the negotiations over the creation of the deputy regency, Bárdossy apparently suggested to Horthy that it would be a good idea to appease those who opposed István Horthy for ideological reasons. He suggested that it would be appropriate, once Horthy's son was safely installed in his new office, to make certain changes in the Cabinet to give it more of a right-wing tilt. Bárdossy gained the impression that Horthy approved this idea, although, in light of later events, it seems more likely that Horthy refrained from an immediate rejection of the proposal only because he wished to avoid any political complications during the negotiations over the creation of the deputy regency.

In a conversation with Horthy in late February, Bárdossy returned to his proposal and presented his ideas for the reconstruction of the Cabinet.[42] He urged the replacement of several moderates, including Keresztes-Fischer, with individuals more acceptable to the right-wing factions. But Horthy proved recalcitrant, rejecting each name put forward by Bárdossy. Some he termed Arrowcross men, others he called totally unacceptable to him personally. Finally, in exasperation, Bárdossy declared that they must not have had an agreement after all. To which Horthy responded: "Well, what do you want then, a dictatorship?" Bárdossy's sarcastic reply surely sealed his fate: "No, but there is in fact a dictatorship here!" After a few more acrimonious exchanges the Prime Minister declared that he wished to resign. Horthy responded that he could not simply resign, but he could step down for reasons of health. On March 6 it was in fact announced that the Prime Minister had resigned and had been admitted to a sanitorium.[43]

Admiral Horthy was determined to replace Bárdossy with someone in whom he could have implicit trust, someone who would remain Prime Minister for the duration of the war. Reviewing the disappointing performances of Gömbös, Imrédy, and Bárdossy, Horthy now concluded that the basic problem was that these men were not sufficiently and genuinely Magyar in their background and political orientation. What was needed in the current crisis was a "real Hungarian." The nation, he had become convinced, would have confidence in and follow only someone who was "blood of their blood." Such a man would be able to stand up to the Germans, neutralize Hungary's noisy right-wing extremists, and protect the country's interests in wartime. One man alone, Miklós Kállay, seemed to fit this description.

Of Miklós Kállay a historian has aptly written: "Neither ancestry, environment nor career could be more Hungarian, nor even physique."[44] A scion of one of the most illustrious of Hungary's aristocratic families, Kállay had played only a minor role in national politics. In his general political outlook he was of the Bethlen school, moderately conservative, hostile to extremist movements of any kind, protective of the interests of the great landowners, and respectful of Hungary's constitutional traditions. On international issues he shared the outlook of Pál Teleki, while realizing the immense difficulties of conducting such a foreign policy in wartime. Although he rarely spoke publicly on domestic political issues, his vote against the third anti-Jewish law drew the ire of the radical right-wingers, who suspected, quite accurately, that on the "Jewish question" he shared the relatively tolerant views of his friend Ferenc Keresztes-Fischer.

A clear indication that Horthy was considering Kállay as a replacement for Bárdossy came in early January, when he arranged to have Kállay join him in a conversation with Ribbentrop. At one point in the talk, to Ribbentrop's obvious annoyance, Kállay suggested that it was a mistake for the Germans to draw small nations like Romania and Hungary into an offensive war. In general, Kállay asserted, "a small nation's radius of activity could never extend beyond its historic frontiers." Kállay's forthrightness pleased Horthy, who afterwards drew him aside and told him that "that was the way to talk to the Germans." Horthy added that "great changes were imminent," and that he, Kállay, should prepare for them.[45]

Shortly after conferring on March 4 with Count Bethlen, Horthy summoned Kállay to the royal palace. Horthy began by declaring that he was "completely disappointed" with his Prime Minister, whose transgressions he proceeded to describe at length and in somewhat exaggerated terms.[46] He had appointed Bárdossy in April 1941 with the sole purpose of having an experienced career diplomat who could guide the country smoothly out of the crisis over Yugoslavia, and he had never thought of him as a Prime Minister for the long run. Yet, contrary to his intentions, Bárdossy had "plunged wholeheartedly into internal politics and even international ideological politics." He had sought "popularity at any price," and had ingratiated himself with the Germans and the radical right-wing factions in Hungary. Bárdossy had confronted him with "one *fait accompli* after another," such as the declarations of war against Russia and the United States. Moreover, he was now trying to force out of the Cabinet people like Keresztes-Fischer, who were loyal and in whom the Regent had complete confidence. And he had even raised the question of another anti-Jewish law and the possible deportation of the Jews.[47]

In short, Horthy continued, Hungary had reached such a "wretched state" that he had decided to dismiss Bárdossy and appoint Kállay as his new Prime Minister. He had "complete confidence" in Kállay, whose views he knew and approved of. As Prime Minister he would have a completely free hand and could proceed as he wished. He, the Regent, would not interfere in the selection of the Cabinet or formulation of policy, except in the realm of military affairs. What's more, this appointment would be for the duration of the war. He wished to work with Kállay "so long as he lived and remained the Regent." If there were ever a problem with Parliament, he would dissolve it and, if Kállay wished, call new elections.

The terms of Admiral Horthy's offer reflected his eagerness to persuade Kállay to undertake a most difficult assignment. Not since the Bethlen era had a Prime Minister been promised such freedom of maneuver. Nonetheless, Kállay, citing the enormous obstacles he would face, respectfully declined the Regent's offer. How would he be able to govern? The majority of the government party did not trust him; the Germans would be hostile; and anti-Semitism had permeated internal politics. Horthy tried, without success, to demonstrate that Kállay was being unduly pessimistic. Germany was very powerful but not invincible. The moment Hitler suffered his first defeat, the Wehrmacht would turn against Nazism and the possibility of a compromise peace would arise. Hungary's position between Russia and Germany was not necessarily hopeless. Surely Great Britain, which had always sought to maintain a balance of power on the continent, would not allow Russia to bolshevize Europe. True, errors had been made by the Hungarian government in the past, but the two of them working in tandem would be able to rescue the country.

The two men parted that day without any agreement. Kállay

explained to a friend why he was loath to take on the responsibility of leading the country. The only foreign policy he would pursue was that of Pál Teleki. But "if Teleki had found no way except suicide of remaining true to his own principles, and suicide at a time when we were not yet at war with anyone, how could one follow this policy now, with Bárdossy's four wars on one's back?" Yet the Regent was persistent, calling Kállay daily to press his case. After a few days Kállay relented. When he appeared in the Regent's office to announce his decision, Horthy embraced him warmly and, tears welling in his eyes, thanked him for undertaking this grave responsibility. As he was leaving the royal palace, Kállay met István Horthy, who, upon hearing the news, exclaimed: "Now everything is all right; everything will be all right!"[48]

In formulating a strategy for coping with the precarious situation in which Hungary found itself, Kállay and Horthy shared certain fundamental principles and assumptions.[49] In the spring of 1942 neither man believed that the war would end in a German defeat.[50] Rather they anticipated that there would be a stalemate that would lead to a compromise peace. Hungary's task, then, was to prepare for this eventuality. In domestic affairs the clamor of the radical right-wing for various totalitarian measures and increased oppression of the Jews would be resisted. Imrédy and his followers were, at Horthy's insistence, to be treated "as national enemies and outside the law."[51] Above all, it was imperative that Hungary conserve its military strength in order to thwart an occupation by either Russian or German troops and to preserve the territorial gains of the past few years. Certainly both men also hoped to maintain the political regime of which they were integral parts, but they were prepared to make certain concessions to moderate and even left-wing forces if circumstances at war's end required it.

Upon assuming office on March 10, Miklós Kállay thus embarked on a pragmatic policy that came to be known variously as a "see-saw policy" (*hintapolitika*) or the "Kállay two-step" (*kállai kettő s*), a reference to a popular Hungarian dance. Both Hungarian terms are appropriate metaphors for Kállay's strategy, for he was prepared to promote the policies described above by a series of back and forth steps that would lead eventually, but not directly, to the desired objectives. The nature of these steps would be determined by the course of the war, and would be cautious enough not only to avoid provoking a German occupation, but also to allow Hungary to coexist with the Third Reich should a negotiated peace leave Germany dominant in Eastern Europe or in the unlikely case of a German victory in the war. Many of Kállay's critics on the right divined what his policy would be and were convinced that he would fail. Bárdossy, who probably spoke for a majority in the political establishment and certainly the bulk of the military officers, warned Kállay that he "would lose the friendship of Germany without gaining that of England, which was committed to Russia and the Little Entente."[52]

Since for the remainder of 1942 Germany remained the paramount power on the continent, and certainly in Danubian Europe, Kállay felt constrained to make certain gestures and concessions to the Germans and their Hungarian supporters. In his maiden speech to Parliament he was careful to affirm Hungary's commitment to fight the war "with all the energies at our disposal."[53] During the remainder of 1942 and for much of 1943 his speeches and statements were filled with pro-Axis, anti-Russian, and anti-Semitic utterances, but he carefully avoided any hostile references to the Anglo-Saxon powers.[54] To pacify his right-wing critics at home, Kállay was prepared to enact certain measures further limiting the role of Jews in Hungarian economic life. He reasoned that the Jews could survive discrimination of this kind, and that any injustices could be made right after the war. However, Kállay and Horthy agreed that there could be no "destructive intolerance" or inhumane treatment of the Jews, and certainly no deportations.[55] When the Germans or Hungarian radical right-wingers demanded more radical steps against the Jews, Kállay and Horthy would procrastinate: such measures would be taken "eventually" or "after the war."[56]

That Admiral Horthy favored a relatively tolerant policy toward the Jews in this period, and not just later as an opportunistic response to Germany's declining fortunes in the war, can be seen from private remarks he made on several occasions in 1942. Early in the year he instructed the new Director of the Hungarian Radio, Antal Náray, to avoid dealing with partisan politics or the "Jewish question" in radio broadcasts.[57] It was wrong, Horthy explained, to think of the Jews as all alike. Among them there were honorable individuals, like Léo Goldberger and Manfréd Weiss, who by themselves had done more for the country's economy than the whole radical right-wing camp put together.

Additional information about Horthy's attitude toward the Jews in 1942 is provided by a German document that records a conversation in July between the Regent and Lajos Reményi-Schneller, the Minister of Finance.[58] A fervent admirer of Nazi Germany, Reményi-Schneller had drafted a proposal for expropriation of Jewish wealth by means of a capital levy. Although a majority of the Cabinet apparently gave its approval, Kállay and Horthy were both opposed.[59] Horthy told Reményi-Schneller that he agreed that the "Galician Jews" would have to be excluded (*ausgeschaltet*) from the life of the country, but all the other Jews who had served Hungary in science, industry, and finance were to be regarded as patriots and were not to be harmed. He would certainly not tolerate mistreatment of Jews who had served as his advisors or as members of the Upper House. Moreover, he would reject all measures that amounted to robbery of the Jews. He agreed that in general Jewish influence should be checked and that Jews should not own farm land, but care had to be taken to prevent the flight of Jewish capital abroad. A better plan, Horthy suggested, was to place the Jewish firms at the service of the state, which would guide production along useful lines and would allot to the Jewish owners a certain percentage of the profits, perhaps 4 percent.[60] Horthy suggested that Reményi-Schneller prepare a plan along these lines, but the Minister of Finance did not do so, for such an idea was totally incompatible with the severe measures being taken against Jews throughout the rest of Nazi-dominated Europe.

On several fronts Regent Horthy thus proved a major obstacle to the introduction of the radical right-wing program for solving the "Jewish problem." On one related issue, however, his attitude was much harsher. In January 1942 Hungarian Army units in the southern province of Bácska had carried out reprisals against partisans who were committing terrorist acts.[61] Under the command of a sadistic commander, this operation became a series of wholesale massacres in the city of Újvidék and its environs. More than three thousand innocent Serbs and Jews, including many women and children, were executed in what came to be known as the Újvidék massacre.[62] When information about these events reached the Hungarian Parliament, several members called for an investigation. In early February, Endre Bajcsy-Zsilinszky, who was emerging as the spokesman for the anti-German faction, sent Horthy a twenty-five page memorandum in which he referred to extensive evidence that horrible atrocities had been committed by units of the Hungarian Army and gendarmerie.[63] But Horthy was unimpressed by this document, even though it made a convincing case against the officers responsible for the massacre. On such matters his attitude remained as rigid as ever: accusations of this kind by civilians were tantamount to defamation of the army. Horthy summoned Bajcsy-Zsilinszky to his office and upbraided him for always looking for the dark side of things.[64] Bajcsy-Zsilinszky left greatly depressed by the fact that Horthy rejected his advice and instead took at face value the account provided by the Hungarian commander of the Újvidék operation, General Ferenc Feketehalmi-Czeydner, who insisted that there had been no massacres but merely justifiable retaliations against terrorists.

In light of the available evidence, Miklós Kállay was less inclined than the Regent to believe the accused officers. Upon accepting Horthy's invitation to become Prime Minister, Kállay argued that in line with their agreement that the nation's "traditional standards of honor and humanity" were to be preserved, the Újvidék case must be investigated. Horthy agreed, with some reluctance, to the establishment of a military review commission, which conducted its investigation over the course of several months. However, this proved to be a whitewash, since the officer in charge of the investigation was a secret member of the Arrowcross. The resulting report fully exonerated the accused officers; it was accepted, albeit with some skepticism, by Kállay and Szombathelyi.[65] Regent Horthy himself apparently had no qualms about formally dismissing all charges against the accused officers, which he did in August 1942.

Aside from the events described above, the Hungarian political scene remained relatively tranquil in the first six months of Kállay's premiership. The first units of the Second Army began their journey to the Eastern Front in May, but the most serious fighting was still some months off. Otherwise, the traditional rhythm of Hungarian political life continued almost unchanged. Horthy's birthday was celebrated on June 18 in the usual fashion. As was his custom, the Regent spent much of the summer at the former royal residence in Gödöllő and at his estate in Kenderes. But he was back in Budapest in mid-August, for it was his duty to lead a procession through Buda as part of the St. Stephen's Day ceremonies on the 20th. For Horthy and his wife this was an occasion for special celebration, since, on the basis of a resolution recently passed, at Kállay's urging, by the Hungarian Cabinet, István Horthy was being recalled from active duty to assume his political responsibilities as Deputy Regent.[66]

This St. Stephen's Day, however, was to end in tragedy for the

Horthy family. As the seventy-four year old Regent made his way along the cobbled streets and acknowledged the cheers of the assembled crowds, he had no inkling of the message that the head of the Regent's Military Chancery had whispered in Miklós Kállay's ear just as the procession got underway: "István Horthy has had a flying accident. He has been killed." Kállay chose not to act on this information during the procession or the mass celebrated at the Coronation Church. Only afterwards, when they had returned to the Royal Palace, did Kállay inform the Regent. Horthy could not cope with this shattering news. He fainted in Kállay's arms, recovered, and then fainted again.[67]

Over the next several days Admiral Horthy's mood swung wildly between apathy and vituperation. At first he blamed himself for allowing his son to go to the Front in the first place. The he decided that the fault really lay with Bárdossy, who, by preventing István from gaining the right of succession, had made it necessary for him to demonstrate his military skills.[68] While Horthy and his wife grieved, however, other members of the family and of Horthy's entourage began almost immediately to search for a way to honor István Horthy's memory in an appropriate way. Already on August 21 a trial balloon was floated to test reaction to the designation of István Horthy's two-year-old son, István Jr., as the deputy regent or, more remarkably, as "heir to the throne."[69] Cardinal Serédi wasted no time in expressing his strong disapproval of these plans. He made it clear to both Kállay and Horthy that he would never crown a "Protestant baby." The idea was absurd and if pursued would tear the country apart.[70]

Nonetheless, throughout September and early October Horthy family members and supporters continued their campaign promoting an immediate coronation of the infant István. In the halls of Parliament once again the complaint was heard that the "female camarilla," led by István Horthy's widow, was engaging in intrigue. Despite the protests of Cardinal Serédi and others, Admiral Horthy refused for several weeks to intervene and call a halt to this activity, which he claimed, somewhat implausibly, "represented the nation's sympathies." Eventually, however, he agreed with Kállay that there were more appropriate ways that the Parliament could honor the memory of his son and secure the future of his grandson. On October 6 Horthy assured Serédi that he did not approve of the more extreme plans that had been proposed. He managed to formulate his decision in self-serving terms that emphasized the contribution of the Horthy family to the nation: "I've sacrificed myself, my wife, and my son. But I will not hand over my grandson. I will not permit him to become the plaything in the hands of others."[71]

By October the tremors set off by the sudden death of István Horthy had subsided and Hungarian political life began to return to its normal wartime concerns. For Admiral Horthy the past three months had been a trying and enervating time that took a toll on him both physically and mentally. He had become thinner and had lost some of the vivacity and robustness that had been his trademarks. Beginning in late 1942 those who had frequent contact with the Regent also noticed an increased inattentiveness and apathy. His tendency in conversations to ramble and lose his concentration, which had been present even in the 1920s, now became more pronounced. Horthy no longer read newspapers on a daily basis; as a result, he began to lose track of developments in Europe and the wider world. He was less attentive to the stream of memorandums and reports that crossed his desk. Few of his papers from 1943 and 1944 contain the kind of personal annotations one finds in the earlier period. By the same token, Horthy now only infrequently had the interest or energy to write down his thoughts in letters or memorandums. This did not mean that his devotion to work diminished in this period. Rather, he now conducted his affairs almost completely through oral communication. Given Horthy's occasional lapses of memory, however, this sometimes led to confusion and misunderstandings.

In one sense, however, Miklós Horthy's stature was strengthened by the dignified way in which he had endured his tribulations in late 1942. Public respect and sympathy for the Regent and his wife reached even higher levels. Who could not feel sorry for a couple who had lost three of their four children? More and more Admiral Horthy was compared with other Hungarian leaders who had suffered great personal tragedies. It was pointed out, for example, that St. Stephen too had lost his favorite son. To be sure, some Hungarians in the political establishment were dismayed by the way in which Horthy had tolerated and perhaps even encouraged those who wanted to establish a Horthy dynasty. In the end, however, Horthy had rejected the grandiose plans put forward by his friends and close family members and made the "statesmanlike" decision.[72] For this he won grudging respect even from some of his critics.

One curious development in the aftermath of the death of István

Horthy was the Regent's decision not to push for the selection of a new deputy regent. He now declared that there were no suitable candidates and that he didn't really need a deputy after all. Horthy's attitude lends credence to the accusation that he had favored the establishment of the deputy regency merely as a way of ensuring that his son István would succeed him. On the other hand, his initial lack of enthusiasm for the idea of having his other son, Miklós Jr., appointed deputy regent suggests that a passion to establish a Horthy dynasty was not his overwhelming motivation. On several occasions in late 1942 Horthy privately expressed doubts about the intellectual abilities of his son Niki, suggesting that he had never fully recovered from head injuries caused by falling off a horse. It seems, also, that Horthy's personal relationship with Niki was not as warm and intimate as it had been with his eldest son. The two sometimes quarreled and were not on speaking terms for days at a time.[73] Nonetheless, Niki had acquitted himself well as Hungary's envoy in Brazil, and upon his return to Hungary in November 1942 Regent Horthy somewhat reluctantly agreed that his son might be of some assistance to him. To the surprise of many, Niki came to play an important political role in the last two years of the war and showed both courage and ingenuity in helping his father deal with the grave crisis that engulfed Hungary in 1944.

In retrospect, one incident connected with the death of Horthy's son can be seen as almost a medieval portent of the string of misfortunes and disasters that would soon strike Hungary. On August 27, the day of the funeral of István Horthy, a group of family members and friends had gathered in a hall of the royal palace. Suddenly an enormous crystal chandelier crashed to the floor, landing only a few feet from the Regent.[74] Horthy no doubt wondered what else could go wrong. He soon discovered that for those countries that had allied with Nazi Germany, much could and would go wrong.

In October 1942 those German officials responsible for the carrying out of the "Final Solution" of the "Jewish question" decided that the time had come to put pressure on Hungary to participate. By this time Jews were being deported "to the East" from all over Europe, including Slovakia. Romanian forces were cooperating with the Germans in large-scale massacres of Jews in occupied areas of the Soviet Union. Hitler, who had once cynically observed that Hungary would be the last country where the Jews would hold on,[75] was losing his patience. Döme Sztójay reported from Berlin that the Germans were now insisting on "appropriate action," including compulsory wearing of the yellow star, expropriation of Jewish wealth, and deportation. Sztójay, who at this time was one of the few Hungarians to know the real purpose of the deportation of Jews, nonetheless advocated full cooperation with the Germans. He warned of "fatal consequences" if the response from Budapest was unsatisfactory, since for the Germans this issue was of the utmost importance.[76]

Ironically, these new German demands came at a time when Admiral Horthy had just taken action to ameliorate the plight of Jews who were serving in Hungarian labor battalions on the Eastern Front. Horthy had had no objection to the creation of these military-style work units, which in fact had been first employed in Horthy's Hungary to deal with "political undesirables" in the immediate post–World War I period. He reasoned that Jewish men, who were barred by law from serving as regulars in the army, should be forced to make sacrifices for the war effort. But beginning in the late summer of 1942 Horthy had begun to receive reports of extremely cruel and sadistic treatment of Jews in the labor battalions.[77] On the basis of these reports, which must have come from sources that Horthy trusted, the Regent acted favorably on a number of petitions he received for the recall of individual Jews (mostly physicians and scholars) who had been conscripted to forced labor battalions. More importantly, these reports prompted Horthy to dismiss the Minister of Defense, General Károly Bartha, whom he held responsible for a breakdown in discipline among the officers. To be sure, Horthy had other reasons for turning against Bartha, who, like Henrik Werth, had come to exhibit pronounced sympathies for Nazi Germany. It is significant, however, that Horthy chose as the new Minister of Defense General Vilmos Nagy, who had a reputation for integrity and humanitarianism. Nagy, who was appointed on September 24, was instructed to restore discipline and end the "political activity that had become fashionable" among the officers. During his tenure over the next ten months, Nagy found it impossible to carry out the first assignment, for he discovered that extremist right-wing and pro-German tendencies were too firmly embedded in the officer corps. His attempts to end the most blatant abuses in the forced labor units did meet with some success, although his orders were often sabotaged by anti-Semitic officers at the lower levels.[78] Nagy reported fully to Horthy on the atrocities that had been committed, on one occasion declaring that the poor Jewish servicemen had in effect "carried their death warrants in their packs."[79]

Having just taken action to end atrocities against Hungarian Jews in the labor battalions, Admiral Horthy was hardly prepared to approve the kinds of anti-Jewish measures the Germans were now demanding. At the time of Kállay's appointment earlier in the year, Horthy had agreed with his new Prime Minister that there would be no "destructive intolerance" toward the Jews. Horthy, of course, had no special fondness or sympathy for the Jews, and he failed to recognize the pernicious and degrading impact the anti-Jewish laws had already had and the extent to which public anti-Semitic sentiments had been inflamed. Moreover, he believed that in wartime cruel and violent acts were inevitable and that much suffering would occur. Nonetheless, Admiral Horthy also subscribed to the notion that those in authority, whether government officials or military officers, were obliged not only to respect the rule of law but to act honorably. Horthy's concept of honor, as has been seen, was in some ways anachronistic and was not always applied in an evenhanded way, but it did lead him to reject the anti-Jewish measures proposed by the Germans as inhumane. By the fall of 1942 there may also have been other, more pragmatic, reasons for pro-Western Hungarians to practice tolerance toward the Jews. It is possible that Horthy learned, perhaps from Kállay or Keresztes-Fischer, of the statements made in September by British statesmen who had learned some of the details of the "Final Solution." Most notable was Winston Churchill's expression of horror at the atrocities committed against Jews in France. The "hour of liberation" would inevitably come, Churchill declared, for those who had lent themselves to the Nazis' "unnatural and perverted passions."[80]

With Regent Horthy's backing, Miklós Kállay thus rejected the demands put forward by the Germans. He raised a variety of objections. Hungary could not act precipitously on this matter because it would disrupt the economy, cause inflation, and hamper deliveries of war material to Germany. He would not allow the Jews to be deported until he had a better idea of the fate of the Jews in the East. Would they have the means to sustain themselves there? Besides, the Jews could be usefully employed on work projects in Hungary. In any case, the "Jewish question" was an internal affair and Hungary would not brook any interference from outsiders.[81]

As the Hungarian government procrastinated on this issue in late 1942 and early 1943, the military fortunes of the Axis powers began a precipitous decline. On November 8 the Allies made a successful landing in North Africa. By the end of the month it was clear that Germany had lost the Battle of Stalingrad. Admiral Horthy saw the military significance of these events. In early January he told a German visitor that he foresaw a complete rout in Africa and the possibility of an Allied landing in the Balkans in the near future.[82]

Emboldened by these military developments, the anti-German camp in Hungary now became more active in the search for ways to extricate the country from the war and ameliorate the condition of the Jews. Those who shared these views came from different parts of the political spectrum, but there was a consensus that the Regent must be won over before significant progress could be made. Accordingly, in December a group of moderate conservatives agreed on the wording of a memorandum that was presented to Horthy on the 17th by a delegation consisting of Count Bethlen, Cardinal Serédi, and Géza Töreky, the president of the Kuria (Hungary's Supreme Court).[83] Horthy's visitors explained that they had chosen this unusual kind of personal intervention because of the "extraordinary dangers threatening our poor country." The memorandum called for action in two main areas. Horthy was urged to find a way to withdraw Hungary's forces from the Eastern Front and to strengthen a home army that would be needed to defend the country as the war came to an end. Secondly, steps should be taken to restore the rule of law and respect for Hungary's tradition of humanism. Those who were responsible for the "godless and inhumane" treatment of the Jews should be called to account, and amends should be made to the Serbs and other victims of the Újvidék massacre. Bethlen added on his own that the exaggerated pro-German orientation of the General Staff and military leadership was a serious danger. Regent Horthy was receptive to the arguments of his distinguished visitors, but he made no commitment to act on their recommendations.[84]

Early in 1943 Horthy received a similar memorandum from other members of the Opposition, including Endre Bajcsy-Zsilinszky, who had once again publicly called for a new investigation of the Újvidék atrocities.[85] By that time, however, the Regent's main concern centered on the deterioration of the situation on the Eastern Front. In December Horthy's military chiefs informed him that the Second Army was in a perilous position. The

Germans had not provided the promised equipment and supplies, and if the Red Army launched a major attack, it was questionable whether the Hungarian forces could hold the battlefront.[86] Horthy must have realized the gravity of the situation when, shortly before Christmas, he received a telegram from Hitler urging him to see to it that the Hungarian troops on the Don River put up a stiff resistance. In his response, Horthy agreed to do everything within his power, but pointed out that the Hungarian troops were not adequately equipped, were assigned to too long a section of the Front, and were not backed up by sufficient reserves. Horthy pleaded for "some assistance in this regard."[87]

Given the unfulfilled German promises of the past and the poor morale of the Hungarian soldiers, nothing could be done to avert the impending disaster. On January 12 the Soviet forces began a massive attack. The Hungarian Second Army, which had been assigned the sector of the Front near Voronezh, was able to offer little resistance and by the 14th was in full, panicky retreat. Within two weeks more than half of the 200,000-man army was listed as dead, wounded, or missing. Furthermore, the Jewish labor battalions, numbering some 40,000, were almost entirely decimated.[88]

In the aftermath of the "disaster at Voronezh," both Horthy and Kállay agreed that an attempt had to be made to withdraw the remnants of the Second Army and to disengage entirely from combat on the Eastern Front. Since, however, the Germans rejected such a notion and Kállay remained wary of taking any step that might provoke a German occupation of Hungary, nothing was accomplished.

In two other areas, however, Kállay was able to take more decisive action. Now that an Allied victory in the war seemed possible, and even probable, it became clear to him that the Horthy regime could not emerge unscathed from the war. If things went badly, the whole system "based on the twin pillars of big capital and big landed estates" would be destroyed.[89] It was his aim, however, to preclude a complete social and political revolution, and to ensure that the aged Admiral Horthy would remain for a time after the war as head of state and symbol of authority. With this in mind and with the hope that he could establish ties between the regime and the more moderate leaders of the left-wing opposition, Kállay began in late 1942 to make conciliatory gestures to the liberal and left-wing parties.[90]

Admiral Horthy supported Kállay's modest "opening to the

left" and even agreed to grant an audience to the leader of the Social Democrats, Károly Peyer. The uniqueness of this event, which was not kept secret, did not escape the notice of political observers either in Hungary or abroad.[91] Not only was Peyer the first Social Democrat to be invited to the Royal Castle since the early 1920s, but it was widely known that for years the Regent had steadfastly refused Ferenc Szálasi's request for an audience. Horthy received his visitor cordially and listened patiently as Peyer recited the needs of the workers and stated the willingness of his party to participate in the "national task" of withdrawing from the war. Horthy promised to fulfill Peyer's requests "as much as possible," and asked in return that the Social Democrats cooperate in maintaining civil order and ensuring a trouble-free harvest. Horthy enthusiastically accepted Peyer's suggestion that the Social Democrats might send to the Labour party in England a memorandum describing Hungary's domestic situation and explaining the country's participation in the war.[92]

In light of Admiral Horthy's long-standing distrust of the Socialists, one can perhaps doubt the sincerity of his friendly words to Peyer.[93] More difficult to explain, however, is his apparent willingness to rethink his position on land reform. For more than two decades Horthy had remained adamantly opposed to further distribution of land. Early in 1943, however, it occurred to him that in the current war many Hungarian soldiers would distinguish themselves and become eligible for induction into the *Vitézi Rend* (Order of Heroes). He therefore asked Kállay to work up a plan for an expansion of what had always been his pet project. The Prime Minister complied, but Horthy was not entirely happy with his suggestions, which apparently focused on offering to future "heroes" rewards other than plots of land.[94] Horthy pointed out to Kállay that the Order of Heroes had become "the nation's most reliable national defense organization and its strongest economic unit." He agreed that in some cases other kinds of inducement could be offered to inductees into the Order, but he insisted that the existing practice of awarding plots of land should be continued and in fact accelerated. Horthy acknowledged that landowners were often reluctant to hand over portions of the family estate to strangers, but he pointed out how critical it was to provide a reward to which the individual soldier could aspire.

Kállay, who did not think it was a propitious time to open up the question of further land reform, even for the creation of "heroes estates," apparently hoped that Horthy's attention would soon turn to other urgent matters. But Horthy must have given further thought to the question and even consulted individuals who were proponents of extensive land reform, for in late January or early February he presented to the Prime Minister a memorandum in which he put forth a remarkable proposal.[95] Pointing out that the country lacked a systematic land distribution policy, Horthy suggested that a new Ministry of Land Reform be established and that consideration be given to an eventual distribution of 5½ million holds (4 million acres), that is, roughly 60 percent of Hungary's arable land.

Although Kállay must have been flabbergasted to receive such a proposal from a man who had always insisted that there just wasn't enough land in Hungary for meaningful land reform, he nonetheless complied with Horthy's wish that the matter be brought before the Cabinet. At a meeting on February 23 Kállay presented Horthy's ideas as well as a set of other less controversial proposals for social and economic reform. These matters had to be discussed, Kállay observed, because "the end of the war would bring a social transformation." It seems, however, that in the ensuing discussion both Kállay and Keresztes-Fischer spoke against the Regent's plan on the grounds that nothing could be accomplished along these lines during the war. Most of the assembled ministers shared this view. Strong opposition also came from Count Bethlen, Gyula Károlyi and other conservative aristocrats who had long been Horthy's trusted advisors.[96]

Kállay reported the results of the Cabinet meeting to Horthy in a diplomatically worded but firm letter dated February 26.[97] He raised all the objections to land reform that, ironically, Horthy himself had always used when someone raised the issue. There was, Kállay reminded the Regent, simply not enough land to go around. He questioned the source of Horthy's claim that 5½ million hold could be distributed. This, he said, would require the breakup of all private and church estates in Hungary. In any case, now was not a good time to force the pace of land reform, since it would disrupt civil order. Furthermore, Kállay added, the funding and proper leadership were not available for such an enterprise. Those individuals suggested by Horthy as leaders of a new Ministry of Land Reform were unsuitable. One, Elemér Kovács, was "a fanatical peasant politician who would want to divide up the land to the last inch." Surely the Regent would not approve of the results of his work.

The manner in which Horthy and Kállay resolved this issue is not known, and it seems likely that it was in fact pushed to the side as other more urgent problems presented themselves in the first months of 1943. One detects an echo of Horthy's initiative, however, in a speech that Kállay made in Szeged in June, in which he adumbrated a plan for land reform after the war that would have turned 90 percent of the country's arable land into small- and medium-sized plots.[98] Horthy apparently did not pursue this issue in the last two years of the war; indeed, when the topic did come up again, he seemed to revert to his traditional opposition. But there is additional evidence from the postwar period that Horthy's initiative in 1943 was a first, hesitant step in what would be a genuine conversion to advocacy of major land reform.[99]

Miklós Kállay's second main initiative in this period was the extension of peace feelers to the Allies. Through most of 1942 Kállay had hesitated to take this risky step, but the decline in the military fortunes of the Axis powers and the belief in an imminent Anglo-American landing in the Balkans prompted him to action. In early 1943 a number of Hungarian emissaries tried to make contact with the Allies.[100] Kállay gave his tacit approval to these diplomatic missions, but only one of the emissaries, György Barcza, was dispatched with specific instructions from him. Kállay explained to Barcza, who was working closely with Bethlen and his colleagues, that Hungary was prepared to distance itself gradually from the Germans, but would not embark on any policy that would likely lead to either a German or Soviet occupation. Barcza was authorized to suggest that Hungary's leaders did not insist on saving the current regime, but to warn that too radical a turn leftward (for example, reliance on Michael Károlyi, who was living in England) would be a disaster. Kállay urged Barcza to argue the case for keeping Horthy as head of state in a postwar government, since he was very popular and was an ardent Anglophile. He was also to put forward the case for maintaining a strong Hungary as a "factor of order" in postwar Eastern Europe.[101]

Most of the other Hungarian emissaries wandering through neutral countries in early 1943 did not have any explicit instructions from Kállay. Some of them, in fact, represented groups within or outside the government that were willing to jettison the current regime in order to make peace with the Allies. Antal Ullein-Reviczky, the anti-German chief of the Press Section of the Prime Minister's office, was responsible for the dispatch of several scholars and journalists with instructions to try their hand at making contact with the Allies. One of them, Ferenc Váli, a historian, received a last-minute, whispered message from Ullein-Reviczky: "If necessary to save the country, you may repudiate Regent Horthy."[102] Another scholar, Albert Szent-Györgyi, recipient of the Nobel Prize for biology, contacted representatives of the Allies in Istanbul and claimed to speak for all democratic forces in Hungary. Szent-Györgyi had met briefly with Kállay before he left Hungary, but the Prime Minister did not inquire about the precise nature of his mission. Of course, Kállay would hardly have been prepared to endorse Szent-Györgyi's program, which called for the toppling of Hungary's "feudal system."[103]

That Hungary was in the process of sending out peace feelers to the Allies was hardly a well-kept secret in Hungary in early 1943. As he waited for final authorization from Kállay to leave the country, György Barcza was asked by many people he met, even by his barber, when he would embark on his mission abroad.[104] Strangely, even as Budapest buzzed with rumors of secret peace negotiations, Hungary's head of state, Miklós Horthy, knew almost nothing about these developments. At the time of his appointment in March 1942, Kállay had suggested to the Regent that at some point he might wish to contact the Allies. Horthy had given him a "free hand" to pursue his policy as he saw fit. Horthy later explained it in this way: "Between him [Kállay] and myself, there was an unspoken agreement that he should have a free hand without referring details to me in taking measures that would, while safeguarding our relations with Hitlerite Germany, draw us closer to the British and Americans without entailing active support of the Soviet Union."[105] When Kállay, Bethlen, and Barcza discussed the plan to establish diplomatic contact with the Allies, it was agreed that the details of the various missions should be withheld from the Regent. This would enhance Horthy's ability to fend off the Germans should they suspect what was afoot and accuse Hungary of treason. Never an adroit liar, Horthy would be able in good conscience to deny any accusations that Hitler might make. Moreover, it was thought best not to brief Horthy thoroughly on the various missions being sent out, since there would then be the danger that in conversation with a German representative or one of Germany's many supporters in Hungary he might inadvertently blurt out some incriminating information.[106]

Miklós Kállay's hesitant peace initiative in early 1943 proved singularly unproductive. On the one hand, those few emissaries who did make contact with the Allies were coldly received. The same message kept coming back to Budapest: so long as Hungary continued to fight against the Soviet Union and to aid the Axis, she could expect "neither sympathy nor consideration."[107] On the other hand, the German counterintelligence service was so efficient and some of the Hungarian missions so inept that Berlin soon had detailed reports about the Hungarian peace feelers. Since Hitler, like the Hungarian leaders, believed that an Allied landing in the Balkans was imminent, it seemed imperative that the "treasonous" Kállay government be replaced by one on which Germany could rely. The Germans were also disturbed by Hungary's unsatisfactory response to the demand that harsher measures be implemented against the Jews. Not only had Kállay dragged his feet on this, but it seemed that the Hungarians were going out of their way to demonstrate tolerance toward the Jews. In early April the German Minister in Budapest reported that two "full Jews" whom Horthy had appointed members of the Upper House had been elected to the important and sensitive Foreign Affairs Committee.[108]

In these circumstances Hitler decided to exert pressure directly on Horthy. It had become the Führer's habit to meet the leaders of Germany's satellites at least once or twice a year on a rotating basis. Marshal Antonescu had been in Germany in October 1942 and was expected again in early April. Since a visit from Horthy was thus overdue, an invitation went out to join Hitler in mid-April at Klessheim Castle near Salzburg. The purpose of the talks would be to discuss the military situation and the fate of the remnant of the Hungarian Army on the Eastern Front.[109] Both Kállay and Horthy realized, however, that the discussions were likely to range over a wide variety of issues, and that Horthy might be called on to explain why Hungary had failed to comply with German demands concerning suppression of the Jews. To assist Horthy in preparing for these talks, the Foreign Ministry drew up for his perusal a detailed memorandum that provided responses to questions and criticisms Hitler was likely to advance. It is not known if Horthy actually made a careful study of this document. In any case, more useful to him was a short brief composed by Ferenc Keresztes-Fischer, some of whose arguments the Regent was actually to use at Klessheim Castle.[110] In addition, Kállay carefully rehearsed Horthy shortly before his departure. Even at this point Kállay apparently did not provide the Regent many details about the peace feelers. Rather, he seems to have hinted that such initiatives had been made, that they had so far been fruitless, and that therefore it would be best simply to assert strongly that Hungary would never commit treason against her ally. In general, if political questions were raised, the Regent was to avoid getting embroiled in arguments and to ascribe all responsibility for political matters to the Prime Minister.

Finally, Kállay implored Horthy to "be firm on the 'Jewish question' and to adhere to our well-known attitude that this was a Hungarian domestic problem. . . ."[111] Horthy resolved to do this, for he had become convinced that Nazi Germany's policy toward the Jews was uncivilized. But at this time did he know the real meaning of the "Final Solution"? Certainly a few Hungarian officials, such as Döme Sztójay, knew in general terms of the horrible fate awaiting the Jews deported "to the East." Some of Horthy's trusted advisors, such as Kállay, Keresztes-Fischer, and Bethlen, must have suspected that atrocities on an unprecedented scale were being committed. Yet this was a subject that apparently was so sensitive that it was rarely discussed among Hungarian officials.[112] All the available evidence suggests that before 1944 Horthy was never given the kind of information that would allow him to grasp the true nature of the unfolding Holocaust, that is, the systematic massacre of the Jews in death camps. As has been seen, Horthy's understanding of events was usually simplistic and unsophisticated. For him an event became "real" and fully entered his consciousness only when it could be described in terms of compelling stories and anecdotes. This had been demonstrated in the case of the Jewish forced labor battalions. In general Horthy was not inclined to believe that his military officers were capable of dishonorable conduct, yet when he was told gruesome stories of specific atrocities that had been committed, he took steps to ameliorate conditions in the Jewish battalions.

10

Two Visits to Klessheim Castle

Schloss Klessheim, a Baroque-era castle on the outskirts of Salzburg, was, according to the prewar Baedeker, once the country residence of the local archbishop but after the Great War came to house the Isadora Duncan School of Dancing. Miklós Horthy was to pay two visits to Klessheim toward the end of World War II, not, of course, as a tourist but as the guest of Adolf Hitler, who chose Klessheim Castle for a series of personal meetings with the leaders of Germany's allies. The first of Horthy's visits, in April 1943, was tense and unpleasant; the second, in March 1944, was the stormy overture to the greatest crisis of Horthy's regency.

Horthy and his entourage arrived at Klessheim early on April 16. Before him lay three exhausting sessions with the Führer and Foreign Minister Ribbentrop.[1] Before the first, which began around 5:00 on the evening of the 16th, Horthy probably did not suspect that anything was amiss, for the usual diplomatic pleasantries were exchanged and the atmosphere was convivial. At that first conversation, however, it did not take long for him to notice a colder, less friendly mood. In their previous meetings Hitler had shown at least some deference to Horthy and had not monopolized the conversations. Now, however, he reverted to his usual style and opened with an hour-long monologue through which Horthy sat in silence. Hitler's opening remarks dealt with the threat of bolshevism and the lessons of the Great War as they could be applied to the current conflict. By stressing the Russian danger and using terms and historical analogies that Horthy himself had previously employed or would be familiar with, Hitler obviously hoped to establish common ground before he launched his attacks on Hungarian policy.

During his opening remarks and at other times during the course of these talks, Hitler emphasized the vital role that Germany was playing in the war against the Bolsheviks, whom he compared with such other Eastern threats to European civilization as the Huns, Mongols, and Turks. If, he argued, Germany's 240 divisions did not fight on with "fanatical determination," Budapest and the other cities of Europe would be quickly overrun by the Soviets. It was senseless to imagine that the Allies would eventually stop the advance of the Red Army, since the Jews of Washington and London would never permit this. Furthermore, the "Bolshevik Jews" would destroy the European intelligentsia and "exterminate millions of people using the most unimaginable methods."[2] On the other hand, if Germany prevailed, Hungary and the rest of Europe would be the beneficiaries of this great victory, which would bring in its wake a magnificent cultural renaissance in Europe.

Horthy had no opportunity to comment on these remarks for the Führer moved quickly into strongly worded recriminations of the Hungarian government.[3] Hitler asserted that Hungary simply was not making the necessary contributions in the "world historic" struggle against bolshevism. Hitler's criticisms, which were brought forward in the first conversation and repeated by him and Ribbentrop in the later discussions as well, focused on three areas: the allegedly poor performance of the Hungarian Army, the "treasonous" policies of Miklós Kállay, and the failure of Hungary to deal properly with its "Jewish problem."

Although Hitler must have known the great pride that the Hungarian Regent took in his armed forces, he nonetheless proceeded to declare that the armies of his allies had, in general, fought poorly in the winter campaign and that the performance of the Hungarian soldiers had been "very bad." This was not, he insisted, because of a lack of proper equipment and munitions: that was a "false accusation." Rather these soldiers were not "emotionally and spiritually" prepared to fight against bolshevism. The mere playing of the Internationale had caused some troops to desert their officers and begin a reckless retreat. He was appalled to hear that Kállay had claimed that the Hungarians had fought as heroically as the Germans. The only units of the satellite armies who had performed "marvelously" were a few Romanian divisions. He knew this was a "bitter truth" for Hungarians, but it was true nonetheless.

As for Kállay, the German government had "concrete evidence" that he was making preparations for a defection to the enemy camp. Hitler pointed out that in the current crisis Germany and her allies were in the same boat on a stormy sea. It was clear that anyone who tried to evacuate the ship would drown, but Kállay did not seem to grasp this. Ribbentrop produced a stack of intercepted diplomatic telegrams and other material that, he claimed, clearly demonstrated that Kállay's emissaries were active in all the neutral capitals. He dwelt at great length on the activities of Albert Szent-Györgyi, about which the Germans were in fact very well informed.[4] All in all, Hitler concluded, the impact of Kállay's negative policies was "catastrophic."

According to Ribbentrop, one of the messages that Kállay asked Szent-Györgyi to convey to the Allies was that he intended to continue to protect the Jews residing in Hungary. This, Hitler declared, was inexplicable to him. Why would anyone want to treat the Jews "with kid gloves"? The Jews were responsible for the Communist Revolution, two world wars, and the current bombing of countless women and children. In those countries where the Jews were not suppressed and expelled, they destroyed the economy and currency. Germany was now "morally secure" because the Jews had been made to "disappear in the East." He did not wish to interfere in Hungary's domestic affairs, but it seemed clear to him that the poor morale of the Hungarian soldiers was due to Jewish influence and propaganda. As proof of this, Ribbentrop pointed to the presence of "full Jews" in the Upper House of the Hungarian Parliament.

Although Admiral Horthy had been primed by Kállay and others to respond to any complaints that the Germans might make at Klessheim, he could not have expected the intense barrage of recriminations that would descend on him. Unaccustomed to conversations in which he seldom got to hold the floor and was forced to sit glumly listening to long, hostile disquisitions by others, Horthy became at times disoriented and, as the drafter of the German protocol observed, often lost track of the trend of the conversation or abruptly changed the topic. Of course, some of Horthy's digressiveness may have been a conscious tactic to avoid a direct response to the accusations Hitler and Ribbentrop were making. For the most part, however, Horthy's confusion reflected the desperate efforts of a seventy-five-year-old man to get through a grueling experience. At times he tried, without much success, to follow his Prime Minister's advice and argue that he was not prepared to deal with political matters. Occasionally he was also able to recall and employ arguments that had been made in the memorandums that had been presented to him before his departure from Budapest. For the most part, however, Horthy had to fend for himself and rely on his own understanding of and attitude toward the issues raised by his hosts. The remarkable result was that, despite the fact that he appeared so disorganized and almost pathetically uninformed, Admiral Horthy on the whole conducted himself in a dignified manner that compares quite favorably with that of the other satellite leaders who had discussions with Hitler in this period.[5]

Although he must have been stung by Hitler's disparaging comments on the Hungarian Army and praise of Romanian soldiers, Horthy refrained from entering into a polemical exchange on this question. He merely pointed out that his country had had a very late start in rearming and was fighting in Russia even though the Hungarians had no territorial claims there. As for the performance of the Hungarian Army, he would leave that for future historians to make a final judgment. He would merely observe that an army that had lost 146,000 regular soldiers, 36,000 labor servicemen, and all its equipment had surely not disgraced itself.

Horthy was more animated in his response to the criticisms of Kállay. In fact, he had tried, without success, to break into Hitler's long-winded introductory remarks to begin his rebuttal. Once he finally got the floor, and on frequent occasions throughout the two days of talks, Horthy vigorously defended his Prime Minister. He insisted that the accusations were "100 percent false." Kállay was completely trustworthy and did nothing that he, the Regent, was not aware of. They were good friends who conversed on a regular basis and he could not imagine that Kállay would hide anything from him.[6] No one in Hungary, Horthy insisted, was thinking of coquetting with the enemy. That would be "absolute idiocy" and would merely result in a new Treaty of Trianon.

Horthy tried whenever possible to change the subject from his Prime Minister to other, sometimes totally unrelated, issues. He complained that Germany had failed to fulfill its promises to supply weapons and military equipment, thus leaving Hungary at a great disadvantage vis-à-vis Romania, which had been rearmed by Britain, France, and Germany. Horthy also did his best, as usual, to create suspicions about the reliability of Romania as an ally. Perhaps Horthy's most pathetic attempt to change the subject came during the first day's conversation when, according to the official German protocol, Horthy "wandered a bit from the main theme" and apprised his hosts of an idea he had come up with during recent bouts of insomnia. It seemed to him that the main weakness of submarines was the fact that one could not see very far from them. He remembered that during his naval service in the Great War a sailor had on one occasion been sent up to the height of one hundred meters on a one-man kite. Why not, Horthy suggested, arrange to have all German submarines launch such one-man kites at a predetermined time? In that way, large areas of the ocean could be surveyed quickly and without undue risk. No doubt amazed at how out-of-touch the Hungarian Regent was with recent developments, Hitler patiently explained the technology of radar. Besides, he pointed out, the men sent up on such kites would doubtless be in grave danger in case of attack by enemy aircraft.

Despite Horthy's efforts to defend his Prime Minister, Hitler and Ribbentrop returned again and again to the argument that Kállay was sabotaging the war effort of the Axis. Horthy held his ground even when Ribbentrop produced extensive documentation that he claimed directly implicated Kállay in treasonous activity. The most that he would concede was that Kállay sometimes talked "a bit too much" (*ein bisserl zu viel*), for which he had chided him. When, on the second day of the talks, Hitler tried to build on this admission and persuade Horthy that he must appoint a new Prime Minister, Horthy cleverly responded: "You know, I'm very hard of hearing. It seems I only understood half of what you were saying yesterday." Hitler was not fooled: he privately complained that Horthy was obviously trying to avoid making any commitments.[7]

Admiral Horthy's responses to Hitler's complaints about the lenient treatment of Jews in Hungary produced some of the most significant exchanges of the Klessheim talks. Horthy conceded that the large number of Jews in Hungary created problems, but he refrained from employing the vulgar anti-Semitic language that he had often used earlier in his career and that flowed so effortlessly from Hitler's lips. Horthy pointed out that the Magyars had traditionally regarded money-making as a vulgar occupation and were thus partly responsible for the fact that Jews played so vital a role in Hungary's economy. There simply was no easy way to replace the Jews, who were involved in economic life in far greater percentages than had been the case in Germany. Nonetheless, Hungary had been the first country in Europe to take action against the Jews in the form of the *numerus clausus*. As for the Jews in the Upper House of Parliament, he could do nothing about that without violating the constitution. Besides, there were many converted Jews who were very valuable to Hungarian society. In sum, "he had done everything he could against the Jews within the limits of decency, but he could hardly murder them or do away with them in some other way." Hitler replied that that wouldn't be necessary. Hungary should follow the example of Slovakia and place the Jews in concentration camps or at least put them to work in mines. In that way many positions in the economy would be opened up for non-Jews. This elicited from Horthy a remark so incongruous that it must have startled both Hitler and Ribbentrop: "he was ashamed to have to confess that he had sent 36,000 Jews in labor battalions to the Front, and that most of them had been killed in the Russian advance." Hitler immediately retorted that the Regent had nothing to be ashamed of, since the Jews had unleashed the war and therefore deserved no sympathy. Besides, he was convinced that the Jewish laborers were not killed, but had surrendered to the Soviets.

The "Jewish question" came up again on the morning of the 17th. A comment by Horthy that he had been unable to control the black market in Hungary led Hitler to declare that just as in the Great War the Jews were once again responsible for the black market. This prompted Horthy to ask: "What am I supposed to do with the Jews then, after I have taken from them all possibility of making a living? After all, I can't have them shot." Ribbentrop thereupon interjected that "the Jews must either be killed or sent to concentration camps. There was no other possibility." Hitler followed up this remarkable statement with an equally candid allusion to the "Final Solution." The Jews, he said, were "pure parasites." In Poland if they refused to work, they were shot. If they were unable to work, they must die. They had to be handled like the tuberculosis bacillus that attacked a healthy body. Animals such as hares and deer sometimes had to be killed if they became pests. Why should mercy be shown to the "beasts who would bring us bolshevism?" Nations that did not defend themselves against the Jews would perish.[8] The German protocol gives no indication of any response by Horthy to these extremely harsh statements.

As these Klessheim talks came to an end on April 17, the Germans clearly were unhappy with the results. Horthy had been stubborn in his defense of his Prime Minister, had tried to use "humanitarian counterarguments" to defend his policy toward the

Jews,[9] and at one point had annoyed Ribbentrop by disagreeing with his assertion that there could be no diplomatic solution to the war. In the final conversation Horthy tried to appease his hosts by promising that he would make "an honorable investigation" of the accusations against Kállay and would report the results to Berlin. Moreover, he insisted that "as long as he lived Hungary would remain a loyal ally of Germany." This was hardly convincing, however, especially when just before his departure Horthy balked at the wording of an official communiqué to be issued to the press. The proposed communiqué, which was identical to one published several days earlier after the visit of Marshal Antonescu, called for a continuation of the struggle against bolshevism and the Anglo-American Allies "until the final victory." Horthy preferred not to make such a direct reference to the Western Allies, and refused to give his approval.[10] As Horthy's train was departing Döme Sztójay made one last appeal to the Regent, who responded with a hand gesture indicating disgust. This was interpreted by Sztójay to mean a reluctant approval, and the communiqué was duly put out. Upon arriving in Budapest, however, Horthy denied that he had given his consent, and the Hungarians issued their own communiqué without the objectionable passage.[11]

In the aftermath of the Klessheim visit the German attitude toward Horthy became uniformly negative. Hitler and Ribbentrop regarded Horthy as a "cunning rogue" who had no intention of making a break with Kállay, whose "defeatist" policies he actually approved.[12] Their suspicions were by no means allayed by the report that was subsequently sent to Hitler in fulfillment of the Regent's promise to make a full investigation of the charges that had been leveled against Kállay. Dated May 6, this long letter was signed by Horthy but was apparently written by Kállay and other government officials. At great length each of the accusations that had been made against the Hungarian government, and especially against Kállay, was rebutted. In the last paragraph, which Horthy wrote out in long-hand, he tried to reassure Hitler that "in my country nothing can happen against my will, and that I shall maintain quiet and order in all circumstances."[13]

At about the same time a much different picture of the attitude of the Hungarian government and the role of the Regent reached Berlin. Edmund von Veesenmayer, an S.S. officer who had been sent by Ribbentrop to Budapest to make an on-the-scene investigation, reported back that Hungary was an "arrogant nation" that was contributing only a fraction of what it could to the war effort.[14] He lamented the fact that Hungary had become "the asylum of European Jewry" and that "the present Hungarian regime, the Jews, and wide sectors of the bourgeoisie neither believe in nor desire the victory of the Axis powers." As for Admiral Horthy, Veesenmayer described him as reliably anti-Bolshevik but living "an isolated existence, surrounded by his one-sided clique of Jews, aristocrats related to Jews, and clerical politicians." Among those who had a "nefarious influence" on Horthy were Kállay, Bethlen, Goldberger, and Ferenc Chorin. The key to toppling the current regime, Veesenmayer concluded, was the elimination of the clique surrounding Horthy. However, this could be accomplished "only with, and not against, the person of the Regent."

Veesenmayer's conclusions seem to have reinforced a strategy that Hitler and Ribbentrop had already decided on. So long as the military situation in the Balkans remained stable and Hungary continued to supply Germany with industrial and agricultural goods, no attempt would be made to undermine Horthy's position or to force an immediate solution to the "Jewish problem" in Hungary. As in the past, the Regent was to be flattered and treated with courtesy. At the same time intense pressure was to be put on Kállay in an effort to topple his government. Accordingly, German officials in Budapest were instructed to ostracize the Hungarian Prime Minister and to encourage the Hungarian radical right-wing parties to attack the government even more vehemently. As a result, throughout this period Horthy was importuned by the extremist right-wing parties to jettison Kállay, Keresztes-Fischer, and Nagy and appoint a government that would cooperate fully with the Germans. Horthy brushed aside such demands, and memorandums sent to him by the followers of Szálasi and Imrédy went unanswered and probably unread. He did agree, with great reluctance and only after Mussolini had joined the chorus of criticism, to drop General Nagy from the Cabinet, but the new Minister of Defense was General Lajos Csatay, also a Horthy loyalist.[15] In this period political debates in Parliament grew increasingly acrimonious, and on one vote the government survived by a margin of only nine votes. This ominous indication of the strength of pro-German sentiments prompted Kállay to request that the Regent prorogue Parliament, which he did on May 4.

That Admiral Horthy had not fallen completely out of Hitler's good graces was demonstrated by the exceedingly warm greetings he received from the German leader on his seventy-fifth birthday in June. Hoping to exploit Horthy's vanity and love of the sea, Hitler informed Horthy that his gift, a new yacht, would be sailed down the Danube to Budapest in the near future. Horthy responded at the time, and later when Admiral Erich Raeder delivered the yacht, with effusive letters of thanks for this "colossal maritime token of attention" that "nearly took my breath away." Privately, however, he scoffed at Hitler's gauche ways: "What the hell can I do with a yacht? Cross over to Pest? Does he think he can win me over with presents of this kind? . . . If he were a gentleman, he would send me a riding horse or a team of horses. . . ."[16]

Even though Hitler's birthday gift turned out to be impractical and unappreciated, the basic German strategy toward Horthy in this period was not totally misconceived. Horthy detested the Nazis and harbored increasing doubts about Germany's ability to win the war. He was prepared to conceal from the Germans the fact that Kállay was discreetly making overtures to the Allies. He refused to heed Hitler's advice about how to treat the Jews. But when Horthy insisted, as he had at Klessheim, that he would never betray his ally, he sincerely meant it. Horthy was convinced that throughout its history Hungary had never once committed treason against an ally, in contrast to Romania which, in his opinion, had elevated treasonous behavior to a national virtue. For Horthy this was a matter of principle: an honorable person would never betray a friend. Thus, in June when Horthy told the German Minister that he "would stand unconditionally" at Germany's side,[17] he was not consciously lying. What Horthy meant was that he would never approve a sudden, unannounced defection of Hungary to the enemy camp. Hungary would never stab Germany in the back.

Horthy's concept of national honor proved to be a complicating factor for the Hungarian government when it was forced to deal with the consequences of the successful Allied landing in Sicily on July 10, which neither Kállay nor Horthy had anticipated.[18] Equally unexpected was the fall of Mussolini two weeks later. Immediately the anti-German political forces in Hungary mobilized and pressed the government to take advantage of the situation to withdraw from the war and return to Teleki's policy of neutrality.[19] Count Bethlen and the conservative dissidents also urged a renewed effort to seek an armistice with the Anglo-American powers. Kállay's reaction was equivocal; if the German position in Italy had rapidly collapsed, he might have been willing to consider taking bold action. But the Wehrmacht maintained its hold on most of the Italian peninsula, and furious combat developed as the Allied troops inched slowly northward. By early September, when the new Italian government formally capitulated, the Germans had firm military control over most of Italy. This did not set an encouraging example for the Hungarians. In any case Admiral Horthy made it clear that he would not approve a sudden "jumping out" of the war. For Horthy this episode revived unpleasant memories of Italy's "treachery" in abandoning the Triple Alliance in 1915. He would never permit his country to engage in such despicable behavior. It was not that Horthy failed to see the significance of the Allied landing in Italy. He agreed with Kállay that Hungary must adjust to the new situation and he gave him a free hand to continue exploring a separate peace with the Allies, but not, of course, with Soviet Russia. He insisted, however, that he would never stab Germany in the back as Italy had supposedly done. If it came to the point where Hungary in its own interests chose to end its cooperation with Germany and withdraw from the war, he would feel honor-bound to inform Hitler beforehand of his intentions.[20]

In July, with Horthy's approval, Kállay thus intensified his efforts to make fruitful contact with the Allies to ascertain on what terms Hungary could sue for peace. At the same time he and Horthy pondered the knotty problem of how to withdraw from the war in an "honorable" way but without provoking a German occupation of Hungary. At this time Allied forces were closer to Hungary than the Red Army, so it seemed reasonable to assume that Hungarians would be able to surrender to American or British troops advancing northward from Italy or from the Balkans. One potential problem was that Hungarian military officers, the great majority of whom were staunchly pro-German, might not obey an order to capitulate to Allied forces. Earlier in the year Horthy had been urged by Bajcsy-Zsilinszky and others to purge the General Staff of those officers who were fanatical adherents of Nazi Germany.[21] Horthy found it difficult to imagine any situation in which a Hungarian officer would fail to obey his orders. His belief in the loyalty of his officers was no doubt reinforced by the praise showered on him by the generals who gathered in mid-June to help the Regent celebrate his birthday and at a gala banquet in February 1944.[22] Nonetheless, Horthy had observed that some of the higher officers, especially those of German-Hungarian background like

General Werth, sometimes seemed unable to see that German and Hungarian national interests were not necessarily identical. He therefore instructed Szombathelyi to remove from the officer corps the most egregious of the Germanophiles. And in July, as matters became more urgent, he summoned a group of General Staff officers, reminded them of their oath of loyalty to the Regent, and warned them to refrain from right-wing politics.[23] As later events would demonstrate, however, these attempts to reduce pro-German sentiments in the officer corps were totally ineffective, and Horthy did nothing further to remedy the problem.[24]

In the effort to identify capable army officers who could be relied on to support a decision to seek a separate peace, the Regent's son, Niki, played an important role. Like his late brother, Niki was an Anglophile who abhorred Nazi Germany and its Hungarian sympathizers. Although Kállay apparently disapproved,[25] Niki began to serve as the unofficial liaison between his father and pro-Western Hungarians in the government and the army and quickly gained attention as one of the more vocal advocates of withdrawal from the war. At some point in the summer of 1943, probably in July, Niki arranged for his father to meet with Colonel Gyula Kádár, one of the few General Staff officers deemed trustworthy enough to participate in secret negotiations with the Allies. Horthy spoke openly to Kádár of his hopes and frustrations. He was bitter toward Hitler and outspoken against the war. "What's the purpose of further bleeding the nation?" he asked. Many people were urging him to withdraw from the war, but unfortunately this was not a simple matter. "Should I step out on the balcony of the Castle and shout: 'I have changed sides! I have changed sides!'" That would do no good, for within twenty-four hours the Germans would install Szálasi.[26]

Horthy's pessimistic analysis of the immediate prospects of turning against the Germans was based in part on his fear that any plans along these lines that were submitted to the Cabinet would quickly be leaked to Berlin by Reményi-Schneller or one of the other Germanophile ministers. As a result, when in mid-August Horthy wished to consult with trusted advisors about the possibilities of withdrawing from the war, he turned not to the Cabinet but to his camarilla, the unofficial council from whom he had often received advice on an individual basis in the past. In mid-August he summoned to Gödöllő those former prime ministers of Hungary whom he trusted (Kállay, Bethlen, Károlyi, and Esterházy, but not, of course, Imrédy or Bárdossy), Kálmán Kánya, and two members of the current Cabinet (Keresztes-Fischer and Jenő Ghyczy, the recently appointed Foreign Minister). The result of this discussion was an informal decision to proceed with negotiations for a separate peace on the following conditions: (a) a guarantee from the Allies that Hungary would not be occupied by Russian troops; (b) a binding declaration from the Allies about Hungary's future borders; and (c) recognition of the present Hungarian government, which would be broadened by the addition of the Social Democrats.[27]

That the Regent and some of Hungary's most experienced statesmen felt justified in putting forward such conditions in the summer of 1943 despite the fact that the Allies had already enunciated the principle of "unconditional surrender" is a reflection of the kind of wishful thinking that still prevailed in Budapest. To be sure, Kállay and Bethlen realized that Hungary was not in a position to drive a hard bargain. But Admiral Horthy seemed truly to believe that, despite her participation in the war, Hungary could now find a way to emerge relatively unscathed. This despite the fact that Horthy was not yet prepared to sanction any direct defiance of the Germans of the kind that the Allies were likely to demand, because, as he explained to Bajcsy-Zsilinszky in late August, such rash steps would bring on even greater dangers, such as a German occupation of the country or, even worse, an invasion by the Romanians, Slovaks, and Croatians. "Withdrawal from the war," he insisted, "must be done with the consent of the Germans. We are so intertwined with them that this sort of step could only be done with them."[28] This attitude led Horthy to reject the specific proposals put to him by Bajcsy-Zsilinszky as spokesman for the anti-German groups. Horthy was urged, for example, to declare Budapest an "open city" in which no significant military operations would take place. This, proponents argued, would likely spare the capital city the intensive bombing raids that the Allies had threatened. But Horthy retorted that such an action "would hardly be acceptable to the Germans." Besides, Hungary's factories were now producing weapons and airplanes that were necessary for the national defense. He hoped the Allies would realize that it was not in their interest to bomb Budapest. In any case, he told Bajcsy-Zsilinszky, "I can reassure you that we are in touch with the Anglo-Saxons on this matter."[29]

Admiral Horthy apparently had no clear strategy in mind for

achieving what would seem to have been the impossible: withdrawing from the war "with the consent of the Germans." To those who continued to urge him to take decisive action to demonstrate Hungary's independence of Germany, Horthy recommended patience: "We must wait and have faith." Much now depended, of course, on the fate of the renewed Hungarian initiatives for a separate peace. These, in contrast to the earlier peace feelers, met with a more hopeful response from the Allies. The Hungarian Minister in Bern, Switzerland, was able to establish fruitful contact with Royall Tyler, an American economist and diplomat who had served for many years as the League of Nations financial advisor to the Hungarian government. Of the various Hungarian attempts to establish contact with the Allies in this period, this is the only one that Horthy is known personally to have authorized and supported.[30] He apparently regarded Tyler, who knew Hungary well and had even learned the Magyar language, as a friend who would empathize with Hungary's leaders. Establishing contact with the Americans seemed all the more important because Tibor Eckhardt was reporting from Washington that Archduke Otto had won the confidence of President Roosevelt and had been assured that he would be restored to the Hungarian throne after the war.[31]

Although the secret contacts with the Americans in Switzerland were to prove important over the next year, it was in Istanbul that one of Kállay's secret emissaries achieved the most dramatic results. Sensing that it would be pointless to put forward at the outset the conditions decided on by the Regent's camarilla, Kállay instructed his envoy, László Veress, to inform the British that Hungary was prepared to accept unconditional surrender. This quickly paved the way for substantive talks that led, on September 9, to the signing of a preliminary armistice on board a British ship in the Sea of Marmara. This "Istanbul agreement," the first of its kind involving one of Hitler's allies, stipulated that Hungary would capitulate to Anglo-American troops when they reached the Hungarian frontier. At that time the Hungarian government would make a public announcement of its acceptance of unconditional surrender. In the meantime the Allies expected evidence of Hungarian goodwill in the form of obstruction and even sabotage of the German war effort.[32]

Although Admiral Horthy's attitude toward these decisions and the terms of the preliminary armistice, of which he was apprised in mid-September, is not recorded in the contemporary documentation, there is reason to believe that his approval was not unequivocal. He apparently gave Kállay a free hand to implement these decisions, but he remained extremely wary of provoking the Germans. Kállay, who seemed surprised by the speed with which the "Istanbul agreement" had been reached, was also cautious. No doubt both men were influenced by General Szombathelyi, who warned that even though the Germans were in a difficult situation, Anglo-American forces were still far from Hungary, the Wehrmacht was largely intact, and German discipline was unparalleled. In short, Germany still possessed sufficient power to deal with both her opponents and recalcitrant allies.[33]

As a result, in late 1943 Kállay did very little to comply with the terms of the preliminary armistice calling for Hungarian efforts to obstruct the German war effort. His policy of "progressive disentanglement" from the German alliance proceeded at an almost imperceptible pace. Several small steps were taken to prepare for the time when the actual defection would be feasible. With Horthy's approval a secret radio transmitter was set up in the Castle to maintain contact with the British government; it was to be put to good use later for other purposes. The one significant Hungarian contribution to the Allied cause was the decision to allow free use of Hungarian air space to Allied aircraft, including Soviet planes supplying Tito's partisans. The Germans were powerless to interfere with this, since they had never been granted air bases in Hungary. The Allies reciprocated by refraining from conducting bombing raids on Hungary.[34] Otherwise, Kállay tried to impress the British by emphasizing long-standing Hungarian policies that thwarted the German war effort, such as granting asylum to large numbers of Polish refugees, protecting the Jews, and treating Allied prisoners of war with respect. Among the latter was Colonel Charles Howie, a South African officer who had managed to escape from a German POW camp in Breslau. Howie made his way to Hungary in 1943, where he was treated as an honored guest and was received on more than one occasion by the Regent. Howie was encouraged to work out a plan for the occupation of Hungary by British troops.[35]

Neither Kállay nor Horthy, however, was prepared to risk provoking Hitler by withdrawing Hungarian troops from the Eastern Front without German approval. On three occasions in late 1943 and early 1944 Szombathelyi was sent to Hitler's headquarters to request the return of the remnants of the Second Army, which, the Hungarian Chief of Staff argued, were needed to establish a defense line on the Carpathian Mountains. Each time he was rebuffed. Hungarian forces, however meager, thus remained on the Eastern Front as the Red Army continued its relentless westward advance.

One other initiative of Kállay in this period could be seen as a gesture to the Atlantic Democracies, although strong domestic pressures were at work as well. On October 11, two weeks before the Allies announced their intention of prosecuting war criminals, Kállay reopened the investigation of the Újvidék massacres. How he persuaded the Regent to assent to this is not known. But even Horthy, who had up to then stubbornly defended the accused officers, could not dismiss the impartial findings of this new investigation and the judgment of the subsequent court martial.[36] In December eight officers were found guilty and sentenced to long prison terms. Any lingering doubts Horthy might have felt about these proceedings, which one historian has aptly dubbed the first trial in Europe of World War II war criminals,[37] were doubtless extinguished by the "ungentlemanly" behavior of the defendants. Released temporarily by the court on their own recognizance, General Feketehalmi-Czeydner and three of his accomplices fled to Germany, where they were welcomed as heroes.[38]

By the end of 1943 and early 1944 the possibility that the "Istanbul agreement" would form the basis for Hungary's withdrawal from the war seemed increasingly remote. The fundamental problem was that the armies of the Western powers were making very slow progress northward in Italy, while the Red Army was moving ineluctably westward. Furthermore, contrary to the expectations of both Hitler and Horthy, the Allies had made no attempt to land in the Balkans. But the Hungarians continued well into 1944 to base their planning on the assumption that somehow the Soviet forces would not be the first reach the Hungarian frontier. For Horthy, especially, the thought of Red Army soldiers and Stalin's minions swarming across Hungary was too horrible to contemplate.[39]

There were, to be sure, unpleasant indications that, regardless of the manner in which the Allied victory was secured, the West had reconciled itself to the creation of a Soviet sphere of influence in Eastern Europe. The terms of the Teheran Conference of November 1943 were not announced, but soon thereafter Eduard

Beneš visited Moscow and signed a Czechoslovak-Soviet Pact of Friendship. In the same period came word that Britain had given recognition to Tito and his Partisan movement. All this caused great despondency in the Hungarian political establishment, for it suggested that the arbiters of Hungary's destiny might be the diabolical triumvirate of Stalin, Beneš, and Tito. Such a prospect seemed all the more likely when Mihály Károlyi, the *bête noire* of right-wing Hungarian society, was granted air time on the BBC to call for the destruction of "the feudal and Fascist regime" of Admiral Horthy. Károlyi seriously undermined the position of pro-Westerners in Hungary when he added flattering words about the positive role that Soviet Russia would play in liberating Danubian Europe.[40] Miklós Kállay was deeply depressed by these developments and for a time seemed to be moving toward a rapprochement with Imrédy, who kept insisting that "in the event of an Anglo-Saxon victory all Eastern Europe would be handed over to Russia." Privately Kállay declared that so long as Anglo-American troops were far from Hungary, "it cannot be in Hungary's interest to weaken the German Army, which is, after all, holding up the Bolsheviks."[41]

The unfavorable turn of international events in late 1943 caused a great stir in the Hungarian Parliament, which Horthy had recalled in September. In the fall session a furious debate erupted in which voices from all points of the political spectrum, including the left, were heard. In an almost eerie fashion, here, in the heart of Hitler's Europe during the fifth year of the war, the combatants in interwar Europe's ideological civil war were given one last chance to defend their positions. Béla Imrédy could now confidently proclaim that he had been right all along in his analysis of the course of the war. Hungary thus had to remain firmly on Germany's side come what may, for the alternatives were Pan-Slav imperialism and bolshevization. Although the moderate and liberal opposition attempted to refute these arguments, they found it difficult to explain away the mounting evidence that Great Britain and the United States had abandoned Hungary to the Soviets. Among the delegates there was virtual unanimity on one point: Hungary would never willingly accept a new, let alone a harsher, Trianon Treaty. Bajcsy-Zsilinszky, the most vociferous of the anti-Nazis, declared that even while he and his colleagues demanded the democratization of Hungary, they stood on the basis of "historic Hungary, both ideal and geographic."[42]

In a sense, the competing ideological forces that were disrupting Parliament were waging a struggle within Regent Horthy as well. The unfavorable international developments of the past few months had made the task of extricating Hungary from its dilemma seem to him even more daunting. Although Horthy continued to insist to German envoys that he would always act honorably and in the spirit of Hungary's thousand-year history of fealty to its allies, he finally had to admit to himself that Germany was not going to win the war.[43] It must have been even more depressing to hear that Hitler was now describing the war as a long struggle comparable in European history to the Thirty Years War.[44] But what could Horthy do to avert the disaster toward which Hungary seemed to be plunging? At some point in late 1943 Count Bethlen became the first of the Regent's advisors to suggest that contact should be made with the Russians, but neither Kállay nor Horthy was as yet prepared to think the unthinkable. Nor did Horthy show much interest in intensifying cooperation with the Social Democrats and other anti-German parties and individuals who would be logical partners of the government if and when Hungary attempted to seek an armistice. Horthy's one step in this direction was designed merely to keep open lines of communication with such groups and to appease his son Niki, who was pressing for a bolder anti-German policy. In January 1944, the Regent arranged for his son to be given an inconspicuous office in the Castle ostensibly to deal with the repatriation of Hungarians from abroad, but with the real purpose of maintaining contact between the government and the various resistance and dissident groups.[45] Few Hungarians were fooled by this subterfuge, and soon both friends and foes were referring to Niki's office as the "defection bureau." Admiral Horthy himself was skeptical that his son could accomplish much and worried that Niki would just get into trouble.[46]

In early 1944 Miklós Horthy was frustrated by the situation, but by no means fatalistic. In fact, at times he spoke with a defiant optimism that seemed hardly grounded in reality, as can be seen in a conversation that Colonel Kádár had with the Regent early in 1944. Kádár had asked for an audience in order to try to persuade Horthy to prepare for a possible occupation of the country by the Germans and to consider approaching the Soviets with peace feelers. But Kádár hardly had a chance to touch on these concerns, for Horthy launched into a *tour d'horizon* in which he spoke almost nonstop for two and a half hours.[47]

In his monologue Horthy jumped from one topic to the next without much continuity. He provided brief character sketches of a host of individuals. Hitler was "a half-witted house painter" who did not know how to act like a gentleman. It was not Szálasi but Imrédy who was the "truly dangerous person" in Hungary, since the latter had gained support from a segment of the intelligentsia. There were few people left in Hungary, Horthy lamented, whom he could fully trust. He even had doubts about some of his generals. To Kádár's suggestion that General Szombathelyi could be relied on, Horthy replied: "Yes, yes, I trust him, but you know, he's a Schwab too."

When Kádár tried to raise the question of withdrawal from the war, Horthy declared that the time was not yet ripe. He wasn't too worried about it though, because he was on good terms with President Roosevelt. In the meantime, he was confident that he would be able to deal with any pressure the Germans would exert on him. He would continue to resist their demands for further actions against the Jews, since "inhumanity was alien to the Magyar character." If the Germans would try to occupy Hungary, he would lead the resistance and "personally stand at the head of the troops." Even if the resistance lasted just two days, it would be useful for the country's future. Horthy ended the conversation by suggesting that Kádár should visit him more often, "but there was no need to dress so nicely."

Colonel Kádár left this perplexing audience with the sad impression that Hungary was led by a very old man who would be swept away by events. Perhaps Kádár was also struck by the irony of the Regent's boast of his good relationship with the American President, since Hungary's most famous wartime joke, with which Kádár was probably familiar, was based on a quite different premise. According to the joke, which may have originated on a BBC broadcast to Hungary, the following exchange occurred between President Roosevelt and Secretary of State Hull (or, in some versions, the Hungarian Minister in Washington):[48]

> Hull: "I am sorry to announce, Mr. President, that Hungary as declared war on us."
> Roosevelt: "Hungary? What kind of country is it?"
> Hull: "It is a kingdom."
> Roosevelt: "Who is the king?"
> Hull: "They have no king."
> Roosevelt: "A kingdom without a king! Who is the head of state?"

Hull: "Admiral Horthy."

Roosevelt: "Admiral? Now, after Pearl Harbor, we have another navy on our neck!"

Hull: "No, Mr. President. Hungary has no navy, not even a seacoast."

Roosevelt: "Strange. What do they want from us? Territorial claims, perhaps?"

Hull: "No, sir. They want territory from Romania."

Roosevelt: "Did they declare war also on Romania?"

Hull: "No, Mr. President. Romania is their ally."

Actually, though Franklin Roosevelt had only a sketchy understanding of East Central European political affairs, he certainly knew of Miklós Horthy and his exploits as a Habsburg naval officer in World War I. In the 1930s the American Minister in Budapest, John Montgomery, had kept Roosevelt abreast of developments in Hungary through correspondence and personal conversations.[49] It was Montgomery who had persuaded Roosevelt to send an autographed photograph to the Hungarian Regent in 1940. There is no evidence, however, that Roosevelt had any special sympathy for Horthy, and the latter's belief that he was on good terms with the American President was clearly an illusion.

Miklós Kállay realized, of course, that Hungarian policy had to be constructed on more realistic assumptions. By early 1944 it had become apparent to him that Anglo-American forces were not likely to reach Hungary in the near future. Groping for a strategy to meet this unexpected development, Kállay now proposed that all Hungarian military forces be concentrated on the country's frontier along the Carpathian Mountains. The Hungarian government would confidentially inform the Allies of its intention of defending its territory but otherwise withdrawing from participation in the war. It was Kállay's hope (in the circumstances an inordinately optimistic one) that Stalin would conclude that no purpose would be served in attacking Hungary proper and would move the Red Army along a northerly route directly into Germany. The major problem remained, however, to convince the Germans to agree to the withdrawal from the Ukraine of the remnants of the Hungarian Second Army. Since previous requests had been ignored, Kállay decided that a direct appeal from the Regent was called for. In a letter to Hitler dated February 12, Horthy gave his assurance that his country would "defend against a possible Russian invasion with all forces and means at its disposal." If all Hungarian forces were concentrated on the Carpathian ridge, Hungary could mount a formidable defense without requiring any assistance from Germany. Horthy thus requested, "most emphatically, in accordance with our agreement," that all Hungarian units currently on the Eastern Front be withdrawn.[50]

For the Germans this impertinent letter was merely further proof that Horthy was the "mainspring" of the anti-German movement in Hungary.[51] In late 1943 and early 1944 numerous reports had reached Berlin of the continuing unsatisfactory situation in Hungary and the unreliability of both Kállay and Horthy. Although the ubiquitous German military intelligence agents had somehow failed to learn of the "Istanbul agreement," they did obtain information on a plan to drop a small Allied parachute unit into Hungary in March. Hitler, it seems, feared that this was the opening salvo of the long-expected Allied landing in the Balkans.[52] His patience finally exhausted, the German leader decided that he must use military force to prevent Hungary from defecting to the enemy camp. Later he would explain to a group of German officers that he had to move against Hungary because that country had become "corrupt and corroded, with Jews everywhere, Jews and more Jews even in the highest places, and the whole state overrun by an unbroken network of agents and spies. . . ."[53] In early March the plan for a German occupation of Hungary, codenamed "Margarethe," was worked out. In the meantime the Hungarians were put off with the explanation that Hitler could not immediately respond to the Regent's letter, since he was ill with influenza and any letter he wrote might carry germs that would infect Horthy.[54]

Hitler's decision and the nature of the subsequent German invasion of Hungary were greatly influenced by a report submitted by Edmund Veesenmayer after a second fact-finding mission to Hungary in December 1943.[55] Veesenmayer argued that the desired changes in Hungary could be obtained only by "the threat of German divisions and fighter planes." However, as in his previous report eight months earlier, Veesenmayer suggested that every effort be made to work with rather than against the Regent. Horthy, he wrote, "is a good soldier but a miserable politician" who has no understanding of domestic or foreign policy. An effort should therefore be made to separate him from "the pseudo-Jewish, legitimist clique" that advised him and turn him into "a soldier of the Führer." Veesenmayer believed that this could be achieved if the proper inducements were offered to Horthy, such as German support for the establishment of a Horthy dynasty and assurances that his "castle Jews" would be protected. If Horthy were appeased in this way, and hints were dropped that he might also realize his lifelong dream of gaining the title of prince, the Regent would, Veesenmayer concluded, accept any Prime Minister the Führer recommended, even Imrédy.[56]

By mid-March 1944 the plan for a German military occupation of Hungary was in place.[57] Hitler's strategy was to invite Horthy once again to Klessheim Castle and there to use a mixture of intimidation and cajolery to gain his assent to the German occupation. If Horthy went along, the whole operation would doubtless go smoothly. If not, his absence from Hungary on the day set for the intervention, March 19, would help thwart any attempts the Hungarians might make to resist.

Although Hungarian military intelligence noticed unusual Wehrmacht movements in the first two weeks of March, few in the Hungarian government or military suspected what was afoot. Horthy and his advisors found it psychologically impossible to believe that Hitler would divert troops badly needed elsewhere to attack an ally in such a treacherous way.[58] Nonetheless, uneasiness about German intentions and alarm over the relentless advance of the Red Army, which was now only one hundred miles from the Hungarian frontier, created a mood of impending crisis in the country. The government thus sought in various ways to steel the people for the enormous sacrifices that would be required in defending the country. Several events, including the premiere of an opera dedicated to the revered poet and national hero Sándor Petőfi, were designed to appeal to Hungarian patriotism and to strengthen the will to resist foreign domination. As a contribution to these efforts Regent Horthy drafted a speech that he proposed to deliver on March 15, Hungary's most important national holiday. What Horthy planned to say to his countrymen was almost completely unoriginal: a recitation of the glories of Hungarian history and the injustices of the peace treaties.[59] In addition, however, Horthy seemed intent on refuting the "calumnies" of Mihály Károlyi and other critics of Hungary abroad. In the country over which he presided there was not, Horthy suggested, a trace of feudalism or social backwardness. Rather, Hungary stood "in the first line of social progress in Europe" and the government remained committed to "freedom, constitutional life, parliamentarianism, and equality before the law." In Hungary, he added, political parties could operate freely and "there is no discrimination against anybody for his ideological or political convictions."

Fearing that the proposed speech, which also included a veiled plea for a negotiated end to the war, might make a bad impression in Germany, Kállay dissuaded Horthy from delivering it.[60] Nonetheless, the draft speech remains an interesting artifact of the last days of the Horthy regime. Although objective observers will find it difficult to accept Horthy's jaundiced description of Hungarian history and the nature of the interwar regime, some of the self-serving formulations of Horthy's draft do contain a modicum of truth. In March 1944, Horthy's Hungary was an anomaly, for nowhere else in the heart of Hitler's Europe had such visible traces of liberalism, political pluralism, and cultural freedom survived. This is a relative judgment, of course, for in comparison with peacetime Western Europe, Hungary in World War II was a land of severe political repression and racial intolerance. Nonetheless, it is remarkable how openly such enemies of Nazi Germany as Polish military officers and escaped British and French prisoners of war moved about in Hungary. Books long ago condemned and burned in Germany, such as Mikhail Sholokhov's *And Quiet Flows the Don* and Thomas Mann's *The Magic Mountain,* were best sellers in the bookstores of Budapest. The poetry and musical works of Jewish artists were still heard on Hungarian National Radio broadcasts. The concept of parliamentary government was still honored, even if the voices of the conservative, moderate, and left-wing parties were usually drowned out by the thunder from the extremist right. The Social Democratic party was not only tolerated but, beginning in 1943, was permitted to expand its activities. In early 1944 *Népszava,* the only surviving press organ of social democracy in Nazi or Soviet-dominated Europe, managed to gain 10,000 new subscribers. Indeed, the circulation of anti-German, moderate, or left-leaning newspapers far exceeded that of extremist right-wing, pro-German organs.[61]

Perhaps the most remarkable thing about Horthy's Hungary up to March 1944 is that it had become a haven for Jews in Hitler's Europe. Of the approximately 825,000 Jews residing in Hungary in early 1944, some 15,000 were refugees from Slovakia and Poland. Many of the approximately 200,000 Jews who had become Hungarian citizens as a result of the territorial provisions of the two Vienna Awards counted themselves lucky, for they believed that

Regent Horthy would somehow protect them from persecution by the Germans.[62] Conditions for Jews in Hungary were, of course, far from humane. The anti-Jewish laws had caused great humiliation and economic misery. But even though they were second-class citizens and were subject to conscription into the forced labor detachments, Hungarian Jews enjoyed a certain amount of security and their property was for the most part not endangered.[63] Especially in Budapest Jews continued to have considerable freedom of movement. They frequented the theaters, coffee houses, and swimming pools. Vulgar anti-Semitic propaganda was commonplace in the press and publications of the radical right-wing groups, but such scurrilous German films as *Jud Süss* and *The Wandering Jew* were banned by the Ministry of the Interior. Moreover, Jewish organizations of various kinds, even a Zionist League, continued to function freely in Hungary.[64]

That Hungary should have become a last refuge for East European Jews was not something that Admiral Horthy, the self-proclaimed anti-Semite, had consciously planned. Yet it was nonetheless his firm insistence that "inhumanity is alien to the Magyar character" that set limits on the persecution of the Jews. Horthy did not devote much of his time or attention to the plight of the Jews. He was probably unaware, for example, that a Zionist League existed in Hungary. As in the past, Horthy continued to have little direct contact with individual Jews, aside from prominent financiers and industrialists like Ferenc Chorin and Leó Goldberger. But by his adamant refusal to withdraw his support for the beleaguered Kállay and Keresztes-Fischer, despite the venomous attacks on them by the Nazis and their Hungarian sympathizers, Horthy in effect gave his imprimatur to their policies, which, in the circumstances, were remarkably tolerant and humanitarian.

On the evening of March 15 Admiral Horthy and his wife were in the Regent's special box at the Budapest Opera House for the premiere of the work based on the exploits of Sándor Petőfi. Horthy's opportunity to ponder the lessons of Hungarian resistance to the Habsburg dynasty in 1848–1849 was interrupted, however, by a message delivered by the German Minister, who requested an urgent meeting to hand over a personal letter from the Führer. This letter, it turned out, was a belated response to Horthy's request in February for the immediate withdrawal of Hungarian forces from the Eastern Front. Now, Hitler wrote, he was prepared to discuss this matter personally with the Hungarian Regent. Would Horthy kindly meet him at Klessheim Castle before the 20th, when he would need to depart for his military headquarters near the Front?

On the morning of March 16, Horthy met with Kállay, Ghyczy, Csatay, and Szombathelyi to discuss how to respond to Hitler's invitation. Kállay strongly urged that the Regent not travel once again to Klessheim.[65] His absence from the country could lead to disorder and arbitrary actions by Germany and her Hungarian sympathizers. Horthy seemed persuaded and agreed to the suggestion that the Chief of Staff be sent instead. General Szombathelyi expressed a willingness to take on this assignment if necessary, but argued that only the Regent himself could achieve the desired result of getting Hungarian troops withdrawn from the Front. For twenty-five years Horthy "had shouldered every burden for the nation's sake." He could not now refuse to undertake this difficult task. He, the Chief of Staff, would see to it that the Regent was not harmed.[66]

Admiral Horthy found it impossible to resist this appeal to his sense of duty and courage. He was quickly convinced that if he did not gamble on this personal confrontation with Hitler, he "would never see his divisions again."[67] He ordered that plans be made for his train to depart for Salzburg on the next day. In the short time available, Kállay tried to brief the Regent on the various issues that Hitler might raise and how Hungary might respond in various contingencies. Kállay suggested that if the Germans were adamant that he must be dismissed, Horthy should agree, but only in exchange for the return of all Hungarian troops and the maintenance of the current domestic policies. But Horthy refused to consider sacrificing his Prime Minister. He declared that he would not tolerate any interference with his rights or those of the Parliament.[68] On the crucial issue of what to do if Hitler threatened a German military intervention, Horthy and Kállay agreed, apparently without intensive discussions, that no resistance would be offered. In the past Horthy had on occasion boasted that he would preserve the nation's honor by leading the Hungarian Army against an invading German force even if resistance was futile. Now, however, the matter appeared to him in a different light. General Szombathelyi reported that there was no possibility of a successful resistance. In Budapest and western Hungary there was not a single military unit capable of action against the Germans.[69]

Previous plans for the organization of paramilitary groups drawn from members of the *Vitézi Rend* and various patriotic societies had gotten nowhere. Horthy was not inclined to attempt to rally the workers and left-wing forces for a national resistance, and in any case there was now insufficient time to mobilize the nation in this way. The only major precaution taken by the government was to alert Hungarian envoys in neutral states that in case of a German occupation they were to seek contact with American or British legations. Otherwise Horthy left behind no signed proclamation that might be issued in his absence and no specific plan of action.[70]

When late on Friday, March 17, Admiral Horthy boarded his train, the Turán, he did so with some trepidation. Not only was he uncertain about Hitler's intentions, but he also found himself violating an old naval tradition. According to a superstition that Horthy had always heeded during his career in the Habsburg Navy, journeys that began on a Friday always ended in misfortune.[71] But there was no alternative, for Hitler's timetable was rigid. By the morning of the 18th the Hungarian party, which consisted also of Szombathelyi, Ghyczy, and Csatay, was safely in Salzburg, where they were welcomed by Hitler and taken by car to Klessheim. Already during the ride to the meeting site Horthy noticed, however, that the atmosphere was more strained than during previous visits. He did not suspect, however, what an uneven match the confrontation with Hitler would be. The German leader had a detailed plan for the invasion of Hungary, which was set to begin at 5:00 P.M. that day. The Hungarian Regent arrived with virtually no plans for responding to such a German threat.[72]

The first discussion between Hitler and Horthy occurred late that morning.[73] At this critical talk no one else was present, not even Paul Schmidt, who had drawn up the stenographic protocol at the Klessheim talks a year earlier.[74] At first, Horthy later recollected, Hitler was uncharacteristically hesitant. For a few minutes he "hemmed and hawed" before deciding on the tack he would take. He began by referring not to the disposition of the Hungarian forces on the Eastern Front, the ostensible purpose of Horthy's visit, but to the catastrophic condition that had been created for Germany when Italy had attempted its "betrayal in the summer of 1943." He regretted not having taken preemptive action to clarify that situation, the more so because he now suspected that Hungary too was preparing to defect to the enemy. He "would not tolerate such treason by an ally." He had expressed his concerns in their previous meeting at Klessheim, but had received no satisfactory response from Hungary.

Horthy was gravely insulted by Hitler's accusations, which he denied vigorously. "Never in its thousand-year history," he asserted, "had Hungary ever committed such a dishonorable act." Hungarians had never been traitors and never would be so long as he was at the helm. "Should events force my hand one day," he added, "I assure you that I shall openly and honestly inform the German Government of such negotiations beforehand. Hungary would never be the first to take up arms against its German comrades."[75]

Hitler was unmoved by Horthy's protestations of innocence. "Ich habe meine Beweise!" ("I have my proofs"), he insisted. "Ich kenne Ihre Beweise!" ("I know your proofs"), Horthy replied sarcastically.[76] Berlin, the Regent argued, relied on traitorous German-Hungarians for information, but it was he who knew best what was happening in his own country. Horthy argued in vain that Hungary remained a loyal ally and had placed a large percentage of its industry and transportation network at Germany's disposal. Hitler, however, was unmoved and declared that he had to take precautionary measures. He had decided on a military occupation of Hungary so that the destructive elements there could be purged. To Horthy's remark that German forces could surely be put to better use in fighting the Russians, Hitler responded that he had plenty of reserve units to use in an occupation of Hungary. Besides, he could also call on the Romanians, Slovaks, and Croatians for assistance. This statement infuriated Horthy, who declared that such an action would be both injudicious and criminal, and "would cause unparalleled hatred for your regime to flare up" in Hungary. He, the Regent, would have no other recourse but abdication. Hitler replied blandly that he hoped that the Regent would consent to the occupation, but if not he would carry it out anyway. Horthy could tolerate no more of this insolence: "If everything has been decided upon already, there is no point in protracting the discussion. I am leaving!"[77]

To the astonishment of those gathered in the hall outside the conference room, the door now flew open and Horthy, "very red in the face," burst out and began to climb the stairs to his room. Hitler, "looking angry and embarrassed," chased after him. The German *chef de protocole*, Freiherr von Dörnberg, managed to slow the Hungarian Regent's progress sufficiently to allow Hitler to catch up and show his visitor to his room. Hitler thereupon retreated angrily to his conference room to consult with Ribbentrop.[78]

The members of Horthy's entourage, as well as Sztójay and Sándor Homlok, the Hungarian military attaché in Berlin, quickly assembled to hear the Regent's account of his dramatic confrontation. So agitated was Horthy that, to the dismay of his advisors, he was unable to give a completely lucid account of what had happened. They urged him not to break off the talks entirely; perhaps it would be possible to discover what concessions the Germans were seeking and whether in fact Hitler's decision to invade Hungary was irrevocable. Horthy agreed. When an invitation to lunch was delivered, he replied that he would attend only if talks would continue in the afternoon. At the luncheon itself, however, the atmosphere was frigid. Hitler "picked nervously at his vegetarian food" and such conversation as occurred was strained and nonpolitical.

At the second conversation between Horthy and Hitler, which began around 3:30 in the afternoon, the Hungarian Regent took the offensive. He had never imagined that Germany would try something like this. Hitler should reconsider his decision in light of the fact that the Hungarians were the only people who still harbored friendly feelings toward Germany. The Germans had behaved so badly all over the world that even the Hottentots and Lapplanders hated them.[79] There had been no sabotage in Hungary, not "a single explosion, a single strike, or any action whatever." A German invasion of Hungary could not possibly be helpful to Germany. It would result only in massive new air raids by the Anglo-Saxons and a guerrilla movement might even arise. What exactly were the allegations against Hungary that had led Hitler to consider such drastic action?

Hitler perfunctorily presented his case, which amounted to little more than a rehashing of the accusations he had made at Klessheim a year earlier. Kállay, he insisted, was in contact with the Allies. The Szent-Györgyi incident was proof of this. He was also disturbed by many signs that the Hungarian press was not totally committed to the Axis cause. Recently some Hungarian newspaper had reported favorably on the Finnish peace negotiations. Germany had protested against this, but nothing had been done. Hungary's air defense was totally inadequate. Enemy planes seemed to fly over Hungary with impunity. Pro-British and even pro-Communist sentiments were spreading rapidly. Furthermore, the Hungarian government seemed unwilling to "settle accounts with the large Jewry in Hungary." Finland had only six thousand Jews, and look at the subversive and defeatist activity they carried out. He could not permit one million Hungarian Jews to continue their destructive work and spying so close to the Front.

These were the problems, Hitler continued, that he wished to rectify by sending his troops to Hungary. As for the objectives of the German occupation, these were listed in a protocol that he now placed before his guest. This document, which Horthy apparently read only cursorily, called for the appointment of a new Hungarian government, with Imrédy as Prime Minister and General Jenő Rátz as Minister of Defense. To assist the new government a German plenipotentiary would be sent to Budapest along with the occupying German Army. The Regent would issue a proclamation instructing the Hungarian people and army to receive the Wehrmacht in a friendly way.[80]

Admiral Horthy indignantly refused Hitler's request that he sign the proposed protocol. Never in his life, he declared, had he ever told a lie and he would not do so now. Besides he could not legally sign such a document because it required the signature of the Prime Minister as well. In desperation Horthy now tried a different, more unconventional, tack. If Hitler refrained from attacking Hungary, he, the Hungarian head of state, would give his solemn promise that his country would not defect to the enemy or act in some other dishonorable way. If this promise were broken, he would feel honor bound to use his revolver to commit suicide. To which Hitler could only reply with disgust: "But what good would that do me?"[81]

On this bizarre note the conversation ended in deadlock at 5:25. Horthy returned to his room, changed into his traveling clothes, and announced his intention of departing immediately for Budapest. But Hitler was not about to permit the Hungarian party to leave until "Operation Margarethe" was well under way. There are indications that he was even prepared to have Horthy formally arrested if he continued to be obstreperous.[82] To delay Horthy's departure Ribbentrop went so far as to stage a fake air raid, which included a convincing smoke screen over the Castle. Horthy's efforts to reach Kállay by telephone were futile, for the telephone lines had unfortunately been "badly hit" in the air raid. Admiral Horthy was thus closeted with his entourage for several hours in the evening. It was during this interval that he decided, for reasons that remain obscure, to give his grudging consent to the German occupation. Although Horthy had throughout the day remained adamant in his opposition to Hitler's plans, the other Hungarians present had been almost frantic to find some compromise solution. As military officers, Szombathelyi, Csatay, Sztójay, and Homlok were convinced that any resistance to a German occupation would entail disastrous consequences for Hungary. Sztójay, Homlok, and perhaps even Szombathelyi believed that a temporary German occupation might even have some salutary effects.[83]

It was apparently General Szombathelyi who persuaded Horthy to make one final effort to find common ground with Hitler. During the day Szombathelyi had had discussions with both Hitler and Ribbentrop, both of whom hinted that some compromise was possible. If only Horthy abandoned his opposition to the occupation, there would perhaps be no need for him to sign an official protocol at Klessheim. He could return to Budapest where he would be expected to appoint a new government acceptable to Germany. Once he had achieved the necessary guarantees, Hitler told Szombathelyi, he would withdraw his troops from Hungary.[84] This "promise" made by the Führer may have begun to tip the balance in Horthy's calculations. No doubt the others in the Hungarian party reminded him of Hitler's threat that Hungary's neighbors would join in the occupation. This would be a catastrophic repetition of events after World War I, when Romanian, Czechoslovak, and Yugoslav forces gobbled up Hungarian territory and set the stage for a Communist regime. If the Kállay government had to be jettisoned in order to avert this catastrophe, perhaps this was a sacrifice, however abhorrent to Horthy, that had to be made. Szombathelyi may also have used an argument that had been persuasive in convincing Horthy to travel to Klessheim in the first place. Only Regent Horthy, Hungary's courageous leader for more than two decades, could hope to find some way out of what seemed to be a hopeless situation. The important thing now was for Admiral Horthy to remain at the helm, return to Budapest, and then work for a rapid end to the German occupation.

Horthy seemed to be leaning toward acceptance of a solution along these lines when, around 8:00 in the evening, Ribbentrop appeared and declared that Hitler was prepared for a further discussion with the Hungarian Regent. Horthy proceeded once more to the conference room and, wishing to put the onus of a compromise on Hitler, asked: "Do you want to speak to me?" Hitler, no doubt prompted by Ribbentrop, made an effort to seem conciliatory. He began by imploring Horthy to remain at his post; by no means did he want him to abdicate. He had always liked the Magyars very much, and it was ridiculous to imagine he wished to turn Hungary into a German "Gau" like Bohemia. "I will never," he solemnly declared, "violate Hungary's sovereignty." He emphasized again that Kállay was the main stumbling block, for the Germans simply did not trust him. "I give you my word," Hitler said, "that German troops shall be withdrawn as soon as a new Hungarian Government that has my confidence has been formed."[85] In other words, the German occupation would be temporary, lasting at most a couple of months, and if the Regent cooperated there was really no need to involve Hungary's neighbors.[86]

From these statements Horthy deduced that Hitler indeed wished "to improve the situation."[87] Horthy's exact response to the Führer's overture is not recorded in any documentation, and no formal agreement was drafted. But subsequent developments make it clear that Horthy, perhaps in a muddled and indirect way, accepted the terms of the compromise that Szombathelyi had worked out earlier. He apparently gave Hitler an assurance that there would be no resistance to the German occupation and that upon returning to Budapest he would dismiss Kállay and appoint a government acceptable to the Germans. It was implicitly understood that the Hungarian Army, including the units on the Eastern Front, would continue the fight against the Soviet Union.[88] Hitler expressed great satisfaction at Horthy's willingness to cooperate. Now, he declared, he would be able to inform Antonescu that he could deploy all his divisions against the Red Army, since there was no need to worry about Hungary.

Neither Hitler nor Horthy seemed intent on filling in the blank spaces of the compromise solution they had reached. Thus, there was no discussion, let alone specific agreement, on how the "Jewish problem" would be dealt with, what role, if any, the Gestapo would play in Hungary, and which individuals would be acceptable members of the new government to be appointed by the Regent. The agreement was thus verbal and, to an extent, even tacit, but Horthy's assurances were sufficient to convince Hitler that the occupation would be accomplished without major complications. Around 9:00 Hitler accompanied the Hungarian party to their train and sent them off "with a friendly smile." He then ordered certain changes in "Operation Margarethe." The previous plans for a military seizure of the Castle and dropping of leaflets over Budapest were called off. The number of units to be used in the operation was somewhat reduced, though the occupation force remained formidable. Hungarian troops were to be confined to barracks until further notice, but their weapons were not to be confiscated.[89]

Once en route to Budapest, Admiral Horthy made no attempt to renege on the concessions he had made to Hitler. He and Szombathelyi sent off telegrams instructing that there be no resistance to the entry of German troops, and in fact the occupation took place in the early hours of March 19 without even token opposition from Hungarian armed forces. Strangely, during the journey back to Budapest Horthy did not act like a man who had been intimidated and who faced a bleak future. There is no evidence that he made any effort to consult with his entourage in order to devise a strategy of action to be employed when the train reached its destination. Instead, Horthy invited Paul Schmidt, who had been assigned to accompany the Regent and accord him "full honors," to a late dinner. Long into the night Horthy regaled his guest with his favorite stories and anecdotes. Schmidt later marveled at how Horthy was able to be so congenial despite the painful experience he had just undergone.[90] One suspects, however, that Horthy's attempt to take his mind off his troubles was only briefly successful. His sleep that night could hardly have been peaceful, for he must have given anxious thought to the critical days that lay ahead. How could he extricate his country from this grave crisis? What would be his fate and that of his family?

Little did Admiral Horthy suspect the kaleidoscopic events that would unfold in the coming months. He would be forced to contend with a cadre of Hitler's cruel and efficient minions, including Adolf Eichmann. He would finally be confronted with the reality of the "Final Solution." For a time he would become the focus of world attention: messages would arrive from the pope, several European kings, the American President, and other world dignitaries. The most unlikely things would happen. He would receive Ferenc Szálasi in audience. He would write Stalin a personal letter and beg his forgiveness. In the end he would abdicate and appoint Szálasi as the new Prime Minister. No, not even in his wildest dreams during that night of March 19–20 could Horthy's mind have produced such a bizarre scenario.

11

Between Hitler and Stalin

When Admiral Horthy awoke on the morning of March 19, he was surprised to discover that he was still several hours from Budapest and that a number of new passengers, including Edmund von Veesenmayer, the new German Minister and Reich Plenipotentiary in Hungary, and Ernst Kaltenbrunner, the Chief of the Gestapo, had boarded the train during the night.[1] This initial encounter with the new Nazi German representatives in Hungary must have alerted Horthy to the seriousness of the situation and the grave trials that lay ahead. As he emerged from the train around 11:00 A.M. at the station in Budapest, he seemed to Kállay, who was there to greet him, "deathly pale" and "worn out."[2] As they were being driven to the Castle, Horthy related his experiences at Klessheim. He tried to explain that he had made no promises to Hitler and that he had insisted that he could take no definitive action until he was back in Budapest. He did, however, inform his Prime Minister of Hitler's promise that if a pro-German government in which he could have confidence were appointed, he would see to it that Hungary's sovereignty was not violated and that German troops would be withdrawn. Sensing what Horthy was hinting at and not wishing to place his friend in the embarrassing position of asking for his resignation, Kállay now offered it himself and declared that this was the only viable course of action.[3]

At a Crown Council that began at noon, Horthy and the other members of the delegation described their conversations at Klessheim.[4] Horthy declared that Hungary simply did not possess the necessary military power to resist the German occupation, especially in light of the fact that Hitler had threatened to invite Romanian, Croatian, and Slovak troops to join in an attack. Although he had full confidence in Miklós Kállay and had avoided making any definite commitments to the Germans, in the present circumstances he was compelled to accept the resignation of the govern-

335

ment. The Germans would now put forward all kinds of demands and would interfere in everything. But "the war will not last forever," and "with the help of God we shall cope with the difficult situation." Besides, if the Russians invaded the country things would be even worse. The Council ended with an alarming report from Ferenc Keresztes-Fischer, who informed the group that the Gestapo had already arrested forty-five prominent Hungarians, including some members of Parliament. Severe measures against the Jews were apparently being planned: not a single Jew was permitted to leave Budapest.

Through the afternoon of the 19th Horthy agonized over the critical decisions he now had to make. Kállay and several of his advisors, shocked by a spate of reports of brutal actions by the Gestapo, now tried to persuade him to resign and completely dissociate himself from any government the Germans might install. Perhaps a way could still be found for Horthy to appoint a government that would function abroad. At the very least he should retire to Kenderes and thus make it clear that he would have nothing to do with any German puppet state, as King Christian X of Denmark had done. But Horthy resisted such solutions, which seemed to him dishonorable and counterproductive. In the past, he said, he could have boarded an airplane and escaped into exile, as the queen of Holland, the king of Norway, the Regent of Yugoslavia, and even President Beneš had. But, Horthy insisted, he simply could not run away, even just to Kenderes, and abandon the Hungarian people in this time of extreme emergency.[5] He explained it this way to Kállay:

> I cannot let a usurper sit in this place. I have sworn to the country not to forsake it. I am still an admiral. The captain cannot leave his sinking ship; he must remain on the bridge to the last. Whom will it serve if Imrédy sits here? Who will defend the army? Who will save a million Magyar lads from being dragged away to the Russian shambles? Who will defend the honorable men and women in this country who have trusted me blindly? Who will defend the Jews or our refugees if I leave my post? I may not be able to defend everything, but I believe that I can still be of great, very great, help to our people. I can do more than anyone else.[6]

Kállay's counterarguments proved unavailing. Horthy listened but his response, which reminded Kállay of similar words often spoken by Emperor Francis Joseph, was always the same: "I have weighed everything; I have considered everything. I cannot act otherwise." Kállay departed in a mood of deepest pessimism. The two men would not meet again until 1948.

Horthy's fateful decision to remain at his post did, however, receive support from members of the Jewish establishment. Shortly after his return from Klessheim a delegation headed by Ferenc Chorin and Móric Kornfeld visited the Castle and implored Horthy not to abdicate or withdraw completely from the political scene. He should appease the Germans by appointing a new government; otherwise, the Jews would face certain extermination.[7] On the other hand, just before his escape Count Bethlen implored the Regent not to appoint a new Prime Minister and thereby contribute to the formation of a German puppet regime. "If there is no government," he asserted, "the Germans have no opposite number with whom to negotiate. Hence, public opinion at home as well as abroad will clearly see that an end has been put to legitimate government."[8]

As Horthy struggled with the conflicting advice he had received, he discovered how difficult it was for a captain to navigate in stormy, uncharted waters without the aid of most of his crew and fellow officers. Within the first few days of the German occupation Ferenc Keresztes-Fischer, Endre Bajcsy-Zsilinszky, and many others known to be pro-Western or sympathetic to the Jews were apprehended and sent to prison camps in Germany. Miklós Kállay escaped arrest only by seeking asylum at the Turkish Legation, where he remained completely isolated until November. Count Bethlen managed to leave Budapest in disguise and went into hiding in the countryside. Over the coming months Horthy would have to rely increasingly on his family and on members of his dwindling entourage in the Castle for advice and moral support.

In Edmund von Veesenmayer Horthy faced a truly formidable opponent, whom Budapest pundits would soon be calling the *Reichsverwesenmayer,* a play on the name of Hitler's envoy and the German word for regent. During their first extensive conversation Veesenmayer demanded that Horthy appoint a government headed by Béla Imrédy and that the Cabinet consist of members drawn from all the radical right-wing parties with the exception of the Arrowcross. Horthy scoffed at this idea: "What? You want Imrédy, the Jew?" He suggested instead that he appoint a kind of caretaker government to be run by high-ranking civil servants. But Veesenmayer angrily rejected the notion of a transition government as "politically false and untimely." The era of constant procrastination and "endless compromises" was past. It was obvious, he said, that the Regent was merely trying to gain time. Horthy was flustered by his visitor's intimidating and relentless manner, and after trying in vain to change the topic and obfuscate the issue, finally blurted out that his visitor was just too intelligent and articulate for him. Nonetheless, he must stand by his decision to form a transition government. At that Veesenmayer expressed regret at Horthy's stubbornness and warned that it would very likely lead to severe consequences, for the Führer would not permit his plans to be thwarted in this way.

In reporting on March 20 to his superiors in Berlin Veesenmayer expressed the exasperation he felt after his first few conversations with the Hungarian Regent in Budapest:

> . . . Horthy is either a chronic liar or else he is physically not up to his tasks any more. He repeats himself constantly, often contradicts himself within a few sentences, and sometimes is at a loss how to continue. What he has to say sounds like a memorized formula, and I fear that he will be difficult to convince, much less to win over.[9]

As Veesenmayer had predicted, Hitler was in no mood for further negotiation or delay. Accordingly, Horthy was informed on the 21st that if a government acceptable to the German Reich was not appointed within thirty-six hours, energetic military measures would be taken, including the seizure of the Castle.[10]

But even as gun-toting S.S. soldiers in their tan raincoats patrolled menacingly in the courtyard of the Castle, Admiral Horthy stubbornly resisted the German demand that he appoint Béla Imrédy as his new Prime Minister. Finally, early on March 23, Veesenmayer, who himself preferred to avoid a break that would lead to Horthy's resignation, worked out a compromise. Instead of Imrédy, the new Prime Minister would be Döme Sztójay, whom both Ribbentrop and Hitler trusted and who had been mentioned as a possible candidate even at the Klessheim meeting. Although in the negotiations Horthy attempted to veto the names of proposed Cabinet members whom he found objectionable, in the end he managed only one minor victory. The Sztójay Cabinet was to consist of reliably pro-German right-wing extremists, except for General Lajos Csatay, whom Horthy succeeded in retaining as Minister of Defense.

When asked later why he had agreed to appoint the Sztójay government, Horthy explained that his main objective had been to avoid "even greater misfortune" for Hungary. Horthy was aware of Sztójay's pronounced pro-German sympathies, but he apparently thought that as an army officer, Sztójay would be more likely than a pro-German politician like Imrédy to obey the Regent's commands.[11] Actually, Sztójay, who was in ill health, was not eager to undertake the task and did so only after Horthy made an emotional appeal to his patriotic duty.[12] On March 23 the new government was thus appointed in a legal manner. In a communiqué published at the same time it was stated that the entry of German troops into Hungary had occurred "by mutual consent" in order to help mobilize the country for the struggle against bolshevism. Although Hitler remained intensely suspicious of Horthy, the German press and radio were now instructed to lavish praise on him: "It is no accident that the man who saved Hungary in 1919 has done so again."[13] György Barcza, observing events from abroad, saw a different historical analogy. Horthy, he wrote in his diary, has in a "cowardly, unpatriotic, and degrading way handed over the country to the Nazis just as twenty-five years earlier, almost to the day, Károlyi handed the country to Béla Kun and the Soviets."[14] Count Károlyi himself, interviewed in London, also drew on historical events to condemn the Hungarian Regent: "Horthy is a new Count Tisza and the fate of his people today is no more favourable than in 1918."[15]

Few of the prominent members of Hungary's interwar political establishment, whether Barcza and other dissident diplomats abroad or Kállay, Bethlen, and their colleagues in hiding or in prison in Hungary, had much hope that the seventy-five-year-old Admiral Horthy could on his own find a way to maneuver between Hitler and Stalin and extricate the country from its horrible predicament. They knew all too well Horthy's political naiveté and limited diplomatic skills. Yet Admiral Horthy remained convinced that by stubbornly clinging to power and patiently observing the unfolding events, he could eventually find a way to thwart the Germans and hold off the Bolsheviks. Through most of April and May Horthy remained secluded in the Castle. In part this was a self-imposed isolation, for Horthy indeed wished to dissociate himself as much as possible from the Sztójay government and to emphasize his political impotence. But this also served German interests, since Ribbentrop had instructed that Horthy's political role be reduced to the barest minimum. Horthy's assertion that he was a prisoner in his own home was, however, belied by two public appearances he made in his capacity as head of state: once, on April 8, when he accompanied Sztójay on a visit to a heavily bombed section of Budapest; and a second time, on May 9, when he observed military maneuvers.

The best evidence of Horthy's strategy in this period comes, ironically, from comments he made during a conversation with Ferenc Szálasi in early May. Horthy agreed only with great reluctance to grant an audience to the one man whom he in the past had adamantly refused to meet. Perhaps Horthy reasoned that this was just another unpleasant chore he had to undertake in order to appease the Germans and persuade Hitler to withdraw his troops. Horthy, who broke down and wept several times during the conversation, told Szálasi that the Germans had "tricked him into going to Klessheim."[16] Hitler now had the government he wanted in Hungary, but he would have nothing to do with it: "they can do what they want . . . but my sole concern will be to keep the army in my own hands." He was convinced that the English would never permit the Russians to play a leading role in Europe. His objective was therefore to ensure that Hungary had a powerful army at the end of the war, because "that and nothing else will be the decisive trump card." All in all, he thought the best policy for Hungary was, as the English would say, "to wait and see."

At several points in the conversation Szálasi tried to convince Horthy that the time was ripe to forge a political alliance between the Hungarist movement, which was the true voice of the Hungarian people, and the Regent. A policy of "wait and see" might have merit, Szálasi observed, but Hungarian society was ready and eager to embrace the principles of national socialism. Horthy listened courteously to Szálasi's exposition of the principles of his movement, but politely rejected his proposed alliance, pointing out that he would never act in such an unconstitutional manner. Besides, he said, he found it difficult to grasp the meaning of national socialism: no one had ever given him a satisfactory definition. Nationalism he understood and approved. But how could this be combined with socialism? As for the Jewish problem, Horthy continued, the fault lay not so much with the Jews as with the nation as a whole. Too many Hungarians looked down on economic activity, while a Jew like Goldberger created more wealth for the country than anyone else. For this reason, Horthy concluded, a distinction had to be made between "the revolutionary Communist Jews" and "the useful Jews."

From Horthy's remarks to Szálasi on May 3, one can deduce elements of the political strategy he had adopted after the formation of the Sztójay regime. Horthy apparently reasoned that the only way to get Hitler to honor his promise to end the military occupation of Hungary was by cooperating with the military effort against the Red Army and by allowing the Germans and their Hungarian lackeys to carry out a *Gleichschaltung* of Hungarian life. Horthy was not averse to a fuller mobilization of the Hungarian Army, since he continued to believe that a Soviet occupation of Hungary would be even more frightful and damaging than the German occupation. But he suspected that the "nazification" of the country would mean the institution of violent and inhumane measures that he had resisted for many years. His way of protesting this was to remain secluded in the Castle and to assert that he was a prisoner of the Germans.[17]

Throughout the spring of 1944 Admiral Horthy's main objective was to preserve his authority as Supreme War Lord over an autonomous Hungarian Army. In late March he told Veesenmayer and a group of German military officers that he was prepared to cooperate in "striking a blow at the Bolsheviks," but only if Hungarian troops were treated "in the spirit of the traditional comradeship of arms." On April 15 Horthy authorized the publication of an "order of the day" in which he appealed to Hungarian soldiers to "continue to resist bolshevism shoulder to shoulder with the German comrades, our true and honorable allies. . . ."

Having made this initial overriding concession, Horthy hoped that he might be able to obstruct the Germans by ensuring that men in whom he had confidence occupied key positions in the Hungarian military command. But aside from protecting General Csatay, who remained Minister of Defense, Horthy had little success. By mid-April Colonel Gyula Kádár and a number of other officers known for their anti-Nazi sentiments had been incarcerated and repeated demands for their release went unheeded. Meanwhile, the renegade Hungarian officers responsible for the Újvidék massacres returned from Germany and were reinstated and promoted. When the Germans proposed that Horthy appoint General János Vörös as Chief of Staff, Horthy demurred: "I do not know this person." But the Germans flatly rejected Horthy's nominee, General Géza Lakatos, and after delaying the matter for a week, Horthy saw no alternative to accepting the German nominee.

Horthy's suspicion that General Vörös would be too pro-German were well-founded. Soon after assuming his office Vörös began to press for the recall from retirement of those Hungarian officers of high rank who had been forced out earlier because of their pro-Nazi views.[18] Also disconcerting to the Regent was his Chief of Staff's ready acquiescence in a German demand that the first Cavalry Division, an elite unit that Horthy had intended to keep as a "last reserve" under a commander loyal to him, be mobilized and sent to the Front. In late April, when the German demand was first made, Horthy rejected it with the explanation that such a move would harm agricultural production.[19] When Vörös insisted that the Germans would not tolerate resistance in this matter, Horthy gave his approval, only to rescind it a few days later. Horthy managed to procrastinate on this issue for more than a month, at times giving in, then abruptly withdrawing his consent. As late as the beginning of June the cavalry division had not been sent to the Front. This represented one of Horthy's few, albeit fleeting, victories over the Germans in this period.

Meanwhile, however, a crisis of monumental proportions was looming on another front. When, in late March, Horthy had decided that he would focus on maintaining control of his army but would otherwise allow the Germans to "do what they wanted," he had certainly realized that the Jews would now be subjected to severe persecution. Wishing to dissociate himself from the inhumane measures the Nazis would likely implement, Horthy had informed Sztójay that any measures enacted against the Jews would have to be in the form of ministerial decrees, which would not require the Regent's signature. Like Pontius Pilate, Horthy thus hoped to wash his hands of this distasteful matter.[20]

It is true that on several occasions in April and May Horthy privately expressed uneasiness over certain vulgar aspects of the unfolding anti-Jewish campaign. When invited to the Hungarian premiere of *Jud Süss*, the notorious anti-Jewish propaganda film, Horthy declined and recommended that Sztójay also not attend.[21] In the larger sense, however, Horthy's attempt to remain head of state but avoid being implicated in the persecution of the Jews was a dismal and tragic failure. Despite all the evidence that he had at his disposal, Horthy failed to realize that Hitler intended to carry out a systematic massacre of Hungary's Jews. Certainly he knew from his conversations with Hitler and Ribbentrop at Klessheim in 1943 that the Germans had been utterly ruthless in their treatment of the Jews, but it seemed beyond his capacity at this time to imagine the true nature of the "Final Solution." No one had ever told him of the gas chambers or other details of the grisly mechanism of extermination in Auschwitz and other death camps. As so often in the past, Horthy could comprehend the true nature of an event only when it was related to him in compelling personal stories or specific detail. In late March 1944 Horthy knew that Hungarian Jews would probably be consigned to a cruel, uncertain fate, but this was a matter so painful to contemplate that he preferred not to dwell on it. Psychologically it was much easier for him to focus on other pressing issues, especially the threat from the Red Army that was now poised at Hungary's eastern frontiers. Horthy was certainly not alone in responding with moral ambivalence and cynical indifference to the fate of the Jews. In the first two months of the German occupation even the leaders of the Hungarian Jewish community, who were better informed than Horthy of what had happened to the Jews in Hitler's Europe, complied with the demands of Adolf Eichmann and his Hungarian collaborators. Some wealthy Jews, including Ferenc Chorin, even seized the opportunity to make a deal with the Germans and escape with their families to Portugal.[22]

There is no convincing evidence to support the argument that Admiral Horthy had made an agreement at Klessheim concerning the deportation of Hungarian Jews.[23] This issue was apparently raised only in early April, when Veesenmayer proposed to Sztójay that Hungary provide a substantial number of "Jewish workers" (*Arbeitsjuden*) for use in German war production. Although it is possible that Veesenmayer and certain other German leaders initially believed that the Jews would indeed be employed in this way, it quickly became evident that the true destination of the deported Jews would be Auschwitz. Sztójay and the two officials placed in charge of the anti-Jewish campaign, László Baky and László Endre, were indifferent to the actual fate of the Jews. Their single-minded objective was to cooperate with the Germans in order "to rid the country of Jews." Although Horthy had indicated that he did not wish to be consulted on these matters, Veesenmayer and Sztójay apparently thought it best to apprise the Regent of the deportations and perhaps even gain his tacit approval. Thus, Baky and Endre, two former Szeged officers, appeared before the Regent some time in early April. No contemporary account of this important conversation was made, but from fragmentary evidence it seems that Baky explained to Horthy that "several hundred thousand" Jews would be sent to Germany as workers. Playing on the Regent's well-known dislike for the "Galician Jews," he suggested that the required Jews would most easily be found in such areas of the country as Ruthenia and Transylvania. In any case, for reasons of "national security" it would be necessary to evacuate Jews from these areas that had become, or would soon be designated, combat zones. Jews, he argued, could not be allowed to remain too close to the Front, since they were all pro-Communist and would constitute a dangerous "fifth column."[24]

Horthy apparently accepted these explanations at face value.[25] According to Baky's testimony at his postwar trial, however, Horthy did express some reservations:

> Baky, you are one of my old Szeged officers. The Germans have cheated me. Now they want to deport the Jews. I don't mind. I hate the Galician Jews and the Communists. Out with them, out of the country! But you must see, Baky, that there are some Jews who are as good Hungarians as you and I. For example, here are little Chorin and Vida—aren't they good Hungarians? I can't allow these to be taken away. But they can take the rest.[26]

There is no contemporaneous evidence to corroborate Baky's account of his conversation with Horthy,[27] and it is possible that he gave false testimony at his trial in order to shift responsibility for the deportation of the Jews away from himself and on to the Regent. Still, it is not implausible that Horthy, in the company of some of his former officers, would revert to the vulgar anti-Semitic language of his Szeged days. Subsequent events confirm that Horthy did in fact approve the deportation of the "Galician Jews" in the belief that this was just one of the many distasteful concessions he had to make to appease Hitler and hasten a German withdrawal.[28] In Horthy's callous and naive way of thinking, what he was sanctioning was the dispatch of "revolutionary Communist Jews" to do forced labor in Germany. Horthy was incapable of imagining that, with the war at such a critical stage, the Germans would simply kill these Jews rather than use them as workers. Perhaps he recalled that during their first Klessheim meeting Hitler had told him that the Jews in Poland who would not work were killed. This could be interpreted by someone seeking to ease his conscience to mean that Jews who did work were spared.

Although Admiral Horthy's attitude to the deportations was ambivalent, Veesenmayer was nonetheless able to report to his superiors on April 14 that both the government and the Regent had approved the dispatch of more than 100,000 Jews to do forced labor in the Reich.[29] Under the supervision of Adolf Eichmann and his Special Operational Commando, Baky and Endre now began to carry out, in an exceedingly brutal fashion, the ghettoization of the Jews throughout eastern and northeastern Hungary. This process was accompanied by such ugly manifestations of vulgar anti-Semitism as widespread denunciations of Jews by their neighbors, pitiless cruelty on the part of the Hungarian gendarmes, and the looting of property.[30] The first trainloads of Jews departed for Auschwitz in mid-May. Among them were Jews who up to the last moment believed that they would somehow be spared, because "our great benefactor the Regent of Hungary will protect us."[31]

Already in the first days of the process of ghettoization, reports began to reach Budapest of horrible atrocities being committed against Jews in the northeastern provinces. Bishop László Ravasz, the spiritual leader of the Reformed Church, was among the first to alert the Regent. As early as April 12 he appeared at the Castle and warned Horthy that he might have to bear the responsibility for any cruelties. "The desperadoes," he said, "will not fail to make an attempt at having their own accounts paid out of the moral capital of others."[32] In response to the bishop's warning, and perhaps other reports he was receiving, Horthy summoned Andor Jaross, the Minister of the Interior, and instructed that he make an investigation. Jaross, who was a staunch pro-Nazi, duly sent off Endre on an "inspection tour." Endre, who was accompanied by Baky and Eichmann, subsequently submitted a report to Horthy that was filled with outlandish lies. He asserted that everything was now in order in the provincial ghettoes, which had the character of sanitoria. The Jews were being given the opportunity to exchange their former life-style for a healthier one in the open air.[33] Horthy, who labored under the illusion that Hungarian gendarmes would never commit atrocities, was able to convince himself that the reports of alleged atrocities were "the usual gossip of cowardly Jewish sensation-mongers."[34]

In the meantime, however, Bishop Ravasz had become so alarmed by new accounts of the cruelties of the ghettoization process that he requested a second audience with the Regent. He did so with considerable uneasiness, for he had never before intervened in such a direct and persistent way in governmental affairs. In their meeting on April 28,[35] Ravasz again implored the Regent to ensure that his name was not associated with atrocities against the Jews. Horthy, who seemed to be irritated by this clerical "meddling," explained that he had responded to the first reports of atrocities by making a commotion and ordering an investigation. He was now convinced that any scandalous treatment of the Jews had been ended. Horthy proceeded to explain that the Jews being pressed into labor service were the ones who could not be considered for military service. Their families would accompany them, "so that they can remain together." As a result, "a few hundred thousand Jews would leave the country, but not a hair on their heads would be harmed, just as is the case with the several hundred thousand Magyar workers who since the beginning of the war have been working in Germany." Ravasz, who was deeply saddened by the Regent's apparent gullibility and moral callousness, did not press the issue.[36]

For most of the month of May, Admiral Horthy tried to put the problem of the Jews out of his mind and to focus on developing a plan to end the German occupation. Among the ideas he began to mull over was one in which he would confront the Germans with a *fait accompli* by dismissing Sztójay and appointing a new Cabinet consisting exclusively of high military officers. As Prime Minister he had in mind General Géza Lakatos, who had been a recipient of the German *Ritterkreuz* but, as a "pure Magyar," would perhaps be more likely than Hungary's "Swabian" officers to remain loyal to the Regent.[37] In a conversation on May 12 with the Swiss Minister, Maximillian Jaeger, Horthy expressed confidence that within a short time he would be able to arrange for the German troops and the Gestapo to leave.[38] However, Horthy soon discovered that his own political fate was deeply intertwined with that of Hungary's Jewish community. Soon after the actual deportations to Auschwitz began on May 15, new efforts were made to inform the Regent of the inhumane treatment of the Jews. Desperate requests were made of members of the Horthy family to intercede with the Regent.[39] Ernő Pető, a leading member of the Jewish Council who for years had had a friendly relationship with the Horthy family, met surreptitiously with the Regent's son several times in May and June. Niki became convinced of the gravity of the situation and offered to serve as a liaison between his father and the Jewish Council.[40] In late May he arranged for Count Móric Esterházy, an elder statesman in whom Horthy had great confidence, to deliver a detailed memorandum that Pető and other members of the Jewish Council had drafted.

In this important document, dated May 25, the leaders of the Jewish community warned that unless countermeasures were quickly taken, the current persecutions would end in the destruction of Hungary's entire Jewish community.[41] The memorandum included a graphic account of the brutal deportation of sick people, the aged, pregnant women, and children. Seventy or eighty Jews were crammed into railway cars and provided only one bucket of water to drink and one bucket for sanitary purposes. Prominent citizens, including members of the Jewish Council in Munkács, had been publicly whipped. Aware of Horthy's tendency to distinguish between "good" and "bad" Jews, the authors of the memorandum pointed out that in some cases fully assimilated Jews, even war heroes from the Great War, were the victims of atrocities.

It was this memorandum, with its vivid details and persuasive arguments, that finally convinced Admiral Horthy that the Jews were being treated inhumanely. On many future occasions he would cite examples from this document as evidence of the depravity of the Nazis and their Hungarian collaborators.[42] But Admiral Horthy still did not grasp the true purpose of the deportations, for the authors of the May 25 memorandum, who surely knew the grisly truth, chose not to describe the fate of the deportees. As a result, during the first weeks of June, as the remaining Jewish communities outside of Budapest were being relentlessly dispatched to Auschwitz, Horthy was slow to move to action. He now made an effort not to end the deportations outright, but merely to mitigate the harshness of the process. Horthy's unwillingness to take bolder steps also reflected his continuing belief that any attempt on his part to challenge Hitler directly would be doomed to failure because of Germany's military superiority. He was also concerned that a confrontation with the Germans would undermine the defense of the country against the Red Army. He told the Swiss military attaché that he was ashamed of the treatment of the Jews in Hungary and of the large number of denunciations, which "threw a sad light on the morality of those who were responsible." He could never forgive the Germans for invading the country, but for the moment he had to focus his attention on the Communist threat, since the Bolsheviks were "at the gates of Hungary."[43]

Horthy's initiatives in early June seem, in retrospect, exceedingly timid and ineffective. In a letter to Sztójay drafted at the beginning of the month, Horthy took special pains to exonerate himself from any responsibility for the "cruel and in many cases inhumane" treatment of the Jews.[44] Circumstances had forced him into a passive position since March, but now he felt compelled to protest against measures that "did not conform to the Hungarian mind" and that, in many cases, were even more brutal than what had occurred in Germany. Horthy demanded that the government grant exemptions to Jews of "special merit," including those who had converted to Christianity, those who were indispensable to the economy, and in general those who had performed significant services for the country. Horthy also requested that Baky and Endre be dismissed from their positions, since these were the officials whom the public identified with the "exaggerated measures."

At the same time Horthy asked Sztójay, who was scheduled to make a trip to Germany on June 6, to deliver a letter he had written to Hitler.[45] In his letter Horthy reminded the Führer of the promise he had supposedly made at Klessheim, namely that the occupation of Hungary would end when a government was formed in which the Germans could have confidence. His "poor, mutilated, and looted country" was contributing all it could to the anti-Bolshevik struggle, but the Germans were treating Hungary like enemy territory. The Gestapo and S.S. had unlawfully imprisoned thousands, and German occupation troops were enjoying a "comfortable, carefree life" while Hungarian soldiers were sacrificing their lives in combat. For all these reasons, Horthy argued, the time had come for the German occupying forces to be withdrawn. Surely the 250,000 German troops in Hungary could be put to better use at the Front.

Horthy's two letters had no effect. Sztójay's immediate response was an offer to resign, but the Regent was not yet prepared to challenge Hitler by dismissing his Prime Minister.[46] He was still convinced that he was powerless to deal with likely German reprisals. As a result, his intervention yielded no immediate results. Sztójay and Veesenmayer concluded that Horthy's protests were not to be taken seriously; his letter, they believed, was merely "an alibi to be used with the English and Americans in case the war ends badly."[47]

As a result, for most of June nothing came of Horthy's attempt to mitigate the severity of the anti-Jewish measures and to end the German occupation. The deportations continued unabated. The Regent's weak position vis-à-vis the Germans was demonstrated when, after over a month of procrastination and resistance, Horthy finally saw no alternative but to yield to German pressure and approve the mobilization of his prized Cavalry Division. On June 12 it was dispatched to the Pripet march area on the Eastern Front, where it soon suffered devastating losses.[48] This setback deepened Horthy's despondence and feeling of impotence as he waited in vain for a response to his letter to Hitler and for action by Sztójay on the directives he had given. Among his dwindling number of confidantes Horthy expressed his frustration and bitterness. The private comments he made in this period suggest that he was truly appalled by the atrocities that had been committed. In a conversation with a visitor in mid-June, after describing the measures against the Jews as "beyond mere inhumanity," he became silent and then wept uncontrollably. Horthy frequently railed against Sztójay, whom he now referred to contemptuously by his former Serb name, Sztojakovics. It was this "stupid man" who was "the main cause of all his troubles." As for Baky, and Endre, he had at first trusted them because they had been his officers at Szeged, but now he concluded that they had disobeyed his orders. The country would have to be liberated from such sadistic madmen.[49] Nonetheless, Baky, Endre, and Jaross continued their deadly work unimpeded through the month of June.

Admiral Horthy, who only months earlier had possessed almost unchallenged political authority in Hungary, was thus reduced to a state of paralysis. Never a creative thinker or a clever strategist, he had to face this crisis, the most severe in his entire regency, virtually alone. The advisors to whom he had always turned for counsel in critical times, such as Bethlen, Kállay, Kánya, and Keresztes-Fischer, were unavailable. Yet by the middle of June developments were underway that would dramatically transform the situation. The essential catalyst was the arrival in Budapest around June 10 of a report on the Auschwitz death camp that had been composed by two Jewish inmates who had managed to escape and make their way to Slovakia. The Jewish Council arranged for copies of these so-called Auschwitz Protocols to be sent abroad and to key individuals in Hungary, including church leaders. On June 19 or 20 Sándor Török, a well-known writer and member of the Jewish Council, delivered a copy to the Regent's daughter-in-law. She and Magda Horthy wept as they read this detailed account of the systematic murder of the Jews in the gas chambers of Auschwitz. Shocked by these revelations, Magda Horthy showed the report to her husband and convinced him that this could not be mere exaggeration.[50] Moreover, on June 23, through the intercession of Niki Horthy, the Jewish Council was able to send another memorandum to the Regent. In it they implored him, "in the twelfth hour of our tragedy," to call an immediate halt to the continuing deportations of "hundreds of thousands of innocent people." They warned Horthy that the Germans intended to deport the Jews of Budapest in the near future.[51]

By the last week of June 1944, an unprecedented international campaign was being mounted on behalf of Hungary's Jews. On June 25 Admiral Horthy received a telegram from Pope Pius XII, in which the pontiff, without specifically mentioning the Jews, called on him "to do everything possible to ensure that the sufferings which had to be borne for so long by numerous unfortunate people in the bosom of this noble and chivalrous nation because of their nationality or racial origins shall not be prolonged or made worse."[52] In the next few days Horthy received similar messages of concern and admonition from King Gustav of Sweden, Franklin Roosevelt, and other world dignitaries. The American President backed up his appeal for an end to the deportations with a clear threat of grave reprisals: "I rely not only upon humanity, but also upon the force of weapons."[53]

The Auschwitz Protocols and the messages from abroad helped to galvanize Horthy's conscience and to embolden him to risk defying the Germans. His willingness to do so was increased by two other developments. The Allies had landed at Normandy on June 6 and by the end of the month had gained a secure foothold on the continent. This may have persuaded Horthy that his freedom of maneuver would be enhanced as Hitler focused his attention on Western Europe. At the same time Horthy was greatly angered when he received a report that the Germans were showing a propaganda film in Switzerland that attributed the cruelties against the Hungarian Jews to the Hungarian authorities.[54] Horthy, who had convinced himself that the Germans, along with a handful of Hungarian "sadists" like Baky and Endre, bore sole responsibility for all the atrocities that had been committed, was indignant at what he regarded as a calumny of the Hungarian nation.[55]

When Horthy learned that the Hungarian Cabinet at meetings on June 21 and 23 had failed to act on his previous directives to the Prime Minister, he realized that only his personal intervention would bring results. On June 26, shortly after the arrival of Roosevelt's sharply worded note, Horthy thus summoned and presided over a Crown Council, the first to be held since the early days of the German occupation.[56] Horthy began by informing the ministers of the protests with which he had been bombarded. He went on to denounce Baky and Endre as "sadistic scoundrels who cannot be kept under control," and to mention several places where atrocities had been committed against Jews. When called on to account for the behavior of his troops, Gábor Faraghó, the Commander of the Gendarmerie, insisted that the Germans bore sole responsibility for the atrocities that had been committed. This sparked a prolonged debate, with Sztójay, Imrédy, and Reményi-Schneller defending the Germans. Finally Horthy lost patience and closed the discussion in an irritated voice:

> I won't stand it any longer! I won't allow the deportations to bring more shame upon Hungary. The Government shall take measures to remove Endre and Baky from their positions. The deportation of the Budapest Jews shall be stopped. The necessary steps shall be taken by the Government.

Horthy's directive did not, and probably was not intended to, bring a halt to the deportation of the last Jewish communities outside of the capital city. Perhaps he was simply not aware that this deadly process had not yet been completed; more likely, he had drawn the pragmatic conclusion that the only Jews he had a reasonable chance of protecting were those in Budapest, where he could more easily assert his authority. In the last days of June and the first of July, freight trains crammed with Jews thus continued to depart from Szeged, Sopron, and other cities in southern and western Hungary. On the other hand, Sztójay and Veesenmayer agreed that certain temporary concessions should be made to pacify the Regent. On June 30 Baky and Endre were temporarily "relieved of their duties," although in reality they continued to carry on as before. The date for the beginning of deportations from Budapest, originally set for June 30, was postponed until the completion of the operations elsewhere in Hungary. In addition, the Regent was to be permitted to exempt a small number of his favored Jews from the anti-Jewish laws. Veesenmayer believed that these measures would satisfy Horthy and that the deportation of the Budapest Jews could commence in the near future.

It did not take long for Horthy to realize that the minor concessions offered to him did not fundamentally alter the situation. Baky,

Endre, and other pro-German Hungarians were intent on thwarting the Regent's will, even if that required eliminating by force members of Horthy's entourage who were thought to have a baneful influence on him. Horthy began to sense the ruthlessness and fanaticism of his opponents when, on June 29, an unsuccessful attempt was made to assassinate his friend István Bárczy, the keeper of the Cabinet minutes. Meanwhile, Baky, who continued to cooperate closely with Eichmann, was arranging to bring into Budapest those gendarme brigades that had "distinguished" themselves in the anti-Jewish operations in the countryside. By early July several thousand gendarmes, armed with bayonets, were patrolling the streets of the capital city in groups of two or three.[57] July 6 was set as the day for the beginning of a rapid liquidation of what the fanatical German and Hungarian anti-Semites regarded as the last bastion of European Jewry.

Admiral Horthy now realized that if he was to assert his political will, he would have to find a way to bring to Budapest a sizable contingent of troops loyal to him. Over the past three months he had regarded such an action on his part as impossible, since the Germans closely supervised all Hungarian military operations. Furthermore, he worried that he might not be able to count on the unquestioning obedience and cooperation of his Chief of Staff, General Vörös. In late June, however, a pretext for action arose precisely because of the menacing concentration of gendarme units in Budapest. On June 29 Horthy summoned Vörös and told him he had reliable evidence that Baky had met secretly with representatives of the Gestapo and S.S. and was scheming to topple the government. He ordered Vörös to take appropriate military countermeasures.[58]

Although Horthy apparently believed that Baky and his clique were desperate enough to contemplate a coup d'état, it is possible that he deliberately exaggerated the danger in order to justify his taking the military initiative. When General Vörös, whose investigation of the situation uncovered no plans for a seizure of power, procrastinated in carrying out the Regent's order, Horthy decided to act unilaterally. Perhaps inspired by a memorandum from Count Bethlen that reached him in early July,[59] Horthy now proceeded with uncharacteristic boldness, discretion, and skill.[60] Bypassing Vörös, he authorized Károly Lázár, the commander of his personal guard, to assume military command in Budapest and to take measures to prevent both a coup d'état and deportation of the

Jews. On July 5 Horthy summoned Colonel Ferenc Koszorús, commander of the First Armored Division, which was stationed north of Budapest, and ordered him to remove the gendarmerie from the capital city. In meetings on July 5 and 6 Horthy informed Vörös that he intended to stop the deportations of the Jews, so that at least those of Budapest would be spared. Vörös tried to dissuade him. Bringing units of the army to Budapest would, he argued, merely cause greater anxiety among the people. Furthermore, the Germans would never stand for such unilateral action. They would simply take complete responsibility for solving the "Jewish problem" and the results would be even more horrible for the Jews. What's more, the wealth of the Jews would then fall into German hands.[61]

Although he briefly wavered, Admiral Horthy finally ignored the warnings of his Chief of Staff and on July 6 gave a formal order for the withdrawal of the gendarme units from Budapest and for the dismissal of Baky and Endre. Late on the same day, without informing Vörös, he had Colonel Koszorús deploy his battalion at the main train station and other key points in Budapest.[62] Then he waited, with considerable anxiety, to see whether his gamble would succeed. On July 7 and 8 there was an atmosphere of crisis in the capital city. Air raid sirens sounded constantly and rumors circulated of the imminent entry into the city of German military units. By late on the 7th, however, it seemed that Horthy's gamble was succeeding. General Faraghó was unwilling to disobey a direct command from the Regent, and the Germans, caught off guard, were in fact not prepared to risk a direct confrontation. In the circumstances Döme Sztójay felt compelled to carry out Horthy's wishes. As a result the gendarmes began an orderly withdrawal that was completed by July 8, Baky and Endre were relieved of their duties, and the deportation of the Jews of Budapest was called off.[63] By this time, however, over 400,000 Hungarian Jews had been transported to the Auschwitz death camp.

Horthy's action was unprecedented in the history of the Holocaust: never before had a leader successfully used the threat of military force to halt the deportation of Jews to the death camps. Yet on first hearing of this development, Veesenmayer professed not to be overly concerned. "It's the same old eternal song with the Regent," he concluded. "The last person to see him is the one who is right." He seemed satisfied with Horthy's assurance that he would stand by the Germans "for better or for worse," and that he would soon approve a resumption of the deportation of the Jews, albeit without the harshness of the previous actions. Veesenmayer reported to Berlin that the situation was under control and that no military reinforcements need be sent.[64] But Adolf Eichmann, whose operations were directly affected, was more alarmed: "In all my long practice this is the first time such a thing has happened to me; this won't do at all. It's contrary to all agreements. I can't get over this."[65] Eichmann moved quickly to test the resolve of the Regent. With the cooperation of Andor Jaross, who was prepared to thwart Horthy's will and find a way to "to carry out the complete de-Jewification of Budapest," he initiated in mid-July a rapid action to deport a group of 1500 Jews being held at a camp on the outskirts of Budapest. But, alerted by the Jewish Council, Horthy managed to dispatch troops in time to intercept the train and return the transport safely back to the camp.[66]

Buoyed by these initial successes, Admiral Horthy tried to move quickly to exploit his newly discovered freedom of maneuver. For some time he had been toying with the idea of replacing the Sztójay government with one comprised of military officers loyal to him. In late May he had hinted strongly to General Géza Lakatos that "one fine day" he would summon him to take the reins of the government.[67] His confidence no doubt bolstered by the detailed, step-by-step plan of political action drawn up by Count Bethlen and delivered to him in early July,[68] Horthy now determined that that "fine day" had arrived. He even began to give serious thought to a possible military clash with the Germans. In a conversation with Vörös on July 7, Horthy sketched his plan for the creation of a military government. How would Hungary fare, he asked, if it came to a military confrontation with Gestapo and S.S. units in Hungary? Vörös replied that Hungarian forces were too weak to deal with the Germans, who might be having their troubles at the Front but could easily put down any resistance in Hungary. Furthermore, Hungary's position on the Carpathians would be gravely weakened and the Soviets would be able to break through. The result would be "the annihilation of our country, which would in the end resemble Hungary after the invasion of the Mongols."[69]

Undaunted by his Chief of Staff's bleak assessment of the situation, Horthy summoned General Lakatos, who for the past month had been on leave at his country home awaiting word from the Regent. In a conversation on the afternoon of July 8, Horthy briefed Lakatos on the events of the past month and his plan to create an "apolitical government" of generals. He implored Lakatos to agree to serve as Prime Minister. But Lakatos, who was concerned about how the Germans would respond to such a change, asked for and was granted twenty-four hours to make a full assessment of the situation. Lakatos was able to confer with Bethlen, who managed to return to Budapest and enter the Castle without being detected by the Germans. Bethlen urged Lakatos for patriotic and moral reasons to accept the task assigned to him by Horthy. "This is a question," Bethlen stressed, "of preserving the Regent's position for the postwar era." When, however, Lakatos and Bethlen were briefed by General Vörös on the military situation, they became convinced that Horthy's planned action was in fact too great a gamble. In a conference late on July 9 they convinced him that a move at that point would be premature and doomed to failure.[70] Horthy accepted their advice and agreed to bide his time and wait for more propitious conditions.

Almost immediately, however, Horthy regretted that he had not seized what he regarded as a most favorable opportunity. In contrast to his passive and even timid conduct in the first three months of the German occupation, he now seemed gripped by a compulsion to move boldly and rapidly. On July 10 or 11 he composed a letter to Hitler in which he repeated the arguments used in his letter of June 6 and asked once again that Wehrmacht and Gestapo units be withdrawn from Hungary. Citing the ineffectiveness of the Sztójay government and the corruption and traitorous activities of certain right-wing elements, Horthy announced that he planned to ban all political parties and appoint a military Cabinet headed by a three-star general who had recently received a German military order. The new government, Horthy insisted, would not "deviate a hair's breath" from the current orientation. He promised that the "Jewish question" would continue to be addressed, but "without the unnecessarily brutal and inhumane methods" of the past.[71]

Horthy entrusted his letter to the head of his Military Bureau, General Béla Miklós, and informed Veesenmayer that Miklós wished to meet immediately with Hitler in order to deliver an important communication. But Hitler was "unavailable at the Front" and as the days passed Horthy grew impatient. He summoned Vörös daily and issued a flurry of orders to move army units to Budapest to deal with "impending domestic disturbances."[72] He drew up a list of proposed Cabinet members, which was based largely on suggestions made by Bethlen in his earlier memorandum.[73] Finally, Horthy could wait no longer. Early on July 15 he explained to Sztójay that he must resign since he no longer enjoyed his confidence. At the same time he sent an urgent message to Lakatos, asking him to return immediately to Budapest. Finally, he summoned Veesenmayer and bluntly informed him that since General Miklós had been kept waiting so long, he was forced to act even before formally informing the Führer of his plans. He had made a "final decision" and had already signed the appropriate decree for the appointment of a new government of a "military-administrative character." It would be headed by General Lakatos and would be sworn in the next day, July 16.

After reporting to Berlin and receiving instructions from Ribbentrop, Veesenmayer met with Horthy again in the Castle on the afternoon of July 17.[74] Lakatos waited in an adjoining room, expecting to be called in at the appropriate time and introduced as the new Prime Minister. But before Horthy could proceed, Veesenmayer declared that he had been instructed to convey an important message from the German government. Hitler and Ribbentrop, he said, had reacted with "utter consternation" to the news that Horthy planned to dismiss the Sztójay government and those officials, notably Baky and Endre, responsible for the measures against the Jews. Any such actions would be regarded as a break with the course set on March 19. It seemed to the Führer that the "same clique of traitors" that had brought Hungary at that time to the brink of disaster was at work again. If the contemplated changes were made, the Reich Minister would be recalled from Hungary and those traitors who had misled the Regent, "whether found inside or outside the Castle," would be immediately arrested by the SD and "would be brought to justice within twenty-four hours." Furthermore, Hitler expected that the measures against the Budapest Jews would be carried out as planned. If there were any continued procrastination, the Führer would withdraw his approval of the exemptions that Horthy had been allowed to grant to selected Jews. In this connection Horthy should ignore the "ridiculous Jewish-American threats," for when the war ended Germany and her allies, not America, would stand victorious.

Horthy had listened in stunned silence to the lengthy indictment presented by Veesenmayer. Only once, at the mention of how his advisors "would be brought to justice," had he managed an interjection: "That would be a severe measure." Once he gained the floor, Horthy tried, in vain, to justify his actions. Surely Hitler had been misinformed about the situation in Hungary, he argued, or he would not have sent such an ultimatum. Hungary had in fact been a faithful ally; it was the German Reich that had not kept it promises. In the circumstances he would now have to resign, even though he was confident that 90 percent of the country was behind him. Veesenmayer allowed the Regent to "talk himself out" and then, like a skillful prosecuting attorney trying to persuade a defendant to turn state's evidence, returned to the attack. The German government, he said, made "a sharp distinction" between Horthy and his entourage. Bethlen and his clique were intent on committing treason and were concealing this from the Regent. The Führer had been "magnanimous" in allowing Horthy's image to remain untarnished. Would Horthy now want "his historical reputation to be besmirched with treason?" To help Horthy free himself from his dangerous entourage, he, Veesenmayer, was prepared to make daily visits to the Castle and offer advice and counsel. In any case, the Regent should keep in mind that Germany still had sufficient reserves and many friends in Hungary to enable it restore order if necessary.

At the end of this grueling two-hour conversation, Horthy was, according to the German envoy, "completely finished; his whole body trembled and he was an old, broken man." So shattered was Horthy that when he rejoined Lakatos he found it impossible to relate the details of the ultimatum Veesenmayer had just delivered. All he could recall was that the Germans were threatening to execute Bethlen. The only course left to him, Horthy declared, was resignation. Over the next few days, however, Horthy slowly regained his poise and determination. Those of his former advisors who were available managed to assemble in the Castle on July 19 as a privy council.[75] They convinced Horthy that he must remain at his post and continue his pragmatic policy of "wait and see." The consensus seemed to be that some smaller successes might be gained without provoking German military reprisals, which the Hungarian General Staff wished fervently to avoid, especially in light of the fact that two additional German Panzer divisions had been sent to back up Hitler's threats and were being ostentatiously paraded around Budapest.[76]

Now resigned to the reality that for the time being he would have to continue to deal with the Sztójay government, Horthy told

Lakatos that he should return to his country home, but to be ready at a moment's notice because "I will still need you."[77] In late July and early August Horthy concentrated his efforts on placing reliable individuals in key positions in the army. Given the thoroughly pro-German orientation of the General Staff, however, he could hardly make much progress in this respect, although he did manage to appoint General Béla Miklós commander of the First Army. Taking Miklós's place as head of the Regent's Military Bureau was General Antal Vattay, who, along with Gyula Ambrózy, head of the Cabinet Bureau, was to be one of Horthy's key collaborators in the coming months.

In this period there was one issue on which Horthy was resolved not to yield to German threats. Having intervened successfully on behalf of the Budapest Jews, he now considered it a matter of personal honor that the deportations not be resumed. Moreover, despite the fulminations of Veesenmayer, Horthy probably realized that both his historical reputation and his political future would be destroyed if he once again capitulated to the Germans on an issue that had so aroused the conscience of the world. He made his position clear in a speech at the Ludovika Military Academy: "Regrettable mistakes must be put right and the injury done to Hungarian honor must be wiped out."[78] During the summer of 1944 Admiral Horthy thus lent his support to a variety of projects aimed at ameliorating conditions for Hungarian Jews. In July he cooperated with Miklós Mester, an official in the Ministry of Culture, in exempting prominent Jews from wearing the yellow star and from other prejudicial provisions of the anti-Jewish laws. By late August over six hundred prominent Jews, including the members of the Jewish Council, had received what became known as "Horthy exemptions," and over thirty thousand additional applications were received. As a symbolic gesture, exemptions were even granted to a number of Jews who had been deported and had presumably perished in Auschwitz.[79]

In terms of its worldwide impact, the most important initiative on behalf of the Hungarian Jews was an agreement reached on July 18 between the Sztójay government and the International Red Cross to "permit a very considerable number of Jews to emigrate to neutral countries" and to Palestine.[80] Horthy approved this plan, but neither at the time nor in the postwar period did he realize the enormous stir it caused in the Allied capitals in the summer of 1944. The Allies and neutral countries had earlier felt compelled to voice their indignation over the persecution of the Hungarian Jews and to threaten reprisals against those in Hungary who were responsible for the atrocities. The problem was seen in a different light when Allied officials learned the details of what became known as the "Horthy offer." "It is clear," a British diplomat wrote, "that the floodgates of Eastern Europe are now going to be opened and that we shall in a very short time have masses of East European Jews on our hands."[81] Although the American government proved more forthcoming, the British were concerned that acceptance of the "Horthy offer" would severely damage their position in the Arab world. The matter was thus treated in a dilatory fashion and was soon overtaken by the rapid course of events in East Central Europe.

The importance of Horthy's various interventions in this period on behalf of the Jews of Budapest was recognized by Raoul Wallenberg, a Swedish diplomat who arrived in Budapest in mid-July to provide humanitarian aid to the Jews. In early August Wallenberg was granted an audience with the Regent in order to explain his mission. Horthy assured Wallenberg that he intended to protect the Jewish community and would support his rescue plans. These should be drawn up in a memorandum and, for security reasons, submitted to him anonymously and without a letterhead. Horthy spoke flattering words about Sweden and its king, and in general left his visitor with the impression that he was a sincere person "whose power has to be reckoned with."[82]

That the Budapest Jews enjoyed a reprieve in the middle of the summer was due not only to the Regent's intervention but to the temporary paralysis of the German authorities in Hungary. But Adolf Eichmann was not prepared to admit defeat. Through the summer he continued to marshal his forces for a renewed attempt to deport the remaining Jews, and by mid-August began again to take the offensive. The Hungarian government was informed that since Jewish workers were still needed in Germany, the deportations must resume immediately. On August 17 Eichmann showed his determination by having three members of the Jewish Council, including the president, Samu Stern, arrested. At the same time, S.S. units surrounded the city and a huge German military parade was staged.

These actions created panic among the Jews and prompted immediate protests to the Regent. Moving quickly, Horthy immediately ordered the release from prison of the members of the Jewish

Council and on August 22 firmly informed the Germans that he would permit no further deportations. Horthy's determination, and the weakening of Germany's strategic position to be described below, led at the end of the month to the final recall to Germany of Eichmann's commando.

In late August 1944 there began a rapid, kaleidoscopic series of events that would lead within two months to the end of the Horthy era in Hungarian history. On August 23, just as Horthy had always predicted, Romania suddenly surrendered to the Allies and turned its troops against the Germans. Some Hungarian officials now urged that Hungary at least consider taking advantage of the chaotic situation and follow Romania's example. But Admiral Horthy was incapable of such opportunistic maneuvering. In his eyes, Romania, by immediately attacking its former ally, had perpetrated the worst kind of "stab in the back." For Hungary to surrender in that way would not only be dishonorable but would be "a leap in the dark," since Romania had declared war not only against Germany but also against Hungary, and a combined Soviet-Romanian advance into Transylvania had to be reckoned with.[83] Horthy now realized that Germany had lost the war and that there were no "miracle weapons" that could transform the situation.[84] Hungary, too, would soon need to drop out of the war, but he preferred to follow the model of Finland, which on September 2 signed an armistice with the Allies that allowed for the German troops to withdraw unmolested from the country. Thus, Horthy believed that even while moving to regain its sovereignty and preparing for an armistice, Hungary must continue its active cooperation with Germany in the struggle against the Soviet and Romanian troops. Moreover, he still felt honor-bound to inform the Germans of his intentions beforehand.[85]

The defection of Romania did, however, prompt Horthy to take two decisive steps. On August 28 he had a telegram sent to György Bakách-Bessenyey, a dissident Hungarian diplomat residing in Switzerland, empowering him to explore an armistice with the Anglo-American powers. Horthy suggested that territorial issues were no longer of concern; rather, Hungary was seeking "independence with democratic guarantees."[86] On that same day Horthy summoned Veesenmayer and announced that since the problem confronting Hungary was now a "purely military one," he had decided to ban all political parties and appoint General Lakatos to head a new government. Although Germany's position in Hungary had been significantly weakened and Veesenmayer realized he must yield some ground, he nonetheless insisted on haggling over the composition of the new government and managed to persuade Horthy and Lakatos to keep two reliable friends of Nazi Germany, Reményi-Schneller and Béla Jurcsek, in the Cabinet.[87] One result of this unfortunate concession was that in the coming weeks the Germans continued to receive confidential information about discussions and decisions of the Hungarian government.

Admiral Horthy's frame of mind and his determination to seek an honorable way out of the war are reflected in a comment he made in early September to the new Foreign Minister, Gusztáv Hennyey:

> As head of state I am responsible for my country and people. It is my foremost duty to rescue the country and its citizens from destruction, especially as there is not the slightest prospect of victory. I want to avoid unnecessary bloodshed and prevent my country from becoming a theater of war.[88]

If Horthy had finally come to the conclusion that the war was lost, he still could not bring himself to accept the inevitability of Soviet domination in Hungary after the war. He, along with the great majority of Hungarian military officers, clung to the hope that the Germans and Hungarians could hold off the Red Army long enough to allow Anglo-American troops to reach western or southern Hungary. This would ensure that the occupation of Hungary would be a joint Allied rather than exclusively Soviet operation, and would make it possible for Horthy to fulfill his promise to Hitler and inform the Germans that Hungary was seeking a separate peace. The Wehrmacht would then be allowed to withdraw unmolested. In this way, Horthy thought, Hungary would follow the "honorable" example of Marshal Mannerheim in Finland rather than the "treasonous" policy of King Michael in Romania.

Given the strategic and military realities in Europe at the time, it is difficult to imagine how even a far more capable statesman than Horthy could have carried out such a chimerical plan. As several historians have suggested, Horthy committed many blunders as he struggled to hold off the inevitable. Yet, given the unpropitious circumstances and the very small number of advisors on whom he could confidently rely, even the minor successes that Horthy was able to achieve in September and early October were noteworthy.

Shortly after the swearing in of Lakatos's government in late

August, Horthy began to take an active role in preparing for Hungary's withdrawal from the war. Hoping to prevent the Arrowcross party from obstructing this process, Horthy summoned Ferenc Szálasi, informed him that the war would soon be over, and implored him to act in a patriotic and constructive way in the coming crisis. Szálasi paid no attention to Horthy's appeal, but instead repeated his long-standing suggestion that Regent appoint him Prime Minister. Horthy once again rejected this idea, as well as Szálasi's proposal that he be sent as the Regent's special emissary to mediate with Hitler. Concluding that Szálasi was either "an idiot or a fantast," Horthy then abruptly dismissed his visitor with the excuse that he had no more time for him. Horthy later complained to Ambrózy that Szálasi kept repeating himself and "it was impossible to talk sense with the man; he saw himself in everything." More significantly, Szálasi left this meeting convinced that the Regent had lost faith in a German victory and was a "puppet in the hands of Bethlen and the Anglo-Jewish gang." He no longer felt obliged to seek power only in cooperation with Horthy, and he resolved that he would not "fall with him into the fatal depths of dishonor."[89] By early September Szálasi was discussing with Veesenmayer and S.S. representatives the possibility of coming to power with German support. When in mid-September Horthy began to suspect what was afoot, he ordered Szálasi's arrest, but the Arrowcross leader was quickly offered a safe haven in the German legation.

Meanwhile military developments in the first week of September were creating a critical situation for the newly installed Hungarian government and forcing Admiral Horthy's hand. When informed that the defensive line in Transylvania was collapsing and that the Red Army seemed to be preparing to move directly into Hungary in the direction of Temesvár and Szeged, Horthy called a Crown Council for September 7 to consider the possibility of an armistice.[90] He opened the Council by declaring bluntly that the enemy was at the gates of Hungary and that he intended to seek an armistice similar to the one Finland had negotiated. He had no wish to betray the Germans and would inform them beforehand of his decision. But he was now convinced that one must not sacrifice the nation on the altar of loyalty to an ally. It was clear, Horthy added, that Hungary could obtain less severe terms if an agreement were made beforehand with the Russians. Only in this way could the youth of the country be spared.

Horthy was unpleasantly surprised by the negative, and even unsympathetic, comments of some of the ministers, who raised a variety of objections. Lakatos suggested that a decision of this magnitude should be taken before Parliament. But Horthy stated his unwillingness to follow that procedure. He as Supreme War Lord had the authority to negotiate an armistice, and in any case the Hungarian Parliament was no longer sovereign because so many of its members had been arrested and many who remained feared to speak openly. Thus, he would assume responsibility for this matter.

The strongest opposition to Horthy's proposal came from the two pro-Nazi ministers, who argued that the situation was not so bleak as to require such a drastic solution. Reményi-Schneller went so far as to accuse the Regent of wanting to sacrifice the Hungarian middle class in favor of the peasantry. To this accusation Horthy replied firmly: "This is not a matter of saving one social class. We are talking about saving the whole nation."[91] But even those ministers not known for their pro-German sentiments expressed concern about a repetition of the armistice in 1918, when the soldiers gave up their arms and the result was political catastrophe. Sensing that the overwhelming sentiment of the Cabinet was opposed to the Regent's proposal, General Csatay proposed a compromise that the ministers found acceptable. The Germans would be sent an ultimatum demanding that within twenty-four hours they send five tank divisions to help stem the Soviet advance. Unless the German response was positive, Hungary would sue for peace.

Horthy apparently accepted this decision only because he thought it highly unlikely that the Germans could comply with the terms of the ultimatum.[92] However, Veesenmayer informed Lakatos on September 8 that Hitler, who intended to defend Hungary as if it were Reich territory, had issued orders for the dispatch of the necessary troops and equipment. It might take a few days, but the Hungarians could count on this support. This German promise, though hedged, was sufficient to satisfy Lakatos, Vörös, and most of the ministers. At a long Cabinet meeting that day it was agreed that Hungary must fight on and avoid at all costs surrendering to the Russians, for, as initial reports from Romania indicated, that would mean the bolshevization of the country. If a military collapse occurred, everything should be done to ensure that Anglo-American, and not Soviet, troops occupied the country. Lakatos's view was typical: "If I can spare just three-fourths of the country from a Soviet invasion, then I will not have lived in vain. . . ."[93] This profound fear of a Soviet occupation was widespread in the Hungarian political establishment, but especially so among the military officers, who were convinced that if Stalin triumphed they and their families would meet the same fate as the Polish officers in the Katyn forest massacre.

By September 9 Admiral Horthy was beginning to realize that his strategy for restoring Hungary's sovereignty by appointing a "government of generals" had backfired. Most of the senior military officers, including Lakatos, did not really share Horthy's view that continued participation in the war was futile and that a diplomatic solution must be sought. In an effort to construct a counterweight to the government, Horthy thus decided to seek the advice of his privy council. The group he assembled, which included four current Cabinet ministers, three retired generals, and several senior statesmen, met on September 10.[94] Horthy opened the proceedings by declaring that Germany had lost the war. There was thus no purpose in waiting for Hitler to send the five Panzer divisions that had been promised. Instead Hungary had to seek an armistice in order not to remain at the loser's side when the war ended. Horthy informed the group that he had received a message from Switzerland urging Hungary to seek an armistice from the Allies, including Russia, for Hungary would likely be in the Soviet sphere of influence.[95] He proposed that Hungary move quickly to seek an armistice modeled on the one the Finns had achieved. By changing sides Hungary would, he argued, help the Allies and shorten the war.

Count Bethlen, who had again managed to enter the Castle without being observed by the Germans, strongly supported the Regent's proposal. "Hungary must get out of the war," he declared, "or it will be wiped off the map." The Regent should that very day dispatch a delegation to Moscow to open negotiations. Any further delay would be a "crime against the nation." There then ensued a long discussion in which no one directly challenged Horthy's analysis of the situation, but various reservations were nonetheless raised. Some of the military officers were clearly uneasy about the idea of abandoning the Germans and trusting in a diplomatic agreement made with Soviet Russia. Nonetheless, at the end of the more than five-hour meeting a broad consensus was apparently reached: Hungary should quickly seek to contact the Allies, preferably the British and Americans, and negotiate an armistice that would permit German troops to leave the country unmolested. One final question remained: should approval for this momentous action be sought from the Cabinet? Bethlen strongly opposed this, arguing that there were traitors in the government who would immediately inform the Germans of what was happening. But Lakatos and several others raised strenuous objections, and it was decided that the Cabinet would be told simply that the Regent had made "a final and unalterable decision" to ask for an armistice. Those who objected to the decision would then be dismissed, thus leaving a Cabinet willing to support the Regent.[96]

Count Bethlen's strong reservations about the advisability of consulting the Cabinet were soon proved justified. Late on September 11 Lakatos reported that the Cabinet had discussed the issue of an armistice and had unanimously rejected the idea, preferring instead to carry on the fight against the Red Army. In the circumstances, Lakatos added, he and his fellow ministers had decided that the only course open to them was resignation. Horthy was incredulous: "No one stood by me? Not Rakovszky? Not even Csatay?" When questioned separately by the Regent about the decision of the Cabinet, General Vörös expressed the opinion that if an armistice were signed, there would be a split in the army as well in society as a whole. Some officers would order their troops to fight on in order to avoid certain death or exile.[97]

Some of Horthy's advisors, including Bárczy, Kánya, and Bethlen, urged him to take advantage of this turn of events to appoint a new Cabinet that would be unquestionably loyal to him. Horthy mulled over this idea, but soon decided that there was not enough time to form a new government, and in any case the Germans would be obstructive. Thus, Horthy informed Lakatos that he would "bow to the wishes of the Cabinet," although he hinted strongly that he intended nonetheless on his own authority to explore the possibility of a separate peace. Horthy's true intentions were revealed only to his family and a few loyal members of his entourage, including Vattay and Ambrózy. He told them that he was determined to forge ahead on his own, informing the government only when unavoidable. He planned to take personal responsibility for contacting the enemy by sending an emissary to Italy and, if necessary, to Russia as well.[98]

Admiral Horthy, who was a virtual dilettante in the art of diplomacy, faced a formidable task in seeking to negotiate an armistice. He had to keep his moves secret not only from the vigilant

Germans and their Hungarian sympathizers, but even from his own Prime Minister, Foreign Minister, and Chief of Staff. Yet, with the help of his wife, son, daughter-in-law, and a handful of aides, Horthy managed to carry it off. In late September he informed the Allies, through the Swedish legation, that he was prepared to sue for peace. He then sent off two secret peace missions, one to the Western Democracies and the other to the Soviet Union. The former was entrusted to General István Náday, who was instructed to contact the British or American authorities in Italy and to deliver a letter to the pope. Although Náday, accompanied by Colonel Howie, miraculously evaded detection by the Germans and arrived safely at the Allied headquarters at Casserta in Italy, his mission was quickly overtaken by the rapidly changing events in Hungary.[99]

Admiral Horthy's second peace initiative had a much greater impact on the course of events. Even before the departure of General Náday, Horthy, at the urging of his son and Géza Teleki, the son of the late Prime Minister, had approved the dispatch to Russia of a small delegation to sound out the Soviet government about its willingness to negotiate with the Hungarian Regent. This mission, headed by a maverick left-wing aristocrat, Baron Ede Aczél, managed to reach Moscow and return on September 24 with a favorable report. The Soviet leaders, Horthy was told, would welcome an authoritative Hungarian negotiator. They had no intention of establishing a Communist regime in Hungary, were prepared to leave all frontier decisions to an eventual peace conference, and would not automatically regard all Hungarian military officers as war criminals. This information would surely have been viewed by Horthy and his colleagues with considerable skepticism were it not consistent with assurances contained in the two "Makarov letters" that had reached Budapest a few days earlier. These documents were thought by Horthy's aides to be Stalin's preliminary peace terms as transmitted by Colonel Makarov, the Soviet liaison with the partisans in Slovakia. Horthy was "overjoyed" to learn from these documents that Stalin was prepared to guarantee the full independence and territorial integrity of Hungary.[100]

Several days were spent in finding a suitable person to head the mission to Moscow. Several candidates, including Albert Szent-Györgyi, were apparently approached, but finally General Faraghó, the head of the gendarmerie, was chosen. Faraghó had been for a time military attaché in Moscow and spoke Russian fluently. Although he had played an unsavory role in the deportation of the Jews, Faraghó had shown his loyalty to the Regent by turning against Baky in the critical days of early July. Furthermore, it may have occurred to Horthy that the Germans and pro-Nazi Hungarians would not suspect that someone like Faraghó would be entrusted with peace negotiations, and his prolonged absence from Budapest would thus go unnoticed.

In the presence of Vattay and Ambrózy, who were to be Horthy's main advisors in the last days of his regime, the Regent gave a final briefing to the delegation on September 27. They were urged to gain Soviet acceptance of an immediate end of hostilities and participation of British and American troops in the occupation of Hungary. Horthy stated his preference for following the Finnish rather than the Romanian model: that is, he still hoped that the Soviets would allow German troops to withdraw from Hungary without being attacked. Faraghó was entrusted with copies of the "Makarov letters" and a personal, hand-written letter from Horthy to Stalin. Composing that letter must have caused Horthy a good deal of anguish. What language should he use? It could not be Russian, for that was the only major European language he had never thought to master. He chose English as the least objectionable alternative. What could he say to appease the victorious leader of a country that over the past twenty-four years he had excoriated as a cancerous plague and an evil empire?

Addressing Stalin as "Field Marshal," Horthy began with an unconvincing attempt to exonerate Hungary from blame for the war:

> In the name and for the sake of my people in their extreme danger, I address myself to you. Doing so in the name of the Hungarian people, who has no responsibility for this war. For thousand years and particularly during this last decade, the fate of our people has been influenced by the neighbouring German Collosus. It was again under this influence that we were carried to this unfortunate war with the Soviet Union.[101]

Horthy went on to assert that, unlike Romania, Hungary had never aspired to gain any territory "that was not ours by right." Moreover, because of the powerful German "fifth column" in Hungary, important news and reports had never reached him. Thus, he had learned only recently that during a conversation with the Hungarian minister in June 1941, Molotov had emphasized Russia's peaceful intentions. "If this was really so," Horthy suggested, "it is fatal, for it did not reach me at the time."[102] In informing Stalin that the Hungarian delegation was fully authorized to negotiate an armistice, Horthy begged him "to spare this unfortunate country which has its own historic merits and the people of which has so many affinities with the Russian people."

The Hungarian peace delegation departed Budapest on September 28, arrived in Moscow three days later, and began sending daily coded telegraphic messages that were received on a secret radio transmitter in the Castle. These were laboriously transcribed and encoded by a group of amateurs (Gyula Ambrózy, Niki Horthy, Ilona Horthy, and Gyula Tost, Horthy's aide-de-camp) and then taken immediately to the Regent.[103] The most important telegram arrived shortly after the Hungarian delegation met with Molotov on October 8. Faraghó, who had earlier reported that the delegation had been received in a friendly manner, now had disconcerting news: Molotov disclaimed any knowledge of the "Makarov letters" and was insisting on stern peace terms. Hungary would have to withdraw its military forces to the pre-1938 frontiers, break all ties with Germany, and declare war on its former ally. The Soviet Union preferred to leave all political questions to the eventual peace conference.[104]

With Hungarian villages falling one after another into Soviet hands and major cities like Debrecen and Szeged in grave danger, Admiral Horthy finally realized that any further attempt to avoid acceptance of the Soviet terms, which amounted to unconditional surrender, was futile. On October 10 Horthy thus summoned Lakatos, Hennyey, and Vörös, and, with Vattay and Ambrózy at his side, revealed that a Hungarian peace delegation was in Moscow.[105] Although the Soviet terms for an armistice were severe, Hungary had no alternative but to accept and make the best of a horrible situation. The Germans were clearly not able to fulfill their promise of assistance, and Náday's mission to the Western Allies had been unsuccessful. Horthy suggested that if an agreement were in fact reached with the Soviets, it would be a preliminary armistice that would later be superseded by a formal agreement negotiated with the victorious powers. He hoped in that way to halt, at least temporarily, the westward advance of the Red Army and gain time to bring the Anglo-Americans into the negotiations and perhaps obtain somewhat more favorable conditions. Above all, he wished to find a way to avoid complying with the Russian demand that Hungary declare war on Germany.[106]

Military developments in late September and early October persuaded even Lakatos, Vörös, and Csatay that Hungary must now consider dropping out of the war. All present at the meeting of October 10 were shocked when Lakatos reported that, according to the latest information he had received, the Germans planned to establish a defense line running from the town of Esztergom to Lake Balaton, which in effect would abandon most of Hungary, including Budapest, to the Red Army.[107] The military chiefs were now prepared to support the Regent's diplomatic efforts; they urged, however, that Horthy insist that, as a gesture of goodwill, the Soviets halt their attacks on Hungarian forces.

Having received preliminary support from key members of the government, Admiral Horthy proceeded early on October 11 to send a telegram to the Hungarian peace delegation in Moscow authorizing them to sign a preliminary armistice. Once the document was duly signed by Faraghó later that day, the Soviet officials became surprisingly friendly. Molotov agreed to a temporary, unannounced truce at the Front to allow time for the Regent to make final preparations for Hungary's defection. Stalin, who was apparently impressed by Horthy's personal letter and his willingness to surrender to a hated enemy, seemed willing to retain him as head of state in a transitional Hungarian government. He jokingly told the Hungarian delegates that this would be the first war in four centuries in which Hungary would finish on the side of the victors.[108]

Horthy's remarkable success in arriving at the preliminary armistice of October 11 did not, unfortunately, extend to the actual implementation of that agreement. Not only were there formidable obstacles still to be overcome, but the old admiral had, in fact, reached the limits of his capabilities. His plan for the actual withdrawal of Hungary from the war proved to be muddled and his preparations woefully inadequate. Without informing the Russians, Horthy set October 20 as the day on which he would announce that Hungary was suing for peace. Shortly before the proclamation he intended to fulfill his promise to the Germans by informing Veesenmayer of his intentions. The commanders of the two main Hungarian Army groups, Generals Miklós and Veress, would then be sent a prearranged coded message that would instruct them to cease fighting and make friendly contact with the Red Army. In the meantime some troops would have been brought to Budapest to maintain order and deal with the Germans should they refuse to withdraw peacefully. Contact would be made with representatives of the workers so that a general strike could be staged.[109]

As events would soon demonstrate, Admiral Horthy's plan was based on several false assumptions. He believed, for example, that the majority of Hungarian military officers would remain loyal to him. Thus, there was no reason to arm the workers and rely on a broadly based national resistance to the Germans. He clung to the naive hope that, just as had happened in Finland, the Germans would honor a request for a rapid evacuation of the country once the armistice was announced. In general, Admiral Horthy greatly underestimated the extent to which a fanatical anticommunism, which he himself had of course nurtured, continued to motivate broad segments of the Hungarian middle class, the officer corps, and even the Hungarian Cabinet. Many such Hungarians even at this point preferred to share the German Armageddon rather than accept the likely bolshevization of the country.

One unfortunate decision made by Admiral Horthy as he prepared to withdraw from the war was his refusal to consider fleeing Budapest and announcing Hungary's defection from the safety of the headquarters of the First or Second Armies. Even in retrospect, it is difficult to imagine how he could have managed to carry out his plan from his precarious base in the Royal Castle. After Romania's defection and the consequent retreat of the Wehrmacht from Romania, the number of German troops in and around Budapest grew steadily, reaching nearly 500,000 by mid-October. By contrast, the forces readily available to Regent Horthy were, in the judgment of one historian, "ridiculously weak."[110] Moreover, although the Germans never learned about the Hungarian mission to Moscow, they were actively working by early October to prepare for any unpleasant surprises that Horthy might try to spring. On October 2 Veesenmayer informed Ferenc Szálasi that Horthy would not remain much longer in office. He would be replaced by a three-person Regent's Council and Szálasi would become Prime Minister. Szálasi thereupon proceeded with eager anticipation to prepare to take power.[111]

Meanwhile in Berlin Hitler was devoting an inordinate amount of his time to studying maps of the Hungarian Royal Castle and its labyrinth of tunnels to determine how best to deploy the crack commando of Otto Skorzeny, which he dispatched to Hungary in early October. In Budapest, Skorzeny joined with Otto Winkelmann, the S.S. chief, in making plans to abduct key members of Horthy's entourage and to seize and occupy the Castle.[112] On October 8, as the armistice negotiations began in earnest in Moscow, General Szilárd Bakay, who had been entrusted with the defense of Budapest, was arrested by the S.S. and taken to Germany. The Castle was placed under increased surveillance, and the activities of Niki Horthy, who was suspected of being in contact with Marshal Tito through intermediaries, were closely monitored.

As the Germans tightened the vise on Horthy, he struggled to thwart the countermeasures of his opponents and to make all the necessary preparations for the "changeover" on October 20. Sensing the physical danger now confronting him and his closest collaborators, Horthy ordered increased security for Vattay and his son Niki. He also appointed General Veress as his stand-in (*homo regius*) should he be incapacitated or arrested by the Germans.[113] Veress was in fact a Horthy loyalist, but some of the other military officers on whom the Regent was planning to rely were not fully committed to the course on which he had embarked. As events would soon demonstrate, General Vörös was playing a double game, outwardly collaborating with Horthy but maintaining his former intimate ties with the Germans. Lakatos was at best lukewarm in his support of a preliminary armistice with the Russians. The events of October 1944 thus demonstrated that Admiral Horthy in fact was unaware of the extent to which pro-German and radical right-wing ideas had permeated the officer corps. Despite frequent warnings over the past few years from Bárczy and other advisors, he had always dismissed the thought that "his" officers were capable of disloyalty. Certainly he never imagined that large numbers would support a German puppet state under Szálasi. When, around October 10, Hennyey warned the Regent not to have any illusions about the officer corps, Horthy blithely responded: "Never fear, I have a firm hold over the army."[114]

Beginning on October 11, the day on which the preliminary armistice was signed, the pace of events in Budapest greatly accelerated. Pressed by his son, Horthy agreed finally to receive Zoltán Tildy, a Smallholder, and Árpád Szakasits, a Social Democrat, who represented the main parties that comprised the oppositional group known as the March Front.[115] In a meeting late on the 11th Horthy assured his guests that preparations for ending the war were far along and would be announced "within a week, possibly even sooner." He agreed in general to most of the suggestions made by his visitors, including arming of the workers and release of any remaining left-wing prisoners. The detailed planning, he said, would be taken care of by his aides. On the question of the political orientation of the government to be formed once Hungary had withdrawn from the war, Horthy spoke equivocally, although he agreed that a coalition government under Count Bethlen could be considered.

Admiral Horthy's willingness to cooperate with the March Front in withdrawing from the war and forming the postwar government was in fact never put to the test, and it may be that he retained to the end his distaste for the moderate and left-wing parties.[116] Two days later, without consulting anyone outside his immediate entourage, Horthy suddenly decided to announce the preliminary armistice on October 15. It is not known precisely what prompted this acceleration of the Regent's timetable, although he may have been alarmed by reports that the Germans were reinforcing their troops around Budapest to support an impending coup d'état by the Arrowcross.[117] Increasingly desperate and overwhelmed by the complexities of the situation, Horthy decided to gamble that a bold, early move on his part would discomfit the Germans and clarify the situation.

When informed that the Regent intended to issue his proclamation early on the afternoon of the 15th, both Lakatos and Vörös warned that all the necessary preparations had not been made and that the attitude of the officer corps remained unclear. Lakatos expressed serious concern when shown the draft of the Regent's proclamation, which he regarded as too harsh and anti-German. He suggested several changes in the text, one of which proved to be crucial. The following sentence was deleted from the draft proclamation: "From this point on Hungary is in a state of war with Germany."[118] Late on the 14th Horthy told his Chief of Staff that on the next day "he would break with the Germans." Vörös strongly urged Horthy to accompany him to the town of Huszt, the location of the headquarters of the Second Hungarian Army. There he could issue his proclamation in relative security. If, however, the Regent tried to carry out his plan in Budapest, within two hours the two of them would be prisoners of the Germans. But Horthy was unpersuaded and gave his familiar response: "I am a naval officer and have never abandoned a sinking ship. In this most difficult of times I will not abandon my country."[119]

Two developments on the morning of October 15 strengthened Horthy's resolve to follow through on his revised plan. His daughter-in-law, who had been deciphering the latest messages from the peace delegation in Moscow, informed him that the Russians, who were growing increasingly impatient at the lack of concrete steps by Horthy, had issued an ultimatum demanding that by 8:00 A.M. on October 16 the Hungarian government take immediate steps to break with Germany. Later in the morning, shortly before a meeting at which Horthy intended to reveal his plans to the government, Horthy was outraged to learn that his son had been lured from the Castle by the Gestapo and had been abducted.[120]

Shortly before 11:00 A.M. on October 15 the Hungarian Cabinet and Horthy's aides assembled in the Castle for a meeting of the Crown Council, the last such gathering of the Horthy era.[121] The atmosphere was charged with high emotion and a deepening fatalism. His face flushed and his demeanor somber, Horthy declared that Germany was on the verge of collapse and there was the danger that the victorious Allies would treat Hungary as Hitler's "last remaining ally." Germany had plundered Hungary and committed many atrocities, the most recent being the kidnapping of his son. Having determined that Hungary would receive acceptable terms from the enemy, he had thus decided to withdraw the country from the war. A continuation of the "hopeless fight" would place Hungary in the greatest jeopardy and perhaps lead to its complete destruction. Of course, there would likely be ruthless reprisals by the Germans, but he could see no other alternative: "We must decide to sue for an armistice."

It is notable that Admiral Horthy chose at the beginning of the proceedings not to inform the Cabinet of the secret negotiations in which he had been engaged. Clearly he still doubted that he could gain government approval for the preliminary armistice that had been signed with the Russians.[122] When Reményi-Schneller had the temerity to ask what exactly were the "acceptable terms" for an armistice that the Regent had been offered, Horthy replied with indignation that he would talk about that later. For now, he wanted to determine who was with him and who against. Following a scenario that Lakatos and Vattay had agreed on earlier, the Prime Minister declared that he and the Cabinet would offer their resignation. He felt honor-bound to do so because he had promised the leaders of the Hungarian Parliament that the legislature would be consulted before the conclusion of an armistice. Horthy accepted the Cabinet's resignation, but rejected the idea that Parliament must be consulted about an armistice. The Parliament, he argued, no longer represented the country. He, as Supreme War Lord, would assume all responsibility for this action before the nation and before history. He was willing to reappoint Lakatos and all other Cabinet ministers who agreed to support him in his endeavor. To the astonishment of both Lakatos and Horthy, all the ministers, even Jurcsek and Reményi-Schneller, agreed to serve in the Cabinet on these terms.

Perhaps it was at this point that Horthy intended to apprise the new Cabinet of the results of the negotiations in Moscow and the text of his proclamation that would soon be read out on the radio. But the Crown Council had already lasted almost an hour, and Veesenmayer had arrived for a noontime meeting that had been arranged the day before. The Council was thus adjourned, and Horthy, accompanied by Hennyey and Lakatos, retired to the Regent's office to receive the German Minister. As soon as Veesenmayer sat down in his chair, Horthy launched into angry recriminations, as if he had been waiting for months for this opportunity.[123] Germany, he said, had plundered Hungary, interfered blatantly in domestic affairs, failed to keep a single promise, and committed one treacherous act after another. Angrily throwing a German cartridge belt on the desk in front of Veesenmayer, Horthy declared that this belonged to the Gestapo officer who had attacked and abducted his son, his only surviving child. Veesenmayer interjected that he had nothing to do with that affair, but Horthy refused to listen and threatened to keep the German Minister as a hostage in the Castle until his son had been returned. Having vented his spleen in this way, Horthy turned to the original purpose of the meeting. The military situation, Horthy declared, was now hopeless and the war was lost. Therefore, in accordance with the promise he had made to Hitler, he was now giving notice that Hungary was about to withdraw from the war. Sensing that no purpose would be served by a detailed rebuttal, Veesenmayer briefly expressed dismay at the Regent's decision and then announced that he would be departing, since his mission in Hungary was clearly at an end.[124]

As Veesenmayer was leaving the Castle shortly before 1:00, Horthy's proclamation was already being read out over the state radio. This first reading came shortly before 1:00. Most Hungarians were preparing to begin their Sunday dinners when normal programming on the radio was interrupted and an announcer, speaking in the name of the Regent, declared that "it is obvious to any sober-minded person that the German Reich has lost the war."[125] The proclamation contained a brief and largely tendentious account of Hungary's role in the war and a bitter indictment of Germany, which was accused, among many other sins, of trying "to rob the Hungarian nation of its greatest treasure—its freedom and independence." Citing Otto von Bismarck's maxim that "no nation ought to sacrifice itself on the altar of an alliance," Horthy announced that he had informed the Germans that Hungary was "about to conclude a military armistice with our former enemies and to cease all hostilities against them." He called on all soldiers to obey the commanders he had appointed, and on "every honest Hungarian to follow me on this path, beset by sacrifices, that will lead to Hungary's salvation."

The Regent's proclamation did not have the electrifying impact that some in Horthy's entourage had apparently anticipated. There were scattered instances of celebrating in the streets and a few cries of "hurrah for the Regent!" Some Jews tore off their identifying patches in anticipation of their imminent liberation. It may well be, as a Hungarian writer later suggested, that at no other time was Admiral Horthy more popular as he was in the last full day of his regency. In general, however, the reaction of the Hungarian public was subdued and apprehensive. How would the Germans respond to Horthy's bold move? More importantly in the long run, how would the Soviets act when they gained control of the country? Most Hungarians seemed at this critical moment to adopt the Regent's favorite slogan: "Wait and see."[126]

Those Hungarians who had long urged the Regent to withdraw from the war and had been preparing to play a part in the resistance against the Germans, especially members of the March Front, were caught totally unaware by Horthy's proclamation, which they had been led to believe was still a week off. Frantic efforts were made on the afternoon of October 15 to patch together a plan of action, but the workers had not yet been provided weapons and the calling of a general strike on a Sunday was unlikely to have much effect. The success of Horthy's endeavor now hinged entirely on the attitude of the military leadership. Around 1:30, after the second reading of the Regent's proclamation over the radio, Horthy's order to the army was read out.[127] In it he called on the soldiers to remain true to their oaths and to obey all of his orders as given by their commanders. However, largely because of Lakatos's objections, neither of Horthy's two proclamations that afternoon made it clear that Hungary had already signed a preliminary armistice and that Hungarian troops were expected to cooperate with the Red Army. A good deal of confusion about the true state of affairs thus prevailed not only among officers in the field but at General Staff headquarters in Budapest. Fearing a demoralization of the troops and a general collapse at the Front, General Vörös thus took a fateful step that in effect sabotaged Horthy's enterprise. Shortly before 3:00 he authorized the dissemination of a message to all field commanders in which they were told that the Regent's proclamation meant only that armistice negotiations would be embarked on. In the meantime the war would go on and Hungarian troops were to defend themselves "in the fact of attack from any quarter." In effect, this meant a continuation of the fight against the Red Army. This order was broadcast on the radio later in the afternoon.[128]

Vörös's message may have been decisive for those officers who otherwise would have sided with the Regent if they had realized his true intentions. In fact, however, the majority of officers were appalled when they heard of Horthy's radio proclamation, which they regarded as treason against the Germans. They were not prepared to stab a former ally in the back, and preferred to fight on even in a hopeless struggle.[129] Horthy's belief that the loyalty of the commanders of the two main army groups would help him carry the day also proved unfounded. Upon receiving the prearranged coded message that Horthy had sent out shortly after his radio proclamation, Generals Miklós and Veress did in fact endeavor to establish contact with their Soviet counterparts. Veress, however, was quickly arrested by the Germans. Miklós did manage to cross into Soviet-held territory with several of his aides, but the only immediate result was that his army unit fell under the command of officers who remained loyal to the Germans.

For most of the afternoon of October 15 Admiral Horthy remained unaware that his attempt to withdraw Hungary from the war was miscarrying. At a reconvened meeting of the Crown Council at 2:30, Horthy reported on his negotiations with Veesenmayer and his instructions to the army commanders, and declared that he had "burned all the bridges behind me." He regretted that this decision could mean "bitter hours and much suffering for the members of the government." Inexplicably, however, Horthy still did not reveal that an armistice had already been signed. The ministers, most of whom had been unpleasantly surprised by the Regent's proclamation, were uneasy about the absence of detailed plans for dealing with likely German countermeasures. After the meeting Lakatos, reflecting the opinion of most of his colleagues, commented privately that Hungary was truly making "a leap in the dark."[130]

Horthy first began to realize that things had gone wrong late in the afternoon when the Hungarian radio, which had been seized by German forces, began broadcasting a "war command to the armed nation" by Ferenc Szálasi and General Vörös's order that the troops continue to fight on. From this point on all the incoming reports indicated that the Germans were seizing the initiative. By late evening it seemed that only the Royal Castle, with its 300-man force, remained securely under the Regent's command. Around 7:00 Vattay and Ambrózy reported the latest events to Horthy and recommended that Lakatos be authorized to approach the Germans and try to find a compromise. Horthy reluctantly agreed, but only if there were guarantees that no harm would come to his family or aides. For the next several hours Horthy vacillated between bouts of despondency and sudden optimism. Though conceding that "the situation was lost," he nonetheless vowed that "he would go on trying to the last."[131] In a discussion with István Szent-Miklósy, whom he was thinking of sending to Szeged to negotiate with Marshal Vasili Malinovsky, Horthy even suggested that Hungary would have to attack Germany. But the situation continued to deteriorate and reports were received that the Germans would soon attack the Castle.[132]

Around 9:00 Lakatos and Hennyey returned to the Castle with a report on their attempt to reach a compromise with Veesenmayer. It was only now, as they discussed this matter with Horthy, Vattay, and Ambrózy, that the Prime Minister and Foreign Minister learned that a preliminary armistice had already been signed and that the Soviets had sent an ultimatum that expired at 8:00 A.M. on October 16. Lakatos expressed alarm at the "putsch-like" manner in which the armistice had been arrived at without the knowledge or approval of the Cabinet. He suspected that the Cabinet would never accept such severe terms. Admiral Horthy, looking extremely weary and dejected, made no attempt to defend his initiative; indeed, he now apparently agreed that the armistice terms were unacceptable.[133]

Hoping to salvage what they could from what had become a disastrous situation and to ensure at least the personal safety of the Regent, Lakatos, Vattay, and Ambrózy now retired to the Prime Minister's office and, after extensive discussions, agreed on a new offer to make to the Germans. The Cabinet would resign and the Regent would abdicate, thus allowing the Germans to appoint a government they approved of. At the same time, Horthy would ask that he and his family be taken under the protection of the Reich and be given asylum in Germany.[134] However, Lakatos was willing to approach the Germans with this proposal only if Horthy was consulted and gave his explicit approval. Vattay thus returned to the Castle shortly after midnight and had the Regent, who had retired after an exhausting day, roused from sleep. Irritated and perhaps a bit disoriented, Horthy angrily rejected Vattay's proposal and refused even to discuss the matter. When Vattay, supported by Ambrózy and the Regent's aide de camp, Gyula Tost, persisted, Horthy abruptly dismissed them: "We'll talk it over in the morning."[135]

Horrified that a German attack on the Castle would endanger the lives of Horthy and family, Vattay decided that, in these extraordinary circumstances, loyalty to the Regent demanded that he take the initiative. He thus reported to Lakatos that the Regent approved the proposed diplomatic settlement "in its entirety."[136] This set in motion renewed negotiations between Lakatos and the Germans that lasted for several hours. In the meantime S.S. troops had surrounded the Castle and final preparations were made for the launching of Operation Panzerfaust at 6:00 A.M. When around 4:00 A.M. General Lázár, who was in charge of the 300-man force defending the Castle, realized that an attack was imminent, he awakened the Regent and persuaded him to send his wife, daughter-in-law, and grandson to safety in the residence of the papal nuncio. Unaware of the negotiations that Lakatos was still conducting, Horthy decided that if the Germans attacked, he would order resistance. At around 5:00 he and Vattay were sitting in the early morning fog on the steps of the Castle, loading their pistols, and contemplating the grim possibility of a heroic death. Scattered gunfire and the muffled roar of approaching tanks indicated that the battle would soon begin. Suddenly, however, Lázár appeared and reported that Lakatos had phoned and directed that a military conflict should be avoided at all costs.[137]

Several minutes later Lakatos, accompanied by Veesenmayer,

arrived in a German military car at the main entrance to the Castle. After Lakatos reported that a tentative agreement had been reached with the Germans, both he and Vattay urged Horthy to call off all resistance. Veesenmayer stressed the urgency of the matter: "It is my unpleasant task to take charge of your security, since in twelve minutes the attack will begin." Seeing no other alternative, Horthy relented and declared to Lázár: "I don't want any shedding of blood. There will be no resistance. Cease all resistance!" Veesenmayer then suggested that the Regent be taken to nearby Hatvany Castle, so that he "would be spared the painful sight of the occupation of the Castle." Horthy went along meekly, and the whole event proceeded with such formality and politeness that those Hungarian officers who observed it from a distance did not realize that they were witnessing the arrest of the Regent and his colleagues.[138]

Horthy spent the rest of the morning confined with Lakatos and members of his entourage in a gloomy room in Hatvany Castle. He snatched a few hours of sleep and otherwise remained deep in thought, speaking little. The mood of despondency was deepened when Horthy and his colleagues learned that Gyula Tost, who was being held in a nearby room, had taken his own life. Admiral Horthy had been shattered by the course of recent events, but he did not consider suicide a way out of his personal crisis. His sole remaining concern now was to be reunited with his family, especially with his son. He thus authorized Lakatos to negotiate his abdication on this basis and agreed to sign a communiqué in which he declared his proclamation of October 15 to be "null and void."[139]

Horthy drew the line, however, at appointing Szálasi as the new Prime Minister. When the Arrowcross leader appeared before him at noontime in the belief that the Regent had already agreed to entrust the formation of a new government to his party, Horthy immediately dismissed him, declaring that he would be the last person in Hungary whom he would make Prime Minister. Horthy's reaction was the same when Szálasi showed up once again at 7:00 P.M. Yet Lakatos had discovered that the Germans preferred, even in the waning days of the Nazi regime, to preserve a facade of constitutional procedure. Thus they insisted that the safety of Horthy and his family could not be guaranteed unless the Regent appointed Szálasi and abdicated. If the Regent did not come around, Germany would use "the most brutal methods" and the life of the Regent's son would be in danger. Lakatos thus did his best to persuade Horthy that it would not be dishonorable to comply with all the German requests, since "the country and the world would realize that he had acted under German pressure." Horthy finally gave in only when he received Veesenmayer's word of honor that his son would join him on his train the next day in Vienna or Linz. However, he made it a point to declare that he was abdicating and appointing Szálasi under duress; later he would describe this document as a mere "scrap of paper."[140]

The next day, October 17, was, Horthy later recalled, the "saddest day of my life."[141] In the afternoon he, his family, and a few members of his entourage were taken under guard to the Western train station for their transport to Germany. Horthy was dressed incongruously in his hunting attire, since the rest of his clothing had been stolen from his apartment by German soldiers. His official train, the Turán, now retraced the path that Admiral Horthy had followed on that fateful day twenty-six years earlier, when he had returned to Hungary after the collapse of the Austro-Hungarian Empire. Now he was leaving a Hungary that had become one of the main battlefields of the most devastating war in European history. Shortly before midnight the Turán crossed the border into Austria. Though he would live for thirteen more years and outlast his nemeses, Hitler and Stalin, not to mention Szálasi, Miklós Horthy would never again set foot on Hungarian soil.

12

The Admiral on Horseback: An Assessment

In the wake of Admiral Horthy's forced departure from his homeland on October 17, 1944, the Szálasi government made desperate and futile attempts to hold off inevitable defeat. Adolf Eichmann returned to Hungary and the Jews of Budapest were subjected to renewed persecution and terror, but most managed to survive these last months of the war. For a time the Soviet attitude toward Horthy and his regime remained relatively favorable. Ironically, General Vörös, who had helped to torpedo Horthy's attempt to withdraw from the war, now himself defected to the Russians and volunteered to make propaganda broadcasts urging the Hungarian people to turn against the Germans and cooperate with the Red Army. His radio message from Moscow on November 10 ended with the words: "Long live free democratic Hungary under the leadership of Regent Horthy!" Despite the incongruous nature of these words, Vörös's appeal was picked up by the BBC in London and sent out frequently in its programs.[1]

Miklós Horthy knew nothing of this development, since he and his family remained under German custody in a castle near Weilheim in Bavaria. In April 1945, however, the S.S. contingent guarding the castle melted away as American troops approached the area. Liberation by Allied troops did not, however, mean personal freedom for Horthy. To his dismay he now found himself a prisoner of the victorious Allies, who viewed him as a possible war criminal. Horthy was dumbfounded and shocked by this, since he not only denied that he had committed or condoned any war crimes, but even tried to portray himself as the mastermind of Hungarian resistance to Nazi Germany.[2] In his postwar interrogations Horthy insisted that his abdication had been invalid because it took place "in the presence of the tommy guns of fifty-five S.S.

soldiers."[3] Thus, he remained Hungary's legal head of state. The new Hungarian government, Horthy asserted, was dominated by Communist Russia and did not represent the people of Hungary, who "stand 99 percent behind me, as one man." He urged the Allies to free him so that he could play his rightful role in the reconstruction of Hungary and at the peace conference that would determine Hungary's future "for centuries."

Admiral Horthy pleaded his case in letters to President Harry Truman and the British Foreign Secretary Ernest Bevin, but it was clear to Allied statesmen that there was no place for a seventy-eight-year-old Habsburg admiral in the postwar Hungarian government. Now, more than ever, Horthy seemed to be an anachronism. One finds in these letters the very same arguments that Horthy had used repeatedly over the past twenty-five years: Hungary before World War I had not discriminated against its ethnic minorities; simple justice dictated that Hungary be restored to its millennial frontiers; Hungary's neighbors, especially the Romanians, were unreliable; and so on.[4] Although no one took these arguments seriously, British and American officials were unsure what to do with the former Regent. The new Yugoslav government under Marshal Tito was pressing vigorously for Horthy to be put on trial for the atrocities committed at Újvidék, but the balance was tipped in Horthy's favor by Joseph Stalin, who advised the leaders of the new Hungarian government not to request his prosecution. Horthy, he suggested, was "an old man" who had at least made an effort, albeit an inept one, to reach a preliminary armistice. For that reason he should not be regarded as a war criminal. The Hungarian government thus advised the Allies against making Horthy a defendant at the war crimes trials, since that would just make a martyr of him. On the other hand, it was made clear that there was no place for a "living Horthy" in the new democratic Hungary.[5]

It was just as well that Horthy was not placed on trial, for when he did appear as a witness at the Nuremberg trial of Veesenmayer, his testimony was confused and at times incoherent. Released from captivity in 1946 and finally reunited with his son Niki, Admiral Horthy remained in Weilheim before moving to Portugal in 1948. There he lived with his family in obscurity and, in the beginning at least, in near poverty, for such wealth as he had possessed remained in Hungary and during his career he had never taken the precaution of sending money abroad. Eventually friends of the family established a "Horthy fund" that secured a reasonably comfortable life style. Ironically, two of the major contributors to this fund were Hungarian Jewish financiers who had survived the war and were living in the West.[6]

In his retirement years Admiral Horthy made little attempt to play an active role in émigré politics. He corresponded occasionally with friends, especially members of the Order of Heroes, and spoke up from time to time when he believed his honor to be sullied. Thus, in 1954 he wrote to Konrad Adenauer, the German Chancellor, to refute the accusation that Hungary had been prepared in October 1944 to comply with a Soviet demand to declare war on Germany. "That," Horthy declared, "would have been unthinkable, for at no time in its thousand-year history had Hungary ever been a traitor or broken its word."[7] On only one issue, land reform, did Horthy change his long-held views. Following up on his hesitant initiative in 1943, Horthy now concluded that the breakup of the large estates was necessary and desirable, although he insisted that the new smallholders would have to be carefully chosen and educated.[8]

Not surprisingly, in his last years Horthy remained rigidly hostile toward bolshevism, all the more so since the existence of a Communist regime in Hungary made it impossible to realize his desire to spend his last days in his native land and be buried near his home in Kenderes. In October 1956 it seemed for a time that the revolution that erupted in Hungary would sweep away the Communist government and that Horthy's fondest hopes would be realized. But when the Red Army crushed the revolution, it was as if Horthy himself had been dealt a mortal blow. He died three months later on February 9, 1957, and was laid to rest in a cemetery in Lisbon.[9]

In assessing the twenty-four year political career of Miklós Horthy, most historians have concentrated on his numerous personal foibles, sympathy for extremist right-wing ideas, narrow-minded views, and ineptness as a leader. Certainly the list of Horthy's assorted character weaknesses and misguided and intolerant policies is lengthy. Horthy's Hungary was notorious for its attempts to discriminate against the Jews, from the *numerus clausus* of 1920 to the anti-Jewish legislation of the World War II era. Under Horthy's tutelage Hungary took advantage of German aggression to regain territory from her neighbors. In 1944 Horthy acquiesced in the deportation of the majority of Hungarian Jews, and at the end of the war Hungary stood alone as Hitler's last ally. The Hungarian government's belated attempt to follow the example of Romania and Finland and defect from the war failed miserably, in part because Horthy lacked the shrewdness and diplomatic skill of Marshal Mannerheim or King Michael.

Even contemporary Hungarian political observers who sympathized with Admiral Horthy bemoaned his naiveté, malleability, and susceptibility to manipulation by those who could gain access to him. One unfortunate result of these character flaws was that in times of political or social crisis, such as the immediate post–World War I period, the onset of the Depression, or the first months of the German occupation in 1944, Horthy was persuaded to condone repressive policies by right-wing extremists who were able to play on his deepest prejudices and antipathies. A sophisticated analysis of political and social problems was simply beyond Miklós Horthy's capacity, for he lacked political acumen and was ignorant of basic political concepts and movements. He knew what ideas appealed to him, but he probably could not have defined or explained such terms as the "Szeged idea," liberalism, or fascism.[10] Because he had difficulty fathoming complex ideas of any kind, he often became confused when forced to speak extemporaneously in a political or diplomatic exchange or engage in a logical debate of issues. He also lacked the ability to formulate efficacious long-term political strategies, and as a consequence sometimes clung to policies and beliefs that were not grounded in reality. Thus, in World War II he believed almost to the end that, despite its close collaboration with Nazi Germany, Hungary would somehow manage to stay in Great Britain's good favor and keep the territorial gains it had made.

One of Admiral Horthy's least admirable personal characteristics was his tendency to blame others for his own failures or mistakes. He was simply incapable of honest introspection or critical self-analysis. When Count Teleki committed suicide in 1941 and indirectly blamed the Regent for the horrible crisis into which Hungary had been plunged, Horthy refused to concede that he might share responsibility for these events. In 1944 when the true nature of the Holocaust finally became evident, he placed all the blame on the Germans and a few sadistic Hungarians. Horthy never recognized that his own earlier anti-Semitic policies had contributed to the creation of a climate of intolerance. Indeed, Horthy truly believed that his own motives were always pure and honorable, and that he never told a lie or betrayed a friend. Yet the disinterested historian can identify numerous occasions on which Horthy told untruths. Already in the 1920s, in the face of much contrary evidence, he was explaining to visitors that he had never aspired to be Regent and had hoped that Count Apponyi would be elected. Likewise, he insisted after 1942 and in his memoirs that he had played no role in the election of his son as Deputy Regent. And when, during interrogations after World War II, he was asked who was responsible for the catastrophe that had engulfed his country, Horthy placed the blame on the Germans of Hungary, who, he asserted, had come to dominate the officer corps and served the interests of Nazi Germany rather than of their native land.[11]

Miklós Horthy's concepts of honor and gentlemanly behavior were at times applied in ways that concealed his or his friends' responsibility for sordid acts. During the "White Terror" of 1919–1920, Horthy was aware that Prónay and the other commanders of special detachments were committing atrocities, but he refused to acknowledge this and protected these officers from prosecution. He did so in part because it had been ingrained in him during his naval training that the conduct of officers must never be subject to criticism by civilians. Thus when journalists reported on the outbreak of terror, Horthy's instinctive reaction was not to determine the truth of the matter but to fulminate against the "Jewish scribblers" who were making such insulting accusations and calling into question the honor of the officer corps. Horthy thus contributed to the atmosphere of terror that led to numerous atrocities in 1919 and 1920, even if his own complicity in individual crimes was indirect or absent. Horthy's rigid adherence to the concept of *Ehrennotwehr* also determined his initial reaction to reports of atrocities committed by Hungarian troops at Újvidék in 1942.

Admiral Horthy often claimed that he and his country always engaged in honorable behavior in international affairs. In particular, he was wont to assert that Hungary had always carried out its treaty obligations and had never in its entire history engaged in treacherous behavior. Yet Horthy failed to apply these principles in a systematic way, and the results often were deleterious for Hungary. On the one hand, he did refuse to accept a German offer to join in the attack on Poland in 1939. Poland was regarded as a traditional ally of Hungary, and, Horthy argued, it would be a dastardly act to betray such a friend. He even incurred Hitler's wrath by granting a safe haven in Hungary to many Polish officers and officials. Yet two years later Horthy had no qualms about approving an attack on Yugoslavia, with which Hungary had recently signed the Treaty of Eternal Friendship. The difference, of course, was that Hungary had territorial claims on its neighbor to the south. Thus Horthy employed various sophistries to explain why Hungary's apparent betrayal of an ally was in this case not dishonorable conduct. Likewise, Horthy insisted to the very end of his regency that he was honor-bound to give Germany, Hungary's ally, advance notice when plans were being completed to withdraw from the war. The fact that Hitler had intimidated him on many occasions and that Germany had carried out an exceedingly brutal occupation in Hungary did not alter his conviction that he must honor his promises to Hitler. At the same time, in seeking to withdraw from the war Horthy made certain commitments in the preliminary armistice signed in Moscow on October 11, 1944, that he immediately tried to evade. In particular, he hoped that he would not have to fulfill that provision of the armistice calling for Hungary to join in the attack on Germany. It is symptomatic of Horthy's warped sense of honor that at that critical turning point of the war he still worried more about betraying Nazi Germany than about cooperating in good faith with the great powers from whom he was requesting an armistice and a fair hearing for Hungary's territorial claims.[12]

The various character weaknesses described above combined with an ardent nationalism and a fervent anticommunism to create a number of "blind spots" in Admiral Horthy's approach to public affairs. So convinced was he that the Magyars were a noble, superior people, especially in comparison with their inferior neighbors, that he found it psychologically impossible to comprehend the possibility that a Hungarian could be capable of dishonorable conduct. Thus, in 1944 he refused to believe reports that Hungarian gendarmes had committed atrocities against Jews. Likewise, despite strong warnings from his advisors about growing pro-Nazi sentiments in the Hungarian officer corps, he could not imagine that in a time of crisis a Hungarian officer would refuse to carry out commands of the Supreme War Lord. Horthy's feelings of revulsion for communism led him to remain intensely suspicious of the Social Democrats; as a result, he was unable to bring himself fully to cooperate with those opposition groups who could have been his most useful domestic allies against Nazi Germany in 1944. Finally, Horthy's chauvinist assumptions and frequent denigration of the other nations of Danubian Europe made it impossible for him to embrace a program of limited territorial revisionism. Horthy paid no heed to Count Teleki's warnings about the dangers of relying on Nazi German power to effect a restoration of Hungary's historic frontiers. To Horthy all that mattered was that Hungary had been treated unfairly in the Treaty of Trianon. His simple-minded approach can be seen in the argument that he saw fit to employ both in his letter to Stalin in 1944 and in postwar interrogations: Hungary had done nothing wrong in World War II, for she had sought to annex only those territories that were rightfully hers and had been stolen in 1920.

The preceding catalogue of Miklós Horthy's shortcomings confronts the historian with a very basic question: How could such a person achieve lasting political success? How was it possible for an admiral with no political experience and such shallow and intolerant views not only to become a prominent political leader but to enjoy one of the longest tenures in power of any twentieth-century European statesman? Horthy's critics have explained this apparent paradox by arguing that Horthy succeeded in his military career largely through good luck, rode to power on a wave of a "White Terror," and solidified his power by brutally suppressing all democratic and progressive forces.

To arrive at more satisfactory and persuasive explanations of the paradoxes of Miklós Horthy's career, however, one must recognize that he in fact possessed some remarkable personal qualities and that he enjoyed considerable popularity in Hungary. Moreover, he was not so inept as his popular image would suggest, and he was able to use even some of his shortcomings to his advantage. Perhaps the most striking of Miklós Horthy's attributes was his congenial personality. In this respect the Hungarian Regent compared favorably with many other European leaders. In terms of political astuteness, diplomatic skill, or leadership qualities in general, Horthy bears no comparison with Winston Churchill, who also came to prominence in World War I as First Lord of the Admiralty. Yet he nonetheless possessed one quality that Churchill, who remained a political pariah for much of his career, lacked: the ability to ingratiate himself with virtually everyone he met. Horthy had an uncanny ability to make every guest feel comfortable and welcome. One might disapprove of his policies or be disconcerted by his indiscreet manner and sometimes bizarre utterances, but almost everyone who encountered the Hungarian Regent was impressed by his sincerity, gentility, linguistic virtuosity, and the aura of authority that he seemed to exude. The roster of individuals who succumbed to Horthy's charm is a long and ideologically diverse one, ranging from the British pacifist George Lansbury to the American envoy Joseph Davies and, for a time at least, to Adolf Hitler himself. Even that most stern judge of men, Joseph Stalin, managed from afar to form a relatively favorable image of the Hungarian Regent, certainly far more favorable than that held by the Hungarian Communists.[13]

Despite his deep-seated suspicion of democratic procedures, Admiral Horthy might well have been elected chief of state even if the interwar Hungarian regime had been based on a more liberal franchise. The Parliament that elected him regent in 1920 was not fully representative of the nation, and military coercion was certainly a factor in that election, but a plebiscite based on universal suffrage would probably have yielded the same result. After the turbulent events of 1918–1919 and the humiliating peace treaty imposed on Hungary, many Hungarians yearned for an authoritative leader who would preside over a restoration of order and stability and champion national interests. Like General Dwight Eisenhower in the United States after World War II, Horthy was an apolitical war hero around whom patriots could rally. Horthy had the added advantage of being able to project himself as the embodiment of anticommunism, anti-Semitism, and extreme nationalism, which were powerful currents in Hungary during this period. To an extent his popularity was artificially stimulated by Gyula Gömbös and later propagandists, but Horthy contributed to his own success through his activities as an effective orator or "itinerant preacher." Although he had had little experience in public speaking, Miklós Horthy developed in the immediate postwar period a small set of stock speeches that he continued to give throughout his regency. Unlike the emotional, impromptu speech that had launched his career in Szeged in July 1919, these were patriotic sermons delivered in a grave but sincere tone. Again and again Horthy emphasized the conservative values of hard work, national pride, and devotion to family and church. His successful broadcast to the nation in April 1938, which acquainted a wider audience with many of the pet theories he routinely spoke of in private conversation, suggests that Admiral Horthy might have been capable of establishing an even more extensive rapport with the masses had he thought to make greater use of modern media, especially radio.

Nor was Horthy completely lacking in leadership qualities. As a Habsburg naval officer in World War I he demonstrated the ability to supervise complicated operations and gain the confidence of his subordinates. These skills served Horthy in good stead when he organized the National Army in Szeged and later as regent. He was at his best when, as in the Bethlen era, he could stay above the fray, delegate authority to the most capable people he could find, and serve as a symbol of legitimacy and stability. The creation of a stable, authoritarian government in Hungary after World War I was, of course, the work of Count István Bethlen, but it was Horthy who early on recognized Bethlen's abilities and persisted until he succeeded in persuading him to accept appointment as Prime Minister.

On the other hand, during the German occupation in 1944, when Horthy had few trusted advisors available to him and he had to fend for himself, he floundered and made numerous mistakes. At times he was his own worst enemy. His lack of discretion led him at times to blurt out his confidential plans to Veesenmayer.[14] His insistence that a captain must not abandon his ship made it impossible for him to accept the idea that he leave Budapest and make his proclamation to the nation from the headquarters of the First Army. That might have been the only real chance for a successful defection. In general, Horthy badly managed the last stage of the attempted withdrawal from the war. He failed to ensure coordination between the government and the military leadership, and badly bungled preparations for the actual withdrawal on October 15.

Yet one wonders if any Hungarian statesman, let alone the seventy-six-year-old Regent, could have found a way to extricate the country from the nearly hopeless situation in which it found itself in World War II and particularly during the German occupation. Even in retrospect it is difficult to conceive a strategy Horthy might have pursued in 1944 that would have fundamentally altered the course of events. Horthy might, of course, have taken Kállay's advice in late March to retire to his estate in Kenderes and withdraw totally from any contact with the government, à la King Christian X of Denmark. Had he done this, the Regent's historical reputation might have been enhanced, but the only practical result in Hungary would likely have been a more rapid deportation and annihilation of the Jews, including those of Budapest. Indeed, it might be more fruitful to rephrase the standard question about

Horthy's conduct in 1944 by asking: What did he manage to accomplish against stupendous odds? Although he initially acquiesced in the deportation of the Jews, when the reality of the "Final Solution" finally penetrated his consciousness he acted in a forceful and courageous way that protected the Jews of Budapest. No other European leader caught in such a dilemma, with the military equation so heavily in Germany's favor, had ever defied Hitler so directly. Likewise, once Horthy determined that the only way to spare the Hungarian nation further bloodshed was to seek an armistice, he swallowed his pride and even humbled himself to beg for Stalin's mercy. In doing so Horthy parted company with the great majority of Hungarian officials and military officers, including some whom he had heretofore regarded as entirely loyal to him. It was a truly remarkable achievement to enter negotiations with the Russians and reach a preliminary armistice without the knowledge and cooperation of the Hungarian Cabinet and without the vigilant Germans discovering what was afoot.

That episode suggests that, despite his garrulous nature and shallow understanding of international affairs, Admiral Horthy could at times outwit his opponents and score a diplomatic success. One of the great ironies of his career was that, up until the disasters of 1944, he was one of the few statesmen to hold his own against Adolf Hitler. With his propensity for outlandish statements, his rigid sense of honor, and his discursive conversational style, Horthy proved to be an exasperating interlocutor. Horthy was quite capable of walking out on the German leader, as he did on two occasions when he felt that he was being treated in an insulting manner. He surely baffled Hitler at the Klessheim meeting of 1943 when he spoke in such a moderate and humanitarian way about the Jews. Hitler never quite figured out what to make of the Hungarian Regent: was he a hopelessly uninformed political innocent, or was he a shrewd calculator who feigned ignorance and confusion in order to avoid responding to German complaints?

Of course, Horthy was in fact uninformed about many things, and in certain circumstances could become confused and disoriented. On the other hand, when he had time to prepare and was in control of the situation, Horthy was capable of speaking in an organized and persuasive manner. This can be seen, for example, in the various councils over which he presided during World War II. In the minutes of these meetings there is no evidence that the Regent, despite his advanced age, became discursive or was uninformed about the issues being discussed. At the Crown Councils of June 26 and October 15, 1944, for example, Horthy demonstrated that he could present issues in a clear manner and keep the conversation focused even when other participants digressed and sought to evade confronting the key issues. This suggests that although Horthy's apparent befuddlement when pressed by Hitler, Veesenmayer, or other hostile inquisitors was in part genuine, it is also likely that he deliberately exaggerated his confusion in order to avoid having to discuss the issues at hand. Even when persuaded against his better judgment to go along with a plan to which he had been objecting, Horthy later sometimes would cleverly wriggle out of a commitment by claiming that his hearing was bad and he had not really understand the issue.

It is also worth noting that despite Admiral Horthy's limited education and his narrow intellectual horizons, his pronouncements about European affairs and diplomatic arrangements were at times quite insightful. Skeptics might suggest that this merely demonstrates the truth of the cliché that even a stopped clock is accurate twice each day. Nonetheless, some of Horthy's ideas, especially those not directly touching on Hungarian interests, were insightful, and some of his predictions were prescient. Horthy knew enough European history to be able, from time to time, to apply useful examples from the past to support his arguments. On one occasion, for example, in attempting to lecture Hitler on the need to avoid vindictiveness after victory in war, Horthy made a perceptive reference to Bismarck's restraint after the Austro-Prussian War of 1866.[15] In the 1920s when many statesmen seemed to take seriously the idea that the Kellogg-Briand Pact would make a real contribution to the preservation of peace, Horthy refused to play along with this charade. During the Ethiopian War in the mid-1930s he correctly predicted that the British and French would not seek a final confrontation with Italy. Although he wavered for a time when Germany was at its ascendancy in 1940–1941, Horthy never abandoned his fundamental belief that the Western powers, with their mighty navies, could never be defeated in war. Finally, his insistence that Czechoslovakia and Yugoslavia were artificial states that could never last seemed outlandish and self-serving at the time, but the transformation of the map of Eastern Europe in the last decade of the twentieth century might be seen as a confirmation of the validity of Miklós Horthy's analysis.

Horthy's ambivalence about so many of the critical political and social issues of his time led to an inner turmoil that was manifested in his frequent indecisiveness, malleability, and contradictory policies. In normal circumstances Horthy preferred the kind of traditional moderate conservatism espoused by Count Bethlen. In the Bethlen era he seemed content to play the role of a ceremonial head of state in a pluralist system in which parties of the center and moderate left had room to operate. But when there arose a threat of political upheaval, economic crisis, or revolutionary change, his darker impulses came to the surface. Then he was open to proposals from the right-wing extremists for radical measures and violence against those whom he suspected of fomenting trouble and promoting communism. Although Horthy came to sense that his power was based in large part on balancing between the two major right-wing camps, he never fully understood this dichotomy in his political makeup. Many of his actions in the late 1930s and during World War II seemed to be instinctive attempts to suppress his own radical tendencies. It was as if he subconsciously sensed that unless he surrounded himself with moderate advisors, he would find it difficult to resist the temptation to embark on dangerous policies that he would later regret. Thus, even as the Third Reich was extending its hegemony on the European continent and right-wing radicalism and extreme anti-Semitism were advancing steadily in Hungarian society, Horthy attempted to bolster those individuals who sought to preserve constitutional procedures and maintain ties with the Western powers.

This process began in 1936 when Horthy decided to dismiss Gyula Gömbös because he was not acting like a "true gentleman," which in the circumstances meant that Horthy suspected he aimed ultimately to establish a totalitarian dictatorship. Subsequent prime ministers appointed by Horthy were expected to show respect for Magyar political traditions of constitutionalism and pluralism and to combat the Arrowcross movement. Each was asked to keep on good terms with Great Britain even while seizing all opportunities for the recovery of territory lost after World War I. That such otherwise capable men as Darányi, Imrédy, and Bárdossy not only failed to fulfill the assignment the Regent had given them but in fact ended up as proponents of increased cooperation with Nazi Germany and appeasement of the radical right-wing in Hungary reflected not so much Horthy's lack of foresight but the political realities of the times. The conversion of these men, and indeed the majority of the Hungarian political establishment, to a pro-German position was primarily the result of a pragmatic calculation that Hitler's Germany would for the foreseeable future dominate the European continent. For most of World War II it required a great leap of faith for any realistic political observer in Hungary to imagine that the Western democracies would somehow play an important role in Eastern Europe in the postwar world. To many Hungarians Béla Imrédy's warning that Hungary would end up in the sphere of influence of either Nazi Germany or Bolshevik Russia was compelling. Yet Horthy persisted well into 1944 in his belief, or perhaps forlorn hope, that, just as in World War I, West European troops would be landed on the Adriatic coast and make their way toward Vienna and Budapest. His calculation proved faulty, but it was not entirely farfetched. Winston Churchill had pressed for just such an attack on the "soft underbelly" of Hitler's Europe, and as late as September 1944 the British Prime Minister proposed to Stalin that in the allocation of spheres of influence in East Central Europe, Hungary be divided 50-50 between the two countries.[16] But the same geopolitical and military realities that frustrated Churchill's attempt to limit Soviet expansionism in Eastern Europe doomed Horthy's attempt to preserve Hungary's independence.

One ironic result of this massive shift to the radical right in Hungary during World War II was that Admiral Horthy, who had risen to prominence in 1919 under the banner of the "Szeged idea," found himself decidedly less extremist in his views than the majority of Hungarian politicians, government officials, and military officers. Horthy's instinctive response was to gravitate toward the dwindling minority of Hungarian officials who believed a way could still be found for Hungary to avoid succumbing to either Nazi barbarism or a brutal Soviet occupation. Horthy's rigid and deeply held convictions prevented him from turning to the Social Democrats or Smallholders for political support. In any case, though they had the potential to win widespread support in Hungary in the post-1945 era, they were exceedingly weak in the prevailing conditions of wartime Hungary. As a result Horthy turned for assistance to such men as Miklós Kállay, Ferenc Keresztes-Fischer, István Bethlen, and General Vilmos Nagy, who were among the most moderate and humane members of Hungary's interwar political elite. By the standards of Hitler's Europe they were, indeed, "liberals at heart" who fought courageously to preserve a pluralist political system and to prevent the implementation of the "Final Solution" in Hungary.[17]

Where does Miklós Horthy stand in relation to contemporary European leaders? What does a study of his career reveal about Hungarian, and in a broader sense, European history in the era of the two world wars? Although in some ways Horthy as a statesman was *sui generis*, he does resemble other Europeans who were products of the political and intellectual milieu of the late nineteenth century and for whom World War I and its revolutionary aftermath were a traumatic experience. Horthy came to prominence as a military leader who vowed to rid his country of all revolutionary influences. He never actually led his National Army against Béla Kun's government, but he was able to exploit the widespread revulsion for the Communist government to further his own political objectives. Horthy's visceral hatred for bolshevism and desire to launch a crusade to destroy the revolutionary regime in Russia were shared by the White Generals in Russia and by such prominent European military leaders as Marshal Foch and General Ludendorff. Unlike most of these other early warriors against Bolshevik Russia, Horthy managed to gain power and forge a successful political career. In this respect he most closely resembled Marshal Mannerheim, who served for a time as Regent of Finland and was at hand in 1941, with Horthy, to join Hitler's European crusade against Soviet Russia. A fruitful comparison might also be made between Horthy and other war heroes who made a successful transition to a political career, such as Marshal Pilsudski in Poland and, in a different and later context, General Dwight Eisenhower in the United States.

In his passionate advocacy of Hungarian national goals and his stereotypical views of other ethnic groups, Admiral Horthy was a typical East European nationalist of the interwar period. Though his language was perhaps cruder and his arguments less sophisticated, Horthy's nationalistic views mirrored those held by almost all politically conscious Hungarians. He uncritically accepted all the myths that helped sustain the belief that the Treaty of Trianon was a grave injustice and that the Magyars were destined to exercise hegemony in the Danubian Basin. But it would be a mistake to assume that in his intolerant nationalism Miklós Horthy was unique among East European leaders. In fact chauvinism infected the political life of the entire region, and the only reason the statesmen of the Successor States sometimes seemed more moderate and reasonable was that they had the luxury of being able to pose as defenders of the status quo against the bellicose Magyars.

Intractable nationalism was to be found even in Czechoslovakia. When, for example, Eduard Beneš negotiated with Soviet leaders in Moscow in 1943, he made vituperative attacks on the Magyars and employed national stereotypes every bit as crude and chauvinist as those Horthy frequently used.[18]

In reviewing Admiral Horthy's relationship to the Jews and the insight it provides into the nature of European anti-Semitism, the historian must confront the irony that a man who was a self-proclaimed anti-Semite, who after World War I became notorious as a persecutor of the Jews, emerged in World War II as an apparent protector of Jews. It seems quite clear that Horthy felt uncomfortable with, and ultimately rejected, the violent racial anti-Semitism of the Hungarian and German radical right-wing. His attitude toward the Jews was a more traditional one, shaped, in large part, by his experiences in prewar Austria-Hungary. One historian has noted that in late nineteenth- and early twentieth-century Austria it was not uncommon for educated, well-respected members of society to express in private strong, even vulgar prejudices against the Jews, yet act tolerantly toward, and even socialize with, Jews in public.[19] This description would seem to fit Miklós Horthy, who might well have adopted the philosophy attributed to Karl Lueger, the popular mayor of fin de siècle Vienna: "I decide who is a Jew." For those he considered "good, indigenous Jews," Horthy developed a grudging respect and, for certain individuals, even affection.

Horthy's policies towards the Jews were also influenced by the example of Emperor Francis Joseph, whom the Hungarian Regent tried whenever possible to emulate. Certainly Horthy never went so far as to declare, as had Francis Joseph, that "there will be no Jew-baiting in my land."[20] But Horthy's increasing tolerance toward the Jews during the 1920s, his refusal to allow Gömbös to enact anti-Semitic legislation, and his insistence during World War II that he would not inflict "senseless humiliations" on the Jews did seem to echo the sentiments of his former emperor/king.

That Admiral Horthy nonetheless contributed greatly to the intensification of anti-Semitism in Hungary after the Great War and was implicated in several repressive actions against Hungarian Jews can be attributed largely to the exaggerated nationalism and fervent anticommunism that pervaded his thinking. The example of the Hungarian Soviet Republic seemed to him conclusive proof that Jews seemed perversely attracted to communism. Of course,

Horthy was far from alone in making this facile deduction. In the wake of the revolutionary outbreaks beginning in 1917 political elites all over the Western world were becoming wary of "revolutionary Jews." It is noteworthy that in 1919, even before Admiral Horthy led his National Army into Budapest, Winston Churchill was disturbed by what he regarded as the "astonishing" number of Jews involved in revolutionary activity and publicly urged British Jews to stand up against "Jewish-led bolshevism."[21] The position of a Hungarian nationalist and anti-Communist was complicated by the profound indignation over Hungary's loss of the war and humiliation at the Paris Peace Conference by her victorious neighbors. This led Horthy and many of his compatriots to resent and suspect any remaining foreign or alien elements in rump Hungary. This was the assumption that underlay Horthy's callous attitude toward the "Galician Jews," whom he regarded as latecomers who had never fused into the Magyar nation. At the same time, it helps explain Horthy's more protective view of the assimilated Jews, whom he came to regard as real patriots who had made important contributions to national life. Horthy's attitude in this regard was also influenced by his ability to break with certain traditional views held by many Hungarians of his generation. Like his contemporaries, Horthy placed a high value on such virtues as honor, sacrifice, and courage, but he also extolled entrepreneurial skills, business success, and hard work. He thus came to admire the many Jews who had succeeded in the world of finance, engineering, and business, and to believe that the Christian Magyars, who for the most part shunned such endeavors, were in part responsible for the Jewish domination of these fields.

Miklós Horthy did sanction drastic action against Jews on those occasions when communism seemed to pose a direct threat to Hungary. But in both the "White Terror" of 1919 and the deportations of 1944, Horthy's main motive was to strike a blow against communism, not to torment the Jews. Thus his attitude in both cases was ambivalent and he ultimately rejected the most radical plans of the fanatical German and Hungarian anti-Semites. Some historians have interpreted Admiral Horthy's relatively tolerant attitude toward the Jews during World War II and his belated intervention on behalf of the Budapest Jews in July 1944 as blatant opportunism aimed at creating an insurance policy should the Axis powers lose the war, a way of demonstrating to the victorious Western powers that Hungary had not been Hitler's lackey.

Thus it has been asserted that Horthy's policies were designed "for the benefit of London and Washington" and did not represent "a honest attempt to remedy the abuses which had long since been officially sanctioned and carried out rather pitilessly."[22] But this ascribes to Admiral Horthy a degree of calculation and cleverness that he did not possess. His refusal to comply with the most radical of Nazi Germany's demands was not a pragmatic response to Germany's declining fortunes in the war, but rather a matter of principle to which he stubbornly clung from the late 1930s on.

Horthy's vulgar anti-Jewish comments are found most often in casual conversations he had in the 1920s, when he knew that his words were not likely to have any political or diplomatic impact. On the other hand, not once in his entire career did he ever make scurrilous comments about the Jews in a public forum. Furthermore, in later years when he talked with individuals whom he knew to have violent intentions toward the Jews, he usually exercised great caution. Thus, in his conversations at Klessheim the Hungarian Regent refrained from joining Hitler and Ribbentrop in attacks on the Jews and responded to criticisms of his leniency toward the Jews with a decency and dignity that contrasted sharply with the tawdry behavior of the leaders of Germany's other allies. It is striking that during World War II Horthy even attempted to convince both Hitler and Szálasi that there were "useful Jews" who were indispensable to the welfare of Hungary.[23] There is no reason to think that on those occasions Horthy was thinking of enhancing his postwar reputation, since he had no reason to think a record of such conversations would ever be published.

Frustrated by the Hungarian government's refusal in 1943 to take harsher measures against the Jews, Joseph Goebbels grumbled that Horthy was too tangled up with the Jews and mistakenly tried to employ humanitarian and liberal arguments. Admiral Horthy was by no means a liberal, but the historian can detect a spark of humanitarianism in his policies toward the Jews. This was not based on religious principles, although it should be noted that Horthy's attitude toward the Jews was basically the same as the spiritual leaders of the Christian churches in Hungary. Rather, like a "latter-day knight,"[24] Horthy seemed ultimately guided by an archaic sense of chivalry, a code of honor to which an officer and gentleman had been expected to adhere. This code prohibited gratuitous violence against one's enemy, not to mention against women and children. In Admiral Horthy, it produced a limited kind of humanitarianism that enabled him, a self-proclaimed anti-Semite, to protect at least some Hungarian Jews from the Nazi "Final Solution." Miklós Horthy's career is a reminder that anti-Semites have represented a wide range of attitudes and types and that in grave crises, such as the Dreyfus Affair, it has sometimes been precisely someone with a reputation for anti-Semitism who was able to intervene on behalf of beleaguered Jews.[25]

As this study demonstrates, Miklós Horthy's career was filled with paradoxes and ironies. He was one of Europe's earliest and most persistent anti-Communists, yet during the interwar period the life of a Hungarian Communist was probably more secure in Horthy's Hungary than Stalin's Russia. After the "White Terror" of 1919–1920, very few political executions took place in Hungary. Of course, active Communists were hounded by the police, and some, like Mátyás Rákosi, spent many years in Horthy's prisons. Yet, Rákosi survived to become the leading Communist in postwar Hungary; by contrast, many Hungarian and other East European Communists perished during the 1930s in Stalin's purges. Horthy's bitter hatred of communism, his "bolshevism on the brain," struck many of his contemporaries as obsessive. Yet during the Cold War that developed in the decades after World War II, many Western statesmen were to echo Horthy's words condemning the "evil Soviet Empire." During his lifetime Horthy's prediction that the Soviet Union would never last and would eventually have to be broken down into its constituent parts seemed to be hopelessly unrealistic. However, within fifty years of the ignominious end of his career in 1944, Horthy was apparently vindicated by the totally unexpected collapse of Communist regimes in Eastern Europe.

Toward the end of his long career Admiral Horthy was tempted for a time by the idea of having his son István succeed him as regent and thereby laying the foundation for a "Horthy dynasty." In large part this reflected Horthy's intense devotion to his family and his uncritical admiration of his elder son. However, the Regent's initiative dovetailed with his strategy for combating the radical right-wingers, since, given the European balance of power at the time, there was no other way Horthy could have arranged for an individual with such a pro-Western and anti-German orientation to become Deputy Regent or Prime Minister. Horthy himself, however, was sincere in his frequently repeated assertion that he did not wish to be crowned king. Yet over the years and without any conscious planning on his part, he became for all practical purposes a constitutional monarch, one might say the last king of Hungary. Like many successful monarchs, he became a symbol of authority and a link with a more glorious national past. Perhaps he satisfied a certain yearning among Hungarians for a return to a time when kings really did ride on horseback and Hungarians dominated the Danubian Basin. Although he consistently sought and obtained an extension of his powers, Horthy rarely made use of this power and always observed constitutional procedures. He carried out his responsibilities in a dignified and dutiful manner, and put his modest talents unreservedly at the service of his country. When the European crisis deepened in the late 1930s and war came, Horthy rejected any suggestion that he flee and set up a government in exile. To the end he remained the captain who refused to abandon a sinking ship.

Miklós Horthy can be faulted for failing to use his immense power to promote necessary social reforms in Hungary. In his social views he was very much a product of the nineteenth-century gentry class. Once the traditional order had been reestablished in 1920, Horthy had no inclination to tamper with it. He regarded the great disparities in the distribution of wealth as part of the natural order, although he made no objection to the expansion of social welfare measures benefiting the workers. On the other hand, he believed that the peasants understood the need to be deferential to the landowners and he was oblivious to the misery of the "people of the puszta." Yet even on the issue of land reform Horthy in time showed a certain amount of flexibility. His pet project, the Order of Heroes, effected a limited expansion of the class of smallholders. And his interest in even more significant land reform during World War II and in the postwar period suggests that, had he come to power in Hungary as a younger man, he might well have become a cautious advocate of social and economic reform in the countryside.

As the "last king" of Hungary, Horthy faced enormous problems that few of his predecessors in the thousand-year history of the Kingdom of Hungary had ever confronted. Interwar Hungary had to balance precariously between the two most sinister totalitarian regimes of world history. In the ultimately hopeless task of preserving Hungarian independence while at the same time working toward a revision of the hated Treaty of Trianon, Horthy at times tilted dangerously toward Nazi Germany. But in the end he always shrank from the employment of totalitarian methods in

Hungary. Several times in the late 1930s and at any point in World War II, Horthy could have used his immense power and authority to establish a pro-German, radical right-wing government in Hungary. So strong was pro-Nazi and anti-Semitic sentiment in the civil service, officer corps, and Parliament that a decision by Horthy in 1942 or 1943 to accede to the German demand for deportation of the Jews would surely have meant the annihilation of the entire Hungarian Jewish community. But Horthy did not do this, for he believed that "inhumanity is alien to the Hungarian character." A nod of approval from Horthy could have led to the crushing of the Social Democrats and other opposition parties. But he did not give his approval, for he had a fundamental, if sometimes grudging, respect for Hungarian political traditions. It was largely through his influence that in early 1944 Hungary was such an anomaly: an island in the heart of Hitler's Europe where a semblance of the rule of law and a pluralistic society had been preserved in a sea of barbarism. And this was the basis of Horthy's most important legacy to Hungarian history. Though for the most part he did not share their views or approve their objectives, Horthy made it possible for the adherents of democratization, liberalism, parliamentary government, and social reform to maintain a precarious foothold in Hungarian society, so that when the totalitarian tide eventually receded from Hungary, they would be on hand to take part in the rebuilding of the country.

Note on Sources

Whenever a book or article exists in both a Hungarian and a Western language version, the latter is cited. Since in some cases the translated version is garbled or awkward (as, most conspicuously, in *The Confidential Papers of Admiral Horthy*), more readable translations have been provided by the author of this study. When public statements are cited in the text without a footnote, it may be assumed that the source is the contemporary press.

Abbreviations

ADAP	*Akten zur deutschen Auswärtigen Politik*
CPAH	*The Confidential Papers of Admiral Horthy*
DBFP	*Documents on British Foreign Policy*
DDF	*Documents Diplomatiques Français*
DGFP	*Documents on German Foreign Policy*
DIMK	*Diplomáciai iratok Magyarország külpolitikájához*
FO	Foreign Office (London)
FRUS	*Foreign Relations of the United States*
GFM	German Foreign Ministry (Berlin)
HFP	*Hungarian Foreign Policy*
HHWH	*Hungarian History-World History*
HMTI	*Horthy Miklós titkos iratai*
IET	*Iratok az ellenforradalmi történetéhez*
NA	National Archives (Washington, D.C.)
NAM	National Archives Microcopy
NPA	Neues Politisches Archiv (Vienna)
OF	*October Fifteenth*
OL	Országos Levéltár (Budapest)
POG	*Politics of Genocide*
PRO	Public Record Office (London)
USSD	United States State Department (Washington)

Notes

Preface

1. The Hungarian term for the office to which Horthy was elected, *kormányzó*, has traditionally been translated as "regent," and that usage will be employed in this study. However, this is an inadequate rendering in that the Hungarian term has the more general meaning of "governor" and does not imply allegiance to a monarch.

2. Lily Doblhoff, *Horthy Miklós* (Budapest: Athenaeum, 1938). An English language biography, based in part on Doblhoff's, is that of Owen Rutter, *Regent of Hungary. The Authorized Life of Admiral Horthy* (London: Rich and Curran, 1939).

3. Gordon Brook-Shepherd, *The Last Habsburg* (London: Weidenfeld and Nicolson, 1968).

4. Typical of such works were Zoltán Vas, *Horthy* (Budapest: Szépirodalmi, 1975) and István Pintér, *Ki volt Horthy Miklós?* (Budapest: Zrinyi, 1968).

5. Among the most important works of these historians are: Gyula Juhász, *Hungarian Foreign Policy, 1919–1945* (Budapest: Akadémiai, 1979). Cited hereafter as *HFP*); György Ránki, *Unternehmen Margarethe. Die deutsche Besetzung Ungarns* (Vienna: Hermann Böhlaus, 1984); and Ignác Romsics, *Bethlen István. Politikai életrajz* (Budapest: Magyarságkutató Intézet, 1991).

6. C. A. Macartney, *October Fifteenth. A History of Modern Hungary, 1929–1945*, 2nd edit., 2 vols. (Edinburgh: Univ. of Edinburgh, 1961). Cited hereafter as *OF*.

7. Mario Fenyő, *Hitler, Horthy, and Hungary. German-Hungarian Relations, 1941–1944* (New Haven: Yale U. P., 1972); Péter Gosztony, *Miklós von Horthy. Admiral und Reichsverweser* (Göttingen: Musterschmidt, 1973); Randolph L. Braham, *The Politics of Genocide. The Holocaust in Hungary*, 2 vols. (New York: Columbia U. P., 1981). Cited hereafter as *PoG*.

8. Nicholas Horthy, *Memoirs* (New York: Robert Speller, 1957).

9. *The Confidential Papers of Admiral Horthy* (Budapest: Corvina, 1965). Hereafter cited as *CPAH*. Some items of importance from the Horthy archive that were not published in this collection were made available to the author by archivists of the Országos Levéltár (Hungarian State Archives).

10. Miklós Kállay, *Hungarian Premier* (New York: Columbia U. P., 1954).

Chapter One

1. Pál Csaba, "Kenderes, a családi birtok," *Historia*, 12, nos. 5–6 (1990), pp. 12–13. A brief genealogical study of the Horthy family was composed in 1932 and is found in Országos Levéltár (hereafter OL), Horthy Iratai, K565-III-0-7.

2. The school in Sopron is reported to have been one that readily accepted children of gentry families who were not progressing well in other schools. István Pintér, *Ki volt Horthy Miklós?* (Budapest: Zrinyi, 1968), pp. 13–14.

3. Pintér, *Ki volt*, pp. 13–14.

4. Zoltán Vas, *Horthy* (Budapest: Szépirodalmi, 1975), p. 15. Vas also suggests that Francis Joseph wished to encourage more Hungarians to enter military service, and Horthy was thus a kind of "token" Hungarian.

5. For a good description of military training in the Habsburg lands in this era, see Anton Lehár, *Erinnerungen: Gegenrevolution und Restaurationsversuche in Ungarn, 1918–1921* (Munich: R. Oldenbourg, 1973), pp. 26–32; and Gyula Kádár, *A Ludovikától Sopronkőhidáig. Visszaemlékezések* (Budapest: Magvető, 1978), pp. 48–49.

6. For a discussion of the concept of *Ehrennotwehr*, see István Deák, *Beyond Nationalism. A Social and Political History of the Habsburg Officer Corps* (New York: Oxford, 1992), p. 127.

7. Nicholas Horthy, *Memoirs* (New York: Robert Speller, 1957), p. 13.

8. Horthy's four years at the naval academy are recounted in Doblhoff, pp. 29–31. See also Lawrence Sondhaus, "The Austro-Hungarian Naval Officer Corps, 1867–1918," *Austrian History Yearbook*, 24 (1993), pp. 63–66.

9. Adam Wandruszka and Peter Urbanitsch, *Die Habsburgermonarchie, 1848–1918*, Vol. 5: *Die Bewaffnete Macht* (Vienna: V. der Österreichischen Akademie der Wissenschaften, 1987), p. 746.

10. Edgar von Schmidt-Pauli, *Nikolaus von Horthy. Admiral, Volksheld, und Reichsverweser*, 2nd. edit. (Hamburg: P. Toth, 1942), p. 44; Péter Sipos, "A kormányzó," *Historia*, 12, nos. 5–6 (1990), p. 3.

11. Horthy, *Memoirs*, p. 31.

12. Richard Ellman, *James Joyce* (New York: Oxford, 1982), p. 186. Might Horthy have been Joyce's source for the many Hungarian obscenities in *Ullyses*?

13. Vas, pp. 19, 53.

14. Horthy, *Memoirs*, p. 56.

15. Sipos, p. 3.

16. Vas, p. 53; Gosztony, *Miklós von Horthy*, p. 11.

17. Horthy, *Memoirs*, p. 68.

18. John F. Montgomery, *Hungary. The Unwilling Satellite* (New York: Devin-Adair, 1947), p. 41. A photo of Horthy's painting of Francis Joseph is found facing p. 3 of his *Memoirs*.

19. Kálmán Csatho et al., *Horthy Miklós*, 2nd edit. (Budapest: Singer és Wolfner, 1943), p. 218.

20. Horthy, *Memoirs*, p. 49.

21. Gárdos, p. 13; Horthy, *Memoirs*, p. 59.

22. Thomas Sakmyster, "Horthy and the Jews of Hungary," in ed. Richard Frucht, *Labyrinth of Nationalism, Complexities of Diplomacy. Essays in Honor of Barbara and Charles Jelavich*, (Columbus: Slavica, 1992), p. 122.

23. Ernst Rudiger Starhemberg, *Between Hitler and Mussolini* (New York: Harper, 1942), p. 139.

24. Gosztony, p. 14; Rutter, p. 116.

25. Paul G. Halpern, *The Naval War in the Mediterranean, 1914–1918* (Annapolis: Naval Institute Press, 1987), p. 70.

26. Gosztony, p. 15; Horthy, *Memoirs*, pp. 80–86. For the best treatment of the Battle of Otranto, see Halpern, pp. 357–61, where the battle is described as "both a tactical and, to a lesser extent, strategic success for the Austrians." A medical report describing Horthy's wounds and minor gas poisoning is found in OL, Horthy iratai, K569-III-E-3.

27. See, i.a., Vas, pp. 87–127, part of a chapter entitled "The Legend of the Naval Hero."

28. Mark Kerr, *The Navy in my Time* (London: Rich and Cowan, 1933), p. 196.

29. Schmidt-Pauli, p. 113; Vas, 122–23.

30. Glatz, p. 3.

31. Halpern, p. 449.

32. Rutter, p. 131.

33. Richard Georg Plaschka, *Nationalismus, Staatsgewalt, Widerstand* (Vienna: V. fur Geschichte u. Politik, 1985), pp. 344–45.

34. Richard Georg Plaschka et al, *Innere Front. Militärassistenz, Widerstand, und Umsturz in der Donaumonarchie 1918*, 2 vols. (Munich: R. Oldenbourg, 1974), II: 238.

35. Hans Hugo Sokol, *Österreich-Ungarns Seekrieg, 1914–18*, 2 vols. (Vienna: Akademische Druck, 1967), II: 737.

36. For a good firsthand account of the dilemma of the Habsburg officers in late 1918, see Lehár, p. 57.

37. Oscar Jászi, *The Dissolution of the Habsburg Monarchy* (Chicago: Univ. of Chicago, 1929), p. 142.

38. Boriviczény, pp. 13, 16.

39. Boriviczény, p. 16.

40. Paul Ignotus, *Hungary* (New York: Praeger, 1972), p. 145.

41. Horthy, *Memoirs*, p. 99; Rutter, p. 155.

42. Miklós Kozma, *Az összeomlás, 1918–19* (Budapest: Az Athenaeum, 1933), p. 128.

43. József Révay, *Gömbös Gyula élete és politikája* (Budapest: Franklin, 1934), p. 115; Horthy, *Memoirs*, p. 99.

44. Peter Pastor, *Hungary Between Wilson and Lenin: The Hungarian Revolution of 1918–1919 and the Big Three* (Boulder: East European Quarterly, 1976), pp. 126–27; Jászi, pp. 73–81.

45. Nicholas M. Nagy-Talavera, *The Green Shirts and the Others. A History of Fascism in Hungary and Rumania* (Stanford: Hoover Institution, 1970), p. 24.

46. For an excellent treatment of the domestic policies of the Hungarian Soviet Republic, see Bela Kovrig, *Communism in Hungary from Kun to Kádár* (Stanford: Hoover Institution,1979), pp. 44–55.

47. István Deák, "Budapest and the Hungarian Revolutions of 1918–1919," *Slavonic and East European Review*, 46, no. 106 (1968), p. 129.

48. Jászi, p. 136; Deák, pp. 137–38; Ignác Romsics, *A Duna-Tisza köze hatalmipolitikai viszonyai 1918–19-ben* (Budapest: Akadémiai Kiadó, 1982), pp. 36, 78–79.

49. For the "Red Terror," which has not yet been adequately studied, see Nagy-Talavera, pp. 24–25; Kovrig, pp. 50–52; and Dezső Sulyok, *A magyar tragédia* (Newark: by the author, 1954), p. 242.

50. Doblhoff, pp. 198–99; Andrew János, *The Politics of Backwardness in Hungary, 1825–1945* (Princeton: Princeton U.P., 1982), p. 199.

51. Horthy, *Memoirs*, p. 95.

52. Ezra Mendelssohn, *The Jews of East Central Europe between the World Wars* (Bloomington: Indiana U. P., 1983), p. 95.

53. Horthy, *Memoirs*, pp. 99–100.

54. Letter of Prince Lajos Windischgraetz, June 29, 1920, in *The Confidential Papers of Admiral Horthy*, Miklós Szinai and László Szűcs, eds. (Budapest: Corvina, 1965), p. 4. Hereafter cited as *CPAH*.

55. *Shvoy Kálmán titkos naplója és emlékirata, 1918–1945*, ed. Mihály Perneki (Budapest: Kossuth, 1983), pp. 47–48. Hereafter cited as Shvoy, *Diary*; Béla Kelemen, *Adatok a szegedi ellenforradalom és a szegedi kormány történetéhez (1919)* (Szeged: Mars grafikai műintézet, 1923), p. 206; Sipos, p. 3.

56. Seniority is referred to as the determining factor in Horthy's selection in Kádár, p. 114.

57. Kozma, p. 269.

58. Shvoy, *Diary*, p. 50. Several contemporary renderings of Horthy's words of acceptance were recorded. For the most colorful, see Kozma, p. 277. In a short time the story was circulating even among the peasants. Ferenc Nagy, *Ahogy én láttam* (Budapest: Gondolat, 1965), p. 47.

59. Mária Ormos, *Padovától Trianonig, 1918–1920* (Budapest: Kossuth, 1983), pp. 314–16; and Eva Balogh, "The Road to Isolation: Hungary, the Great Powers, and the Successor States, 1919–1920," Ph.D. diss., Yale Univ., 1974, p. 33. See also Leslie C. Tihany, "The French Army and the Rightist Restorations in Hungary, 1918–1919," in *Revolutions and Interventions in Hungary and its Neighboring States, 1918–1919*, ed. Peter Pastor (Boulder: Social Science Monographs, 1988), pp. 388–89.

60. Shvoy, *Diary*, p. 50.

61. Percival Dodge's report, June 17, 1919, United States State Department Records, National Archives, 864.01/19. Hereafter cited as USSD followed by identification number.

62. Kádár, p. 114. For a more iconoclastic view of Horthy in Szeged, see Vas, pp. 178–84.

63. Kelemen, p. 519.

64. Gárdos, p. 26; Jenő Pilch, *Horthy Miklós* (Budapest: Athenaeum, 1929), p. 132.

65. István I. Mócsy, *Hungarian Refugees and Their Impact on Hungary's Domestic Politics, 1918–1921* (New York: Brooklyn College Press, 1983), pp. 112–16.

66. For an authoritative study of István Tisza and his peculiar blend of "liberal tolerance and limited authoritarianism," see Gabor Vermes, *István Tisza. The Liberal Vision and Conservative Statecraft of a Magyar Nationalist* (New York: East European Monographs, 1985).

67. Gyula Gömbös, *Egy magyar vezérkari tiszt biráló feljegyzései a forradalomról és ellenforradalomról* (Budapest: Budapesti Hírlap, 1920), pp. 5–8; Révay, p. 211.

68. Prónay, *Diary*, p. 70.

69. Shvoy, p. 52; Mócsy, p. 116.

70. Lehár, p. 159.

71. On this, see the perceptive comments of George Barany in his essay "Hungary: From Aristocratic to Proletarian Nationalism," in *Nationalism in Eastern Europe*, eds. Peter Sugar and Ivo J. Lederer (Seattle: Univ. of Washington,1969), pp. 290–292.

72. Zadravecz, 117. At a dinner in his honor, Horthy gave a toast to Zadravecz, his first ever in Hungarian. Zadravecz, p. 237.

73. There are several vivid eyewitness accounts of Horthy's speech: Kelemen, p. 335; Kádár, p. 117; Shvoy Diary, p. 51; Zadravecz, p. 239; and Kozma, pp. 303–04.

74. Kádár, p. 117; Kelemen, p. 336; Kozma, p. 325; Gusztáv Gratz, *A forradalmak kora. Magyarország története 1918–1920* (Budapest: Magyar Szemle, 1935), pp., 218–19.

75. Mócsy, p. 124.

76. Kozma, p. 380.

77. Denis Sinor, *History of Hungary* (New York: Praeger, 1959), pp. 140–41.

78. Prónay, pp. 102–03.

Chapter Two

1. Eva Balogh, "The Road to Isolation: Hungary, the Great Powers, and the Successor States, 1919–1920," Ph.D. diss., Yale Univ., 1974, p. 211; Gratz, p. 248.

2. Istvan Pataki, *Az ellenforradalom hadserege, 1919–1921* (Budapest: Zrinyi, 1973), p. 10. Accurate estimates of the number of victims of the "White Terror" are notoriously difficult to make. A recent estimate, probably overstated, suggests that at least 5,000 were killed and 70,000 imprisoned. Ervin Hollós and Vera Lajtai, *Horthy Miklós a fehérek vezére* (Budapest: Kossuth, 1985), p. 266.

3. Prónay, 113. For a detailed treatment of the "White Terror," see Mócsy, pp. 225–65; Hollós, pp. 136–72; and Prónay's own candid account, Prónay, pp. 102–13.

4. Horthy, *Memoirs*, p. 106.

5. Robert Seton-Watson, "Hungary in the Grip of Reaction," *New Europe* (Nov. 27, 1919), pp. 212–13; Horthy, *Memoirs*, pp. 106–07.

6. Prónay, p. 131. As a result of Horthy's support, the commanders of the special detachments denied accusations that they had committed criminal acts. As Prónay said privately at the time: "As soldiers we have only been obeying orders, so we are not murderers." Lehár, p. 111.

7. Lehár, p. 146.

8. Dezső Nemes, ed., *Iratok az ellenforradalom történetéhez* (Budapest: Szikra, 1956), vol. 1, p. 180. Hereafter cited as *IET*.

9. Kozma, p. 371.

10. Mócsy, pp. 143–44.

11. Horthy's directive of August 28, 1919, in *IET*, I: 180–81; Horthy's letter of Sept. 12 to Friedrich, *IET*, I:183–85.

12. Pilch, pp. 244–47.

13. Ferenc Pölöskei, *Hungary after Two Revolutions (1919–1922)* (Budapest: Akadémiai Kiadeo, 1980), p. 37.

14. Sipos, p. 4; Pölöskei, pp. 37–38; Benigna von Krusenstjern, *Die Ungarische Kleinlandwirte-Partei, 1909–1922/1929* (Munich: Trofenik, 1981), p. 140.

15. Ormos, pp. 358, 372.

16. Unpublished portions of diary of General Harry Bandholtz, Nov. 19, 1919, U.S. Army Historical Research Collection, Carlisle Barracks, PA.

17. Col. Yates' report of late September, 1919, in Records of the American Military Mission in Hungary, National Archives Microcopy (NAM) M820, 185/523–24. Hereafter cited as American Military Mission.

18. Unpublished Bandholtz diary, August 30, Sept. 4, 1919. The Hungarian Army numbered approximately 30,000 in mid-October. Balogh, p. 257.

19. In September an American officer, himself a Jew, concluded after a cursory investigation that the reports of the "White Terror" were exaggerated and that law-abiding Jews of Budapest had nothing to fear from Horthy's army. This report is in *Papers Relating to the Foreign Relations of the United States. The Paris Peace Conference, 1919* (Washington: Govt. Printing Office, 1947), 12: 695. Hereafter cited as *FRUS*.

20. Beniczky's account is in *IET*, I: 195–96. See also Pataki, pp. 63–64.

21. Jászi, p. 162; Hollós, p. 157.

22. Prónay, pp. 131–32, 160.

23. Ernő Garami, *Forrongó Magyarország: Emlékezések és tanulságok* (Vienna: Pegazus, 1922), p. 175; Gratz, p. 256.

24. In mid-October Horthy had told a member of the American Military Mission that he intended to put *Népszava* and *Az Est* out of business, leaving only Christian papers in Budapest. American Military Mission, NAM, M820, 189/586.

25. The following is based on the accounts of two of the participants: Garami, pp. 175–78; Varjassy, p. 116. See also Pölöskei, p. 38.

26. Garami, p. 136.

27. Varjassy, p. 116.

28. Balogh, p. 357. Balogh calls the results of the Clerk mission a "victory for Horthy." p. 330.

29. Gosztony, *Nikolaus von Horthy*, pp. 25–26; József Patai, "A fő vezérnél és a kormányzónál. Visszaemlékezés a tízéves jubileum alkamából," *Múlt és Jövő*, (April, 1930), pp. 140–42.

30. Pilch, pp. 327–32.

31. Vargyai, p. 65.

32. In August 1919, Horthy told Lehár, who was a fervent legitimist, that he still got emotional shivers when he heard the Austrian imperial anthem, the "Gott Erhalte." Lehár, p. 123. See also Boroviczény, pp. 46–47.

33. Zadravecz, p. 243.

34. Maxwell H. H. Macartney, *Five Years of European Chaos* (London: Chapman & Hall, 1923), p. 47.

35. The term used by Horthy, *bünös*, means both "guilty" and "sinful." On this see John Lukacs, *Budapest 1900. A Historical Portrait of a City and its Culture* (New York: Weidenfeld & Nicolson, 1988), p. 179.

36. For Horthy's speech, see *Források Budapest multjából*, ed. Ágnes Ságvari (Budapest: Főváros Levéltárának Kiadványa, 1972), III: 21. Also Horthy, *Memoirs*, pp. 104–05.

37. Robert Seton-Watson, "Hungary in the Grip of Reaction," *New Europe*, Nov. 27, 1919, p. 213; Pölöskei, p. 41.

38. "Hungarians Back in Budapest," Nov. 18, 1919, *London Times*.

39. Zadravecz, pp. 100–01; Pilch, pp. 279–80.

40. Prónay, p. 150; American Military Mission, NAM, M820/189/570–1.

41. Clerk's reports are in *Documents on British Foreign Policy, 1919–1939*, ed. E. L. Woodward, First Series (London: Her Majesty's Stationery Office, 1947), II: 444–51; VI: 284, 290. Hereafter cited as *DBFP*.

42. These internment camps, the most notorious of which was in Zalaegerszeg, are estimated to have held as many as 60,000 prisoners at their peak. Mócsy, p. 157.

43. Prónay, p. 149. Horthy had sent Prónay to Austria to investigate the possibility of kidnapping or assassinating Béla Kun and his comrades being held in protective custody. This "special mission" may have been

devised by Horthy to keep the volatile Prónay away from Budapest during November, when any outrages that would alarm the Allies would have to be avoided.

44. *DBFP*, 1/6/291.

45. Protocol of conference of Hungary's political parties, Nov. 17, 1919, Public Record Office (hereafter PRO), London, Foreign Office 371/3517/159121.

46. Elek Karsai, *A budai Sándor-palotában történt, 1919–1941* (Budapest: Táncsics, 1967), p. 27.

47. Vas, p. 443.

48. Bandholtz, p. 297; Vas, pp. 448–49.

49. Miklós Szinai, *Ki lesz a kormányzó? A Somogyi-Bacsó gyilkosság hátere* (Budapest: Kossuth, 1988), p. 36; Lehár, pp. 148–49; Vargyai, pp. 264–303.

50. Memorandum from Hungarian Supreme Command, Dec. 26, 1919, American Military Mission, NAM, M820/189/616–26.

51. Report of General Reginald Gorton of Jan. 9, 1920, PRO, FO371/3518/173953.

52. In his report of Jan. 9 to the Foreign Office, Hohler suggested that a military dictatorship under Horthy would "really tend to the safety of the country and the preservation of order," although Horthy would probably refuse the task unless he was sure of the approval of the Peace Conference. *DBFP*, 1/ 6/412.

53. Horthy, *Memoirs*, p. 110.

54. Prónay, pp. 159–60; Lehár, p. 159; Vas, p. 455.

55. Miklós Szinai points out that this was a distorted interpretation of the agreement with Sir George Clerk. Szinai, *Ki lesz*, p. 37.

56. Nagy-Talavera, p. 53; Pölöskei, p. 69; Ignác Romsics, *Ellenforradalom és konszolidáció. A Horthy-rendszer első évtizede* (Budapest: Gondolat, 1980), p. 85.

57. For a sample of such articles, see Györgyi Markovits, ed., *Magyar pokol. A magyarországi fehérterror betiltott és üldözött kiadványok tükrében,* (Budapest: Magvető, 1964).

58. Sulyok, p. 28. In reference to Horthy's conduct in Kecskemét, one moderate officer noted in his diary: "If I hadn't seen all of this myself, I wouldn't have believed it." Shvoy, p. 62.

59. Pataki, p. 71. Horthy had been given a memorandum by István Bárczy in which the crimes and excesses of the Héjjas detachment were described, but he apparently did not believe such accusations, or perhaps did not even read the document. Vas, pp. 491–92.

60. *Bethlen István titkos iratai*, eds. Miklós Szinai and László Szűcs (Budapest: Kossuth, 1972), p. 9. Hereafter cited as *Bethlen Papers*.

61. In his memoirs Horthy gave a totally misleading account of his election as regent. For example, he stated that he hoped that Apponyi, "one of the worthiest and most brilliant figures in our public life," would be elected. Horthy, *Memoirs*, pp. 110–11.

62. Prónay, p. 171.

63. Ernő Gergely and Pál Schönwald, *A Somogyi-Bacsó gyilkosság*, pp. 106, 181–82; *IET*, vol. 1, p. 253.

64. During the Communist era Hungarian historians generally branded Horthy as guilty of murder. For example, Ernő Gergely (p. 106) concluded that Horthy "pronounced Béla Somogyi's death sentence." In a more recent study, however, Miklós Szinai argues convincingly that Horthy was probably not the person who gave the final impetus to the assassinations. Szinai, *Ki lesz*, p. 19. Still persuasive is C. A. Macartney's suggestion that Horthy's guilt was similar to that of Henry II's in the death of Thomas à Becket. Macartney, *October Fifteenth. A History of Modern Hungary, 1929–1945*, 2nd edit. (Edinburgh: Edinburgh U.P., 1961), I: 494. Cited hereafter as *OF*.

65. Prónay, p. 171.

66. See Horthy's explanations to the American envoy, Grant Smith, in the latter's report of Feb. 24, 1920, NAM, M708/3/596.

67. Gergely, p. 32; *IET*/1/251–53; András Fehér, *A Magyarországi Szociálpolitika Párt és az ellenforradalmi rendszer 1919 Augusztus-1921* (Budapest: Akadémiai Kiadó, 1969), pp. 111–12.

68. A good summary of the powers of the regent is provided in Macartney, *OF*, I: 49–51.

69. Karsai, *A budai*, p. 40.

70. Grant Smith's report, Feb. 24, 1920, NAM, M708/3/596.

71. Grant Smith's report, March 5, 1920, NAM, M708/4/4.

72. Two other candidates received one vote each, and one ballot, thought to be Apponyi's, was left blank. Vargyai, p. 298. For the view that the majority of the parliamentary delegates favored Apponyi, see Ervin Hollós, *Horthy Miklós a fehérek vezére* (Budapest: Kossuth, 1985), p. 249.

73. Vargyai, pp. 299–300; Grant Smith's report of March 1, 1920, NAM, M708/13/222.

74. Vargyai, pp. 300–01.

75. Kádár, p. 137; Romsics, p. 88; Lehár, p. 152.

76. Prónay, p. 179.

Chapter Three

1. István Deák, "Hungary," in *The European Right: A Historical Profile*, ed. Hans Rogger and Eugen Weber (Berkeley: Univ. of California, 1965), p. 373.

2. See, i.a., Grant Smith's report of July 7, 1920, NAM, M708/4/324.

3. In November 1919, Lehár jotted in his diary: "Horthy apparently acts only in ways suggested by his wirepullers. To what extent he has an orientation, his own orientation, to what extent he is only being misused by others, only the future will tell." Lehár, p. 135.

4. Charles von Werkmann, *The Tragedy of Charles of Habsburg* (London: Philip Allan, 1924), pp. 178–79.

5. Boroviczény, pp. 77–78; *CPAH*, pp. 14–16.

6. In this vein Gordon Brook-Shepherd has written that "once the Regent settled down in the gilt and brocade chairs on the Buda hill, his ambitions quickened." Brook-Shepherd, p. 254.

7. Boroviczény, p. 77; Lehár, p. 155; Prónay, p. 180.

8. Many of these plans were first articulated in a memorandum of October 28, 1919, which was signed by Horthy but not likely composed by him. *IET*, I/200–202.

9. See Horthy's comments to General Massow, a visiting German officer, as recorded in NAM, T-120, L532/L155099-100.

10. Lehár, pp. 126, 160.

11. Bruno Thoss, *Der Ludendorff-Kreis, 1919–1923. München als Zentrum der mitteleuropäischen Gegenrevolution zwischen Revolution und Hitler-Putsch* (Munich: Stadtarchiv München, 1977), p. 398.

12. Trebitsch-Lincoln was a Hungarian Jew whose chameleon-like character and career are treated in Bernard Wasserstein, *The Secret Lives of Trebitsch Lincoln* (New Haven: Yale, 1988).

13. The following is based on Elek Karsai, ed., *Számjeltávirat valamennyi magyar királyi követségnek* (Budapest: Táncsics, 1969), pp. 60–62; and Thoss, pp. 396–99.

14. For the attitude of Teleki and Kánya, see the report of Theodor Hornbostel, Austrian chargé d'affaires in Budapest, August 6, 1920, Austrian State Archives, Neues Politisches Archiv, K883/567-70, hereafter cited as NPA, followed by carton and item number. See also Ferenc Boros, *Magyarcsehszlovák kapcsolatok, 1918–1921-ben* (Budapest: Akadémiai, 1970), p. 181.

15. Zadravecz, p. 135; Karsai, *Számjeltávirat*, pp. 108–09.

16. Horthy, *CPAH*, p. 26; Wasserstein, pp. 167–68; Thoss, p. 399.

17. Thoss, p. 399; Karsai, *Számjeltávirat*, p. 73.

18. Prónay, p. 216; Karsai, *Számjeltávirat*, pp. 74–78. Horthy requested that the recipients destroy his letter. Thus, no copy of his letter to Ludendorff has survived.

19. *CPAH*, pp. 26–28.

20. Wasserstein, pp. 175–97. Prónay had been hostile to Trebitsch-Lincoln from the start, arguing that no Jew could be trusted. Prónay, pp. 200–01. Horthy seems not to have shared this skepticism toward Trebitsch-Lincoln.

21. Report of Sir George Clerk, Oct. 28. 1920, PRO, FO371/4841/C9951/7208/18; also C11957/7208/18, in which Clerk describes the case against Horthy as "pretty black."

22. Vargyai, pp. 64–69; Boros, p. 177; Lehár, pp. 163–64.

23. Karsai, *Számjeltávirat*, pp. 112–13.

24. Loránt Tilkovszky, *Teleki Pál. Legenda és valóság* (Budapest: Kossuth, 1969), p. 69.

25. Prónay, p. 219.

26. Hohler's report of Jan. 6, 1920, *DBFP*, 1/6/410. See also Horthy's

comments to Athelstan Johnson in the latter's report of Sept. 14, 1920, PRO, FO371/C6776/5/21.

27. Gyula Juhász, *Hungarian Foreign Policy, 1919–1945* (Budapest: Akadémiai, 1979), pp. 54–55; Magda Ádám, "France and Hungary at the Beginning of the 1920's," in *Total War and Peacemaking: A Case Study of Trianon*, eds. Béla Király et al. (New York: Brooklyn College, 1982), pp. 145–82.

28. Lehár, P. 159. Horthy explained to the German General Massow that the Hungarians would have to be smarter than the French and "rescue ourselves from this desperate situation without being dependent on them." GFM, NAM T120/L532/L155099.

29. Ádám, "France and Hungary," pp. 151–53; Kalervo Hovi, *Alliance de revers. Stabilization of France's Alliance Policies in East Central Europe, 1919–1921* (Turku: Turun Yliopisto, 1984), p. 58.

30. Horthy had written to Pilsudski to express his "profound sympathy and affection" for the Poles. Pilsudski reciprocated these sentiments, but was hardly in the position to provide military assistance to deliver Slovakia to the Hungarians. See Horthy's letter of June 6, 1920, Francis Deák and Dezső Újváry, eds. *Papers and Documents Relating to the Foreign Relations of Hungary*, 2 vols. (Budapest: Royal Hungarian University, 1939, 1946), I: 321.

31. Hohler's report, Nov. 7, 1920, *DBFP*, 1/12/268.

32. Shvoy, p. 63.

33. Gratz, *A forradalmak kora*, p. 317.

34. *Papers and Documents*, I: 889; Sulyok, p. 286.

35. Tilkovszky, p. 63.

36. The delegation, which was in Hungary in May 1920, concluded that the terror was anti-Communist rather than anti-Semitic in nature and that the government could not control it. However neither the government nor the Regent was accused of direct complicity in atrocities. Joint Labour Delegation for Hungary, ed., *Report on the White Terror in Hungary* (London: Trade Union Council and the Labour Party, 1920), pp. 23–24.

37. When told by members of the British Labour Delegation that they had convincing evidence that Prónay, Héjjas, and Ostenburg were guilty of outrages, Horthy blithely replied that this could not be true, since these were his "best officers." *Ibid.*

38. Pataki, pp. 210–12; Pölöskei, p. 92.

39. Grant Smith's report of July 7, 1920, NAM, M708/4/324.

40. Ignác Romsics, *Bethlen István. Politikai életrajz* (Budapest: Magyarságkutató Intézet, 1991), pp. 108–09.

41. Prónay, pp. 165, 169, 196; Zadravecz, p. 134.

42. Hohler's report of July 27, 1923, PRO, FO371/C13048/54/21.

43. Prónay, pp. 225–26.

44. Prónay, pp. 226–27.

45. Lehár tried to explain why such an operation would be logistically im-

possible, but Horthy insisted he would definitely be able to pull it off. Lehár may have had some impact when he then pointed out that such methods were as reprehensible as the poisoning of wells. Lehár, pp. 167–68.

46. *Papers and Documents*, II: 240.

47. Juhász, *HFP*, pp. 57–58; Boros, pp. 284–85.

48. Lehár, p. 169. Similarly, for a time in late 1920 Horthy became enthusiastic about prospects for recovering Transylvania in cooperation with Turkey under Enver Pasha, "an old friend from my Constantinople days." Zadravecz, p. 246.

49. Horthy, *Memoirs*, p. 109.

50. Andrew C. Janos, *The Political Backwardness of Hungary, 1825–1945* (Princeton: Princeton U.P., 1982), p. 204.

51. Ezra Mendelsohn, *The Jews of East Central Europe between the World Wars* (Bloomington: Indiana U.P., 1983), p. 101.

52. Tilkovszky, p. 78.

53. Mendelsohn, p. 105; Nathaniel Katzburg, *Hungary and the Jews. Policy and Legislation, 1920–1943* (Jerusalem: Bar-Ilan, 1981), pp. 60–64.

54. 34.5 percent of all peasant households now owned land, in effect a doubling of the number of smallholders. Joseph Held, ed., *The Modernization of Agriculture: Rural Transformation in Hungary, 1848–1975* (Boulder: East European Monographs, 1980), pp. 217–19; See also Gyula Borbándi, *Der ungarische Populismus* (Mainz: v. Hase & Koehler, 1976), p. 491.

55. Horthy, *Memoirs*, p. 109.

56. For the *Vitézi Rend*, see Pölöskei, pp. 96–98; Gosztony, *Miklós von Horthy*, pp. 54–55; Janos, pp. 252–53; Vas, pp. 622–23; Horthy, *Memoirs*, p. 132.

57. Pölöskei, p. 98; Janos, p. 252.

58. See the report of Athelstan Johnson, Sept. 14, 1920, PRO, FO371/4854/753.

59. See, for example, his comments as recorded in Lehár, pp. 163, 169.

60. Lehár, pp. 163, 167. Horthy told Lehár that only four other people knew of his plan.

61. Athelstan Johnson's report, July 12, 1920, *DBFP*, 1/12/188. For an earlier meeting between Horthy and Miakits, see András Fehér, *A Magyarországi Szocialpolitika Párt és az ellenforradalmi rendszer 1919 augusztus-1921* (Budapest: Akadémiai, 1969), pp. 125–26.

62. The American Minister in Budapest, Grant-Smith, reported his conviction that "the number of Jews who have been made away with has been grossly exaggerated." Report of March 12, 1920, NA, M708/20/31.

63. Athelstan Johnson's report, Oct. 11, 1920, PRO, FO371/4861/C9029/283/21.

64. Beneš's comments were recorded in a report of the Austrian chargé d' affaires in Prague on Sept. 8, 1920, NPA, K882/2684.

65. *CPAH*, pp. 17–18.

66. Zadravecz, p. 208.

67. *Számjeltávirat*, p. 128.

68. Romsics, *Bethlen István*, p. 126; Pölöskei, p. 102.

69. On one occasion Horthy tried to convince Lehár that Charles had

released him (Horthy) from his oath. But from his later actions it is clear that Horthy did not really believe this. Lehár, p. 167.

70. Lehár, p. 162.

71. Zadravecz, p. 206. Horthy seems to have assumed, erroneously, that the delegation was intent on offering him the crown. Lehár, p. 167.

72. Reports of Athelstan Johnson on Nov. 7, 1920, *DBFP*, 1/12/268; and Dec. 8, 1920, PRO, FO371/C13698/283/21. See also Mária Ormos, *"Soha, amig élek!" Az utolsó koronás Habsburg puccskisérletei 1921-ben* (Budapest: Pannónia, 1990), pp. 25–27.

73. Following in a tradition established by such legitimists as Karl Werkmann and Aladár Boroviczény in their memoirs, Gordon Brook-Shepherd surely oversimplified the matter when he wrote: "Like many a political adventurer before and after him, Horthy . . . so identified ambition with patriotism, egoism with idealism, and even luxury with sacrifice that he probably no longer knew them apart." Brook-Shepherd, p. 238. Some Marxist historians adopted a similar position. See Dezső Nemes, *Az ellenforradalom története Magyarországon, 1919–1921* (Budapest: Akadémiai, 1962), p. 448. For a contrasting view more favorable to Horthy, see Gosztony, *Miklós von Horthy*, pp. 37–41.

74. Lehár, p. 164.

75. *CPAH*, pp. 29–31.

76. See Charles's letter of December 14, 1920, to Cardinal Csernoch, Hungary's Prince Primate, in which he dismissed as irrelevant the anti-Habsburg declarations made by the Entente representatives in Budapest and asserted that the policy of the great powers had not yet been clarified. *Számjeltávirat*, pp. 137–38.

Chapter Four

1. The evidence suggests that Briand deviated from his government's official policy and pursued a private line of diplomacy aimed at restoring the Habsburg monarchy in Budapest and Vienna. See Brook-Shepherd, p. 259; Magda Ádám, "A két királypuccs és a kisantant," *Történelmi Szemle*, no. 4 (1982), pp. 681–83; Lajos Windischgraetz, *My Adventures and Misadventures* (London: Barrie and Rockliff, 1965), pp. 119–20; Mária Ormos, *"Soha, amig élek!"* pp. 43–50.

2. Lehár, p. 177.

3. A historian otherwise sympathetic to Charles suggests that his attitude to the perils of a restoration attempt was one of "remarkable blindness." Heinz Rieder, *Kaiser Karl. Der letzte Monarch Österreich-Ungarns, 1887–1922* (Munich: Callwey, 1981), p. 310.

4. Karl Werkmann, *Aus Kaiser Karls Nachlass* (Munich: Verlag für Kultur-Politik), p. 39. Cited hereafter as Werkmann, *Nachlass*. See also Lehár, p. 180.

5. Lehár, p. 181.

6. Zadravecz, p. 211.

7. Prónay, p. 243; Hohler's report, March 29, 1921, PRO, FO371/

6102/C6851/180/21. The following reconstruction of the confrontation between Charles and Horthy is based on the accounts, sometimes conflicting, that were later given by the two protagonists. The memoirs of Charles, dictated to his secretary, Karl Werkmann, and published posthumously in 1924 under the title *Aus Kaiser Karls Nachlass*, are an invaluable source. However, there is reason to suspect that Werkmann or Queen Zita may have edited the memoirs in some places to sharpen the indictment against Horthy. Charles also gave a description of his encounter to Boroviczény (pp. 116–19) and Lehár (p. 183). The account in Horthy's memoirs, published many years later, is important only for certain minor details. More significant are his contemporary comments to Prónay (pp. 243–45), Boroviczény (pp. 172–73), and Zadravecz (pp. 211–12). Also valuable is an article in *The Times* of London, April 16, 1924, entitled "A Bid for the Throne. King Charles and Hungary. The Regent's Case," which is based in part on interviews with Horthy and Bethlen. See also Bruno Brehm, *Weder Kaiser noch König. Der Untergang der Habsburgischen Monarchie* (Munich: R. Piper, 1933), pp. 390–428.

8. Prónay, p. 243.

9. Zadravecz, p. 211.

10. Werkmann, *Nachlass*, p. 52.

11. Charles had forgotten that only Catholics were eligible for the Order of the Golden Fleece. According to Werkmann (pp. 45–46), Horthy, in his inordinate greed and vanity, was the one to take the initiative in demanding from Charles some tangible rewards for his cooperation in the restoration. Charles is depicted as responding to Horthy's demands with a feeling of deep physical revulsion. However, this version of the event seems unlikely, since Charles had planned beforehand to offer Horthy these inducements and had even brought along the appropriate medals with him to Budapest. See Edgar von Schmidt-Pauli, *Nikolaus von Horthy. Admiral, Volksheld, und Reichsverweser* (Hamburg: I.P. Toth, 1942), pp. 187–89.

12. Lehár, p. 210.

13. Prónay, p. 244; Werkmann, *Nachlass*, p. 52.

14. Prónay, p. 172; Zadravecz, p. 212. Werkmann (*Nachlass*, p. 53) has Horthy suggesting a postponement of the restoration for ten years.

15. Zadravecz, p. 213.

16. Werkmann, *Nachlass*, p. 57; Schmidt-Pauli, p. 185.

17. Werkmann, *Nachlass*, p. 57; Brook-Shepherd, p. 268.

18. Werkmann, *Nachlass*, p. 59.

19. Zadravecz, p. 212.

20. Boroviczény, pp. 119, 173.

21. Prónay, p. 243.

22. Windischgraetz, p. 121.

23. Lehár, pp. 184–85. Since Horthy later vigorously denied that he had sent this telegram, it may have been inspired by Gömbös or some official in the General Staff. See *The Times*, April 16, 1924, p. 16.

24. Lehár, p. 185.

25. Lehár, p. 186; Werkmann, *Nachlass*, p. 82. The Hughes telegraph system made possible the rapid exchange of telegraphic messages dictated by the two communicating parties.

26. *The Times*, April 16, 1924, p. 16.

27. Lehár, p. 190; Werkmann, *Nachlass*, pp. 82–83.

28. In accounts sympathetic to Charles, Horthy is accused of violating a promise of confidentiality by disclosing to the Entente envoys the fact that Charles had spoken of private support from Briand. Boroviczény, p. 186; Brook-Shepherd, p. 269.

29. Ádám, "A két királypuccs," p. 682; Henry Bogdan, *La question royale en Hongrie au lendemain de la Premiere Guerre mondiale* (Louvain: Institut de recherches de l'Europe Centrale, 1979), pp. 36–37; and Hovi, p. 114.

30. Hohler's report, March 29, 1921, PRO, FO371/6102/C6851/180/21; and *DBFP*, 1/22/66.

31. Ádám, "A két királypuccs," p. 674.

32. Lehár, p. 195; Hohler's report, March 29, 1921, *DBFP*, 1/22/66.

33. Lehár, p. 195.

34. *The Times*, April 16, 1924, p. 16.

35. Lehár, pp. 201–02.

36. On April 2 Eduard Beneš spoke of a possible Czechoslovak march on Budapest with five divisions. Bogdan, pp. 37–38; Ádám, "A két királypuccs," pp. 676–77.

37. *IET*, 1/404; Rieder, p. 326.

38. Zadravecz, p. 213.

39. *Számjeltávirat*, p. 190.

40. Werkmann, *Nachlass*, pp. 113–14; Emilio Vasari, *Ein Königsdrama im Schatten Hitlers* (Vienna: Europa Verlag, 1968), p. 85.

41. *Számjeltávirat*, p. 195.

42. Historians sympathetic to the Habsburgs have been unanimous in perpetuating this hostile view of Admiral Horthy. Thus one historian has written: "There is no doubt that it was Horthy, and he alone, who caused the failure of Charles's attempt." Emilio Vasári, p. 81. For an account more favorable to Horthy, see Gosztony, *Miklós von Horthy*, pp. 38–39.

43. Sándor Hegedűs, *Az utolsó trónfosztás* (Budapest: Kossuth, 1970), pp. 154–55.

44. The Austrian envoy in Budapest, Hans Cnobloch, reported that he and most other diplomats in Budapest believed that Horthy's position had been noticeably strengthened by his tactful conduct in a difficult situation. Cnobloch's report of April 2, 1921, NPA, K17/1331.

45. *DBFP*, 1/22/98.

46. Prónay, p. 221.

47. Romsics, *Bethlen István*, p. 118.

48. Miklós Surányi, *Bethlen. Történetpolitikai tanulmányok* (Budapest: Singer és Wolfner, 1927), pp. 17–18. In a more recent study the suggestion is made that this story is apocryphal. Romsics, *Bethlen István*, p. 204.

49. *IET*, 2/23–28; Romsics, *Bethlen István*, p. 115.
50. Statement of Béla Kovrig in letter of July 6, 1955, in Macartney Archive, All Souls College, Oxford University. Referred to hereafter as Macartney Archive.
51. Horthy had privately alluded to this plan already in late 1920. Lehár, pp. 166–67.
52. Romsics, *Bethlen István*, pp. 115–16.
53. Horthy's attitude may have been affected by his wife, who also had the greatest admiration for Count Bethlen. Zadravecz, p. 214.
54. Prónay, pp. 319–20.
55. For good analyses of this strategy, see Romscis, *Bethlen István*, pp. 133–34; *Bethlen Papers*, pp. 14–16; and William M. Batkay, *Authoritarian Politics in a Transitional State. István Bethlen and the Unified Party in Hungary, 1919–1926* (New York: East European Quarterly, 1982), pp. 24–27.
56. Lehár, pp. 213–14. On April 19 Horthy told Boroviczény that someday, perhaps in ten years, His Majesty would realize that he had done him an injustice. Boroviczény, pp. 173–74; Zadravecz, p. 213.
57. *Számjeltávirat*, p. 210.
58. Boroviczény, pp. 240–41; Somogyi, p. 155.
59. *Számjeltávirat*, pp. 210–11. The text of the letter is in Werkmann, *Nachlass*, pp. 250–53.
60. Boroviczény, p. 245.
61. Boroviczény, p. 245; *Számjeltávirat*, pp. 219–21; Brook-Shepherd, p. 282; Prónay, p. 336; Lehár, p. 268.
62. The following is based on Prónay, p. 317; Zadravecz, pp. 134–35, 249.
63. Zadravecz, p. 249.
64. Prónay, pp. 262–65.
65. Katalin Soós, *Burgenland az európai politikában (1918–1921)* (Budapest: Akadémiai, 1971), pp. 136–38. See the report of the Austrian chargé d'affaires in Budapest, April 26, 1921, NPA, K19/1773.
66. Romsics, *Bethlen István*, pp. 134–35; Boroviczény, pp. 359–61.
67. Ormos, *Soha*, pp. 100–01; Boroviczény, p. 255.
68. Boroviczény, p. 258.
69. An American officer in Sopron witnessed this event. See NAM, M708/15/250. See also Hegedűs, p. 164.
70. Brook-Shepherd, p. 189.
71. *Számjeltávirat*, p. 235.
72. Zoltán Speidl, "A legitimista-szabad király-választó harc és a 'nemzeti hadsereg' (1919–1921)" *Hadtörténelmi Közlemények*, 18, no. 2 (1971), p. 310.
73. Hegedűs, p. 166.
74. *Számjeltávirat*, p. 244.
75. Ádám, "A két királypuccs," p. 688.
76. Ádám, "A két királypuccs," p. 688; *Számjeltávirat*, p. 235.
77. *Számjeltávirat*, p. 239.

78. Hohler's report, Oct. 22, 1921, PRO, FO371/6105/C20207/180/21; *Számjeltávirat*, pp. 240–41.
79. Hohler's report, Oct. 23, 1921, PRO, FO371/6105/C20165/180/21.
80. Boroviczény, p. 300.
81. Andor Ladányi, *Az egyetemi ifjúság az ellenforradalom első éveiben* (Budapest: Akadémiai, 1979), p. 217.
82. *Számjeltávirat*, pp. 230, 246.
83. Ladányi, pp. 219–20; Révay, p. 237; Boroviczény, p. 302; report of Grant-Smith, Oct. 31, 1921, NAM, M708/14/382.
84. Hohler's report, Oct. 23, 1921, PRO, FO371/6106/C20324/180/21; *Számjeltávirat*, p. 246; Lehár, pp. 222–23.
85. Fehér, p. 187; *Számjeltávirat*, p. 249.
86. Hohler's report, *DBFP*, 1/22/467–8.
87. Lajos Kerekes, "A Habsburg-restaurációs kisérletek és az osztrák-magyar viszony 1921-ben," *Századok*, 110, no. 1 (1976), p. 35.
88. Brook-Shepherd, p. 296.
89. *Számjeltávirat*, p. 252.
90. Brook-Shepherd, p. 297; Boroviczény, pp. 311–12.
91. Ormos, *Soha*, pp. 123–25, pp. 130–31, 134–48. Also see Beneš's statements in PRO, FO371/6106/C20367/180/21 and *DBFP*, 1/22/456–57.
92. Ádám, "A két királypuccs," p. 700; Hohler's report, Oct. 26, 1921, PRO, FO371/6106/C20584/180/21.
93. Hohler's report, Oct. 29, 1921, *DBFP*, 1/22/504–05.
94. Hohler's reports of Oct. 31 and Nov. 1, 1921, PRO, FO371/6108/C20905/C20907/21.
95. Zadravecz, pp. 174–75; Prónay, p. 118.

Chapter Five

1. Boroviczény, p. 353.
2. The Hungarian émigrés were particularly disheartened by Beneš's unwillingness to take military action against Hungary. One of them, Lajos Biró, complained that "the Little Entente seems to regard Horthy as preferable to a Hungarian democracy." Nagy, p. 74.
3. Zadravecz, p. 227.
4. Romsics, *Bethlen István*, pp. 143–45.
5. Fehér, pp. 187–88; Pölöskei, pp. 127–28.
6. Horthy's comments as recorded by Col. Gossett of the Inter-Allied Military Commission, Oct. 18, 1921, PRO, FO371/6115/C20229/182/21; and by Thomas Hohler, March 12, 1924, PRO, FO371/9902/C4501/21/21.
7. Romsics, *Bethlen István*, pp. 145–47. One historian notes that compared to pre-1918 conditions Bethlen's franchise could actually be regarded as "a relatively progressive achievement." William M. Batkay, *Authoritarian Politics in a Transitional State. István Bethlen and the United Party in Hungary, 1921–1926* (Boulder: East European Quarterly, 1982), p. 55.

8. The "Party of Unity" was to undergo numerous name changes over the years. Henceforth it will be referred to as the government party.

9. Joseph Rothschild, *East Central Europe between the Two World Wars* (Seattle: University of Washington, 1974), p. 160.

10. István Bethlen, *Bethlen István beszédei és irásai* (Budapest: Génius, 1933), I, pp. 156–68. Cited hereafter as *Bethlen Speeches*.

11. Report of General Csáky, May 21, 1921, *Bethlen Papers*, pp. 77–78.

12. When asked to free Iván Héjjas, who had been imprisoned because of atrocities committed during the "White Terror," Bethlen refused: "Just as I will not tolerate destructive activities, I will also not tolerate arbitrary, illegal acts done from patriotic motives." Surányi, p. 141.

13. It may be, as C.A. Macartney suggested, that Bethlen subscribed to "a quiet anti-Semitism," but in public life he was one of the most outspoken critics of the anti-Semites. Macartney, *OF*, I:38. See also Romsics, *Bethlen István*, p. 156 and Pándi, p. 38.

14. Mócsy, p. 136; Erős, p. 122; Romsics, pp. 163–68.

15. Unpublished memoirs of György Barcza, p. 331. The papers of Barcza, a Hungarian diplomat, are held in the Hoover Institution Archives.

16. Letter of Béla Kovrig to C.A. Macartney, July 6, 1951, Macartney Archive.

17. Zadravecz, p. 247.

18. Zadravecz, p. 258.

19. Zadravecz, pp. 247, 257–58; Kádár, p. 219.

20. *IET*, 2/104–5.

21. Batkay, p. 73.

22. *IET*, 2/105, 329.

23. Horthy had apparently learned through emissaries that the Fascists were eager for cooperation with Hungary and were prepared to help with armaments shipments. Zadravecz, p. 247.

24. Romsics, *Bethlen István*, p. 159

25. Miklós Kozma's account of a conversation with Horthy, Aug. 23, 1923, *IET*, 2/325.

26. *Ibid.*

27. On this see Thoss, pp. 472–74; Kurt G. W. Lüdecke, *I Knew Hitler* (New York: Scribner's, 1937), pp. 139–40; and the reports from the Austrian Legation, which was well informed on the activities of the radical right-wing conspirators. See especially Hornbostel's report of Sept. 1, 1923, NPA, K8888/154–161/2333.

28. *IET*, 2/330–31.

29. Ulain's memo is in *IET*, 2/329–30.

30. *Bethlen Papers*, pp. 170–71.

31. Macartney, *OF*, I: 62–63; Mócsy, pp. 140–41.

32. I. T. Berend and G. Ránki, *Hungary. A Century of Economic Development* (New York: Barnes and Nobles, 1974), pp. 105–10. Joseph Rothschild (p. 169) concludes that "Hungary's rulers invited her exploitation

and maximized her vulnerability by soliciting foreign credits that were too high relative to the current productive capacity of her economy—a capacity kept limited by sociopolitical considerations."

33. Marginal note of M.W. Lampson in March, 1924 on PRO, FO371/9902/C4501/21/21. See also Nagy, pp. 82–83.

34. György Markovits, *Magyar pokol. A magyarországi fehérterror betiltott és üldözött kiadványok tükrében* (Budapest: Magvető, 1964), pp. 92–113.

35. Pándi, p. 136.

36. For the forged francs scandal, see Romsics, *Bethlen István*, pp. 169–72, Nagy, pp. 88–89, and the colorful account in Paul Ignotus, *Hungary* (New York: Praeger, 1972), pp. 162–63.

37. Romsics, *Ellenforradalom*, pp. 199–200.

38. *CPAH*, pp. 39–42.

39. As possible successors Bethlen mentioned Count Klébelsberg, the Minister of Culture, Count Hadik, Béla Scitovszky, József Vass, and Count Gyula Károlyi, all of whom he deemed "more or less suitable for the role." *CPAH*, p. 41.

40. Romsics, *Ellenforradalom*, p. 203.

41. Macartney, *OF*, I: 69. Andrew Janos points out that in 1929 Hungarian workers had a larger share of GNP than their counterparts in Germany or even Great Britain, although in absolute terms they of course remained substantially behind. Janos, pp. 238–39.

42. Miklós Surányi, *Bethlen. Történetpolitikai tanulmányok* (Budapest: Singer és Wolfner, 1927), p. 140; Romsics, *Ellenforradalom*, pp. 123–24.

43. Horthy, *Memoirs*, p. 127.

44. *CPAH*, pp. 36–39.

45. Karsai, *A budai vár*, p. 180.

46. Nicholas Roosevelt, *A Front Row Seat* (Norman: Oklahoma U.P., 1953), p. 192.

47. A notable exception was an American left-wing writer, Eugene Bagger, who sarcastically described Horthy as "Turanian Khan who speaks with a German accent, Count Salm's friend and protector, Calvinist who renounced his faith, Admiral who abandoned his ship, Regent who betrayed his King." Eugene Bagger, *Eminent Europeans. Studies in Continental Reality* (New York: G.P. Putnam's, 1922), p. 283.

48. Shvoy, p. 89.

49. Barcza, "Diary," pp. 141–42.

50. For the "Horthy cult," see Tibor Dömötörfi, "A Horthy-kultusz elemei," *Historia*, 12, no. 5–6 (1990), pp. 23–26. See also Vas, p. 111.

51. Shvoy, p. 79.

52. Janos, p. 217.

53. József Kardos, *A szentkorona-tan története (1919–1944)* (Budapest: Akadémiai, 1985), p. 178; Janos, p. 214.

54. Barcza, "Memoirs," p. 334. Horthy's salary was 100,000 pengős plus expenses.

55. Rothschild, p. 153.

56. *Manchester Guardian*, Feb. 1, 1929.

57. Ignotus, p. 158.

58. Charles Ira Stastny, "The Hungarian Communist Party, 1918–1930: Days of Power and Years of Futility," (diss. Harvard University, 1967), pp. 326–32.

59. Gyula Borbándi, *Der ungarische Populismus* (Mainz: v. Hase & Koehler, 1976), pp. 43–44; Nagy, p. 83.

60. One historian has written of the literary scene in the interwar period: "Never before had Hungary had such a number of fine writers and poets; many among them . . . made no secret of their criticisms of the régime." Sinor, p. 293. See also Ignotus, pp. 174–84.

61. See Horthy's comment as recorded in Athelstan Johnson's report of Sept. 14, 1920, in PRO, FO371/4854/C6776/5/21.

62. Jay Leyda, *Kino. A History of the Russian and Soviet Film* (New York: Collier, 1960), p. 218.

63. Macartney, *OF*, I: 55, fn. 2.

64. Mária M. Kovács, "Hungarian Women in the Professions: Interwar Feminism on the Right," (unpublished paper), p. 7.

65. William McCagg, "The Role of the Hungarian Nobility in Modern Jewish History, *East European Quarterly*, 20, no. 1 (March, 1986), pp. 43–44. This phrase was used by the influential Hungarian historian, Gyula Szekfű, in his *Három Nemzedék*. Horthy is unlikely to have read Szekfű's work, but this concept of the "good Jew" was prevalent in many quarters of Hungarian society.

66. George Clare, *Last Waltz to Vienna. The Rise and Destruction of a Family, 1842–1942* (New York: Holt Rinehart, 1982), p. 83.

67. No confirmation of the incident has been found in YMCA records held at the Yale University Library or the YMCA world headquarters in Geneva, Switzerland.

68. Among the books Horthy is known to have read is Friedrich Burgdörfer, *Sterben die weissen Völker? Die Zukunft der weissen und farbigen Völker im Lichte der Statistik* (Munich: Georg D. W. Callwey, 1934).

69. The following paragraph is based on reports prepared by several diplomats and military officials who were received by Regent Horthy in the 1920s, including that of Hans Cnobloch, July 21, 1922, NPA, K885/2–4/21594; Amtsvermerk of Legionsrat Seeman, June 5, 1928, NPA, K885/18–20/22799; report of Major Parry Jones, PRO, FO371/12180/C5330/58/21.

70. In 1936 Horthy told the British Minister that the recent acts of sabotage in the English naval stockyards were a natural consequence of the admission of Jewish refugees. PRO, FO371/R2315/84/21.

71. Major Parry's report, PRO, FO371/12180/C5330/58/21. Some officials of the British Foreign Office showed a certain understanding for Horthy's views. In a marginal comment on Parry's report, one suggested that "Admiral Horthy undoubtedly overrates Jewish influence, but as regards the Continent we are apt to underrate it." PRO, FO371/12180/C5330/58/21/.

72. Report of Hans Cnobloch, July 21, 1921, NPA, K885/2–4.

73. Andrew Handlery, *From the Ghetto to the Games. The Jewish Athletes in Hungary* (Boulder: East European Monographs, 1985), pp. 64–101.

74. Béla Vágó, "Budapest Jewry in the Summer of 1944. Otto Komoly's Diaries," *Yad Vashem Studies on the Jewish Catastrophes and Resistance,* 8 (1970), p. 99.

75. Marginal note by Oliver Harvey on PRO, FO371/1927/12180/58/21.

76. Horthy to the Austrian Minister in 1937: NPA, K21/96632.

77. See his remarks as recorded in the report of the American Minister, J. Butler Wright, July 8, 1927, USSD, 864.00/74. Occasionally, but not as a consistent theme, Horthy equated Jews directly with communism. See his remarks in 1937 to the French envoy as recorded in *Documents diplomatiques français,* 2nd. Series (Paris: Imprimerie Nationale, 1983), 4: 448.

78. *IET,* 3/742; Ignác Romsics, "A kormányzó és a 'gazda'," *Historia,* 12, nos. 5–6 (1990), p. 16.

79. Juhász, *HFP,* pp. 75–76; *Számjeltávirat,* pp. 319–23; Karsai, *A budai vár,* pp. 125–26.

80. Lajos Kerekes, *Az osztrák tragédia* (Budapest: Kossuth, 1973), p. 100; J. F. Montgomery, *Hungary. The Unwilling Satellite* (New York: Devin-Adair, 1947), p. 41.

81. Report of Hans Cnobloch, July 21, 1922, NPA, K85/2–4/211594.

82. Report of Major Parry Jones, PRO, FO371/12180/C5330/58/21.

83. Report of Sept. 14, 1920, PRO, FO371/4854.

84. Jean Nouzille, "Ausztria és Magyarország új határa (1919–1921)," *Történelmi Szemle,* 39, no. 3 (1987–88), p. 336.

85. Report of Jan. 3, 1924, *DBFP,* 1/26/4.

86. For Horthy's most colorful version of this anecdote, see PRO, FO371/12180/C5330/58/21.

87. *CPAH,* pp. 83–84, 192.

88. *CPAH,* p. 192. As late as 1945, when being interrogated by Allied officers, Horthy was still telling his favorite anecdote about the corruption of Romanian officials. See NAM, M679/1/0292.

89. Horthy in a radio speech in 1938: "Without exception, every wealthy, happy, and powerful nation owed and owes its prosperity to merchant shipping. Think of the Phoenicians, Carthage, Athens, the Normans, the Spaniards; think of Venice, the Netherlands, and Britain." *CPAH,* p. 99.

90. Although their informal contacts in Hungary had been limited mostly to hunting parties, Nicholas Roosevelt later wrote a flattering introduction to the English language edition of Horthy's memoirs.

91. See his comments as recorded in Geoffrey Knox's report, April 9, 1936, PRO, FO371/R2315/84/21.

92. Horthy's letter of Oct. 22, 1925, NAM, T120, R3949/K319/109080. Hindenburg's reply of Nov. 10, 1925 is full of similar sentiments. T120, R3949/K319/109084.

93. NAM, T120, R3949/K319/109080.

94. See Horthy's comments to Hans Lindeiner-Wildau recorded in *ADAP*, B/5/198.

95. Macartney, *OF*, I: 83; Thomas L. Sakmyster, *Hungary, the Great Powers, and the Danubian Crisis, 1936–1939* (Athens: University of Georgia, 1980), pp. 36–37.

96. Ignác Romsics, "Bethlen István és a forradalmak kora," *Történelmi Szemle*, 23, no. 4 (1985), pp. 567–68.

97. Juhász, *HFP*, pp. 85–86.

98. Minutes of a Cabinet meeting of August 1, 1921, cited in *Bethlen Papers*, p. 57, fn. 80.

99. For Hungary's orientation toward Italy in the late 1920's, see Juhász, *HFP*, pp. 84–86.

100. *CPAH*, p. 42.

101. See, i.a., the report of Col. Gossett, Oct. 18,1921, PRO, FO371/6116/ C20229/182/21)

102. *IET*, 4/132.

103. For Mayer-Csekovits' memorandum and Horthy's comments on it, see *CPAH*, pp. 43–48.

104. Von Seeckt's diary entries for October, 1927, as cited in Hans Meier-Welcker, *Seeckt* (Frankfurt: M. Bernard u. Graefe, 1967), pp. 373–75.

105. Report of Hans von Schoen, June 11, 1929, *ADAP*, B/12/23. Von Schoen added that Horthy's statement should probably not be taken seriously, since he was very garrulous and occasionally spoke in ways that caused the responsible Hungarian authorities some anxiety.

106. On this, see Romsics, *Bethlen István*, pp. 182–85 and Sakmyster, *Hungary*, pp. 42–44.

107. Detailed plans for military action against Czechoslovakia were presented to Horthy in October, 1929, and January, 1931. *CPAH*, pp. 74–81.

108. Barcza, "Memoirs," p. 335.

109. Barcza, "Memoirs," p. 332; Loránd Dombrády, *A legfelsőbb hadúr és hadserege* (Budapest: Zrinyi, 1990), pp. 84–85.

110. Vargyai, 142, fn 160

111. Macartney, *OF*, I: 75.

112. *Manchester Guardian*, Oct. 14, 1929; March 1, 1920. A less generous but uninformed assessment was given at the same time in an editorial entitled "Horthy and Hoover—Fascists," published in the Communist party newspaper in the United States, *Daily Worker*, Oct. 30, 1929.

113. *London Times*, Feb. 28, 1930.

114. Romsics, *Bethlen István*, p. 206.

115. See Tibor Hetés and Mrs. Tamás Morva, eds., *Csak szolgálati használatra! Iratok a Horthy-hadsereg történetéhez, 1919–1938* (Budapest: Zrinyi, 1968), p. 494. Cited hereafter as *CSH*.

116. Romsics, *Bethlen István*.

117. Macartney, *OF*, I: 94.
118. Romsics, *Bethlen István*, p. 228; László Márkus, *A Károlyi Gyula-kormány bel-és külpolitikája* (Budapest: Akadémiai, 1968), p. 38.
119. The minutes of the Crown Council of February 20, 1931, which was continued at a second session on March 5, are found in *Horthy Miklós titkos iratai*, pp. 82–96. Hereafter cited as *HMTI*.
120. *HMTI*, p. 110; Macartney, *OF*: I, 94; Romsics, *Bethlen István*, pp. 234–35.
121. *HMTI*, pp. 110–11.
122. Romsics, *Bethlen István*, pp. 235–36.

Chapter Six

1. See De Vienne's comments to Károlyi in *IET*, 4/311.
2. On one occasion in 1925 Gömbös had declared publicly that Hungary should never rely on France, since that country "always kicked Hungary like a ball." Lajos Székely, "Gömbös Gyula külpolitikai koncepciójának kialakulása," *Valóság*, 5 (1962), p. 84.
3. Rothschild, *East Central Europe*, pp. 170–71.
4. Macartney, *OF*, I: 102.
5. *Ibid*, p. 100.
6. Report of Nicholas Roosevelt, Nov. 24, 1930, NAM, M1206/1/122–26.
7. Miklós Stier, "Politikai újraorientálódás az 1920-as és 30-as évek fordúlóján," *Századok*, 120, no. 2 (1986), p. 296.
8. Macartney, *OF*, I: 102; Kónya, 36.
9. Gömbös's letter of Sept. 20, 1932 to József Somkuthy, head of Horthy's Military Bureau, *CPAH*, pp. 51–53.
10. Vargyai, *A hadsereg*, p. 144, fn. 104.
11. Macartney, *OF*, I: 103, fn. 1.
12. Kónya, p. 42.
13. Romsics, *Bethlen István*, pp. 263–64. In 1934 Gömbös told Ferenc Szálasi that he could not have Parliament dissolved because the Regent refused to authorize it. Unpublished diary of Ferenc Szálasi, p. 15. Macartney Archive.
14. Macartney, *OF*, I: 100–01, 117.
15. 20. Braham, *POG*, I: 48; János, p. 260; Révay, p. 276.
16. Macartney, *OF*, I: 117; Braham, *POG*, I: 48.
17. Kónya, p. 95.
18. Minutes of the Cabinet meeting of March 18, 1933, CPAH pp. 61–64.
19. Horthy's draft letter to Gömbös, undated (probably early 1933), *CPAH*, pp. 66–68.
20. Kónya, p. 62, fn. 95.
21. See Horthy's remarks to the French Minister, Maugras, in the latter's report of Feb. 15, 1937, *DDF*, 2/4/448.

22. Székely, p. 84. For the development of Gömbös's foreign policy program, see Pál Pritz, *Magyarország külpolitikája Gömbös Gyula miniszterelnöksége idéjén, 1932–1936* (Budapest: Akadémiai Kiadó, 1982). Gömbös is thought to have coined the term "axis" to describe a Rome-Berlin alliance.

23. Vargyai, *A hadsereg*, p. 84, fn. 122.

24. Mackensen's report of March 21, 1934, *Documents on German Foreign Policy, 1918–1945*, eds. Paul Sweet et al., Series C (Washington, D.C., 1959) II: 346. Cited hereafter as *DGFP*.

25. *DGFP*, C/2/444.

26. *CPAH*, pp. 54–58.

27. Maurice Paléologue, *La Russie des Tsars pendant la grande guerre* (Paris: Plon Nourit, 1921).

28. *CPAH*, p. 57.

29. No trace of such a memorandum was found by the author in the British, German, Austrian, or United States archives.

30. Pritz, *Magyarország kulpolitikája*, pp. 143–44; NPA, K20/301112.

31. *CPAH*, p. 83.

32. See Horthy's comments to the British Minister, Sir Patrick Ramsay, in the latter's report, July, 7, 1934, PRO, FO371/18406/R3917/52/21.

33. *CPAH*, p. 83.

34. Juhász, *HFP*, pp. 118–21.

35. Romsics, *Bethlen István*, p. 257; Kónya, p. 122.

36. Montgomery's report of April 17, 1934, NAM, M1206/1/393–6; Kónya, p. 114, fn. 101.

37. Macartney, *OF*, I: 125. See also Kállay's comments as recorded in the report of John Montgomery, Jan. 16, 1935, NAM, M1206/1/460–67.

38. Lóránd Dombrády, *A legfelsőbb hadúr és hadserege* (Budapest: Zrinyi, 1990) p. 89.

39. Macartney, *OF*, I: 125–26.

40. Kónya, p. 143.

41. Romsics, *Bethlen István*, p. 260; Kónya, pp. 144–45.

42. Kónya, pp. 146–47.

43. Horthy, *Memoirs*, p. 140.

44. Romsics, *Bethlen István*, p. 258. It is worth noting that the decision to call new parliamentary elections was supported by most Hungarian newspapers, even the relatively moderate *Pester Lloyd*.

45. Macartney, *OF*, I: 130.

46. *Ibid.* p. 148, fn. 4.

47. Mackensen's reports of Oct. 7 and Oct. 10, 1935, *DGFP*, C/4/337.

48. Macartney, *OF*, I: 148. See also György Ránki and Iván Berend, *Magyarország a fasiszta Németország "életterében," 1933–1938* (Budapest: Kossuth, 1960), pp. 131–33.

49. Peter Sugár, ed., *A History of Hungary* (Bloomington: Indiana U.P., 1990), p. 334; Kónya, p. 153.

50. Report of H. Hennet, Oct. 21, Oct. 1934, NPA/K20/46711.

51. Ignác Romsics, "A kormányzó és a 'gazda'," *Historia*, 12, no. 5–6 (1990), p. 17.

52. Miklós Stier, "A kormánypart fasiszta jellegű átszervezésének csödjéhez (1935–1936)," *Századok*, 105, nos. 3–4 (1971), p. 706. Gömbös learned that Lajos Keresztes-Fischer had tried to persuade Horthy that he aimed to "make a grab for the regency." Ferenc Rajniss's diary, March 18, 1945, in Tibor Zinner and Péter Róna, eds., *Szálasi bilincsben*, (Budapest: Lapkiadó Vállalat, 1986), I: 38.

53. Macartney, *OF*, I: 133.

54. *Ibid.*, p. 173, fn. 2. See also Montgomery's report of January 17, 1936, NA, State Department records, 864.00/840.

55. Romsics, *Bethlen István*, pp. 265–66.

56. Pritz, *Magyarország külpolitikája*, p. 235.

57. Knox's report, April 9, 1936, PRO, FO371/20395/R2315/84/21.

58. Sakmyster, *Hungary*, p. 81.

59. PRO, FO371/20396/R3210/470/21. Apologizing for his inability to write fluently in English, Horthy composed his letter in German.

60. In a letter to Marshal Pilsudski of Oct. 10, 1934, Horthy had also referred to a dismemberment of Soviet Russia in which Britain and the "Mohammedan countries" would participate. *CPAH*, pp. 72–73.

61. Robert Vansittart's marginal note on PRO, FO371/20396/R3210/470/21.

62. *CPAH*, pp. 79–80.

63. Hitler's letter dated May 13, 1935, *CPAH*, pp. 80–81. Horthy's earlier letter has not survived.

64. *CPAH*, pp. 83–90.

65. For secondary accounts of Horthy's visit, see Macartney, *OF*, I: 150; Pritz, *Magyarország külpolitikája*, pp. 266–69.

66. Memo of Foreign Minister Neurath, Aug. 24, 1936, *DGFP*, C/6/516.

67. Horthy, *Memoirs*, p. 147. Horthy was to give similar advice to Ciano and Mussolini during his visit to Italy several months later. Barcza Diary, Jan. 30, 1938.

68. *CPAH*, p. 84.

69. Hugh Trevor-Roper, ed., *Hitler's Secret Conversations, 1941–1944* (New York: Farrar, Strauss, 1953), p. 542.

70. Horthy, *Memoirs*, pp. 147–48.

71. *Ibid.*, p. 142.

72. Macartney, *OF*, I: 173. Macartney described Horthy's turn against Gömbös as perhaps "the most important single event in Hungarian interwar politics." (p. 135).

73. Horthy, *Memoirs*, p. 142.

74. Macartney, *OF*, I: 174, fn. 3.

75. Sugár, p. 335.

76. Horthy's comments to the British Minister, Sir P. Ramsay, July 7, 1934, PRO, FO371/18407/R3917/52/21

77. Barcza diary, Nov. 28, 1936.

78. No less a propagandist than Joseph Goebbels observed that during his visit to Warsaw in February, 1938, Horthy was treated "like an emperor." *Die Tagebücher von Joseph Goebbels. Sämtliche Fragmente*, ed. Elke Fröhlich (Munich: K.G. Saur, 1987), 3: 433. For Horthy's state visits in the period 1936–1938, see Gosztony, *Miklós von Horthy*, pp. 62–66.

79. Davies's report of Sept. 29, 1937, NAM, M1206/1/670–81. A British visitor in this period, Sir Frederick Leith-Ross, found Horthy to be "a very sensible and level-headed man" with a fervent desire to safeguard his country's independence. Frederick Leith-Ross, *Money Talks. Fifty Years of International Finance* (London: Hutchinson, 1968), p. 262.

80. See Eckhardt's comments to a member of the American Legation, NA, USSD, 864.00/868.

81. Macartney, *OF*, I: 190.

82. Horthy's draft letter to Darányi of June 14, 1937, *CPAH*, pp. 94–95.

83. For an account that stresses Horthy's intention of forming a dynasty, see Hans Georg Lehmann, *Der Reichsverweser-Stellvertreter: Horthys gescheiderte Planung einer Dynastie* (Mainz: v. Hase und Koehler, 1975), pp. 164–66.

84. PRO, FO371/18407/PCH/52.

85. *CPAH*, p. 94.

86. *Ibid.*, p. 185.

87. For sketches of Szálasi, see Macartney, *OF*, I: 160–67; Miklós Lackó, *Nyilasok, Nemzetiszocialisták, 1935–1944* (Budapest: Kossuth, 1966), pp. 43–55; Margit Szöllösi-Janze, *Die Pfeilkreuzlerbewegung in Ungarn: Historischer Kontext, Entwicklung und Herrschaft* (Munich: Oldenbourg, 1989), ff.; and Elek Karsai, "Szálasi," in Ferenc Glatz, ed., *Reformists and Radicals in Hungary* (Budapest: MTA Történettudományi Intézet, 1991), pp. 191–210.

88. Karsai, "Ferenc Szálasi," p. 195.

89. Szálasi diary, pp. 21–27.

90. Szálasi diary, p. 27.

91. Péter Sipos, *Imrédy Béla és a Magyar Megújulás Pártja* (Budapest: Akadémiai, 1970), p. 21.

92. Sakmyster, *Hungary*, p. 90.

93. Sipos, pp. 21–23.

94. Sakmyster, *Hungary*, pp. 95–96.

95. *Ibid.*, pp. 95–96; Sipos, pp. 21–22; Barcza Diary, Jan. 30, 1938, pp. 6–7.

96. See Eckhardt's comments to the American Chargé d'Affaires, as recorded in NAM, M1206/1/646–53.

97. For further details, see Macartney, *OF*, 1: 183–84.

98. Neurath's memo, Nov. 25, 1936, *DGFP*, C/5/556.

99. Montgomery's report, Dec. 3, 1937, NA, State Department, 864.00/882.

100. Szálasi diary, pp. 40–41. See also Macartney, *OF*, I: 188.

101. Karsai, "Ferenc Szálasi," p. 196.

102. See, i.e., Szálasi's statement to an American diplomat as recorded in an enclosure to NA, State Department, 864.00/882.

103. Sakmyster, *Hungary*, pp. 110–11.

104. Eberle's report, Nov. 23, 1937, NPA, K21/96526.

105. Baar's report is found in GFM, NAM, T-120, 2935/568512–3.

106. GFM, NAM, T-120, 2935/568516–17.

107. Baar's report of Dec. 1, 1937, NPA, K21/96549.

108. Von Erdmannsdorff's report of Dec. 1, 1937, *DGFP*, D/5/152.

109. Bohle's report, Feb. 3, 1938, GFM, NAM, T-120, 3626/028046–47.

110. Sipos, p. 70.

111. Sipos, p. 72.

112. Soós's account of his meetings with the Regent and the text of his memorandum are found in Szálasi's diary, pp. 42–54.

113. For a further discussion of this episode, see Macartney, *OF*, I: 212–14.

114. Szálasi diary, p. 54.

115. Sipos, p. 75.

116. See Horthy's comments to the British Minister, Geoffrey Knox, in the latter's report of Feb. 13, 1938, PRO, FO371/C1240/62/18. Knox thought that in response to recent events Horthy spoke with unaccustomed moderation and objectivity.

117. *Pesti Napló*, Feb. 10, 1938.

Chapter Seven

1. Sakmyster, *Hungary*, p. 135.

2. Nagy-Talavera, p. 135; Kádár, p. 295.

3. Miklós Kozma's comment on the speech: "It is evident at the first glance that it is the personal wording of Horthy and that it contains his most cherished ideas." *CPAH*, p. 101.

4. Barcza Diary, April 4, 1938. See also Montgomery's report of April 7, 1938, NAM, M1206/1/911–15.

5. Szálasi Diary, p. 59.

6. Lackó, p. 138.

7. Szálasi Diary, pp. 55, 69–70. See also Lackó, pp. 106–07; Macartney, *OF*: I: 215.

8. Lackó, p. 107.

9. Shvoy, p. 166.

10. Braham, *POG*, I: 123.

11. Barcza Diary, Jan. 30, 1938.

12. See Horthy's comments recorded in Barcza Diary, Jan. 20, 1938.

13. Sakmyster, *Hungary*, pp. 115–16.

14. Kádár, p. 295.

15. Szálasi Diary, p. 72.

16. Nagy-Talavera, p. 137; Braham, *POG*, I: 128.

17. For the "weekend crisis" and its importance for Hungary, see Sakmyster, *Hungary*, pp. 167–68. For the European context, see Gerhard Weinberg, *The Foreign Policy of Hitler's Germany: Starting World War II* (Chicago: Univ. of Chicago, 1980), pp. 367–77.

18. Barcza Diary, June 1, 1938, p. 141.

19. Sakmyster, *Hungary*, pp. 147–48.

20. Barcza Diary, June 1, p. 142; Montgomery's report of June 2, 1938, *FRUS*, 1938, I: 55–56; and Knox's report, June 26, 1938, PRO, FO371, R5926/626/21.

21. Sakmyster, *Hungary*, p. 177.

22. Helmuth Groscurth, *Tagebücher eines Abwehroffiziers, 1938–1940*, ed. Helmut Krausnick and Harold C. Deutsch (Stuttgart: Deutsches Verlagsanstalt, 1970) 102; *Diplomáciai iratok Magyarország külpolitikájához, 1936–1945*, ed. László Zsigmond (Budapest: Akadémiai Kiadó, 1965), II: 102. (Cited hereafter as *DIMK*).

23. János Csima, "Adalékok a horthysta vezérkarnak az ellenforradalmi rendszer háborús politikájában betöltött szerepéről," *Hadtörténelmi Közlemények* 15 (1968), p. 495; *CPAH*, p. 131.

24. Horthy had revised his earlier negative judgment of Eckhardt and since the beginning of 1938 had begun to seek his advice. Montgomery's report of March 10, 1938, NAM, M1206/1/886.

25. Collection of Hungarian Political and Military Records, 1909–1945, NAM, T973/15/345. Also a report of John Montgomery on the basis of information from Eckhardt, Nov. 16, 1938, NAM, M1206/1/1091.

26. Groscurth, *Tagebücher*, p. 102.

27. Goebbels, *Tagebücher*, Part 1, 3: 517.

28. Elemér Ujpétery, *Végállomás Lisszabon. Hét év a magyar külügyi szolgálatban* (Budapest: Magvető, 1987). p. 101. The French Ambassador in Berlin, François-Poncet, declared that "the king of Italy or England would not have been afforded greater respect or pomp" than that given Horthy. *DDF*, 1932–1939, 2/10/503.

29. Ufa Tonwoche, no. 416, Aug. 24, 1938. On deposit at the Film and Recording Division, Library of Congress, Washington, D.C.

30. For a detailed treatment, see Sakmyster, *Hungary*, pp. 179–81.

31. József Lipski, *Diplomat in Berlin, 1933–1939*, ed. Wacław Jedrzejewicz (New York: Columbia U.P., 1968), p. 396.

32. See Horthy's recollection of the incident related to the British Minister Geoffrey Knox, in the latter's report of April 24, 1939, in PRO, FO371/C6314/350/21. See also Macartney, *OF*, I: 242.

33. PRO, FO371/C9178/1941/18.

34. Sakmyster, *Hungary*, p. 179; Macartney, *OF*, I: 242.

35. *DGFP*, D/2/402.

36. As a way of demonstrating Hungary's independence of Germany, Kánya on August 20 had approved the signing of an ambiguously worded

nonaggression pact with the Little Entente. See Sakmyster, *Hungary*, p. 178. For Horthy's attitude, see *Lipski Papers*, p. 380.

37. Goebbels, *Tagebücher*, Part 1, Vol. 3, p. 516. See also Leonidas E. Hill, ed., *Die Weizsäcker Papiere, 1933–1950* (Frankfurt: Propyläen, 1974), p. 138; *DGFP*, D/2/283.

38. Horthy, *Memoirs*, p. 165.

39. Memoirs of István Bárczy, p. 22, in Macartney Archive.

40. Erdmannsdorff's letter of Aug. 29, 1938, *DGFP*, D/2/402.

41. Memorandum of George Lansbury, Sept. 1, 1938, on deposit at British Library of Political and Economic Science (London). See also PRO, FO371/C9283/1941/18 and Jonathon Schneer, *George Lansbury* (Manchester: Manchester U.P., 1990), pp. 186–95.

42. Sakmyster, *Hungary*, p. 213.

43. *DIMK*, 2/430–431.

44. *DIMK*, 2/486.

45. *CPAH*, pp. 109–110.

46. Sakmyster, *Hungary*, p. 212.

47. *CPAH*, pp. 105–07.

48. For Darányi's mission to Berlin, see Macartney, *OF*, I: 290–91; Juhász, *HFP*, pp. 143–44.

49. For a visual record of Horthy's entry into Kassa, see the Hungarian propaganda film "Észak felé!" (To the North!), a copy of which is on deposit at the Museum of Modern Art, New York City. See also Erdmannsdorff's report of Nov. 12, 1938, NAM, T120, R1688/023153–56.

50. Romsics, *Bethlen István*, p. 275.

51. Erdmannsdorff's report of Nov. 15, 1938, *DGFP*, D/4/118.

52. For a full discussion of this incident, see Sakmyster, *Hungary*, pp. 215–18; Macartney, *OF*, I: 310–13.

53. Rudolf Andorka, *A madridi követségtől Mauthausenig* (Budapest: Kossuth, 1978), p. 72.

54. Barcza, "Memoirs," p. 100.

55. In late 1938 London was informed, apparently by György Barcza, that Regent Horthy would welcome an invitation for a state visit to England. The Foreign Office was not opposed in principle, but the diplomatic crises of 1939 rendered such a visit impossible. Katzburg, p. 156.

56. Goebbels, who found Imrédy to be "very energetic and clear-headed," records that he "was deeply impressed by his conversation with Hitler." *Tagebücher*, Part 1, Vol. 3, p. 516.

57. For Imrédy's metamorphosis, see Sakmyster, *Hungary*, pp. 208–09.

58. Goebbels, *Tagebücher*, Part 1,Vol. 3, p. 516.

59. Sipos, p. 63; Shvoy, p. 176.

60. Shvoy, p. 179; Sipos, p. 72.

61. Montgomery's report of Dec. 1, 1938, NAM, M1206, 1/1125–36. See also Macartney, *OF*, I: 315–16.

62. Shvoy, p. 184; Sipos, p. 74.

63. For a full discussion of the second Jewish law, see Braham, *POG*, I: 147–56; and Katzburg, p. 118.

64. Mrs. Imrédy's account of her meeting with Horthy is found in the Macartney Archive.

65. Andorka, p. 72.

66. In late 1938 and early 1939 General Werth, the Chief of Staff, complained that the officer corps was losing confidence in the Regent, because Horthy and his sons maintained "intimate ties" with the Jews. Andorka, pp. 78, 82.

67. Andorka, p. 83.

68. For Montgomery's reports, see NA, USSD, 762.64/128, 133. For Knox's report, see PRO, FO371/C821/129/21. See also Katzburg, pp. 129–31.

69. See Erdmannsdorff's report of Feb. 22, 1939, NAM, T-120, 1881/424677–78.

70. Romsics, *Bethlen*, p. 274.

71. See the comments of Horthy and Eckhardt to Montgomery recorded in his report of Feb. 11, 1939, NA, M1206, 1/1251–56.

72. For Horthy's talk with Imrédy, see the account in Bárczy (p. 13), who was present, and Erdmannsdorff's report of Feb. 22, 1939, GFM, NAM, T120/1881/424677–8.

73. Bárczy, p. 13.

74. Macartney, *OF*, I: 328.

75. Horthy, *Memoirs*, p. 175. Imrédy's wife believed that Horthy had forced her husband to resign because he was striving for National Socialist reforms that were unsuitable for Hungary. *A Wilhelmstrasse és Magyarország. Német diplomáciai iratok Magyarországról 1933–1944*, eds. György Ránki et al (Budapest: Kossuth, 1968), p. 749.

76. This analysis is based in part on conversations Montgomery had with Bethlen as recorded in his report of Dec. 1, NA, USSD, 864.00/932. See also the discussion in Katzburg, p. 233.

77. Unlike Imrédy, Teleki viewed the "Jewish question" in racial terms that he believed were grounded in scientific principles. Katzburg, p. 134.

78. For these provisions, see Braham, *PoG*, I: 153–56.

79. Horthy's comment to Montgomery as recorded in NA, USSD, 762.64/133.

80. Macartney, *OF*, I: 331; Sakmyster, *Hungary*, p. 221; Nandor A. F. Dreisziger, *Hungary's Way to World War II* (Toronto: Weller, 1968), pp. 106–08.

81. NA, USSD, 762.64/133, 135; PRO, FO371, 23111/C821/129/21. About Horthy's tirade Knox reported to London: "It was a pathetic occasion and made the more so by his intense niceness and sincerity."

82. PRO, FO371/23111/821/129/21.

83. Macartney, *OF*, I: 331.

84. *DGFP*, D/4/199.
85. *DGFP*, D/4/199.
86. Knox's report of March 16, 1939, PRO, FO371/C3274/166/21.
87. Rothschild, *East Central Europe*, p. 181.
88. *Ciano Diaries, 1937–38*, p. 207; FRUS, 1939, 1/85–86.
89. Gyula Juhász, *A Teleki-kormány külpolitikája* (Budapest: Akadémiai Kiadó, 1964), pp. 35–36; Macartney, *OF*, 1: 348.
90. Montgomery's reports of March 21 and April 24, 1939, *FRUS*, 1939, 1/85–86; NA, USSD, 740.00/1109. Knox's report of April 24, 1939, PRO, FO371/23113/C6314/350/21. Knox, who left Budapest on April 24 for a new assignment, thought Horthy in this period spoke more moderately and sensibly than at any other time in the past.
91. Macartney, *OF*, I: 348; Juhász, *HFP*, p. 159.
92. The idea of the pope acting as president of such a conference seems to have originated with Bethlen. Macartney, *OF*, 1: 356.
93. PRO, FO371/23842/R5250/140/37.
94. On a number of previous occasions Horthy had suggested to Polish interlocutors that they voluntarily cede Danzig and the Corridor to Germany. See Anna Cienciala, *Poland and the Western Powers, 1938–1939* (London: Routlege and Kegan Paul, 1968), pp. 61, 104.
95. See Lansbury's letter to the *Times*, June 20, 1939.
96. This episode is well described in Macartney, *OF*, 1: 358–59.
97. Macartney, *OF*, 1: 359.

Chapter Eight

1. Ciano, *Diaries*, p. 123. In November Horthy told the American Minister that Hitler had made a "monumental blunder" in waging war with "a disunited country containing large number of racial and religious malcontents." Montgomery's report of Nov. 18, 1939, USSD, 864.00. PR/170.
2. Vilmos Nagybaczoni Nagy, *Végzetes esztendők, 1938–1945* (Budapest: Körmendy, n.d.), p. p. 35.
3. Juhász, *HFP*, p. 162.
4. Macartney, *OF*, I: 367.
5. Horthy, *Memoirs*, p. 177.
6. Macartney, *OF*, 1: 367; Horthy, *Memoirs*, p. 177. *Allianz Hitler-Horthy-Mussolini. Dokumente zur ungarischen Aussenpolitik (1933–1944)*, ed. Magda Ádám *et al*, eds. (Budapest: Akadémiai, 1966), pp. 248–50. Hereafter cited as *Allianz*. There is no evidence that Horthy's harsh, personal warning was actually passed on to the Germans.
7. Horthy, *Memoirs*, p. 177. At the time Horthy did express regret that the Poles had chosen to send their gold and aircraft to Romania rather than to Hungary. Montgomery's telegram of Oct. 5, 1939, NA, USSD, 740.0011/700.

8. Goebbels, *Tagebücher*, Part 1, vol. 3, p. 609. Six months later Hitler was still complaining of Hungary's insolent behavior in September 1939. "England and Hungary," he said, were "one heart and one soul." Mario D. Fenyő, *Hitler, Horthy, and Hungary. German-Hungarian Relations, 1941–1944* (New Haven: Yale U.P., 1972), p. 7.

9. Erdmannsdorff's report of Oct. 14, 1939, NAM, T-120, R3626/028134–5. See also an OKW report of Oct. 20, 1939, T-77, R1026/2498922–23.

10. *CPAH*, pp. 126–28.

11. Montgomery's telegram of Nov. 17, 1939, NA, USSD, 740.0011 European War 1939/1045; and O'Malley's report of Nov. 8, 1939, PRO, FO371/23113/C18609/166/21.

12. In public speeches in late 1939 and early 1940, Teleki denounced the Soviet attack on Finland and called for the creation of a united anti-Soviet bloc of states. Juhász, *HFP*, p. 167.

13. Tilkovszky, *Pál Teleki*, p. 48.

14. Barcza, "Memoirs," p. 161.

15. In April 1940 the German propaganda film "Campaign in Poland" made a "profound impression" on an invited audience of 1,200 officers and government officials, including Csáky, Werth, and Bartha. It is not known whether the Regent was on hand, but the officers surely conveyed their impressions to him. Report of German Air Attaché, April 30, 1940, NAM, T-77, R976/446432.

16. Barcza, "Memoirs," p. 278. Barcza regarded this as "a naive and completely baseless illusion."

17. Roosevelt's photograph arrived, with a warm letter of congratulations from the president, only in April, after Horthy had privately expressed his disappointment that he had received no message or gift from the United States President. See the material in PPF6575, Franklin D. Roosevelt Library (Hyde Park, New York).

18. PRO, FO371/23113/C18609/166/21; Goebbels, *Tagebücher*, Part 1, vol. 3, p. 515.

19. Macartney, *OF*, 1: 383.

20. Barcza, "Memoirs," p. 166.

21. O'Malley's report of Nov. 8, 1939, PRO, FO371/23113/C18609/166/21.

22. Macartney, *OF*, I: 376.

23. The Hungarian Government lodged an official protest against the cartoon because of its defamation of the Regent. See PRO, FO371/C5334/949/21.

24. O'Malley's report of March 1, 1940, PRO, FO371/24427/C37661/529/21.

25. Horthy later criticized Britain's "flabby handling" of the opening phase of the Norwegian campaign. He suggested that if the British Navy had attacked with greater determination, the Germans would have suffered a disaster. O'Malley's report of Oct. 19, 1992, PRO, FO371/24428/C11325/529/21.

26. Bárczy, pp. 44–46.

27. Bárczy, pp. 46–47.

28. Bárczy, p. 47. Teleki showed a copy of the letter in which he threatened to resign to the American economist, Royall Tyler. See NA, USSD, 740.0011 EW, 1940/3001.

29. Nagy, p. 124.

30. Macartney, *OF*, I: 402.

31. Sipos, pp. 163–64.

32. Dombrády, *A legfelsőbb hadúr*, p. 130.

33. Horthy, *Memoirs*, p. 179.

34. *CPAH*, pp. 130–32.

35. Macartney, *OF*, I: 405–07; Juhász, *HFP*, pp. 173–74. Also *DIMK*, 5/129, 147, 149.

36. Kádár, p. 353.

37. Juhász, *A Teleki kormány*, p. 215.

38. *CPAH*, pp. 133–49. See also Macartney, *OF*, 1: 432–33.

39. Macartney, *OF*, I: 433; Juhász, *A Teleki kormány*, p. 217.

40. Montgomery's report of Oct. 7, 1940, on the basis of information from Eckhardt, NA, USSD, 864.00/1000.

41. Ferenc Keresztes-Fischer was so opposed to the concessions described below that he threatened to resign. But Horthy would not hear of this; he insisted that at all costs he must have both Teleki and Keresztes-Fischer in the Cabinet. Dezső Saly, *Szigorúan bizalmas! Fekete könyv, 1939–1944* (Budapest: Anonymus, 1945), p. 253.

42. Braham, *PoG*, 1: 173; Juhász, *HFP*, p. 175. When he met Hitler on November 20, Teleki volunteered that "when peace was concluded the Jews would have to be moved out of Europe." *DGFP*, D/11/633.

43. Count István Bethlen, *Hungarian Politics during World War Two. Treatise and Indictment*, ed. Ilona Bolza (Munich: Rudolf Trofenik, 1985), p. 10.

44. Lackó, pp. 228–29.

45. *CPAH*, pp. 149–52. As he explained in this letter, Horthy preferred to convey his thoughts to his colleagues orally rather than in writing. For this reason only a handful of candid letters of this kind are known. "Bóli" was the affectionate nickname used by Teleki's closest friends.

46. This statement suggests that Horthy did not consider the Jews and converts with whom he continued to socialize at the bridge table to be "real Jews."

47. Horthy based this argument on information contained in an unsigned memorandum on the influence of the Arrowcross that was submitted to him in early October. OL, Horthy iratai, K585, I-D-10.

48. Here, as was his habit, Horthy used a colorful German proverb to make his point.

49. In the first draft of his letter Horthy suggested even more drastic measures, including an adjournment of Parliament sine die and transfer of its powers to the Regent. He did not raise this possibility in the actual letter to Teleki.

50. Two days after Hungary's adherence to the Tripartite Pact,

Goebbels wrote in his diary: "Report from Hungary: there everyone, under the leadership of Horthy, is anti-German. A corrupt feudal regime. . . . With this Hungary we will never get anywhere. It must be overthrown one day." Goebbels, *Tagebücher*, pp. 406–07.

51. Ciano, *Diary*, p. 313.

52. PRO, FO371/24428/C11020/529/21.

53. The Yugoslav diplomatic record of this conversation, during which Horthy expressed his hope that the British would win the war, was passed on by Prince Regent Paul to the British Foreign Office. PRO, FO371/24427/C6327/529/21.

54. Horthy's comments to the Yugoslav and American Ministers in November 1940, recorded in PRO, FO371/25036/XC/B 968; and USSD, 740.0011/EW/1939/7284.

55. N. F. Dreisziger, "Bridges to the West: The Horthy Regime's 'Reinsurance Policies' in 1941," *War and Society*, 7, no. 1 (May, 1989), pp. 2–3.

56. O'Malley's report of Jan. 26, 1941, PRO, FO417/43/C837/837/6; O'Malley's recollection of the plan in a memorandum of April 1, 1944, FO371/39246/C4287/1/2/9. See also Sir Owen O'Malley, *The Phantom Caravan* (London: John Murray, 1954), p. 211.

57. Remarkably, the New York *Daily News* reported as early as December 28, 1940, that Eckhardt would soon arrive in the United States as Horthy's emissary to establish a government-in-exile in Pittsburgh, the "second largest Hungarian city in the world." The story was accompanied by a photograph of Admiral Horthy, probably the only such appearance of the Hungarian Regent in America's largest mass circulation newspaper.

58. Bárczy, p. 48.

59. Teleki's letter of March 3, 1941, to the Hungarian representatives in London and Washington, *Allianz*, p. 289.

60. See, i.e., Horthy's comments to O'Malley in the latter's report of Oct. 19, 1940, PRO, FO371/24428/C11325/529/21.

61. Ciano, *Diary*, p. 313.

62. Horthy's letter of Oct. 23, 1940, *DIMK*, 5/431.

63. *DIMK*, 5/652; Macartney, *OF*, I: 474.

64. No copy of this draft letter has survived. It is referred to in a letter Teleki wrote to a friend on April 2. See Richard V. Burks, "Two Teleki Letters," *Journal of Central European Affairs*, 7, no. 1 (April, 1947), p. 73.

65. Macartney, *OF*, I: 475; Zinner, *Szálasi bilincsben*, p. 162.

66. Tilkovszky, *Pál Teleki*, p. 63; Márton Himler, *Igy néztek ki a magyar nemzet sirásói* (New York: St. Marks, 1958), p. 48.

67. Macartney, *OF*, I: 475.

68. Burks, "Two Teleki Letters," p. 72.

69. *DGFP*, D/12/227.

70. *DIMK*, 5/705; Macartney, *OF*, I: 477.

71. Himler, p. 49; Macartney, *OF*, I: 480; Juhász, *A Teleki-kormány külpolitikájához*, pp. 302–03.

72. Burks, "Two Teleki Letters," p. 71.

73. Juhász, *A Teleki-kormány*, pp. 296–99. On April 11 Bethlen declared in a speech to Parliament that failure to intervene militarily in Yugoslavia would be "a renunciation of our nation's honor and our thousand-year historical calling." Romsics, *Bethlen István*, p. 286.

74. Count Móric Esterházy, one of Hungary's elder statesman and a man for whom Horthy had a high regard, apparently wrote a letter to the Regent and described the coming war in "fearfully severe terms." Macartney, *OF*, I: 482.

75. For the minutes of this meeting see Antal Náray, *Náray Antal visszaemlékezése 1945* (Budapest: Zrinyi, 1988), pp. 44–53.

76. It is noteworthy that, seven months before Pearl Harbor, the Hungarian statesmen regularly spoke as if the United States were already a full war partner of Great Britain.

77. Dombrády, *A legfelsőbb hadúr*, pp. 156–57.

78. Tilkovszky, *Pál Teleki*, p. 63.

79. *Allianz*, no. 681.

80. Juhász, *HFP*, p. 182; Burks, "Two Teleki Letters," p. 73.

81. Teleki referred here to the speech that Horthy had given at Mohács in 1926, in which he had called for a rapprochement with Yugoslavia.

82. *MHTI*, p. 292.

83. Barcza, "Memoirs," p. 240.

84. Interrogation report of László Bárdossy, Sept. 9, 1945, NA, RG332, 7th Army Interrogation Center.

85. Juhász, *HFP*, p. 185; Macartney, *OF*, II: 3.

86. *DGFP*, D/12/261.

87. Fenyő, 21–22; Travers' report of April 7, 1941, *FRUS*, 1941, 1: 302–03.

88. See his remarks to General Himer, the OKW liaison to the Hungarian Army, in the latter's report of April 9, 1941, NAM, T-77, 1423/000303.

89. Károly Urbán and István Vida, "Barcza György. Budapest. 1941 május—1943 március," *Századok*, 121, nos. 2–3 (1987), pp. 360–61. Heeding a warning from Bethlen that Horthy was too much the narrowminded soldier to understand political arguments, Barcza avoided any further discussions with the Regent. Barcza, "Diary," May 23, 1941. Barcza did state his case in a long memorandum of May 8, 1941, but there is no evidence that Horthy read it. *DIMK*, 5/779.

90. *CPAH*, pp. 354–56. Horthy had begun to draft this letter in response to a long letter that Hitler had sent at the conclusion of the Yugoslav campaign. Hitler's letter has not survived.

91. David Irving, *Hitler's War* (New York: The Viking Press, 1977), p. 229. Irving's account is based on the unpublished diary of Walther Hewel, a diplomat assigned to Hitler's headquarters.

92. *DIMK*, 5/888; Macartney, *OF*, II: 17.

93. Sakmyster, "Army Officers," p. 34; Dombrády, *A legfelsőbb hadúr*, pp. 162–66.

94. Gostony, p. 119; Macartney, *OF*, II: 18–21; Dombrády, *A legfelsőbb hadúr*, pp. 167–68.

95. Dombrády, *A legfelsőbb hadúr*, pp. 167–68.

96. Erdmannsdorff's report of June 22, 1942, NAM, T-120, 93/10372; Macartney, *OF* II: 21.

97. When General Himer tried to get an audience with the Regent, he was told that Horthy was at a polo match. Peter Gosztony, *Hitlers fremde Heere. Das Schicksal der nichtdeutschen Armeen im Ostfeldzug* (Düsseldorf: Econ, 1976), p. 119.

98. Kádár, p. 391; Dombrády, *A legfelsőbb hadúr*, p. 170.

99. On the 23rd Molotov had told the Hungarian Minister that he saw no reason for war between Hungary and Soviet Russia. Moreover, if Hungary remained neutral, she could expect future Soviet support for the return of all of Transylvania. Zinner, *Szálasiék*, I: 187–88. See also Himler, p. 49; Macartney, *OF*, II: 26.

100. Macartney, *OF*, II: 28.

101. Nicholas Kállay, *Hungarian Premier. A Personal Account of a Nation's Struggle in the Second World War* (New York: Columbia U.P., 1954) p. 8.

102. Horthy, *Memoirs*, pp. 190–91.

103. The mystery of who bombed Kassa has never been unravelled. The most recent treatment of the subject is in Julian Borsányi, *Das Rätzel des Bombenangriffs auf Kauschau*, 26 Juni 1941 (Munich: Ungarisches Institut, 1978). See also Thomas Sakmyster, "Magyar katonatisztek és Kassa bombazása," *Történelmi Szemle*, no. 2 (1985), 368–373.

104. *DIMK*, 5/891; Macartney, *OF*, II: 30.

Chapter Nine

1. Pell's report of August 22, 1941, NA, USSD, 864.00/1025. For a fuller discussion of this document, see Fenyő, p. 42.

2. Bárdossy's letter is in *HMTI*, pp. 300–12.

3. Juhász, *HFP*, pp. 199–200; Fenyő, p. 30; Peter Gosztony, "Hungary's Army in the Second World War," (in) *Hungarian History/World History*, ed. György Ránki (Budapest: Akadémiai Kiadó, 1984). Hereafter cited as *HHWH*.

4. Another reason, it seems, was Horthy's belief that Werth was the only prominent Hungarian officer who spoke German so fluently that he could deal on an equal basis with the Germans. Macartney, *OF*, II: 274, fn. 1.

5. The German Minister, Ernst von Jagov, shared this view: "There is no doubt that he [István Horthy] is outspokenly friendly to the English and that he fundamentally rejects National Socialism." NAM, T-120, 92/104586.

6. Ferenc Szombathelyi, *Visszaemlékezései* (Washington: Occidental, 1980), p. 14; Kádár, p. 124.

7. Kádár, p. 424.

8. Gosztony, "Hungary's Army," p. 238; Dombrády, p. 177.

9. Gosztony, *Hitlers Fremde Heere*, pp. 159–60.

10. Gosztony, *Hitlers Fremde Heere*, p. 160; Dombrády, p. 178; Fenyő, p. 32.

11. Fenyő, p. 33.

12. Braham, *PoG*, I: 194–95; Katzburg, p. 177.

13. For the most authoritative treatment of what became known as the Kamenets-Podolsk massacre, see Braham, *PoG*, I: 199–207.

14. John Lukacs, *The Last European War. September 1939/ December 1941* (Garden City: Anchor Press, 1976), p. 160.

15. Macartney, *OF*, II:

16. Montgomery, p. 153.

17. *ADAP*, E/1/64. See also Gostony, *Hitlers Fremde Heeren*, pp. 197–99; Fenyő, p. 36; Juhász, *HFP*, p. 206.

18. Elek Karsai, *A budai vártól a gyepűig 1941–1945* (Budapest: Táncsics, 1965), p. 96; Gostony, *Hitlers Fremde Heere*, p. 204.

19. *CPAH*, pp. 187–94, 356–62. At the end of the letter Horthy apologized for having "unburdened my heart in this long-winded manner."

20. Horthy used similar arguments in a conversation with Count Ciano, who visited Hungary in mid-January. *Ciano Diaries*, pp. 477–78.

21. Fenyő, 38–40; Juhász, *HFP*, pp. 207–08.

22. Gosztony, *Hitlers Fremde Heere*, pp. 160–61.

23. Fenyő, pp. 38–40.

24. The account of this episode in Horthy's *Memoirs* (pp. 196–98) is misleading on several points. For a thorough account largely unsympathetic to Horthy, see Hans Georg Lehmann, *Der Reichsverweser-Stellvertreter: Horthys gescheiderte Planung einer Dynastie* (Mainz: v. Hase und Koehler, 1975).

25. Kádár, pp. 410–13; *Serédi Justinián hercegprimás feljegyzései 1941–1944*, eds. Sándor Urbán and István Vida (Budapest: Zrínyi, 1990), pp. 57, 133. Cited hereafter as *Serédi*.

26. *Serédi*, pp. 57–58.

27. He was concerned not only about István Horthy's "moral character," about which he had received several unfavorable reports, but about his marriage in a Protestant ceremony to Countess Ilona Edelsheim, who had been raised a Catholic. *Serédi*, pp. 57, 133.

28. *CPAH*, pp. 184–85.

29. Cardinal Serédi declared that "in the background it was the women (the Regent's wife, István Horthy's wife, and, especially, the latter's mother) who were behind this intrigue." *Serédi*, p. 76.

30. Lehmann, p. 89; *Serédi*, pp. 138–44.

31. *Serédi*, p. 63.

32. In requesting an audience with Hitler, Albrecht promised his obedience and loyalty to the Führer if Germany supported his candidacy.

Hitler declined, pointing out that it would be an insult to Horthy "to whom he felt a close personal connection." *A Wilhelmstrasse,* pp. 641, 646; Nagy-Talavera, p. 175.

33. Lehmann, pp. 78–79.

34. Horthy was so infuriated that he wanted immediately to expel Imrédy from the Order of Heroes. Bárczy, p. 78.

35. Kádár, p. 474.

36. Trevor-Roper, p. 485.

37. Goebbels, *Diaries,* p. 95.

38. István Vida, "A lengyel emigrans kormány lisszaboni követségének magyar vonatkozású iratai (1942–1945)." *Történelmi Szemle,* 32, no. 4 (1987–88), p. 444.

39. *The Ciano Diaries,* p. 478.

40. Macartney, *OF,* II: 82.

41. Nicholas Kállay, *Hungarian Premier* (New York: Columbia U.P., 1954), p. 5.

42. Lehmann, pp. 84–85. See also Macartney, *OF,* II: 80–81.

43. Fenyő, p. 57; Lehmann, p. 85.

44. Macartney, *OF,* II: 84. The following sketch of Kállay is based in part on Macartney's perceptive analysis (pp. 83–86).

45. Kállay, p. 6, fn. 7.

46. The only detailed account of this important conversation is that provided by Kállay, pp. 7–11. Horthy's *Memoirs* (p. 203) are not helpful.

47. There is no other evidence to confirm that Bárdossy had in fact made suggestions along these lines.

48. Kállay, p. 7.

49. The following is based on a critical reading of Kállay's own account in his memoirs (pp. 14–17). See also the somewhat sympathetic account in Macartney, *OF,* II: 86–88; and the more skeptical analyses in Fenyő, pp. 64–66 and Ránki, *Unternehmen Margarethe,* pp. 11–12.

50. In a postwar interrogation Horthy admitted that in this period he, unlike his son, did not believe that Germany would lose the war. NA Record Group 59, DeWitt Poole Interrogations, Sept. 1, 1945. In 1942 even the most vociferous anti-Nazis, such as Bethlen and György Barcza, believed that the war would end in a stalemate, not in an outright German defeat. Károly Urbán, "Barcza György," pp. 397–98.

51. Kállay, p. 16.

52. Macartney, *OF,* II: 88.

53. Macartney, *OF:* II: 91.

54. Kállay, p. 72.

55. Kállay, p. 15.

56. Kállay, p. 99; Macartney, *OF,* II: 100. For a detailed and balanced treatment of Kállay's policies toward the Jews, see Braham, *PoG,* I: 222–54.

57. Náray, pp. 63, 66.

58. Undated and unsigned S.D. report, GFM, NAM, T-120, 1096/452385–

87. Horthy's interlocutor is identified in the document only as "a Hungarian economic expert," but from the context the reference is to Reményi-Schneller.

59. Katzburg, p. 209. Kállay does not mention this episode in his memoirs, but see Saly, p. 561.

60. Horthy may have picked up this idea from Lipot Baranyai, President of the National Bank, who opposed Reményi-Schneller's plan on both economic and political grounds. Katzburg, pp. 209–10; Saly, 561.

61. Horthy referred to the beginning of this operation in his letter to Hitler of January 10, 1942, *HP*, p. 188.

62. For a full treatment, see Braham, *PoG*, pp. 207–15; also Fenyő, p. 70–1; Macartney, *OF*, II: 70–74.

63. Karsai, *A budai vár*, pp. 116–19; Braham, *PoG*, I: 212. Horthy received a similar memorandum from Géza Szüllő, a member of the Upper House. Saly, p. 469.

64. Károly Vígh, "Horthy és Zsilinszky," *História*, 12, nos. 5–6 (1990), p. 19.

65. Macartney, *OF*, II: 74.

66. Macartney, *OF*, II: 110.

67. Kállay, 102–03.

68. S.D. report of Aug. 29, 1942, NAM, T-120, 2090/452388–9.

69. Lehmann, p. 93.

70. *Serédi*, pp. 78–79.

71. Serédi, pp. 78–80, 86–91.

72. Hans Lehmann, whose attitude toward Miklós Horthy was generally critical, concluded that ultimately Horthy "placed the welfare of the state over the plans of his family and the camarilla." (p. 55)

73. Kádár, p. 478.

74. Károly Urbán, "Barcza György," p. 387; *Serédi*, p. 83.

75. Hitler to Marshal Sladko Kwaternik on July 21, 1941, in *Staatsmänner und Diplomaten bei Hitler. Vertrauliche Aufzeichnungen über Unterredungen mit Vertretern des Auslandes 1939–1941*, ed. Andreas Hillgruber (Frankfurt: Bernard & Graefe, 1967), I: 615. Cited hereafter as *Staatsmänner*.

76. Thomas L. Sakmyster, "A Hungarian Diplomat in Nazi Berlin: Döme Sztójay," in *HHWH*, pp. 300–01.

77. Braham, *PoG*, I: 285, 320.

78. Nagy, *Végzetes esztendők*, p. 77; Macartney, *OF*, II: 114; Fenyő, pp. 76–77; Braham, *PoG*, I: 321–25.

79. Nagy, *Végzetes esztendők*, p. 139.

80. Martin Gilbert, *The Holocaust. A History of the Jews of Europe during the Second World War* (New York: Holt, Rinehart, and Winston, 1985), pp. 450–51.

81. Fenyő, pp. 72–74; Kállay, pp. 113–21.

82. S.D. report of Jan. 2, 1943, GFM, PRO, T-120, 231/E310753–6.

83. Andorka, p. 271. For the text of the memorandum see Saly, pp. 600–07. See also Romsics, *Bethlen István*, p. 289.

84. Andorka, p. 278; Romsics, *Bethlen István*, p. 289.

85. Loránt Tilkovszky, "Ellenzéki törvényhozók memorandum-akciója 1942–43 telén," *Századok*, 119, no. 1 (1985), pp. 152–223; Andorka, p. 283.

86. Dombrády, *A legfelsőbb hadúr*, p. 187.

87. Fenyő, pp. 102–03; Dombrády, *A legfelsőbb hadúr*, pp. 189–90.

88. Fenyő, pp. 106–08; Gosztony, *Hitlers Fremde Heere*, pp. 343–44.

89. Macartney, *OF*, II: 132.

90. István Pintér, *A Sociáldemokrata Párt története 1933–1944* (Budapest: 1980), pp. 195–96.

91. Upon learning of this incident, Mussolini expressed his astonishment that the Hungarian Regent would grant a "three hour audience" to a socialist while at the same time refusing to meet with the leader of the Hungarian Nazis. *ADAP*, E/5/326.

92. Pintér, pp. 195–96; Saly, p. 615.

93. Peyer and his colleagues apparently believed the Regent's gesture to be sincere and believed that they might be asked to join a coalition government soon to be formed. Pintér, p. 196.

94. Kállay's suggestions are known only from Horthy's response in a letter of Jan. 13, 1943. OL, Horthy iratai, K589, I/H/14.

95. Horthy's memorandum is known only from references to it in Kállay's response of Feb. 26, 1943, *HMTI*, pp. 356–60.

96. *HMTI*, p. 356; Romsics, *Bethlen István*, p. 295.

97. *HMTI*, pp. 356–60.

98. Kállay, p. 195; Macartney, *OF*, II: 157, fn. 2.

99. See Ignác Romsics, "Horthy Miklós levelei Zsitvay Tiborhoz," *História*, 12, nos. 5–6 (1990), pp. 33–35.

100. For the details, see Juhász, *HFP*, pp. 220–21.

101. Károly Urbán, "Barcza György," p. 417; Kállay, pp. 384–85; Juhász, *HFP*, p. 217.

102. Ferenc Váli, *A Scholar's Odyssey* (Ames: Iowa St., 1990), pp. 11–12.

103. Juhász, *HFP*, pp. 222–23; Fenyő, pp. 122–24.

104. Károly Urbán, "György Barcza," p. 411.

105. Horthy, *Memoirs*, p. 204; Kállay, p. 136.

106. Károly Urbán, "Barcza," p. 408; Macartney, *OF*, II: 123.

107. Juhász, *HFP*, pp. 220–21.

108. Braham, *PoG*, I: 252, fn. 57.

109. Fenyő, p. 125.

110. For these memorandums, see *CPAH*, pp. pp. 221–23, 231–44.

111. Kállay, pp. 178–79.

112. For a full discussion of this issue, see Braham, *PoG*, II: 716–18.

Chapter Ten

1. This is the best documented of their six meetings, since a detailed protocol was drawn up by Hitler's interpreter, Paul Schmidt: *Staatsmänner*, II: 234–63. The following account is based on this source except where noted. Hitler

had insisted that Schmidt attend the sessions even though no interpreter was needed: "I want to have you there today when I talk to Horthy, so that we can have an independent report made; otherwise Horthy distorts what I say." Paul Schmidt, *Hitler's Interpreter*, ed. R.H.C. Steed (London: William Heinemann, 1951), p. 248.

2. This remark may have been prompted by the fact that Hitler just days earlier had received the first report of the Katyn Forest massacres that the Soviet secret police had committed two years earlier.

3. In his diary Goebbels wrote of the Klessheim talks: "The Führer minced no words and especially pointed out to Horthy how wrong were his policies both in general and especially with reference to the conduct of the war and the question of the Jews. The Führer was very outspoken." Goebbels, *Diaries*, p. 335.

4. Fenyő, p. 124.

5. On this see the perceptive comments of György Ránki, "Hitler and the Statesmen of East Central Europe, 1939–1945," in Steven Béla Várdy and Ágnes Huszár Várdy, *Society in Change. Studies in Honor of Béla K. Király* (Boulder: East European Monographs, 1983), p. 648.

6. Bárczy, p. 65.

7. Irving, *Hitler's War*, p. 612, fn. 5. Although Horthy had a slight hearing problem as a result of the injuries he incurred in the Battle of Otranto, the American doctors who examined him after World War II found no significant hearing impairment. NA, USSD, 740.0016, EW/1-2247.

8. This is the only recorded instance in which Hitler spoke so openly of the need to kill the Jews.

9. Goebbels wrote in his diary: "Horthy . . . is badly tangled up with the Jews through his family, and will continue to resist every effort to tackle the Jewish problem aggressively. . . . You cannot talk humanitarianism when dealing with the Jews. Jews must be defeated. The Führer made every effort to win Horthy over to his standpoint but succeeded only partially." Goebbels, *Diaries*, p. 357.

10. Goebbels, *Diaries*, p. 335.

11. Bárczy, 65; Juhász, *HFP*, p. 239.

12. *ADAP*, E/6/56; Irving, p. 612, fn. 5.

13. *CPAH*, pp. 248–57. Mario Fenyő (p. 139) called this document "one of the Regent's more courageous letters."

14. Veesenmayer's report, dated April 30, is found in NAM, T-175, 65/2581460–73. See also Elek Karsai, "Edmund Veesenmayer's Reports to Hitler on Hungary in 1943," *New Hungarian Quarterly*, 5 (1964), pp. 146–53.

15. *HMTI*, p. 371; *CPAH*, pp. 244–48. Nagy, *Végzetes esztendők*, pp. 141–42.

16. *CPAH*, pp. 258–60; 379–81; Kádár, p. 635.

17. Von Jagov's report of June 21, 1943 in *ADAP*, E/6/108.

18. In his conversation with Jagov in late June, Horthy had predicted that there would be no Allied landing in Italy. Rather, there would be an attempt to pass through the Turkish Straits and to seize the Romanian oil fields. *ADAP*, E/16/108.

19. The Smallholders party made these recommendations in a memorandum that was presented to Kállay and Horthy in late July. Pintér, *A Szociáldemokrata Párt*, pp. 249–50.

20. Kállay, p. 205; Juhász, *HFP*, pp. 255–56.

21. Dombrády, *A legfelsőbb hadúr*, p. 194. Dombrády (p. 195) estimates that about two-thirds of the field generals could have been counted on to support a surrender to the Allies, but not even one-third of the the General Staff officers.

22. Dombrády, *A legfelsőbb hadúr*, p. 197. Of the fifty generals in attendance at the banquet in February, 1944, only six were to remain loyal to the Regent in October, 1944. Károly Vígh, *Ugrás a sötétbe* (Budapest: Magvető, 1984), pp. 219–20.

23. Kádár, p. 529; Kállay, p. 319.

24. Dombrády, p. 198.

25. He thought "loony Niki" shouldn't stick his nose into political affairs, because he would just cause trouble. Kádár, p. 534.

26. Kádár, p. 529.

27. This meeting of Horthy's "camarilla" is known only from a German intelligence report, which appears, however, to be accurate: NA, T-120, 2090/452456–60. See also Romsics, *Bethlen István*, p. 291; Juhász, *HFP*, p. 257.

28. Károly Vígh, "Horthy és Zsilinszky," *História*, 12, nos. 5–6 (1990), p. 20; György Ránki, *Unternehmen Margarethe. Die deutsche Besetzung Ungarns*, p. 13; Pintér, *A Szociáldemokrata Párt*, pp. 256–58.

29. Pintér, *A Szociáldemokrata Párt*, pp. 259–60.

30. Ránki, *Unternehmen Margarethe*, pp. 32–33.

31. Macartney, *OF*, II: 198–99; Ránki, *Unternehmen Margarethe*, pp. 74–75.

32. Juhász, *HFP*, pp. 264–65.

33. Gosztony, *Hitlers Fremde Heere*, p. 367.

34. Kállay, p. 376.

35. Kállay, p. 343.

36. In a draft of a proposed speech that Horthy composed in March, 1944, he referred to the "unpardonable and condemnable events" that had taken place at Újvidék. *CPAH*, p. 272.

37. Gostony, *HHWH*, p. 248.

38. Fenyő, pp. 71–72. Feketehalmi-Czeydner's postwar claim that Horthy had abetted his escape is not plausible. Szombathelyi publicly condemned the fugitives and the Regent's Military Bureau issued orders that an energetic effort be made to locate them. The evidence suggests that the escape of the four officers was arranged by Archduke Albrecht. Kádár, pp. 646–47.

39. In 1942 Horthy had apparently been so outraged by reports of atrocities committed by the Red Army on the Eastern Front that he proposed to General Wilhelm Keitel that poison gas be used in retaliation. GFM, NAM, T-120, Roll 93 93/104884-5.

40. Ránki, *Unternehmen Margarethe*, pp. 87–88, 93–94.

41. Macartney, *OF*, II: 210.

42. Macartney, *OF*, II: 208.

43. Horthy admitted this to his friend Franz von Papen in December, 1943, and even confided that he had sent out peace feelers to the Western powers. Franz von Papen, *Memoirs* (New York: E. P. Dutton, 1953), p. 509.

44. Hitler spoke in these terms to General Nagy in late 1943. See Nagy, *Végzetes esztendők*, p. 182.

45. Macartney, *OF*, II: 203; Juhász, *HFP*, p. 272.

46. Kádár, p. 636.

47. Kádár, pp. 635–37.

48. The earliest written version of this joke seems to be that found in Ciano, *Diaries*, p, 484. The version cited here is found in Váli, p. 6.

49. Roosevelt had once told Montgomery to tell Horthy that "we sailors must stick together." Montgomery, pp. 26, 45. See also Ignác Romsics, "A State Department és Magyarország, 1942–1947," *Valóság*, 3, no. 2 (Nov., 1991), p. 56.

50. *CPAH*, pp. 267–69.

51. Thus Goebbels in his diary (p. 507): "Influential circles are at work for a direct break with us. The Regent is trying to create the impression that he is neutral about these efforts. That is, however, in no wise the case."

52. Macartney, *OF*, II: 233, fn. 1.

53. Hans Heinrich Wilhelm, "Hitlers Ansprache vor Generalen und Offizieren am 26. Mai 1944," *Militärische Mitteilungen*, 20 (1976), p. 156.

54. This from a later survey of events leading to the German occupation to be found in PRO, FO371/39261/67515.

55. NAM, T-120, 94/106873–910. Also printed in *A Wilhelmstrasse*, pp. 743–55.

56. For a good analysis of Veesenmayer's report, see Ránki, *Unternehmen Margarethe*, pp. 62–69.

57. For a full discussion of German planning, see Fenyő, pp. 158–63.

58. By contrast, the Swiss diplomatic mission in Budapest concluded by March 16 that a German occupation of Hungary was imminent and that no resistance was expected. Péter Gosztony, *Magyarország a második világháborúban*, 2 vols. (Munich: HERP, 1984), p. 34.

59. *CPAH*, pp. 269–72.

60. See his letter to Horthy of March 8, 1944, *CPAH*, pp. 273–76.

61. Gyula Juhász, "Some Aspects of Relations between Hungary and Germany during the Second World War," *HHWH*, p. 212.

62. Leni Yahil, *The Holocaust. The Fate of European Jewry, 1932–1945* (New York: Oxford U.P., 1990), p. 184.

63. Writing shortly after the war, Jenő Lévai concluded that Hungary's Jews "were able to maintain themselves satisfactorily, even if they did have to draw largely on their own reserves for this purpose." Jenő Lévai, *Zsidosors Magyarországon* (Budapest: Magyar Téka, 1948), p. 37.

64. Gestapo report of Dec. 22, 1943, NAM, T-175, 59/574568.

65. Bethlen apparently also advised Horthy not to leave the country. He correctly suspected that the Germans had laid a trap. Romsics, *Bethlen István*, p. 296.

66. Kállay, p. 414.

67. Interview of Horthy in 1945 by C. A. Macartney, in Macartney Archive.

68. Kállay, p. 416.

69. Macartney, *OF*, II: 230.

70. Macartney, *OF*, II: 233; Juhász, *HFP*, p. 288. Juhász also suggests that a message was sent by Horthy to Otto via Lisbon investing him with full authority in case of a German occupation and asking him to take over as legitimate king of Hungary. Although such a message may have been sent, it is very unlikely that Horthy had knowledge of it or would have approved it.

71. Horthy, *Memoirs*, p. 212.

72. Ránki, *Unternehmen Margarethe*, p. 144.

73. No stenographic record was made of any of the discussions at Klessheim. The following account is based primarily on recollections from the Hungarian side. Horthy told his story a number of times: to Kállay (pp. 428–30); at the Crown Council of March 19, *CPAH*, pp. 280–88; several months later to Antal Náray (pp. 107–10); in postwar interviews; and in his *Memoirs*, pp. 212–16. General Szombathelyi's report on his role is in *Allianz*, pp. 375–81. An official of the Foreign Office, Andor Szentmiklóssy, prepared an account that reached the British Foreign Office in April, PRO, FO371/39261/C5182/15/21. In addition to other scattered primary sources cited in the footnotes below, there are good accounts in Macartney, *OF*, II: 232–41 and Ránki, *Unternehmen Margarethe*, pp. 145–55.

74. Horthy insisted that since he had brought none of his entourage with him to the conference room, all of Hitler's aides, even Schmidt, must leave also.

75. Horthy, *Memoirs*, p. 213.

76. Náray, p. 108.

77. In writing his memoirs several years later, Horthy recalled this incident with bitterness and anger. He even hinted that he might have used his revolver against Hitler had he not, after considerable deliberation, left it in his train compartment. Horthy, *Memoirs*, pp. 213–14.

78. Schmidt, p. 270.

79. Horthy interrogation in 1945, NA, World War II War Crimes Records, 6824, DIC (MIS).X-P7, p. 16.

80. Fenyő, pp. 165–66.

81. *Allianz*, p. 378.

82. Paul Schmidt was told by Ribbentrop that if Horthy did not give way, he would return to Hungary "as a prisoner." Schmidt, p. 271.

83. Later Sztójay told the German military attaché in Budapest that he

had no objection to the entry of German troops. In fact, both he and Homlok were glad that there would now be a radical solution to the "Jewish question." NAM, T-78, 451/426889.

84. *Allianz*, p. 379–80.

85. Horthy, *Memoirs*, p. 214. Horthy referred to Hitler's promise in a draft letter of June 6, 1944, *CPAH*, pp. 384–85.

86. Náray, p. 109; Kállay, p. 431. Horthy gained the impression that Hitler intended for the German occupation to last at most two or three months. Ránki, pp. 152–53.

87. *CPAH*, p. 284.

88. An OKW document seems to overstate the case in reporting that Horthy at this time declared "that he understood the views of the Führer fully and therefore will comply with his requests." Fenyő, p. 167.

89. Ránki, pp. 154–56; Fenyő, p. 168.

90. Schmidt, p. 271.

Chapter Eleven

1. Kaltenbrunner was introduced to Horthy by Peter Hain, the Regent's personal detective, who, it turned out, had for years been sending secret reports to the Gestapo. Eugene Lévai, *Black Book on the Martyrdom of Hungarian Jewry* (Zürich: Central European Times, 1948), p. 99.

2. Kállay, p. 439.

3. Kállay, pp. 431–32.

4. *CPAH*, pp. 280–88.

5. Bárczy, p. 82; Horthy, *Memoirs*, pp. 214–15.

6. Kállay, p. 433.

7. An unsigned memo (probably drafted by Móric Kornfeld) entitled "A Zsidókérdés Magyarországon," in Macartney Archive.

8. István Bethlen, *Hungarian Politics*, p. 2.

9. Veesenmayer's report of March 20, 1944, *ADAP*, E/7/277.

10. Juhász, *HFP*, p. 292.

11. Náray, p. 106; Fenyő, p. 177, fn. 10.

12. At his postwar trial Sztójay recalled that on March 22, 1944, Horthy had promised to put up a statue of him "on the finest site in Budapest" if he succeeded in regaining the confidence of the Germans. Macartney, *OF*, II: 250.

13. Ránki, *Unternehmen Margarethe*, p. 179.

14. Barcza, Diary, March 25, 1944.

15. *The Times*, March 24, 1944.

16. Szálasi wrote a meticulous, almost verbatim, account of the conversation for his diary. See *Szálasi naplója. A Nyilasmozgalom a II. Világháború idején*, ed. Elek Karsai, (Budapest: Kossuth, 1978), pp. 189–97.

17. Bárczy, p. 82.

18. Péter Gosztony, "Das private Kriegstagebuch des Chefs des ungari-

schen Generalstabes vom Jahre 1944," *Wehrwissenschaftliche Rundschau*, no. 11 (1970), p. 642 (Cited hereafter as Vörös, "Diary"); Fenyő, pp. 179–80; Géza Lakatos, *Ahogyan én láttam. Visszaemlékezések* (Munich: Aurora, 1981), pp. 83–85.

19. Kádár, p. 701; Vörös, "Diary," pp. 638–39.

20. Jenő Lévai, ed., *Eichmann in Hungary. Documents* (Budapest: Pannonia, 1961), pp. 66–67; Macartney, *OF*, II: 275.

21. Sztójay and other members of his Cabinet did attend, despite Horthy's advice against it. *A Wilhelmstrasse*, pp. 844–45. See also Lévai, *Black Book*, p. 170.

22. Braham, *PoG*, I: 691–716. Chorin's letter of explanation to Horthy dated May 17, 1944, is in *CPAH*, pp. 291–93.

23. For an opposing view, see Braham, *PoG*, I: 372; Macartney, *OF*, II: 280.

24. Lévai, *Black Book*, p. 113; Braham, *PoG*, I: 379–80. See also Macartney, *OF*, II: 282–83.

25. In early July, 1944, Horthy told the Swedish Minister that it had been his understanding that the Jews of "the eastern operational zone" had been deported as war workers because among them were "numerous Communist elements who during the last few decades had insinuated themselves into society and who don't have a good deal in common with the Hungarian people." Gilbert Joseph, *Mission sans retour. L'Affaire Wallenberg* (Paris: Albin Michel, 1982), p. 74.

26. Braham, *PoG*, I: 379.

27. At his postwar trial Veesenmayer claimed that Horthy told him he wanted to protect "the economically valuable Jews in Budapest, those who were well off." As for the other Jews, and here Horthy allegedly used "a very ugly term," he was not interested in them "and was quite prepared to have them go to the Reich or elsewhere for labor." Braham, *PoG*, I: 379; Ránki, pp. 318–19. On the other hand, if Horthy had in fact spoken in this way, it seems Veesenmayer would have mentioned the conversation in his otherwise detailed reports from that period.

28. At his postwar trial Endre testified that Horthy told him that the faster the deportations occurred, the sooner the German occupation would end. Ránki, *Unternehmen Margarethe*, p. 319.

29. Braham, *PoG*, I: 378.

30. Yahil, p. 509.

31. Debórah Dwork, *Children with a Star. Jewish Youth in Nazi Europe* (New Haven: Yale U.P., 1991), pp. 159–60.

32. Lévai, *Black Book*, p. 117.

33. Lévai, *Black Book*, p. 125.

34. Lévai, *Black Book*, p. 250.

35. For this meeting, see Jenő Lévai, *Zsidosors*, p. 100; Ernő Munkácsi, *Hogyan történt? Adatok és okmányok a magyar zsidóság tragédiájához* (Budapest: Renaissance, 1947), p. 168; Braham, *PoG*, I: 380.

36. When asked at a postwar trial whether he believed Horthy to be telling the truth in this conversation, Ravasz responded: "I believe that the Regent had been misled, and in this way was trying to ease his conscience." Munkácsi, p. 168.

37. Lakatos, p. 90; Kádár, p. 720.

38. Gosztony, *Magyarország a második világháború*, II: 35–36.

39. On May 17 Mrs. Samuel Gotterer, head of the Jewish Women's Association of Kassa, managed to dispatch a letter to Horthy's wife, who was asked to work to have the deportations halted, at least for children and old people. Munkácsi, pp. 82–83.

40. Munkácsi, p. 172.

41. *CPAH*, pp. 296–99.

42. See Horthy's comments in a postwar interrogation, NA, World War II War Crimes Records, 6824, DIS (MIS), X-P7, p. 17.

43. Arieh Ben-tov, *Facing the Holocaust in Budapest. The International Red Committee of the Red Cross and the Jews in Hungary, 1943–1945* (Dondrecht: Nijhoff, 1988), p. 157; Gosztony, *Magyarország a második világháborúban*, p. 38. See also PRO, FO371/39263/C7464/15/21.

44. The draft of Horthy's letter is in *CPAH*, pp. 301–03.

45. This letter, dated June 6, is found in *CPAH*, pp. 305–06.

46. Horthy did tell Sztójay that he had little confidence in him. Náray, p. 111.

47. Veesenmayer's report of June 21, 1944, GFM, NA, T-120, 3579/E025114–5.

48. Vörös, "Diary," p. 648.

49. Náray, p. 106; Munkácsi, pp. 169, 172.

50. Tsvi Erez, "Hungary. Six Days in July, 1944," *Holocaust and Genocide Studies*, 3, no. 1 (1988), p. 51, fn. 32. For the Auschwitz Protocols, see Braham, *PoG*, II: 708–16.

51. Lévai, *Black Book*, pp. 192–96; Yahil, p. 513.

52. Jenő Lévai, *Hungarian Jewry and the Papacy. Pope Pius XII Did Not Remain Silent* (London: Sands, 1968), pp. 25–26. This direct cable from the pope was "the first of its kind during the Holocaust period." Yahil, p. 640.

53. Lévai, *Black Book*, p. 229; Erez, "Six Days," p. 38.

54. Péter Bokor, *Végjáték a Duna mentén. Interjúk egy film sororzathoz* (Budapest: RTV-Minerva, 1982), p. 158; Braham, *PoG*, II: 610–12.

55. Horthy told the Swedish Minister on July 3: "Since the Germans came, Hungary has no longer been a sovereign state. The Germans are behind all the measures taken against the Jews. They are carrying out this filthy work. . . . That which has been reported about the excesses committed by the Hungarian gendarmerie is untrue. The gendarmerie is impeccable and above all suspicion." Joseph, p. 74.

56. The minutes of this key meeting have not survived. The following is based on Vörös, "Diary," p. 653; Lévai, *Black Book*, p. 243; Munkácsi, pp. 173–74; Braham, *PoG*, II: 754–55.

57. Macartney, *OF*, II: 303; Lévai, *Black Book*, pp. 247–48; Erez, "Six Days," p. 42.

58. Vörös, "Diary," p. 655. Ernő Pető may have been the first to alert Horthy to the possibility that Baky would use the gendarmes to stage a coup d'état. Erez, "Six Days," p. 43. See also Macartney, *OF*, II: 305.

59. Among other things, Bethlen deplored the "inhuman, foolish, and cruel persecution of the Jews" and warned that the "incredible corruption and moral depravity" of the current government would inevitably "pave the way to Bolshevism." *CPAH*, pp. 308–14.

60. During a two-hour conversation with Veesenmayer on July 5, Horthy complained bitterly that he was being treated like an "object of ridicule" (*Popanz*) in his own country, but he gave no indication of the bold action he was planning. *ADAP*, E/8/102.

61. Vörös, "Diary," pp. 657–59.

62. Erez, "Six Days," p. 45. Vörös did not learn of these moves until the morning of July 7. When he questioned Lázár, the latter explained that he, the Chief of Staff, had not been informed earlier because they did not wish to disturb his sleep. Vörös, p. 659.

63. Lévai, *Black Book*, pp. 248–49; Fenyő, pp. 203–04.

64. Veesenmayer's reports of July 8 and 9, 1944, *ADAP*, E/8/105; GFM, NA, T-120, 1757/3579/E025088–89.

65. Lévai, *Black Book*, p. 252.

66. Lévai, *Black Book*, p. 255; Erez, "Six Days," p. 514.

67. Lakatos, p. 90.

68. *CPAH*, pp. 308–14.

69. Vörös, "Diary," p. 703.

70. Lakatos, pp. 91–92; Romsics, *Bethlen István*, p. 299.

71. Horthy's letter was subsequently dated July 17, but was clearly composed a week earlier. For the text, see *CPAH*, pp. 316–18.

72. Vörös, "Diary," p. 705.

73. Most of the proposed ministers, including General Kálmán Hardy (as Foreign Minister) and Iván Rakovszky, were known for their pro-Western and anti-Nazi sentiments.

74. See *ADAP*, E/8/121; and Veesenmayer's report of July 17, 1992, GFM, NA,T-120, 1757/3579, E025080–81. See also Ránki, *Unternehmen Margarethe*, pp. 355–57; Fenyő, p. 209.

75. It was too dangerous for Bethlen to come to Budapest, but Kálmán Kánya, Gyula Károlyi, and Zsigmond Perényi were able to join Lakatos, Csatay, and Gyula Ambrózy, the chief of the Regent's Cabinet Bureau.

76. Lakatos, pp. 94–95; Ránki, *Unternehmen Margarethe*, pp. 362–63; Macartney, *OF*, II: 308.

77. Lakatos, p. 95.

78. Lévai, *Black Book*, p. 325.

79. Lévai, *Black Book*, pp. 296–99.

80. Bela Vágo, "The Horthy Offer. A Missed Opportunity for Rescuing

Jews in 1944," in *Contemporary Views on the Holocaust*, ed. Randolph L. Braham (New York: , 1983), p. 27.

81. Vágo, "The Horthy Offer," p. 29.

82. Joseph, p. 126; see also Éva Szabó, "A magyarországi svéd mentő-akció történetéhez (1944), *Történelmi Szemle*, 30, no. 3 (1987–88), pp. 379–94.

83. Macartney, *OF*, II: 319.

84. Heinz Guderian, who was in Budapest in late August, confided to Horthy that Hitler had no "Wunderwappen" that could alter the course of the war. Heinz Guderian, *Panzer Leader* (New York: Dutton, 1952), p. 368. See also Gustav Hennyey, *Ungarns Schicksal zwischen Ost und West* (Mainz: Von Hase-Koehler, 1975), p. 65.

85. Lakatos, p. 97. In his memoirs (p. 223) Horthy wrote that in the fall of 1944 he no longer felt a responsibility to honor his promises to Hitler, but he did not want to act dishonorably toward the German people, who were themselves victims of Hitler and later of Russia.

86. Macartney, *OF*, II: 335; Hennyey, p. 79; Juhász, *HFP*, p. 302.

87. Bárczy, p. 93.

88. Hennyey, p. 73.

89. Macartney, *OF*, II: 330–31; *A Szálasi per*, pp. 543–44; Margit Szöllösi-Janze, *Die Pfeilkreuzlerbewegung in Ungarn: Historische Kontext, Entwicklung, und Herrschaft* (Munich: Oldenbourg, 1989), p. 305.

90. The following is based on *Vattay Antal naplója 1944–1945*, ed. Károly Vígh (Budapest: Zrínyi, 1990), pp. 48–49; Lakatos, pp. 111–13; Vörös, "Diary," p. 717.

91. Vattay, p. 78.

92. For a different interpretation of Horthy's motives, see Juhász, *HFP*, p. 304.

93. Vörös, "Diary," p. 720; Lakatos, pp. 86, 114–15; Károly Vigh, *Ugrás*, p. 7; Macartney, *OF*, II: 339.

94. The following is based on Romsics, *Bethlen István*, pp. 302–03; Vigh, *Ugrás*, pp. 77–83; Macartney, *OF*. II: 342–43; Lakatos, p. 118; Vörös, "Diary," p. 721. Those present at the meeting included Lakatos, Hennyey, Csatay, Vörös, Röder, Sónyi, Náday, Kánya, Perényi, Károlyi, Esterházy, and Bethlen.

95. Horthy was referring here to the initial response he had received from Bakách-Bessenyey. Macartney, *OF*, II: 335–36.

96. Macartney, *OF*, II: 342.

97. Lakatos, p. 118; Bárczy, p. 102; Vörös, "Diary," p. 722.

98. Vattay, p. 49; Hennyey, p.83; Vígh, *Ugrás*, p. 87; Zinner, *A Szálasi per*, p. 40.

99. Náday brought with him a personal letter from Horthy to the pope in which the Regent made an attempt to depict Hungary as an innocent victim of a rogues' gallery of Hungarophobes, including the peacemakers after World War I, the Little Entente, the Nazis, and the Bolsheviks. *Actes et Documents du Saint Siège Relatifs à la Seconde Guerre Mondiale*, ed. Pierre

Blet et al. (Vatican City: Libreria Editrice Vaticana, 1981), II: 546–47. See also Macartney, *OF*, II: 351–52.

100. Macartney, *OF*, II: 354; Gosztony, *Magyarország a második világháborúban*, pp. 112-13.

101. The text of Horthy's letter is found in László Szűcs, "Horthy levele Sztálinhoz 1944 őszén," *Századok*, no. 4 (1970), pp. 987–88.

102. In fact, Horthy had learned of the report of the Hungarian Minister, which Bárdossy had suppressed at the time, only in August 1944, when Bárczy brought it to his attention .

103. Vattay, p. 83. The encryption of the messages was not carried out by a General Staff communications specialist, because none could be identified who was considered completely trustworthy. Vígh, *Ugrás*, p. 149.

104. Ignác Ölvedi, *A Budai Vár és a debreceni csata. Horthyék katasztrófapolitikája 1944 őszén* (Budapest: Zrinyi, 1974), pp. 158–59; Macartney, *OF*, II: 372. It has been determined that the "Makarov letters" were in fact composed independently by Col. Makarov as propaganda material for use in Slovakia and had not been authorized by Moscow. Vígh, *Ugrás*, pp. 136–42.

105. The following is based on Vattay, p. 81; Hennyey, p. 85; and Lakatos, pp. 128–29.

106. Mihály Korom, *Magyarország ideiglenes nemzeti kormánya és a fegyverszünet (1944–1945)* (Budapest: Akadémiai, 1981), pp. 134–35.

107. Vattay, p. 81.

108. Ölvedi, p. 161. Stalin later told a group of Hungarian Communists that he would have been prepared to retain Horthy as head of a transitional Hungarian government if he had been able to carry out the terms of the armistice. Korom, p. 189.

109. The following is based on the excellent exposition in Macartney, *OF*, II: 381–82, as well as Fenyő, p. 225;

110. Macartney, *OF*, II: 363. See also Szöllösi, p. 302 and Hennyey, pp. 92–93.

111. Szöllösi, p. 314.

112. Winkelmann's report to Himmler of Oct. 25, 1944, NAM, T-175, 59/574485–96; Macartney, *OF*, II: 359–60.

113. Vigh, *Ugrás*, pp. 199–200; Vattay, p. 55.

114. Gosztony, *HHWH*, p. 249; Kádár, pp. 742, 745.

115. Macartney, *OF*, II: 383; Pintér, *Szociáldemokrata Párt*, p. 375; Vígh, *Ugrás*, pp. 203–05. Horthy refused to meet with the Communist delegate on the March Front, László Rajk, although he agreed that Niki and others in his entourage should maintain contact with Rajk.

116. Horthy later wrote that he regarded Tildy and Szakasits as "minor political figures" and his discussion with them as having "no practical results." *Memoirs*, p. 226.

117. Macartney, *OF*, II: 391.

118. Lakatos, pp. 137–38; Gosztony, *Magyarország és a második világháborúban*, pp. 93–94. The proclamation had been drafted by Ambrózy and was edited by Vattay. Vattay, p. 91.

119. Zinner, *Szálasi per*, p. 590; Macartney, p. 396; Vörös, p. 731; Vígh, p. 253.

120. The Gestapo lured Niki from the Castle by sending him a message that led him to believe that an emissary from Tito would meet him at a designated place in Pest. Macartney, *OF*, II: 399.

121. The minutes of the Crown Council are found in Bárczy, pp. 107–15. See also Horthy, *Memoirs*, pp. 230–31; Macartney, *OF*, II: ; Vígh, *Ugrás*, p. 265; Vattay, pp. 90–91; Hennyey, pp. 94–95.

122. Horthy was correct in suspecting that the Cabinet remained opposed to armistice negotiations with the Russians, as can be seen in the long discussion of the issue at the Cabinet meeting of October 14. *Allianz*, pp. 391–400.

123. The following is based on Bárczy, pp. 111–12; Hennyey, pp. 96–97; Lakatos, pp. 141–42; Macartney, *OF*, II: 402; and Veesenmayer's testimony at Szálasi's postwar trial, Zinner, *Szálasi bilincsben*, II: 225.

124. Horthy did agree, at Veesenmayer's request, to meet with Rudolph Rahn, who had just arrived in Budapest as Hitler's special emissary. Horthy's conversation with Rahn was surprisingly friendly but had no impact on the course of events. Macartney, *OF*, II: 406–07; Hennyey, p. 97; Lakatos, p. 144.

125. The Hungarian text of the proclamation, which took about five minutes to read and was repeated two times on the afternoon of October 15, is found in Vattay, pp. 109–10. An English translation is in Horthy, *Memoirs*, pp. 259–60.

126. Vígh, *Ugrás*, pp. 272, 276–78.

127. The text is in *Allianz*, p. 402. See also Szöllösi, p. 315 and Fenyő, p. 233. Horthy's order that his proclamation to the troops be sent directly to all soldiers was thwarted by the General Staff. Hennyey, p. 98.

128. Vígh, p. 282; Juhász, *Hungarian Foreign Policy*, p. 329; Macartney, pp. 416–19; Ölvedi, pp. 180–81; and József Borus, "Vörös János és Nádas Lajos 1944. Október 15-i szerepéről," *Történelmi Szemle*, 91, nos. 3–4 (1991), p. 253.

129. Szöllösi, p. 315.

130. Vígh, p. 288; Bárczy, 99, 114–15; Korom, pp. 138–39.

131. Macartney, *OF*, II: 428; Vattay, p. 96.

132. Vattay, p. 96; István Szent-Miklósy, *With the Hungarian Independence Movement, 1943–1947. An Eyewitness Account* (New York: Praeger, 1988), pp. 64–65.

133. Lakatos, pp. 148–49; Hennyey, p. 105.

134. Hennyey, pp. 106–07; Lakatos, pp. 150–51.

135. Macartney, *OF*, II: 432, 487; Juhász, *HFP*, p. 327; Hennyey, p. 107; Lakatos, pp. 150–51.

136. Lakatos, p. 151. Strangely, Vattay did not mention this incident in his memoirs.

137. Vattay, p. 22.

138. *Szálasi per*, p. 556; Hennyey, p. 171; Lakatos, p. 154; Szent-Miklosy, p. 68.

139. Lakatos, p. 155–56.

140. Lakatos, pp. 156–57, 166; *Szálasi per*, pp. 522–530; Szöllösi, p. 317.

141. Horthy, *Memoirs*, p. 238.

Chapter Twelve

1. PRO, FO371/39267/C15601/15/21.

2. Horthy in a letter of June 14, 1945, to the American diplomat Robert Murphy: "I may declare with a quiet conscience that I am one of the majority of those Hungarians who never sided with the German party system. . . ." USSD, 864.00/4-2346.

3. ASHCAN interrogation of Horthy on June 13, 1945, NA, RG 332, EI0, G2 section.

4. Horthy's letter of May 19, 1945 to Truman, USSD, 864.00/7-545; to Robert Murphy of April 14, 1946, USSD, 864.00/4-2346; and to Ernest Bevin, PRO, FO371/59016/R7683/569/21.

5. PRO, FO371/59016/R9446/568/21; USSD, 864.00/5-1845. See also Gosztony, *Miklós von Horthy*, p. 113 and Éva Harászti-Taylor, "Why Was Admiral Horthy not Considered a War Criminal?" *New Hungarian Quarterly*, 30, no. 113 (1988), pp. 133–43.

6. Gosztony, *Miklós von Horthy*, p. 114. On Horthy's exile in Portugal, see Vajnai Lajos, "Horthy Lisszabonban," *História*, 12, nos. 5–6 (1990), p. 36.

7. For Horthy's letter and Adenauer's polite but brief reply, see Hennyey, pp. 176–78.

8. Ignác Romsics, ed., "Horthy Miklós levelei Zsitvay Tiborhoz, 1949–1951," *História*, 12, nos. 5–6 (1990), p. 33.

9. In 1993 the remains of Miklós Horthy were returned to Hungary and were buried in Kenderes. The ceremony, conducted on September 4, was broadcast on state television and was attended by several representatives of the government.

10. During his conversation with Ferenc Szálasi in May 1944, Horthy confessed that no one had ever been able to explain to him what the phrase "national socialism" really meant.

11. See, i.e., Horthy's interrogation on June 14, 1945, NA, RG332, ETO, G2 section, CCPWE, 32IX-P12.

12. On this see Korom, pp. 136–37.

13. Mátyás Rákosi, who at the end of World War II published a short pamphlet condemning Horthy as "the guilty man of Hungary," was said to have turned red with embarrassment when in a conversation in the Kremlin in 1945 Stalin suggested that the Regent was an old man who should be allowed to live in peace in the West. "Horthy's Responsibility," *The Hungarian Observer*, 5, no. 2 (1992), p. 26.

14. An egregious example occurred on July 7, when Horthy intimated

that he was thinking of dropping Sztójay and forming a Cabinet of military officers. On this, see Ránki, *Unternehmen Margarethe*, pp. 381–83.

15. See Horthy's ruminations in *CPAH*, p. 192.

16. Vojtech Mastny, *Russia's Road to the Cold War. Diplomacy, Warfare, and the Politics of Communism, 1941–1945* (New York: Columbia U. P., 1979), pp. 207–09.

17. For a discussion of these "liberals at heart," see the comments of István Deák and William McCagg in "Hungary: An Exchange," *New York Review of Books*, May 27, 1982, p. 56.

18. Mastny, pp. 137–38.

19. On this phenomenon, see Sigurd Paul Scheichl, "The Contexts and Nuances of Anti-Jewish Language. Were all the 'Antisemites' Antisemites?" in Ivar Oxaal et al, eds., *Jews, Antisemitism and Culture* (New York: , 1987), pp. 89–110.

20. Robert S. Wistrich, *The Jews of Vienna in the Age of Franz Joseph* (New York: Oxford U.P., 1989), p. 176.

21. Sharman Kadish, *Bolsheviks and British Jews. The Anglo-Jewish Community, Britain and the Russian Revolution* (London: Frank Cass, 1992), p. 136.

22. Zvi Erez, "The Jews of Budapest and the Plans of Admiral Horthy, August–October, 1944," *Yad Vashem Studies*, 16 (1984), p. 618.

23. Horthy told Szálasi during their conversation on May 3, 1944, that the main reason for the "Jewish problem" was that too many Christian Hungarians looked down on economic activity. As a result, Jews like Léo Goldberger created more wealth for the country than anyone else. Karsai, *Szálasi naplója*, p. 193.

24. This term in used by István Deák in his *Beyond Nationalism. A Social and Political History of the Habsburg Officer Corps, 1848–1918* (New York: Oxford U. P. , 1992), pp. 126–38.

25. See the provocative treatment of this question by Albert S. Lindemann, *The Jew Accused. Three Anti-Semitic Affairs: Dreyfus, Beilis, Frank, 1894–1915* (Cambridge: Cambridge U.P., 1991), pp. 110–20, 276–82.

Bibliography

I. Unpublished Primary Sources
(listed alphabetically by country of provenance)

Austria

Records of the Neues Politisches Archiv, Austrian State Archives (Vienna)

Germany

Documents of the German Foreign Ministry, Reich Leader of the S.S., and Oberkommando Wehrmacht, National Archives Microcopy, T-77, T-120, T-175 (Washington, D.C.)

Great Britain

Papers of George Lansbury, British Library of Political and Economic Science (London)

Records of the British Foreign Office, FO371, Public Record Office (London)

Hungary

Collection of Hungarian Political and Military Records, 1909–45, National Archive Microcopy T-973 (Washington, D.C.)

Diary and Memoirs of György Barcza, Hoover Institution on War, Revolution and Peace (Stanford, Calif.)

Macartney Archive, Bodleian Library (Oxford, England)

Papers of Miklós Horthy, Országos Levéltár (Budapest)

United States

Files of the Department of State, RG59, National Archives (Washington, D.C.)

Papers of General Harry Bandholtz, U.S. Army Historical Research Collection (Carlisle Barracks, Pa.)

Records of American Military Mission in Hungary, National Archives Microcopy M820 (Washington, D.C.)

II. Published Document Collections and Official Papers

Actes et documents du Saint Siège relatifs à la seconde guerre mondiale. Vol. 11: *Le Saint Siège et la guerre mondiale, Janvier 1944–Mai 1945.* Vatican City: Libreria Editrice Vaticana, 1981.

Adatok a szegedi ellenforradalom és a szegedi-kormány történetéhez (1919). Edited by Béla Kelemen. Szeged: Mars grafikai műintézet, 1923.

Allianz Hitler-Horthy-Mussolini. Dokumente zur ungarischen Aussenpolitik (1933–1944). Edited by Lajos Kerekes et al. Budapest: Akadémiai, 1966.

Auswärtiges Amt. *Akten zur deutschen auswärtigen Politik, 1918–1945*. Series A, B, and E. Göttingen: Vandenhoeck u. Ruprecht, 1972- .

Bethlen, István. *Bethlen István beszédei és irásai*. 2 vols.. Budapest: Genius, 1933.

Bethlen, István. *Bethlen István titkos iratai*. Edited by Miklós Szinai and László Szűcs. Budapest: Kossuth, 1972.

Ciano, Galeazzo. *Ciano's Diplomatic Papers*. Edited by Malcolm Muggeridge. London: Odhams, 1948.

Csak szolgálati használatra! Iratok a Horthy-hadsereg történetéhez. Edited by Tibor Hetés and Mrs. Tamás Morva. Budapest: Zrinyi, 1968.

The Confidential Papers of Admiral Horthy. Budapest: Corvina, 1965.

Diplomáciai iratok Magyarország külpolitikájához, 1936–1945. Budapest: Akadémiai, 1962- .

Diplomat in Berlin, 1933–1939. Papers and Memoirs of József Lipski, Ambassador of Poland. Edited by Wacław Jedrzejewicz. New York: Columbia U. P., 1968.

Documents diplomatiques français, 1932–1939. First and Second Series. Paris: Imprimerie Nationale, 1963- .

Documents on British Foreign Policy, 1919–1939. Edited by E. L. Woodward et al. First, Second, and Third Series. London: H. M. Stationery Office, 1949- .

Documents on German Foreign Policy, 1918–1945. Edited by Bernadotte Schmitt et al. Series C and D. Washington: Government Printing Office, 1949- .

Eichmann in Hungary. Documents. Edited by Jenő Lévai. Budapest: Pannonia, 1961.

Források Budapest történetéhez, 1919–1945. Edited by József Szekeres. Budapest: Főváros levéltárának kiadványa, 1972.

Iratok az ellenforradalom történetéhez, 1919–1945. Edited by Dezső Nemes. 5 vols. Budapest: 1953–1976.

Magyar pokol. A magyarországi fehérterror betiltott és üldözött kiadványok tükrében. Budapest: Magvető, 1964.

Papers and Documents Relating to the Foreign Relations of Hungary. 2 vols. Budapest: Royal University Press, 1939–1946.

Papers Relating to the Foreign Relations of the United States. Washington: Government Printing Office, 1955–1972.

Staatsmänner und Diplomaten bei Hitler. Vertrauliche Aufzeichnungen über Unterredungen mit Vertretern des Auslandes, 1939–1941. Edited by Andreas Hillgruber. Frankfurt: Bernard & Graefe, 1967.

A Szálasi per. Edited by Elek Karsai and Lászlo Szűcs. Debrecen: Reform, 1988.

Szálasiék bilincsben. Edited by Tibor Zinner and Péter Róna. 2 vols. Budapest: Lapkiadó, 1986.

Számjeltávirat valamennyi magyar királyi követségnek. Budapest: Táncsics, 1969.

The White Terror in Hungary. Report of the British Join Labour Delegation to Hungary. London: Trade Union Congress, 1920.

Wilhelm, Hans-Heinrich. "Hitlers Ansprache vor Generalen und Offizieren am 26. Mai 1944. *Militärische Mitteilungen* 20 (1976): 123–70.

A Wilhelmstrasse és Magyarország. Német diplomáciai iratok Magyarországról 1933–1944. Edited by György Ránki et al. Budapest: Kossuth, 1968.

III: Memoirs and Diaries

Andorka, Rudolf. *A madridi követségtől Mauthausenig.* Edited by Zsuzsa Lőrincz. Budapest: Kossuth, 1978.

Bandholtz, Harry H. *An Undiplomatic Diary.* New York: Columbia U.P., 1933.

Bethlen, Count István. *Hungarian Politics during World War II. Treatise and Indictment.* Edited by Ilona Bolza. Munich: Rudolf Trofenik, 1985.

Ciano, Galeazzo. *The Ciano Diaries, 1939–1943.* Edited by Hugh Gibson. New York: Doubleday, 1946.

Ciano, Galeazzo. *Ciano's Hidden Diary, 1937–1938.* Edited by Andreas Mayor. New York: Dutton, 1953.

Ciano, Galeazzo. *Ciano's Diplomatic Papers.* Edited by Malcolm Muggeridge. London: Odhams, 1948.

Garami, Ernő. *Forrongó Magyarország: Emlékezések és tanulságok.* Vienna: Pegazusz, 1922.

Goebbels, Joseph. *The Goebbels Diaries, 1939–1941.* Edited by Fred Taylor. New York: G. P. Putnam's Sons, 1983.

Goebbels, Joseph. *Die Tagebücher von Joseph Goebbels. Sämtliche Fragmente.* Edited by Elke Fröhlich. Munich: K. G. Saur, 1987- .

Gömbös, Gyula. *Egy magyar vezérkari tiszt bíráló feljegyzései a forradalomról és ellenforradalomról.* Budapest: Budapesti Hírlap, 1920.

Gosztony, Péter. "Das private Kriegstagebuch des Chefs des ungarischen Generalstabes vom Jahre 1944." *Wehrwissenschaftliche Rundschau.* (1970): 634–59; 703–32.

Guderian, Heinz. *Panzer Leader.* New York: Dutton, 1952.

Hennyey, Gustav. *Ungarns Schicksal zwischen Ost und West.* Mainz: Von Hase-Koehler, 1975.

Hitler's Secret Conversations, 1941–1944. Edited by Hugh Trevor-Roper. New York: Farrar, Strauss, 1953.

Horthy, Nicholas. *Memoirs.* New York: Robert Speller, 1957.

Kádár, Gyula. *A Ludavikától Sopronkőhidáig. Visszaemlékezések.* Budapest: Magvető, 1978.

Kállay, Nicholas. *Hungarian Premier.* New York: Columbia, 1934.

Kerr, Mark. *The Navy in My Time.* London: Rich & Cowan, 1933.

Kozma, Miklós. *Az összeomlás, 1918–1919*. Budapest: Az Athenaeum, 1933.

Lakatos, Géza. *Ahogyan én láttam*. *Visszaemlékezések*. Munich: Aurora, 1981.

Lehár, Anton. *Erinnerungen: Gegenrevolution und Restaurationsversuche in Ungarn, 1918–1921*. Munich: R. Oldenbourg, 1973.

Leith-Ross, Frederick. *Money Talks. Fifty Years of International Finance*. London: Hutchinson, 1968.

Montgomery, John F. *Hungary. The Unwilling Satellite*. New York: Devin-Adair, 1947.

Nagy, Ferenc. *Ahogy én láttam*. Budapest: Gondolat, 1965.

Nagy, Vilmos. *Végzetes esztendők, 1938–1945*. Budapest: Körmedy, n.d.

Náray, Antal. *Náray Antal visszaemlékezése, 1945*. Edited by Sándor Szakály. Budapest: Zrinyi, 1988.

O'Malley, Owen. *The Phantom Caravan*. London: John Murray, 1954.

Papen, Franz von. *Memoirs*. New York: E. P. Dutton, 1953.

Patai, József. "A fővezérnél és a kormányzónál. Visszaemlékezés a tízéves jubileum alkamából." *Múlt és jövő* (April, 1930) 140–42.

Páter Zadravecz titkos naplója. Edited by György Borsányi. Budapest: Kossuth, 1967.

Prónay, Pál. *A határban a halál kaszál. Fejezetek Prónay Pál feljegyzéseiből*. Edited by Ágnes Szabó and Ervin Pamlényi. Budapest: Kossuth, 1963.

Roosvelt, Nicholas. *A Front Row Seat*. Norman: Oklahoma U. P., 1953.

Saly, Dezső. *Szigorúan bizalmas! Fekete könyv, 1939–1944*. Budapest: Anonymus, 1945,

Schmidt, Paul. *Hitler's Interpreter*. Edited by R. H. C. Steed. London: William Heinemann, 1951.

Shvoy Kálmán titkos naplója és emlékirata, 1918–1945. Edited by Mihály Perneki. Budapest: Kossuth, 1983.

Serédi Jusztinián hercegprimás feljegyzései, 1942–1944. Edited by István Vida. Budapest: Zrinyi, 1989.

Starhemberg, Ernst Rüdiger. *Between Hitler and Mussolini*. New York: Harper, 1942.

Sulyok, Dezső. *A magyar tragédia*. Newark: by the author, 1954.

Szálasi naplója. A Nyilasmozgalom a II. Világháború idején. Edited by Elek Karsai. Budapest: Kossuth, 1978.

Szent-Miklósy, István. *With the Hungarian Independence Movement, 1943–1947*. New York: Praeger, 1988.

Szombathelyi, Ferenc. *Visszaemlékezései*. Washington: Occidental, 1980.

Tagebücher eines Abwehroffiziers, 1938–1940. Edited by Helmut Krausnick and Harold C. Deutsch. Stuttgart: Deutsches Verlagsanstalt, 1970.

Trebitsch-Lincoln, J. T. *The Autobiography of an Adventurer*. New York: Henry Holt. 1932.

Újpétery, Elemér. *Végállomás Lisszabon. Hat év a magyar királyi külügyi szogálatában*. Budapest: Magvető, 1987.

Urbán, Károly and István Vida, eds. "Barcza György. Budapest 1941 május–1943 március. Részlet Barcza György 'Diplomata emlékeim' c. emlékiratainak II. kötetéből." *Századok* 121 (1987): 355–420.

Vágó, Béla. "Budapest Jewry in the Summer of 1944. Otto Komoly's Diaries." *Yad Vashem Studies* (1970): 81–105.

Váli, Ferenc. *A Scholar's Odyssey*. Ames: Iowa St. U. P., 1990.

Vattay Antal naplója 1944–1945. Edited by Károly Vígh. Budapest: Zrinyi, 1990.

Die Weizsäcker Papiere, 1933–1950. Edited by Leonidas E. Hill. Frankfurt: Propyläen, 1974.

Werkmann, Karl. *Aus Kaiser Karls Nachlass*. Munich: Verlag für Kultur-Politik, 1924.

Windischgraetz, Lajos. *My Adventures and Misadventures*. London: Barrie, 1965.

IV: Secondary Sources

Ádám, Magda. "France and Hungary at the Beginning of the 1920s." In *Total War and Peacemaking: A Case Study of Trianon*. Edited by Béla Király et al., pp. 145–82. New York: Brooklyn College Press, 1982.

Ádám, Magda. "A két királypuccs és a kisantant." *Történelmi Szemle* 25 (1982): 665–713.

Bagger, Eugene. *Eminent Europeans. Studies in Continental Reality*. New York: G. P. Putnam's, 1922.

Balogh, Eva. "The Road to Isolation: Hungary, the Great Powers, and the Successor States, 1919–1920." Ph.D. dissertation, Yale University, 1974.

Barany, George. "Hungary: From Aristocratic to Proletarian Nationalism." In *Nationalism in Eastern Europe*. Edited by Peter F. Sugár and Ivo J. Lederer. Seattle: University of Washington Press, 1969.

Batkay, William M. *Authoritarian Politics in a Transitional State. István Bethlen and the Unified Party in Hungary, 1921–1926*. Boulder: East European Monographs, 1982.

Ben-tov, Arieh. *Facing the Holocaust in Budapest. The International Committee of the Red Cross and the Jews of Hungary, 1943–1945*. Dondrecht: Nijhoff, 1988.

Berend, I. T. and G. Ránki. *Hungary. A Century of Economic Development*. New York: Barnes and Noble, 1974.

Bogan, Henry. *La question royale en Hongrie au lendemain de la Premiere Guerre mondiale*. Louvain: Institut de recherches de l'Europe Centrale, 1979.

Bokor, Péter. *Végjáték a Duna mentén. Interjúk egy filmsoroszathoz*. Budapest: RTV-Minerva, 1982.

Borbándi, Gyula. *Der ungarische Populismus*. Mainz: Hase & Koehler, 1976.

Borus, József. "Vörös János és Nádas Lajos 1944. Október 15-i szerepéről." *Történelmi Szemle* 91 (1991): 249–54.

Boroviczény, Aladár von. *Der König und sein Reichsverweser*. Munich: Verlag für Kulturpolitik, 1924.

Boros, Ferenc. *Magyar-csehszlovák kapcsolatok, 1918–1921-ben.* Budapest: Akadémiai, 1970.

Borsányi, Julián. *Das Rätzel des Bombenangriffs auf Kauschau.* Munich: Ungarisches Institut, 1978.

Braham, Randolph L. *The Politics of Genocide. The Holocaust in Hungary.* 2 vols. New York: Columbia U. P., 1981.

Braham, Randolph L., ed. *The Tragedy of Hungarian Jewry. Essays, Documents, Depositions.* Boulder: Social Science Monographs, 1986.

Braham, Randolph L. and Béla Vágó, eds. *The Holocaust in Hungary: Forty Years Later.* Boulder: East European Monographs, 1985.

Brehm, Bruno. *Weder Kaiser noch König. Der Untergang der Habsburgischen Monarchie.* Munich: R. Piper, 1933.

Brook-Shepherd, Gordon. *The Last Habsburg.* London: Weidenfeld and Nicolson, 1968.

Burks, Richard V. "Two Teleki Letters." *Journal of Central European Affairs* 7 (1947): 68–73.

Cienciala, Anna. *Poland and the Western Powers, 1938–1939.* London: Routlege and Kegan Paul, 1968.

Clare, George. *Last Waltz in Vienna. The Rise and Destruction of a Family, 1842–1942.* New York: Holt Rinehart, 1982.

Csathó, Kálmán et al. *Horthy Miklós.* Budapest: Singer és Wolfner, 1943.

Csima, János. "Adalékok a horthysta vezérkarnak az ellenforradalmi rendszer háborús politikájában betöltött szerepéről." *Hadtörténelmi Közlemények* 15 (1968): 486–512.

Deák, István. *Beyond Nationalism. A Social and Political History of the Habsburg Officer Corps.* New York: Oxford U. P., 1992.

Deák, István. "Budapest and the Hungarian Revolutions of 1918–1919." *Slavonic and East European Review.* 46 (1968): 129–40.

Deák, István. "Hungary." In *The European Right: A Historical Profile.* Edited by Hans Rogger and Eugen Weber, pp. 364–407. Berkeley: Univ. of California, 1965.

Doblhoff, Lily. *Horthy Miklós.* Budapest: Athenaeum, 1938.

Dombrády, Loránd. *A legfelsőbb hadúr és hadserege.* Budapest: Zrinyi, 1990.

Dombrády, Loránd. "A Kormányzó Katonai Irodája." *História* 12 (1990), 29–30.

Dömötörfi, Tibor. "A Horthy-kultusz elemei." *História* 12 (1990): 23–26.

Dósa, Rudolf Mrs. *A MOVE. Egy jellegzetes magyar fasiszta szervezet, 1918–1944.* Budapest: Akadémiai, 1972.

Dreisziger, Nándor. "Bridges to the West. The Horthy's Régime's Reinsurance Policies in 1941." *War and Society* 7 (1989): 1–23.

Dreisziger, Nándor A. F. *Hungary's Way to World War II.* Toronto: Weller, 1968.

Dwork, Debórah. *Children with a Star. Jewish Youth in Nazi Europe.* New Haven: Yale U. P., 1991.

Ellman, Richard. *James Joyce.* New York: Oxford U. P., 1982.

Erez, Tsvi. "Hungary. Six Days in July, 1944." *Holocaust and Genocide Studies* 3 (1988): 37–53.

Erős, J. "Hungary." In *European Fascism*, edited by S. J. Woolf. New York: Random House, 1969.

Fehér, András. *A magyarországi Szociálpolitika Párt és az ellenforradalmi rendszer 1919 augusztus-1921.* Budapest: Akadémiai, 1969.

Fenyő, Mario. *Hitler, Horthy, and Hungary. German-Hungarian Relations, 1941–1944.* New Haven: Yale U. P., 1972.

Gárdos, Miklós. *Tengerész a várban.* Budapest: Kosmosz, 1969.

Gergely, Ernő and Pál Schönwald. *A Somogyi-Bacsó gyilkosság.* Budapest: Kossuth, 1978.

Gilbert, Martin. *The Holocaust. A History of the Jews of Europe during the Second World War.* New York: Holt, Rinehart, and Winston, 1985.

Gosztony, Péter. *Hitlers fremde Heere. Das Schicksal der nichtdeutschen Armeen im Ostfeldzug.* Düsseldorff: Econ, 1976.

Gosztony, Péter. "Hungary's Army in the Second World War." In *Hungarian History/World History*, edited by György Ránki. Budapest: Akadémiai, 1984.

Gosztony, Péter. *Miklós von Horthy. Admiral und Reichsverweser.* Göttingen: Musterschmidt, 1973.

Gosztonyi, Péter. *Magyarország a második világháborúban.* 2 vols. Munich: HERP, 1984.

Gratz, Gusztáv. *A forradalmak kora. Magyarország története, 1918–1920.* Budapest: Magyar Szemle, 1935.

Halpern, Paul G. *The Naval War in the Mediterranean, 1914–1918.* Annapolis: Naval Institute Press, 1987.

Handlery, Andrew. *From the Ghetto to the Games. The Jewish Athletes in Hungary.* Boulder: East European Monographs, 1985.

Hegedűs, Sándor. *Az utolsó trónfosztás.* Budapest: Kossuth, 1970.

Held, Joseph, ed. *The Modernization of Agriculture. Rural Transformation in Hungary, 1848–1975.* Boulder: East European Monographs, 1980.

Himler, Márton. *Igy néztek ki a magyar nemzet sirásói.* New York: St. Marks, 1958.

Hollós, Ervin and Vera Lajta. *Horthy Miklós a fehérek vezére.* Budapest: Kossuth, 1985.

Hovi, Kalervo. *Alliance de revers. Stabilization of France's Alliance Policies in East Central Europe, 1919–1921.* Turku: Turun Yliopisto, 1984.

Ignotus, Paul. *Hungary.* New York: Praeger, 1972.

Irving, David. *Hitler's War.* New York: Viking, 1977.

János, Andrew C. *The Politics of Backwardness in Hungary, 1825–1945.* Princeton: Princeton U. P., 1982.

Jászi Oscar. *The Dissolution of the Habsburg Monarchy.* Chicago: Univ. of Chicago, 1929.

Jászi, Oscar. *Revolution and Counter-Revolution in Hungary.* London: P. S. King, 1924.

Joseph, Gilbert. *Mission sans retour. L'affaire Wallenberg*. Paris: Albin Michel, 1982.

Juhász, Gyula. *A Teleki-kormány külpolitikája, 1939–1941*. Budapest: Akadémiai, 1964.

Juhász, Gyula. *Hungarian Foreign Policy, 1919–1945*. Budapest: Akadémiai, 1979.

Kadish, Sharman. *Bolsheviks and British Jews. The Anglo-Jewish Community, Britain and the Russian Revolution*. London: Frank Cass, 1992.

Kardos, József. *A szentkorona-tan története (1919–1944)*. Budapest: Akadémiai, 1985.

Karsai, Elek. *A budai Sándor-palotában történt, 1919–1941*. Budapest: Táncsics, 1967.

Karsai, Elek. "Edmund Veesenmayer's Reports to Hitler in Hungary in 1943." *New Hungarian Quarterly* 5 (1964): 146–53.

Karsai, Elek. "Szálasi." In *Reformists and Radicals in Hungary*, edited by Ferenc Glatz, pp. 191–210. Budapest: MTA Történettudományi Intézet, 1991.

Katzburg, Nathaniel. *Hungary and the Jews. Policy and Legislation, 1920–1943*. Jersusalem: Bar-Ilan Press, 1981.

Kerekes, Lajos. "A Habsburg-restauraciós kisérletek és az osztrák-magyar viszony 1921-ben." *Századok* 110 (1976): 3–50.

Kónya, Sándor. *Gömbös kisérlete totális fasiszta diktatúra megteremtésére*. Budapest: Akadémiai, 1968.

Korom, Mihály. *Magyarország ideiglenes nemzeti kormánya és a fegyverszünet (1944–1945)*. Budapest: Akadémiai, 1981.

Kovács, Mária. "Hungarian Women in the Professions: Interwar Feminism on the Right." Unpublished paper.

Kovrig, Bennett. *Communism in Hungary from Kun to Kádár*. Stanford: Hoover Institute, 1979.

Krusenstjern, Benigna von. *Der Ungarische Kleinlandwirte-Partei, 1909–1922/1929*. Munich: Trofenik, 1981.

Lackó, Miklós. *Nyilasok, Nemzetiszocialisták, 1935–1944*. Budapest: Kossuth, 1966.

Ladányi, Andor. *Az egyetemi ifjúság az ellenforradalom első éveiben*. Budapest: Akadémiai, 1979.

Lehmann, Hans Georg. *Der Reichsverweser-Stellvertreter: Horthys gescheiderte Planung einer Dynastie*. Mainz: von Hase und Koehler, 1975.

Leyda, Jay. *Kino. A History of Russian and Soviet Film*. New York: Collier, 1960.

Lévai, Jenő. *Black Book on the Martyrdom of Hungarian Jewry*. Zürich: Central European Times, 1948.

Lévai, Jenő. *Hungarian Jewry and the Papacy. Pope Pius XII Did Not Remain Silent*. London: Sands, 1968.

Lévai, Jenő. *Zsidosors Magyarországon*. Budapest: Magyar Téka, 1948.

Lukacs, John. *Budapest 1900. A Historical Portrait of a City and its Culture*. New York: Weidenfeld & Nicolson, 1988.

Lukacs, John. *The Last European War, September 1939/ December/1941*. Garden City: Anchor Press, 1976.

Macartney, C. A. *October Fifteenth. A History of Modern Hungary, 1929–1945*. 2nd edit. 2 vols. Edinburgh: Edinburgh U. P., 1961.

Macartney, Maxwell H. H. *Five Years of European Chaos*. London: Chapman & Hall, 1923.

Márkus, László. *A Károlyi Gyula kormány bel- és külpolitikája*. Budapest: Akadémiai, 1968.

McCagg, William. "The Role of the Hungarian Nobility in Modern Jewish History." *East European Quarterly* 20 (1986):

Mendelsohn, Ezra. *The Jews of East Central Europe between the World Wars*. Bloomington: Indiana U. P., 1983.

Meier-Welcker, Hans. *Seeckt*. Frankfurt: M. Bernard, 1967.

Mócsy, István. "Count István Bethlen (1874–1947)." In *Hungarian Statesmen of Destiny (1860–1960)*. Edited by Paul Bődy. Highland Lakes, N.J.: Atlantic Research and Publications, 1989.

Mócsy, István. *Hungarian Refugees and Their Impact on Hungary's Domestic Politics, 1918–1921*. New York: Brooklyn U. P., 1983.

Munkácsi, Ernő. *Hogyan történt? Adatok és okmányok a magyar zsidóság tragédiájához*. Budapest: Renaissance, 1947.

Nagy, Zsuzsa. "Amerikai diplomaták Horthy Miklósról, 1920–1944." *Történelmi Szemle* 32 (1990): 173–96.

Nagy, Zsuzsa. *The Liberal Opposition in Hungary, 1919–1945*. Budapest: Akadémiai, 1983.

Nagy-Talavera, Nicholas M. *The Green Shirts and the Others. A History of Fascism in Hungary and Rumania*. Stanford: Hoover Institute, 1970.

Nouzille, Jean. "Ausztria és Magyarország új határa (1919–1921)." *Történelmi Szemle*. 30 (1987–88): 330–38.

Ölvedi, Ignác. *A budai vár és a debreceni csata. Horthyék katasztrófa politikája 1944 őszén*. Budapest: Zrinyi, 1970.

Ormos, Mária. *Padovától Trianonig, 1918–1920*. Budapest: Kossuth, 1983.

Ormos, Mária. *"Soha, amig élek!" Az utolsó koronás Habsburg puccskisérletei 1921-ben*. Budapest: Pannónia, 1990.

Pál, Csaba. "Kenderes, a családi birtok." *História* 12 (1990): 12–13.

Pándi, Ilona. *Osztályok és pártok a Bethlen-konszolidáció időszakában*. Budapest: Kossuth, 1966.

Pastor, Peter. *Hungary Between Wilson and Lenin. The Hungarian Revolution of 1918–1919 and the Big Three*. Boulder: East European Quarterly, 1976.

Pataki, István. *Az ellenforradalom hadserege 1919–1921*. Budapest: Zrinyi, 1973.

Pilch, Jenő. *Horthy Miklós*. Budapest: Athenaeum, 1929.

Pintér, István. *Ki volt Horthy Miklós?* Budapest: Zrinyi, 1968.

Pintér, István. *A Szociáldemokrata Párt története, 1933–1944*. Budapest: Kossuth, 1980.

Plaschka, Richard Georg. *Nationalismus, Staatsgewalt, Widerstand*. Vienna: V. für Geschichte u. Politik, 1985.

Plaschka, Richard Georg et al. *Innere Front. Militärassistenz, Widerstand, und Umsturz in der Donaumonarchie 1918.* 2 vols. Munich: R. Oldenbourg, 1974.

Pölöskei, Ferenc. *Horthy és hatalmi rendszere (1919–1922).* Budapest: Kossuth, 1977.

Pölöskei, Ferenc. *Hungary after Two World Revolutions (1919–1922).* Budapest: Akadémiai, 1980.

Pritz, Pál. *Magyarország külpolitikája Gömbös Gyula miniszter-elnöksége idején, 1932–1936.* Budapest: Akadémiai, 1982.

Ránki, György. "Hitler and the Statesmen of East Central Europe, 1939–1945." In *Society in Change. Studies in Honor of Béla K. Király,* edited by Steven Bela Vardy and Agnes Huszar Vardy, pp. 641–71. Boulder: East European Monographs, 1983.

Ránki, György. *Unternehmen Margarethe. Die deutsche Besetzung Ungarns.* Vienna: Hermann Böhlau, 1984.

Ránki, György and Iván Berend. *Magyarország a fasiszta Németország 'életterében,' 1933–1938.* Budapest: Kossuth,1960.

Révay, József. *Gömbös Gyula élete és politkája.* Budapest: Franklin, 1934.

Rieder, Heinz. *Kaiser Karl. Der letzte Monarch Österreich-Ungarns 1887–1922.* Munich: Callwey, 1981.

Romsics, Ignác. *Bethlen István. Politikai életrajz.* Budapest: Magyarságkutató Intézet, 1991.

Romsics, Ignác. *Ellenforradalom és konszolidáció. A Horthy-rendszer első évtizede.* Budapest: Gondolat, 1982.

Romsics, Ignác. "Horthy Miklós levelei Zsitvay Tiborhoz." *História* 12 (1990): 33–35.

Romsics, Ignác. "A kormányzó és a 'gazda.'" *História* 12 (1990): 15–18.

Romsics, Ignác. "A State Department és Magyarország, 1942–1947." *Valóság* 34 (1991): 32–67.

Rothschild, Joseph. *East Central Europe between the Two World Wars.* Seattle: Washington U. P., 1974.

Rutter, Owen. *Regent of Hungary. The Authorized Life of Admiral Nicholas Horthy.* London: Rich and Cowan, 1939.

Sakmyster, Thomas L. *Hungary, the Great Powers and the Danubian Crisis, 1936–1939.* Athens: Univ. of Georgia, 1980.

Sakmyster, Thomas. "Magyar katonatisztek és Kassa bombazása." *Történelmi Szemle* (1985): 368–73.

Sakmyster, Thomas. "Miklós Horthy and the Jews of Hungary." In *Labyrinth of Nationalism, Complexities of Diplomacy. Essays in Honor of Charles and Barbara Jelavich,* pp. 121–42. Edited by Richard Frucht. Columbus: Slavica, 1992.

Scheichl, Sigurd Paul. "The Contexts and Nuances of Anti-Jewish Language: Were All the 'Antisemites' Antisemites?" In *Jews, Antisemitism, and Culture,* pp. 89–110. Edited by Ivár Oxaal et al. New York: Oxford U. P., 1987.

Scheer, Jonathon. *George Lansbury*. Manchester: Manchester U. P., 1990.

Schmidt-Pauli, Edgar von. *Nikolaus von Horthy. Admiral, Volksheld und Reichsverweser*. Hamburg: I. P. Toth, 1942.

Seton-Watson, Robert. "Hungary in the Grip of Reaction." *New Europe* (Nov. 27, 1919): 212–13.

Sinor, Denis. *History of Hungary*. New York: Praeger, 1959.

Sipos, Péter. *Imrédy Béla és a Magyar Megúulás Pártja*. Budapest: Akadémiai, 1970.

Sipos, Péter. "A kormányzó." *História* 12 (1990): 3–10.

Sondhaus, Lawrence. "The Austro-Hungarian Naval Officer Corps, 1867–1918." *Austrian History Yearbook* 24 (1993), pp. 51–78.

Soós, Katalin. *Burgenland az európai politikában (1918–1921)*. Budapest: Akadémiai, 1971.

Stastny, Charles Ira. "The Hungarian Communist Party, 1918–1930: Days of Power and Years of Futility." Pd.D. dissertation, Harvard University, 1967.

Stier, Miklós. "Politikai újraorientálódás az 1920-as és 30-as évek fordúlóján." *Századok* 120 (1986): 260–300.

Sugar, Peter F., ed. *A History of Hungary*. Bloomington: Indiana U. P., 1990.

Sugar, Peter and Ivo Lederer, eds. *Nationalism in Eastern Europe*. Seattle: Univ. of Washington, 1969.

Surányi, Miklós. *Bethlen. Történetpolitikai tanulmányok*. Budapest: Singer és Wolfner, 1927.

Szabó, Éva. "A magyarországi svéd mentő-akció történetéhez (1944)." *Történelmi Szemle* 30 (1987–88): 379–94.

Szinai, Miklós. *Ki lesz a kormányzó? A Somogyi-Bacsó gyilkosság hátere*. Budapest: Kossuth, 1988.

Szöllösi-Janze, Margit. *Die Pfeilkreuzlerbewegung in Ungarn. Historische Kontext, Entwicklung und Herrschaft*. Munich: Olderbourg, 1989.

Szűcs, László. "Horthy levele Sztálinhoz 1944 Őszén." *Századok* 104 (1970): 983–89.

Thoss, Bruno. *Der Ludendorff-Kreis 1919–1923. München als Zentrum der mitteleuropäischen Gegenrevolution zwischen Revolution und Hitler-Putsch*. Munich: Stadtarchiv München, 1977.

Tihany, Leslie C. "The French Army and the Rightist Restorations in Hungary, 1918–1919." In *Revolutions and Interventions in Hungary and its Neighboring States, 1918–1919*. Edited by Peter Pastor, pp. 377–91. Boulder: East European Monographs, 1988.

Tilkovszky, L. *Pál Teleki (1879–1941). A Biographical Sketch*. Budapest: Akadémiai, 1974.

Tilkovszky, Loránt. "Ellenzéki törvényhozók memorandum-akciója 1942-43 telén." *Századok* 119 (1985): 152–223.

Tilkovszky, Loránt. *Teleki Pál. Legenda és valóság*. Budapest: Kossuth, 1969.

Vágó, Béla. "The Horthy Offer. A Missed Opportunity for Rescuing Jews in 1944." In *Contemporary Views of the Holocaust*. Edited by Randolph L. Braham, pp. 23–45. Boston: Kluwer-Nijhoff, 1983.

Vajnai, Lajos. "Horthy Lisszabonban." *História* 12 (1990): 36.

Vargyai, Gyula. *Katonai közigazgatás és kormányzói jogkör (1919–1921)*. Budapest: Közigazdasági és Jogi Kiadó, 1971.

Varjassy, Louis. *Révolution, Bolshevisme, Réaction: Histoire de l'occupation français en Hongrie, 1918–1919*. Paris: Jouve, 1934.

Vas, Zoltán. *Horthy*. 2nd edit. Budapest: Szépirodalmi, 1975.

Vasari, Emilio. *Ein Königsdrama im Schatten Hitlers. Die Versuche des Reichsverwesers Horthy zur Gründung einer Dynastie*. Vienna: Europa, 1968.

Vermes, Gabor. *István Tisza. The Liberal Vision and Conservative Statecraft of a Magyar Nationalist*. Boulder: East European Monographs, 1985.

Vida, István. "A lengyel emigrans kormány lisszaboni követségének magyar vonatkozásu iratai." *Történelmi Szemle* 32 (1987–88): 438–79.

Vígh, Károly. "Horthy és Zsilinszky." *História* 12 (1990): 18–20.

Vígh, Károly. *Ugrás a sötétbe*. 2nd. edit. Budapest: Magvető, 1984.

Wandruszka, Adam and Peter Urbanitsch. *Die Habsburgermonarchie, 1848–1918*. Vol. 5: *Die Bewaffnete Macht*. Vienna: V. der Österreichischen Akademie der Wissenschaften, 1987.

Weinberg, Gerhard. *The Foreign Policy of Hitler's Germany: Starting World War II*. Chicago: Univ. of Chicago, 1980.

Werkmann, Charles von. *The Tragedy of Charles of Habsburg*. London: Philip Allan, 1924.

Yahil, Leni. *The Holocaust. The Fate of European Jewry, 1932–1945*. New York: Oxford U. P., 1990.

Index